LIONEL MARCH

ARCHITECTONICS OF HUMANISM

ESSAYS ON NUMBER IN ARCHITECTURE

I dedicate this book to my mother, Rose,
in her ninetieth year

LIONEL MARCH

ARCHITECTONICS OF HUMANISM
ESSAYS ON NUMBER IN ARCHITECTURE

ACADEMY EDITIONS

Front cover: Scheme for Leonardo Mocenigo on the Brenta. Andrea Palladio, *I Quattro Libri Dell'Architettura,* Dominico de' Franceschi, Venice, 1570. Courtesy The Elmer Belt Library of Vinciana, University of California, Los Angeles.

Back cover: Design of the Zodiac, attributed to Andrea Palladio. Daniele Barbaro. *M. Vitrvvii Pollionis: De Architectvra Libri Decem cvm Commentariis,* Franiscum Franciscium Senensem & Ioan. Crugher Germanum, Venice, 1567. Courtesy The Elmer Belt Library of Vinciana, University of California, Los Angeles.

Cover design: Mario Bettella, Artmedia, London

Typeset by Florencetype Ltd, Stoodleigh, Devon

Published in Great Britain in 1998 by

ACADEMY EDITIONS
a division of
JOHN WILEY & SONS LTD
Baffins Lane
Chichester
West Sussex PO19 1UD

ISBN 0-471-97754-3

Other Wiley Editorial Offices
New York • Weinheim • Brisbane • Singapore • Toronto

Printed and bound in China

CONTENTS

PROLOGUE vii

A GROUND 1
    I Classical Arithmetic 3
    II Euclidean Arithmetic 9
    III Cosmogonic Arithmetic 13
    IIII Gendered Number 15
    V Ethical Number 20
    VI Shapeful Number 22
    VII Theological Number 31
    VIII Occult Number 38
    VIIII Playful Number 49
    X Right Triangular Number 53
    XI Rational Proportion 58
    XII Inexpressible Proportion 65
    XIII Empowered Proportion 70
    XIIII Proportionality 72
    XV Composite Proportion 78
    XVI Euclidean Regular Figures 85
    XVII Scales of Proportion 91
    XVIII Prisoners of Number 103

B FOUNDATION 113
    XVIIII Judaic Heritage 115
    XX Greek Experience 124
    XXI Roman Wonders 132
    XXII Christian Works 143

C EDIFICE 151
    XXIII Centralized Design 153
    XXIIII Leon Battista Alberti 182
    XXV Sebastiano Serlio 206
    XXVI Andrea Palladio 216

EPILOGUE 267

APPENDICES 272
    1 Canons of Proportion 272
    2 Ratios Used in Plans by Palladio: Tables 277

ACKNOWLEDGEMENTS 279

INDEX 281

NON MOLTO lungi dalle Gambarare fopra la Brenta è la feguente fabrica delli Magnifici Signori Nicolò, e Luigi de' Foscari.   Questa fabrica è alzata da terra undici piedi, e fotto ui fono cucine, tinelli, e fimili luoghi, & è fatta in uolto cofi di fopra, come di fotto. Le ftanze maggiori hanno uolti alti fecondo il primo modo delle altezze de' uolti. Le quadre hanno i uolti à cupola: fopra i camerini vi fono mezati: il uolto della Sala è à Crociera di mezo cerchio: la fua impofta è tanto alta da piano, quanto è larga la Sala: la quale è ftata ornata di eccellentiffime pitture da Meffer Battifta Venetiano.   Meffer Battifta Franco grandiffimo difegnatore à noftri tempi hauea ancor effo dato principio à dipingere una delle ftanze grandi, ma foprauenuto dalla morte ha lafciata l'opera imperfetta. La loggia è di ordine Ionico: La Cornice gira intorno tutta la cafa, e fa frontefpicio fopra la loggia, e nella parte oppofta.   Sotto la Gronda vi è vn'altra Cornice, che camina fopra i frontefpicij: Le camere di fopra fono come mezati per la loro baffezza, perche fono alte folo otto piedi.

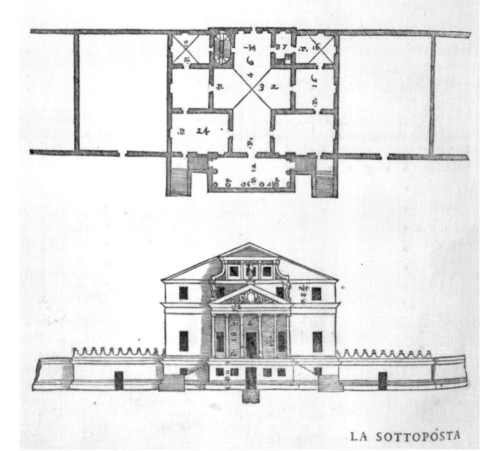

LA SOTTOPOSTA

Villa for Signori Niccolo and Luigi de' Foscari, known as La Malcontenta, Gambarare on the Brenta. Andrea Palladio, *I Quattro Libri Dell'Architettura*, Dominico de' Franceschi, Venice, 1570, p. 50. Courtesy The Elmer Belt Library of Vinciana, University of California, Los Angeles.

Tulle numerum omnibus rebus et omnia pereunt.
Remove number from everything, and all
will come to nothing.

ISODORE OF SEVILLE (560–636CE)

PROLOGUE

These essays would not have been written but for the lasting influence of Rudolf
Wittkower's lectures first published by the Warburg Institute in 1949 as *Architectural
Principles in the Age of Humanism.* As an architectural student in the 1950s at
Cambridge, with a mathematical background, his essays intrigued me. The matter
was reinforced by Colin Rowe's celebrated essay, 'The Mathematics of the Ideal
Villa' which was advertised on a notice announcing his appointment to the faculty
of the School of Architecture, Cambridge University, in my second year.[1] In my
final examination, one of the questions concerned Wittkower's thesis on proportional design. I wrote about Palladio's Villa Malcontenta and struggled over the
length of the cruciform hall – 46½P. This was an unusual dimension. How did this
relate to the width of the hall – 32P. In neither Wittkower's nor Rowe's understanding of simple ratios was there an explanation, and especially in the musical
analogy. The puzzle remained with me. At the time I was involved in the musical
circles of Cambridge life and I recall giving a talk to musicians on Alberti's theories of proportion which Wittkower had done so much to revive. In turn, I learned
of developments in composition from my musician colleagues. Darmstadt was the
centre of innovation and *Die Reihe* was the journal of choice. Leon Lovett, the
conductor, drew out a numerical matrix on a table napkin: 'This is how they write
music in Darmstadt.' Then, once in the corridor of the School of Architecture, Colin
St John Wilson spoke to me of 'architecture by numbers'. The mathematician in
me was challenged. If musicians could use numbers to compose, why not architects?[2] I was taken back to why I was studying architecture at all. At a grammar
school science society meeting, my mathematics master, Leslie 'Tabby' Tabrett, had
delivered a talk on Christopher Wren, mathematician and architect. That was where
the connection was made. The talk made an indelible impression on me and largely
determined my future career.

When I arrived in Los Angeles in 1984, I was known for my mathematical and
computational studied in architecture and urban design.[3] I soon found that the grad-
uates were ill-prepared historically and my classes began to include more historical
material. This took me to the Elmer Belt Library, one of the extraordinary treasures
of the University of California, Los Angeles. When in Florence during the 1920s,
Dr Belt had become fascinated by the medical studies of Leonardo da Vinci and
then had the idea of reconstituting Leonardo's library with editions as close to those
that Leonardo himself had acquired. The result is a unique collection which has

1 Reprinted in C. Rowe, *The Mathematics of the
Ideal Villa and Other Essays*, The MIT Press,
Cambridge MA:, 1976, 1–28.
2 I contributed a statement at this time – 'Serial Art',
Architectural Design, February 1966 – which paral-
leled these developments in music.
3 For example, *The Geometry of Environment* with
Philip Steadman, RIBA Publications, London, 1971,
the edited volumes, *Urban Space and Structures*, with
Leslie Martin and *The Architecture of Form*,
Cambridge University Press, 1972 and 1976 respec-
tively; and papers such as 'On Counting Architectural
Plans' with Christopher Earl, *Environment and
Planning B*, 4, 1977, 57–80, 'Dynamic Urban Models
Based on Information-Minimizing' with Michael
Batty, Martin R. L., Bennett R. J., Thrift N., eds,
Towards a Dynamic Analysis of Spatial Systems,
Pion, London, 1978, 'On Enumerating Certain Design
Problems in Terms of Unlabelled Bi-coloured Graphs'
with Frank Harary and R. Robinson *Environment
and Planning B* 5, 1978, 31–44, and 'Design
Machines' and 'Spatial Systems in Architecture and
Design: Some History and Logic', with George Stiny,
Environment and Planning B, 8, 1981, 245–55, and
Planning and Design, 12, 1985, 31–53.

4 P. L. Rose, *The Italian Renaissance of Mathematics: Studies on Humanists and Mathematicians from Petrarch to Galileo*, Librairie Droz, Genève, 1975. C. V. Palisca *Humanism in Italian Renaissance Musical Thought*, Yale University Press, New Haven CT, 1985.

5 D. H. Fowler, *The Mathematics of Plato's Academy: a New Reconstruction*, Clarendon Press, Oxford, 1987. M. Daly Davis, *Piero della Francesca's Mathematical Treatises*, Longo Editore, Ravenna, 1977.

6 W. Elders, *Composers of the Low Countries*, Clarendon Press, Oxford, 1991. The musicologist, Joscelyn Godwin, has also influenced my thinking: *Harmonies of Heaven and Earth: the Spiritual Dimensions of Music*, Thames and Hudson, London, 1987, ed., *Cosmic Music: Musical Keys to the Interpretation of Reality. Essays by Marius Schneider, Rudolf Haase, Hans Erhard Lauer*, Inner Traditions International, Rochester VT, 1989, ed., *The Harmony of the Spheres: a Sourcebook of the Pythagorean Tradition in Music*, Inner Traditions International, Rochester VT, 1993.

7 G. Hersey, *Pythagorean Palaces: Magic and Architecture in the Italian Renaissance*, Cornell University Press, Ithaca, NY, 1976. F. A. Yates, *The Occult Philosophy in the Elizabethan Age*, Routledge & Kegan Paul, London, 1979, and *Giordano Bruno and the Hermetic Tradition*, Routledge & Kegan Paul, London, 1964.

8 I was first alerted to this magical world in discussions, as President of the Cambridge University Opera Group, with the composer Alexander Goehr who, with librettist Christopher Logue, was contemplating a new opera 'Kelly and Dee' based on the lives of the Elizabethan magus Dr John Dee and his companion Edward Kelly.

9 In this context, M.J.B. Allen, *Nuptial Arithmetic: Marsilio Ficino's Commentary on the Fatal Number in Book VIII of Plato's Republic*, University of California Press, Los Angeles, CA, 1994. It was Michael Allen, as Director of the Centre for Medieval and Renaissance Studies, who brought me to the periphery of a remarkable circle of scholars at UCLA in this area. I do not, however, claim to be such a scholar myself. The present essays are speculative and circumstantial, rather than historical and factual. They are based on my design interests and mathematical background. Nevertheless, I have tried to bring my design interests in line with the *mentalité* of the Renaissance – particularly the multifaceted understanding of number, so different from our own – as best I am able to reconstruct it from sources readily at hand.

10 C. Ginzburg, *The Enigma of Piero: Piero della Francesca. The Baptism. The Arezzo Cycle. The Flagellation*, Verso, London, 1985. B.P. Copenhaver 'Astrology and Magic' in Q. Skinner, E. Kessler, *The Cambridge History of Renaissance Philosophy*, Cambridge University Press, Cambridge, 1988, B. P. Copenhaver, ed. *Hermetica: The Greek Corpus Hermetica and the Latin Asclepius in a New English Translation*, Cambridge University Press, Cambridge, 1996.

11 A. W. Crosby, *The Measure of Reality: Quantification and Western Society 1250–1600*, Cambridge University Press, Cambridge, 1997.

enjoyed the scholarly care of Carlo Pedretti, Armand Hammer Professor of Leonardo Studies, and librarians Anne Hartmere and Alfred Willis in recent years. To handle fifteenth- and sixteenth-century architectural books and related materials directly fires the imagination and awakens the passion to enter into the *mentalité* of that period.

Paul Lawrence Rose and Claude V. Palisca provided a new canvas on which to rework the Wittkowerian themes.[4] Their scholarship on mathematical and musical developments in the fifteenth and sixteenth centuries was not available to Wittkower when he wrote. David Fowler transformed my thinking on classical arithmetic and the arithmetization of geometry for which Margaret Daly Davis' examination of the mathematical treatises of Piero della Francesca has forewarned me.[5] Willem Elder confirmed my suspicions that artists played number games in a symbolic language during the Renaissance: particularly the composers, Johannes Ockeghem and Josquin des Pres.[6] With references to Marsilio Ficino, George Hersey opened up new architectural interpretations and these found corroborative support in Dame Frances Yates' writings on the occult philosophy and the hermetic tradition.[7] This element of the magical, the occult, the hermetics, is missing in Wittkower: his fellow Warburg colleague did not publish her findings for some years after his original lectures.[8]

At the University of California, Los Angeles, I have enjoyed the charismatic presence of Michael Allen whose works on Ficino's Platonic commentaries are legendary.[9] While physical proximity is a fact, it was the conscious propinquity of Carlo Ginzburg's writings on Piero della Francesca and Brian Copenhaver's on astrology, magic and hermeticism in the Renaissance that contributed to a conducive intellectual ambience for my speculations.[10] Speculations which, I acknowledge, are mine alone, and cannot match the intellectual rigour of these established scholars of Renaissance thought and practices.

Recently, Alfred Crosby has sketched in a history of number in the middle ages and the Renaissance.[11] He is especially concerned to portray a shift from a qualitative to a quantitative perception over this period. The essays in GROUND, the first part of the present book, are designed to give a feel for the many 'qualitative' interpretations of number in this same period without regard to the historian's interest in how we arrived at our modern 'quantitative' terms. Compared to the ambivalent poetics of number of the humanist period, modern number is positively gradgrind.

Paul F. Grendler's penetrating survey of Renaissance schooling reminded me of the influence of schooling on my own thought formations.[12] Mr Reynolds had taught me to read music as a choirboy; my first grammar school headmaster, Mr Norden, had personally introduced me to the theory of harmony and counterpoint at a time when he was writing a symphony for the school orchestra in which my father, a Master Organ Builder, played clarinet; and Mr Campbell had struggled against all natural habits to teach me Latin – 'There may come a time when mediaeval Latin will prove useful to you' – instead I learned translations of Caesar and Ovid off by heart for the examinations. So much for my school education, but Grendler's exceptional work gave me insights to the formation of a humanist's mind-set. In the Renaissance, beyond schooling, there was the quadrivium: arithmetic, geometry, music and astronomy. Beyond my schooling there was mathematics and then architecture. Alan Turing had recommended me to Dennis Babbage at Magdalene College to read mathematics. Both mathematicians had served during WWII at Bletchley Park and had worked in the teams that cracked the Nazi's Enigma code.[13] Unknowingly, I came to take almost all human activity as forms of encipherment and decipherment in some symbolic or iconic system. With the arrival of Leslie Martin as Professor of Architecture, I transferred to architecture.

Philosophically, since the 1960s, I have found an empathetic voice in the writings of Charles Sanders Peirce. He raised the aesthetic to a sovereign position among the normative sciences. As a young man, he had found the works of Schiller inspirational, and would later except Schelling from the crowd. There was a time when I read Schiller's *On the Aesthetic Education of Man* annually, and recently it had been extremely valuable to have access to an English translation of Schelling's *Philosophy of Art*.[14] I was aware of Umberto Eco's interest in Peirce during this period, and recently I was amused by the citations in *Foucault's Pendulum* which follow so closely my own readings and preoccupations.[15] Schelling provides the equation 'architecture = music', but close by he also states that 'architecture necessarily proceeds in its constructions according to arithmetical or, since it is music in *space*, geometric relationships'. A little further on appears the aphorism: 'The harmonic part of architecture refers primarily to proportions or relationships and is the ideal form of this art.'

One of Schelling's works is entitled *Bruno* after the humanist magus, Giordano Bruno.[16] It reveals a metaphysics sympathetic to Renaissance neo-platonism: and one that certainly does not exclude the divine. When Leon Battista Alberti applies the same rules to the country, as he does to the region, and then to the platform of a building – or says that a room is a small house is a small city – he is reciting the idea that Bruno Giordano is to reiterate a century later in the statement quoted by Schelling: 'Thus every single thing exhibits the universe, each in its own way.' At the very end of the dialogue, Schelling's Bruno quotes the magus Bruno again: 'To penetrate the deepest secrets of nature, one must not tire of inquiring into the opposed and antagonistc . . . . To discover their points of union is not the greatest task, but to do this and then develop its opposite elements out of their point of union, this is the genuine and deepest secret of art.

Here are two notions that I perceive as important in appreciating creative acts among humanists. The first is the idea of the artist working as second Nature, so that an artefact is designed as a microcosm of the universe. If the universe has mathematical origins – Pythagorean, or even more precisely, Timaean, after Plato – then so should the highest creations of humankind. The second idea is that opposites are to be resolved in the union of an artwork, but that emerging from this union should be new contrasts and oppositions. This is particularly evident in the mannerist architecture of Michelangelo, Giulio Romano, and their younger contemporary, Palladio. Both these notions find expression through the play of number. As Johann Reuchlin wrote in *De arte cabalistica*: 'The world is more perfect, the more it contains many modes of numbering'.[17] A third theme emerges from these two and that is that none of this play should be obvious: it is to be occult and esoteric for the digestion of those in the know. Certainly not for the vulgar. My refrain to students is: 'know your numbers.'

An architectonic study seeks an order beyond appearances. A formal study of humanist architectural production attempts to uncover the 'many modes of numbering' employed in each work, looks for the 'warring and opposite elements' which go to make an original microcosm echoing universal harmony. Such studies are simultaneously limited – ignoring almost all the most contingent characteristics of architecture – and yet expansive in drawing attention to the hard intellectual light which illuminates each work from the viewpoint of an eternal world of intelligibles, angels, gods. Again, I recall

12 P. F. Grendler, *Schooling in Renaissance Italy: Literacy and Learning 1300–1600*, John Hopkins University Press, Baltimore MD, 1989.

13 A. Hodges, *Alan Turing: The Enigma*, Burnett Books, London, 1983. As a boy I had briefly corresponded with Turing, then a Professor at Manchester University, over a generalization of complex numbers that had exercised me. In the present instance, it was G. Ifrah, *From One to Zero: a Universal History of Numbers*, Viking Penguin, New York NY, 1985, in his section 'Numerals and Letters' that directed my attention to the possibilities of number-letter encoding in architecture. He cites Arabic examples of chronograms in which a phrase represents a commemorative date on a building or monument. G. Scholem, *Kabbalah*, Dorset Press, New York NY, 1974, encouraged me in this same direction. I have probably been over-enthusiastic, but I sense there is some veracity in at least some of my speculations.

14 E. M. Wilkinson, L. A. Willoughby, *Friedrich Schiller: On the Aesthetic Education of Man in a Series of Letters*, Clarendon Press, Oxford 1967. D. W. Stott, *The Philosophy of Art: Friedrich Wilhelm Joseph Schelling*, University of Minnesota Press, Minneapolis MN, 1989.

15 U. Eco, *Foucault's Pendulum*, Harcourt Brace Jovanovich, San Diego CA 1989. I first encountered Eco in his writings on Charles Sanders Peirce. In this context, his *Art and Beauty in the Middle Ages*, Yale University Press, New Haven CT, 1986, has proved a valuable supplement to an essay that had a profound influence on me as a student – E. Panofsky, *Gothic Architecture and Scholasticism*, Archabbey Press, Latrobe PA, 1951. Even more relevant is Eco's *The Search for the Perfect Language (The Making of Europe)*. Blackwell, Oxford, 1997, which provides an appropriate linguistic background to this study.

16 M.G. Vater, *Bruno or On the Natural and the Divine Principle of Things: F.W.J. Schelling*, State University of New York Press, Albany NY, 1984.

17 M. and S. Goodman, *Johann Reuchlin: On the Art of the Kabbalah. De Arte Cabalistica*, Abaris Books, New York NY, 1983.

18 A sentiment supported by E. Panofsky, *Idea: A Concept in Art History*, Harper & Row, New York NY, 1986.

19 As a prominent leader in the field, Bruce Martin had introduced the concepts of modular coordination to us as students.

20 Original texts published since Wittkower include G. Zorzi's monumental documentation of the works and projects of Palladio, Neri Pozza Editore, Venice, 1958–68, M. Baxandall, *Painting and Experience in Fifteenth Century Italy*, Oxford University Press, Oxford, 1972, especially the essay 'Intervals and Proportions', L. Puppi, *Andrea Palladio*, Electa Editrice, Milan, 1973, H. Burns, B. Boucher, L. Fairbairn, *Andrea Palladio 1508–1580: The Portico and the Farm-yard*, Arts Council of Great Britain, London, 1973, F. Borsi, *Leon Battista Alberti*, Electa Editrice, Milan, 1975, D. Lewis, *The Drawings of Andrea Palladio*, The Foundation, Washington DC, 1981, J. Onians, *Bearers of Meaning: the Classical Orders in Antiquity, the Middle Ages, and the Renaissance*, Princeton University Press, Princeton NJ, 1988, M. Tafuri, *Venice and the Renaissance*, The MIT Press, Cambridge MA, 1989, J.S. Ackerman, *Palladio*, Penguin Books, Harmondsworth, 1966, and *Distance Points: Essays in Theory and Renaissance Art and Architecture*, The MIT Press, Cambridge MA, 1991, J. Rykwert, A. Engel, eds., *Leon Battista Alberti*, Olivetti/Electa, Milan, 1994, B. Boucher, *Andrea Palladio: The Architect in his Time*, Abbeville Press, New York NY, 1994, H. A. Millon, V. M. Lampugnani, eds., *The Renaissance from Brunelleschi to Michelangelo: the Representation of Architecture*, Rizzoli, New York NY 1997, J. Rykwert, *The Dancing Column: On Order in Architecture*, The MIT Press, Cambridge MA, 1997, and R. T. Tavernor, *Palladio and Palladianism*, Thames and Hudson, London, 1991, and *On Alberti and The Art of Building*, Yale University Press, New Haven CT, 1998. The last decade has seen new, annotated translations of Alberti's *De re aedificatoria* (1989), Serlio's *Tutte l'opere d'architettura et prospetiva* (1996) and Palladio's (1997) *I quattro libri dell'architettura* – these are fully referenced later.

21 E. Wind, *Pagan Mysteries in the Renaissance*, Faber and Faber, London, 1968.

Schelling who did not see art in the mere need and utility of architecture: 'architecture can appear as free and beautiful only inasmuch as it becomes the expression of ideas, an image of the universe and of the absolute'.[18] I am not speaking of architecture today. I use Schelling because, writing in a period of exquisite neo-classicism, he seems closest at recalling the motivations of the humanists and their classical groundings.

Wittkower did a great deal more than raise questions concerning proportional theory in the Renaissance. He made us – at least the English – look again at Alberti, Serlio and Palladio. He suggested affinities between the researches of Le Corbusier and modular coordination in the twentieth century, and the humanistic approaches of the fifteenth and sixteenth centuries which contemporary British architects like Alison and Peter Smithson were able to exploit.[19] At the time, few texts existed in print in the English language on Renaissance humanist architect-theoreticians. An Italian facsimile of Palladio's *I Quattro Libri dell'Architettura* was published in 1951, and a reproduction of James Leoni's 1726 English translation of Alberti's *Ten Books on Architecture*, edited by Joseph Rykwert, was published by Alec Tiranti in 1955. I acquired both of these as a student and had them bound in navy blue hard-covers along with Louis Sullivan's *Kindergarten Chats*. These three volumes with their uniform gilt lettering that I commissioned from the binder became, for me, the voices of true architecture. The 'powers' of Sullivan have turned out to be relatives of the 'potencies' of Schelling and the connections with Renaissance thought are not as distant as might first be imagined. Certainly, Sullivan's idea of functionalism includes the functions of satisfying the cultural and higher spiritual necessities of humankind, not just the utilitarian needs for which 'form follows function' has often, and very mistakenly, been cited.

The year 1999 celebrates the fiftieth anniversary of Rudolf Wittkower's *Principles of Architecture in the Age of Humanism* which began a renewal of Renaissance studies in architecture now coming to fruition.[20] These new editions and commentaries on primary sources are significant works in which English scholars – Joseph Rykwert, Robert Tavernor, Neil Leach, Vaughan Hart, Peter Hicks, and Richard Schofield – and their American publishers have made truly significant contributions to Renaissance architectural studies.

The four essays in the second part of this book, FOUNDATION, examine architectural practices before the Renaissance. It is understood that Roman architecture was the model. The archaeological studies of Palladio affirm this. Yet the Roman, if the author of *De architectura* is to be believed, owed much to the Greek. Then again, the Roman and Greek cultures were pagan, while that of the Renaissance was ostensibly Christian.[21] The Judaeo-Christian tradition had to be influential. While the northern Gothic style in Italy might have been suppressed after Milan Cathedral, the architectonics of Christian and Hebrew thought were necessarily retained and amalgamated in practice: especially the cabalistic tendencies of Spanish Jews and Christians. For this reason, I have re-examined the Biblical accounts of the Ark, the Tabernacle and the Temples. This Judaic tradition seems to have been neglected, yet it must surely be taken into account. The consequence of this preliminary study is that proportional techniques attributed to the Greeks and their followers, were already understood and appreciated a millennium earlier at the time of Moses, and then with Solomon. Pythagoras, indeed, was the transmitter of ancient knowledge which Plato transcribed, but neither Pythagoras nor Plato were arithmetical and geometrical originators: at least this is the conclusion to be drawn from the Biblical descriptions, and my interpretations, of Judaic architectural practices.

These four essays show a persistent interest in evoking some, or all, of the classical problems of the diagonal of the square, the altitude of an equilateral triangle, duplicating the cube, and squaring the circle in architectural form. It is as if these problems hold the secret of the universe which must be present in any artificial 'small world' for it to mimic universal harmony: the moral imperative to be at one with Nature. Another theme is that of the primacy of 'the word'. Starting with the Tabernacle and the Solomon's Temple, numbers are associated with words, and names in particular. An examination of Vitruvius' basilica in the Julian colony of Fano reveals that the author of *De architectura*, Marcus Vitruvius Pollio, may well be a fiction of the Roman polymath, Marcus Terentius Varro. This is the most extreme speculation to come out of the architectonic analyses undertaken in these essays, but one to which circumstantial evidence gives plausible credence.

The third part of the present book, EDIFICE, comprises four essays in which I discuss the architectonics of Renaissance architecture. I revisit the matter of centrality which Wittkower had addressed and examine in detail projects by Alberti, Serlio and Palladio. The manner in which I do this may seem to be overly complicated by the standards of current architectural studies. Architectural students, in my experience, rarely look at literature in other arts. Go into a music library and see the shelves of musical scores. Ask in an architectural library for architectural drawings of masterworks and the question is likely to be answered by puzzlement. A musician rarely listens to a piece of music without a score in hand. An architect looks at a building without drawings. A literary scholar learns poetry by heart, a musician remembers a musical score note by note, yet most architects are unable to draw the plans, section and elevations of a work of architecture not their own. There is no architectural writing, to my knowledge, equivalent in technical depth of the kind to be found in the field of music.[22] Or imagine a book on Palladio's villas to match Helen Vendler's study of Shakespeare's sonnets. She quotes W.H. Auden whose interests in a poem are two: the technical aspects of a 'verbal contraption' and the moral question 'what kind of guy inhabits this poem?' As Vendler says, the question cannot be addressed until the technical issues are appreciated: 'It is the workings of the verbal construct that give evidence of the moral stance of the poet.'[23] Even the formal studies of languages themselves have far more to offer than vague and shallow metaphors appropriated by architectural apologists.[24] Where are the musicologists or the linguists of architecture?[25]

The essays in *Architectonics of Humanism* attempt one such beginning: their obsessive interest is the 'architectural contraption'. Others have dealt with the social and political issues of architecture in the Renaissance, or the psychological aspects of Renaissance art, or the perceptual, especially the matter of perspective theory with its relation to geometrical developments.[26] These are not my concerns, although they are part and parcel of the living art of the period.

While it has been common analytical practice to overlay geometrical figures on architectural schemata, with all the incumbent inaccuracies of small scaled drawings and thick pencils, the approach taken here relies essentially on counting, not estimating. Numbers are taken from drawings, or are given by counting the modules indicated by the designer or from individual building elements, about which there can be little argument. Nor is there any ambivalence about the arithmetic rational convergents to geometric figures even though they are multivalued: classical algorisms and Renaissance methods of computation limit the set of options among such values. This approach to analysis has a methodological advantage over prejudiced

22 For example, a mainstream text such as L. B. Meyer, *Style and Music: Theory, History and Ideology*, University of Pennsylvania Press, Philadelphia PA, 1989. I am unaware of anything in contemporary architectural writing to match Kathryn Bailey, *The Twelve-note Music of Anton Webern: Old Forms in a New Language*, Cambridge University Press, Cambridge, 1991, or of an architect approaching his or her art with the keen, reflective intellectuality of Pierre Boulez, *Boulez on Music Today*, Faber and Faber, London, 1971, or *Orientations: Collected Writings*, Harvard University Press, Cambridge MA, 1986, especially his essays in the section 'Frenzy and Organization'. Perhaps, the architect, O.M. Ungers, comes closet today.

23 H. Vendler, *The Art of Shakespeare's Sonnets*, The Belknap Press, Harvard University Press, Cambridge MA, 1997.

24 I have in mind the tedious and indolent dropping of names – the recitation of Peircian syntax, semantics and pragmatics, Saussurian langue and parole, Chomskian deep or surface structures, the semiology of Barthes, the semiotics of Eco, the différances of Derrida, Gadamar's hermeneutics, or psycho-poetics derived from Lacan – in architectural writings over the last half century unaccompanied by the difficult, focused and cumulative work needed to investigate the subject, in and of itself, as these scholars of linguistics have pursued their own enquiries.

25 Terry Knight suggests a possible direction that such discussion might take in her *Transformations of Style: a Formal Approach to Stylistic Change and Innovation in the Visual Arts*, Cambridge University Press, Cambridge, 1994. In a different vein, J. P. Steadman, *Architectural Morphology: an Introduction to the Geometry of Architectural Plans*, Pion, London, 1983. George Stiny's original writings on shape grammars, which mark fundamental and logical differences between symbolic languages and languages of shape, are exceptional. A synoptic advertisement for his forthcoming book appears in the journal, *Planning and Design*, 25, 1998, G. Stiny, 'Shape'.

26 Especially J. White, *The Birth and Rebirth of Pictorial Space*, Faber and Faber, London, 1957, M. Kemp, *The Science of Art: Optical Themes in Western Art from Brunelleschi to Seurat*, Yale University Press, New Haven CT, 1990, J. V. Field, *The Invention of Infinity: Mathematics and Art in the Renaissance*, Oxford University Press, Oxford, 1997. R. Evans *The Projective Cast: Architecture and its Three Goemetries* MIT Press, Cambridge MA, 1995.

eye-balling, where the zealot has a preconceived view that triangles, or squares, or golden sections will be found uniformly applied throughout a work of a particular period or style.

My approach is pluralistic and makes the assumption that designers use whatever knowledge they have available to them, and may well want to display their learning in a spirit of intellectual generosity. In truth, the Renaissance might be called the era of conspicuous erudition in which patrons, scholars and artists displayed their breadth of classical learning in various works and commissions. Such polymathic expression will have been conspicuous only to the learned of the day. Its immediacy is lost to modern commentators since the intellectual ground has shifted – arithmetic is no longer governed by Nicomachus, or geometry by Euclid's thirteen books, or music by Boethius, or astronomy by Ptolemy. The period under review is the very same historic moment when this ground is ruptured irrevocably. Our everyday eyes no longer see with the *mentalité* of the age of humanism: indeed, for seeing their works, such eyes are no better than those of the uncouth of that time.

Today, any attempt to reconstruct the vision of that age requires an effort to appreciate the body of learning, which comprised the mental set of its actors; a set in which the heritages of Greek, Roman, Arabic and Hebrew cultures are stewed in a pot of mediaeval cast, under the heady spells of the Holy Roman Empire, rising Protestantism, Eastern Orthodoxy, the conquering Ottomans, and the Jewish diaspora subsequent to the defeat of the Moors in Spain.

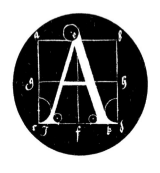

GROUND

1

CLASSICAL ARITHMETIC

Among the writers before 1000CE who may have influenced humanist design computations are Euclid, Archimedes, Nicomachus, Theon of Smyrna, Heron of Alexander, Ptolemy, Pappus, Iamblichus, Boethius, al-Khindi. After 1000CE, Leonardo of Pisa, Nicole Oresme, Regiomontanus, Piero della Francesca, Nicholas Cusanus, Nicholas Chuquet, Luca Pacioli, Cosimo Bartoli, Giovanni-Battista Benedetti, Silvio Belli might be included among mediaeval and Renaissance writers.

There are several themes that may be extracted from these writings. From Euclid comes a particular view of ratio and proportion which is no longer current. In the modern view, the concept of fraction runs together with ratio, and this was simply not true of the classical position. Number, too, in classical terms, is conceived in very different ways from the modern sense: this is to be seen in the writings of the neo-Pythagoreans: Nicomachus, Theon of Smyrna and Iamblichus. The comparison of ratio with musical harmony is far more generous in the classical contribution of Ptolemy, than in the modern view just then emerging in the sixteenth century. Boethius in Latin, and al-Khindi in Arabic, sustained many of these ideas in the intervening mediaeval period.

It is generally agreed that Leonardo Pisano, also known as Fibonacci, initiated the process of modernizing arithmetic notation in Europe by adopting Arabic numerals. Yet two centuries later, Alberti, in his Latin texts, remains reluctant to use the new characters; while another century on, Palladio is quite comfortable with them. Alberti's close contemporary, Piero della Francesca, certainly reflects some of Leonardo Pisano's mathematical interests, but the sequence which bears Fibonacci's name today is not one of them and is unlikely to have played any part in Renaissance design computations. The chief contribution of Piero della Francesca is the arithmetization of geometry. This theme was made popular by Luca Pacioli's printed edition of Piero della Francesca's manuscripts. Both Nicholas Cusanus and Regiomontanus were known to Alberti in Rome in the court of Nicholas V. The outstanding mathematician of this mathematically numerate trio was undoubtedly Regiomontanus whose trigonometrical work is foundational.

Another mathematical interest, closely related to the arithmetization of geometry, involved the solution of quadratic and higher degree equations. To arrive at numerical solutions required the extraction of roots: square roots, cubic roots and so on. In fact, Nicole Oresme had developed notation to handle fractional powers of a number in the fourteenth century, probably building on earlier work by Thomas Bradwardine who had investigated ratios between differently powered numbers.

Archimedes had published excellent values of quantities such as π and the square root of 3, but his method for doing so was never made explicit and remains obscure. Several classical algorisms were known for extracting square roots. In particular, Theon of Smyrna published the algorism for extracting the square root of 2, and Heron of Alexander provides formulæ for any integer. Towards the end of the fifteenth century, the French mathematician, Nicholas Chuquet, described in manuscript a general algorism for extracting the square root of any non-square number, and Chuquet's algorism was appropriated and published in printed form by Estienne de la Roche at the beginning of the sixteenth century.

In the sixteenth century, Cosimo Bartoli, translator of Alberti's *De re aedificatoria*, published *Del modo di misurare* which is mainly translations into the vernacular of Latin texts by writers such as Oronce Finè, Albrecht Dürer, and Alberti himself. Bartoli was known to Palladio. The work of the mathematician Benedetti is altogether more original, but his influence among designers is unclear, although the pictorial manner of depicting the composition of ratios is 'designerly'. Finally, Silvio Belli was a close acquaintance of Palladio. His *Proportione, et Proportionalità* contains similar arithmetical materials to be found in Daniele Barbaro's commentary on Vitruvius.

The mathematicians

Euclid (*c*330–275BCE) was author of *The Elements*. Mediaeval translations from Arabic version into Latin include manuscripts by the Englishman Athelhard of Bath (*c*1130), Gherard of Cremona (1114–1187) and Johannes Campanus of Novaro (*c*1270). The Campanus translation was eventually printed in Venice in 1482. According to Heath it was 'the first printed mathematical book of any importance'.[1] In 1471, or a few years earlier, the German mathematician Regiomontanus saw some manuscripts in Greek which may have been in the collection of his friend Bessarion – former Metropolitan of Nicea and by then a distinguished Cardinal of the Roman church. The first direct translation from the Greek was published in Venice by Bartolomeo Zamberti in 1505, with subsequent editions in 1510, Paris, 1516, and Basle, 1537, 1546, 1558. Zamberti (1473-post 1530) attacked the Campanus version, 'ille interpres barbarissimus'. Unfortunately the unidentified Greek manuscripts from which he worked appear to have been poor, with many interpolations. In defence, Luca Pacioli (*c*1445–1517) produced a revised version of the Campanus edition 'interpres fidissimus', Venice 1509. He had delivered a much acclaimed lecture on Euclid's Book V concerning the proportional theory of magnitudes in the previous year to a group of patricians and scholars at the church of San Bartolomeo di Rialto. The first Greek edition was printed in 1533 in Basle and this was the chief text used in the most successful translations by Frederico Commandino (1509–1575), in Latin 1572 and Italian 1575.

Archimedes 287–212BCE enumerated the semi-regular polyhedra which carry his name today as well as making major contributions to mechanics and hydrostatics. Translations of his works were actively solicited from the middle of the fifteenth century, especially by Pope Nicholas V. Commandino provided the standard Latin versions in the sixteenth century.[2]

Nicomachus of Gerasa is thought to have lived in the metropolitan area of Decapolis (in what is now Israel) in the second century CE. He probably received his mathematical education from the school at Alexander. His *Introduction to*

1 T. L. Heath, *Euclid: the Thirteen Books of the Elements*, Cambridge University Press, Cambridge, 1926.
2 R. L. Rose, *The Italian Renaissance of Mathematics: Studies of Humanists and Mathematicians from Petrarch to Galileo*, Librairie Droz, Genève, 1975, also T. L. Heath, *A History of Greek Mathematics*, Clarendon Press, Oxford, 1921, II, pp. 16–109.

Arithmetic became the standard Greek arithmetical text of the Western world well into the eighteenth century. It was translated into Latin by Boethius and in this accessible form became a primary influence throughout the mediaeval period, into the Renaissance and beyond.[3]

Leonardo Pisano was born in 1170 and died sometime after 1240. 'Fibonacci' is a nineteenth-century sobriquet never used by Leonardo. He did, however, use the Latin expression *filius Bonacci* after his father Guglielmo Bonaccio. His *Liber abacci* (1202 and 1228) is a remarkable compendium of arithmetical and algebraic knowledge for its time which set the curriculum for mediaeval schools of abaccists, cossists and rechen-meisters. It begins with the revolutionary declaration: 'Nouem figure indorum he sunt

9, 8, 7, 6, 5, 4, 3, 2, 1.

Cum his itaque nouem figuris, et cum hoc signo 0, quod arabice zephirium appellatur, scribitur quilibet numerus.' With these words, the Hindu/Arabic numerals, including zero, were formally introduced to the West. His *Liber abacci* (1228) includes the famous rabbit-breeding problem with its pattern of population growth 1, 1, 2, 3, 5, 8, 13, ... Leonardo does not make a specific study of this sequence: for him, it is a solution to a problem, not a subject of interest in itself. The connection of this sequence with the 'golden section' is first made by Kepler in the seventeenth century. Examples of Leonardo's, from the *Liber abacci*, his *Practica geometriae* (1220) – based on Euclid and Heron of Alexander, and largely concerned with the measurement of figures and shapes – and *Liber quadratorum* (1225), are to be found in works by Piero della Francesca and Luca Pacioli in the fifteenth century.[4] Theon of Smyrna, who wrote *Mathematics Useful for Understanding Plato* was a close contemporary of Nicomachus and their works parallel one another.[5]

Heron of Alexander flourished in the third century CE. His reputation was well regarded in the Renaissance, but few of his original works were available. His *Metrica* remained an unrecognized manuscript in Constantinople until 1896, yet materials from it seem to have been known to writers in the fourteenth century, and Luca Pacioli and others used a method, similar to his, of extracting the square roots of non-square numbers in the sixteenth century. The *Metrica* also enumerated the thirteen Archimedean semi-regular solids which were to prove so fascinating to Dürer, Pacioli, and Barbaro.[6]

Claudius Ptolemaeus was of Alexander and produced his mathematical and astronomical works during the first half of the second century. It is the Arabic translation *Almagest* which is best known, and it was not until 1538 that the Greek *Syntaxis* was printed in Basle. An unsatisfactory Arabo–Latin version was made for Pope Nicholas V in 1451 by Georgius Trapezuntius. A revised edition by Lucas Gauricus was printed in Venice in 1528. The *Syntaxis* contains an exact construction for the regular pentagon as well as a table of chords. Ptolemy's other influential works include his *Harmonics* which was translated by Nicolò Leoniceno in 1499 at the request of the musical authority Franchino Gaffurio, by Giovanni Battista Augio in 1545 for the maestro di canto of San Petronio in Bologna, and the first printed edition by Antonio Gogava (Venice, 1546 and 1547). Gogava is known to have consulted Daniele Barbaro on this edition which also included translations of Aristoxenus – the authority whom Vitruvius had used. Barbaro used Ptolemy to counter the Vitruvian musical view in his commentaries. Ptolemy's *Tetrabiblos* provided a considered approach to astrological matters, some of which is to be found

3 M. L. D'Ooge trans, *Nicomachus of Gerasa: Introduction to Arithmetic* with studies in Greek arithmetic by F. E. Robbins and L. C. Karpinski, University of Michigan Press, Ann Arbor, 1938; also A. Barker, *Greek Musical Writings Volume II: Harmonic and Acoustic Theory*, Cambridge University Press, Cambridge, 1989, pp. 245–69 for an English translation of Nicomachus' *Enchiridon*, a manual on musical harmonics; F. R. Levi, *The Harmonics of Nicomachus and the Pythagorean Tradition*, American Philological Society, University Park PA, 1975. On a recent assessment of the Pythagorean content of Nicomachus' philosophical position refer to D. J. O'Meara, *Pythagoras Revived: Mathematics and Philosophy in Late Antiquity* Clarendon Press, Oxford, 1989, pp. 14–22.
4 Fibonacci's work was not published in print until B. Boncompagni, *Scritti di Leonardo Pisano*, Rome, 1857–62. Most scholars continue to defer to Boncompagni. For a short biography see L. E. Sigler, *Leonardo Pisano Fibonacci: The Book of Squares*, Academic Press, Boston, 1987. Also N. N. Vorob'ev, *Fibonacci Numbers*, Pergamon Press, Oxford, 1961.
5 M. J. B. Allen, *Nuptial Arithmetic: Marsilio Ficino's Commentary on the Fatal Number in Book VIII of Plato's Republic*, University of California Press, Los Angeles, 1994, for remarks on Ficino's unpublished Latin translation. Ficino's commentary provides an excellent summary and understanding of the chief contents of both Nicomachus' and Theon's arithmetic tracts. There is an English translation from the 1892 Greek/French edition of J. Dupuis by R. and D. Lawlor Wizard's Bookshelf, San Diego, 1979, also note Barker, *op. cit.*, pp. 209–13.
6 *Op. cit.* Heath, *History*, II pp. 298–354.

in later sections of *Harmonics*. Theoretical concepts in his *Geographia*, upon which Regiomontanus had written a *Commentaria Magna* in the mid-fifteenth century, may well have influenced Alberti's cartographical studies, perspective theories, and sculptural mensurations.[7]

Pappus lived at the end of the third century. He wrote a commentary on Ptolemy's *Syntaxis*, but is best known for his own *Synagoge*, or *Collection* in eight books. Greek versions of Pappus were in all the principal Renaissance collections. Its contents, which included material on the classical means, a curious statement on the geometrical sagacity of bees, new constructions for the five Platonic polyhedra, and a recounting of the Archimedean semi-regular solids, seem to have been well known before Commandino translated the *Synagoge* into Latin and its posthumous publication in Venice, 1589.[8]

Iamblichus flourished in the fourth century. He may be the author of *Theologumena arithmetica* which, in any case, is a compilation of writings by Nicomachus and others. He did much to direct neo-Platonism back towards the tenets and mysteries of Pythagoras. Allen believes that *Theologumena arithmetica* may have been known to Ficino; it is certain that its general contents were well known in some form or other during the Renaissance.[9]

Anicius Manlius Severinus Boethius (*c*480–524) is arguably one of the most influential Latin philosophers during the scholastic middle ages, especially in lending authority to the quadrivium as the subjects of higher education: arithmetic, geometry, music and astronomy. Here, the interest is in his Latin versions of Nicomachus: the treatises on arithmetic and music in particular.[10]

Ya'qub ibn Isbaq al-Khindi, styled the 'Philosopher of the Arabs', thrived during the first half of the tenth century. It is probable that Daniele Barbaro's interest in al-Khindi arose from a common concern in optics – in a translation by Gherard of Cremona, al-Khindi's *De aspectibus* was widely known. Barbaro has been labelled the father of the modern camera. His *La Pratica della Perspettiva* (Venice, 1569) demonstrates his profound and skilful interest in optics. Al-Khindi developed a theory of emanations through light which gave physical substance to neo-Platonic speculations of an astrological kind. A mathematical work on proportion translated into Latin as *Libellum sex quantitatum* is used by Daniele Barbaro in his Vitruvian commentaries.[11]

Nicole Oresme (*c*1325–1382) contributed *De proportionibus proportionum* which developed concepts first found in Thomas Bradwardine *Tractatus de proportionibus* (1328, Venice edition 1505). Bradwardine tackles certain problems raised by the Aristotelian approach to velocity. He builds on the proportional theories of Euclid and Boethius, but finds essentially that he needs to deal with geometric proportionalities rather than the standard arithmetic ones: thus instead of the linear relation $p = mq$ between p and q, he examines what we would call the exponential relation $p = q^m$. All the numbers in these cases being understood to be rational. Oresme some thirty years later takes the next step and allows for incommensurable, irrational numbers. By the fifteenth century, the upshot of these developments is that it was understood that powers of numbers could be fractional or irrational. It was also understood that 'parts' might be, for example, $2^{1/3}$ and $2^{2/3}$ rather than simply ⅓ and ⅔. All this was to lead to Simon Stevin's 1585 dismissal of the classical distinctions between number and magnitude in favour of the modern view of a continuum of number, and in particular, to his mathematical description of what musicians call equal temperament – the division of the octave into twelve equal–intervals.[12]

7 For English translations of *Syntaxis* see Heath, *ibid.* pp. 356–439; of *Geographia* see E. Luther trans, *Claudius Ptolemy: Geography*, New York Public Library, New York, 1932; and of *Harmonics* see Barker trans, *op. cit.* pp. 270–391. For Aristoxenus see Barker, *ibid.* pp. 119–189.

8 *Op. cit.*, Heath, *History*, II, pp. 355–439.

9 *Op. cit.*, Allen, n.79, p. 34. See the English translation by R. Waterfield trans, *The Theology of Arithmetic: On the Mystical, Mathematical and Cosmological Symbolism of the First Ten Numbers*, Phanes Press, Grand Rapids, 1988; also O'Meara, *op. cit.*, especially Part 1, 'The Revival of Pythagoreanism in the Neoplatonic School', pp. 9–108.

10 M. Masi trans, *Boethian Number Theory: a translation of the 'De institutione arithmetica'*, Rodopi, Amsterdam, 1983, and C. Bower trans, *Fundamentals of Music*, Yale University Press, New Haven, 1989.

11 For al-Khindi's occult influence during the sixteenth century, see N. H. Clulee, *John Dee's Natural Philosophy: Between Science and Religion*, Routledge, London, 1986, pp. 52–8. On his optical theory see D. L. Lindberg 'Alkindi's Critique of Euclid's Theory of Vision', *Isis* 62, 1979, pp. 469–89.

12 H. L. Crosby Jr, *Thomas of Bradwardine: His 'Tractatus de proportionibus'*, University of Wisconsin Press, Madison, 1955; G. Molland, *Thomas Bradwardine, Geometria Speculativa*, Franz Steiner Verlag, Stuttgart, 1989; E. Grant, *Nicole Oresme: 'De proportionibus proportionum' and 'Ad pauca respicientes'*, University of Wisconsin Press, Madison, 1966; A. D. Fokker, ed., *The Principal Works of Simon Stevin: Music*, C. V. Swets & Zeitlinger, Amsterdam, 1966.

Regiomontanus, Johann Müller (1436–1476), adopted his Latin name from that of his home town of Königsberg . He was brought to Rome by Pope Sixtus IV and was an acquaintance of L. B. Alberti, and Nicholas Cusanus. His *De triangulis* is considered to be the first treatise to establish trigonometry as an independent subject. He played a central role in the renaissance of mathematics.[13]

Piero della Francesca (*c*1410–1496) is best known today as the painter of the frescoes at Cappella Maggiore, San Francesco, Arezzo, among other exceptional works. In the Renaissance, Vasari remembers him first as a distinguished arithmetician and geometer whose original manuscripts had been plagiarized by a younger colleague – Luca Pacioli. There is little doubt that Piero possessed a fine mathematical intelligence, and a comparison of his *Trattato d'abaco* and *Libellus de quinque corporibus regularibus* with Alberti's *Ludi rerum mathematicarum* shows him to be more than an adequate amateur. Unlike Piero, Alberti leaves no evidence of original mathematical skills beyond what might be expected from a well-trained graduate of the quadrivium. Piero builds on the tradition established by predecessors such as Leonardo Pisano and Thomas Bradwardine. In *Trattato*, Piero describes over fifty algebraic forms including cubic equations, biquadratics and equations of the fifth degree.[14]

Nicholas Cusanus (1401–1464) was a critic of scholastic Aristotelianism and a protagonist of Platonism. He was made a Cardinal in 1446 and was at the Papal court of Pius II in 1458. He was a tireless advocate of the mathematical approach to natural philosophy, but his mathematical abilities were more enthusiastic than professional. A tract on squaring the circle was described by Regiomontanus as being the work of a 'geometra ridiculus'. Nevertheless, Nicholas' philosophical drive gave initial impetus to the new science movement.[15]

Nicholas Chuquet lived in France during the fifteenth century. He died in Lyon in 1487 or 1488. He is considered to be the most distinguished and original French mathematician of his generation. His manuscript *Triparty en la science des nombres* was written in 1484. The work is in three parts: the first deals with traditional arithmetic matters although Chuquet concludes this section with 'a rule of intermediate numbers' which is used in the second part where an algorism for determining the roots of non-square numbers is presented. The third part of the manuscript presents Chuquet's approach to algebra. Chuquet does not deal with fractional powers in the manner of Oresme. A partial version of this work was published without acknowledgement by Estienne de la Roche, *Laritsmethique nouellement . . .* (Lyons, 1520).[16]

Luca Pacioli (*c*1445–1517) published three significant mathematical texts: *Summa de Arithmetica, Geometria, Proportione et Proportionalità* (Venice,1494), *De divina proportione* (Venice, 1509), and an edition of Campanus' Latin translation of Euclid (Venice, 1509). The first has been described by D. E. Smith as 'a remarkable compilation with almost no originality', and by P. L. Rose as 'scarcely an improvement on the mediaeval Fibonacci *corpus*' which nevertheless 'succeeded in laying out the boundaries of contemporary mathematical knowledge and so supplied a programme of sorts for the renaissance of mathematics'. The first part of the *Summa* is devoted to arithmetic derived from Leonardo Pisano and Piero della Francesca, and the second part is largely a recapitulation of Leonardo's *Practica Geometria*. Girolamo Cardano devotes a whole chapter of his *Practica Arithmeticae, & Mensurandi singularis* (1539) to correcting Pacioli's errors. *De divina proportione* has established a cult status among sacred geometry followers. It really is three unrelated books. The first sets out to demonstrate an analogy between the properties of the extreme and

13 Chapter 4, 'Regiomontanus in Italy', pp. 90–117 in Rose, *op. cit.*

14 M. D. Davis, *Piero della Francesca's Mathematical Treatises*, Longo Editore, Ravenna, 1977 ; R. Lightbown, *Piero della Francesca*, Abbeville Press, New York, 1992; S. A. Jayawardene, 'The *Trattato d'abaco* of Piero della Francesca' in *Cultural Aspects of the Italian Renaissance: Essays in Honor of Paul Oskar Kristeller*, C. Clough ed., Manchester, 1976; G. Vasari, *Lives of the Painters, Sculptors and Architects*, Alfred A. Kopf, New York, 1996, first published in Venice in 1550 and in a second edition 1568. For Piero's closeness to Alberti see F. Borsi, *Leon Battista Alberti*, Phaidon, Oxford, 1975, p. 199. An excellent contextual ground is C. Ginzburg, *The Enigma of Piero – Piero della Francesca: The Baptism, The Arezzo Cycle, The Flagellation*, Verso, London, 1985.

15 P. M. Watts, *Nicholas Cusanus: A Fifteenth Century Vision of Man*, Leiden, 1982; also Rose *op. cit.*

16 G. Flegg, C. Hay, B. Moss, *Nicholas Chuquet, Renaissance Mathematician*, D. Reidel, Dordrecht, 1985.

mean ratio – later to be known as the 'golden section' among other names – and the divine nature of God; the second is a summary of Vitruvius in which the extreme and mean ratio plays no aesthetic part whatsoever; and the third is mostly based on Piero della Francesca, *Libellus de quinque corporibus regularibus*, with the famous illustrations and alphabet design by Leonardo da Vinci. Pacioli's edition of Euclid revives the mediaeval translation of Campanus in a deliberate attack on the more recent version of Zamberti (see Euclid, n.1). Pacioli's chief contribution was to bring the works of Fibonacci and Piero della Francesca – without due acknowledgement – to the attention of his contemporaries, since neither was to receive independent publication until the nineteenth century, and thereby to set the benchmark for the rapid development of algebra in the sixteenth century.[17]

Cosimo Bartoli (1503–1572) is chiefly remembered as the translator of Alberti's works and particularly *Dell'architettura* (Florence, 1550) in the 'Florentine vernacular'. His *Del modo di misurare* (Venice, 1564) is essentially a translation of other practical texts including Oronce Finè, *Protomathesis*, illustrating the uses of various measuring instruments, some materials from Alberti, *Ludi Matematici,* a little from Dürer, *Underweysung der Messung*, and some materials from Gemma Frisius, *Libellus de locorum describendorum ratione*, on triangulation in surveying. The book includes a table of square roots up to 662 borrowed from the Spaniard, Rojas Sarmiento.[18]

Giovanni-Battista Benedetti (1530–1590) is said to have provided the mathematical prelude to Galileo's 'general overthrow of Aristotelian science'.[19] His *Diversarum Speculationem Liber* provides a contemporary source of illustrations for numerical factors and the composition of ratios.[20]

Silvio Belli (d.1575) wrote two books, the popular *Libro del mesurar con la vista* (Venice, 1565) which went through five more editions up to 1595, and *Proportione, et Proportionalità* (Venice, 1573). Both books are elementary, and neither advance the mathematical field. The first covers much of the ground found in Bartoli's *Del modo di misurare*, and the second could almost be said to be an arithmetical companion to Barbaro's commentary on Vitruvius' Book III and proportional theory. Belli, like Bartoli, does not get a mention in Rose's magisterial survey of Renaissance mathematics. They are clearly minor figures. But they relate to architectural activities: Bartoli through his work on Alberti, and Belli through his friendship with Palladio. Palladio consulted Silvio Belli when writing his report around 1570 on the completion of Milan Cathedral. Earlier, the two had received remunerations for their work on the wooden theatre in the Roman style built for the Olympic Academy in 1561.[21]

17 M. D. Davis, *op. cit.*, especially Appendices I and II, pp. 98–123, where exact comparisons are drawn between Pacioli's text and the manuscripts of Piero della Francesca. Also E. Giusti, C. Maccagni, *Luca Pacioli e la Matematica del Rinascimento*, Giunti, Florence, 1994.

18 J. Bryce, *Cosimo Bartoli: The Career of a Florentine Polymath,* Librairie Droz, Genève, 1983.

19 Rose, *op. cit.*, p. 38.

20 *Ibid.*, Chapter 7, 'The New Science of Tartaglia and Benedetti', pp. 151–58.

21 On Belli and Palladio, see R. Wittkower, *Architectural Principles in the Age of Humanism,* Tiranti, London, 1952, p. 129; also L. Puppi, *Andrea Palladio*, p. 21, p. 28, n.115, pp. 185–6, p. 242.

EUCLIDEAN ARITHMETIC

There are effectively three distinct approaches to proportional theory in Euclid. There is a geometric theory which hinges on theorems of similarity and especially those about similar triangles. Illustrations of these theorems occur, for example, in Alberti and are later reiterated in Bartoli. (Figs. 1, 2).

Then there are two arithmetic theories of proportion. Heath has commented on the essential redundancy of having two theories.[1] In Book V, Euclid deals with relations between magnitudes, while in Book VII the propositions are confined to relations between numbers. Some magnitudes behave just like numbers, but other magnitudes like the incommensurable diameter of a square do not.[2] The theory for magnitudes developed in Book V is thus the more general of the two theories, while Book VII sets out the special theory for numbers only. The special theory is the one that is computable in practice.

For Euclid, a number is a multitude of units, and a magnitude 'is a part of another magnitude, the less of the greater, when it measures the greater.'[3] In the case of the square and its diameter, the magnitude of the side is not a part of the magnitude of the diameter since it does not measure it. In fact, the side goes into the diameter just once, leaving something over. This remainder is another magnitude. Does this third magnitude measure the side? The answer is no. It goes into the side just twice with yet another, fourth magnitude left over. In turn, this fourth magnitude is found not to measure the previous, third magnitude although it too goes into the leftover magnitude twice. There is no end to this procedure. There is no ultimate 'unit' which measures the diameter of the square in relation to its side. The two magnitudes are incommensurable. The diameter is said to be irrational with respect to the side.[4]

Suppose on the other hand two multitudes had been compared, say, the numbers 17 and 12. The number 12 goes into 17 once with 5 leftover. The number 5 goes into 12 twice with 2 leftover. The number 2 goes into 5 twice again with 1 leftover. This unit 1 goes into 2 exactly twice. The algorism concludes within practical limits with the discovery of a unit which measures the number 17 with respect to the number 12. These two numbers are not incommensurable. The same unit measures 17 seventeen times, and 12 twelve times. It will be noted that the pattern is the same in the two examples. This way of comparing one magnitude, or one number, against another, is said to be *anthyphairetic*, after the Greek, which implies successive subtractions.[5] In the case of the numbers 17 and 12 the anthyphairesis 'once, twice, twice, twice', expressed today as [1, 2, 2, 2], describes how successive

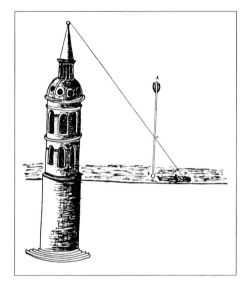

Fig. 1. Using similar triangles to measure the height of a tower from Alberti, *Ludi matematici.*

1 T. L. Heath, *Euclid: The Thirteen Books of The Elements*, Cambridge University Press, Cambridge, 1921, II, p. 113.
2 That is, natural numbers or rational numbers.
3 Euclid V, Definition 1. Heath, *ibid.*, p. 113.
4 Discussion occurs, for example, in Plato, *Meno* 82–87, *Theaetetus* 147c-148b, and *Republic VIII*, 546c4–5. See A. Szabó, *The Beginnings of Greek Mathematics*, D. Reidel, Dordrecht, 1978, Part 1, 'The early history of the theory of irrationals', pp. 33–98; also D. H. Fowler, *The Mathematics of Plato's Academy: A New Reconstruction*, Clarendon Press, Oxford,1987, particularly Chapter 1, pp. 3–30.
5 See Fowler, *ibid.*, Chapter 2, pp. 31–66.

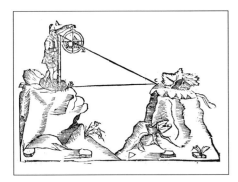

Fig. 2. Using similar triangles to estimate the width of a river from Bartoli, *Del modo di misurare*.

magnitudes measure against their immediate predecessor. Against this, the side of the square measures the diameter in the unending sequence [1, 2, 2, 2, . . .]. By cutting short the infinite sequence, the practitioner establishes a rational convergent to the problem of determining a numerical value for $\sqrt{2}$. The sequence [1, 2, 2, 2] does just that, and therefore $17 : 12$ is a rational convergent to $\sqrt{2} : 1$. But then, so would the curtailments [1], [1, 2] and [1, 2, 2] be rational convergents, and these correspond to $1 : 1$, $3 : 2$, and $7 : 5$. It is clear that the first two ratios make poor proxies for $\sqrt{2} : 1$, but $7 : 5$ is really quite good although Alberti cautions against its use to determine a right-angle in the isosceles 5, 5, 7 triangle.[6] A right-angled triangle would satisfy Pythagoras' theorem, but it is clear that the sum of the squares of the two sides $5^2 + 5^2 = 25 + 25 = 50$ exceeds the square on the hypotenuse $7^2 = 49$ by 1. It must be understood that all this comes about by comparing one magnitude with another. On its own the diameter of a square is neither rational nor irrational. It becomes one or the other by comparison with the side of the square. If the side is taken as the unit of measure, the diameter is irrational. If the diameter is taken as the unit, then the side is irrational. Without comparison, a solitary magnitude is just another unit. By contrast, numbers assume a base unit from which all others are constructed as multitudes.

Euclid defined transformations of ratios in the form $p : q$. The first term he defined as the antecedent; the second, as the consequent. By replacing the antecedent by the consequent, and the consequent by the antecedent, the 'inverse' ratio $q : p$ is constructed.[7] The ratio $p + q : q$ is defined as 'composition'.[8] The ratio $p - q : q$ is defined as 'separation'.[9] The ratio $p : p - q$ is called 'conversion'.[10] Euclid does not give a name to the ratio $p + q : p$ which is the composition of the inverse ratio $q : p$. It seems appropriate to call this the 'inverse composition'. For example, if the ratio is $5 : 3$, the inverse is $3 : 5$; the composition is $5 + 3 : 3$, or $8 : 3$; the separation is $5 - 3 : 3$, or $2 : 3$; the conversion is $5 : 5 - 3$, or $5 : 2$. The inverse composition of $5 : 3$ would be $8 : 5$. In all, ten different individual ratios may be produced from this one progenitor: $3 : 2$, $8 : 5$, $5 : 3$, $5 : 2$, $8 : 3$, all greater than $1 : 1$; and their inverses $2 : 3$, $5 : 8$, $3 : 5$, $2 : 5$, $3 : 8$, all less than $1 : 1$. Architecturally, inversion is equivalent to changing the orientation of a room whose dimensions are p from front to back, and q side to side, to one whose dimensions are q from front to back, and p from side to side. Composition adds a square to the short side of the room. Inverse composition adds a square to the long side of the room. Separation takes a square away from the short side of the room. Conversion takes a square away from the long side of the room, which is only possible in a positive sense, if the square on the long side is depleted by the room when long sides are matched. (Fig. 3).

Euclid defines a ratio as a relation in respect of size between two magnitudes of the same kind: that is, length to length, area to area, volume to volume, and so on. What Euclid meant by magnitudes in the same ratio was certainly misunderstood by Campanus, and was criticized by Galileo, yet modern commentators have demonstrated that it satisfies the exacting requirements of number theorists such as Weierstrass and Dedekind. Nevertheless, the concept of sameness, as de Morgan wrote, 'is one of the most common acts of the mind, since it is performed on every occasion where similarity or dissimilarity of figure is looked for or presents itself'.[11] Whether the idea was communicated clearly or not by Euclid's translators in the Renaissance, there can be little doubt that its implications were accepted pragmatically. The notion of proportionality then follows. A ratio involves a relation between two magnitudes, $p : q$. A proportion involves a relation between two ratios, and

6 L. B. Alberti, ed., R. Rinaldi, *Ludi matematici*, Guanda, Milan, 1980, p. 52, *'Sono alcuni che misurano il filo cinque e poi pur cinque e poi sette, e fanno come noi un triangulo. Questi errano, però che i quadrati loro non rispondono a pieno: màncavi delle cinquanta parti l'una'*.
7 Book V, Definition 13.
8 *Ibid.*, Definition 14.
9 *Ibid.*, Definition 15.
10 *Ibid.*, Definition 16.
11 For a discussion, see Heath, *op. cit.*, pp. 120–29.

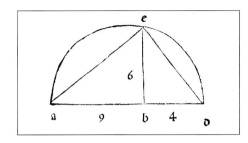

Fig. 4. Figure showing the determination of the mean proportional. From Campanus-Pacioli *Euclid*, VI.13.

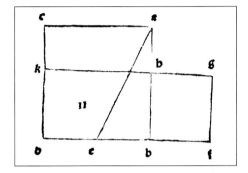

Fig. 5. Geometric construction of the extreme and mean ratio. From Campanus-Pacioli, *Euclid*, II.11.

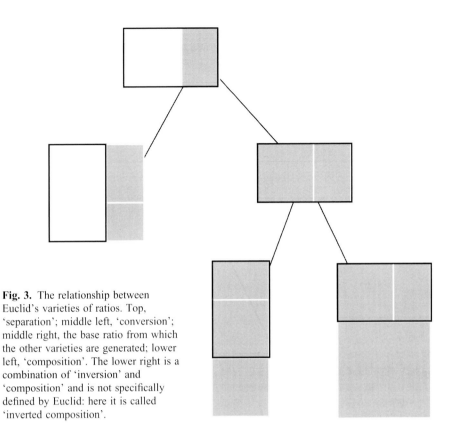

Fig. 3. The relationship between Euclid's varieties of ratios. Top, 'separation'; middle left, 'conversion'; middle right, the base ratio from which the other varieties are generated; lower left, 'composition'. The lower right is a combination of 'inversion' and 'composition' and is not specifically defined by Euclid: here it is called 'inverted composition'.

potentially between four magnitudes, $p : q :: r : s$.[12] The definition of *alternate* ratio really applies to proportion.[13] By taking the antecedent in relation to the antecedent, and the consequent in relation to the consequent, the alternate ratio $p : r :: q : s$ is made. Euclid's Definition 8 in Book V states that 'a proportion in three terms is the least possible.'[14] Such a relation is $p : q :: q : r$, and it is then said that the first magnitude to the third magnitude is in duplicate ratio. The terms are said to be in continuous proportion.[15] Clearly it is not twice in the modern sense of duplicate, but rather that the result is the original ratio to the second power, $p : r :: p^2 : q^2$. Euclid extends the definition indefinitely to the third power and beyond as in the triplicate ratio $p : q :: q : r :: r : s$, where $p : s :: p^3 : q^3$, or the original ratio to the third power.[16] Hippocrates had signalled the existence of two mean proportionals in continued proportion as a solution to the Delic problem of duplicating the cube, and Plato reflects this observation.[17] It is evident that Barbaro and his collaborator, Palladio, were aware of these definitions and their implications.

In Book VI.13, Euclid gives the geometric construction for determining a mean proportional, that is, finding the geometric mean. (Fig. 4).

This is a version of an earlier proposition in Book II.14. In Book II there are specific propositions referring to problems such as estimating the ratio of the diameter of the square to its side, II.9 and 10,[18] and of cutting a line into extreme and mean ratio, II.11, although this specific terminology is not used until VI.30. (Fig. 5).

12 *Ibid.*, Definitions 5 and 6.
13 *Ibid.*, Definition 11.
14 *Ibid.*, Definition 8.
15 *Ibid.*, Definition 9.
16 *Ibid.*, Definition 10.
17 Heath, *op. cit.*, p. 133. Plato, *Timaeus* 32A-B is interpreted by Nicomachus in this sense, see d'Ooge, *op. cit.*, p. 272 n.2; but other interpretions are possible, see F. M. Cornford, *Plato's Cosmology*, Routledge & Kegan Paul, London, 1937, pp. 44–52. Cornford, having reviewed the other possibilities, tends to agree with Heath.
18 Heath, *op. cit.*, p. 397–402, following Proclus' exegisis, shows that these propositions – not couched specifically in such terms – nevertheless, lead directly to the 'side' and 'diagonal' numbers of the square. These numbers are discussed in more detail *infra*, 'Inexpressible Proportion'.

Both problems are related to Euclid's proportional transformations, (Fig. 3 above). If the base ratio is made equal to its inverse composition, then $p/q = (p + q)/p$, which is satisfied if $p : q :: \sqrt{5} + 1 : 2$. Today this is called the golden section, but for Euclid and for those who read his works in the Renaissance it was known as the extreme and mean ratio. Also, if there were to be equality between the base ratio and its separation, this condition would need to be satisfied, $p/q = q/(p - q)$, which leads to the same extreme and mean ratio. Such equalities cannot exist for finite values, but only emerge over the unbounded, long run. In our depiction, the transformations involve either the addition or subtraction of a square preserving the base ratio. This is the familiar spiral of squares associated with the golden section. Similarly, the equality of the separation of a ratio with its composition, can only occur if $(p + q)/q = q/(p - q)$, which implies that $p : q :: \sqrt{2} : 1$, the irrational ratio of the diameter of a square to its side. In these ways, Euclid's system of proportional transformations is seen to be intimately bound to classical problems involving incommensurability.

An application of the Euclidean transformations to the Palladian canon, the ratios $1 : 1, 4 : 3, \sqrt{2} : 1, 3 : 2, 5 : 3, 2 : 1$, shows that a small number of other ratios, found in Palladio's works, may be derived this way. Some of these do not have musical associations. Also, the ratios in the canon themselves are closely interconnected through the transformations: for example, the separation of $3 : 2$ is $2 : 1$, of $5 : 3$ is $3 : 2$ and $2 : 1$ is $1 : 1$.[19]

Table 1 Palladio's base ratios and their Euclidean transformations. The equality $1 : 1$ is not tabulated. It has no separation, and its composition and inverted composition are the same, $2 : 1$. The *diagon*, $\sqrt{2} : 1$, is represented by the rational convergents $7 : 5, 17 : 12, 24 : 17$ used by Palladio. Only ratios which are found in Palladio's drawings are indicated. It should be noted that twelve derived ratios are not found in his work.

base ratio	composition	inverted composition	separation	conversion
4 : 3		7 : 4		
7 : 5	12 : 5	12 : 7	5 : 2	
17 : 12	29 : 12		12 : 5	
24 : 17				
3 : 2	5 : 2	5 : 3	2 : 1	
5 : 3	8 : 3	8 : 5	3 : 2	5 : 2
2 : 1		3 : 2	1 : 1	2 : 1

19 *Vide infra*, Appendix I, for a fuller discussion of the Palladian canon. A. Palladio, *I quattro libri dell'architettura*, Venice, 1570, I.xxi, p. 52 gives these six preferred ratios for rectangular rooms.

COSMOGONIC ARITHMETIC

Two contemporaries, alive in the second century CE, are responsible for transmitting the Pythagorean arithmetic tradition: Nicomachus and Theon of Smyrna.[1] The former's contribution was written to stand alongside his introductions to geometry, music and astronomy, although these texts have not survived.[2] Theon's work addresses the knowledge required to understand mathematical constructs in Plato, and also covers aspects of the quadrivium. The two texts parallel one another's contents. Here, with one exception, the account of Nicomachus is used. In part, this is done since Alberti mentions Nicomachus, rather than Theon, as an arithmetician.[3]

Nicomachus does not make the contribution to mathematics that Euclid does. His work is really a philosophical tract, in which arithmetic relations are proposed as models of cosmic order. He commences by drawing attention to the eternal qualities of mathematical entities against the fitful corruptibility of the corporeal world. He writes:

> The bodiless things, however, of which we conceive in connection with or together with matter, such as qualities, quantities, configurations, largeness, smallness, equality, relations, actualities, dispositions, places, times, all those things, in a word, whereby the qualities found in each body are comprehended . . . those things are immaterial, eternal, without end, and it is their nature to persist ever the same and unchanging, abiding by their own essential being, and each of them is called real in the proper sense. But what are involved in birth and destruction, growth and diminution, all kinds of change and participation, are seen to vary continually, and while they are called real things, by the same term as the former, so far as they partake of them, they are not actually real by their own nature; for they do not abide for even the shortest moment in the same condition, but are always passing over in all sort of changes.[4]

Things, Nicomachus continues, are of two kinds:

> some of them unified and continuous, for example, an animal, the universe, a tree, and the like, which are properly and peculiarly called 'magnitudes'; others are discontinuous, in a side-by-side arrangement, and, as it were, in heaps, which are called 'multitudes', a flock, for

1 M. L. D'Ooge, *Nicomachus of Gerasa: Introduction to Arithmetic*, University of Michigan Press, Ann Arbor, 1938, R. Lawlor, D. Lawlor, *Mathematics Useful for Understanding Plato*, Wizard's Bookshelf, San Diego, 1979. Thomas Taylor *Theoretic Arithmetic* London, 1816, new edition Samuel Weiser, York Beach, 1983, is an amalgam of Nicomachus, Theon, and later commentators.
2 Although a short piece on music, *Enchiridon*, has survived, it is not the companion book to *The Introduction to Arithmetic*.
3 Alberti, *On the Art . . .* p. 317.
4 D'Ooge, *op. cit.*, p. 182.

instance, a people, a heap, a chorus, and the like. . . . Since, however, all multitude and magnitude are by their own nature of necessity infinite – for multitude starts from a definite root and never ceases increasing; and magnitude, when division beginning with a limited whole is carried on, cannot bring the dividing process to an end, but proceeds therefore to infinity – and since sciences are always sciences of limited things, and never of infinites, it is accordingly evident that a science dealing either with magnitudes, *per se*, or with multitudes, *per se*, could never be formulated, for each of them is limitless in itself, multitude in the direction of the more, and magnitude in the direction of the less. A science, however, would arise to deal with something separated from each of them, with quantity, set off from multitude, and size, set off from magnitude.[5]

Four sciences are proposed, the quadrivium.[6] Concerning multitude: arithmetic deals with quantity in itself, music with quantity in relation to something else. Concerning magnitude, geometry deals with size at rest, astronomy with size in motion. This classification is not strictly adhered to by Nicomachus and, despite his authorship of monographs on all four subjects, his introduction to arithmetic includes aspects of music, and some geometry. Nicomachus discusses the ordering of these four subjects and declares that arithmetic rules sovereign over the others and 'not solely because we said that it existed before all others in the mind of the creating God like some universal and exemplary plan, relying upon which as a design and archetypal example the creator of the universe sets in order his material creations and makes them attain to their proper ends. . . .'[7] Nicomachus finally argues for this order of priority: arithmetic first, and then in order, geometry, music and astronomy. Arithmetic, he says, is the 'mother and nurse of the rest'.[8]

What Nicomachus presents is an organic view which transcends appearances, reaching beyond the superficial to principles – abstract, arithmetic principles which govern formative processes and physical form. This is the neo-Platonic tradition of creative activity within which many humanist patrons and designers operated. No deep appreciation of their achievements is possible without a thorough understanding of this underlying, arithmetic metaphor. The metaphor is a double one. God creates the material world by analogy to an arithmetic design, the play of numbers. In parallel, an individual creates a work, in harmony with the God-made universe, by acting as second Nature, also through the play of numbers. Determined and ordered in accordance with number: a pattern 'fixed like a preliminary sketch . . . as to an artistic plan'.

All that has by nature with systematic method been arranged in the universe seems both in part and as a whole to have been determined and ordered in accordance with number, by the forethought and the mind of him who created all things; for the pattern was fixed like a preliminary sketch, by the domination of number preexistent, in the mind of the world-creating God, number conceptual only and immaterial in every way, but at the same time the true and eternal essence, so that with reference to it, as to an artistic plan, should be created all things, time, motion, the heavens, the stars, all sorts of revolutions.[9]

5 *Ibid.*, pp. 183–84.
6 The latinate 'quadrivium' is a later neologism of Boethius, who contrasts it with 'trivium' for grammar, rhetoric and dialectic. Together these constitute the seven liberal arts.
7 *Ibid.*, p. 187.
8 *Ibid.*, pp. 188–89, Chapters 4–5.
9 *Ibid.*, p. 189, Chapter 6. This is the kind of sentiment to be found in the writings of Alberti's acquaintance, Nicholas Cusanus. See C. H. Lohr, 'Metaphysics', in C. B. Schmitt, Q. Skinner, *The Cambridge History of Renaissance Philosophy*, Cambridge University Press, 1988, p. 535: of Cusanus, he writes: 'With respect to the creator, man is a "human god" or a "second god", because of the creative power of his mind. Just as God is active *ad extra*, creating real things and natural forms, so also man can bring forth rational things and artificial forms – mathematical ideas, instruments and tools and works of art.'

GENDERED NUMBER

They realized that numbers were either odd or even; they employed both, but the even in some places, the odd in others. Taking their example from Nature, they never made the bones of the building, meaning the columns, angles, and so on, odd in number – for you will not find a single animal that stands or moves upon an odd number of feet. Conversely, they never made openings even in number; this they evidently learned from Nature: to animals she has given ears, eyes, and nostrils matching on either side, but in the center, single and obvious, she has set the mouth.[1]

Much of Nicomachus' monograph is concerned with the classifications of the natural numbers starting with one and two which are treated more as progenitors and not so much as typical numbers.[2] One, the monad, is identified with Platonic 'sameness', while 2, the dyad, is identified with 'otherness'.[3] It is from these contrarieties that the natural number series is constructed in harmony with the doctrine of 'the unification of the diverse and concord of the discordant'.[4] The first proper number, 3, conjoins the monad with the dyad, the 'same' with the 'other'. The primal dichotomy of number is odd (O) and even (E).[5]

O   1   3   5   7   9   11   13   15   17   19   . . .

E   2   4   6   8   10   12   14   16   18   20   . . . .

An even number can be divided into two equal halves without remainder. An odd number can have two equal parts removed until only a unit is left. Take the numbers 5 and 6, for example

5   ‖ I ‖

6   ‖‖ ‖‖.

The analogy – attributed to the Pythagoreans – that odd numbers are male and the even numbers are female arises from this graphic observation, although this distinction is not made by Nicomachus.[6]

The even numbers (E) are divided into three classes. The even-times even (EE) numbers are powers of two in modern terms. The even-times odd (EO) numbers

1 J. Rykwert, N. Leach, R. Tavernor. trans, *Leon Battista Alberti: The Art of Building in Ten Books*, MIT Press, Cambridge, 1988, XI.5, p. 303.
2 The classification of Nicomachus is somewhat different from that given in T L Heath, *Euclid: The Thirteen Books of the Elements*, Cambridge University Press, 1921, VII, pp. 277–344. Likewise there are some distinctions between Nicomachus and Theon of Smyrna.
3 D'Ooge, p. 259, II.xviii, where Nicomachus cites Plato (is he referring to *Timaeus* 35A?) on 'the same' and 'the other'. This distinction between the 'One' and the 'Indefinite Dyad' is discussed in W. Burkert, *Lore and Science in Ancient Pythagoreanism*, Harvard University Press, Cambridge MA, 1972, Part I, 'Platonic and Pythagorean Number Theory', pp. 15–96. Another valuable introduction to Pythagorean, Platonic and Neoplatonic number theories is to be found in J. Klein, *Greek Mathematical Thought and the Origin of Algebra*, MIT Press, Cambridge, 1968, Part I, pp. 3–116.
4 Nicomachus cites the Pythagorean writer Philolaus, D'Ooge, *op. cit.*, p. 259, II.xix. This aphorism probably derives from fragment 6: 'It is not things that are alike or of the same kind that need harmony, but things unlike and different and of unequal speed; such things must be bonded together in harmony, if they are to be held together in the cosmos. . . .' In Burkert, *op. cit.*, p. 252.
5 D'Ooge, *op. cit.*, pp. 190–91, I.vii . Note that the numbers 1 and 2 are included here in the modern manner. 'One' was often held to be both odd and even among Pythagoreans. Both Nicomachus and Theon are ambivalent on this question of whether 1 and 2 are numbers: the usual way out was to assume a special status for the monad and the dyad in some eternal realm, and to make them manifest in practical terms as numbers 1 and 2 in the immediate world.
6 Aristotle, *Metaphysics*, 985b.22ff. discusses the Pythagorean approach to number. According to

are twice the odd numbers, and the odd-times even (OE) numbers are all the rest. Nicomachus takes some length to distinguish these three types and to draw attention to their distinctive properties.[7]

E		2	4	6	8	10	12	14	16	18	20	22	24	26	28	30	32	34	36	38	40	42	44
EE	2	4		8					16								32						
EO			6		10		14			18		22		26		30		34		38		42	
OE						12					20		24		28				36		40		44.

Concerning the even-times even numbers, Nicomachus shows, in an odd-numbered set of successive terms, that the product of a pair of terms equally spaced about the centre will be equal to the square of the central term, or the mean term. In the case of an even number of terms, the product of the two central means will be equal to those placed symmetrically about them.

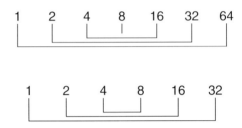

The description of these relationships draws attention to the size of the number and the quantities involved: that 4 is one-eighth of 32, 2 is one-sixteenth, and 1 is one thirty-second. Nicomachus sees in this the rule of opposition: that as size increases, quantity decreases, and vice-versa. For him, this opposition is what necessarily gives rise to harmony. He also shows that the sum of successive terms from unity, 1, 2, 4, 8, . . . , is always one less than the next term. The sum to 8 is 15, the next term being 16; the sum to 16 is 31, the next term being 32, and so on. Of course, Nicomachus is describing the properties of what we now call a geometric series.

Opposed to the even-times even numbers are the even-times odd.[8] These two types are the extremes among even numbers. Unlike the even-times even numbers which may be divided in half as many times as possible until unity is reached, the even-times odd may only be so divided just once. 'It is possibly for this reason that it received such a name, that is, because, although it is even, its halves are at once odd.' In the even-times odd number there is opposition between quantity and size: Nicomachus gives the number 18 as an example: the half is 9 – an even quantity and odd size; the third is 6 – an odd quantity and even size; the sixth is 3 – an even quantity and odd size; and a ninth is 2 – an odd quantity and even size. Again, Nicomachus points out relationships between numbers symmetrically placed about the single mean in a series where there are an odd number of terms, and those about the two mean values where there are an even number of terms. Today, this is called an arithmetic series:

Aristotle, some members of the school 'say there are ten principles, which they arrange in two columns of cognates –

limit	unlimited
odd	even
one	plurality
right	left
male	female
resting	moving
straight	crooked
light	darkness
good	bad
square	oblong'.

Lists similar to this are adopted by later Pythagorean commentators, for example, Plutarch, *De Iside et Osiride*, (trans J. Gwynn Griffiths, University of Wales Press, Cambridge, 1970, p. 195). The Pythagorean community at Croton is generally supposed to have been something of a model of sexual equality in the ancient world. Aristotle does not cite his source for the table. Perhaps it reflects his own misogynistic tendency, and is a pseudo-Pythagorean fabrication. Later 'Pythagorean' writers provide similar, but shorter, dichotomous lists. Most leave out the male–female pair and are therefore sexually unprejudiced. However, the identification of odd numbers with the male, and even numbers with the female persists into the Renaissance. See Burkert, *op. cit.*, p. 52 n. 119. Also M. Wertheim, *Pythagoras' Trousers: God, Physics and the Gender War*, Times Books, New York, 1995, a provocative, but salutary, cultural history of the exclusion of women from the mathematical sciences.

7 D'Ooge, *op. cit.*, pp. 192–96, I.viii. Nicomachus' classification may be compared with Euclid's definitions, Book VII, Heath, *Euclid* II, pp. 277–78.

8 D'Ooge, *op. cit.*, pp. 196–98, I.ix.

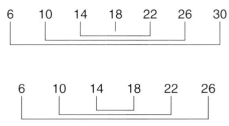

This relationship, however, is additive with symmetrically placed pairs summing to either twice the single mean in the case of an odd number of terms, or the sum of the two means in the case of an even number of terms. Nicomachus states that the even-times odd are 'opposite in properties' to the even-times even, 'in particular because in the former case the reciprocal arrangement of the parts from extremes to mean term or terms make the product of the former equal to the square or product of the latter; but in this case by the same correspondence and comparison the mean term is one half the sum of the extremes, or if there should be two means, their sum equals that of the two extremes'.[9]

Having established this opposition, Nicomachus can then claim that the odd-times even numbers are the mean of these two: 'belonging in common to both the previously mentioned species like a single mean between two extremes.'[10] 'Now in admitting more than one division, the odd-times even is like the even-times even and unlike the even-times odd; but in that its subdivision never ends with unity, it is like the even-times odd and unlike the even-times even. ... This number is produced by a somewhat complicated method, and shows, after a fashion, even in its manner of production, that it is a mixture of both other kinds. For whereas the even-times even is made from even numbers, the doubles from unity to infinity, and the even-times odd from the odd numbers from 3, progressing to infinity, this must be woven together out of both classes, as being common to both.'[11]

	4	**8**	**16**	**32**	**64**	**128**	**256**
3	12	24	48	96	192	384	768
5	20	40	80	160	320	640	1280
7	28	56	112	224	448	896	1792
9	36	72	144	228	576	1152	2304
11	44	88	176	352	704	1408	2816.

This Table excites Nicomachus: 'Now when you arrange the products of multiplication by each term in its proper line, making the lines parallel, in marvellous fashion there will appear along the breadth [the height] of the table the peculiar property of the even-times odd, that the mean term is always half of the extremes, if there should be one mean, and the sum of the means equals the sum of the extremes if two. But along the length of the table the property of the even-times even will appear; for the product of the extremes is equal to the square of the means, should there be one mean term, or their product, should there be two. Thus this one species has the peculiar properties of them both, because it is a natural mixture of them both.'[12]

Next, Nicomachus describes three species of the odd.[13] Only two of these actually partition the odd numbers. The third is fabricated to satisfy Nicomachus' sense of

9 *Ibid.*, p. 198, I.ix.
10 *Ibid.*, p. 198, I.x.
11 *Ibid.*, p. 199, I.x.
12 *Ibid.*, pp. 200–1, I.x.
13 *Ibid.*, pp. 201–2, I.xi.

symmetry – that both even and odd should have three divisions. The two primary divisions of odd numbers (O) are between the incomposite, odd primes (OP) and the secondary, odd composite numbers (OC):

O	3	5	7	9	11	13	15	17	19	21	23	25	27	29	31	33	35	37	39	41	43	45
OP	3	5	7		11	13		17	19		23			29	31			37		41	43	
OC				9			15			21		25	27			33	35		39			45.

The aliquot parts of the primes have a denominator which is the number itself and no other: 3 has a third, 5 a fifth, 7 a seventh, and so on, 'and all of these parts are unity'. The secondary, composite odd number is one produced by combining odd primes. 'It is characteristic of the secondary number to have, in additional to the fractional part with the number itself as denominator, yet another part or parts with different denominators, the former always, as in all cases, unity, the latter never unity, but always that number or those numbers by the combination of which it was produced.'[14] Thus 9, in addition to the ninth part which is unity, has a third part which is 3; 15 has a fifteenth part which is unity, a fifth part which is 3, and a third part which is 5, and so on.

The third species of odd numbers is relational and properly belongs to the next section on ratio. Thus, 49 is relatively prime to 23, and 49 and 21 are secondary and composite relative to each other – examples given by Nicomachus. Theon of Smyrna draws attention to the obvious fact that odd and even numbers may be relatively prime, or secondary, and that this is not a property of odd numbers only: respectively, 49 and 25, and 49 and 28 would be such examples. In part, the problem arises because Nicomachus does not rank the number 2 as a prime: it is of course the only even prime. In discussing the third class of the odd, Nicomachus deals with both the sieve of Eratosthenes and the algorism of Euclid for finding the greatest common divisor of two numbers.[15] The sieve sorts the prime and incomposite odd numbers from the secondary, composite odd numbers.[16]

3	5	7	9	11	13	15	17	19	21	23	25	27	29	31	33	35	37	39	41	43	45
3		*9*				15			*21*			*27*			33			39			45
	5					*15*					*25*					35					*45*
		7							*21*							*35*					
				11											*33*						
					13													*39*			
							17														
								19													
										23										
													29								
														31							
																	37				
																			41		
																				43.	

14 *Ibid.*, pp., 202–3, I.xii.
15 Heath, *Euclid*, II, pp. 296–97, VII.1: 'Two unequal numbers being set out, and the less being continually subtracted in turn from the greater, if the number which is left never measures the one before it until an unit is left, the original number will be prime to one another.'
16 *Ibid.*, pp. 203–7, I.xiii.

Nicomachus observes that the numbers are spaced along each row by an even number of separating terms: 2 for the row starting with 3, 4 for the row starting with 5, 6 for the row starting with 7, 10 for the row starting with 11, and so on to infinity. Again, Nicomachus takes the opportunity to show how opposites, evens and odds, interact in a process.

He then describes Euclid's algorism of successive subtraction, anthyphairesis. His first example is 45 and 23. In this case, 23 from 45 leaves 22, 22 from 23 leaves 1, unity, and 1 may be subtracted from 22 that number of times. We would say $45 : 23 = [1, 1, 22]$. Nicomachus claims that 49 and 23 are 'prime and incomposite to one another'. His second example is 49 and 21. Here, 21 may be subtracted twice from 49 leaving 7, and 7 may be subtracted from 21 exactly three times. 7 is found to be a common factor. We would say that $49 : 21 = [2, 3]$. Nicomachus declares that 49 and 21 are 'secondary and composite relatively to each other'.

Later, in the second book, Nicomachus remarks on another property of the odd and even numbers.[17] Successive sums of the odd numbers amount to square, or equilateral, numbers; while successive sums of the even numbers amount to heteromecic numbers. Ficino comments on this: the offspring, *filii*, of good parents are equilateral, those of bad parents are heteromecic.[18] The argument appears to follow the Pythagorean dichotomy, yet it is surely perverted. On the one hand, square numbers are the product of either two male numbers, or two female numbers: the equation seems to be that things produced by the same are good, whether or not the things are in themselves good or bad by the Pythagorean dichotomy. On the other hand, heteromecic numbers are bad since they are the issue of a male and female number. This suggests that mixing good and bad is necessarily bad.[19] Despite the unusual sexual propagation implied, this is an ethical version of even plus even and odd plus odd is always even (bad), and odd plus even or even plus odd is always odd (good). Nicomachus further observes that the sums of adjacent square and heteromecic numbers amount to the triangular numbers. These numbers are in turn the issue by addition of good, equilateral parents and bad, heteromecic parents.

17 D'Ooge, *op. cit.*, p. 260.

18 M. J. B. Allen, *Nuptial Arithmetic: Marsilio Ficino's Commentary on the Fatal Number in Book VIII of Plato's 'Republic'*, University of California Press, Los Angeles, 1994, pp. 85–86, and Ficino's Chapter xiii 'On good or bad offspring through the observance of numbers and figures', pp. 210–13. This discussion is taken up in more detail in the section 'Shapeful Number', *infra*.

19 Such a view contradicts Nicomachus who introduces his discussion on equilateral and heteromecic numbers with the statement that 'harmony is the unification of the diverse and the reconciliation of the contrary-minded': it would follow that the heteromecic numbers – the product of two neighbouring numbers such as 3 and 4, or 4 and 5 – always exhibit harmony while the equilaterals often do not. Allen, *ibid.*, p. 85, points to the fact that an equilateral such as $6 \times 6 = 36$ may also be expressed as 4×9.

V

ETHICAL NUMBER

The seduction of symmetry is so great for Nicomachus that he breaks with categorical logic to accommodate the third, but relative, form of odd number.[1] His argument concerning absolute number, number in itself, is interrupted by a premature discussion of relative number. Theon of Smyrna avoids this rupture. Theon's discussion of absolute number is entirely dealt with under the heading of arithmetic, whereas relative number is assigned to his subsequent section on music. This, too, is not entirely satisfactory, since many aspects of relative number have no relevance to musical theory. Here, the discussion concerning number in itself will be completed first before moving on to relative number: ratio, proportion and means.

In a different manner, numbers may be divided into three classes: 'some are superabundant, some deficient, like extremes set over against each other, and some are intermediary between them and are called perfect.'[2] Nicomachus uses the Aristotelian moral comparison of excess and deficiency with the vices, and the mean with the virtues.[3] He describes the extremes in terms of 'evil, disease, disproportion, unseemliness'. The mean corresponds to the virtues 'wealth, moderation, propriety, beauty, and the like.' This ethical classification depends on comparing a number with the sum of its factors including unity, but excluding the number itself: in other words its proper aliquot parts. For example, the number 12 has twelfths of 1, sixths of 2, fourths of 3, thirds of 4, and halves of 6 units. The sum $1 + 2 + 3 + 4 + 6$ is 16 which is larger than 12. The number 12 is said to be superabundant. The number 14 has fourteenths of 1, sevenths of 2, and halves of 7. The sum $1 + 2 + 7$ is 10 which is less than 14. The number 14 is deficient. The number 6 has sixths of 1, thirds of 2, and halves of 3. The sum $1 + 2 + 3$ is 6 – the number itself. Such a number is declared to be perfect. Superabundant and deficient numbers are extremes. Perfect numbers are the mean. A superabundant number is compared to an animal 'created with too many parts or limbs, with two tongues, as the poet says, and ten mouths, or with nine lips, or three rows of teeth, or a hundred hands, or too many fingers on one hand'.[4] A superabundant number 'oversteps the symmetry which exists between the perfect and its own parts'. A deficient number is 'as if some animal should fall short of the natural number of limbs or parts, or as if a man should have but one eye, as in the poem, "And one round orb was fixed in his brow"; or as though one should be one-handed, or have fewer than five fingers on one hand, or lack a tongue, or some such member'.[5] A deficient number whose factors are less than itself is 'so to speak maimed'. These numbers are comparable with monsters.

1 M. L. D'Ooge, *Nicomachus of Gerasa: Introduction to Arithmetic*, University of Michigan Press, Ann Arbor, 1937, I.xiii, pp. 203–7.
2 *Ibid.*, I.xiv, p. 207.
3 Aristotle, *Nicomachean Ethics*. D. J. O'Meara, *Pythagoras Revived: Mathematics and Philosophy in Late Antiquity*, Clarendon Press, Oxford, 1989. O'Meara discusses this issue in reference to excerpts by Psellus on a text assumed to be Iamblichus, *On Pythagoreanism VI: On Ethical Arithmetic*, pp. 70–76 and Appendix I, p. 223ff.
4 *Ibid.*, I.xiv, pp. 207–8.
5 *Ibid.*, I.xv, p. 208.

'While these two varieties are opposed after the manner of extremes, the so-called perfect number appears as a mean, which is discovered to be in the realm of equality. . . . For the equal is always conceived of as in the mid-ground between greater and less, and is, as it were, moderation between excess and deficiency. . . . '[6] Nicomachus notes that 'as fair and excellent things are few and easily enumerated, while ugly and evil ones are widespread, so also the superabundant and deficient numbers are found in great multitude and irregularly placed – for the method of discovery is irregular – but the perfect numbers are easily enumerated and arranged with suitable order; for only one is found among the units, 6, only one other among the tens, 28, and a third in the rank of the hundreds, 496 alone, and a fourth within the limits of the thousands, that is, below ten-thousand, 8,128'.[7] Unfortunately, this pattern does not, in fact, continue. Nevertheless, Nicomachus does restate the law, without proof, for deriving perfect numbers.[8] He sets out the even-times even numbers and takes successive sums from unity. He has already shown that these sums are always one less than the next term in the series. Only the prime numbers are selected from the sums. A product is then formed from the prime and the final term in the series which has been summed. Such products are perfect numbers. Nicomachus includes unity in the list of perfect numbers since it is at once its own sum as well as the last – and only – term taken into the summation.

Even-times even	1	2	4	8	16	32	64	128	. . .
Sums	1	3	7	15	31	63	127	256	. . .
Primes	1	3	7		31		127		. . .
Perfect numbers	1	6	28		496		8128		. . . .

6 *Ibid.*, I.xvi, p. 209.

7 Unfortunately, the search for perfect numbers goes hand in hand with the search for the irregularly distributed prime numbers. The next perfect number is 33,550,336 which occurs with the prime $1 + 2 + 4 + \ldots + 1024 + 2048 + 4096 = 8191$. Primes made from the sums of even-even numbers, powers of 2, are today known as Mersenne primes, J. H. Conway, R. K. Guy, *The Book of Numbers*, Springer-Verlag, 1996, pp. 135–37. The subject was a matter of lively investigation among some mathematicians at the turn of the seventeenth century and beyond. Theon of Smyrna only records 6 and 28 as perfect numbers. Unlike Nicomachus, he also mentions 3 and 10 as perfect numbers, but in other, nonarithmetical senses. R. Lawlor, D. Lawlor, *Mathematics Useful for Understanding Plato*, Wizard's Bookshelf, San Diego, 1979, II.xxxii, pp. 30–31. *Vide infra*, 'Theological Number'.

8 Both Theon and Nicomachus give the law for the formation of perfect numbers, which is given and proved in Euclid IX.36: 'If as many numbers as we please beginning from an unit be set out continuously in double proportion, until the sum of all becomes prime, and if the sum multiplied into the last makes some number, the product will be perfect.' Heath, *op. cit.*, II, pp. 421–26.

VI

SHAPEFUL NUMBER

The classical arithmetician saw number in three distinct ways as shape. One visualizes the factors of a number in distinct dimensions, another sees a certain circularity when some numbers are multiplied by themselves, and the third depiction arranges the units making up the number in the form of either a planar polygonal figure, or a solid pyramidal figure.

A cube number such as 8 can be visualized as an actual $2 \times 2 \times 2$ cube with edges of length 2, square faces of area 4, and volume of 8; the cube number 27 can be visualized as an actual $3 \times 3 \times 3$ cube with edges of length 3, square faces of area 9, and volume of 27. Plato had drawn attention to two means between cube numbers: between 8, $2 \times 2 \times 2$, and 27, $3 \times 3 \times 3$, the means are 12, $2 \times 2 \times 3$, and 18, $2 \times 3 \times 3$.[1] The latter two numbers may be visualized as blocks with two square faces. In one case the square faces are separated by a length more than the side of the square, and in the other this same length is less than the side of the square. The first kind is seen as a 'beam', and the second kind as a 'brick'.[2] (Fig. 1).

In another sense – and such multiple readings are typical – the beam and brick are means between the perfect symmetry of the cube and the asymmetry of the scalene parallelepiped with three different dimensions along its orthogonal axes which depict a number like $2 \times 3 \times 5$, 30. Nicomachus calls such numbers 'scalene'.[3] (Fig. 2).

In this depiction many numbers may be visualized in one of four ways as cube, brick, beam and scalene. That not all numbers may be so classified is due to the fact that unity is not normally accepted as a separate dimension. Thus the number 6, $1 \times 2 \times 3$, is not viewed as a scalene solid, but is treated as a planar, 2×3 rectangle. Also a prime number, like 7, is not depicted as a $1 \times 1 \times 7$ solid beam, nor as a planar, 1×7 rectangle, but as a line of length 7. All primes are lines. All even-times odd

1 This is not just a matter of vulgar arithmetic! The notion is filled with cosmogonic significance. In considering the body of the world, Plato argues for not less than four primary elements – fire, air, water, and earth. He does so on an *a priori* argument that involves the consideration of two means between two cube numbers. One of these represent earth and the other fire – the primary element of the heavens. These two elements are mediated by the means which are water and air in 'continuous proportion'. The single mean between two square numbers, implying just three primary elements, would not prove satisfactory because the square numbers lack the solidity, the three dimensionality that the world requires. The whole matter is discussed by F. M. Cornford, *Plato's Cosmology*, Routledge & Kegan Paul, London, 1937, in his commentary on *Timaeus* 31B-32C, pp. 43–52. Thomas of Bradwardine concludes his tract on proportion with a calculation of the radii of the spheres related to the four elements based partly on comments by Averroes concerning Aristotle's *De caelo et mundo*. Within some minor tolerance, Bradwardine demonstrates that the element 'water' occupies a sphere 33 times the radius of 'earth', 'air' a sphere 33 times the radius of 'water', and 'fire' 33 times that of 'air'. Thus, Plato's model of continuous proportionality – two means between two cubes – among the elements is still very much alive in the thirteenth century, but now attributed to the scholastically appropriate authority of Aristotle. See H. L. Crosby, *Thomas of Bradwardine: His 'Tractatus de Proportionibus'*, University of Wisconsin Press, Madison, 1955, pp. 47–48, pp. 133–41.

2 M. L. D'Ooge, *Nicomachus of Gerasa: Introduction to Arithmetic*, University of Michigan Press, Ann Arbor, 1937, II.xvii, p. 256. The depiction of numbers in this way, as rectangular, hyper-parallelepipeds, is the germ of the modern Hasse diagram for modular lattices setting out the factors of a number.

3 *Ibid.*, II.xvi, p. 253.

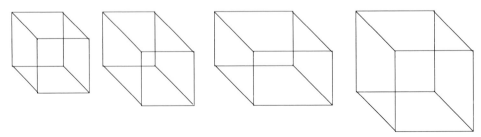

Fig. 1. The two means between two cubes depicted as three-dimensional blocks. From left to right: cube, beam, brick, cube.

numbers are rectangles with one even side of length 2 and one odd side with the length of a prime. Rectangular numbers in which one side is just one unit longer than the other are said to be heteromecic: 2×3, 3×4, 4×5, and so forth. Heteromecic numbers are obtained additively by summing successive even numbers from 2:[4]

$$2, \quad 2 + 4 = 6; \quad 2 + 4 + 6 = 12; \quad 2 + 4 + 6 + 8 = 20; \quad \dots$$

All other rectangular numbers are described as oblongs.[5] With the single exception of the number 6, 2×3, even-times odd numbers are oblongs. As is shown below, tetragonal numbers are obtained by successively summing odd numbers.[6]

Unity, the monad, is taken to be a point. There is considerable room for metamorphosis in these depictions. Nicomachus gives the example of the odd-times even, scalene number $3 \times 5 \times 12$.[7] This particular scalene may be transformed into beams like $2 \times 2 \times 45$ and $3 \times 3 \times 20$, a $5 \times 6 \times 6$ brick, and some seven or so scalene variations, such as $4 \times 5 \times 9$. Another example is the scalene number $2 \times 4 \times 8$ made up from even-times even terms, which might also be viewed as a $4 \times 4 \times 4$ cube, or a $2 \times 2 \times 16$ beam.

The classical writers do not suggest how higher powers beyond the cube might be visualized. By the Renaissance, however, fourth, fifth and sixth powers and beyond were given visual expression.[8] (Fig. 3).

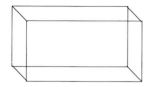

Fig. 2. A number depicted as a scalene parallelopiped, or a block with three distinct dimensions.

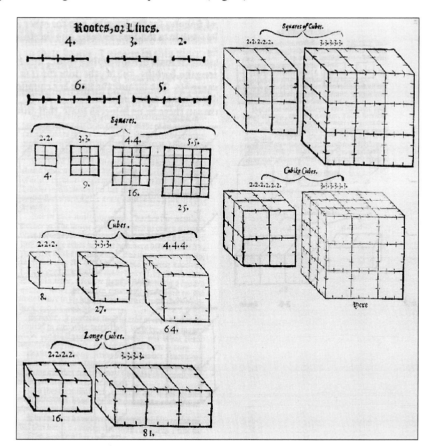

Fig. 3. The powers of numbers illustrated by three-dimensional forms. From Robert Recorde, *The Whetstone of Witte.*

4 *Ibid.*, II.xvii, p. 256.
5 *Ibid.*, II.xvii, p. 254. Otherwise called promecic.
6 *Ibid.*, II.xvii, p. 256. Much is made of the 'sameness' and the 'otherness' of numbers derived from the odd series such as squares and cubes, and numbers derived from the even series such as the heteromecic forms.
7 *Ibid.*, II.xvi, p. 253.
8 For example, the Welsh mathematician Robert Recorde, *The Whetstone of Witte*, London, 1557, shows such a scheme.

Fig. 4. Illustration from T. and L. Digges, *Arithmeticall Militare Treatise, named Stratioticos.*

Take the $2 \times 2 \times 2$ cube depicting the number 8. Place two such cubes side by side to give a $2 \times 2 \times 4$ beam depicting the number 16; then add another beam alongside the first to form a $2 \times 4 \times 4$ brick depicting the number 32; and finally add one brick on top of the other to create a new $4 \times 4 \times 4$ cube. From then on, the process may be repeated. It was not necessary for the Renaissance arithmetician to imagine hyperspace, everything could be visualized in three-dimensional space. It is possible to imagine a unit cube as origin; two unit cubes in a line representing 2; four unit cubes in a square representing 4; and eight unit cubes forming a $2 \times 2 \times 2$ cube, 8. Abstractly, since the monad was generally considered to be analogous to a point, the sequence goes from a point, 1, to a line, 2, to a plane, 4, and then to a solid in the cube, 8. Significantly, this cube is the one that Alberti chooses for his proportional demonstration involving roots and powers.[9]

A number ending in a 5 has the special property that its square will also end in 5, and so too will its cube. Such a number is said to be circular, or spherical. A term ending in 6 will also behave in this way.[10] Today, we would expect a number ending in zero to be recognized in the same way, but with no notation for zero the classical writer could not see this. Neither in Greek, nor later in Roman Latin, could this be observed.[11] The numbers 10, 100, 1000 use different symbols in Greek and Latin.

10	$\bar{\iota}$	X
100	$\bar{\rho}$	C
1000	$\bar{\Lambda}$	M.

Whereas, the numbers 6, 36 and 216, like numbers ending in 5, show the constancy to which classical writers draw attention

6	$\bar{\varsigma}$	VI
36	$\bar{\gamma\varsigma}$	XXXVI
216	$c\iota\,\bar{\varsigma}$	CCXVI.

This example demonstrates that patterns among numbers are, to a degree, dependent on notation. The reader should not read into modern transliterations patterns which would not have been discernible to persons in another historical period using different notational devices.

The third description of number as a polygonal figure is, perhaps, the most developed in classical writings.[12] The previous descriptions rely on factorization. The new description depends on a construction which is additive, although the result has implications for factoring. It is thought that very early computations were conducted with pebbles – or the like of bean counters, and inexorably it was found that the pebbles could be arranged to form simple shapes such as triangles and squares. The technique survives today in formal table settings with arrangements for wine glasses, and during the Renaissance it had relevance for military formations.[13] (Fig. 4).

Arithmeticians developed a method for generating numbers to form any polygonal figure. The method essentially determines appropriate arithmetical series. If the natural numbers are set out in order, the trigonal numbers are found by summing successive terms from unity:

$$1, \quad 1 + 2 = 3, \quad 1 + 2 + 3 = 6, \quad 1 + 2 + 3 + 4 = 10, \quad \ldots\ldots$$

9 J. Rykwert, N. Leach, R. Tavernor trans. *Leon Battista Alberti: The Art of Building*, MIT Press, Cambridge MA, 1988, IX.6, p. 307.
10 D'Ooge, *op. cit.*, II.xvii, p. 257.
11 *Vide infra*, 'Occult Number', for numerical equivalence of Greek letters and numbers.
12 *Ibid.*, II.vii–xiv, p. 239ff.
13 See, for example, L. and T. Digges, *An Arithmeticall Militare Treatise, named Stratioticos*, London, 1572.

The tetragonal numbers are found by summing successive, alternate terms from unity, that is to say the odd numbers:

$$1, \quad 1 + 3 = 4, \quad 1 + 3 + 5 = 9, \quad 1 + 3 + 5 + 7 = 16, \quad \ldots.$$

The pentagonal numbers are found by successively summing every third term from unity; the hexagonal numbers are the successive sums of every fourth term; the heptagonal every fifth term; and so on. The end term of each summation is known as a gnomon.[14] (Table 1.)

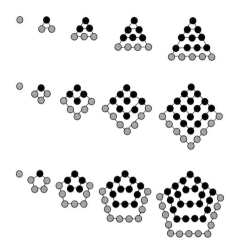

Fig. 5. Planar polygonal numbers. Top, the first five trigons; middle, the first five tetragons; and bottom the first five pentagons. The grey dots show the gnomon added to the prior figure.

Table 1 Gnomons of polygonal numbers from trigonal to heptagonal

△	1 2 3 4 5 6 7 8 9 10 11 12 13 14 15 16 17 18 19 20 21 22 23 24
◇	1 3 5 7 9 11 13 15 17 19 21 23
⬠	1 4 7 10 13 16 19 22
⬡	1 5 9 13 17 21
⬡	1 6 11 16 21

Nicomachus gives a table for polygonal numbers from the triangle to the heptagon for the first ten terms which represent polygons of side lengths from 1 to 10.[15] (Table 2.)

Table 2 Planar polygonal numbers from the trigonal to heptagonal. The numbers are obtained by summing the gnomons in Table 1.

△	1	3	6	10	15	21	28	36	45	55
◇	1	4	9	16	25	36	49	64	81	100
⬠	1	5	12	22	35	51	70	92	117	145
⬡	1	6	15	28	45	66	91	120	153	190
⬡	1	7	18	34	55	81	112	148	189	235

In modern notation, the *n*-gon of side length *r* depicts the number $\frac{1}{2}((r-1)(n-2)+2)$ which is a composite number – factorizable – for values of *r* greater than 2. In his tabulation, Nicomachus notices that the difference of two terms, one above the other in a column, is a trigonal number: in the second column it is the first trigonal number; in the third column, the second trigonal number, and so on. (Fig. 5.) It will also be observed that unity, the monad, is common to all polygonal numbers. Like God it is omnipresent. A term in the second column is always equal to the number of sides

14 Figurate numbers are colourfully described in J. H. Conway, R. K. Guy, *The Book of Numbers*, Springer-Verlag, New York, 1996, pp. 27–58. In this present book, the convention is adopted that figurate numbers are indicated by open polygons if they are planar, and by solid black polygons if they are pyramidal.
15 D'Ooge, *op. cit.*, II.xii, p. 248.

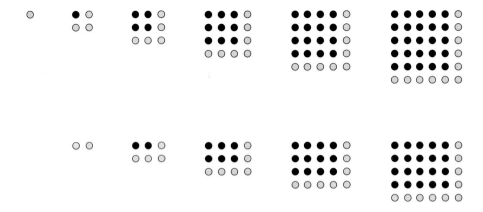

Fig. 6. Top row, the generation of tetragonal numbers by the successive addition of odd numbers indicated by the gnomons shown in grey. Bottom row, the gnomons are now even numbered and the successive summation of even numbers leads to the heteromecic variety.

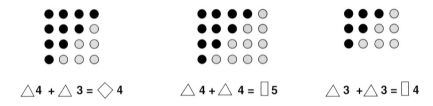

Fig. 7. Left, the sum of two adjacent trigonal numbers is a tetragonal number. The case of 6 + 10 = 16. Centre and right, the sum of two equal triangles build an heteromecic number: the cases of 10 + 10 = 20 and 6 + 6 = 12. The notation indicates the third and fourth trigonal numbers, the fourth tetragonal number and the fifth, 5 × 4, and fourth, 4 × 3, heteromecic numbers. The latter are depicted by □.

16 Figurate numbers continued to be a topic of interest in number theory into the nineteenth century. E. T. Bell, *Men of Mathematics*, The Scientific Book Club, London, undated, p. 261, reports that Carl Friedrich Gauss (1777–1855) wrote in his diary July 10, 1796: 'EYPHKA! num = Δ + Δ + Δ' having proved that every positive integer may be expressed as the sum of three trigonal numbers.

In 1815, Augustin-Louis Cauchy (1789–1857) 'created a sensation by proving one of the great theorems which Fermat had bequeathed to a baffled posterity: every positive integer is a sum of three "trigons", four "tetragons", five "pentagons", six "hexagons", and so on, zero being in each case being counted as a number of the kind concerned. . . . This was not easy to prove. In fact it had been too much for Euler, Lagrange and Legendre. Gauss had early proved the case of "triangles"'. Bell, p. 321.

17 D'Ooge, *op. cit.*, II.xii, p. 248.

18 The numbers 6, 10, 16 are cited in Vitruvius II. i. '*Postea quam animadverterunt utrosque numeros esse perfectos, et sex et decem, in unum coiecerunt et fecerunt perfectissimum decusis sexis.*' trans F. Granger, *Vitruvius: De architectura*, Harvard University Press, Cambridge, 1933 , pp. 164–65: 'But afterwards they perceived that both numbers were perfect, both the six and ten; and they threw them together, and made the most perfect number sixteen.' It seems that this is a play on Pythagorean arithmetic. Both 6 and 10 are perfect numbers – 6 arithmetically and 10 'theologically' – and they are the third and fourth trigonal numbers respectively. Together they make the fourth tetragonal number 16. Only Vitruvius seems to think that 16 is 'the most perfect number'.

19 D'Ooge, *op. cit.*, II.xix, pp. 259–62.

20 D'Ooge, *op. cit.*, II.xiii-xiv, pp. 249–252.

of the polygon which depicts it. Every number, in this sense, is a polygon, and vice-versa.[16]

Another way of visualizing this relationship is to imagine that a triangle is added to the side of a polygon. 'Naturally, then, the triangle is the element of the polygon both in figures and in numbers . . . .'[17] Of special note is the relationship that two successive trigonal numbers form a tetragonal number: for example, the third and fourth trigonal numbers form the fourth tetragonal number, 6 + 10 = 16.[18] Nicomachus argues that triangularity arises from the primal contrariety of odd and even. That the successive summations of odd numbers build the tetragonal numbers, while the successive summations of the even numbers build the heteromecic.[19] (Fig. 6.) The addition of adjacent tetragonal numbers and heteromecic numbers in Fig. 6 then give rise to the trigonal variety. (Figs. 7, 8, 9.)

Polygonal numbers are planar. By heaping successive polygonal numbers upon one another, pyramidal numbers are constructed like piles of cannonballs. Effectively these numbers are found by summing successive terms from unity in the table given by Nicomachus for polygonal numbers.[20] (Table 3.) For the trigonal pyramid, the numbers are:

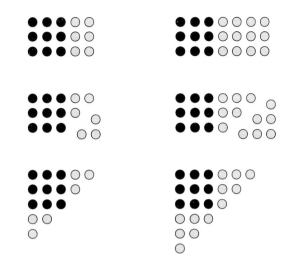

Fig. 8. (Right) Top row, the addition of a tetragonal number and compatible heteromecic numbers. Centre row, the heteromecic is decomposed into its two equal, trigonal components. Bottom row, these trigonal components are redistributed around the tetragonal base to make trigonal numbers.

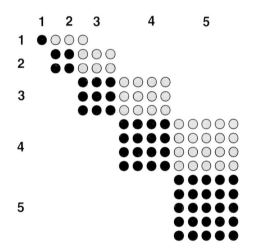

Fig. 9. (Right) Square, black, and heteromecic, grey, numbers follow the diagonal of the multiplication table (see Pythagorean Table p. 62). The trigonal numbers, black and grey, alternate with the reading of horizontal and vertical rectangles.

Table 3 Solid pyramidal numbers from the trigonal pyramid to the heptagonal pyramid obtained by summing polygonal numbers in Table 2.

▲	1	4	10	20	35	56	84	120	165	220
◆	1	5	14	30	55	91	140	204	285	385
⬠	1	6	18	40	75	126	196	288	405	550
⬡	1	7	22	50	95	161	252	372	525	715
⬣	1	8	26	60	115	196	308	456	645	880

Fig. 10. Detail from Raphael's 'School of Athens' showing *tetraktys*.

$$1, \quad 1+3=4, \quad 1+3+6=10, \quad 1+2+6+10=20 \quad \dots;$$

and for the tetragonal pyramid,

$$1, \quad 1+4=5, \quad 1+4+9=14, \quad 1+4+9+16=30 \quad \dots.$$

'From this too it becomes evident that triangles are the most elementary; for absolutely all of the pyramids that are exhibited and shown, with the various polygonal bases, are bounded by triangles up to the apex.' Nicomachus then states that 'we are sure to encounter in scientific writings' truncated versions of these pyramidal numbers in which the top layers are removed: one layer, truncated; two layers, bi-truncated; three layers, tri-truncated; 'and so on as far as you care to carry the nomenclature'.[21]

It will be observed that a number may have several guises as a figurate number. For example, the number 55 is the tenth trigonal number, the fifth heptagonal number, and the fifth tetragonal pyramid.[22] We may represent this as:

$$55 = \triangle\, 10 = \bigcirc\, 5 = \blacklozenge\, 5.[23]$$

Alberti's description of the decad is unusual. Vitruvius writes: 'Plato considered that number perfect, for the reason that from the individual things which are called monades among the Greeks, the decad is perfected.'[24] The Pythagoreans refer to the *tetraktys*, made up of the number 1, 2, 3, 4, which add up to 10. Wittkower shows a detail from Raphael's *School of Athens* in the Vatican, but he does not draw attention to the tetraktys on the slate held by the Pythagorean follower.[25] Note that the Pythagoreans' oath – mentioned above by Alberti – was 'by the *tetraktys*'. The tetraktys is depicted as a triangular figure:[26]

```
        I
      I   I
    I   I   I
  I   I   I   I.
```

Or:

$$1 + 2 + 3 + 4 = 10.$$

Alberti presumably finds this observation trite. In modern notation, he prefers the more esoteric:

$$1^3 + 2^3 + 3^3 + 4^3 = 10^2.$$

This equality may not be pellucid to modern eyes, but to a Renaissance mathematician versed in Nicomachus it is patent. According to Nicomachus square numbers are generated by summing successive odd numbers.[27] For example, the first ten odd numbers sum to the square of ten:

$$1 \quad 3 \quad 5 \quad 7 \quad 9 \quad 11 \quad 13 \quad 15 \quad 17 \quad 19.$$

21 *Ibid.*, II.xiv, p. 252. It is remarkable that, while visiting Paris, Gottfried Wilhelm Leibniz (1646–1716) actually copied by hand a manuscript of René Descartes (1596–1650) *De solidorum elementis*, in which Descartes extends the idea of polyhedral numbers to include those based on Platonic solids. This indicates the continuing fascination of the classical figuration of number among the finest of mathematicians. See P. J. Federico, *Descartes on polyhedra: a study of the 'De solidorum elementis*, Springer-Verlag, New York, 1982, an edition based on the only surviving manuscript – Leibniz's copy.
22 Another example: the number 30 is the fourth tetragonal pyramid, the third octagonal pyramid, and the third hendecagonal number.
23 The play on 5 and 10 in this depiction is important in the theological characterization of number, *vide infra*, 'Theological Number'.
24 Vitruvius III.i.5. Plato did not enter into such a consideration, see F. Cornford, *Plato's Cosmology*, Routledge & Kegan Paul, London, 1937, p. 69. Aristotle mentions that the Pythagoreans thought the number 10 perfect, *Metaphysics* I.v.986a 7–12.

Taking pairs of terms symmetrically placed about the centre, the larger may be reduced to ten by subtracting an amount which when added to the smaller term of the pair makes that term up to ten:

(1+9) (3+7) (5+5) (7+3) (9+1) (11–1) (13–3) (15–5) (17–7) (19–9)

10   10   10   10   10   10   10   10   10   10.

The Nicomachean arithmetician would visualize this as a tetragon, or a square formation of one hundred monads:[28]

```
I  I  I  I  I  I  I  I  I  I
I  I  I  I  I  I  I  I  I  I
I  I  I  I  I  I  I  I  I  I
I  I  I  I  I  I  I  I  I  I
I  I  I  I  I  I  I  I  I  I
I  I  I  I  I  I  I  I  I  I
I  I  I  I  I  I  I  I  I  I
I  I  I  I  I  I  I  I  I  I
I  I  I  I  I  I  I  I  I  I
I  I  I  I  I  I  I  I  I  I.
```

Yet Nicomachus shows that the cube numbers are also generated from the series of odd numbers: 'The first one makes the potential cube; the next two, added together, the second; the next three, the third; the four next, the fourth; the succeeding five, the fifth; the next six, the sixth; and so on.'[29] The sum of the first ten odd numbers may be arranged in the pattern of the *tetraktys*:

```
            1
          3   5
        7   9   11
     13   15   17   19.
```

Making the rows symmetrical, as in the previous example, gives:

```
            1
          4   4
        9   9   9
     16   16   16   16.
```

25 R. Wittkower, *Architectural Principles in the Age of Humanism*, Academy Editions, London, 1998, p. 119.

26 W. Burkett, *Lore and Science in Ancient Pythagoreanism*, Harvard University Press, Cambridge MA, 1972, p. 72.

27 D'Ooge, *op. cit.*, pp. 242–43, also Boethius, trans M. Masi, *Boethian Number Theory*, Rodopi, Amsterdam, 1983, pp. 151–52.

28 Such figures are common in both Nicomachus where the monad is represented by the Greek numeral α, and in Boethius where the Roman numeral I is used, as in Raphael's painting.

29 D'Ooge, *op. cit.*, pp. 263–64.

This suggest a reconfiguration of the one hundred monads:

```
                                    I

                              I  I    I  I
                              I  I    I  I

                     I  I  I    I  I  I    I  I  I
                     I  I  I    I  I  I    I  I  I
                     I  I  I    I  I  I    I  I  I

            I  I  I  I    I  I  I  I    I  I  I  I    I  I  I  I
            I  I  I  I    I  I  I  I    I  I  I  I    I  I  I  I
            I  I  I  I    I  I  I  I    I  I  I  I    I  I  I  I
            I  I  I  I    I  I  I  I    I  I  I  I    I  I  I  I.
```

So that the first row is the cube of one. The second row shows two squares of two, each with four monads, which placed one above the other make a cube of two containing eight monads. Similarly, the third row shows three squares of three which placed one above the other make a cube of three. The fourth row shows four squares of four which placed one above the other make a cube of four. Notice that little modern computation is necessary to verify the equality. Two distinct patterns are compared and found to be equivalent. The arithmetic is concrete and pictorial.

The treatment of the numbers six and ten illustrate the difference between modern arithmetic and calculation, and the classical system within which Alberti operated. Not only were numbers imbued with extranumeric qualities, but they were often visualized as geometric figures, combinations of which generated other figures. The square of four is seen as two successive triangular numbers, six and ten:[30]

```
            I  I  I  I
            I  I  I  I
            I  I  I  I
            I  I  I  I.
```

A square number conjoined to its immediately preceding triangular number, makes a pentagonal number; a pentagonal number conjoined to its immediately preceding triangular number makes an hexagonal number; and so forth.[31] A modern student who ignores such number attributes will fail to appreciate the nicety of their usage in the Renaissance, and particularly in a work such as Alberti's.

30 For example, Nicomachus, *op. cit.*, p. 247, shows how a triangular number and its immediate successor produce a square number. This seems to be the import of Vitruvius' remark that mathematicians had 'perceived that both numbers were perfect, both six and ten; and they threw both together and made the most perfect number sixteen'. Vitruvius III.i.8.
31 D'Ooge, *op. cit.*, pp. 243–44.

VIII

THEOLOGICAL NUMBER

Nicomachus wrote *Theologumena arithmeticae*, but this text has not survived. There are mentions of the work in later writings, and a work of the same title has been attributed to Iamblichus who cites Nicomachus along with Anatolius and others.[1] Indeed, it is said that the Iamblichean treatise is a compilation 'based almost entirely upon Nicomachus, aside from the obvious citations of Anatolius'.[2] The book examines the decad, the 'numbers' from one to ten, although the author follows neo-Pythagorean practice and does not count the monad and the dyad as numbers in themselves, but as the 'source' of all numbers. The first true number, then, is considered to be the triad, followed by the tetrad, pentad, hexad, heptad, octad, ennead and the decad itself. In a sense, none of these are numbers, but rather the qualities associated with number: with the quality of threefoldness, of fourfoldness, and so on; and the manifestation of these qualities internally among numbers themselves, and externally among divine essentials, ethical situations and physical objects. In arithmology, to mention a number is to draw attention to its qualities, and in turn to conjure up a theatre of allegories.[3]

I

The MONAD is identified with 'intellect,' resembling God in its creative principle as the source of all number. It is 'androgyne' in that it is both male and female. It is 'artificer' since its transformations model the corporeal world. 'If the potential of every number is in the monad, then the monad would be intelligible number in the strict sense, since it is not yet manifesting anything actual, but everything is conceptually together in it.' The monad is form without matter. Like God it stands for sameness and changelessness. A number multiplied by one is not changed. One multiplied by one remains the same. The monad is likened to the geometrical point. The monad, however, is potential everywhere: it is a potential square, a potential cube, and so on.[4]

II

The DYAD is an element opposed to the monad. The dyad is corporeal matter, in contrast to the monad's purely intelligible form. The dyad is matter without form.

1 D. J. O'Meara, *Pythagoras Revived: Mathematics and Philosophy in Late Antiquity*, Clarendon Press, Oxford, 1989, questions the attribution to Iamblichus on the grounds that the anonymous *Theologoumena arithmeticae*, whoever its compiler might be, is not based on *On Pythagoras VII* – a text known to have been authored by Iamblichus, p. 15, n. 24. An excerpt from this text, by the prolific eleventh-century Byzantine scholar Michael Psellus, is translated by O'Meara in Appendix I, p. 223ff. See 'Ethical Number' n.1, *supra*. The Nicomachus original is only known through a summary produced by the Byzantine Patriarch Photius in the ninth century.
2 M. L. D'Ooge, *Introduction to Arithmetic*, University of Michigan, Ann Arbor, 1938, p. 83. See also the introduction in R. Waterfield trans, *Theology of Arithmetic*, Phanes Press, Grand Rapids, 1988, pp. 23–27, who writes: '. . . the author of our treatise is unknown.'
3 O'Meara, *ibid.*, p. 22 and n. 49, comments: 'To judge by the approach he takes, it seems that Nicomachus regards the proliferating Greek pantheon as a manner of referring to numbers; *his* gods and goddesses are the monad, dyad, triad. Or, as Photius expressed it, Nicomachus sought to make the numbers gods.'
4 Summaries from Waterfield *op. cit.*, pp. 35–40. K, Critchlow provides a thoughtful forward pp. 9–21.

The dyad is two halves of the monad, but the monad is a dyad of halves. Neither is sovereign over the other, although the monad is prior. Both must coexist. While multiplicands of the monad stand still, multiplication by the dyad extends to the infinite sequence of even-even numbers. The dyad is likened to the geometrical line. Neither monad, nor dyad exhibit shape which is first to be found in the triad's triangularity, the copula of the monad and the dyad.[5]

III

That Nature is composed of threes all philosophers agree.[6]

The TRIAD is the first actual number. It is the first to exhibit the 'primary perfection' of having end, middle, and beginning, $1 + 1 + 1$. Being the only number which is equal to the numbers that precede it, $1 + 2 = 3$, the number three is special. It is the number associated with the most primitive geometrical figure – the triangle with three sides and three vertices. There are three kinds of triangle – acute, right and obtuse; three dimensions – length, breadth and height; three configurations of the moon – waxing, full and waning; three original means – arithmetic, geometric and harmonic – with three terms in each, with three intervals which are the differences between the terms, and three reversals of ratio which generate three subcontrary means. The triad is called 'wisdom' for 'when people act correctly as regards the present, look ahead to the future, and gain experience from what has already happened in the past: so wisdom surveys the three parts of time, and consequently knowledge falls under the triad'.[7]

IIII

Some philosophers maintain that the fourfold is consecrated to divinity, and that the most solemn oaths should be based on it.[8]

The TETRAD is associate with all manner of foursomes: with the four elements – fire, air, water, and earth; the four powers – heat, cold, dryness and wetness; the four directions – north, east, south and west; the four seasons spring, summer, autumn and winter; the four parts of the body – head, trunk, legs and arms; the four kingdoms of the universe – angels, demons, animals and plants. The tetrad is the first solid, the tetrahedron with four faces and four vertices. There are four spatial limits – point, line, plane and solid. The quadrivium is a tetrad of sciences: 'Four are the foundations of wisdom – arithmetic, music, geometry, astronomy – ordered 1, 2, 3, 4.'[9] It also completes the tetraktys, the summation of the monad, the dyad , the triad and the tetrad which form the decad: $1 + 2 + 3 + 4 = 10$. Within the tetraktys are to be found the principal concords of harmony – the octave in the doubles $2 : 1$ and $4 : 2$; the fifth in the sesquialter, $3 : 2$; the fourth in the sesquitertian ratio, $4 : 3$. 'If the universe is composed out of soul and body in the number 4, then it is also true that all concords are perfected by it.' The tetrad is the first actual tetragonal number. The area of the 2×2 square is equal to its semiperimeter $2 + 2$. It is the only square with this property: square with shorter sides have semiperimeters larger than the

5 Waterfield, *ibid.*, pp. 41–48.
6 J. Rykwert, N. Leach, R. Tavernor trans, *Leon Battista Alberti: The Art of Building in Ten Books*, MIT Press, 1988, IX.5, p. 304.
7 Waterfield, *op. cit.*, pp. 55–64.
8 J. Rykwert, N. Leach, R. Tavernor, *op. cit.*, p. 304.
9 This is a different ordering than that implied by Nicomachus, 1, 3, 2, 4, in D'Ooge, *op. cit.*, I.iv,v, pp. 187–89.

area, and those with longer sides have semiperimeters smaller than the area. Such an argument is typical of the arithmologists' favourite threefold division: equality, the inequality of excess and the inequality of deficiency.[10]

V

> And as for the number five, when I consider the many varied and wonderful things that either themselves relate to that number or are produced by something that contains it – such as the human hand – I do not think it wrong that it should be called divine, and rightly be dedicated to the gods of the arts, and Mercury in particular.[11]

The PENTAD combines the dyad, the first even number, with the triad, the first odd number. The pentad is the marriage of male and female, and is reckoned a 'marriage' number. There are five regular solids – the tetrahedron, the octahedron, the hexahedron, or cube, the icosahedron, and the dodecahedron which respectively represent fire, air, earth, water, and the 'universe', or aether. Typical of the arithmologists' zeal is the computation that the sum of the faces of the five solids $4 + 8 + 6 + 20 + 12$ amounts to 50, or the product of decad with the pentad. Similarly, within the decad the observation is made that $1 + 9 = 2 + 8 = 3 + 7 = 4 + 6 = 5 + 5 = 10$, and that the pentad is its own conjugate, the arithmetic mean of the extremes and the average of the sum $1 + 2 + 3 + 4 + 5 + 6 + 7 + 8 + 9$, that is, $\frac{1}{9} \times 45$, or 5. The pentad is identified with justice, since pure justice demands equality – the balance of five with five stands for the rational and divine soul. The other partitions of the decad show excess against deficiency, the mortal and irrational inequalities. The greater aspect reflects the cornucopean passionate soul, the lesser the hungry appetitive soul. The number 5 is the length of the hypotenuse in the Pythagorean triangle with sides of 3 and 4. The Greek letter theta stands at the end of the first course of numbers from one to nine. In the middle is epsilon for the number five. The character for the letter epsilon is appropriately half of the letter theta when divided along the vertical axis

The number 5 is both circular, $5 \times 5 = 25$, and spherical $5 \times 5 \times 5 = 125$. The pentad is called 'Pallas', after Athena, because it reveals the quintessential aether.[12]

VI

> The sixfold is one of the very few which is called 'perfect', because it is the sum of its integral divisors.[13]

The HEXAD is the progeny of the first female and male numbers, 2 and 3, by multiplication. A balance of genders, it is said to be androgenous. Like the pentad it is also a marriage, but by product not addition. 'It is called "marriage" because it is equal to its own parts, and it is the function of marriage to make offspring similar to parents.'

10 Waterfield, *op. cit.*, pp. 55–64.
11 J. Rykwert, N. Leach, R. Tavernor, *op. cit.*, p. 304. The accepted order of the 'wandering stars' was Saturn, Jupiter, Mars, Venus, Mercury. Mercury appears fifth in this list. Vitruvius discusses the planets in reverse order according to the time each planet takes to complete a cycle through the signs of the zodiac – Mercury taking the least amount of time at 360 days and Saturn the longest at almost thirty years. Vitruvius IX.i.
12 Waterfield, *op.cit.*, pp. 65–74.
13 J. Rykwert, N. Leach, R. Tavernor. *op. cit.*, p. 304.

The primary perfection is having beginning, middle and end, $2 + 2 + 2$. The secondary perfection is being equal to its own parts, $1 + 2 + 3 = 6$. Whereas the triad possesses primary perfection, it does not possess the secondary; but the hexad is characterized by both perfections. Examining successive triads of numbers 1, 2, 3; 4, 5, 6; 7, 8, 9; and so on, it is observed that their sums are 6, 15, 24,. . . . In turn, adding the digits, 6, $1 + 5$, $2 + 4$, the hexad, 6, is produced. This procedure knows no end: 'all number is formed by the dependence of triad on hexad; and since number is formative of the formlessness in matter, we would not be wrong in considering the hexad to be the form of forms.' There are six extensions to a solid body – up, down, left, right, front and back. There are six incomposite proportions – multiple, superparticular, superpartient, submultiple, subsuperparticular and subsuperpartient. The hexad is at the root of harmony. The double of the hexad, 12, is in the octave relation to 6. Between lies the sesquioctave $9 : 8$. Nine is the arithmetic mean and eight is the harmonic mean. This proportion, $6 : 8 :: 9 : 12$, is the perfect proportion which concludes Nicomachus' *Introduction to Arithmetic*. Now, $6 + 8 + 9 + 12 = 35$ and six times 35 is 210. The classical month is 30-days long, so that 210 days is seven months. This is one of the periods of gestation which engender healthy living beings. Taking the triple ratio from 6 to 18, the two intervening means are 9 and 12. Their sum, $6 + 9 + 12 + 18$ is 45 which, multiplied by the hexad, gives 270, or nine months. This is the second propitious gestation period to be found often in classical arithmology. Upon such arguments it is said that the hexad is 'soul-like'. The multiplicative triad $6 \times 6 \times 6$ is 216, 'the period pertaining to seven-month offspring, when the seven months are added to the six days in which the seed froths up and germinates', is also the number for the transmigration of the soul which recurs in cycles of 216 years.[14]

VII

> And as for the number seven, it is clear that the great maker of all things, God, is particularly delighted by it, in that he has made seven planets to wander the heavens, and has so regulated man, his favorite creature, that conception, formation, adolescence, maturity, and so on, all these stages are reducible to seven. According to Aristotle, when a child was born, the ancients would not give it a name for seven days. For both the seed in the womb and the new born baby are at grave risk for the first seven days.[15]

The HEPTAD 'is not born of any mother and is a virgin.' Within the decad it is not composed of any preceding numbers, but unlike 3 and 5 it cannot mate with a number in the decad to produce another number within the decad: $2 \times 3 = 6$, $3 \times 3 = 9$, $2 \times 5 = 10$, whereas $2 \times 7 = 14$. It is thus a virgin. Being an odd prime, it has no other factors other than 1 and 7 neither of which is purely female. It has no mother. It is called 'Athena' because it is a virgin and like Athena is born solely from the head of the monad, Zeus, and not from the womb of a mother. Athena is sometimes known as the Hebdomad. There are seven elementary sounds, those of the 'seven vowels and seven alterations of voice', those of the musician's heptachord and those of the seven heavenly bodies. There are seven apertures in the head – two eyes, two ears, two nostrils, and one mouth. There are seven geometrical entities – point, line, surface, angle, shape, solid, and plane – which is a thoroughly confusing classification, but is in no way untypical of the arithmologists' attempt to categorize and to force number

14 Waterfield, *op. cit.*, pp. 75–86. The number 216 occurs in Vitruvius V. Introduction 3, F. Granger trans, *Vitruvius: De Architectura*, Harvard University Press, Cambridge MA, 1931, I p. 253: 'Pythagoras also, and those who followed his sect, decided to write their rules, cube fashion, in their volumes, and fixed upon a cube 216 lines – and they thought that not more than three cubes should be in one treatise. Now a cube is a body with all its sides square and their surfaces equal. When a cube is thrown, on whatever part it rests, it retains its stability unmoved so long as it is untouched, like the dice, which players throw in a tray. Now this analogy they seem to have taken from the fact that this number of verses, like a cube upon whatever sense it fall, makes the memory there stable and unmoved.' D. Barbaro, *M. Vitrvvii Pollionis De architectura libri decem cum commentariis* . . . Venice, 1567, p. 157, shows that the number 216 may also be expressed as the sum of the cubes on the three sides of the 3, 4, 5 Pythagorean triangle $3^3 + 4^3 + 5^3 = 6^3$.

15 J. Rykwert, N. Leach, R. Tavernor, *op. cit.*, p. 304.

patterns on the world. There are seven aspects of the triangle – the three edges, the three vertices, and its area. There are several examples of the use of the hebdomad in medicine especially in conception, pregnancy and birth as well as the various cycles of fever. Seven is the length of the two sides of the 3, 4, 5 Pythagorean triangle. Seven is the ages of man. Seven the number of planets. The sum of the first seven numbers $1 + 2 + 3 + 4 + 5 + 6 + 7 = 28$, the cycle of the moon in nights, and 28 is perfect in its parts $1 + 2 + 4 + 7 + 14 = 28$. Starting with the monad and doubling seven times, the first number which is both square and cube, 64, is produced. While trebling seven times produces the second square-cube number, 729. The hebdomad represents actual corporeality consisting of three dimensions – length, breadth and height – and four limits – point, line, plane and solid.[16]

VIII

It is clear that eightfold exerts a great influence on Nature. Those born in the eighth month will not survive, we have observed, except in Egypt. They say also that a pregnant woman who gives birth to a stillborn baby in the eighth month will herself soon die. If the mother lies with a man during the eighth month, the child will be full of thick mucus and will have a foul skin full of thoroughly unpleasant scabs.[17]

The OCTAD is the first actual cube. 'All the ways it is put together are excellent and equilibrated tunings.' It is the sum of the only two numbers within the decad which are neither engenderers nor engendered, $1 + 7$, the monad and the heptad; the sum of the only two even odd numbers in the decad, the one potential and the other actual, $2 + 6$, the dyad and the hexad; and the sum of the first two actual odd numbers, $3 + 5$, the triad and the pentad. The latter is the first actual summation of odd numbers which define the cubes: $(1) = 1$, $(3 + 5) = 8$, $(7 + 9 + 11) = 27$, and so on. It is also twice the tetrad, and four is the only number which – unlike the heptad – both engenders and is engendered within the decad: $2 \times 4 = 8$ and $2 \times 2 = 4$. The ogdoad is 'untimely for birth' since, according to fable, labour in the eighth month is without issue. Yet the number eight is the source of harmony in the universe:

the 9 of the Moon is in sesquioctaval relation to 8	$9 : 8$;
the 12 of Mercury is the sesquialter of 8	$3 : 2$;
the 16 of Venus is double 8	$2 : 1$;
the 21 of Mars is the double sesqitertian of 9	$7 : 3$;
the 24 of Jupiter is the double of 12, the sesquialter of 8	$2 : 1$;
the 32 of Saturn is quadruple 8	$4 : 1$;
the 36 of the fixed stars is quadruple 9, and the sesquioctave of 32	$9 : 8$.[18]

VIIII

Another popular odd number was nine, that of the orbs which Provident has set in the sky. Then again the physicians are all agreed that many

16 Waterfield, *op. cit.*, pp. 87–100.
17 J. Rykwert, N. Leach, R. Tavernor, *op. cit.*, p. 304.
18 Waterfield, *op. cit.*, pp. 101–4.

of the most important things in Nature are based on the fraction one ninth. For one ninth of the annual solar cycle is about forty days, the length of time, according to Hippocrates, that it takes the fetus to form in the uterus. And we notice as a rule that it takes forty days to recover from a grave illness. Menstruation ceases forty days after conception, if the child is to be a boy, and starts a similar time after birth, if a boy has been born. And during the first forty days you will not see the child laughing or crying while he is awake, although he will do both while asleep – so they say.[19]

The ENNEAD is the greatest of numbers within the decad. After it comes 10 which is reduced to 1 when 9 is subtracted, 11 becomes 2, and 20 becomes 2 after two subtractions of 9. This is the 'rule of nine' by which all numbers greater than 9 are brought into equivalence with one of the nine numbers between 1 and 9, 'so that it is no means possible for there to subsist any number beyond the nine elementary numbers'. It is called 'Oceanus' because, like the bounding ocean, it is the furthest limit of number. 'It is called "Prometheus", because it prevents any number from proceeding further than itself, as is reasonable, since it is thrice perfect $[3 \times 3]$.' Recall that three is a primary perfect number because it has a beginning, middle, and end. The ennead is also the combination of two cubes, $1 + 8 = 9$, the first example of the general rule that the sums of cubes from 1 are tetragonal numbers. It is the first number to have a square root which is trigonal.[20]

X

> Aristotle thought the tenth the most perfect number of all; perhaps because, as some interpret, because its square equals the cube of four consecutive cube numbers.[21]

The DECAD is the starting point for nine more entities in the tens – 10, 20, 30, 40, 50, 60, 70, 80, 90 – beyond which lie the hundreds beginning with 100, and then the thousands from 1000. The author writes that ' number recurs and circles back, in a sense, to the decad; for a hekatontad is ten decads, and a chiliad is ten hekatontads, and a myriad is ten chiliads, and similarly any other number recurs and retrogresses either to the decad or some number within the decad. Anyway, the reduction and returning of numbers to it is manifold.' The decad is the monad of the second course, the hekatonad the monad of the third course, the chiliad, of the fourth course: an analogy in which the circuits of a horse track are evoked. Speusippus, Plato's nephew and successor as head of the Academy, is quoted as describing ten as a perfect number – in the theological, not arithmetical, sense. A theologically perfect number ought to be even so that it contains an equal number of even and odd numbers. There are four odd numbers 3, 5, 7, 9 and four even numbers 4, 6, 8, 10; leaving the 'sources', the monad and dyad, aside. A theologically perfect number should contain an equal number of prime and incomposite numbers, and secondary and composite numbers. The primes are 1, 2, 3, 5, 7 and the composite numbers are 4, 6, 8, 9, 10. No number less than ten has this property. Also no arithmetically perfect number, equal to the sum of its parts, has this property: consider 6 and 28. Forcing the matter further, Speusippus, argues that the decad

19 J. Rykwert, N. Leach, R. Tavernor, *op. cit.*, p. 304.
20 Waterfield, *op. cit.*, pp. 105–8.
21 J. Rykwert, N. Leach, R. Tavernor, *op. cit.*, p. 304. For $1^3 + 2^3 + 3^3 + 4^3 = 10^3$ *vide supra*, 'Shapeful Number'.

is balanced about the number 5, since there are four numbers, 1, 2, 3, 5, which are not composite below and including five, and four numbers above and excluding five which are composite, $6 = 2 \times 3$, $8 = 2 \times 2 \times 2$, $9 = 3 \times 3$, $10 = 2 \times 5$, – all products of the incomposite numbers. The numbers 4 and 7 are excused from this observation since they otherwise end up in the wrong camp. 'Furthermore, all the ratios are contained by 10 – that of the equal, and the greater and the less, and the super-particular and all the remaining kinds are in it, as are the linear, plane and solid numbers. For one is a point, two a line, three a triangle, and four a pyramid: these are all primary and are the sources of the things which are of the same category as each of them. In these numbers is also seen the first of proportions, which is the one where the ratios of excess are constant and the limit is ten.' This is a reference to the tetraktys where the elements sum to ten: $1 + 2 + 3 + 4 = 10$. Another occasion used to illustrate the decad is afforded by a classification of triangles. The equilateral triangle has one angle size and one line length and is identified with the monad. The right isosceles triangle has two angle sizes and two side lengths and is identified with the dyad. The third triangle is the half-triangle (half of the equilateral) in which there are three angle sizes and three side lengths. The system is then broken with the intrusion of a solid figure, 'going up to four', to complete the tetraktys and the decad. The same analogies do not, in fact, hold for the tetrahedron and the reader is offered an arithmologist's sleight of hand to conjure forth the number four.

Another author cited is Iamblichus' mentor, Anatolius, who reiterates these earlier remarks. Most probably in a lost reference to the pyramidal number $20 = (1) + (1 + 2) + (1 + 2 + 3) + (1 + 2 + 3 + 4)$, Anatolius notes that twice the tetraktys sums to twenty. It has already been observed that the decad has an equal division in $5 + 5$. This is likely to be the reason for this extended play on the number 55. Under the rule of nine 55 has an equivalence with the monad, $55 - 54 = 1$ and the decad, $55 - 45 = 10$.[22] The decad generates the trigonal number $55 = 1 + 2 + 3 + 4 + 5 + 6 + 7 + 8 + 9 + 10$, 'which encompasses wonderful harmonies'. From the Pythagorean lamda, the sums of 1, 2, 4, 8 and 1, 3, 9, 27 amount to 55, and these are Plato's sequences concerning the generation of the soul. The numbers of the decad squared give the sum $385 = 1 + 4 + 9 + 16 + 25 + 36 + 49 + 64 + 81 + 100$, which is 7×55. Factors of the hexad squared 36 sum to $55 = 18 + 12 + 9 + 6 + 4 + 3 + 2 + 1$, and this relates the arithmetically perfect hexad to the theologically perfect decad through the shared number 55. The truncated, trigonal pyramid made from the five trigonal numbers starting with the triad also comes to $55 = 3 + 6 + 10 + 15 + 21$, while the tetragonal pyramid built from the first five squares also amounts to $55 = 1 + 4 + 9 + 16 + 25$. Anatolius sees this as corroboration of Plato's claim that the universe is generated out of triangle and square.[23]

Alberti rehearses the theology of arithmetic associated with the decad. He takes the odd numbers first, and then the even numbers.[24] Following the Pythagorean tradition the numbers one and two are not mentioned. The monad and the dyad are not, in this tradition, strictly numbers, they are seen as the prime genitors of number.[25] The numbers properly start with three, the triad, generated by the union of the male monad with the female dyad. Alberti associates the numbers, among other things, with five fingers on a hand, seven planets in the heaven, nine orbs in the sky, the 'holy fourfold' oath, and the dire consequences of a stillbirth, or of coition during pregnancy, in the eighth month. The numbers six and ten are described as 'perfect'. Six because it is the sum of its factors, and ten because 'its square equals the cubes of the first four numbers'.[26]

22 $9 \times 6 = 54$, $9 \times 5 = 45$, and $5 + 5 = 10$ and $1 + 0 = 1$.
23 Waterfield, *op. cit.*, pp. 109–15. For Anatolius see O'Meara, *op. cit.*, pp. 23–25.
24 J. Rykwert, N. Leach, R. Tavernor, *op. cit.*, p. 303. Alberti points out the obvious: that, in a building, elements such as columns are even in number, while the openings between them are odd. Even and odd coexist in such configurations.
25 W. Burkert, *Lore and Science in Ancient Pythagoreanism*, Harvard University Press, Cambridge MA, 1972, p. 432.
26 See 'Shapeful Number' *supra*.

VIIII

OCCULT NUMBER

Fig. 1. The characters of the Hebrew alphabet distributed among nine chambers. From Agrippa, *De occulta philosophia*, 1533.

The Greeks had no special symbols for number, but used the letters of the alphabet instead. In the same way, the Hebrew and the Arabic languages at one time had no special symbols for the numerals.[1] The Hindu numbering system, which we use today, was introduced from Arabic sources to the West in the early stages of the mediaeval period.[2] Thus a Greek number might actually spell out a name, and all Greek words could be read as numbers. The Greeks used the pythmen, or base, which is a number within the decad equivalent to the sum of the digits in modern notation.[3] In the *Theologumena arithmeticae*, there are several examples where a word is read as a number to support an arithmological argument. The word monas, μουας, is equivalent to the number $40 + 70 + 50 + 1 + 200 = 361$. The monad 'reveals its kinship with the sun in the summation of its name, for the word "monad" when added up yields 361, which are the degrees of the zodiacal circle'. The pythmen of 361 is $10 = 3 + 6 + 1$, which reduces to one by the rule of casting out nines, the remainder when divided by nine.[4] The word cosmos, κοσμος, is found to be equivalent to the hexad of the second course $600 = 20 + 70 + 200 + 40 + 70 + 200$: 'for the universe [κοσμος], like 6, is often seen as composed of opposites in harmony, and the summation of the word 'universe' is 600. For this reason, the hexad is sometimes known as "universe"'.[5] In the section on the decad itself, the word 'hen', εν, for the number one, is noted as being equivalent to $55 = 5 + 50$, a number with many arithmetical guises, and $5 + 5 = 10$, which has the pythmen one when nines are cast aside.[6]

The twenty-four letter Greek alphabet with its numerical equivalencies is tabulated in *De occulta philosophia* by Henry Cornelius Agrippa, along with tables for the twenty-two letter Hebrew alphabet and the twenty-three letter Latin alphabet.[7] Names and words may be encoded into numbers. Numbers may be decoded as words and names. (Table 1 and Fig. 1.)

Agrippa also gives tables, or scales, for the decad with the addition of a scale for the dodecad in order to include the twelve apostles of Christ. These scales incorporate Hebraic and Christian references beyond the classical information provided in *Theologumena arithmeticae*. The scales are hierarchically organized in six 'worlds': the exemplary world, the world of the intelligibles, the celestial world, the elementary world, the lesser world, and the infernal world.[8]

For the monad: the highest world which is exemplary contains 'one divine essence' and the 'most simple letter', the Hebrew letter YOD ; the world of the intelligibles embraces the 'soul of the world', the celestial world holds the Sun, the elementary

1 See F. Cajori, *A History of Mathematical Notations: Notations in Elementary Mathematics* Open Court, La Salle, 1928, I, pp. 19–30; G. Ifrah, *From One to Zero: a Universal History of Numerals*, trans L. Bair, Viking, New York, 1985, Part IV, 'Numerals and letters', pp. 249–310. Also K. Menninger, *Number Words and Number Symbols: a Cultural History of Numbers*, trans P. Broneer, MIT Press, Cambridge, 1969, 'Alphabetical Numerals', pp. 257–76.
2 Cajori, *ibid.*, 'Hindu-Arabic Numerals' pp. 45–70; Ifrah, *ibid.*, 'The Origin of Hindu-Arabic Numerals' pp. 428–90; Menninger *ibid.*, 'Our Own Numerals' pp. 389–446.
3 T. L. Heath, *A History of Greek Mathematics*, Clarendon Press, Oxford, 1921, I, pp. 115–17, who cites Saint Hippolytus, *Refutation of all Heresies*, iv.c.14 as a source.
4 R. Waterfield, *Theology of Arithmetic*, Phanes Press, Grand Rapids, 1988, p. 39. The classical system of counting frequently double counts ends, thus 361 and not 360.
5 *ibid.*, p. 80.
6 *ibid.*, p. 115.
7 The letters of the Hebrew alphabet are partitioned into three groups: 'Three Mothers, Seven Doubles, Twelve Elementals'. See G. Scholem, *Kabbalah*, Dorset Press, New York, 1974, pp. 23–25A, for a summary. A. Kaplan, *Sefer Yetzirah: the Book of Creation in Theory and Practice*, Samuel Weiser,

Table 1 Greek and Hebrew numeral-alphabets and the Latin derivative with letters assigned to single digits 1–9, tens 10–90, and hundreds 100–900. After Henry Cornelius Agrippa, *De occulta philosophia*, 1533.

1	2	3	4	5	6	7	8	9
α	β	γ	δ	ε	ς	ζ	η	θ
ALPHA	BETA	GAMMA	DELTA	EPSILON	DIGAMMA	ZETA	ETA	THETA
א	ב	ג	ד	ה	ו	ז	ח	ט
ALEPH	BETH	GIMEL	DALETH	HE	VAV	ZAYIN	HETH	TETH
A	B	C	D	E	F	G	H	I

10	20	30	40	50	60	70	80	90
ι	κ	λ	μ	ν	ξ	ο	π	ϙ
IOTA	KAPPA	LAMDA	MU	NU	XI	OMICRON	PI	KOPPA
י	כ	ל	מ	נ	ס	ע	פ	צ
YOD	KAPH	LAMED	MEM	NUN	SAMEKH	AYIN	PE	TSADE
K	L	M	N	O	P	Q	R	S

100	200	300	400	500	600	700	800	900
ρ	σ	τ	υ	φ	χ	ψ	ϖ	ϡ
RHO	SIGMA	TAU	UPSILON	PHI	KHI	PSI	OMEGA	SAN
ק	ר	ש	ת	ך	ם	ן	ף	ץ
QOPH	RESH	SHIN	TAV	*KAPH	*MEM	*NUN	*PE	*TSADE
T	V	X	Y	Z	I	V	HI	HV

York Beach, 1990, gives a full discussion. *Sefer Yitzirah* 2:2 reads in Kaplan's translation, p. 100: 'Twenty-two Foundation letters:/ He engraved them,/ He carved them,/ He permuted them,/ He weighed them,/ He transformed them,/ And with them, He depicted all that was formed and all that would be formed.' On the three mothers 3.1, p. 139, reads: 'Three Mothers: Alef Mem Shin (אמש)/ Their foundation is/ a pan of merit/ a pan of liability/ and the tongue of decree deciding between them.' The dialectic of thesis, antithesis and synthesis is made very clear in 6:5, p. 230, which starts: 'Three:/ Each one stands alone/ one acts as an advocate/ one acts as an accusor/ and one decides between them.' The seven doubles with their two contrasting sounds are defined in 4:1, p. 159: ' . . . A structure of soft and hard,/ strong and weak.' The seven letters are assigned in a variety ways, but typical is 4:7, p. 174, 'Seven planets in the Universe:/Saturn, Jupiter, Mars,/ Sun,/ Venus. Mercury, Moon./ Seven days in the Year:/ The seven days of the week./ Seven gates in the Soul, male and female:/ Two eyes, two ears, two nostrils, and the mouth'. With twelve elementals, in 5:3, p. 209, ' . . . He formed/ twelve constellations in the Universe, twelve months in the Year/and twelve directors in the Soul,/ male and female.' Kaplan, p. 252, associates the numbers with the triangle, the square and the pentagon: 3 is the triangle, 7 is the triangle and the square, 12 is the triangle, square and pentagon. A simpler explanation might be the Pythagorean triangle, 3, 3 + 4 = 7, 3 + 4 + 5 = 12.

The twenty-four letters of the Greek alphabet are not organized in such a way although they clearly play distinctive linguistic roles. In both cases the letters stand for numerals in the absence of separate symbols for the latter. The placement of the letters into nine chambers, one each for the units, the tens and the hundreds – twenty-seven cells in all – makes room for the possibilty of five more Hebrew letters and three more Greek. Hebrew does this by having five 'finals', or alternative characters for existing letters. Greek does it by having a special symbol 'digamma' for the perfect number six, a symbol 'koppa' for 90 and 'san' for 900.

The Latin alphabet has twenty-three letters. It does not have characters for J., U., W. required to complete the modern twenty-six lettered English alphabet. H. C. Agrippa von Nettersheim, *Three Books of Occult Philosophy*, trans 'J. F.', London, 1651 (first published in Latin, 1533) explains how the Latin alphabet is extended, II, p. 235: 'And seeing in the Roman alphabet there are wanting four to make up the number twenty-seven Characters, their places are supplied with I and V simple consonants, as in the names Iohn and Valentine, and hi and hu aspirate consonants as in Hierom and Huihelme . . . '

8 *Ibid.* Each number from one to twelve is treated in a separate descriptive chapter together with a Table, II, p. 174–225. For background, see F. A. Yates, *Giordano Bruno and the Hermetic Tradition*, Routledge & Kegan Paul, London, 1964, particularly Chapter VII 'Cornelius Agrippa's Survey of Renaissance Magic', pp. 130–43; and F. A. Yates, *The Occult Philosophy in the Elizabethan Age*, Routledge & Kegan Paul, London, 1979, Chapter V, 'The Occult Philosophy and Magic: Cornelius Agrippa', pp. 37–48.

The Scale of the Number six.

In the examplary world.	אל גבור אלותים						Names of fix Letters.
In the intelligible World.	Seraphin.	Cherubin.	Thrones.	Dominations	Powers.	Vertues.	Six orders of Angels, which are not fent to inferiours.
In the Celeftiall World.	Saturn.	Jupiter.	Mars.	Venus.	Merchry.	The Moon.	Six planets wandring through the latitude of the Zodiack from the Eclyptick.
In the Elemental world.	Reft.	Thinnefs.	Sharpnefs.	Dulnefs.	Thicknefs.	Motion.	Six fubftantificall qualities of Elements.
In the leffer world.	The Intellect.	Memory.	Senfe.	Motion.	Life.	Effence.	Six degrees of men.
In the Infernall World.	Afteus.	Megalefius,	Ormenus,	Lycus,	Nicon.	Mimon.	Six divels, the authors of all calamities.

Fig. 2. The scale of the number six from Agrippa, *Three Books of Occult Philosophy*, English translation, 1651.

world contains 'the philosopher's stone'; the lesser world is home to 'the heart – first living, and last dead' and the infernal world is the abode of Lucifer.[9]

For the tetrad: the highest world is associated with the Tetragrammaton יהוה, while the world immediately below God is inhabited by, among others, 'the four triplicities of intelligible hierarchies' – the Seraphim, Cherubim, Thrones; the Dominations, Powers, Virtues; the Principalities, Archangels, Angels; and the Innocents, Martyrs, Confessors. The celestial world contains 'the four triplicities of signs [of the zodiac]' – first, Aries, Leo, Sagittarius; next, Gemini, Libra, Aquarius; then, Cancer, Scorpio, Pisces; and finally, Taurus, Virgo, Capricorn. The elementary world includes the four elements – fire, air, water, earth; the four qualities – heat, moisture, cold, dryness; the four seasons – summer, spring, winter, autumn; and the four corners of the world – east, west, north, south. The lesser world provides haven for the 'four elements of man' – mind, spirit, soul, body. The infernal world is environs for the four princes of darkness – Samael, Azazel, Azael, Mahazel; and the four rivers of Hades – Phlegeron, Cocytus, Styx, Acheron. These readings are the horizontal ones across Agrippa's table. Vertically, extraordinary correlations are set up from world to world. Consider this column from Agrippa's scale of four: one of the four angels ruling over the corners of the world – Michael; one of the rulers of the elements – Seraphim; one of the four consecrated animals – the Lion; one of the four triplicities of the tribes of Israel – Dan, Asher, Naphtali; one of the four triplicities of Apostles – Mathias, Peter, Jacob the Elder; one of the four Evangelists Mark; one of the four triplicities of signs – Aries, Leo, Sagittarius; one of the stars and planets related to the elements – Mars and the Sun; one of the four qualities of the celestial elements – Light; one of the four elements – Fire; one of the four qualities – Heat; one of the four seasons – Summer; one of the four corners of the world – the East; one of the perfect kinds of mixed bodies – Animals; one

9 Agrippa *op. cit.*, II, pp. 174–76.

of four kinds of animals – Walking; one of what answers the elements in plants – Seeds; one of what answers the elements in metals – Gold and Iron; one of what answers the elements in stones – Bright and Burning; one of four elements of man – the Mind; one of four powers of the soul – the Intellect; one of four judiciary powers – Faith; one of four moral virtues – Justice; one of the senses answering to the elements – Sight; one of the four elements of man's body – Spirit; one of the fourfold spirits – Animal; one of the four humors – Choler; one of the four manners of complexion – Violence; one of the four princes of devils – Samael; one of the four infernal rivers – Phlegeron; one of the four princes of spirits upon the four angles of the world – Oriens. Agrippa's scales and their curious correlations signal just how foreign the Renaissance world can be to us today.[10]

For the dodecad, the scale of twelve is headed, in the exemplary world, by the twelve permutations of the Tetragrammaton, **יהוה** YOD-HE-VAV-HE, the unspeakable name of God **ההוי היוה היהי יההו ההיי היהי ויהה היוה ההוי יהוה וההי יהוה** in which 'the great name [is] returned back into twelve banners'.[11] In the intelligible world are the twelve orders of the blessed spirits, the twelve angels ruling over the zodiacal signs, the twelve tribes of Israel, the twelve prophets, and the twelve apostles. In the celestial world reside the twelve signs of the zodiac. The elemental world is inhabited by the twelve months, the twelve plants, and the twelve [precious] stones. In the elementary world dwell the twelve principal members of the body – 'the head, the neck, the arms, the breast, the heart, the belly, the kidnies, genitals, the hams, the knees, legs, feet.' In the infernal world are 'twelve degrees of the damned, and of divels [sic]' – 'false gods, lying spirits, vessels of iniquity, revengers of wickedness, jugglers, aery powers, furies the sowers of evil, sifters, or triers, tempters, or ensnarers, witches, apostates, infidels.'

Later in this second book devoted to celestial magic, Agrippa enumerates nine magic squares, one for each of the heavenly bodies.[12] The square for Saturn is best known:

4	9	2
3	5	7
8	1	6

In this square all the rows, columns and diagonals sum to 15. The total sum is 45, the ninth trigonal number. The numbers associated with Saturn are, then, 3 for the number of elements in the columns, or the rows; 9 for the number of elements in the square, 15 and 45. Agrippa relates these numbers to Hebrew letters and names. The remaining tables follow the same pattern in which the second number is the square of the first, the fourth number is the trigonal number of the second, and the third number is the fourth divided by the first. To summarize:

Saturn	3	9	15	45
Jupiter	4	16	34	136
Mars	5	25	65	325

10 *Ibid.*, II, pp. 183–87. In his descriptive piece, Agrippa cites the Pythagorean oath: 'I with pure minde byth' number four do swear/ That's holy, and the fountain of nature/ Eternall, parent of the mind –.'

11 *Ibid.*, II, pp. 216–21. Agrippa gives the 'Orphic scale of the number twelve'. The twelve permutations on the Tetragrammaton are discussed by A. Kaplan, *Sefer Yetzirah: the Book of Creation in Theory and Practice*, Samuel Weiser, York Beach, 1990, pp. 197–202; but see the contemporary explanation by J. Reuchlin, *De Arte Cabalistica*, 1517, trans M. and S. Goodman, *Johann Reuchlin: On the Art of the Kabbalah*, Abaris Books, New York, 1983, pp. 304–7.

12 *Op. cit.*, Agrippa, II, Chapter 12, pp. 239–52 'Of the tables of the Planets, their virtues, forms, and what Divine names, Intelligences, and Spirits are set over them.'

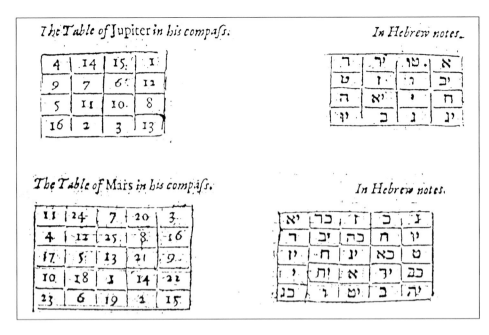

Fig. 3. The magic squares of Jupiter (top) and Mars (bottom) from Agrippa, *Three Books of Occult Philosophy*.

Sun	6	36	111	666
Venus	7	49	157	1252
Mercury	8	64	260	2080
Moon	9	81	369	3321.

In each case, Hebrew letters are associated with the numbers. In particular, the number 5, ה HE , for Mars is 'a letter of the Holy Name', and 65 is numerically equivalent to the speakable name of the Lord 'Adonai', אדני . For the Sun, the number 6, ו VAV , is also marked as 'a letter of the Holy Name'.[13]

Agrippa describes the interrelationships between the planets, the nine Muses – Thalia, Clio, Calliope, Terpsichore, Melpomene, Erato, Euterpe, Polihymnia, Urania – and the modes of ancient music. 'We read them expressed in these verses':

Silent Thalia we to th' Earth compare.
For she by Musick, never does ensnare,
After the Hypodorian Clio sings,
Persephone likewise doth strike the base strings;
Calliope also doth Chord second touch,
Using the Phrygian; Mercury as much:
Terpsichore strikes the third, and that rare,
The Lydian Musick makes so Venus fair,
Melpomene, and Titan do with a grace
The Dorian Musick use in fourth place.
The fift ascribed is to Mars the god
Of War, and Erato after the rare mode

13 The square for Jupiter, *Mensula Jovis*, appears in Dürer's engraving *Melencholia I*. The square is inverted from that shown by Agrippa and the two central columns are exchanged so that the bottom row in Dürer reads 4, 15, 14, 1. The date of the engraving is 1514. E. Panofsky, *The Life and Art of Albrecht Dürer*, Princeton University Press, 1955, remains the outstanding commentator on this enigmatic work. His remarks include references to Agrippa's manuscript version of *De occulta philosophia* which had been in circulation from 1509/10, pp. 156–71.

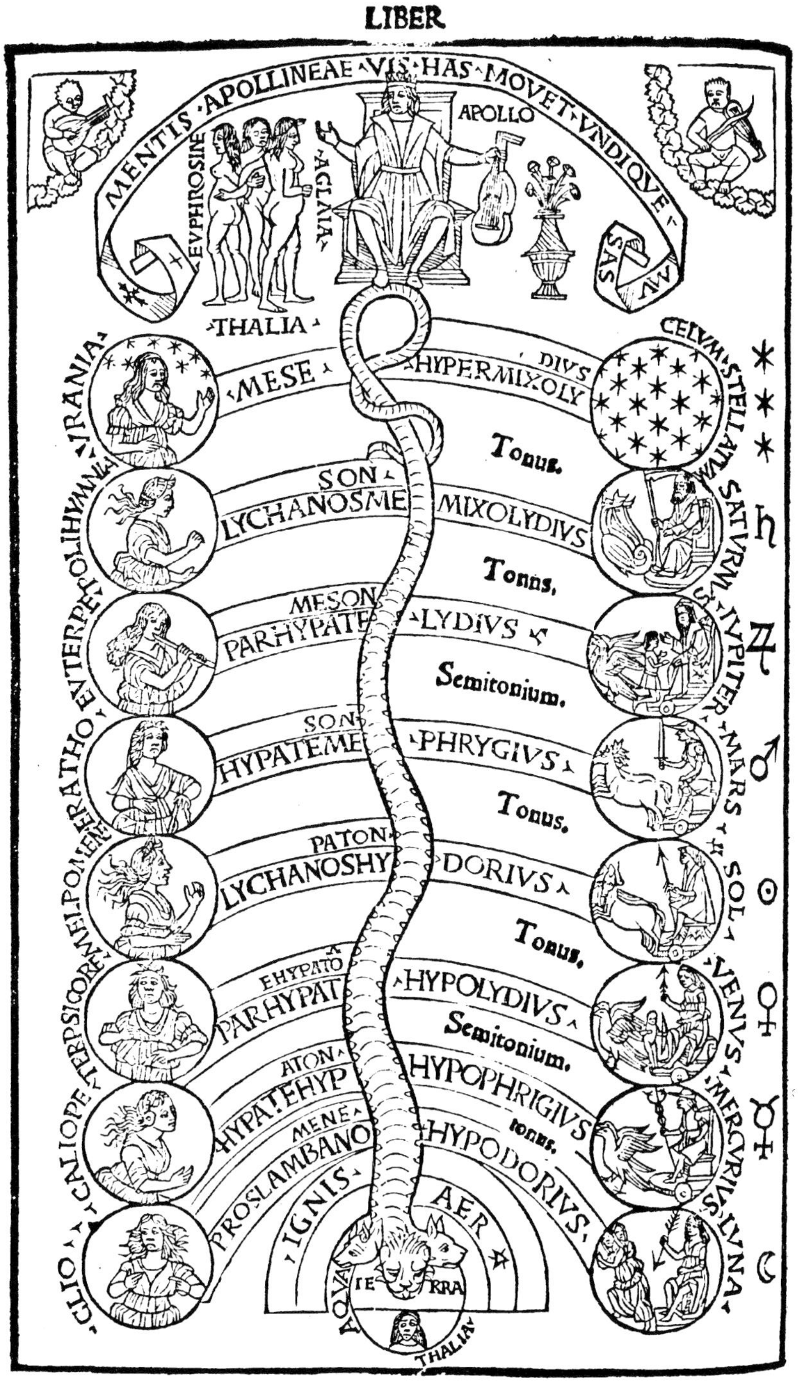

Fig. 4. The relationship of the muses, heavenly bodies, and musical modes under the governance of Apollo and the Three Graces. Woodcut from Franchinus Gaffurius, *De harmonia musicorum instrumentorum opus*, 1518.

14 *Op. cit.*, Agrippa, II, pp. 259–62. The precise attribution of the Muses to the musical modes varies between authors. See J. Godwin, *Harmonies of Heaven and Earth: the Spiritual Dimensions of Music from Antiquity to the Avant-Garde*, Inner Traditions, Rochester VE, 1987, Part III. 11, 'Angelic Orders and Muses: the Great Chain of Being', pp. 167–76. Also, citations from many authors in J. Godwin, *The Harmony of the Spheres: a Sourcebook of the Pythagorean Tradition in Music*, Inner Traditions, Rochester VE, 1993.

15 *Op. cit.*, Agrippa, III, pp. 433–34. The permutational interest of cabalism is asserted in 4:12 of *Sefer Yetzirah*, 'Two stones build 2 houses/ Three stones build 6 houses, Four stones build 24 houses/ Five stones build 120 houses/ Six stones build 720 houses/ Seven stones build 5040 houses/ From here on go out and calculate/ that which the mouth cannot speak/ and the ear cannot hear'. Kaplan, *op. cit.*, pp. 190–93. It is noteworthy that 5040 = 1.2.3.4.5.6.7 is the same number that Plato chooses in *Laws* 737 'The number of our citizens shall be 5040 – this will be a convenient number; and these shall be owners of the land and protectors of the allotment'. For an intriguing exegesis of Plato's arithmetical conceits, see E. G. McClain, *The Pythagorean Plato: Prelude to the Song Itself*, Nicolas-Hays, York Beach, 1978, especially Chapter 8, pp. 97–115.

16 *Vide supra*, 'Prisoners of Number'.

17 *Op. cit.*, Agrippa, II, pp. 263–64. See J. Rykwert, N. Leach, R. Tavernor, *Leon Battista Alberti*, MIT Press, Cambridge MA, 1988, XIII.7, p. 309. Also J. Rykwert, *The Dancing Column: On Order in Architecture*, MIT Press, Cambridge, 1997, p. 369, draws attention to the strange mythology of Noah's Etruscan past which was readily accepted in the Medici court. *Vide supra*, 'Prisoners of Number', and 'Judaic Heritage'.

18 D. P. Walker, *Spiritual and Demonic Magic from Ficino to Campanella*, The Warburg Institute, University of London, 1958, p. 86ff, describes the work of Johannes Trithemius who is generally recognized as having been a mentor to Agrippa. His *Steganographica* which was not published until 1606, but was known in manuscript form well before then, is a treatise on cryptography mixed with angelic magic. In 1506 the magical elements were cause, in part, for the monks at Spanheim to expel Trithemius, their Abbot. In 1518, a book which left aside the magical aspects and concentrated on the cryptography was published: *Polygraphiae libri sex, Ioannis Trithemii . . .* the book was reprinted in 1550 and 1557 during the sixteenth century, and translated into French in 1561. Agrippa's own dedication gives an ample description of 'The Reverend Father in Christ, and Most Illustrious Prince, Hermannus, Earl of Wyda, by the Grace of God Archbishop of the Holy Church of Colonia, Prince Elector of the Holy Roman Empire, and Chief Chancellor through Italy of the Legate of the Holy Church of Rome'. *Op. cit.*, Agrippa, I, p. vii.

19 See L. Geiger, *Johann Reuchlin sein Leben und seine Werke*, B. de Graaf, Nieuwkoop, 1964 (first published Leipzig, 1871). Also M. and S. Goodman trans, *Johann Reuchlin: On the Art of the Kabbalah*,

Of th' Phrygians, Euterpe doth also love
The Lydian, and sixt string; and so doth Jove.
Saturn the seventh doth use with Polymny,
And causeth the mixt Lydian melody.
Urania also doth the eight create.
And musick Hypo-Lydian elevate.[14]

In Book III of *De occulta philosophia*, Agrippa investigates the combinatorial and permutational devices of the cabalistic art in which appear commutation tables of the twenty-two letters of the Hebrew alphabet, combination tables of letter pairs, and tables in which the signs of the seven planetary bodies – Moon, Mercury, Venus, Sun, Mars, Jupiter, Saturn –

☽ ☿ ♀ ☉ ♂ ♃ ♄

and the twelve signs of the zodiac – Pisces, Aquarius, Capricorn, Sagittarius, Scorpio, Libra, Virgo, Leo, Cancer, Gemini, Taurus, Aries –

♓ ♒ ♑ ♐ ♏ ♎ ♍ ♌ ♋ ♊ ♉ ♈

are set against the Hebrew alphabet:

א ב ג ד ה ה ו ז ח ט י כ ל מ נ ס ע פ צ ק ר ש ת

to produce Hebrew words which, reading one way, provide 'entrances' to the good angels. Reading the other way, they offer 'entrances' for the evil angels.[15]

The estimated distances between the heavenly bodies are compared by Agrippa with musical intervals as Iamblichus had demonstrated. The next step in universal harmony is the measure of the human frame compared with regular geometrical figures – the circle, the pentagon, the square and the triangle.[16] Agrippa makes a biblical allusion to the dimensions of the Ark and the dimensions of man: 'Moreover God himself taught Noah to build the Arke according to the measure of man's body; from hence it is called the great world, man's body the less . . . for as the body of man is in length three-hundred minutes, in breadth fifty, and height thirty; so the length of the Arke was three-hundred cubits, the breadth fifty, and the height thirty; that the proportion of the length to breadth be six-fold, to the height ten-fold, and the proportion of the breadth to height about two-thirds . . . there is no member in man which hath not correspondence with some sign, some star, intelligence, divine name, sometimes in God himself the Archetype.'[17]

De occulta philosophia is addressed to two notable churchmen, Abbott John Trithemius, and Hermannus, Archbishop of Colonia.[18] It is a remarkable compendium of magical devices, but the impression is that there is nothing original in Agrippa's effort apart from the very act of collecting somewhat commonplace materials together: commonplace, that is, in esoteric and necromantic circles.

The play of number and alphabet in Hebrew is well illustrated in earlier treatises by the distinguished German humanist and scholar, Johann Reuchlin: in *De verbo mirifico* and *De arte cabalistica*.[19] Reuchlin had met Giovanni Pico della Mirandola in Florence in 1490, just four years after Pico had attempted to present his nine hundred theses reconciling Classical, Christian, Hebraic, Arabic and Hermetic philosophies, and three years after Pico issued his apology and the oration *De hominis dignitate*. Pico sketched his irenic outline of a grand synthesis, but he had little time to delve into the detailed workings. Reuchlin concentrated on the Jewish contribution and the Kabbalah in particular. He was fascinated by the ineffable word for God and its transformation into the word for the Messiah. The words were in Hebrew: the Tetragrammaton יהוה (Jehovah) and the Pentagrammaton יהשיה (Jhesu) in which the letter SHIN ש is inserted between the second and third letters of the four-letter word.[20]

De arte cabalistica is dedicated to Pope Leo X. The argument is a dialogue between a Jew of Frankfurt, Simon, with knowledge of the Kabbalah; a Moslem, Marranus, fom Constantinople, a student of Arabic philosophy including Avicenna and Averroes; and Philolaus from the Caucasus who is 'by persuasion Pythagorean'. Simon asks the other two how they had come to know of him. They reply that the expulsion from Spain had scattered Jews throughout the world and Simon's reputation had travelled with the diaspora. Simon was known worldwide, they tell him, for his erudition concerning the Kabbalah.[21]

Reuchlin's aim, he informs Pope Leo X, is to restore knowledge of Pythagoras through the Kabbalah; just as Marsilio Ficino, he writes, under the patronage of the Pope's grandfather Cosimo de' Medici, had revived Platonic studies; and Jacques Lefèvre d'Etaples had promoted Aristotle. Reuchlin draws special attention to national contributions: Ficino for the Italians, Lefèvre for the French, and himself for the German – 'Capnion ego germanis', Capnion being Reuchlin's assumed Latin name. Reuchlin writes concerning Pythagoras: 'His philosophy, however, I have only been able to glean from the Hebrew Kabbalah, since it derives in origin from Southern Italy into Kabbalistic writings.'[22] The Hebrews, according to this account, absorbed and preserved the esoteric knowledge of the Pythagorean community of Croton in the south of the Italian peninsula. This confusion of Pythagoreanism with the Kabbalah is almost certainly designed to inform an Italian prince about Jewish mysteries under cover of chauvinistic, Latin traditions. There is little substantial information about Pythagoras in *De arte cabalistica*, but considerable technical knowledge about the Kabbalah. The dialogue presents a zealous display of contrived syncretism.[23]

Simon speaks of the fifty gates of intelligence. 'Everything in the universe is classified in five groups, according to their state: the elements and things made of elements, souls, celestial bodies, supercelestial bodies. Each of these is subdivided under ten heads as follows: main groups, subgroups, main species, subspecies, individual things. Not included in these are matter and form, which each relate to each other in ways entailing attributes, properties and qualities. These ten modes of essence and understanding multiplied by five, are the fifty open gates by which we enter creation's secret lairs, following the clues given in the six days grasped fervently by the Kabbalists.'[24] Reuchlin then cites Pico: 'He would know the denary numbers in formal arithmetic, will know the secret of the fifty gates of intelligence, and the great jubilee, and of the thousandth generation, and of the kingdom of all ages.' To unravel this statement, Reuchlin makes use of the description given by Iamblichus in which the numerals from one to nine are arranged around the number five so that diametrically opposite numbers sum to 10. The numbers 1, 2, 3, 6, 9, 8, 7, 4 encircle the 5.

Abaris Books, New York, 1983, and useful 'Introduction' by G. Lloyd Jones, pp. 7–32.

20 Lloyd Jones in Goodman, *ibid.*

21 Goodman, *op. cit.*, pp. 39–45.

22 *Ibid.*, p. 39.

23 *Ibid.*, In Book II, Philolaus and Marranus – without Simon – mainly discuss neo-Platonic authorities as conveyors of the Pythagorean tradition including Iamblichus, Plotinus, Porphyry and Proclus.

24 *Ibid.*, p. 249.

1	2	3
4	5	6
7	8	9

'If you subtract from the greater number the amount by which it exceeds five, the centre of the denary circle, and add to the lesser number the amount by which it is less than five, the pairs of opposite numbers always yield the equalized five and five. If you compare the points of the line in turn, the numerical value of any line is always five and five. The number five, in the ten-circle, is therefore said to be "circular", because as you see, all the numbers on the circle reduce to five, and further there are five lines drawn within the circle which each make up ten.' The 'lines' are $1 + 9$, $2 + 8$, $3 + 7$, $6 + 4$, and the degenerate case $5 + 5$. 'When this circular number is multiplied by ten it makes fifty – gates of understanding or years of the jubilee.' He continues to show how the thousandth year is achieved, and eventually 'the kingdom of all ages'.[25] It is important to realize that such an obvious, almost tautological, computation is laboured over deliberately to emphasize a spiritual meaning higher than a simple grocer's transaction.

Moses is said to have passed through forty-nine gates to find the Law, but was held back from seeing the face of God, or the name of God, the Tetragrammaton, in that 'incomparable world that cannot be made comprehensible by any analogy'. Joshua reached the forty-eighth gate, one step behind Moses.[26]

In all this there may be some allegorical recapitulation of Plato's problems in the *Timaeus*. The ratio $7 : 5$ is a rational convergent to $\sqrt{2} : 1$ since a square of side length 5 has a rational diameter of length 7: as Pythagoras' theorem demonstrates $5^2 + 5^2 = 50$ and $7^2 = 49$, one 'step' less. An equilateral triangle of sides 8, and therefore a halfbase of 4, has a rational altitude of 7. Pythagoras' relation gives $8^2 = 64$ for the square on the hypotenuse, and $7^2 + 4^2 = 63$ for the squares on the sides, again one 'step' less. Now, $7^2 = 49$ and $3 \times 4^2 = 48$ so that $7 : 4$ is a rational convergent for $\sqrt{3} : 1$. In this geometrical way the numbers 50, 49 and 48 are related to rational values of $\sqrt{2}$ and $\sqrt{3}$, each pair missing by one 'step'.[27]

Reuchlin then proceeds to describe each of the gates in turn, the first six 'after God' and then the remaining gates corresponding to events of the 'six day's labor'.[28] He then enumerates 'the thirty-two paths of wisdom' to be found in *Sefir Yetzirah*, the book of creation attributed at the time to Abraham.[29] Simon, Reuchlin's spokesman in the dialogue, speaks: 'For people who long for foreign creeds, I have briefly catalogued our forebear's beliefs concerning the fifty gates of knowledge and the thirty-two paths of wisdom. They dealt with these matters in many books. It is a difficult subject and deserves a better teacher and much hard work. For it has great power to rouse us to near uninterrupted converse with the angels, in meditation on the highest and the divine; if we become closely associated with them, we shall find nothing – in word or deed – difficult. Such close association is achieved by the alphabet, which is its function. If we join the letters of the alphabet to the ten Kabbalistic numerations, straightway we get the number thirty-two. In the book *Yetzirah* it says "There are ten *sephiroth*, . . . and twenty-two letters."'[30] (Fig. 5.)

25 *Ibid.*, p. 251.
26 *Ibid.*, p. 253.
27 *Infra*, 'Inexpressible Proportion'.
28 *Ibid.*, pp. 253–55.
29 *Ibid.*, p. 257–59.
30 *Ibid.*, p. 261.

Simon continues: 'If we pay attention and add this alphabet to the fifty gates, we find the happy ranks of the seventy-two angels. . . . ' Simon then proceeds to show how the seventy-two mnemonics for the angels are found in three letter combinations systematically selected. 'Any Hebrew letter you take stands for a particular number, Thus, in this way, **יהוה** equals seventy-two; **י** [YOD] means ten, **ה** [HE] five, **ו** [VAV] six, **ה** [HE] five again. Put together arithmetically, **י** is ten, **יה** fifteen, **יהו** is twenty-one, **יהוה** twenty-six. Now add ten, fifteen, twenty-one and twenty-six, and the answer is seventy-two.'

'If from the four letters **יהוה**, you posit four YODs, and going down, three HES, two VAVS, one HE, you will soon get the sum seventy-two, which explains the ineffable and incomparable name of God to which all sacred names lead.'[31]

The numbers 10, 15, 21 and 26 are arrived at by summing the rows of the Tetragrammaton. The ratio 21 : 15 is 7 : 5, a rational convergent to $\sqrt{2}$: 1, while the ratio 26 : 15 is a good rational convergent for $\sqrt{3}$: 1. This makes 26 : 21 a rational convergent to $\sqrt{3}$: $\sqrt{2}$, while the ratio of the two top rows is 15 : 10 :: 3 : 2. Arithmetically, then, the Tetragrammaton appears to be a *memoria technica* for the same fundamental geometrical relationships which Plato speaks of in his account of the formation of the world in the *Timaeus*, namely those of the half square and of the half equilateral triangle.

Pico divided the Kabbalah into two parts; knowledge of the ten qualities marked by the sephiroth, and knowledge of letters and numbers, but 'most other Kabbalists follow Solomon the king and believe that the art can be divided into three, both in the speculative and the practical aspects, since there are three states of all – number, shape and weight'.[32]

'What is at issue is allegory. One understands one thing for another by using a third thing, thereby changing the whole sense of the phrase. So we say quite frankly that a word may be substituted for a word, or a letter for a word, or a letter for a letter. So, to begin, a word may be taken for another word either through transposition (called metathesis) or through the numerical equivalence of the letters in the two words. A letter may be posited to stand for a word, whether it lies at the beginning or end, or anywhere else, by a mark placed over it. A letter may be posited to stand for another letter through the alphabetical circle, the whole process assuring that, in the end, every arithmetical, geometrical and musical proportion is achieved.'[33]

Reuchlin, through his interlocutor Simon, goes on to describe three parts to the art of Kabbalah. 'First there is equivalence of numerical calculations. This is called *gematria* or "geometry". Geometry is the numerical measurement of shapes on earth but relies on a sort of arithmetic which, because of its abstract simplicity, cannot be worked on by any of the senses and so is not subjected to the crude efforts of novices. Thus the first part is called geometry rather than arithmetic, although both of them have equal importance in this art. Thereafter one can transfer syllables and thereby create either a transformed expression or a completely altered word. Second is the placing of a letter in the place of an expression. This is called *notarikon* from the marks or notaria on the top of each letter. Any letter may be marked on top to be a sign of another whole word. The third part of the art is the exchange of letters, when one letter is cleverly put in place of another. This called commutation [*temurah*].'[34]

There is not one gematriot for a word, because there is a plurality of ways for assigning numbers to letter. 'The Tetragrammaton, written out to give the full names

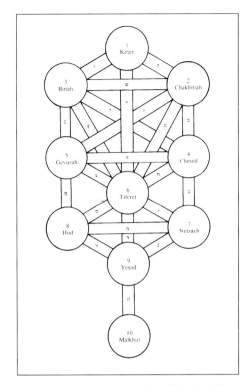

Fig. 5. The ten *Sephiroth* and the 32 paths. The first ten letters of the Hebrew alphabet are distributed among the *sephiroth* and they stand for the first ten numerals. The whole 22-letter alphabet is used to make the connections between the 10 *sephiroth*, which together constitute the 32 paths. After Kaplan, 16th century.

31 *Ibid.*, p. 267. There are many other ways of assigning numbers to the letters in *gematria*. Scholem, *op. cit.*, pp. 341–42 gives seven different methods. He refers to Ms.Oxford 1822 f141–46 which lists 72 different forms of *gematriot*. The word **יהוה** has a value $5 + 6 + 5 + 10 = 26$ in method (1); only the numbers between 1–9 are employed in method (2) so that the value is $5 + 6 + 5 + 1 = 17$; the square of these numbers is taken in method (3) giving two values depending on whether method (1) or (2) is used in the original numerical assignment – $5^2 + 6^2 + 5^2 + 10^2 = 186$, or $5^2 + 6^2 + 5^2 + 1^2 = 87$. Ifrah, *op.cit.*, p. 299, indicates that trigonal numbers may be used in which case the values 106 and 52 are obtained. For the Tetragrammaton the values would be – in the same order above – 72, 36, 572, 176, 322 and 106. Scholem also describes methods of 'filling' in which the letters are spelt out or otherwise expanded. Values for **יהוה**

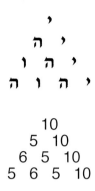

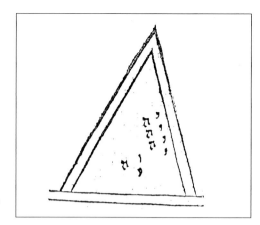

Fig. 7. The Tetragrammaton from Agrippa von Nettersheim, *De occulta philosophia* II.

```
            י
          ה  י
        ו  ה  י
      ה  ו  ה  י

            10
          5  10
        6  5  10
      5  6  5  10
```

Fig. 6. The Tetragrammaton showing the principal numerical interpretation in *gematria*. The rows sum to 10, 15, 21, 26 and the whole amounts to 72.

of the Hebrew letters, signifies Mah through numerical equivalence, since both add up to 45.'[35] Mah is the Hebrew for 'what', so that when Moses asks the question concerning God 'What is his name?', the answer is that 'what' is his name. In this case the names of the letter of the Tetragrammaton are spelt out individually, but those of Mah are not.

י	יהו	YOD	$4 + 6 + 70 = 20$
ה	הא	HE	$1 + 5 = 6$
ו	ואו	VAV	$6 + 1 + 6 = 13$
יהוה		Tetragrammaton	$6 + 13 + 6 + 20 = 45$
מה		Mah	$5 + 40 = 45$

Other key Kabbalistic notions to be aired by Reuchlin are the 42-letter name of God and the 231 permutations of pairs of Hebrew letters from which combinations 'all existence and all speech arises'.[36]

such as 45, 63, 72 are reached in this manner. Method (7) also permits the addition of the number of letters in the word, or the addition of the number 'one'. It is true that almost anything can be demonstrated using *gematria*. It is an extremely licentious system open to many interpretations.

32 Goodman, *op. cit.*, p. 295. Note the variation on the usual Solomonic phrase that the Creator had ordered all things in 'number, weight, and measure', *Wisdom of Solomon* 11.20. M. Allen, *Nuptial Arithmetic: Marsilio Ficino's Commentary on the Fatal Number in Book VIII of Plato's Republic*, University of California Press, Los Angeles, 1994. Appendix III gives a useful summary of Ficino's frequent employment of this notion, for example, in his commentary on *Timaeus*, 'Deum omnia in numero, mensura, pondere perfecisse'. Reuchlin substitutes 'figura' for 'mensura'. The difference is not particularly remarkable: 'figura' may carry the sense of size as well as shape, and Ficino in defining 'mensura' refers to magnitudes as well as figures.

33 *Op. cit.*, p. 295.

34 *Ibid.*, p. 299. Scholem, *op. cit.*, p. 409, cites Joseph Gikattilla of Castile who wrote a work in 1274 (printed in 1615) whose title is based on the first letters GIMEL, NUN, TAV of '*gematria* ("numerology"), *notarikon* 'acrostics', *temurah* ("permutation")'.

35 Goodman, *op. cit.*, p. 301–3.

36 *Ibid.*, The name of 42 letters is described pp. 335–39. 231 is the number of ways of selecting two letters from 22, see p. 331. It is also the twenty-first trigonal number. Kaplan, *op. cit.*, pp. 108–24, discusses and illustrates the number 231 in some detail.

VIIIII

PLAYFUL NUMBER

Rithmomachia, or *ludus philosophorum*, was a number game played during the middle ages and the Renaissance.[1] The name of the game is Latin for 'battle of numbers'. Played on a double chess-like board with 24 pieces on each side, the game provides an extraordinary exercise in Nicomachean arithmetic. Each of the pieces carries a number, but not all the numbers are the same on the two sides.[2] One side is called 'even' and the other 'odd' after the numbers on the leading pieces in the starting position. However, each side has a balance of twelve odd and twelve even numbers. There are circular, square and triangular pieces, and on each side one square pyramidal piece which can be dismantled. In some versions the pieces are bicoloured – black and white – and each side chooses one colour at the beginning of the game. When a piece is captured, it may be reintroduced by the capturer by turning the piece over to show the colour of its new allegiance. To confuse matters, triangular pieces may not be trigonal numbers, or square pieces tetragonal numbers.

On the 'odd' side, the eight circular pieces are numbered 3, 5, 7, 9 and the third, fifth, seventh and ninth tetragonal numbers – 9, 25, 49, 81; the triangular pieces are numbered with the fourth, sixth, eighth and tenth tetragonal numbers – 16, 36, 64, 100, and with the fourth, sixth, eighth and tenth heteromecics – $4 \times 3 = 12$, $6 \times 5 = 30$, $8 \times 7 = 56$, $10 \times 9 = 90$ – which are the geometric means between the tetragonal numbers.[3] The square shaped pieces are numbered with the seventh, eleventh, fifteenth and nineteenth trigonal numbers – 28, 66, 120, 190 – and the tetragonal numbers of the same order – 49, 121, 225, 361. On the even side the circular pieces are 2, 4, 6, 8, and 4, 16, 36, 64; the triangular pieces are 9, 25, 49, 81, and 6, 20, 42, 72; and the square pieces are 15, 45, 91, 153, and 25, 81, 169, 289. The organization of the numbering system is only interpretable in terms of Nicomachean categories.[4] There can be few more compelling examples for the need to decipher the arithmetical usages of the mediaeval and Renaissance period. (Table 1.)

On the even side the pyramid numbered 91, the thirteenth trigonal number, is a pile of pieces made from two squares 36 and 25, two triangles 16 and 9 and two rounds 4 and 1. On the even side the pyramid numbered 190, the nineteenth trigonal number, is a pile of pieces made from two squares 64 and 49, two triangles 36 and 25, and one round 16. The pyramids are 'kings', and the first stage of the game is the capture of the opponent's pyramid.[5] There are several endgames which the players must negotiate at the start, including the 'triumphs' which the victor, like a conquering Caesar, is expected to parade at the conclusion.[6]

All this is complicated enough and illustrates very well the precocious arithmetical

1 See D. E. Smith, *History of Mathematics*, I, Ginn, New York, c1923/1925, pp. 198–200, D. E. Smith and C. C. Eaton, 'Rithmomachia, the Great Medieval Number Game', *Teacher College Record*, XIII.5, November 1912, pp. 413–22, H. J. R. Murray, *A History of Board-Games Other than Chess*, Clarendon Press, Oxford, 1952, pp. 84–87. The description given here is an amalgam of the many different interpretations given in printed versions during the sixteenth century, and is designed solely to give a sense of the arithmetical complexity of the game in general.

2 On the 'odd' side the numbers sum to 1752 and on the 'even' side 1312. The numbers have qualitative value, not quantitative. This is the difference between *arithmetica* and *logistica*, the former concerned with theory and the latter with practical applications.

3 Between the squares $3 \times 3 = 9$ and $4 \times 4 = 16$ lies the geometric mean, the heteromecic $12 = 3 \times 4$; between 25 and 36, the heteromecic 30; 49 and 64, the heteromecic 56; 81 and 100, the heteromecic 90.

4 Smith and Eaton *op. cit.*, p. 414 gives another set of connections between the numbers. This alternate view only emphasizes the multiplicity of interpretations that the classical system permits.

5 The 'odd' king is the eighth tri-truncated tetragonal pyramid, and the 'even' piece is the sixth tetragonal pyramid. Again there are multiple interpretations: each number is both planar and solid at the same time. Note that the 'odd' – male – side has a commanding piece, 190, whose gender is female, while the 'even' –female – side is led by a piece, 91, with a male number. It might be more appropriate to call the first 'queen' and the second 'king'. Both commanders have numbers which reduce to the perfection of the decad: $9 + 1 = 10$ and $1 + 9 + 0 = 10$. *Vide supra*, 'Theological Number'.

6 According to Smith and Eaton *op. cit.*, p. 419 the common endgames that might be chosen were of five kinds: '(a) victory *de corpore*, decided by the number of pieces captured; (b) victory *de bonis*, depending on the value of the pieces; (c) victory *de lite*, not only upon the value of the pieces but upon the number of digits inscribed upon them; (d) victory *de honore*, depending upon both the number of pieces and their value; (e) victory *de honore liteque*, depending upon the number of pieces, their value and the number of

Table 1 Nicomachean organization of the pieces in the game of rithmomachia. Top three rows, the white pieces; next three rows, the black pieces. Bottom left, the black 'king' with its constituent pieces valued at 91; and to its right, the white 'king' whose components sum to 190. Note, reading vertically, the triples, 3, 4, 7, 5, 6, 11, . . . 9, 10, 19 for black, and 2, 3, 5; 4, 5, 9; . . . 8, 9, 17 are Nicomachus X proportionalities.

○	•3	•5	•7	•9	◇3	◇5	◇7	◇9
△	□4	□6	□8	□10	◇4	◇6	◇8	◇10
◇	△7	△11	△15	△19	◇7	◇11	◇15	◇19
●	•2	•4	•6	•8	◇2	◇4	◇6	◇8
▲	□3	□5	□7	□9	◇3	◇5	◇7	◇9
◆	△5	△9	△13	△17	◇5	◇9	◇13	◇17

●	◇1					
●	◇2	○	◇4			
▲	◇3	△	◇5	Punctual number	n	•
▲	◇4	△	◇6	Triangular number	$n(n+1)/2$	△
◆	◇5	◇	◇7	Heteromecic number	$n(n-1)$	□
◆	◇6	◇	◇8	Square number	n^2	◇

mentalité of the period, but the rules of play require quite extraordinary agility in mental computation. It may be assumed that this game was played by the intellectual élite of the period – the patrons and artists responsible for building its monuments, from cathedrals to villas. As in chess, the pieces have specific moves: the round pieces move one step to an adjacent square; the triangle moves two steps in a straight path, diagonally or orthogonally; the square moves three steps in the same way. In each of the last two cases the paths must be free: no piece may jump over another. The pyramid can move according to any of its components.[7]

By the sixteenth century, some six rules for moves had been established. Equality allowed the same value pieces to take one another. Only pieces numbered 9, 25, 49, 81 are involved in applications of this rule. Addition occurs when the moves of two or more pieces could occupy the position of the enemy piece and the sum of the pieces equals the number on the enemy piece. The player removes the captured piece and places whichever attacker he chooses in its place. Multiplication requires that the product of the number of an attacking piece and its diagonal or orthogonal distance is equal to the number on the opponent's piece. There are then similar subtraction and division rules. The last rule was called 'blockade' where the enemy's piece is

digits inscribed upon them.' The number negotiated in each case has to be met by the victor, For example, it might be resolved that, *de corpore*, the capture of twenty-four pieces gives victory; that the player who meets an agreed number, which is the sum of the value, the digits and the number of pieces captured, is the victor under *de honore liteque*.

7 Murray *op. cit.*, pp. 86–87. Not all descriptions agree on these moves. The later game described by the Venetian mathematician Francesco Barozzi sets the pieces against the end four rows at the start and restricts the moves of the circular pieces to those of a chess pawn. Some knight's moves were also entertained.

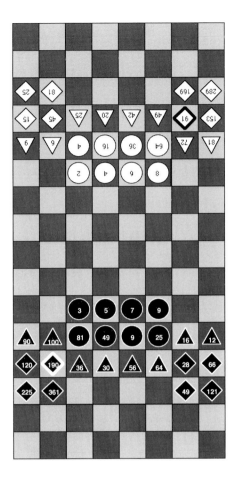

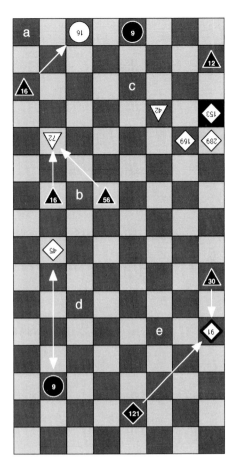

Fig. 1. The opening positions for the game of rithmomachia. The pieces outlined in bold are the 'kings'. They are composite pyramids made up of circular, triangular and square pieces.

Fig. 2. The moves in rithmomachia. Black attacking white. (a) Equality: black 16 may move two places to take white 16, but white sixteen could not take black since it can only move one place. (b) Addition: black 16 and 56 may each move to white 72's position and together they sum to white's value. (c) Blockade: white 153 – shown against a black ground – is under attack from black 9 and black 12. Because of the disposition of the other white pieces, white 153 cannot make a legitimate move and it is thus taken by blockade. (d) Multiplication: black 9 can usually only move one place at a time, but five places away lies white 45. Multiplication allows black to take white. Conversely, by division white 45 could take black 9. (e) Subtraction: white 91 is under attack by black 121 and black 30. Each may make a legitimate move to occupy white's position. Together their difference 121 – 30 is the value of white's king. Black is victorious.

unable to make a legitimate move because of the disposition of the attacking pieces. The attacked piece is removed and any one of the attackers may take its place. The rules also apply to the pyramids only now the individual pieces making up the pyramid are treated separately.[8] (Fig. 2.)

The ultimate object of the game is the complete capture of the enemy pyramid. Victory is then declared, but the game is not over. In Roman manner the victor, playing solo, must celebrate the 'triumphs'. The first triumph, *victoria magna*, requires the victor to line up three pieces in one of the following proportionalities – arithmetical, geometrical or harmonic. The second triumph, *victoria major*, requires that four pieces satisfy two of these proportionalities. The third and final triumph, *victoria excellentissima*, is satisfied when four numbers include all three proportionalities. This occurs either with the 'most perfect proportion' – 2, 3, 4, 6; 4, 6, 8, 12; 6, 8, 9, 12; 12, 15, 16, 20 – or with two variants – 4, 6, 9, 12 where 6, 9, 12 is arithmetic, 4, 6, 9 is geometric, and 4, 6, 12 is harmonic; or 3, 5, 15, 25 where 5, 15, 25 is arithmetic, 3, 5 and 15, 25 are disjoint geometric, and 3, 5, 15 is harmonic.[9]

Among commentators on this 'nobilissimus et antiquissimus ludus Pythagoreus'[10] are Gerbert, Pope Sylvester II, at the first millennium, Richard de Fournival, Chancellor of Amiens at the time of the cathedral's construction; François Rabelais, who accompanied Philibert de l'Orme to Rome and was involved in architectural conservation himself; John Sherwood, who was Bishop of Durham; and the mathematicians, Thomas Bradwardine, who was Archbishop of Canterbury, Nicole Oresme, who became Bishop of Lisieux, Oronce Finè, distinguished in his lifetime as a founding Professor at the Collège de France; Jacques le Fèvre d'Estaples, outstanding humanist tutor to the future Henry II of France; and the Italians, Girolamo Cardano and Francesco Barozzi – the last two moving in Daniele Barbaro's circles.[11]

The connection between the arithmetical mastery required in such a game and the elaborate dimensional and proportional schema of the cathedrals, in particular, has not been explored. Traditional studies have focused on simplistic application of unitary geometrical schemes such as the square or equilateral triangle. The pluralist aphorism 'harmonia est discordia concors' is ignored in attempts to discipline ancient works under some kind of positivistic unitary dogma – much in the same way that the ideal world of the intelligibles which clearly governs intellectual design in the middle ages and Renaissance has too often been reduced to the brute materialistic considerations of our industrial and commercial world.[12]

8 *Ibid.*, pp. 86–87. Smith and Eaton, *op. cit.*, p. 418, give alternative rules. They have the triangle moving three places, and the square four, but this may reflect the classical manner of counting in which both ends are counted. Thus the number 5 is the fifth number from 1, whereas we would normally speak of 5 as being the fourth number from 1 by excluding 1 itself. In this case the different accounts would agree.
9 Smith and Eaton, *ibid.*, p. 421.
10 The title of Claude de Boissière's book on rithmomachia, Paris, 1556. The French mathematician also contributed an arithmetic treatise for actual military purposes during The Hundred Years' War; *L'art d'arythmetique contenant tovte dimention, tressingvlier et commode, tant pour l'art militaire que autres calculations*, Paris, 1554.
11 Some of these authors have been discussed earlier, see 'Classical Arithmetic'. The governing nexus that associates these men over five centuries is undoubtedly the quadrivium.
12 The aphorism appears in the famous woodcut introducing Franchino Gaffurio, *De harmonia musicorum instrumentorum opus*, Milan, 1518. The warring elements of chaos about to be brought into forms of harmony is the opening theme of Ovid, *Metamorphosis*, trans H. Gregory, Viking Press, New York, 1958, p. 31: 'The living elements at war with lifelessness/ . . . Where heat fell against cold, cold against heat – /Roughness at war with smooth, and wet with drought.'

X

RIGHT TRIANGULAR NUMBER

Proportionalities bring three numbers together into relationship. Another triple within the classical tradition is the sides of a rational right triangle of which 3, 4, 5 is the most well known. Many of these integer triples have been recognized from the earliest recorded times and across cultures.[1] The triples satisfy the relationship $p^2 + q^2 = r^2$, for integers $p < q < r$. There are stories concerning the 'harpedonaptai' – rope-stretchers – of ancient Egypt who used ropes marked by knots to stake out right-angles by forming a triangle with sides with lengths proportional to 3 and 4, and an hypotenuse proportional to 5.[2] Problems in the Berlin Papyrus, dated $c1300$ BCE, clearly show a familarity with the properties of the squares on the side of this triangle and the square on the hypotenuse, even though no mention is made of the triangle itself. Vitruvius attributes the discovery of this triangle to Pythagoras – a full eight centuries after the Berlin Papyrus – and explains how a craftsman may make a set-square from rods proportionate in lengths to 3, 4, 5. Vitruvius speaks of the rods being jointed together – the joints then being equivalent to the knots in a rope.[3] From a practical point of view it would seem appropriate to use rods for works on a small scale, and a knotted rope for surveying purposes. Once the ropes or rods are available it makes sense to imagine them used as measuring devices. This implies the use of three primitive modules and their linear combinations. Rods may be arranged in any order, but a rope with two knots (or four if the knotted ends are counted) dividing the three measures requires some predetermination of order, unless a knot is placed at every position at which the measures may be permuted. There are six arrangements of three distinct measures and if the rope is divided into seven sections with six knots (or eight including the ends), then all possibilities of order will be accommodated. Practically, it would have been convenient to place spliced eyes at the knot positions so that stakes could be located precisely. (Fig. 1)

Such a system is very rich in possibilities especially when the dimensions are taken in pairs to form ratios. A rope with two divisions develops three potentially distinct dimensions; a rope with three divisions develops six potentially distinct dimensions; a rope with four divisions develops ten possibilities; and so forth. (Fig. 2)

It will be noted that, in classical terms, these numbers form the trigonal sequence $\triangle 2$, $\triangle 3$, $\triangle 4$, ..., or 3, 6, 10, ... The selection of potential pairs – ratios – from these dimensional sets gives rise to the trigonal numbers $\triangle(3-1) = \triangle 2$, $\triangle(6-1) = \triangle 5$, $\triangle(10-1) = \triangle 9$, ..., or 3, 15, 45, ..., respectively. (Fig. 3)

1 Some earlier historians have been sceptical of prior claims to the theorem known as the Pythagorean, especially in regard to the Egyptians. See R. J. Gillings, *Mathematics in the Time of the Pharaohs*, MIT Press, Cambridge, 1972, especially citations in Appendix 5, 'The Pythagorean Theorem in Ancient Egypt'. Gillings p. 161n cites the Berlin Papyrus 6619 as an instance of the Egyptian use. D. E. Smith, *History of Mathematics*, Ginn, New York, $c1925/6$, II, p. 288, mentions an earlier papyrus dated $c2000$BCE in which four examples of the relation of the sum of two squares equalling another are given. It is possible that this relation was first determined from arithmetical considerations by evoking sums of successive odd numbers to represent the square numbers. For example, $3^2 = 1 + 3 + 5$, $4^2 = 1 + 3 + 5 + 7$ and $5^2 = 1 + 3 + 5 + 7 + 9$. It is then easily seen that $5^2 = (1 + 3 + 5 + 7) + 9 = 4^2 + 3^2$. Other such summations are a little less straightforward. A Babylonian cuneiform tablet, 322 Plimpton Collection, dated 1800–1650BCE shows fifteen right triangular triples expressed in sexigesimal numbers to base 60. The first triple in the list is very good approximation to a rational right isosceles triangle with sides 119, 120, 169, which gives, by summing the sides $120 + 119$, the truly excellent convergent 239 : 169 for $\sqrt{2} : 1$. The fifth listed is the triple 65, 72, 97 and the eleventh shows up as an enlargement of the 3, 4, 5 triple with values 45, 60, 75. The Vedic Indians in the *Sulbasutras* and the Chinese in *Chou Pei* record instances of right triangular triples around 500BCE, and the Chinese author gives a visually demonstrative proof of the theorem. The *Sulbasutras* provide information for the geometric construction of Vedic altars. The topic is conveniently introduced in G. G. Joseph, *The Crest of the Peacock: Non-European Roots of Mathematics*, Penguin Books, Harmondsworth, 1992. The standard Greek tradition is found in T. L. Heath, *A History of Greek Mathematics*, Clarendon Press, Oxford, 1925, I, pp. 144–49, and *Euclid: the Thirteen Books of The Elements*, Cambridge University Press, Cambridge, 1921, I, pp. 350–68.

2 J Gwyn Griffiths trans, *Plutarch: De Iside et Osiride*, University of Wales Press, Cambridge, 1970, pp. 206–9. Plutarch 373F-374A remarks: 'One might suppose that the Egyptians liken the nature of the universe especially to this supremely beautiful

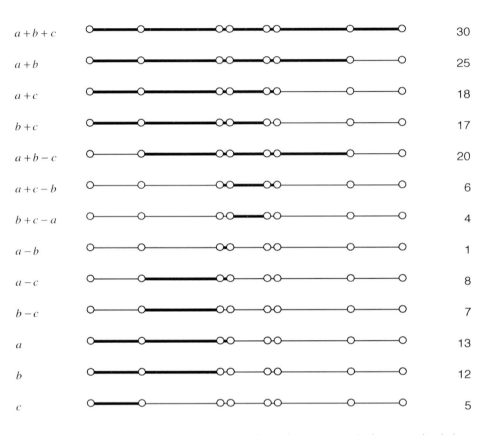

Fig. 1. A rope divided into seven sections which may be used to construct a Pythagorean triangle in any of six symmetrical dispositions. The triangle has an hypotenuse a and sides b and c such that $a > b > c$. Also by the triangular relationship any two sides sum to a length greater than the remaining side. It will be seen that, whereas the original triangle sports three distinct dimensions, the rope displays, between the markers, four dimensions which – with the exception of the 3, 4, 5 triangle – are always distinct. Thirteen simple linear combinations are possible and these are shown for the general case on the left, and the specific 5, 12, 13 triangle on the right. These thirteen dimensions indicate a possible preferred dimensional set which might be expected in a design, if such a rope was used to set out the design.

of the triangles which Plato also in the *Republic* [546A] seems to have used in devising his wedding figure. That triangle has a vertical of three units of length, a base of four, and a hypotenuse of five, which is equal, when squared, to the squares of the other two sides. The vertical should thus be likened to the male, the base to the female, and the hypotenuse to their offspring; and one should similarly view Osiris as the origin, Isis as the receptive element, and Horus as the perfected achievement. The number three is the first and perfect odd number; four is the square of the even number two; five is analogous partly to the father and partly to the mother, being made up of the triad and dyad.'

3 Vitruvius IX, Preface 6. F. Granger, *Vitruvius: De Architectura*, Harvard University Press, Cambridge MA, 1934, II, pp. 200–3.

In the case of right triangular ropes, symmetry plays a part in reducing the possibilities. Instead of there being △7, or 28, distinct dimensions there are only thirteen. In the general case, by laying two ropes end to end, or rotating one rope through 180° about an end, nineteen more potentially distinct dimensions may be generated, including the doubles of the seven dimensions which terminate at one end of the rope. The nineteen additional dimensions are:

$2a + 2b + 2c$

$2a + 2b + c$

$2a + b + 2c$

$a + 2b + 2c$

$2a + b + c$

$a + 2b + c$

$a + b + 2c$

$2a + 2b$

$2a + 2c$

$2b + 2c$

$2a + b$

$a + 2b$

$2a + c$

$a + 2c$

$2b + c$

$b + 2c$

$2a$

$2b$

$2c$.

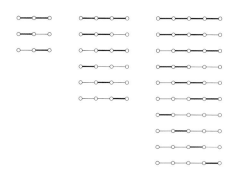

Fig. 2. A rope with two sections will measure $\triangle 2$, or 3, dimensions; a rope with three sections will measure $\triangle 3$, or 6, dimensions; a rope with four sections will measure $\triangle 4$, or 10, dimensions. The drawings are notional and do not show differences in the dimensions of the sections.

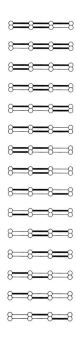

Fig. 3. Six dimensions from a rope with three sections may be arranged in $\triangle 5 = 15$ ratio pairs not all of which need be distinct.

Thus in marking the rope with six internal markings the rope-stretcher is able to generate $13 + 19 = 32$ potentially distinct dimensions. In the case of the 3, 4, 5 rope of length twelve, all the integral dimensions from one to nine may be measured so that ten of the thirteen measures are distinct; and when 'doubled' to span a length of twenty-four, all integral dimensions from one to twenty-one are to be found meaning that twenty-two of the thirty-two measures are distinct. In the case of the 5, 12, 13 triangle all thirteen of the dimensions are distinct in the rope itself, and all thirty-two in the 'doubled' rope.

In any right triangular rope there are $\triangle(13 - 1) = \triangle 12$, or 78, potentially distinct ratios which may be generated; and even then some ratios share the same root. For example, in the 5, 12, 13 triangle, 30 : 20, 18 : 12 and 6 : 4 are each equivalent to the root ratio 3 : 2; the ratios 30 : 18 and 20 : 12 are equivalent to 5 : 3; and the ratio 20 : 4 is equivalent to 5 : 1 which is a root ratio in itself. When the rope is 'doubled' the number of potentially distinct dimensions rises to 32 and the number of ratios thereby increases to an inordinately large palette of $\triangle(32 - 1) = \triangle 31$, or 496, ratios; although some of these can be expected to be equivalent.[4] Two-thirds of the unequal ratios less than 3 : 1, provided by the single 5, 12, 13 rope are used by Palladio, including ratios such as 30 : 17, 25 : 17, 18 : 17, 15 : 4, 18 : 7, 17 : 6 which defy obvious musical interpretation in Wittkower's sense. An architect-builder laying out a design using the 5, 12, 13 rope would find these ratios quite natural. Even Palladio's preferred room ratio of 5 : 3 appears in two of his favourite dimensions 30×18 and 20×12. Further, convergents for ratios involving square roots such as 7 : 5 and 17 : 12 for $\sqrt{2} : 1$; 5 : 3, 7 : 4 and 12 : 7 for $\sqrt{3} : 1$; and 9 : 4 for $\sqrt{5} : 1$; or 10 : 9 for $\sqrt{5} : \sqrt{4}$; 8 : 7 and 7 : 6 for $\sqrt{4} : \sqrt{3}$; 6 : 5 and 5 : 4 for $\sqrt{3} : \sqrt{2}$

are easily constructed using this 5, 12, 13 rope. Palladio uses the ratios 5 : 2 and 12 : 5 for porticoes and the single rope provides these: the double rope gives the ratio 29 : 12 which he also uses for the same purpose. The arithmetic construction of a decagon using the ratio of the radius : side length is attained with the ratios 5 : 3, 8 : 5 and 13 : 8 which are recognized today as terms in the Fibonacci sequence. The ratio 5 : 4 is also a convergent to the cube root of 2 which is central to solving the Delic problem of doubling the volume of a cube: yet, using the double rope the fine convergent 29 : 23 for $^3\sqrt{2} : 1$ is found for the solution of the Delic problem as well as 26 : 23 which represents a good rational solution to squaring the circle – the circle having a diameter twenty-six, and the square having a side length twenty-three. In the case of the 3, 4, 5 rope, it is remarkable that Palladio uses all but two of the twenty-one distinct ratios derived from the single rope, and one of these exceptions is the musical tone, 9 : 8, which is of core significance in classical music theory.

The right triangular rope is a computational device not unlike, for its time, the mechanical slide rule of the age of logarithms. The singular difference is that each right triangular triple has a distinct signature – a preferred set of numbers and ratios – which may perhaps be recognized wherever a particular triangle has been used in setting out a design. Curiously – and this is an ahistorical remark – the nineteenth-century physicist Hermann Helmoltz developed the theory of combinational tones in music which is not dissimilar to the combinatorial possibilities of the right triangular triples.[5] In music two or more distinct pitches sounded together produce tones which are either the differences of the pitch numbers of the generating tones, or the summational tones. An illustration of this is given by James Jeans: 'If tones of of frequency p, q and r are sounded loudly and simultaneously, it can be shewn that we shall hear tones of the frequencies shewn in the table. . . .'[6] (Table 1.)

Thus it may be said that the use of right triangular triples in architectural dimensioning is actually analogous to these musical derivations, but in a completely different way than was ever understood by classical music theorists. Our approach has little to do with the search for psychological consonance, or harmony, or with the physiology of visual perception.[7]

4 Coincidentally this is the third perfect number. *Vide supra*, 'Ethical Number'.

5 H. Helmoltz, *On the Sensation of Tone as a Physiological Basis for the Theory of Music*, (trans A. J. Ellis from the Second German Edition 1877), Dover Publications, New York, 1954. See Part II, 'On the Interruptions of Harmony', pp. 152–233 and particularly Chapter VII, 'Combinational Tones and Beats, Consonance and Dissonance', pp. 152–59.

6 J. Jeans, *Science and Music*, Cambridge University Press, Cambridge, 1937, pp. 235–45, gives a simplified account of combinational tones.

7 Interesting as these issues may be they stand outside the approach taken here. Pragmatically a designer must make choices of how to delineate the design and which dimensions to adopt. Methods of construction and computation will play a large part in configuring the design as conceived, as projected and as built. Such methods will be derived from the cultural norms of the designer's ambience of practice – by the continuance of normative traditions, by their transformation, or by deliberate rejection. The reception of the projected or built design by users and viewers is another matter, too broad and contentious to be considered in this tract.

Table 1 Table of summational and difference tones according to Helmoltz (after Jeans). Higher order summational and difference tones which sound less and less loud are formed from linear combinations of p, q and r.

		Loudest of all:
	$\left.\begin{array}{c} p \\ q \\ r \end{array}\right\}$	the fundamental tones.
Next loudest:		
	$\left.\begin{array}{c} 2p \\ 2q \\ 2r \end{array}\right\}$	the second harmonics of the foregoing.
	$\left.\begin{array}{c} p+q \\ q+r \\ p+r \end{array}\right\}$	the first summation tones.
	$\left.\begin{array}{c} p-q \\ q-r \\ p-r \end{array}\right\}$	the first difference tones, etc.

Some rational right triangles approach the triangles that make up regular polygons. The 20, 21, 29 triangle is almost a half-square cut on the diagonal.[8] The 33, 56, 65 right triangle is very close to half of the equilateral triangle.[9] The 12, 35, 37 triangle is half of the triangle on the base of a decagon with an apex at the centre.[10] Within similar tolerances a dodecagon may be built with twenty-four 16, 63, 65 triangles.[11]

Other rational triangles approach being right-angled. These near-right triangles are those whose sides are convergents to square roots. Thus if the hypotenuse and either side of an isosceles triangle are in the ratio 7 : 5, 17 : 12, 41 : 29, 99 : 71, then they progressively approach a true right isosceles triangle.[12] The rational convergents to $\sqrt{3} : 1$ construct near equilateral triangles: 7 : 4, 19 : 11, 26 : 15, 71 : 41 with sides equal to 8, 22, 30 and 82 respectively.[13] The near right-triangles based on the rational convergents to $\sqrt{5} : 1$, 9 : 4, 29 : 13, 47 : 21, 38 : 17 progressively fit more precisely into the double squares 8×4, 26×13, 42×21, 34×17. [14]

8 Its angles are 46°37′11″and 43°23′49″. The 119, 120, 169 triangle gives a better fit.

9 With angles 59°29′23″ and 60°31′37″. The 8, 15, 17 triangle gives a poorer, but still quite tolerable fit.

10 With angles 71°4′31″ and 18°56′29″ instead of 72° and 18°. This is the same triangle which stands on the base of a pentagon and reaches to the opposite vertex.

11 With angles 75°45′ and 14°15′ instead of 75° and 15°.

12 The 'right' angles are 88°51′14″, 90°11′56″, 89°57′57″ and 90°00′21″ respectively. The last triangle is clearly a very good fit.

13 Applying Pythagoreas' theorem the squares on the sides of the 4, 7, 8 triangle amount to $16 + 49 = 65$ while the hypotenuse is 64, or the squares on the sides of the 15, 26, 30 triangle amount to $225 + 676 = 901$ while the hypotenuse is 900.

14 For example, applying Pythagoreas' theorem in this case, the goodness of fit can be inspected: $4^2 + 8^2 = 80$, while $9^2 = 81$, and $17^2 + 34^2 = 1445$, while $38^2 = 1444$.

XI

RATIONAL PROPORTION

1 M. L. D'Ooge trans, *Nicomachus of Gerasa: Introduction to Arithmetic*, University of Michigan Press, Ann Arbor, 1938, p. 184. Nicomachus, I.iii.1, divides number into absolute quantity and relative quantity: 'it is clear that two scientific methods will lay hold of and deal with the whole investigation of quantity; arithmetic, absolute quantity, and music, relative quantity.' Even so, Nicomachus ignores his own admonition and treats relative number – ratio, proportion, and proportionality – in his tract on arithmetic. Theon of Smyrna (R. Lawlor, D. Lawlor, *Theon of Smyrna: Mathematics for the Understanding of Plato*, Wizard's Bookshelf, San Diego, 1979), however, places the discussion of relative number under music. Unfortunately, the application of proportional theory to music severely limits Theon's understanding of the more general arithmetic issues. Boethius, *De Institutione Arithmetica*, provides a close Latin translation of Nicomachus, *Introduction to Arithmetic*, and reiterates the relevant arithmetic materials in *De institutione musica*, especially in II.i- xvii (M. Masi, *Boethius Number Theory: a translation of the 'De Institutione Arithmetica'*, Rodopi, Amsterdam. 1983; C. M. Bower, *Fundamentals of Music: Anicius Manlius Severinus Boethius'*, Yale University Press, New Haven, 1989. Nicomachus turns to relative quantity in I.xvii D'Ooge, *op. cit.*, p. 212ff.
2 The distinctions become particularly important when numbers are interpreted in their theological or occult sense, *vide supra*, 'Theological Number' and 'Occult Number'.
3 See T. L. Heath, *Euclid: The Thirteen Books of The Elements*, Cambridge University Press, Cambridge, 1921, II, p. 114, V Definition 4: 'A ratio is a sort of relation in respect of size between two magnitudes.' There is no similar definition in VII for ratio between numbers. But *ibid.*, II p. 114, V Definition 6, reads: 'Let magnitudes which have the same ratio be called proportional.' While *ibid.*, II, p. 278, VII definition 20 gives: 'Numbers are proportional when the first is the same multiple, or the same part, or the same parts, of the second that the third is to the fourth.'
4 *Ibid.*, V, Definitions 5 and 7, II, p. 114.
5 *Ibid.*, V, Definitions 8, 9 and 10, II, p. 114.
6 *Op. cit.*, D'Ooge, p. 214ff I.xviii-xxiii. Theon of Smyrna immediately considers whether or not a ratio

Relative number is a number in relation to some other number.[1] The simplest classical relationship is ratio where one number is compared directly with another, $p : q$. An example would be $10 : 6$. These two numbers have a common factor in 2, and the irreducible ratio $5 : 3$ is said to be the root ratio. Note, however, that the numbers 10 and 6 have certain properties which the numbers 5 and 3 do not have. The numbers 10 and 6 are both triangular numbers, and 6 is a perfect number. The numbers 5 and 3 are both primes, and only 3 is a triangular number. Such distinctions may well be important when examining Renaissance usage, and should not be lost in the careless positivism of modern arithmetical computations.[2] A ratio is a relation between two numbers. Proportion is a relation between two or more ratios.[3] The relationship of proportion is either equality – as in the example of $10 : 6$ and $5 : 3$ – or inequality.[4] There are two inequalities: the greater and the less. Given two ratios $p : q$ and $r : s$, if ps is greater than qr, then the first ratio is said to be greater than the second; if ps is less than qr, then the first ratio is said to be less than the second. The ratio $10 : 6$ is greater than $15 : 12$; and, conversely, $15 : 12$ is less than $10 : 6$. The ratios are equal, if ps and qr are equal, which is clearly the case with $5 : 3$ and $10 : 6$. A proportion involving just three numbers, $p : q :: q : r$, is the least possible. In this arrangement the ratios are said to be in continuous proportion.[5]

Equivalent to unity, $1 : 1$, ratios such as $p : p$ are said to be equalities. Among ratios, ancient writers distinguished ten classes of inequalities[6]

multiple	submultiple
superparticular	subsuperparticular
superpartient	subsuperpartient
multiple superparticular	submultiple superparticular
multiple superpartient	submultiple superpartient.

The first column includes ratios which are greater than unity; and the second column includes ratios less than unity. There is an exact reciprocation between the inequalities in the first column and those in the second. For this reason it is not necessary to examine the latter separately. The system of classification is not difficult to appreciate. The multiples are like multitudes ever increasing by addition – double, triple, quadruple . . .:

$$2 : 1 \quad 3 : 1 \quad 4 : 1 \quad 5 : 1 \quad 6 : 1 \quad 7 : 1 \quad 8 : 1 \quad 9 : 1 \quad 10 : 1 \quad \ldots.$$

The submultiples are like magnitudes ever-decreasing by division – one half, one third, one quarter . . .:

1 : 2   1 : 3   1 : 4   1 : 5   1 : 6   1 : 7   1 : 8   1 : 9   1 : 10   . . . .

The equality, 1 : 1, is the divide between the multiples and the submultiples. Within the unit interval 1 : 1 to 2 : 1 lie the superparticulars and the superpartient ratios. For example, the ratio 3 : 2 divides the interval in half, the ratios 4 : 3 and 5 : 3 divide it in thirds, the ratios 5 : 4 and 7 : 4 – together with 6 : 4 whose root ratio is 3 : 2 – divide it in quarters, and so forth. The superparticulars are:

3 : 2   4 : 3   5 : 4   6 : 5   7 : 6   8 : 7   9 : 8   10 : 9   . . . .

The pattern is clear – one and a half to one, one and a third to one, one and a quarter to one, ... The superpartient ratios comprise all the other root ratios in the interval – one and two thirds to one, one and three fifths to one. . . . (Fig. 1.)

The same divisions occur in the intervals 2 : 1 to 3 : 1 where the double superparticulars and double superpartient ratios are located, and in the 3 : 1 to 4 : 1 interval where the triple superparticulars and the triple superpartient ratios are found. The classification continues in this manner without limit. Examples are the double superparticular 5 : 2, or two and a half to one, the double superpartient 8 : 3, or two and two thirds to one; the triple superparticular 7 : 2, or three and a half to one, and the triple superpartient 11 : 3, or three and two thirds to one. The subsuperparticulars and subsuperpartient ratios fill the interval between 1 : 1 and 1 : 2, The subdouble ratios fill the interval between 1 : 2 an 1 : 3, and the subtriple between 1 : 3 and 1 : 4, and so on. (Table 1.)

It will be seen that this system of classification packs as many submultiple ratios in the unit interval from 'zero' to 1 : 1, as are included in the infinite spread of multiple ratios from 1 : 1. (Fig. 2.)

The classificatory system is illustrated by Luca Pacioli at the end of the fifteenth century and partially copied by Leonardo da Vinci. Palladio's friend, Silvio Belli, shows a diagram of the system in his *Proportione et Proportionalità* later in the sixteenth century. (Fig. 3.)

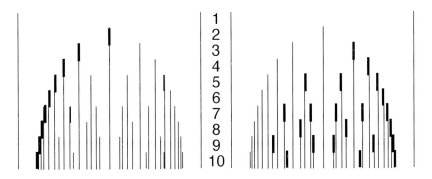

Fig. 1. Dividing a unit interval in aliquot parts – halves, thirds, quarters, . . . tenths – produces (bold lines) the distribution of superparticulars shown left, and the distribution of superpartient ratios shown right.

is an harmonic consonance. His taxonomy is then limited to special multiples 2 : 1, 3 : 1 and 4 : 1 which are consonant; the consonant sesquilalter 3 : 2 and the consonant sesquitertian 4 : 3 among the superparticulars, and then the rest – the 'neutrals' – which include for example the dissonant sesquioctave, or whole tone, 9 : 8 – a superparticular – and ratios such as $256 : 243 :: 2^8 : 3^5$, the Platonic *leimma*, or semitone. Lawlor, *op. cit.*, p. 49, also A. Barker, *Greek Musical Writings: II Harmonic and Acoustic Theory*, Cambridge University Press, Cambridge, 1989, p. 38 n. 36.

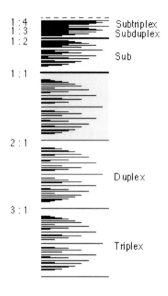

Fig. 2. The superparticular and superpartient ratios are repeated in the multiple intervals to infinity and in the submultiple intervals to 'zero'.

7 *Ibid.*, I.xix, p. 217.

8 *Ibid.*, I.xix, p. 219.

9 *Ibid.*, I.xxiii, p. 225ff. Nicomachus writes: 'There is, however, a method very exact and necessary for all discussion of the nature of the universe which very clearly and indisputably presents to us the fact that that which is fair and limited, and which subjects itself to knowledge, is naturally prior to the unlimited, incomprehensible, and ugly, and furthermore that the parts and varieties of the infinite and unlimited are given shape and boundaries by the former, and through it attain to their fitting order and sequence, and like objects brought beneath some seal or measure all gain a share of likeness to it and similarity of name when they fall under its influence. For thus it is reasonable that the rational part of the soul will be the agent which puts in order the rational part, and passionate and appetite, which find their places in the two forms of inequality, will be regulated by the reasoning faculty as though by a kind of equality and sameness. And from this equalizing process there will properly result for us the so-called ethical virtues, sobriety, courage, gentleness, self-control, fortitude, and the like.' *Ibid.*, pp. 225–26. Once again arithmetic is made analogous to ethical virtues and aesthetic values ('fair' and 'ugly').

Table 1 Nomenclature of relative numbers with respect to the number 10 from 1–30.

RATIO	ROOT	CLASS OF RELATIVE NUMBER		
		EQUALITY	INEQUALITIES	
1 : 10	1 : 10		submultiple	
2 : 10	1 : 5		submultiple	
3 : 10	3 : 10		submultiple superpartient	
4 : 10	2 : 5		submultiple superparticular	
5 : 10	1 : 2		submultiple	
6 : 10	3 : 5		subsuperpartient	
7 : 10	7 : 10		subsuperpartient	
8 : 10	4 : 5		subsuperparticular	
9 : 10	9 : 10		subsuperparticular	
10 : 10	1 : 1	equality		
11 : 10	11 : 10		superparticular	
12 : 10	6 : 5		superparticular	
13 : 10	13 : 10		superpartient	
14 : 10	7 : 5		superpartient	
15 : 10	3 : 2		superparticular	
16 : 10	8 : 5		superpartient	
17 : 10	17 : 10		superpartient	
18 : 10	9 : 5		superpartient	
19 : 10	19 : 10		superpartient	
20 : 10	2 : 1	multiple		
21 : 10	21 : 10		multiple superparticular	
22 : 10	11 : 5		multiple superparticular	
23 : 10	23 : 10		multiple superpartient	
24 : 10	12 : 5		multiple superpartient	
25 : 10	5 : 2		multiple superparticular	
26 : 10	13 : 5		multiple superpartient	
27 : 10	27 : 10		multiple superpartient	
28 : 10	7 : 5		multiple superpartient	
29 : 10	29 : 10		multiple superpartient	
30 : 10	3 : 1	multiple		

Nicomachus chooses to introduce the classification through the multiplication table for numbers from 1 to 10.[7] He then picks out a row and a column in the form of either the Greek letter gamma Γ or chi X and compares two numbers from the marked row and column. (Fig. 4.)

The Table also shows the square numbers along the leading diagonal, flanked on either side by the heteromecic numbers. Nicomachus is keen to show that the corners of the table are monads: the monad 1 and the monad of the third course 100 at the ends of the leading diagonal, and the monad of the second course 10 at both ends of the counter diagonal.[8] This method is copied in one of Leonardo da Vinci's studies from Pacioli's *Summa* . . . (Fig. 5.)

The role of the monad is given further significance in an algorism which Nicomachus cites for generating relative numbers at the conclusion of Book I.[9] Let α, β, γ be numbers in continuous ratio such that $\alpha : \beta :: \beta : \gamma$, then the numbers α, $\alpha + \beta$, $\alpha + \beta$, $\alpha + 2\beta + \gamma$ will also be in continuous ratio. The terms 1, 1, 1, are in continuous ratio 1 : 1, the equality. Applying the algorism, the doubles 1, 2, 4, are generated in continuous proportion through the multiple ratio 2 : 1. Repeating, but now using 1, 2, 4, the triples 1, 3, 9, are next generated in continuous proportion

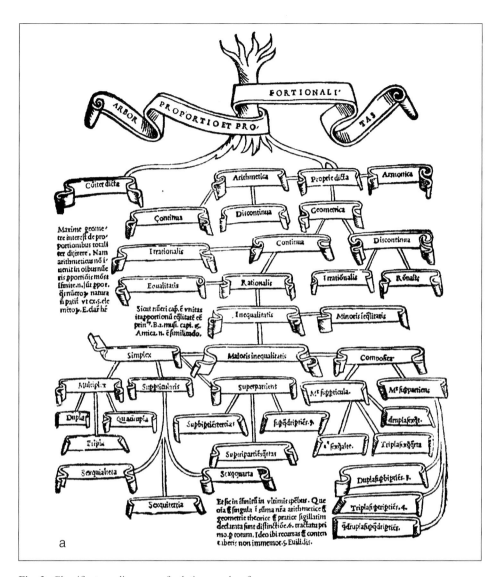

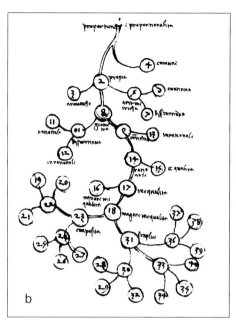

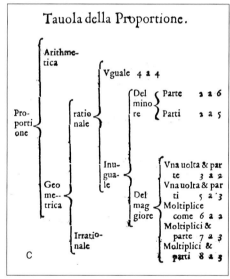

Fig. 3. Classificatory diagrams of relative number from

a. Luca Pacioli, *Summa de arithmetica geometria proportione et proportionalità.*

b. Leonardo da Vinci, *Codex Madrid II folio 78 recto.*

c. Silvio Belli, *De proportione et proportionalità.*

3 : 1. Hence, from equality are produced the multiples by 'following certain rules, like invariable and inviolable natural laws ...'. Now reverse the sequences: 4, 2, 1, generates 4, 6, 9 which is in continuous proportion through the superparticular $3 : 2 - 4 \times \frac{3}{2} = 6$, $6 \times \frac{3}{2} = 9$; and the sequence 9, 3, 1, gives 9, 12, 16, which is in continuous proportion through the superparticular $4 : 3 - 9 \times \frac{4}{3} = 12$, $12 \times \frac{4}{3} = 16$. In this way the superparticulars are born from the ultimate source of equality by way of the multiples. Reversing the superparticular sequences produces superpartient ratios. The sequence 9, 6, 4, generates 9, 15, 25, which is in continuous proportion through the superpartient ratio 5 : 3; the sequence 16, 12, 9, generates 16, 28, 49 in

1	2	3	4	5	6	7	8	9	10
2	4	6	8	10	12	14	16	18	20
3	6	9	12	15	18	21	24	27	30
4	8	12	16	20	24	28	32	36	40
5	10	15	20	25	30	35	40	45	50
6	12	18	24	30	36	42	48	54	60
7	14	21	28	35	42	49	56	63	70
8	16	24	32	40	48	56	64	72	80
9	18	27	36	45	54	63	72	81	90
10	20	30	40	50	60	70	80	90	100

a

1	2	3	4	5	6	7	8	9	10
2	4	6	8	10	12	14	16	18	20
3	6	9	12	15	18	21	24	27	30
4	8	12	16	20	24	28	32	36	40
5	10	15	20	25	30	35	40	45	50
6	12	18	24	30	36	42	48	54	60
7	14	21	28	35	42	49	56	63	70
8	16	24	32	40	48	56	64	72	80
9	18	27	36	45	54	63	72	81	90
10	20	30	40	50	60	70	80	90	100

b

1	2	3	4	5	6	7	8	9	10
2	4	6	8	10	12	14	16	18	20
3	6	9	12	15	18	21	24	27	30
4	8	12	16	20	24	28	32	36	40
5	10	15	20	25	30	35	40	45	50
6	12	18	24	30	36	42	48	54	60
7	14	21	28	35	42	49	56	63	70
8	16	24	32	40	48	56	64	72	80
9	18	27	36	45	54	63	72	81	90
10	20	30	40	50	60	70	80	90	100

c

1	2	3	4	5	6	7	8	9	10
2	4	6	8	10	12	14	16	18	20
3	6	9	12	15	18	21	24	27	30
4	8	12	16	20	24	28	32	36	40
5	10	15	20	25	30	35	40	45	50
6	12	18	24	30	36	42	48	54	60
7	14	21	28	35	42	49	56	63	70
8	16	24	32	40	48	56	64	72	80
9	18	27	36	45	54	63	72	81	90
10	20	30	40	50	60	70	80	90	100

d

1	2	3	4	5	6	7	8	9	10
2	4	6	8	10	12	14	16	18	20
3	6	9	12	15	18	21	24	27	30
4	8	12	16	20	24	28	32	36	40
5	10	15	20	25	30	35	40	45	50
6	12	18	24	30	36	42	48	54	60
7	14	21	28	35	42	49	56	63	70
8	16	24	32	40	48	56	64	72	80
9	18	27	36	45	54	63	72	81	90
10	20	30	40	50	60	70	80	90	100

e

Fig. 4. The Pythagorean multiplication table used by Nicomachus to illustrate the five classes of relative number.
a. The outer row or column is compared with a parallel row or column to produce the multiples, 3 : 1, 2 : 6, 3 : 9, ...
b. Two adjacent rows or columns are compared to give the superparticulars, 3 : 2, 6 : 4, 12 : 8, ...
c. Two nonadjacent rows or columns suitably spaced give the superpartients, 5 : 3, 10 : 6, 15 : 9, ...
d. Two nonadjacent rows or columns suitably spaced give the multiple superparticulars, 5 : 2, 10 : 4, 15 : 6, ...
e. Two nonadjacent rows or columns suitably spaced give the multiple superpartients, 8 : 3, 16 : 6, 24 : 9, ...

continuous proportion through the superpartient ratio 7 : 4. Nicomachus remarks on the fact that the extremes of each sequence are squares. He takes the sequence 9, 15, 25, and repeats the rule to obtain 9, 24, 64, in continuous proportion through the double superpartient 8 : 3, while the reverse order 25, 15, 9, gives 25, 40, 64, in continuous proportion through the superpartient ratio 8 : 5. At the beginning of Book II, Nicomachus reverses the algorism.[10] Given three numbers in continuous proportion α, β, γ, in which, without loss of generality, the first term is the largest and the last term the smallest, a new sequence may be formed γ, $\beta - \gamma$, $\alpha - 2\beta + \gamma$. This process may continue until 1, 1, 1, is reached, the original sequence passing through all the generations of its being from equality. 'Equality is the elementary principle of relative number.'[11]

Nicomachus sets out tableaux for superparticulars in the form of a Greek lambda Λ on its side. He does this for 3 : 2 and 4 : 3, and provides the general construction for any superparticular tableau.[12] The first of these tableaux compares the double ratio in breadth, in the rows, with the triple ratio on the diagonal. In depth, in the columns, consecutive terms are in the sesquialter ratio 3 : 2.

10 *Ibid.*, II.ii, pp. 230–31.
11 *Ibid.*, II.ii, p. 231.
12 *Ibid.*, II.iii, p. 233. Nicomachus writes: 'for other multiples let the manner of your tables be the same'. Boethius sets out the 5 : 4 table in addition to the 3 : 2 and 4 : 3 tables shown by Nicomachus. Masi *op. cit.*, p. 126.

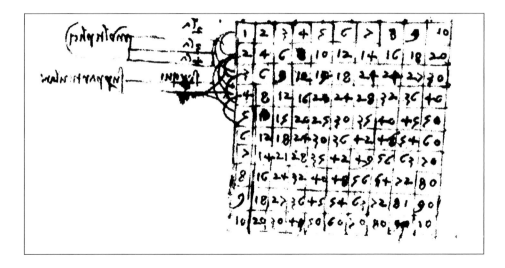

Fig. 5. Pythagoras' table from Leonardo da Vinci, *Codex Madrid folio 48 verso*.

1	2	4	8	16	32	64
	3	6	12	24	48	96
		9	18	36	72	144
			27	54	108	216
				81	162	324
					243	486
						729.

This particular tableau, the Pythagorean lambda, interestingly exhibits properties, having to do with arithmetic, geometric and harmonic means, to which Nicomachus does not draw attention.[13]

Barbaro and Belli both set out examples of relative number. In the commentaries on Vitruvius' third book, Barbaro gives six specific examples (the ratios are read vertically):[14]

I	superparticular	3	4	5	6	7	8	9	10	11	12
		2	3	4	5	6	7	8	9	10	11
II	superpartient	5	7	9	11	13	15	17	19	21	
		3	4	5	6	7	8	9	10	11	
III	duple superparticular	5	7	9	11	13	15	17	19	21	
		2	3	4	5	6	7	8	9	10	
IV	triple superparticular[15]	7	10	13	16	19	22	25	28		
		2	3	4	5	6	7	8	9		
V	duple superpartient	8	11	14	17	20	23	26	29		
		3	4	5	6	7	8	9	10		
VI	triple superpartient	11	15	19	23	27	31	39			
		3	4	5	6	7	8	9.			

13 Possibly because the other tables do not work in the same way. For example, whereas 2, 3, 4 is arithmetic, 3, 4, 9 is clearly not; 2, 3, 6 is harmonic, but 3, 4, 12 is not. However, the geometric relationship is the constructive principle in all tables. Thus, 4, 6, 9 is geometric and so are the triplets 9, 12, 16 and 16, 20, 25.
14 D. Barbaro, *M Vitrvvii Pollionis: De architectvra libri decem cvm commentariis* . . . Venice, 1567, pp. 81–82. The fourth table as printed p. 82:

7	9	11	13	15	17	19	21
2	3	4	5	6	7	8	9

is obviously incorrect, including as it does non-root ratios 9 : 3, 15 : 6 and 21 : 9. Dr Hendrika Buelinckx at the University of California, Los Angeles, first brought these sequences to my attention.
15 Corrected version, LM.

Silvio Belli sets out the multiplex and submultiplex numbers in an interesting manner[16]

9 8 7 6 5 4 3 2 1 A 1 1 1 1 1 1 1 1
1 1 1 1 1 1 1 1 1 1 1 2 3 4 5 6 7 8 9.

In giving the superpartient, unlike Barbaro who gives just the special cases of a unit part less than a multiple, Belli includes all the ratios. Compare Belli's superpartient sequence with Barbaro's sequence II:[17]

5 7 7 8 9 11
3 4 5 5 5 6.

Note the repetition of 5 for the superpartients $1\frac{2}{3}$, $1\frac{3}{5}$, $1\frac{4}{5}$, but not for 6. The only new superparticular is $1\frac{1}{5}$, since four sixths reduce to two thirds, already accounted for by the superpartient $1\frac{2}{3}$, and three sixths reduce to one half and two sixths reduce to one third for the superparticulars $1\frac{1}{2}$ and $1\frac{1}{3}$. Belli also shows sequences in which the multiples vary progressively: $2\frac{1}{2}$, $3\frac{1}{3}$, $4\frac{1}{4}$, and so on.[18]

---

16 Silvio Belli, *De proportione et proportionalità* Venice, 1573, II.iv. Belli appears to follow Thomas of Bradwardine's classes of relative number. Bradwardine has three kinds of superpartient ratio, three kinds of multiple superparticular, and seven kinds of multiple superpartient ratio. Crosby, *op. cit.*, pp. 22–24 and pp. 67–71.

17 Belli II.vi, *op. cit.*

18 *Ibid.*, II.vi. In the terminology of Bradwardine, this series reads 'duplex superbitertia', 'triplex supertriquarta', ... This classification does not take into account reductions of the kind Belli uses. For example, Bradwardine's 'duplex supertritertia' reduces to a simple multiple, the 'triplex', Crosby, *op. cit.*, p. 24. See also the table in T. L. Heath, *A History of Greek Mathematics*, Clarendon Press, Oxford, 1921, I, pp. 101–4 for a convenient summary.

INEXPRESSIBLE PROPORTION

Certain numbers are inexpressible as rational numbers. The diagonal of a square and its sides cannot be compared as a ratio of two natural numbers, no more than the side of a cube of twice the volume of another cube can be so determined.[1] Nicomachus does not address this issue, but Theon of Smyrna does address the former problem. In a brief chapter, Theon discusses diagonal numbers p and side or lateral numbers q using the algorism that if $p : q$ is a rational convergent to $\sqrt{2} : 1$, then $(p + 2q) : (p + q)$ is a better value.[2] In this manner he generates the convergents $3 : 2$, $7 : 5$, and $17 : 12$. The square of the true value of the antecedent $\sqrt{2}$ is 2, or twice the square of the consequent 1. With the rational convergents, the square of the antecedent compared with twice the square of the consequent – $9 : 8$, $49 : 50$, $289 : 288$ – varies by just one unit, alternately more and less. The series may be continued beyond Theon's values to include the ratios $41 : 29$, $99 : 70$, $239 : 169$, and so on. Each estimate is an improvement on the previous value.[3]

Heron of Alexandria provides a general formula for square roots of non-square numbers.[4] Suppose p^2 is the closest square number to n such that there is a quantity r which satisfies $p^2 + r = n$. Thus, if n is 2, p would be 1 and r would be 1, if n is 3, p would be 1 and r would be 2; if n is 5, p would be 2 and r would be 1. The number p is an underestimate for $\sqrt{n}$ and the quantity n / p is an overestimate for $\sqrt{n}$. Heron takes the arithmetic mean of these two estimates to obtain an improved value $p_1 = \frac{1}{2}(p + n / p)$. The process can then be repeated with $p_2 = \frac{1}{2}(p_1 + n / p_1)$. Using this method the following values are obtained:

	p	n / p	p_1	n / p_1	p_2
$\sqrt{2} : 1$	$1 : 1$	$2 : 1$	$3 : 2$	$4 : 3$	$17 : 12$
$\sqrt{3} : 1$	$1 : 1$	$2 : 1$	$7 : 4$	$12 : 7$	$97 : 56$
$\sqrt{5} : 1$	$2 : 1$	$5 : 2$	$9 : 4$	$20 : 9$	$161 : 72$.

This method was known during the fourteenth century and was common practice in the late fifteenth and the sixteenth centuries. It was the method advocated by Luca Pacioli which absorbed the attention of Leonardo da Vinci.[5]

Another method was presented in manuscript by Nicholas Chuquet.[6] A printed work largely based on Chuquet's was published by Estienne de la Roche.[7] The method makes use of the observation that if $p : q$ and $r : s$ are two ratios, then the ratio of the sum of the antecedents to the sum of the consequents $(p + r) : (q + s)$

1 The problem of doubling the cube is known as the Delic problem. Theon of Smyrna mentions it in his Introduction: 'In his work entitled *Platonicus* Eratosthenes says that, when the god announced to the Delians by oracle that to get rid of a plague they must construct an altar double of the existing one, their craftsmen fell into great perplexity in trying to find how a solid could be made double of another solid, and they went to ask Plato about it. He told them that the god had given this oracle, not because he wanted an altar double the size, but he wished in setting this task before them, to reproach the Greeks for their neglect of mathematics and their contempt for geometry.' Translated I. Thomas, *Greek Mathematical Works: From Thales to Euclid*, Harvard University Press, Cambridge,1991, p.257; also R. Lawlor, D. Lawlor, *Theon of Smyrna: Mathematics for Understanding Plato*, Wizard's Bookshelf, San Diego, 1979, pp. 1–2. Thomas gives solutions to this problem by Eutocius, one attributed to Plato, Heron of Alexander, Diocles, Menaechmus, Archytas, Eratosthenes, Nicomedes. Thomas, *ibid.*, pp. 261–309: see also T. L. Heath, *A History of Greek Mathematics*, Clarendon Press, Oxford, 1921, II, pp. 244–70. The solutions of Archytas and Eratosthenes are mentioned in Vitruvius IX, Preface 13–14, F. Granger, *Vitruvius: De Architectura*, Harvard University Press, Cambridge MA, 1934, II, pp. 206–209. D. Barbaro illustrates the solutions of Plato, Archytas, Eratosthenes and Nicomedes in his commentaries on Vitruvius, *vide infra*, 'Euclidean Regular Figures'. Doubling a square is a more tractable problem, but again one mentioned by Vitruvius IX, Preface 2, Granger, *ibid.*, II, pp. 198–201. Another classic problem is squaring the circle. Thomas, *ibid.*, pp. 308–46.
2 Lawlor, *op. cit.*, I.xxxi, pp. 29–30.
3 The matter receives excellent coverage in D. H. Fowler, *The Mathematics of Plato's Academy: a Reconstruction*, Clarendon Press, Oxford, 1987.
4 See Heath, *op. cit.*, II, pp. 323–26.
5 According to Heath, *op. cit.*, II, p. 324, n. 2: 'The method indicated by Heron was known to Barlaam and Nicolas Rhabdas in the fourteenth century. The equivalent of it was used by Luca Paciuolo [Pacioli] ... and it was known to other Italian algebraists of the sixteenth century.' In Leonardo da Vinci *Codex*

lies between. The method proceeds in the same manner as Heron's, but it converges more slowly. The example of $\sqrt{3} : 1$ is used as an illustration: the ratio is known to lie between $1 : 1$ and $2 : 1$. Chuquet's mean estimate $(1 + 2) : (1 + 1)$, or $3 : 2$, lies between the extremes. Now $3 : 2$ is an underestimate and $2 : 1$ is an overestimate. The root must lie between these two values. Chuquet's mean $(3 + 2) : (2 + 1)$, or $5 : 3$, lies between them. The ratio $5 : 3$ is an underestimate. The nearest overestimate is still $2 : 1$. The ratio $(5 + 2) : (3 + 1)$, $7 : 4$, lies between, but it is an over-estimate. The nearest underestimate is $5 : 3$. The ratio $(5 + 7) : (3 + 4)$, or $12 : 7$, lies between, but is an underestimate. Take $7 : 4$ and $12 : 7$ as the new extremes, then $(7 + 12) : (4 + 7)$, or $19 : 11$, lies between, but it underestimates the value. The ratio $7 : 4$ is the nearest overestimate. The new ratio $(19 + 7) : (11 + 4)$, or $26 : 15$, lies between the extremes. The procedure continues. The method leads to the following values:

$$\sqrt{2} \quad 1:1 \quad 2:1 \quad 3:2 \quad 4:3 \quad 7:5 \quad 10:7 \quad 17:12 \quad 24:17 \quad 41:29 \quad 58:41 \ldots$$

$$\sqrt{3} \quad 1:1 \quad 2:1 \quad 3:2 \quad 5:3 \quad 7:4 \quad 12:7 \quad 19:11 \quad 26:15 \quad 45:26 \quad 71:41 \ldots$$

$$\sqrt{5} \quad 2:1 \quad 3:1 \quad 5:2 \quad 7:3 \quad 9:4 \quad 11:5 \quad 20:9 \quad 29:13 \quad 38:17 \quad 47:21 \ldots$$

Another method combines the methods of Heron and Chuquet. It makes use of the the fact that if $p : q$ is an estimate for $\sqrt{n} : 1$, then $nq : p$ is another estimate. One of these estimates will be over and the other will be under. In between will be the estimate $p_1 : q_1 = (p + nq) : (p + q)$. This ratio also has a partner $nq_1 : p_1$ and the process continues. The recursion $p_1 : q_1 = (p + nq) : (p + q)$ is similar to Theon of Smryna's for $n = 2$, although the introduction of $nq_1 : p_1$ now produces intermediate estimates for $\sqrt{2}$ thereby doubling the number of convergents. It makes no difference to the values of $\sqrt{2}$ using Chuquet's method, but some additional values appear for $\sqrt{3}$ and $\sqrt{5}$.

$$\sqrt{3} : 1 \quad 1:1 \quad 3:1 \quad 2:1 \quad 3:2 \quad 5:3 \quad 9:5 \quad 7:4 \quad 12:7 \quad 19:11 \quad 33:19 \ldots$$

$$\sqrt{5} : 1 \quad 2:1 \quad 5:2 \quad 7:3 \quad 15:7 \quad 11:5 \quad 25:11 \quad 9:4 \quad 20:9 \quad 29:13 \quad 65:29 \ldots$$

The pairs of ratios involved in the computation are bracketed. The antecedents and the consequents of a pair are summed to give the leading term of the next pair. Note that derived ratios are reduced. For example, $(11 + 25) : (5 + 11)$, or $36 : 16$, is reduced to $9 : 4$. Arithmetically, Heron's method provides rapid convergence to refined estimates; but architecturally, the slow convergence of latter method provides many distinct rational proxies for the roots which the designer may use. The method given by Chuquet lies between these two.

Nicomachus compares arithmetic and geometric means, pointing out that, in general, the product of the extremes is greater than the square of the mean in the case of the arithmetic, and equal in the case of the geometric. For the harmonic mean, he gives numerical examples in which it is clear that the square of the harmonic mean is less than the product of the extremes, but he does not make a point of this. In fact, this observation – essentially that the product of the arithmetic mean and the harmonic mean is equal to the square of the geometric mean – is the principle which drives the algorisms for square roots. For example, the arithmetic mean between $3 : 2$ and $4 : 3$ is $17 : 12$, and the harmonic mean is $24 : 17$. Such

Atlanticus, fol.120r-d, Leonardo writes: 'Learn the multiplication of roots from Master Luca'. For a convenient summary of Leonardo's mathematical interests, see A. Marinoni 'The Writer' in L. Reti ed., *The Unknown Leonardo*, Abradale Press, New York, 1974, pp. 56–85. Marinoni writes of Leonardo, p. 70: 'In 1501 he was so obsessed by mathematics that he neglected his painting and, writes an observer, "the sight of a brush puts him out of temper"'. His obsessions included the problems of doubling the cube and squaring the circle, but mathematics was definitely not Leonardo's strength.

6 See G. Flegg, C. Hay, B. Moss, *Nicolas Chuquet, Renaissance Mathematician*, D. Reidel, Dordrecht, 1985. There are two problems. One is: given a square number find its square root, or a cube number its cube root. The other is: given a number that is not, say, a true square find its square root. Such a number is 6 which Chuquet uses as a worked example in the section 'The Extraction of Imperfect Roots' in his manuscript, *Triparty en la Science des Nombres*, 1484. This is also an example used by Pacioli in his *Summa*, 1494, but it is evident from the workings that Pacioli uses a method after Heron and not the method advocated by Chuquet. Heron's method converges faster than Chuquet's. In fact Heron's method reaches Pacioli's value for $\sqrt{6}$, $2^{88}\!/_{960}$, in four steps to Chuquet's twelve steps. Both, however, arrive at the same value.

7 Estienne de la Roche, *Larismethique nouellement composée*, Lyons, 1520.

pairs, $p : q$ and $nq : p$, are arithmetic and harmonic means which progressively embrace the inaccessible geometric mean, $\sqrt{n} : 1$, which lies between them.

Chuquet's method also provides a way of estimating cube, and higher, roots. Consider the cube root of two which arises in the Delic problem of doubling the size of an altar.[8] $1 : 1$ is an underestimate, while $2 : 1$ is an overestimate. Chuquet's mean $(1 + 2) : (1 + 1)$, or $3 : 2$, is an overestimate, but one closer to the underestimate $1 : 1$ than the previous overestimate $2 : 1$. The next mean is $(3 + 1) : (2 + 1)$, or $4 : 3$; this too is an overestimate. Again, the mean $(4 + 1) : (3 + 1)$, or $5 : 4$, is formed; this is found to be a new underestimate. The mean between this new underestimate, $5 : 4$, and the closest overestimate, $4 : 3$, is formed, namely $(5 + 4) : (4 + 3)$, or $9 : 7$ – a fresh overestimate. Forming means between the closest overestimates and underestimates, the series of estimates continues with $5 : 4$ the current underestimate:

$$(5 + 9) : (4 + 7), \quad \text{or } 14 : 11, \text{ an overestimate;}$$
$$(5 + 14) : (4 + 11), \quad \text{or } 19 : 15, \text{ an overestimate;}$$
$$(5 + 19) : (4 + 15), \quad \text{or } 24 : 19, \text{ an overestimate;}$$
$$(5 + 24) : (4 + 19), \quad \text{or } 29 : 23, \text{ an overestimate;}[9]$$
$$(5 + 29) : (4 + 23), \quad \text{or } 34 : 27, \text{ a new underestimate;}$$
$$(29 + 34) : (23 + 27), \quad \text{or } 63 : 50, \text{ an overestimate, and so on.}$$

In this manner the inexpressible magnitudes of geometrical figures – such as the diagonal of a unit square, $\sqrt{2}$, the chord of a unit hexagon, $\sqrt{3}$, the diagonal of a unit double square, $\sqrt{5}$, and the side of a double cube, $\sqrt[3]{2}$ – will always be expressible to some degree of rational estimation.

Nicomachus reminds us, 'the cube is harmony'.[10] For Alberti: 'The cube is a projection of the square. The primary cube, whose root is one, is consecrated to the Godhead, because the cube of one remains one; it is, moreover, said to be the one solid that is particularly stable and that rests equally sure and fast on any of its sides.'[11] 'In establishing dimensions, there are certain natural relationships that cannot be defined as numbers, but that may be obtained through roots and powers.' Alberti takes as his model the cube whose side is two. This gives a face area equal to four, and a volume of eight. He introduces 'the relationships that cannot be defined as numbers' by considering the 'diameter' of a square face, and the 'diameter' of the cube. From the first, he obtains the square root of eight; from the second he derives the square root of twelve. Neither of these have a known 'numerical value'. Alberti does not stop there. He considers a right-angled triangle, not directly related to the geometry of the cube, whose sides carry squares of four and twelve, and whose hypotenuse carries a square of sixteen. In this way he returns to a 'numerical value' which can be defined, the square root of sixteen being four. He also deftly moves from the square to the equilateral triangle by way of the cube.[12] Alberti makes it legitimate to use certain transformations of the first four numbers, or *tetraktys*: the identity 1, 2, 3, 4, itself; the squares 1^2, 2^2, 3^2, 4^2; the cubes (recall Alberti's cubic relationship for the decad); the square roots, $\sqrt{1}$, $\sqrt{2}$, $\sqrt{3}$, $\sqrt{4}$; and the cube roots. 'Each should be employed with the shortest line serving as the width of the *area*, the longest as the length, and the intermediate one as the height. But sometimes these may be modified to suit the building.'[13]

Here, Alberti's most innovative contribution is that ratios such as $\sqrt{2} : \sqrt{1}$; $\sqrt{3} : \sqrt{1}$; $\sqrt{3} : \sqrt{2}$ and $\sqrt{4} : \sqrt{3}$ are given 'rational' legitimacy by Euclid's definition, and are

8 See Fowler, *op. cit.*, pp. 117–21. Fowler names the method after Parmenides, pp. 42–44: 'The *Parmenides* proposition . . . is found in Pappus, *Collection* VII.8. It was rediscovered by Chuquet . . . where it is called "la règle des nombres moyens"'.

9 Is it an accident that Nicomachus' work is in two books subdivided into twenty-three and twenty-nine chapters respectively, that is in the Delic proportion? The numerical organization of books may not have been that unusual. St Augustine, *City of God*, VI.3, discusses in detail a work by the Roman polymath M. Terentius Varro who had composed 'forty-one books on *Antiquities*; . . . assigning twenty-five to "anthropology" and sixteen to "theology"' – a division into two square numbers associated with the Pythagorean triangle. Vitruvius, V.Preface 4, writes: 'Pythagoras also, and those who followed his sect, decided to write their rules, cube fashion, in their volumes, and fixed upon a cube – 216 lines – and they thought that not more than three cubes should be in one treatise.' *Vide infra*, 'Roman Wonders'.

10 M. L. D'Ooge, *Nicomachus of Gerasa: Introduction to Arithmetic*, University of Michigan Press, Ann Arbor, 1938, pp. 284–85.

11 J. Rykwert, N. Leach, R. Tavernor, *Leon Battista Alberti: On the Art of Building in Ten Books*, MIT Press, Cambridge MA, 1988, p. 307. The monad is identified with the Godhead by Nicomachus, who is cited for this opinion in *Theologia Arithmetica* attributed to Iamblichus, R. Waterfield, *The Theology of Arithmetic*, Phanes Press, Grand Rapids, 1988, p. 37. That Alberti identifies the Godhead with the unit cube is interesting. For Platonists the cube is associated with the element earth, *Timaeus* 56-D. One possibility is that Alberti is referring to a cabalistic interpretation. Gershom Scholem, *Kabbalah*, Dorset Press, New York, 1974, p. 27, mentions the statement in the *Sefer Yezirah* (I,13) in which the extremities of the world are sealed by the six permutations of the abbreviated Hebrew Name of God, Yod-Hay-Waw. The extremities of the world correspond to the upper and the lower; East and West, North and South. An appropriate model for this would be the six faces of a cube.

12 This is an application of Euclid's Proposition II.10 (Heath I, pp. 395–402) which effectively addresses the question of the diameter of the square, or proposition XIII.14 (Heath, III, pp. 474–77) which directly relates the square on the side of a square with the square on the diameter of the circle within which it is inscribed; and of Proposition XIII.15 (Heath, III, pp. 478–80): 'To construct a cube and comprehend it in a sphere; and to prove that the square on the diameter of the sphere is triple of the square on the side of the cube.' While there are no exact numerical values for these lengths, which in today's language are 'irrational', Piero della Francesca was, nevertheless, interested in giving numerical estimates, or convergents, for such magnitudes in the regular polygons and polyhedra. Luca Pacioli: *De Divina Proportione*, Venice, 1509, presents much of Peiro's earlier manuscript material. An exercise in Book II, iii 2, covers the same ground concerning dimensions in the cube as Alberti does. It is noteworthy that Alberti does not explore the pentagon. Euclid; X,

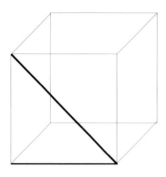

Fig. 1. $\sqrt{2} : \sqrt{1}$.

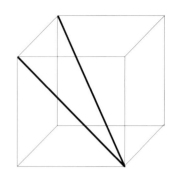

Fig. 2. $\sqrt{3} : \sqrt{2}$.

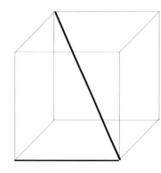

Fig. 3. $\sqrt{3} : \sqrt{1}$.

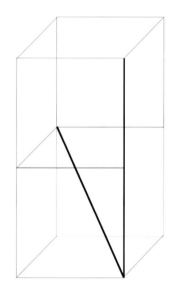

Fig. 4. $\sqrt{4} : \sqrt{3}$.

Definition 2 (Heath, III, pp. 10–11) makes it very clear that 'straight lines are commensurable in square when the squares on them are measured by the same area'. The lines are then said to be 'rational'. This relationship does not hold for sides and diameters in the pentagon. For Euclid XIII.11 (Heath, III, pp. 461–66) these are 'incommensurable', and the lines are 'irrational'. Alberti shows little interest, at least overtly, in the extreme and mean ratio, the golden section. Euclid, Proposition, XIII.13 (Heath, III, pp. 467–73) concerns the relationship of the square on the side of an equilateral triangle to the square on the radius of the circle within which it is inscribed. In the course of the proof Euclid shows that the square on the diameter to the square on the side of the equilateral triangle is in the ratio 4 : 3, so that the lengths involved are in the ratio $\sqrt{4} : \sqrt{3}$.

13 J. Rykwert, et al, *op. cit.*, p. 308. The cube numbers grow very quickly, but Alberti uses the ratio 27 : 8 in determining the limits of the wide category of intercolumniation to column width. The determination of the cube root is a topic in Vitruvius X.xiii – xiv: in particular, the doubling of the cube which involves constructing a cube whose sides are in the ratio, cube root of two to one, with the original cube – the Delic problem.

14 F. Cornford, *Plato's Cosmology*, Routledge & Kegan Paul, London, 1937, p. 211. *Timaeus* 54 B.

15 Alberti quite correctly complains that this is not the way to make a right-angled triangle since a 5, 5, 7 triangle does not satisfy Pythagoras' theorem by one part in fifty. R. Rialdi, *Leon Battista Alberti: Ludi matematici*, Guanda, Milan, 1980, p. 52.

16 A second set of ratios may be derived by taking the conjugates, whereby if $p : q$ is a convergent to $\sqrt{m}:\sqrt{n}$ then the ratio $p' : q' = mq : np$ is its conjugate, since $p/p \cdot p'/q' = m/n$. In the bracketed sets, the left-hand ratio is derived from the anthyphairetic computation and the right-hand ratio is its conjugate. Other algorisms may give rise to different values. For example, an application of Chuquet's method to the second set for $\sqrt{3} : \sqrt{2}$ gives $(11 + 27):(9 + 22) = 38:31$, a perfectly workable value for practical purposes.

acceptable within Alberti's architectonic scheme. The ratios evoke the world-making triangles in the *Timaeus*.[14]

To use these ratios in practice, it is necessary to find arithmetical estimates, or rational convergents. A simple way to find such estimates is to examine two columns of squared numbers and see if one number in one column is very nearly proportional to a number in another column. For example, $7^2 = 49$ is almost proportional to $5^2 = 25$ in the ratio 2 : 1, and so 7 : 5 is a close estimate for $\sqrt{2} : \sqrt{1}$;[15] similarly, $11^2 = 121$ is almost proportional to $9^2 = 81$ in the ratio of 3 : 2, and so 11 : 9 is a close estimate for $\sqrt{3} : \sqrt{2}$. This brute force method was always available, but the algorisms discussed above were also accessible to the mathematically numerate. Some typical values for Alberti's ratios derived from the geometry of the cube have been given above and others are given below:[16]

| $\sqrt{3} : \sqrt{2}$ | 5 : 4 | 6 : 5 | 11 : 9 | 27 : 22 | 49 : 40 | 60 : 49 | . . . |
| $\sqrt{4} : \sqrt{3}$ | 7 : 6 | 8 : 7 | 15 : 13 | 52 : 45 | 97 : 84 | 112 : 97 | . . . . |

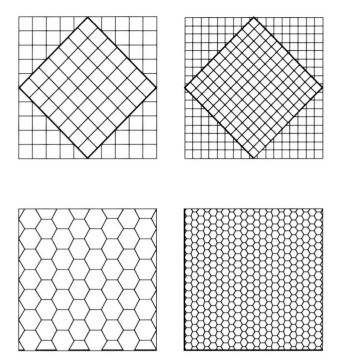

Fig. 5. Top row, square tiles set on the diagonal give rise to the rational convergents to $\sqrt{2} : 1$ such as 7 : 5 (left) and 17 : 12 (right). Bottom row, hexagonal tiles confined to a square give rise to rational convergents to $\sqrt{4} : \sqrt{3}$ such as 8 : 7 (left) and 22 : 19 (right).

Mysterious and esoteric as all this may seem, craftsman laying out tiles in simple patterns would inevitably discover such ratios in everyday practice. Turning square tiles on the diagonal requires being able to place 5 half-tiles against 7 full tiles within the tolerance of the joints, or 12 against 17 and so on. In the case of hexagonal tiles a square area will be packed by an 8 by 7, or 15 by 13, or 22 by 19, array of hexagonal tiles – a reflection of the $\sqrt{4} : \sqrt{3}$ relationship in the geometry of the hexagon.

XIIII

EMPOWERED PROPORTION

1 See H. L. Crosby, *Thomas of Bradwardine His 'Tractatus de Proportionibus'*, University of Wisconsin, Madison, 1955.
2 See E. Grant, *Nicole Oresme: 'De proportionibus proportionum' and 'Ad pauca respicientes'*, University of Wisconsin, Madison, 1966.
3 Euclid VII, Definition 3, 4: '3. A number is a part [*pars*] of a number, the less of the greater, when it measures the greater; 4. but parts [*partes*] when it does not measure.' T. L. Heath, *Euclid: The Thirteen Books of The Elements*, Cambridge University Press, Cambridge, 1921, II, p. 277.
4 See Grant, *op. cit.*, p. 25.
5 Based on the Latin term *radix* for root.
6 G. Flegg, C. Hay, B. Moss, *Nicholas Chuquet, Renaissance Mathematician*, D. Reidel, Dordrecht, 1985, II, pp. 150–54, also pp. 146–49.
7 L. Pacioli, *Summa de arithmetica geometria proportione et proportionalità*, Venice, 1494, II folio 72B, 'reca. 2. ℞. cu. fa. 8' is to be read 'raise 2 to third power; it makes 8'. Pacioli uses ℞. cu. to mean 'cube'. The history of the notation for powers and roots is given by F. Cajori, *A History of Mathematical Notations*, Open Court, La Salle, 1929, I, pp. 335–79.
8 Cajori, *op. cit.*, I.355, notes that the modern notation was introduced by Newton in a letter of June 13, 1676, to Oldenburg, then secretary of the Royal Society.
9 This notation will be used in the analyses below. Its unfamilarity is deliberate. It is used, among other devices, to emphasize that the Renaissance is indeed a 'foreign land' with a *mentalité* concerning numbers quite distinct from our own. Nevertheless, the modern indexical system is preserved for convenience especially since there was no agreement on how to represent powers at the time.
10 There is nothing unique about these classes, Any set of rational numbers which converge on the root may be implied. For example, the root extraction methods of Heron and Chuquet give different convergent series, *vide supra*, 'Inexpressible Proportion'.

By the fifteenth and sixteenth centuries, mathematically informed individuals were familiar with powers of numbers, not only squares and cubes but higher powers beyond these. Sometime in the thirteenth century Thomas of Bradwardine had introduced unit fractional powers such as half for the square root and a third for the cube root.[1] In the fourteenth century, Nicole Oresme, aware of Bradwardine's work, generalized this notion to include any rational power, for example, two-thirds to stand for the cube root of a square number, or three-fifths for the fifth root of a cube number. Indeed, Oresme pushed the frontiers to the point of allowing irrational powers.[2] Also Oresme extends the classical *pars* and *partes* definition, which is arithmetic in nature, to an exponential form.[3] Thus, the fourth root of four is a *pars* of four since the quadruple product of the root equals four, whereas the three-quarter root of four is not a *pars* of four, but *partes* of four, since no product of the root will ever amount to four. In modern notation $4^{1/4}$ is a *pars*, and $4^{3/4}$ is a *partes*. It is now the exponents which are in agreement with the traditional arithmetic sense: 1 is a *pars* of 4, but 3 is *partes* of 4.[4]

Both Bradwardine and Oresme were handicapped by the lack of notation. Chuquet introduced the sign for *radix*, ℞.[5] This sign was then qualified ℞² for square root, ℞³ for cube root and so on. The modern notation for powers appears to be given in Chuquet's description of 'how one can multiply one diversity of number by itself or by another, like it or unlike', where, for example, a table sets 2^0 against 1, 2^1 against 2, 2^2 against 4, 2^3 against 8, and so on.[6] Unfortunately, Chuquet's notation applies to unknowns in algebraic situations, and 2^0 is to be read as $2x^0$, 2^1 as $2x^1$, 2^2 as $2x^2$, and so on. Pacioli uses a similar notation, but he sometimes uses ℞ for powers rather than roots.[7] Chuquet also used negative powers. Another two centuries were to pass before Isaac Newton gave us the modern indexical notation covering both positive and negative powers and roots.[8]

The symbol ℞ is useful in the Renaissance context. It will be used in the form ℞^{n}, where n is a rational power, positive or negative.[9] The notation adopted is designed to remind the reader that roots in the Renaissance were computed either as a class of rational numbers which may be less than or greater than the inexpressible ideal value, or else as a unique rational number. ℞$^{1/5}$32 equals 2, a unique value, but ℞$^{1/6}$32 equals ℞$^{1/2}$2, a value in some infinite class {1/1, 2/1, 3/2, 7/5, 17/12, 41/29, ...}.[10] On the other hand, ℞^{3}2 will stand for 8, and ℞^{2}3 will stand for 9. The ratio of the *tonus*, 9 : 8, may then be represented as ℞^{2}3 : ℞^{3}2. This makes explicit the playful *symmetria* in which the numbers 2 and 3 are exchanged:

a relationship which is merely implicit in the original form. The notation will make clear the *symmetria* between ratios like 25 : 16, 5 : 4, 19 : 17.[11] It will be shown that these ratios may be re-represented as powers and roots:

$$25 : 16 \qquad R^2 5 : R^2 4$$
$$5 : 4 \qquad R^1 5 : R^1 4$$
$$19 : 17 \qquad R^{1/2} 5 : R^{1/2} 4.$$

Earlier it was shown that 5 : 4 is a rational convergent for $\sqrt[3]{2} : 1$.[12] The *symmetria* between the three ratios may be then be re-represented even more fundamentally in terms of powers and roots of the dyad, 2, and the monad, 1:

$$25 : 16 \qquad R^{2/3} 2 : R^{2/3} 1$$
$$5 : 4 \qquad R^{1/3} 2 : R^{1/3} 1$$
$$19 : 17 \qquad R^{1/6} 2 : R^{1/6} 1.$$

11 *Symmetria* is used here in its nonspatial sense of 'mutuality' between 'measures'. It is not to be confused with the modern understanding of symmetry. See Vitruvius I, ii 4, F. Granger, *Vitruvius: De Architectura*, Harvard University Press, Cambridge MA, 1931, I, pp. 26–27. These ratios occur in Palladio, *I quattro libri dell'architettura*, Venice, 1570, II, p. 11. See analysis of Palazzo Della Torre, *infra*, 'Andrea Palladio'.

12 In 'Inexpressible Proportion' *supra*.

PROPORTIONALITY

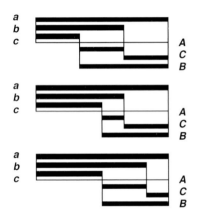

Fig. 1. The three conditions among magnitudes $a > b > c$ and their positive differences $(a - b) = C$, $(a - c) = B$, $(b - c) = A$. In each diagram the three bold lines from the top show the magnitudes in descending order of size a, b, c. The next three bold lines show the differences A, C, B in that order to the bottom line. It is clear from the diagram that $B > A$ and $B > C$ in every case, but the relationship between A and C is ambivalent. Diagrams from top to bottom.

$$C = A$$
$$C > A$$
$$C < A.$$

1 'Proportionality' is used to relate a third medial term to two extremes in a general sense. Unlike proportion, as usually understood, the ratio of the greater to the medial term does not have to be equal to that of the medial term to the lesser, although that arrangement is not excluded. Rather, this arrangement 'is the only one in the strict sense of the word to be called proportion, because its terms are seen to be in the same ratio'. M. L. D'Ooge, *Nicomachus of Gerasa: Introduction to Arithmetic*, University of Michigan, Ann Arbor, 1938, II.xxiv, p. 270. The original three means remain of importance in modern mathematics, E. F. Beckenbach

The most ancient of the known means are the arithmetic, geometric and harmonic.[1] Three more were added: the subcontrary to the harmonic, and two subcontraries to the geometric. The arithmetic is self-contrary. Later still, four more were defined to bring the total to ten. Both Nicomachus and Pappus describe ten means, only each shows one mean that the other omits. Consequently, there are eleven means altogether.[2] It says much for the symbolic power of number that ten, and not eleven, is the preferred count of both authors.[3]

Three numbers are required to define a mean: the greater and less extremes and the medial term in between. Three numbers give rise to three differences: the difference of the greater extreme and the mean, the mean and the lesser extreme, and the difference between the two extremes. (Fig. 1)

The eleven means are derived when the ratios of these differences in pairs are made proportional with the ratios of the original numbers in pairs. Let the numbers in decreasing value be a, b, c.

	a	b	c
a	$a : a$	$a : b$	$a : c$
b	$b : a$	$b : b$	$b : c$
c	$c : a$	$c : b$	$c : c$.

Symmetry dictates that only the ratios in bold type need be compared with the ratios of the differences. The equalities along the diagonal may be compared with just those cases in which the two smaller differences are equal themselves, the condition for the arithmetic mean. The three differences are $a - b$, $a - c$, $b - c$. For convenience, let $C = a - b$, $B = a - c$, $A = b - c$. While it is clear that B is larger than the other two, C, A, it is possible for either of these two to be greater, or less, than the other, and even equal. They are equal when $C : A :: a : a :: b : b :: c : c$, which is the condition for the arithmetic mean.

Among the ratios of differences, the equalities may be ignored as trivial. All the ratios in bold, above, are equal to, or greater than, 1 : 1. Those equal to 1 : 1 have already been taken into account with the arithmetic mean. Any remaining comparison with the ratio of differences must be with ratios greater than, 1 : 1. This leaves just the ratios shown in bold below.

	A	*B*	*C*
A	*A* : *A*	*A* : *B*	*A* : *C*
B	*B* : *A*	*B* : *B*	*B* : *C*
C	*C* : *A*	*C* : *B*	*C* : *C*.

There are three inequalities in the first table and four in the second. This suggests twelve possible means besides the one already accounted for – the arithmetic – in which the two smaller differences are equal.[4] A 3×4 table sets out the means according to the numbering of Nicomachus (Roman) and Pappus (Arabic). The comparison in the top left corner is invalid since the relationship implies that a is equal to b, which defies the original condition that the extremes and the mean be distinct.[5]

	a : *b*	*b* : *c*	*a* : *c*
B : *A*	– –	IX 10	VII –
A : *C*	VI 6	V 5	IV 4
C : *A*	II 2	II 2	III 3
B : *C*	– 8	X 7	VIII 9.

It will be seen that the geometric mean (II) arises in two equivalent ways, although the subcontraries to the geometric ratio (V and VI), obtained by comparing the original ratios with the inverse ratio of the differences in the geometric ratio, give distinct values. The subcontrary to the harmonic (IV) is also produced from the inverse ratio of the differences in the harmonic ratio (III). The arithmetic ratio which is based on equality is invariant under inversion, and is, for this reason, self-contrary. Nicomachus describes the means in detail and provides an arithmetical example of each. If the extremes are given, three of the means (V, VI, IX) are to be found only as solutions to quadratic equations. The geometric mean requires the extraction of a square root.[6] Nicomachus gives numerical examples of his ten proportionalities and these are faithfully recorded by Boethius in his Latin transcription.[7] It will be noted that Nicomachus' examples are confined to numbers within the decad.[8] Table 1 gives all the proportionalities to be found within the decad. It is a fact that the proportionalities are most dense with small numbers and become less dense as the numbers increase in size.[9] Figures 2, 3, 4, 5 (the diagrams are based on the numerical examples provided by Nicomachus).

The algorism which Nicomachus used to develop ratios in continuous proportion – equivalent to determining two extremes and the geometric mean – is transformed by Pappus to create simple additive algorisms for generating eight of his ten means. The remaining means can also be constructed in this manner.[10] If α, β, γ, are in geometric progression, then the eleven means may be constructed as shown in Figs. 6, 7.

The Pythagorean lambda is replete with arithmetic, geometric and harmonic means.[11] Any three closest numbers in a triangular formation with the base of the triangle uppermost and parallel to the row are related as in an arithmetic mean, while those in a triangular formation with the base down are related as in an harmonic mean. (Fig. 8)

and R. Bellman, *Inequalities*, Springer-Verlag, New York, 1971, pp. 16–19. Today, a mean of order t is defined as $M_t(x) = (\sum_{i=1}^{n} x_i)^{1/t}$. For $t = 1$ the mean is arithmetic, for $t \to 0$ the mean is geometric, and for $t = -1$ the mean is harmonic. The other classical means do not belong to this family. In simpler terms, it is seen that if a and c are extremes and b is the mean, then the arithmetic proportionality is given by the equation $a + c = 2b$, the geometric by the equation $\log a + \log c = 2\log b$, and the harmonic by the equation $a^{-1} + c^{-1} = 2b^{-1}$.

2 For a convenient summary see T. L. Heath, *A History of Greek Mathematics*, Clarendon Press, Oxford, 1921, I, pp. 84–90.

3 Boethius writes: 'It is testified to and known among the ancients who have studied the learning of Pythagoras, or Plato, or Aristotle, that these are the three ways to knowledge: arithmetic, geometric, harmonic. After these relationships of proportion there are three others, which are conveyed to us without names but are called fourth, fifth, and sixth, and which are contrasted with the above. Then later thinkers, on account of the perfection of the number ten, which was pleasing to Pythagoras, added four other kinds, so that in these proportionalities they brought together a body of proportions ten in number.' He then reminds us that ten is the same number as there are classes among proportions: 'According to this number we describe the prior relationships and comparisons where there are five in the major proportions, which we call leaders, and with them we put five others, minor terms, which we call followers.' M. Masi, *Boethian Number Theory: a translation of the 'De institutione arithmetica'*, Rodopi, Amsterdam, 1983, II.xli, p. 165.

4 Theon of Smyrna writes: 'There are several means: the geometric, the arithmetic, the harmonic, the subcontrary, the fifth and the sixth, to which six others must be added which are subcontrary to them.' Altogether he suggests twelve means, but he only discusses in detail the first three means since these have musical relevance – an example of the curtailment that music brings to broader arithmetic possibilities. R. & D. Lawlor, *Theon of Smyrna: Mathematics Useful for Understanding Plato*, Wizard's Bookshelf, San Diego, 1979, II.1, p. 70. The comparison of the differences B and A with the magnitudes a and b is not valid since it implies that $a = b$ which contradicts the original assumption that $a > b$. By eliminating this invalid case the number of proportionalities is reduced from Theon's twelve to eleven.

5 D'Ooge, *op. cit.*, II.xxii-xxviii, p. 266ff. For Pappus see T. L. Heath, *A History of Greek Mathematics*, Clarendon Press, Oxford, 1921, II, p. 363–65 where a summary of Pappus, *Synagoge (Collection)*, Book III, Section 2 on means is given.

6 Nicomachus does not address the general question of extracting the square root. Theon does. This is an easy matter, of course, when the two extremes are both square numbers. These are the numerical examples that Nicomachus chooses to illustrate. For further discussion *vide supra*, 'Inexpressible Proportion'.

7 D'Ooge, *op. cit.*, p. 284. Nicomachus' numerical examples: I [arithmetic] 1, 2, 3; II [geometric] 1, 2, 4; III [harmonic] 3, 4, 6; IV [subcontrary to the harmonic]

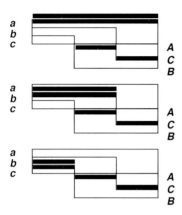

Fig. 2. The arithmetic mean, Nicomachus I, can be represented in three ways according to whether the equality between the differences *A* and *C* is compared with *a* : *a* (top), *b* : *b* (centre), *c* : *c* (bottom). The arithmetic mean is self-contrary.

Table 1 Eighty-four triplets between 1 and 9 including reducible forms. The proportionalities given by Nicomachus are marked I – X with the designation given by Nicomachus. Pappus 8 is represented by the triplet 346.

123	I, IX, X	234	I, VII, VIII	358	
124	II	235	X	359	X, VII
125		236	III	367	
127		237		368	
128		239		378	
129		245	V	379	VIII
134	X	246	I, XI, X	389	
135	I	247		456	I
136		248	II	457	
137	IX	249		458	
138		256	IV	459	IX
139	II	257	X	467	IX
145	X	258	I	468	I, VII, VII
146	VI	259		469	II
147	I	267		478	
148		268		479	
149		269		489	
156		278		567	I
157		279	X	568	
158		289		569	
159	I	345	I	578	
167	X	346	III, Pappus 8	579	I
168		347	X	589	
169		348		678	I
178	X	349		679	VIII
179		356	IV	689	VII
189	X	357	I	789	I

3, 5, 6; V [first subcontrary to the geometric] 2, 4, 5; VI [second subcontrary to the geometric] 1, 4, 6; VII 6, 8, 9; VIII 6, 7, 9; IX 4, 6, 7; X 3, 5, 8. It is to be noted that proportionalities, especially among small numbers, may not be unique. For example, 1, 2, 3 is arithmetic, but it is also satisfies IX and X. The harmonic proportionality 3, 4, 6 satisfies Pappus 8 too – the mean that Nicomachus does not show. 8, 9, 12 is the smallest proportionality to represent Pappus 8 uniquely. Since Pappus ignores Nicomachus VII represented by 6, 8, 9, and Nicomachus ignores Pappus 8 represented by 8, 9, 12, neither is in a position to notice that the 'perfect proportion' 6, 8, 9, 12 embraces both proportionalities. For Boethius see Masi, *op. cit.*, p. 185. Theon does not have such a list.

8 For the decad, numbers from 1 to 9, *vide supra*, 'Theological Number'.

9 An unpublished computer study by Dr Djordje Krstic at the University of California, Los Angeles, shows that within the irreducible triplets 1–10 some 40% are proportionalities, but that among the irreducible triplets 1–100 this falls to less than 3%. The triplet 2, 4, 6 is reducible to 1, 2, 3 and, like similar triplets, is not counted in this study.

10 Heath, *op. cit.*, I, pp. 88–89.

11 *Infra* Figs. 8, 9, 10.

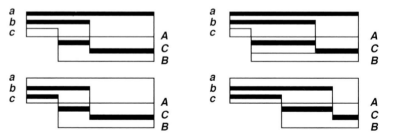

Fig. 3. The geometric mean, Nicomachus II, can be represented in two ways according to whether the ratio *C* : *A* is compared with the ratio *a* : *b* or the ratio *b* : *c* (left). Consequently there are two subcontraries to the geometric where *A* : *C* is compared with *a* : *b*, Nicomachus VI, and then to *b* : *c*, Nicomachus V (right).

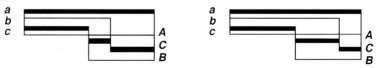

Fig. 4. The harmonic mean, Nicomachus III, is represented in only one way when *C* : *A* is compared with *a* : *c* (left) and there is just one subcontrary to the harmonic, Nicomachus IV, when *C* : *A* is compared with *c* : *a* (right).

Any three numbers in a straight line and equally spaced are related as in a geometric mean (Fig. 9). While the geometric relationship holds true for tableaux based on ratios other than 3 : 2, the same arithmetic and harmonic relationships do not hold.

Two parallelograms define 'the most perfect proportion' of Nicomachus in which two means, one arithmetic and one harmonic, are placed between the two extremes

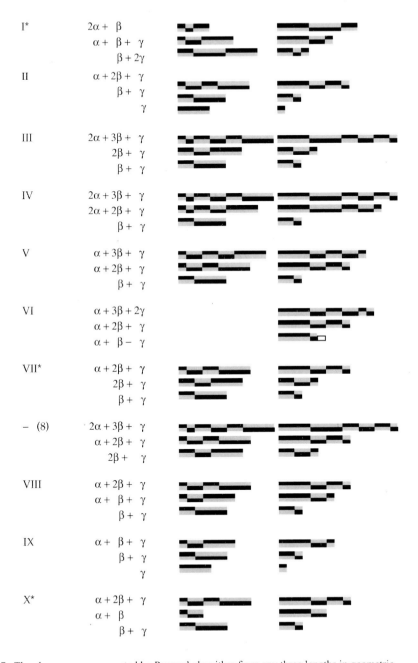

$$I^* \quad 2\alpha + \beta$$
$$\alpha + \beta + \gamma$$
$$\beta + 2\gamma$$

$$II \quad \alpha + 2\beta + \gamma$$
$$\beta + \gamma$$
$$\gamma$$

$$III \quad 2\alpha + 3\beta + \gamma$$
$$2\beta + \gamma$$
$$\beta + \gamma$$

$$IV \quad 2\alpha + 3\beta + \gamma$$
$$2\alpha + 2\beta + \gamma$$
$$\beta + \gamma$$

$$V \quad \alpha + 3\beta + \gamma$$
$$\alpha + 2\beta + \gamma$$
$$\beta + \gamma$$

$$VI \quad \alpha + 3\beta + 2\gamma$$
$$\alpha + 2\beta + \gamma$$
$$\alpha + \beta - \gamma$$

$$VII^* \quad \alpha + 2\beta + \gamma$$
$$2\beta + \gamma$$
$$\beta + \gamma$$

$$- (8) \quad 2\alpha + 3\beta + \gamma$$
$$\alpha + 2\beta + \gamma$$
$$2\beta + \gamma$$

$$VIII \quad \alpha + 2\beta + \gamma$$
$$\alpha + \beta + \gamma$$
$$\beta + \gamma$$

$$IX \quad \alpha + \beta + \gamma$$
$$\beta + \gamma$$
$$\gamma$$

$$X^* \quad \alpha + 2\beta + \gamma$$
$$\alpha + \beta$$
$$\beta + \gamma$$

Fig. 7. The eleven means generated by Pappus' algorithm from any three lengths in geometric progression. Those marked * are not shown in Pappus. Nicomachus VI is the only proportionality to involve a negative sign and in the case illustrated only one solution is possible with positive dimensions.

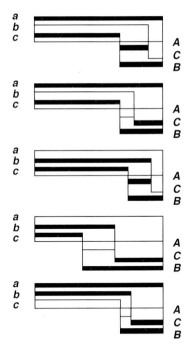

Fig. 5. From top to bottom: Nicomachus VII, VIII, IX, and X. The lowest figure represents Pappus 8.

α

β

γ

Fig. 6. Three lengths in geometric progression. In Pappus' algorithm the extreme values may be exchanged (left and right).

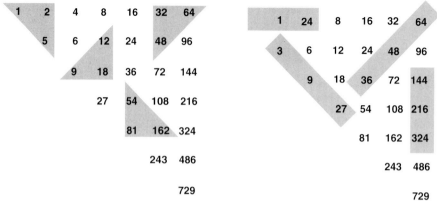

1	2	4	8	16	32	64
	5	6	12	24	48	96
		9	18	36	72	144
			27	54	108	216
				81	162	324
					243	486
						729

Fig. 8. The Pythagorean lambda showing arithmetic and harmonic proportionalities. The two triangles at the top give the formation for arithmetic proportionality. Any three numbers that may be overlayed in this manner will necessarily be in arithmetic progression. The remaining two triangles show the disposition of harmonic proportionalities on the Fig. 8 lambda.

Fig. 9. The Pythagorean lambda showing geometric proportionalities. Any three equally spaced numbers in a straight line are in geometric progression. Only nearest neighbours are shown. The sequences 3, 27, 243, and 1, 8, 64, for example, are also geometric.

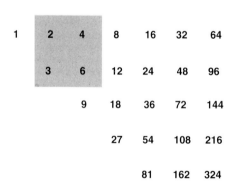

1	2	4	8	16	32	64
	3	6	12	24	48	96
		9	18	36	72	144
			27	54	108	216
				81	162	324
					243	486
						729

1	2	4	8	16	32	64
	3	6	12	24	48	96
		9	18	36	72	144
			27	54	108	216
				81	162	324

Fig. 10. The parallelogram, top, indicates the formation of 'the most perfect proportion' based on the double ratio, and the rectangle, bottom, shows the arrangement for the triple ratio.

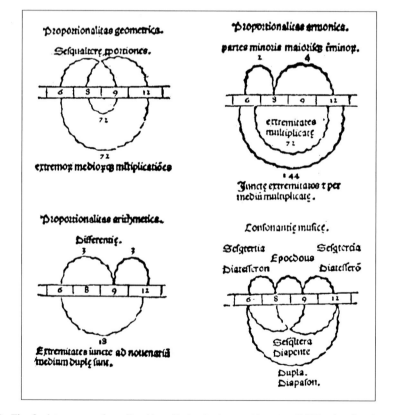

Fig. 11. The final two pages from Boethius, *De institutione arithmetica* (1488), showing the arithmetic, geometric and harmonic relationships present in 'the most perfect' proportion 6, 8, 9, 12.

in such a way that two discontinuous proportions are formed.[12] The first parallelogram is oblique and is made from two triangles, one an harmonic triple and the other an arithmetic triple, joined along their bases; the second parallelogram is rectangular made from a similar two triangles but now joined along their hypotenuses. The first proportion is between extremes in double ratio, the second between ratios in triple ratio.

An example of the first proportion is $6 : 8 : 9 : 12$, in which 8 is the harmonic mean and 9 is the arithmetic mean.[13] The discontinuous proportions are $6 : 8 :: 9 : 12$ which are geometrically related by the sesquitertia ratio $4 : 3$, and $6 : 9 :: 8 : 12$, geometrically related by the sesquialter ratio $3 : 2$. The second proportion is shown by $2 : 3 : 4 : 6$ in which 3 is the harmonic mean and 4 the arithmetic. (Fig. 11). The discontinuous proportions are $2 : 3 :: 4 : 6$, geometrically related by the sesquialter ratio, and $2 : 4 :: 3 : 6$, geometrically related by the duple ratio, $2 : 1$. The former proportion is the example given by Nicomachus. The latter is presented as a 'prime' proportionality by Silvio Belli, Palladio's mathematical companion.[14] Belli also gives specific examples of the first four proportionalities:[15]

arithmetic	5, 7, 9;
geometric	4, 6, 9;
harmonic	3, 4, 6;
contraharmonic	3, 5, 6.

12 D'Ooge, *op. cit.*, II.xxix, pp. 284–86. Nicomachus writes in the concluding chapter of his treatise: 'It remains for me to discuss briefly the most perfect proportion, that which is three dimensional and embraces them all, and which is most useful for all progress in music and in the theory of the nature of the universe. This alone would be properly and truly be called harmony rather than the others, since it is not a plane, nor bound together by only one mean term, but with two, so as thus to be extended in three dimensions, just as a while ago it was explained that the cube is in harmony. . . . When, therefore, there are two extreme terms, both of three dimensions, either numbers multiplied thrice by themselves to be a cube, or numbers multiplied twice by themselves and once by another number so as to be either "beams" or "bricks", or the products of three unequal numbers, so as to be scalene, and between them are found two other terms which preserve the same ratios to the extremes alternately and together, in such a manner that, while one of them preserves the harmonic proportion, the other completes the arithmetic, it is necessary that in such a disposition of the four the geometric proportion appears, on examination, commingled with both mean terms – as the greatest is to the third removed from it, so it is the second to the fourth; for such a situation makes the product of the means equal to the product of the extremes.'

13 *Ibid.*, p. 286. 'Let this be an example of this proportion, 6, 8, 9, 12.' The geometric relation which Nicomachus draws attention to is illustrated in this example by $12 : 8$ and $9 : 6$, both are in discontinuous geometric proportion $3 : 2$. Similarly, $12 : 9$ and $8 : 6$ are in discontinuous geometric proportion $4 : 3$. These are the musical ratios associated with the *diapente* and the *diatesseron* which are then seen to be means between the *diapason* represented by the ratio $12 : 6$, or $2 : 1$. The ratio $9 : 8$ is the *tonus*.

The general formula, for $a < b$, is $2a(a + b) : 4ab : (a + b)(a + b) : 2b(a + b)$. For values of a and b between 1 and 4 there are five distinct 'most perfect proportions' in their root forms:

a	b		
1	2	6, 8, 9, 12	
1	3	2, 3, 4, 6	
1	4	10, 16, 25, 40	
2	3	20, 24, 25, 30	
2	4	6, 8, 9, 12	repeat of $(a, b) = (1, 2)$
3	4	42, 48, 49, 56.	

14 S. Belli, *Della proportione et proportionalità*, Venice, 1573, p. 27, recto, where 2, 3, 4, 6 is presented as '*le prime specie della proportionalità discontinua*'.
15 *Ibid.*, p. 26, recto and verso.

XV

COMPOSITE PROPORTION

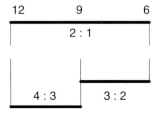

In the process of obtaining roots, two ratios $p : q$ and $r : s$ are combined to form a third ratio $(p + q) : (r + s)$.[1] This is an example of the composition of ratios. In his commentary on Vitruvius, Barbaro shows two other compositions. In classical terms these represent the addition and subtraction of ratios, but to us they are analogous to the multiplication and division of fractions. The system is attributed by Barbaro to four principles given by al-Khindi.[2] (Fig. 1.)

The two compositions are set out by Barbaro in the following way, although in Barbaro's text, the parallel lines, the cross and the colons are not shown, and which multiplicands are involved is left to the reader to infer.

$$
\begin{array}{cc}
p : q & \quad p : q \\
| \quad | & \quad \times \\
r : s & \quad r : s \\
\hline
pr : qs & \quad qr : ps.
\end{array}
$$

Barbaro gives more than two pages of numerical examples for both types of composition. The first is 'additive', the second 'subtractive'. The modern reader will recognize the first as the multiplication of fractions, and the second as division.[3] Take the concrete examples:

$$
\begin{array}{cc}
4 : 3 & \quad 4 : 3 \\
| \quad | & \quad \times \\
3 : 2 & \quad 3 : 2 \\
\hline
12 : 6 & \quad 9 : 8.
\end{array}
$$

These same compositions may be presented diagrammatically in a way that brings out the 'additive' and 'subtractive' qualitites.[4] The first is illustrated as the partitioning of the duple, 2 : 1, into sesquialter, 3 : 2, and sequitertian, 4 : 3, ratios, where the duple is completed by 'addition':

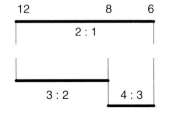

Fig. 1. Page 86 from D. Barbaro, *M. Vitrvvii Pollionis*, showing composite ratios in which two ratios produce a third.

1 *Vide supra*, 'Inexpressible Proportion'.
2 D. Barbaro, *I dieci libri dell'architettura di M. Vitruvio tradutti et commentati . . .* Venice, 1556, and *M. Vitrvvii Pollionis de architectura libri decem cvm commentariis . . .* Venice, 1567. On arithmetical concepts of al-Khindi see Barbaro 1558, p. 60ff for 'Alchindo' and 1567, pp. 85–86 for 'Alchindus'. The subject of composite ratios is not addressed by Euclid. Although Book VI.[Definition5] speaks of the

The second shows that when these two diagrams are superimposed the common difference is the sesquioctave, 9 : 8, as if by 'subtraction' of 4 : 3 from 3 : 2.

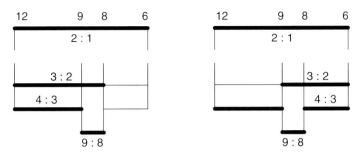

Another representation is suggested by diagrams in Benedetti's work.[5] If a ratio is represented by a rectangle whose length is the antecedent and breadth is the consequent, then an assembly of such rectangles can be made to depict the compositions above. Ratio 'addition' gives a 2 : 1 rectangle in two ways. The first way shows a 4×3 arrangement of 3 : 2 rectangles, and the second shows a 3×2 arrangement of 4 : 3 rectangles:

Ratio 'subtraction' gives a 9 : 8 rectangle in two ways. The first way shows a 3×4 arrangement of 3 : 2 rectangles, and the second shows a 3×2 arrangement of 3 : 4 rectangles:

Essentially Barbaro is investigating the *regula sex quantitatum*, the rule of six quantities, one of the fundamental theorems of Greek trigonometry usually attributed to Menelaus.[6] Take a triangle and cut it by a transversal. The transversal will cut the sides in three points to make six segments:

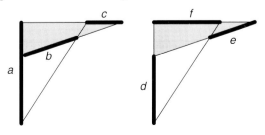

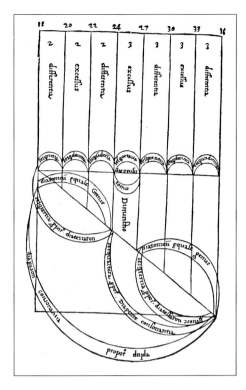

Fig. 2. Figure from Franchinus Gaffurius, *De harmonia musicorum instrumentorum opus*, showing a Renaissance version of the modern diagrams.

multiplication of ratios, it is an interpolation of unknown origin. (Heath, *Euclid: The Thirteen Books of The Elements*, Cambridge University Press, Cambridge, 1921, II, pp. 189–190). GalilEo Galilei's friend and patron, Guidobaldo – Marchese del Monte – made use of Commandino's Latin version of Euclid in his commentary *De Proportione Composita* on this pseudo-Euclidean definition. (P. L. Rose, *The Italian Renaissance of Mathematics: Studies on Humanists and Mathematicians from Petrarch to Galileo*, Librairie Droz, Genève, 1975, p. 230). Commandino was certainly known to Barbaro, and Jacopo Contarini was a mutual acquaintance of both Guidobaldi and Palladio (M. Tafuri, *Venice and the Renaissance*, MIT Press, Cambridge MA, 1989, pp. 130–38). Filippo Pigafetta, Guidobaldi's translator into Italian, mentions among the 'restorers' of mathematics Alberti, Barbaro and Guidobaldi (Rose, *ibid.*).

3 The parallels between multiplication and division, and addition and subtraction, is common at this period. F. Cajori, *A Historical of Mathematical Notations*, Open Court, La Salle, 1928, I, p. 248–49, writes: 'A strange misapplication of the + sign is sometimes found in connection with the "composition" of ratios. If the ratios NP/CN and AN/CN are multiplied together, the product $NP/CN \cdot AN/CN$, according to old phraseology, was "compounded" of the first two ratios. Using

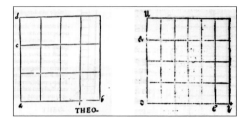

Fig. 3. Figures from G-B Benedetti, *Diversarum speculationum mathematicarum.*

The theorem states that the product of lengths of three segments, *a*, *b*, *c*, having no common endpoints will be equal to the product of the remaining three segments, *d*, *e*, *f*. That is,

$$abc = def.$$

The examples of 'addition' and 'subtraction' given earlier can be depicted as special cases of Menelaus' theorem:

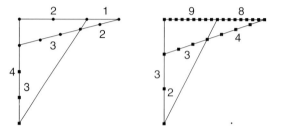

Barbaro cites al-Khindi on the *sex quantitatum*. He gives an arithmetical interpretation of the trigonometrical fact which is based on the permutations of Menelaus' theorem stated in the form:

$$\frac{abc}{def} = 1.$$

Barbaro conceives this as the product of three ratios constituted from one set of numbers 1, 4, 9, and a second set of numbers 2, 3, 6. There are 18 possible pairings of numerator and denominator, the product of six permutations of the denominator, say, and then three of the numerator which do not duplicate pairings already established. An example of one of these in Barbaro's style would be:

$$a - - d$$
$$b - - e$$
$$f - - c.$$

He names each of these permutations a mode. The numbers are derived from the first six terms of the Pythagorean lambda: one set being the square numbers 1, 4, 9, and the other being the means 2, 3, 6. They may be visualized as two disjoint triangles, one for the square numbers and one for the means. The 18 permutations are enumerated by finding all the ways in which the vertices of one triangle may be joined to the vertices of the other triangle in pairs with independent endpoints.

the term "proportion" as synonymous with "ratio", the expression "composition of proportions" was also used. As the word "composition" suggests addition, a curious notation, using +, was at one time employed. For example, Isaac Barrow [*Lectiones opticae*, 1669] denoted the "compounded ratio" *NP/CN · AN/CN* in this manner, "*NP · CN + AN · CN*" That is, the sign of addition was used in place of a sign of multiplication, and the dot signified ratio as in Oughtred" '.

4 Such diagrams, many of them very complex, were popular among music theorists. Fig. 2 is taken from C. A. Miller, *Franchinus Gaffurius: De harmonia musicorum instrumentorum opus*, American Institute of Musicology, Hannsler-Verlag, Neuhausen-Stuttgart, 1977, III.iii, p. 156. See also W. K. Kreyszig, *Franchino Gaffurio: The Theory of Music*, Yale University Press, New Haven, 1993.

5 G.-B. Benedetti, *Diversarum speculationum mathematicarum et physicarum liber*, Turin, 1585.

6 R. Wittkower, *Architectural Principles in the Age of Humanism*, Academy Editions, London, 1998, p. 128 n. 118, cites al-Khindi, *Libellum sex quantitatum*. He suggests that both Lorenzo Ghiberti and Leonardo da Vinci may have been familiar with this work. The *regula sex quantitatum* was well known as a fundamental theorem of Greek trigonometry during the mediaeval period. Menelaus (*c*100CE) *Spherics* was translated from Arabic and Hebrew and published at Messina in 1558, but earlier, Girolamo Cardano, *Practica arithmeticae generalis*, Milan, 1539, contained a Chapter 'Caput 46, de regula 6 quatitatum'. See D. E. Smith, *History of Mathematics*, Constable and Company, 1925, II, pp. 491–92, pp. 606–7. The spherical triangle version of the theorem had important applications in astronomical observations.

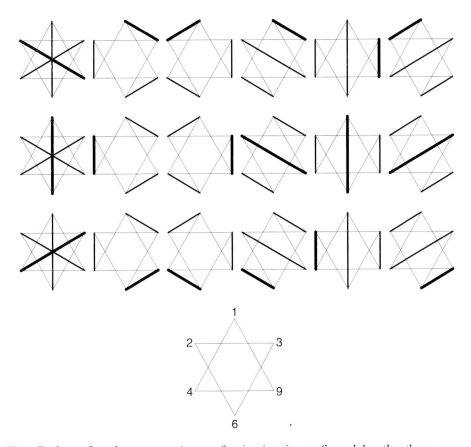

That Barbaro found *sex quantitatum* fascinating is confirmed by the three pages which he devotes to the theme in both his Italian and Latin commentaries on Vitruvius. In fact, the section on *sex quantitatum* is heavily revised in the later Latin version, although the original 1557 edition clearly shows Barbaro's permutational method of deriving the modes. He starts by imagining all possible permutations of six numbers, and removing symmetry, he arrives at 360 possibilities, that is half of $1 \times 2 \times 3 \times 4 \times 5 \times 6$. He then eliminates some of these, eventually arriving at 18 modes in the 1567 Latin edition, having previously cited 36 useful modes and 12 useless modes in the earlier Italian version. He sets up tables to pair the six quantities, which effectively arranges the pairs in this manner:

ab	*ac*	*ad*	*ae*	*af*
	bc	*bd*	*be*	*bf*
		cd	*ce*	*cf*
			de	*df*
				ef.

There are fifteen unordered pairs, and thirty if *ab* and *ba* are considered to be distinct. In doing so, Barbaro is ignoring the separation of the two sets: the denominator and numerator sets. He then takes this into account, eliminating the six denominator-denominator and numerator-numerator pairs from the previous table to obtain:

TABVLA SEX QVANTITATVM
PROPORTIONE RESPONDENTIVM.

Modi comparabiles.	Ordo numerorum.					
	Primus.	Secundus.	Tertius.	Quartus.	Quintus.	Sextus.
Primus modus.	1	2	3	4	6	9
Secundus modus.	1	2	3	9	6	4
Tertius modus.	1	3	2	4	6	9
Quartus.	1	3	2	9	6	4
Quintus.	1	6	2	9	3	4
Sextus.	1	6	2	4	3	9
Septimus.	2	4	1	3	9	6
Octauus.	2	4	1	6	9	3
Nonus.	2	9	1	3	4	6

Modi comparabiles.	Ordo numerorum.					
	Primus.	Secundus.	Tertius.	Quartus.	Quintus.	Sextus.
Decimus.	2	9	1	6	4	3
Vndecimus.	3	4	1	2	9	6
Duodecimus.	3	4	1	6	9	2
Decimus tertius.	3	9	1	2	4	6
Decimus quartus.	3	9	1	6	4	2
Decimus quintus.	4	6	2	1	3	9
Decimus ſextus.	4	6	2	9	3	1
Decimus ſeptimus.	6	9	1	2	4	3
Decimus octauus.	6	9	1	3	4	2

Fig. 4. Table of six quantities from Barbaro, *M. Vitrvvii Pollionis* . . . .

ad *ae* *af*
bd *be* *bf*
cd *ce* *cf.*

This leaves nine legitimate unordered pairs, or 18 pairs when order is taken into account. If numerators are exchanged for denominators throughout, which is of little consequence for the actual relationships, 36 distinct modes would be recorded. Barbaro removes this inconsequentiality from his revised 1567 text and fixes on just 18 distinct modes. The numbers, all of which are from the Pythagorean lambda, possess arithmetic, geometric and harmonic properties, and Barbaro's modes are particularly rich in relationships of this kind. However, the conditions which lead to the 18 modes would also be satisfied by any set of three square numbers and the three means between them. (Fig. 4,[7] Fig. 5.[8])

Palladio's mathematical acquaintance, Silvio Belli, describes nine transformations of ratio.[9] Some are simple permutations of antecedents and consequents, some involve the addition of antecedents and consequents, some their subtraction, and some involve two triples from which a proportion between extremes is derived. All original numbers in Belli's examples come from the Pythagorean lambda: 2, 3, 4, 6, 8, 9, 12. Thus:

in 'la scambiata', or exchange, 6 : 4 :: 3 : 2 goes to 6 : 3 :: 4 : 2;[10]

in 'all'indietro', or backwards, 6 : 3 :: 4 : 2 goes to 4 : 2 :: 6 : 3;

in 'la composita', or mixture, 6 : 3 :: 4 : 2 goes to (6 + 4) : (3 + 2) :: 4 : 2, or 10 : 5 :: 4 : 2;

in 'la simile', or matching, 6 : 3 :: 4 : 2 goes to (6 + 3) : 3 :: (4 + 2) : 2, or 9 : 3 :: 6 : 2;[11]

7 The table is taken from Barbaro, 1567, *op. cit.*, p. 85.
8 The charts are taken from Barbaro, 1558, *op. cit.*, p. 61. In general, if p^2 q^2 r^2 are the square numbers, the means will be *pq qr rp*.
9 S. Belli, *Della proportione et proportionalità*, Venice, 1573, III.ii, pp. 28–9.
10 Euclid V, Definition 12, alternate ratio. *Vide supra*, 'Euclidean Regular Figures'.
11 Euclid V, Definition 14, composition of a ratio.

in 'la divisa', or parting, 6 : 3 :: 4 : 2 goes to $(6-4) : (3-2) :: 4 : 2$, or $2 : 1 :: 4 : 2$;[12]

in 'la stravolta', or disturbed, 3 : 6 :: 2 : 4 goes to $3 : 6 :: (3-2) : (6-4)$, or $3 : 6 :: 1 : 2$.

The last three arrangements involve two triples and demonstrate the *ex aequali* principle of Euclid's Definition 17, Book V, in which the extreme terms may be compared directly having removed the intermediate terms. Thus:

in 'del pari', or alike, 8 : 4 : 6 :: 4 : 2 : 3 goes to 8 : 4 :: 6 : 3;[13]

in 'la ordinata', or ordinate, 6 : 4 : 8 :: 3 : 2 : 4 goes to 6 : 3 :: 8 : 4;[14]

and in 'la turbata', or perturbed, 4 : 6 : 12, 3 : 6 : 9 goes to 4 : 3 :: 12 : 9.[15]

This last transformation appears to follow Euclid's perturbed proportion of Definition 18, Book V, in which 4 : 6 :: 6 : 9 and 6 : 12 :: 3 : 6 produce the perturbed proportion 4 : 12 :: 3 : 9. An application of 'la scambiata' delivers the final result 4 : 3 :: 12 : 9.

It seems that Palladio, in particular, may have used Barbaro's composite ratios to produce ratios which compare the square roots of small numbers 2, 3, 4, and 5. Consider the following computations:

$$
\begin{array}{ll}
21 : 15 & R^{1/2}2 : R^{1/2}1 \\
\quad\times & \quad\times \\
\underline{26 : 15} & \underline{R^{1/2}3 : R^{1/2}1} \\
26 : 21 & R^{1/2}3 : R^{1/2}2.
\end{array}
$$

which uses the rational convergents 21 : 15 :: 7 : 5 for $\sqrt{2} : 1$ and 26 : 15 for $\sqrt{3} : 1$. The compound is a rational convergent to $\sqrt{3} : \sqrt{2}$.

Or take this computation in which the compound is a convergent to $\sqrt[3]{3} : \sqrt[3]{2}$:

$$
\begin{array}{ll}
63 : 50 & R^{1/3}2 : R^{1/3}1 \\
\quad\times & \quad\times \\
\underline{36 : 25} & \underline{R^{1/3}3 : R^{1/3}1} \\
8 : 7 & R^{1/3}3 : R^{1/3}2.
\end{array}
$$

These are empowerments of Palladio's canonic ratio 3 : 2. In fact, we find that Palladio uses all the ratios 27 : 8, 9 : 4, 3 : 2, 11 : 9, 8 : 7 which are rational convergents to $3^3 : 2^3$, $3^2 : 2^2$, 3 : 2, $\sqrt{3} : \sqrt{2}$, $\sqrt[3]{3} : \sqrt[3]{2}$.[16] It is important to note that the computations reduce ratios to their root value, that is to say, 72 : 63 is reduced to 8 : 7. Or take the rational convergent 15 : 13 for $\sqrt{4} : \sqrt{3}$ used by Alberti:[17]

$$
\begin{array}{ll}
26 : 15 & R^{1/2}3 : R^{1/2}1 \\
\quad\times & \quad\times \\
\underline{2 : 1} & \underline{R^{1/2}4 : R^{1/2}1} \\
15 : 13 & R^{1/2}4 : R^{1/2}3.
\end{array}
$$

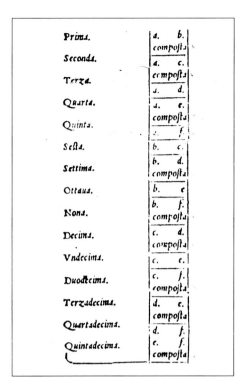

Fig. 5. One of the permutational charts from Barbaro, 1556, used to determine the eighteen proportional modes among six quantities.

12 Euclid V Definition 15, separation of a ratio.

13 Euclid V Definition 17, ratio *ex aequali*.

14 As in n. 13, but the order is inverted.

15 Despite its name this does not appear to be the same as Euclid V, Definition 18, a perturbed proportion. In Euclid, if there are two proportions $a : b :: B : C$ and $b : c :: A : B$, then the perturbed proportion is $a : c :: A : C$.

16 The ratio 27 : 8 is used in the principal hall of the Palazzo Valerio Chiericati $54P \times 16P$ (A. Palladio, *I Quattro Libri dell'Architettura*, Venice, 1570, II, p. 6); the ratio 9 : 4 is used in two schemes, Villa Pogliani (II, p. 58), with two small rooms estimated to be $18P \times 8P$, and four rooms in an invention for Venice (II, p. 72); the canonic ratio 3 : 2 is used in some 40 situations in 18 projects; the ratio 11 : 9 is used in the Villa Angarano where the two principal rooms are $22P \times 18P$ (II, p. 63); and the ratio 8 : 7 is the proportion of the $32P \times 28P$ main hall in the Palazzo Antonini (II, p. 5). It should be noted that the ratio 8 : 7 may also be interpreted as a rational convergent to $\sqrt{4} : \sqrt{3}$ using the estimate 7 : 4 for $\sqrt{3} : 1$ and the identity $\sqrt{4} : 1$ for 2 : 1. This is a good illustration of the licentious ambiguities which classical arithmetic permits.

17 The ratio 15 : 13 occurs in Santa Maria Novella, *vide infra*, 'Leon Battista Alberti'.

Palladio appears to make use of the rational convergent $10:9$ for $\sqrt{5}:\sqrt{4}$ which may be compounded as follows:[18]

$$
\begin{array}{ll}
2 : 1 & R^{1/2}_x 4 \;:\; R^{1/2}_x 1 \\
\quad\times & \qquad\times \\
\underline{20 : 9} & \underline{R^{1/2}_x 5 \;:\; R^{1/2}_x 1} \\
10 : 9 & R^{1/2}_x 5 \;:\; R^{1/2}_x 4.
\end{array}
$$

It has already been noted that Palladio uses the empowerments $5^2:4^2,\ 5:4.$ and $\sqrt{5}:\sqrt{4}$.[19] Another example is this empowerment of Palladio's special ratio $5:3$:

$$
\begin{array}{ll}
12 : 7 & R^{1/2}_x 3 \;:\; R^{1/2}_x 1 \\
\quad\times & \qquad\times \\
\underline{9 : 4} & \underline{R^{1/2}_x 5 \;:\; R^{1/2}_x 1} \\
21 : 16 & R^{1/2}_x 5 \;:\; R^{1/2}_x 3.
\end{array}
$$

The result is that the ratio $21:16$ is a rational convergent for $\sqrt{5}:\sqrt{3}$.[20]

---

18 The ratio $10:9$ is the proportion of the $20P \times 18P$ Olympic Room in the Villa Barbaro at Maser (Palladio, *op. cit.*, II, p. 51), but the same proportion and dimensions are used in two other schemes: two rooms in the invention for Count Francesco and Count Lodovico de Trissino (II, p. 74), and two small rooms in Palladio's reconstruction of an ancient Roman house (II, p. 34).
19 *Vide supra*, 'Empowered Proportion'.
20 The ratio $21:16$ reflects the extreme dimensions of the $42p \times 32p$ central hall to the Villa Pisani (Palladio, *op. cit.*, II, p. 47).

XVI

EUCLIDEAN REGULAR FIGURES

Translations of Euclid's *The Elements* into Latin were in circulation in the fifteenth century. Derived from Arabic and Greek versions they included twelfth-century versions by the Englishman, Aethelhard, and by Gherard of Cremona, and the thirteenth-century translation by Johannes Campanus of Novaro.[1] The mathematician Regiomontanus, who moved in the same circles as Alberti, possessed a copy of the Aethelhard–Campanus translation.[2] However, at the time of *De re aedificatoria*, Alberti names Archimedes as his geometer of choice, and does not mention Euclid.[3] Certainly, Nicholas V had encouraged the translation of Archimedes' works by Jacobus Cremonensis in 1450 around the same time that Alberti was presenting him with *De re aedificatoria*.[4] Nevertheless, it is also certain that Alberti's interest in the regular polygons and Piero della Francesca's investigations of polyhedra derive from Euclidean sources.[5] What Euclid writes about regular polygons and polyhedra is thus worth reciting. Euclid presents the necessary backcloth for specific humanistic actions in the arts, and central planning especially.

Euclid's *The Elements* are in thirteen books. In the Renaissance, a fourteenth and fifteenth book were thought also to be by Euclid. There are many ways of looking at this extraordinary work. There are enunciations – definitions, postulates, common notions, propositions, lemmas – and there are proofs. Some early translations neglected the proofs, and focused on the enunciations. The famous definitions of Book I are the source of illustrations in Sebastiano Serlio, *The First Book on Architecture*, originally published in 1545.[6] Proofs are for mathematicians. The architect is interested in the geometric vocabulary and constructive results. In practice, *The Elements* carries two distinct, but interrelated, themes. First, there is the grand sweep from the construction of a simple equilateral triangle in Book I, Proposition 1, to the astonishing analytical complexities of the climax in Book XIII, Proposition 18, where the sides of the five Platonic regular polyhedra comprehended in the same sphere are compared in a single diagram.[7] This theme may be called the Timaean after Plato's dialogue *Timaeus* in which the five regular solids and the constituent triangles of their faces are cast as elemental worldmakers – fire, air, water, earth, and the 'whole.'[8] It is as if Euclid sets out to write the definitive geometrical commentary on Plato's bold cosmology. The second theme is centred on Book X, and it has been argued, percolates in less comprehensive ways throughout the other books.[9] The theme here is strictly mathematical and concerns the classification of the magnitudes of different kinds of lines. Euclid's taxonomy of lines defines thirteen distinct types.[10] In modern terms, the problem is most easily understood as one in algebra, not geometry. It is

1 T. L. Heath, *Euclid: The Thirteen Books of The Elements*, Cambridge University Press, Cambridge, 1926, Chapter VIII, pp. 91–113. These Latin versions are mostly from prior Arabic translations, not the original Greek.

2 *Ibid.*, I, p. 96. Heath reports on the views of other scholars who perceive a gradual change, through the amendments of copyists with the Arabic in front of them, of Aethelhard's Latin version into the form of Campanus' translation.

Regiomontanus (1436–1476) was born Johannes Müller near Königsberg, the Latin name of which he adopted. He studied Arabic and Greek mathematical texts and was particularly encouraged by Cardinal Bessarion in this activity. In Italy he had contact with Toscanelli, Alberti and Cusanus whom he mentions in his introductory *Oratio* on the history of mathematics and astronomy at the University of Padua in 1464. His account of the history of geometry records his interest in Latin translations of Euclid which also included summaries by Boethius and Alfred. The partnership of the mathematician Paolo Toscanelli and Brunelleschi is well known. In 1439, Alberti had dedicated his *Intercoenales* to Toscanelli. Regiomontanus mentions in a letter of 1464 that he had heard both Alberti and Toscanelli speak of their astronomical observations. Nicholas Cusanus, Cardinal Cusanus, had invited Toscanelli to be an interlocutor in an Archimedean tract on squaring the circle, a work which Regiomontanus subsequently ridiculed. Regiomontanus produced the first major text on modern trigonometry, *De triangulis*, which was to be acknowledged by Copernicus. A contemporary remarks that Regiomontanus began the reconstruction of astronomy that Copernicus completed. He also published *Tabulae Sinuum*, tables which essentially measured the length of a chord suspended by a given angle in a circle. Previous computers of such tables included Ptolemy and Leonardo of Pisa, otherwise known as Fibonacci, in *Practica Geometriae. Op. cit.*, P. L. Rose, *The Italian Renaissance of Mathematics: Studies on Humanists and Mathematicians from Petrarch to Galileo*, Librairie Droz, Genève, 1975, II, Chapter 4, pp. 90–117. *Vide supra*, 'Classical Arithmetic'.

C. Ginzburg, *The Enigma of Piero: Piero della Francesca: the Baptism, the Arezzo Cycle, the Flagellation*,

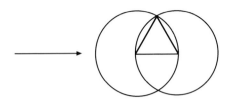

Fig. 1. Proposition I.1. 'On a given finite straight line to construct an equilateral triangle'.

Verso, London, 1985, p. 41ff., suggests that Cardinal Bessarion was actively involved in revising the iconographical program of the Arezzo Cycle around 1459. Given Alberti's acquaintance with Piero della Francesca, the remarkable nexus of intellectuals – leading churchmen, mathematicians and artists – in which Alberti flourished becomes clearer.

3 J. Rykwert, N. Leach, R. Tavernor trans, *Leon Battista Alberti: On the Art of Building in Ten Books*, MIT Press, Cambridge MA, 1988, p. 317. 'For all this I would not expect him [the architect] to be a Zeuxis in his painting, or a Nicomachus in arithmetic, or an Archimedes in geometry.'

4 *Op. cit.*, Rose, p. 39.

5 R. Lightbown, *Piero della Francesca*, Abbeville Press, New York, 1992, mentions the mathematical manuscripts prepared in 1458 for the architect Francesco dal Borgo, including Latin versions of Euclid, Ptolemy and Archimedes. It was most likely Francesco dal Borgo, he suggests, who proposed Piero della Francesca for the commission to decorate the *camera* for Pope Pius II at his consecration in 1458. Alberti and Piero della Francesca both worked for Pius II in Rome. Alberti and Piero della Francesca were together in Urbino in 1447, in Ferrara in 1449, and in Rimini in 1451. *Vide*, F. Borsi, *Leon Battista Alberti*, Phaidon, Oxford, 1977, p. 199.

6 V. Hart, P. Hicks trans, *Sebastiano Serlio: On Architecture*, Yale University Press, New Haven, 1996, p. 7ff. For example, Euclid's 'a point is that which has no part', 'a line is breadthless length', 'the extremities of a line are points', and so on concluding with 'parallel straight lines are straight lines which, being in the same plane and being produced indefinitely in both directions, do not meet one another in either direction'. *Op. cit.*, Heath, I, pp. 153–54.

7 Heath, *op. cit.*, I, p. 241: *The Elements* Book I, Proposition 1: 'On a given straight line to construct an equilateral triangle.' Heath III, p. 503: *The Elements*, Book XIII, Proposition 18: 'To set out the sides of the five figures and to compare them with one another.'

8 Plato, *Timaeus*, 53c–55c. Still one of the most explanatory descriptions is F. Cornford, *Plato's Cosmology: The Timaeus of Plato translated with a running commentary*, Routledge & Kegan Paul, London, 1937, pp. 210–21. The 'whole' refers to the dodecahedron. Plato *Timaeus* 55c, writes: 'There still remained one construction, the fifth; and the god used it for the whole, making a pattern of animal figures thereon.' The animal figures refer to the twelve zodia-

the problem of classifying positive roots of quadratic equations according to relationships between the coefficients. Euclid did not, of course, have available any algebraic methodologies, and had to tackle the issue in terms of geometric entities. His variables were not abstract symbols, but concrete line lengths, rectangular areas, and the sides of squares with the same content as rectangles marked by two distinct lines. It was the comparison of side lengths that was of interest to Euclid. Were the sides commensurable, or incommensurable; rational, or irrational? Were their lengths comparable to numbers, or not? At the heart of the matter is another Platonic question raised in Plato's *Meno*.[11] What is the nature of the diagonal of a square? Or in modern terms, how does the magnitude represented by $\sqrt{2}$ compare with integers such as 1, or 2? Although expressed largely through geometrical constructions, this second theme in *The Elements* focuses on the nature of number and magnitude, ratio and proportion, and is essentially arithmetical. Here, in this particular essay, it is the first Timaean theme that is most relevant. (Fig. 1) Book I of *The Elements* starts with the construction of an equilateral triangle on a line.

Euclid's propositions of interest are shown in this and the following figures in the form of shape rule derivations.[12] On the left is shown the current shape, or figure, – in this case the straight line – and on the right of the arrow is shown the shape which is derived from Euclid's construction. Light lines indicate the construction, heavier lines the result. Serlio calls such construction lines like these *linee occulte*.[13]

Proposition I.46, gives the construction for a square on a given straight line.

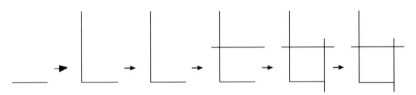

Fig. 2. Proposition I.46. 'On a given straight line to describe a square'.

This proposition immediately precedes the statement and proof of Pythagoras' theorem which Euclid expresses: 'In right-angled triangles the square on the side subtending the right angle is equal to the squares on the sides containing the right angle.'[14] Book III discusses the circle and in Book IV various propositions are proffered concerning inscribed and circumscribed circles in relation to rectilineal figures. Propositions IV.2, 3, 4 and 5 deal with triangles of which the equilateral triangle is a special case illustrated here.

Propositions IV.6, 7, 8 and 9 relate square to circle and circle to square.

Proposition IV.10 provides a construction required to assemble a regular pentagon.

Propositions IV.11, 12, 13 and 14 relate pentagon to circle and circle to pentagon. The equilateral triangle, the square and the regular pentagon relate directly to the faces of the five Platonic solids and their description in the *Timaeus*.[15] The general idea having been established, Euclid concludes with two individual cases. Proposition IV.15 inscribes a hexagon in a circle, while Proposition IV.16 inscribes a 'fifteen-angled figure which shall be both equilateral and equiangular'.

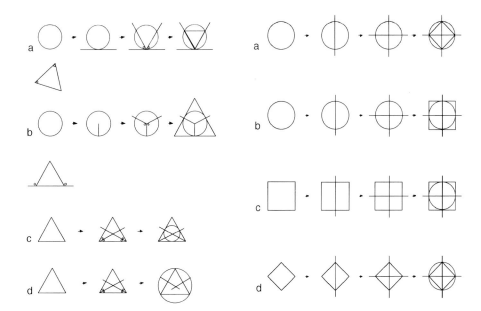

Fig. 3. The propositions illustrated here refer to any triangle, but for more limited purposes the equilateral triangle is taken to be the 'given triangle'.

a. Proposition IV.2. 'In a given circle to inscribe a triangle equiangular with a given triangle'.

b. Proposition IV.3. 'About a given circle to circumscribe a triangle equiangular with a given triangle'.

c. Proposition IV.4. 'In a given triangle to inscribe a circle'.

d. Proposition IV.5. 'About a given triangle to circumscribe a circle'.

Fig. 4. The propositions illustrated relate a square with the circle.

a. Proposition IV.6. 'In a given circle to inscribe a square'.

b. Proposition IV.7. 'About a given circle to circumscribe a square'.

c. Proposition IV.8. 'In a given square to inscribe a circle'.

d. Proposition IV.9. 'About a given square to circumscribe a circle'.

cal constellations, one for each face. The dodecahedron is the regular figure which is closest in volume to the sphere and best suited to represent the whole heaven, or the cosmos. Also D. Lee trans, *Plato: Timaeus and Critias*, Penguin Books, London, 1965.

9 Heath, *op. cit.*, III, p. 8, cites the mathematician De Morgan: 'Euclid investigates every possible variety of lines which can be represented by $\sqrt{(\sqrt{a} \pm \sqrt{b})}$, *a* and *b* representing two commensurable lines. ... This book has a completeness which none of the others (not even the fifth) can boast of: and we could almost suspect that Euclid, having arranged his materials in his own mind, and having completely elaborated the 10th Book, wrote the preceding books after it and did not live to revise them thoroughly.'

10 Heath, *op. cit.*, III, pp. 242–43. As an indication of the elaborate Euclidean taxonomy involved, the names and descriptions of the thirteen irrational lines are quoted here with no further explanation: 'medial, binomial, first bimedial, second bimedial, major, "side" of a rational plus a medial area, "side" of the sum of two medial areas, apotome, first apotome of a medial straight line, second apotome of a medial straight line, minor, producing with a rational area a medial whole, producing with a medial area a medial whole.'

11 W. K. C. Guthrie trans *Plato: Protagoras and Meno*, Penguin Books, London, 1956. A notable contributor to this issue is D. Fowler, *The Mathematics of Plato's Academy: A New Reconstruction*, Clarendon Press, Oxford, 1987, especially the dialogue between Socrates, Meno and the slaveboy, pp. 3–7, and Fowler's additional pretend dialogue, pp. 25–28. Also, Chapter 2, 'Anthyphairetic Ratio Theory'.

12 'Shape rule' is a modern term used in a Stiny Shape Grammar. G. Stiny *Pictorial and Formal Aspects of Shape and Shape Grammars: On Computer Generation of Aesthetic Objects*, Birkhäuser Verlag, Basel and Stuttgart, 1975, p. 21ff.

13 *Op. cit.*, Hart and Hicks, p. xxvii.

14 *Op. cit.*, Heath I, p. 349, Euclid I, Proposition 47.

15 *Ibid.*, I, pp. 97–100 for a mathematical commentary on the relationship of this material to the *Timaeus*.

16 *Ibid.*, III, pp. 461–66, Euclid XIII, Proposition 11, where it is effectively shown that if the radius of the circle is 2 then the length of the side of the inscribed regular pentagon is $\sqrt{(10 - 2\sqrt{5})}$. In the earlier Proposition 9, Euclid shows that if the radius of the circle is 2 then the length of the side of the inscribed regular decagon is $\sqrt{5} - 1$.

Earlier, in Proposition III.30, Euclid has shown how to bisect a given circumference, so that any regular polygon inscribed in or circumscribed by a circle may be replaced by a regular polygon with twice the number of sides – four sides by eight sides, eight by sixteen, and so on; five sides by ten sides, six by twelve, or fifteen by thirty.

Book XI gives definitions for the sphere, the pyramid (of which a special case is the tetrahedron), the cube, octahedron, icosahedron, and dodecahedron. In Book XIII, following some propositions concerning the extreme and mean ratio and the regular pentagon, Euclid gives one of his most celebrated enunciations, Proposition XIII.10, in which the square on the side of the pentagon is equal to the sum of the squares on the side of the hexagon and the side of the decagon given that all these figures may be comprehended by the same circle.

This is immediately followed by a proposition effectively giving the length of the side of an inscribed regular pentagon in terms of the radius of a circle, showing that the side is 'the irrational straight line called minor'.[16] Proposition XIII.12 compares the square on the side of an equilateral triangle with the square on the

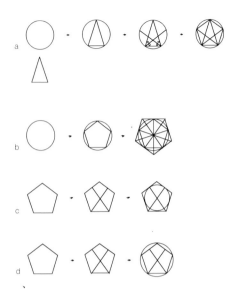

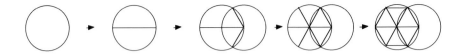

Fig. 6. Proposition IV.15. 'In a given circle to inscribe an equilateral and equiangular hexagon'.

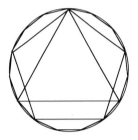

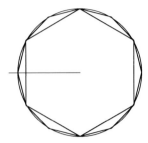

Fig. 5. The propositions illustrated relate a regular pentagon to the circle.
a. Proposition IV.11. 'In a given circle to inscribe an equilateral and equiangular pentagon'.
b. Proposition IV.12. 'About a given circle to circumscribe an equilateral and equiangular pentagon'.
c. Proposition IV.13. 'In a given pentagon, which is equilateral and equiangular, to inscribe a circle'.
d. Proposition IV.14. 'About a given pentagon. which is equilateral and equiangular, to circumscribe a circle'.

Fig. 7. Proposition IV.16. 'In a given circle to inscribe a fifteen-angled figure which shall be both equilateral and equiangular'.

Fig. 8. Doubling the number of sides of a regular polygon. The example illustrated shows a hexagon being used to construct a dodecahedron.

Fig. 9. Proposition XIII.10. 'If an equilateral pentagon be inscribed in a circle, the square on the side of the pentagon is equal to the squares on the side of the hexagon and that of the decagon inscribed in the same circle'.

radius of the circumscribed circle, as a preliminary to stating the first of such theorems involving the Platonic solids. Proposition XIII.13 compares the square on the side of an inscribed regular tetrahedron with the square on the diameter of the sphere which comprehends it, namely that twice the square on the diameter is three times the square on the side. Proposition XIII.14 does the same for the inscribed octahedron. Here the square on the diameter is twice the square on the side of the octahedron. Proposition XIII.15 compares the cube and the sphere within which it is inscribed. Here the square on the diameter is found to be three times the square on the side of the cube. These results for the tetrahedron, octahedron and cube are all rational, involving whole numbers.

It should be noted that the square on the diameter of the circle to the square on the side of the inscribed square, and the square of the diameter of the sphere to the square on the side of the inscribed octahedron are both as 2 : 1. The square on the diameter of the sphere to the square on the side of the inscribed tetrahedron is as 3 : 2, and the diameter of the circle to the square on the side of the inscribed equilateral triangle is as 4 : 3. It is clear that these so-called musical ratios have quite separate and independent geometric origins, in fact they are the very capstones of Euclid's architecture.[17]

The next two propositions, Propositions 16 and 17, deal with the inscribed icosahedron and the inscribed dodecahedron. These comparisons call upon the earlier taxonomy of lines. The results are irrational, involving surds. The squares in the former case are as a 'straight line called minor', and in the latter case as a 'straight line called apotome'.

Euclid extends the use of the term rational to include simple square roots in which the squares are whole numbers, integers. Thus, √2, surprisingly for modern readers, is not considered to be irrational in *The Elements*. Euclid is quite specific about this. In Book X he gives the following definitions:

1. Those magnitudes are said to be **commensurable** which are measured by the same measure, and those **incommensurable** which cannot have any common measure.
2. Straight lines are **commensurable in square** when the squares on them are measured by the same area, and **incommensurable in square** when the squares on them cannot possibly have any area as a common measure.
3. With these hypotheses, it is proved that there exist straight lines infinite in multitude which are commensurable and incommensurable respectively, some in length only, and others in square also, with an assigned straight line. Let then the assigned straight line be called **rational**, and those straight lines which are commensurable with it, whether in length and in square and in square only, **rational**, but those which are incommensurable with it **irrational**.

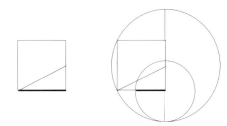

Fig. 11. The side length of the inscribed cube in Euclid's diagram is sectioned in the extreme and mean ratio. The construction follows Proposition VI.30. A square is constructed on the side of the line to be sectioned. A diagonal of the half square is struck. With its centre at the midpoint of the side of the square and radius equal to the length of the diagonal, a circle is drawn. Taking a corner of the square on the diameter of the circle as centre, another circle is drawn to touch the first circle. Where this second circle cuts the original line is the point which sections the line into the extreme and mean ratio.

DODECAHEDRON. The larger section gives the length of the side of the inscribed dodecahedron.

There is a fourth definition concerning the rationality of areas.[18] In general, if k is of the form m/n and is not a square number and if a is an integer, then $a.\sqrt{(m/n)}$ is considered to be rational by Euclid. For example, the side of a tetrahedron, $30.\sqrt{(2/3)}$, inscribed in a sphere of diameter 30 is rational in square, since the square on the side of the tetrahedron has an area of 600, a quantity without surds. However, the side of a dodecagon, $5.(\sqrt{15}-\sqrt{3})$, inscribed in the same sphere is irrational since its square still contains a square root, $150.(3-\sqrt{5})$. Similarly, the square on the side of an icosahedron, $3.\sqrt{(10\ (5-\sqrt{5}))}$, inscribed in this sphere is irrational, $90.(5-\sqrt{5})$.

Finally, the ultimate statement of the *Elements*, Proposition XIII.18, sets out a diagrammatic comparison of the sides of all five Platonic solids with the diameter of the sphere which comprehends them.[19]

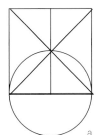 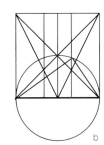 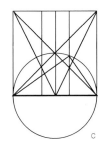 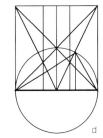

Fig. 10. (Left to right) Exploded view of Euclid's final diagram which compares the lengths of sides of the regular polyhedra comprehended within the same sphere. The diagram comprises an intersecting square and circle. The diameter of the circle is the same as the diameter of the circumscribing sphere.
a. OCTAHEDRON. The diagonal of the square intersects the circle at its midpoint. Half the length of the diagonal is the length of the side of the inscribed octahedron.
b. CUBE. The diagonals of the half squares intersect those of the full square at the third divisions of the diameter. A right triangle is constructed on the diameter with its apex at the point where one of the perpendiculars from the third division cuts the circle. The short side of the triangle gives the length of the side of the inscribed cube.
c. TETRAHEDRON. The longer side of the right triangle containing the right angle gives the length of the side of the inscribed tetrahedron.
d. ICOSAHEDRON. Where a diagonal of the half square cuts the circle defines the apex of another right triangle on the diameter. The short side of this triangle gives the length of side of the inscribed icosahedron.

17 For a fuller discussion of ratios in music, *vide infra*, 'Scales of Proportion'.
18 *Ibid.*, III, p. 10. Also Heath's notes on these definitions pp. 11–13.
19 The exploded diagrams, explaining the individual results which Euclid combines in a single figure, make use of the construction used by Sebastiano Serlio to divide a line in three equal parts. *Op. cit.*, Hart and Hicks, pp. 32–33, also *vide infra*, 'Scales of Proportion'.

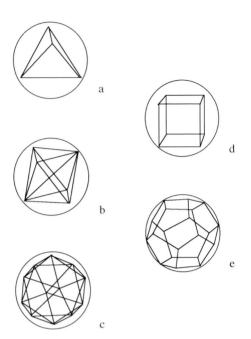

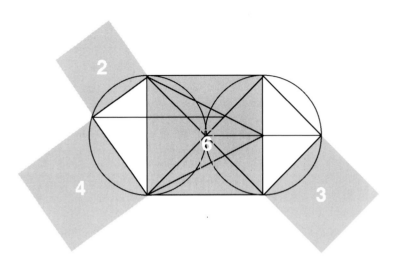

Fig. 13. Diagram showing the 'rational in square' relationship between the diameter of the circumscribing sphere and the lengths of the sides of the tetrahedron, octahedron and cube. If the area of the square on the diameter is 6, then the areas of the squares on the sides of the inscribed polyhedra are 4 for the tetrahedron, 3 for the octahedron and 2 for the cube.

Fig. 12. The five Platonic solids comprehended within spheres of the same diameter.

a. Tetrahedron.

b. Octahedron.

c. Icosahedron.

d. Cube.

e. Dodecahedron.

Comparing the squares on the sides of the cube c^2, the octahedron o^2, and the tetrahedron t^2 with the square on the diameter of the sphere s^2 within which they may be inscribed gives the proportion:

$$s^2 : t^2 : o^2 : c^2 :: 6 : 4 : 3 : 2.$$

This has the classic form of the 'perfect proportion' in which 4 is the arithmetic mean of the extremes 6 and 2, and 3 is the harmonic mean of these extremes. The ratios 4 : 2 and 6 : 3 are both in a geometrical 2 : 1 relationship. Once again relationships among the Platonic figures resonate with the ratios familiar to musicians.[20]

---

20 *Vide supra*, 'Proportionality' for a discussion of the perfect proportion in classical arithmetic.

XVIII

SCALES OF PROPORTION

The principal source of musical theory in the fifteenth century was Boethius, and other texts of that ilk[1]. The theory was based on the relationships of the Pythagorean lambda involving powers of 2 and 3. Plato gave authority to this system in the *Timaeus*. Alberti's acquaintance in the court of Nicholas V, Cardinal Cusanus, was obsessed with attempting to square the circle[2]. In his quest, it seems, he became convinced that the irrational realm was God's territory, and beyond man's ken. His insight was polar to the Pythagorean tradition, and may have derived from Nicole Oresme who had demonstrated that the likehood of relationships in the world being found to be incommensurable was mathematically overwhelming[3]. In the same contrary way, Cusanus found in the 'unlimited' the nature of an infinite God, whereas the Pythagoreans had placed the 'limited' alongside the 'good' in their catalogue of duities[4]. In this vein, Cusanus also speculated on musical harmony in a book that he published at the very time Alberti was completing his manuscript on architecture: 'A simpler [kind of] number than our mind's reason can attain [may be] intuited from the relation [*habitudine*] of the semitone and [from the concept] of the mean between 1 and 2, which is like the ratio of a square to its diagonal.'[5] It has been suggested that Cusanus had in mind the ratio $\sqrt{9} : \sqrt{8}$ which reduces to $3 : 2\sqrt{2}$ and hence the reference to the diagonal of a square[6]. As will be shown later, such a ratio was not foreign to Alberti who – true to Cusanus – gave it Godly purport. Alberti strides the two worlds: the established world of the Pythagoreans with their ratios derived from simple whole numbers, and the emergent world of Oresme and Cusanus with their claim of a higher simplicity for the irrationals.

Following his discussion of number, Alberti turns to ratio, the relationship of one number to another.[7] 'For us [finitio] is a certain correspondence between the line that define the dimensions; one dimension being length, another breadth, and the third height'[8]. He continues: 'I affirm again with Pythagoras: it is absolutely certain that Nature is wholly consistent. That is how things stand.' There then follows his analogy with music: 'The very same numbers that cause sound to have that *concinnitas*, pleasing to the ears, can also fill the eyes and mind with wondrous delight. From musicians therefore who have already examined such numbers thoroughly, or from those objects in which Nature has displayed some evident and noble quality, the whole method [related to *finitio*] is derived.' Alberti then warns that the architect does not have to deal with such musical matters as the modulations of a voice, or the divisions of the tetrachord.[9]

1 Boethius: *De institutione musica*. C. M. Bower, *Boethius' 'The principles of Music': an Introduction and commentary*, PhD Dissertation, George Peabody College for Teachers, 1967, University Microfilms, Ann Arbor, Michigan. Like Boethius' book on arithmetic, *De institutione musica*, is generally taken to be a free translation of a lost work in Greek by Nicomachus. A tract on music by Theon of Smyrna survives and an English version is to be found in R. Lawlor, D. Lawlor trans, *Theon of Smyrna: Mathematics Useful for Understanding Plato*, Wizard's Bookshelf, San Diego, 1979, pp. 32–79. For the Boethian influence and eventual decline see C. V. Palisca, *Humanism in Italian Renaissance Musical Thought*, Yale University Press, New Haven, 1985.

2 *Dialogus inter Cardinalem Sancti Petri et Paulum Physicum de Circuli Quadratura*, 1457. See P. L. Rose, *The Italian Renaissance of Mathematics*, Librairie Droz, Genève, 1975, Chapter 2, pp. 26–75, 'Patrons, Collectors and Translators: Humanist Origins of the Mathematical Renaissance'. According to Rose, Regiomontanus knew the distinguished Florentine mathematician Paolo Toscanelli personally. Toscanelli is forever linked to his friend the architect Filippo Brunelleschi, called by his contemporaries 'the second Archimedes'. The joint astronomical observations of Toscanelli and Alberti, probably made around 1435, received the authoritative praises of Regiomontanus in 1464. Cusanus somewhat misuses Toscanelli as a fictional interlocutor in his tract on squaring the circle. Regiomontanus, who respected Cusanus' intellect, nevertheless described him as 'geometra ridiculus' in regard to his attempts to square the circle in *De triangulis*, Nuremburg, 1533. Rose writes, p. 30 'At Rome in late 1461 these strands all came together at one time. Bessarion was then in Rome and was host to Regiomontanus. Cusanus was in the city and probably entertained Toscanelli. At the same time Alberti was present as apostolic secretary to Pius II.'

3 E. Grant, *Nicole Oresme: De proportionibus proportionum and Ad pauca respicientes*, University of Wisconsin Press, Madison, 1966. Grant discusses this matter in his introduction to *Ad pauca respicientes*. Oresme 'assumes that any two quantities are probably incommensurable . . . [he] demonstrates that no configuration or relationship of celestial bodies can ever

repeat. This constitutes the basis for his repudiation of astrological prediction. . . . The demonstration is given in Chapter 3, Proposition X, *De proportionibus proportionum* (pp. 247–55) which Grant believes was written after *Ad pauca respicientes*. The proposition reads: 'It is probable that two proposed unknown ratios are incommensurable because if many unknown ratios are proposed it is most probable that any [one] would be incommensurable to any [other].' Having supposed that precise observation of heavenly phenomena is impossible, Oresme makes the point that 'we cannot even know about quantities close by because of defective senses', *Ad pauca respicientes*, pp. 386–87.

4 For a refreshing study of the influence of Nicholas Cusanus on Renaissance thought see C. H. Lohr 'Metaphysics as the Science of God' in C. B. Schmitt, Q. Skinner, E. Kessler, *The Cambridge History of Renaissance Philosophy*, Cambridge University Press, Cambridge, 1988 pp. 538–84. Compare an earlier view of E. Cassirer, *The Individual and the Cosmos in Renaissance Philosophy*, Harper & Row, New York, 1963, Chapter 2, 'Cusanus and Italy'.

5 Nicholas Cusanus, *Idiota: de mente*, 1450, cited in M. Lindley, R. Turner-Smith, *Mathematical Models of Musical Scales: a New Approach*, Verlag für systematische Musikwissenschaft GmbH, Bonn, 1993. See particularly their succinct summary of Pythagorean influences in musical thought, Appendix I, pp. 221–42.

6 Lindley, Turner, *ibid.*, p. 230.

7 J. Rykwert, N. Leach, R. Tavernor, *Leon Battista Alberti: On the Art of Building in Ten Books*, MIT Press, Cambridge MA, 1988, p. 305.

8 *Ibid.*, Rykwert, Leach and Tavernor translate *finitio* as 'outline' meaning 'measured outline'. See Grayson, *Leon Battista Alberti: On Painting and Sculpture*, Phaidon, Oxford, 1972. Grayson p. 140 n. 5 keeps the Latin term *finitio* for lack of a precise equivalent in English. In *De statua*, Alberti contrasts *finitio* with *dimensione*. In the terminology of modern mathematics, the former refers to cylindrical coordinates, the latter to a distance between two points. Alberti does not hold to this distinction in *De re aedificatoria*. The English words 'bound' and 'boundary' may come closest to Alberti's concept of *finitio* in the architectural context. Grayson, pp. 36–37, specifically uses the word 'outline' for *fimbria* in his translation of *De pictura*. This accords with common usage.

9 *Ibid.*, p. 305. The most likely text he would have turned to is Boethius, *De institutione musica*, or one based closely on Boethian principles. For a translation see C. Bower, *Boethius' The Principles of Music; an Introduction, Translation, and Commentary*, PhD Thesis, University Microfilm, Ann Arbor, Michigan, 1967.

10 *Ibid.*, p. 305. For convenience, modern notation is used to place the notes. See A. Barker, *Greek Musical Writings, Volume II. Harmonic and Acoustic Theory*, Cambridge University Press, Cambridge, 1989. The absence of the third and sixth is striking, since a characteristic form of music of this period based on the Gregorian chant, the *falsobordone*, was characterized by these intervals between the voices. M. C. Bradshaw, *The Falsobordone: a Study in Renaissance and Baroque Music*, American Institute of Musicology, 1978. Also W. Elders, *Composers of the Low*

We define harmony as that consonance of sounds which is pleasant to the ear.' The length of string gives the pitch of the sound, and certain numbers correspond to relationships between consonant strings. Alberti then lists the consonants:

diapente	*sesquialtera*	3 : 2
diatesseron	*sesquitertia*	4 : 3
diapason	*duplus*	2 : 1
diapason diapente	*triplus*	3 : 1
disdiapason	*quadruplus*	4 : 1
tonus	*sesquioctavus*	9 : 8.

The terms on the left are musical, those on the right are arithmetic. Taking the diatonic scale (A, B, c, d, e, f, g, a), the fourth note (d), counting from and including the key note (A), is at an interval of the *diatesseron* from the key note, the fifth note (e) is at an interval of the *diapente*. The eighth note (a) returns to the key note, but an octave higher: this interval is the *diapason*. The twelfth note (e') is the *diapason diapente*, or at an interval of an octave and a fifth. The fifteenth note (a') is the *disdiapason*, or at an interval of two octaves from the key note. The second note (B) is a *tonus* interval from the key note (A), also the interval between the fourth (d) and the fifth (e). It will be seen that certain notes are not included in Alberti's list. In modern terms these include the third (c), the sixth (f), and the seventh (g).[10]

The Latin arithmetic terms describe the ratios after the manner of Boethius: *sesquialtera*, one and a half; *sesquitertia*, one and a third; *sesquioctavus*, one and one eighth; the *multiplex* terms are more obvious – duple, triple, quadruple. Alberti describes these ratios as divisions of a string, an experiment that Boethius also illustrates. The string of length five divided into three parts and two, the *sesquialtera*; of length seven divided into four and three, the *sesquitertia*; of length three divided into two and one, the *duplus*; and of length four into three and one, the *triplus*. Alberti adds the *quadruplus* and the *sesquioctavus* to the examples given by Boethius[11]. Alberti sums up: 'the musical numbers are one, two, three, and four', the constituents of the Pythagorean *tetraktys*; but 'there is also the tonus . . . where the longer string is one eighth more than the lesser'.

Architects, writes Alberti, use these numbers in pairs to lay out their plans, and in threes to elevate the plans from length and breadth to height. He first examines their use in plan: 'an *area* may be either short, long, or intermediate.' The shortest of all is the square, 1 : 1. Two other short *areae* are the *sesquialtera*, 3 : 2, and the *sesquitertia*, 4 : 3. The three intermediate *areae* are; 'the best of all', the *duplus*; the *duplex sesquialtera*; and the *duplex sesquitertia*. The last two, Alberti constructs in this manner: take a square of side four, extend one side proportionately by the *sesquialtera*, that is by one and a half, to make a length of six; then extend this six by another one and a half to make a length of nine. This will produce a ratio of 9 : 4. (Fig. 1.)

Or, take a square of side nine, extend one side by the *sesquitertia*, that is by one-and-a-third to a length of twelve; then extend this twelve by another one-and-a-third to sixteen. This will produce an area of ratio 16 : 9.[12] (Fig. 2.)

In the first of these two cases, Alberti points out that musically the ratio nine to four gives an octave and one tone more; and the ratio sixteen to nine gives an octave

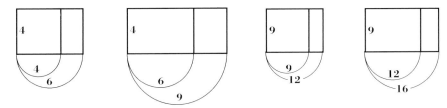

Fig. 1. Derivation of the ratio 9 : 4.   **Fig. 2.** Derivation of the ratio 16 : 9.

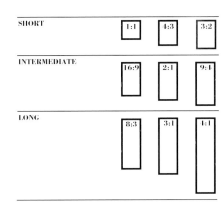

Fig. 3. Alberti's *areae*.

less a tone. The three long areas are derived in the following way: add the *duplus* to the *sesquialtera* to produce the *triplus*; add the *sesquitertia* to the *duplus* to produce the ratio eight to three; or add an octave to the octave, the *quadruplus*, one to four.[13] These nine areas are charted below:

SHORT	INTERMEDIATE	LONG
1 : 1, 4 : 3, 3 : 2	16 : 9, 2 : 1, 9 : 4	8 : 3, 3 : 1, 4 : 1.

The *areae* may be compared by selecting a common width of 36, the smallest number with factors 2, 3, 4, 9.[14] The lengths of the *areae* are then:

SHORT	INTERMEDIATE	LONG
36, 48, 54	64, 72, 81	96, 108, 144.

These *areae* may be depicted as a set of proportioned rectangles. (Fig. 3.)

The arrangement plays on the classical theme of extremes and mean. There are two extreme classes of *areae*, the short and the long. Between them is a mean, the intermediate class. Within each class, there are again two extremes, and between these is a mean. Alberti discusses the concept of mean in an ensuing passage, and this aspect of his classification is best left until that matter has been examined. Meanwhile, it is worth looking at the musical analogy more closely. Alberti is working strictly within the Pythagorean tradition which, as has been noted, had been given additional authority by Plato in the *Timaeus*.[15] The musical aspects were most conveniently available in Boethius' *De institutione musica*.[16] Even fifty years after *De re aedificatoria* was written, this theory of music continued to be promoted, for example by, Franchino Gaffurio; although criticism, by then, was amassing to force a paradigmatic shift towards the modern view.[17] As with arithmetic, the world of music theory in Alberti's time is alien to us today. Music theory was firmly based on Greek sources so that Boethius in his Latin text makes reference to, among others, the Pythagoreans, Aristoxenus, Archytas, Ptolemy, Nicomachus; and there is evidence that he may have used the Euclidian *Sectio canonis*. The prime aim of the theoreticians was to construct *systemata*, ordered arrangements of notes, structured by the tetrachord. Vitruvius mentions the three genera of tetrachord: the diatonic, chromatic and enharmonic.[18] Alberti makes use of the diatonic tetrachord. Such *systemata* were defined over two octaves: the unison and the double octave were the extremes and the octave was the mean, the *mese*. Alberti employs the same two extremes in his classification of *areae*, while the mean of the intermediate class is also the octave, the double square.

Countries, Clarendon Press, Oxford, 1991, pp. 42–44. Many composers from the Netherlands worked in Italy at this time. Alberti's choice of intervals corresponds to the musician's diatonic tetrachord, and certain octave extensions.

11 *Op. cit.*, Bower, pp. 291–93.

12 *Op. cit.*, Rykwert, Leach, Tavernor, p. 306.

13 The 'addition' of ratios is confusing, since the actual arithmetical operation is multiplication. Thus, to 'add' a duplus to a sesquertius is represented arithmetically as:

$$
\begin{array}{c}
4 : 3 \\
|\ \ | \\
2 : 1 \\
\hline
8 : 3
\end{array}
$$

Oresme *op. cit.*, uses the terms 'addition' and 'subtraction' for ratio multiplication and division. F. Cajori, *A History of Mathematical Notation*, The Open Court Publishing Company, La Salle, Illinois, 1928, I p. 249, points to the use of the symbol + as a multiplication sign when dealing with ratios. Already, lurking here is the idea of logarithms.

14 This procedure is common practice in musical theory. See, for example, *op. cit.*, Bower, pp. 137–39, where the sequence 36, 24, 18, 16, 12, 9 is derived. Multiplied by 4 this is seen to be a subsequence of Alberti's: 144, 96, 72, 64,, 48, 36; the remaining terms are 108, 81, 54.

15 For example, F. Cornford, *Plato's Cosmology*, Routledge & Kegan Paul, London, 1937, pp. 66–72, and his commentary on the division of the world-soul into harmonic intervals.

16 Bower, *op. cit.*, According to Palisca, *op. cit.*, p. 36, Boethius' musical treatise 'was revered as having almost infallible and scriptural authority in the field of music'. It was not printed until 1492, but it had 'circulated widely in manuscript copies and could be found in nearly every educational institution and monastery'.

17 Clement A. Miller, *Franchinus Gaffurius: De harmonia musicorum instrumentorum opus*, American Institute of Musicology, 1977. This text is not contemporaneous with Alberti, it does, however, indicate the currency of the Boethian system throughout the

To place notes between the extremes and the mean, a monochord was fabricated and a canon was marked by frets in the manner of lutes, guitars and gambas.[19] Calculating the distances between the frets was a theoretical task. The Pythagorean tradition required that the distances be to one another in ratios based on multiples of the numbers one, two, three and four. Gaffurius provides an excellent diagram, computed on the earlier Boethian scheme, of the *canon* for the diatonic *systema*. A scale change makes it possible to locate Alberti's measures on the *canon* precisely.[20] (Fig. 4.)

	GAFFURIUS	ALBERTI
nete hyperboleon	2304 (64 × 36)	36
nete diezeugemenon	3072 (64 × 48)	48
paranete diezeugemenon	3456 (64 × 54)	54
paramese	4096 (64 × 64)	64
lichanos meson	5184 (64 × 81)	81
hypate meson	6144 (64 × 96)	96
lichanos hypaton	6912 (64 × 108)	108
proslambahomene	9216 (64 × 144)	144.

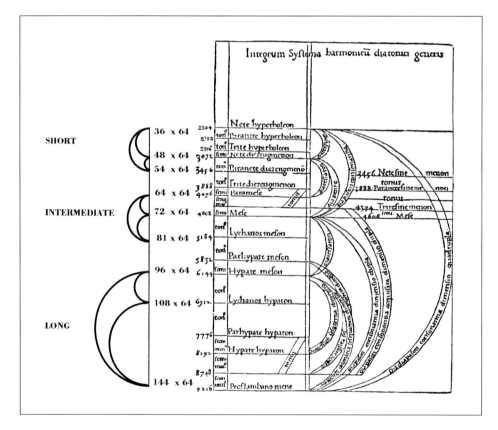

fifteenth century. Gaffurius completed his manuscript in 1500; it was printed in Milan, 1512. The illustrations are particularly compelling, although they are modelled after those found in versions of Boethius.
18 F. Granger, *Vitruvius: On Architecture*, Harvard University Press, Cambridge MA, 1931 V.5 pp. 277–83.
19 The subject is given excellent coverage in M. Lindley, *Lutes, viols and temperament*, Cambridge University Press, Cambridge, 1984.

Fig. 4. Gaffurius' diatonic systemata with Alberti's *areae* dimensions added to the left.

Whereas Alberti's architectural scheme maps onto the musical one, it does so only in part. Comparing the right and left sides of the figure, it will be observed that the important intervals musically (indicated by the arcs) are not those selected for architectural attention. Indeed, while sharing the same arithmetical grounding, Alberti's division of the *disdiapason* cannot be considered 'musical'. The symmetry of Alberti's scheme is emphasized in Fig. 5 where the tones are shown of equal length to one another, and the semitones too. This is like the spacing of notes on the modern keyboard, compared to the variety of string lengths behind, which the Gaffurius diagram suggests.

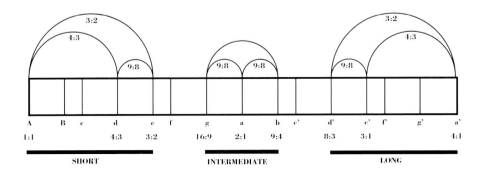

Fig. 5. Alberti's systemata for *areae*.

In three dimensions, Alberti turns away from the musical analogy and directs his attention to a topic in arithmetic. This is the subject of 'means'. Nicomachus concludes his *Introduction to Arithmetic* with an enumeration of the ten known means.[21] Alberti writes of the most familiar three means: the arithmetic, the geometric and the harmonic.[22] His examples are:

ARITHMETIC	8 : 6 : 4
GEOMETRIC	9 : 6 : 4
HARMONIC	6 : 4 : 3.

The first is easily obtained, Alberti explains, by adding the two extremes and by taking a half part of this sum as the mean. The second mean 'is very difficult to ascertain numerically, although it may be found very easily using lines; a subject that I need not discuss here'.[23] The third mean 'is a little more laborious than the arithmetical, yet numbers define it perfectly'. He observes that the ratio of the two extremes is 2 : 1. He sums the antecedent and the consequent to make three. Alberti takes the difference between the extremes, which in his example is $60 - 30 = 30$. This difference is divided into three parts. One of these parts, 10, is added to the lesser extreme to give 40. This is the harmonic mean of 60 and 30. That is to say, Alberti derives the harmonic proportion 60 : 40 : 30 :: 6 : 4 : 3.

Going back to Alberti's classification of *areae*, the pattern of two extremes and a mean in each of the categories suggests that he may have used arithmetical techniques to determine the means:

SHORT	INTERMEDIATE	LONG
$36 : 48 : 54 :: 6 : 8 : 9$	$64 : 72 : 81 :: 8^2 : 8.9 : 9^2$	$96 : 108 : 144 :: 8 : 9 : 12.$

20 *Op. cit.*, Miller, p. 57.

21 M. L. D'Ooge, *Nicomachus of Gerasa: Introduction to Arithmetic*, University of Michigan Press, Ann Arbor, 1938, II. xxi–xxix pp. 264–86. There are, in fact, eleven classical means. Pappus shows the 'eleventh' mean, but also ignores one of the others. He, too, ends up with ten means. See 'Rational Proportion', *supra*.

22 *Op. cit.*, Rykwert, Leach, Tavernor, pp. 308–9.

23 Almost certainly a reference to the porism in Euclid VI. 8: 'if in a right-angled triangle a perpendicular be drawn from the right angle to the base, the straight line so drawn is a mean proportional between the segments of the base.' T. L. Heath, *The Thirteen Books of Euclid's Elements*, Cambridge University Press, Cambridge, 1926, II, pp. 209–11. Theon also shows this geometric method for determining the square root, R. and D. Lawlor, *Mathematics Useful for Understanding Plato by Theon of Smyrna*, Wizard's Bookshelf, San Diego, 1979, pp. 78–79.

Neither the long nor the short case answer to the requirements for arithmetic, geometric, or harmonic means; but the intermediate answers to the conditions for geometric; $81 - 72 = 9$, $72 - 64 = 8$, and $81 : 72 :: 72 : 64 :: 9 : 8$.[24] The three schemes can be characterized by the four numbers 12, 9, 8, 6. It is surely no accident that these are the numbers associated with the concluding chapter of Nicomachus where he discusses the 'most perfect proportion' and gives the example:[25]

$$12 : 9 : 8 : 6.$$

'This alone would be properly called harmony.'[26] What of the proportions $12 : 9 : 8$ and $9 : 8 : 6$? In his penultimate Chapter, Nicomachus summarizes his survey of the ten means and gives an example of each. For the 'seventh' mean he gives $9 : 8 : 6$. All his examples use numbers from the decad, he does not go beyond to, say, 12. However, it is Pappus who replaces this 'seventh' mean by another, not mentioned by Nicomachus. This additional mean in Pappus' list is well illustrated by the example $12 : 9 : 8$.[27] The question arises: could Alberti have known this?[28] Quite possibly, but it is less likely to have governed his actions than the more compelling fact that each of the two proportions $12 : 9 : 8$ and $9 : 8 : 6$ characterize tetrachords. In a sense, Alberti decomposes the 'most perfect proportion':

$$12 : 9 : 8$$
$$9 : 8$$
$$9 : 8 : 6.$$

Much of the order in Alberti's system becomes transparent when a Pythagorean *lambda* is set out. The *lambda* can be extended to any desired size. The string lengths given by Gaffurius all lie on such an extended *lambda*; and Alberti's numbers for *areae* are present too. Interestingly, the distribution of the musical numbers is less tidy than Alberti's compact diamond for his *areae* numbers shown emboldened in Fig. 6.

Alberti exploits the pattern of the *lambda*, elsewhere, when he discusses the rules for the placement of columns. He writes: ' . . . the number of gaps between columns should be odd, the number of columns always even . . . the thickness of the columns [is] restrained by the intercolumniation, and the intercolumniation by the columns, usually according to the following rules; in the "close-set" colonnades, the intercolumniations should be no less than one-and-a-half times the thickness of the columns; in "wide-set" colonnades, it should be no more than three-eighths the thickness of the columns; in "elegant" colonnades, it should be two-and-a-quarter; in the "not-so-close-set", two; and in the "not-so-wide-set", three.'[29] Alberti continues: 'The central gap in the row should be a quarter part wider than the rest.' This refinement will not be discussed here, but it should be recorded that, except in one case, the ratios involved do not lie on the *lambda*.

The 'intercolumniation : column' ratios, reduced to their simplest ratios, characterize the limits of the categories as follows:

CLOSE	not less than	3 : 2
NOT-SO-CLOSE	between 3 : 2 and 2 : 1	
ELEGANT	between 2 : 1 and 9 : 4	

24 D. Barbaro, *M Vitruuii Pollionis: De architectura . . .* Venice, 1567, pp. 175–76, in his commentary of Vitruvius' Book V, concerning music and acoustic applications in architecture.

25 *Op. cit.*, D'Ooge, p. 286. 'Let this be an example of this proportion, 6, 8, 9, 12'. The proportion is illustrated at the end of Boethius (*op. cit.*, Bower, pp. 187–88). This Boethian figure is depicted on the slate held by the Pythagorean follower in Raphael's 'School of Athens', where the proportion is explicitly stated in Roman numerals XII, VIIII, VIII, VI, with the Greek for the musical intervals.

26 *Ibid.*, p. 286.

27 *Synagoge*, see T. L. Heath, *A History of Greek Mathematics*, Clarendon Press, Oxford, 1928, p. 87. This example is the smallest proportionality to be uniquely a Pappus mean. See 'Proportionality', *supra*.

28 The seventh mean of Nicomachus, *op. cit.*, D.'Ooge, p. 283, is defined 'as the greatest term is to the least, so their difference is to the difference of the lesser terms, as 6, 8, 9, for on comparison the ratio of each is seen to be sesquialter': symbolically, $a - c : b - c :: a : c$. A Greek manuscript of Pappus, *Synagoge*, brought back from the East by Giovanni Aurispa was mentioned in a letter by Aurispa to Ambrogio Traversari in 1424. The young Alberti was part of an humanist circle in which Traversari participated. The other great collector of Greek works at this time was Alberti's school friend Francesco Filelfo who also reported to Traversari.

29 *Op. cit.*, Rykwert, Leach, Tavernor, p. 200.

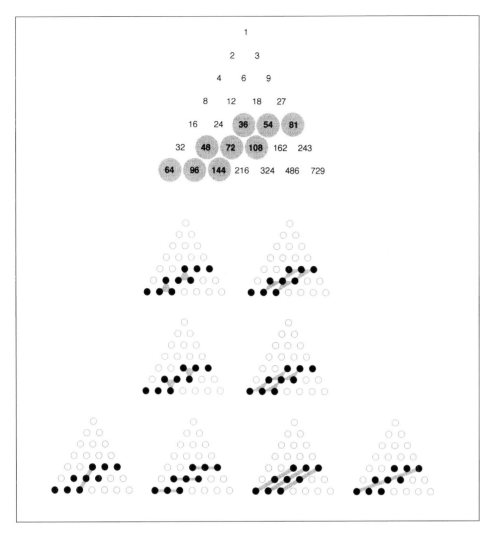

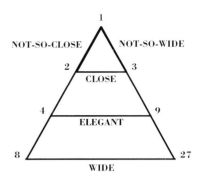

Fig. 7. Alberti's rules for intercolumniations.

Fig. 6. Pythagorean lambda showing Alberti's number diamond highlighted. The three rows below show the arrangement of arithmetic, harmonic and geometric proportionalities on the lambda. Alberti's diamond contains six arithmetic proportionalities (top row) equivalent to 3 : 2 : 1 (left) and 4 : 3 : 2 (right), six harmonic proportionalities (middle row) equivalent to 6 : 3 : 2 (left) and 6 : 4 : 3 (right), and eight geometric proportionalities; one equivalent to 4 : 2 : 1 (far left); three equivalent to 9 : 6 : 4 (left); three equivalent to 16 : 12 : 9 (right); and one equal to 81 : 72 : 64 (far right).

NOT-SO-WIDE   between 9 : 4 and 3 : 1

WIDE   not greater than 27 : 8.

These are all ratios derived from the *lambda*, using just the numbers in Plato's *Timaeus*: Viewed in this way, there is a clear symmetry to the pattern. (Fig. 6).

Any reading of Renaissance music theory will indicate very clearly that it was a period of active dispute and unsettling examination of fundamentals. There is no Renaissance theory, only a plethora of competing theories. To suppose that an architect would latch onto one music theory for emulation over another stretches credulity.

Undoubtedly, Zarlino was one of the foremost theorists of his day and he was a notable humanist in Venetian circles, but there is truly little evidence to suggest that his musical theories influenced, as Wittkower suggests, Palladio. The only musical connection that can be made with Palladio's practice lies with either the Pythagorean adaptions of Alberti, or with the Ptolemaic theories in Barbaro's *Vitruvius*. Claudius Ptolemy, *Harmonics*, espouses views which are both critical of the Pythagoreans and of their most important classical opponent, Aristoxenus.[30] It is Aristoxenus who figures in Vitruvius in the passages concerning 'harmony' which leads to prescriptions for the placing of sounding jars in theatres.[31] Ptolemy's argument against the Pythagoreans rests on his dismissal of their contention that a fourth and an octave are not concordant and that they reason incorrectly about the causes of things to do with concords.[32] Even as late as the seventeenth century this argument continued.[33] Ptolemy 'finds fault with the Aristoxenians, since they neither accepted these [Pythagorean] ratios as clearly established, nor, if they really lacked confidence in them, did they seek more satisfactory ones – assuming that they were genuinely committed to the theoretical study of music'.[34] Barbaro illustrates the Ptolemaic modes: one enharmonic, two chromatic modes, and five diatonic forms.[35] The ratios used by Ptolemy are all, with but one exception, superparticular (The numbers below the fractions refer to the type of tetrachord, for reference see Fig. 8):

5/4	6/5	7/6	8/7	9/8	10/9	11/10	12/11	15/14	16/15	21/20	22/21	24/23	28/27	46/45
1	2	3	4	5	4	6	3	2	7	4	3	1	2	1
				7	6		6		7		5			
				8	7									
				8.										

30 Ptolemy's arguments were communicated first to the mediaeval world and the Renaissance by Boethius before Ptolemy's own work received due attention itself. Palesca, *op. cit.*, pp. 117–22, reports that Nicolò Leoniceno completed a translation of *Harmonics* in 1499. The translation did not receive wide circulation, but, sometime before 1521, it was known to Giangiorgio Trissino since a letter by him suggests that the translation be dedicated to Pope Leo X so that it might become more widely appreciated among music scholars. Trissino, Palladio's mentor, considered *Harmonics* 'the most perfect of all' ancient treatises on music.

31 *Op. cit.*, Granger, V iv–v, pp. 268–83.

32 A. Barker, *Greek Musical Writings: Volume II, Harmonic and Acoustic Theory*, Cambridge University Press, Cambridge, 1989, pp. 284–85.

33 Simon Stevin (1548–1620) follows essentially Ptolemy's argument against contemporary composers and songmasters who considered 'the fourth a dischord'. A. D. Fokker ed., *On the Theory of the Art of Singing* in E. Crone, E. J. Dijksterhuis, R. J. Forbes, M. G. J. Minnaert, A. Pannekoek, *The Principal Works of Simon Stevin*, C. V. Swets & Zeitlinger, Amsterdam, 1966, pp. 451–53.

34 *Op. cit.*, Barker, pp. 293–306.

35 *Op. cit.*, Barbaro, p. 177. F. Granger, *Vitruvius: De Architectura*, Harvard University Press, Cambridge MA, 1931, V iv 3, I, pp. 270–73, mentions just one of each type. The issue centres around the division of a tetrachord, or two and one half tones. According to Vitruvius, the enharmonic division is 2 + ¼ + ¼ tones the chromatic is ½ + ½ + 1½ tones, and the diatonic is 1 + 1 + ½ tones. The problem for musicians is to decide which ratios represents a tone, a semitone and a quarter-tone.

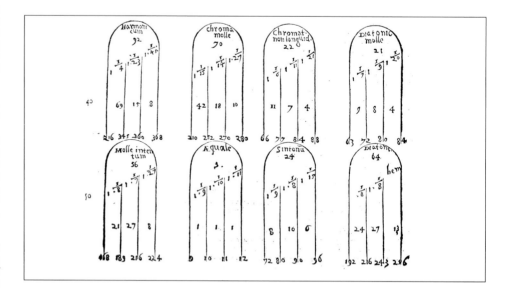

Fig. 8. Ptolemy's eight categories of tetrachord from Barbaro, *Vitruvius*, 1567. Top row: (1) enharmonic, (2) soft chromatic, (3) tense chromatic, (4) soft diatonic; bottom row, (5) tonic diatonic, (6) ditonic diatonic, (7) tense diatonic, (8) even diatonic. In Barbaro the ratios are expressed in the superparticular form 1⅙ : 1 with the consequent 1 being understood. In the second mode there is an error. Barbaro's 1¹⁄₁₅ should read 1⅕ as the numbers 210 and 252 in the bottom line confirm.

The exception is the Pythagorean hemitone $^{256}/_{243}$ (tetrachord 8). The numbers in each tetrachord are arranged:

$$(d - a)$$
$$b:a \quad c:b \quad d:c$$
$$(b - a) \quad (c - b) \quad (d - c)$$
$$a \qquad b \qquad c \qquad d.$$

Architecturally, Palladio makes use of superparticular ratios, but it would be difficult to argue that he does so 'musically'.[36] The occurrence of the ratio 18 : 17 in the project for the Villa Ragona and in the Villa Pogliana, and of the ratio 17 : 16 in the covered entrance court under the raised hall of the Palazzo della Torre suggests some kind of interest in the debate over the equal temperament tuning of fretted instruments. The sixteenth century opened with instruments being fretted with unequal spacing to fit in with Pythagorean theory, but during the course of the century instrument designers and makers began to space the frets proportionately equal in a geometric sequence. This required them musically to divide the octave into twelve equal semitones. Now, a major tone was generally held to be $\frac{9}{8}$ and unison is 1. The arithmetic mean of these two is found to be $\frac{1}{2}(1 + \frac{9}{8}) = {}^{17}/_{16}$ and the harmonic mean is $2.1\frac{9}{8} \div (1 + \frac{9}{8}) = 18/17$. The ratios represent candidates for a semitone. The first rational convergent of $\sqrt{\frac{9}{8}}$ is 17 : 16, and its conjugate is $\frac{9}{8} \cdot 16 : 17 = 18 : 17$.[37] It has been observed that the semitone in one theory or another has ranged over superparticular ratios from the major semitone at 15 : 14 between the tritone and the fifth to a minor semitone at 25 : 24 between the minor third and the major third. It is difficult to see how anyone familiar with music practice and theory in the Renaissance could entertain the absoluteness of Platonic harmony, even more so the consonance of small numbers. Pythagoreans had to deal frequently with ratios like 81 : 80 and 256 : 243, while the moderns such as Girolamo Cardano and Vincenzo Galilei were promoting equal temperament in the only arithmetical way open to them by using rational convergents to $^{12}\sqrt{2}$.[38] Cardano in his *De musica* of c1546 wrote 'a whole tone consists in the proportion of 9 : 8, and either half consists in the proportion of 18 : 17 and is called a minor semitone'. In this context, the major semitone is 17 : 16. Cardano later wrote: 'It is wonderful how the minor semitone [18 : 17] is so nicely suited to the musical performance, but the major [17 : 16] never.'[39]

To find $^{12}\sqrt{2}$ requires the determination of the cube root of 2 and the square root of its square root. Arithmetical methods for finding rational convergents were known in the period under review. Geometrical methods were also available. Vitruvius mentions methods for finding the cube root of a number and cites classical methods. Both Dürer and Barbaro discuss and illustrate methods for determining cube roots. The problem is clearly of physical interest.[40] An illustration in a supplement of Zarlino's shows both the application of Euclid's geometrical method for determining square roots and an application of a method for finding two mean proportionals for the cube root.[41] (Fig. 9.)

Ptolemy describes an 'instrument made by students of mathematics to display the ratios in the concords' called the *helikon* named after Mount Helikon, home of the Muses. This is the figure which is now known to architects as Serlio's construction. The diagram of the *helikon* consists of a square divided by four lines. A remarkable number of musical intervals are defined by this simple geometry.[42] (Fig. 10.)

36 Superparticular ratios not included in Ptolemy's tetrachords for obvious musical reasons include 3 : 2 and 4 : 3, the fifth and fourth respectively (although by definition a tetrachord 'sums' to 4 : 3 when the three ratios that characterize it are multiplied). Palladio makes frequent use of superparticular ratios. However, from Ptolemy's set, he does not use 9 : 8, the standard *tonus*, nor 11 : 10, 12 : 11, 22 : 21, 28 : 27, 46 : 45. He does use 18 : 17 and 17 : 16, which have considerable musical importance in another context discussed below, and ratios 50 : 49, 57 : 56 which appear to have no musical provenance.

37 This issue was raised by Boethius in a Chapter 'Demonstrating that a Superparticular Proportion Cannot Be Divided in Half and for This Reason, Neither Can the Tone', *De institutione musica*, III i, Bower, op. cit., pp. 171–76. Dividing in half refers to finding the geometrical mean which is irrational in the case of $\sqrt{\frac{9}{8}}$. This is easily seen to be $3/2\sqrt{2}$ and thus involves the same problem as the diagonal of the square. The use of 18 : 17 as a minor semitone became a practical matter with the manufacture of fretted instruments in the fifteenth century.

38 Simon Stevin, writing c1585, is generally credited with stating the problem using multiples of the irrational $^{12}\sqrt{2}$. Even then for practical purposes this has to be reduced to a rational convergent. Stevin chooses the value 10 000 : 9 438. In doing so he goes through computations involving fractions such as

$$\frac{96\ 389\ 809\ 968\ 824\ 984\ 468\ 975}{176\ 776\ 695\ 296\ 636\ 881\ 100\ 211}.$$

Stevin writes p. 441: 'Now someone might wonder, according to the ancient view, how the sweet sound of the fifth [$^{12}\sqrt{2^5} = 2^{5/12}$] could consist in so unspeakable, irrational, and inappropriate a number. To this we might give a detailed answer. However, since it is not our intention to teach the unspeakable irrationality and inappropriateness of such a misunderstanding of the speakability, rationality, appropriateness, and natural wonderful perfection of these numbers, we shall leave it at that because we have proved it elsewhere [in a work on arithmetic]'. His views can be traced back to Oresme and Cusanus who effectively recover rationality in the rationality of power indices. In the case of the notes of the equally tempered octave these are the fractional powers of 2 – $\frac{1}{12}$ $\frac{1}{6}$ $\frac{1}{4}$ $\frac{1}{3}$ $\frac{5}{12}$ $\frac{1}{2}$ $\frac{7}{12}$ $\frac{2}{3}$ $\frac{3}{4}$ $\frac{5}{6}$ $\frac{11}{12}$ $\frac{1}{1}$. Stevin then confidently shows p. 447, 'how far amiss were the erroneous divisions of Pythagorus, Boethius and Zarlino'.

39 Op. cit., Lindley, p. 21. Also C. Miller, *Hieronymus Cardanus: Writings on Music*, American Institute of Musicology, 1973.

40 Ibid., pp. 24–27. See supra, 'Inexpressible Proportion'. Barbaro op. cit., pp. 270–281, expands a paragraph by Vitruvius on solutions to the Delic problem – determining a cube root – into a twelve-page commentary with three elaborate full-page illustrations, possibly by Palladio, showing methods by Archytas, Nicomedes and Eratosthenes.

41 Op. cit., Lindley, p. 26. The method of finding two mean proportional used by Zarlino, 1588, is attributed by Söhne to Philon of Byzantium. The method comes from the same family of solutions to which those by Apollonius and Heron belong. Albrecht Dürer, *Underweysung der Messung mit dem Zirkel uñ Richtscheyt*,

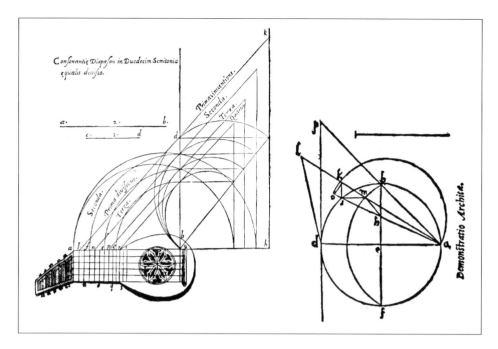

Fig. 9. Method for setting out the frets on a lute for equal temperament, Zarlino 1588 (left). Archytas's method for determining a cube root, Barbaro 1567 (right).

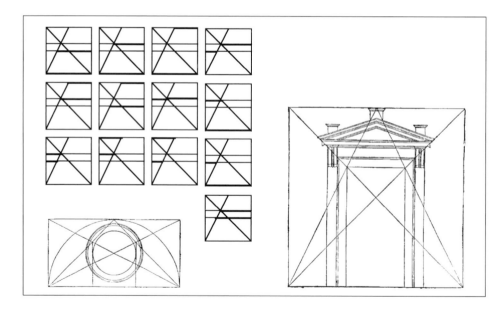

Fig. 10. Top left, Ptolemy's *helikon* diagram (2 CE) marked in bold with the lines indicated in his text. First column shows line in the epitritic ratio, 4 : 3; the second columns shows lines in the hemiolic ratio, 3 : 2; the third column illustrates the duple ratio, 2 : 1; the fourth column, from top to bottom, shows the octave and fourth, 8 : 3, the octave and fifth, 3 : 1, the double octave, 4 : 1, and the epogdoic ratio, 9 : 8. Bottom right and left two design using the *helikon* diagram from Serlio, 1545. On the right, the diagram is applied directly. On the left, the square is transformed into a double square. All ratios of either horizontal lengths, or of vertical lengths, remain in the original *helikon* proportions. Ratios formed from one horizontal and one vertical dimension will involve a doubling or halving.

Finally, instrument makers employed arithmetic and geometry in laying out their designs. Gerhard Söhne examines a lute design described and illustrated in a manuscript by Henri Arnaut *c*1440.[43] This would be contemporary with Alberti and a few years before *De re aedificatoria*. The construction of the design is similar to some of Serlio's vases a century later. It consists of a circle with a radius of 5. The ends of a diameter are taken as centres for two arc which are struck with a radius of 10 – the diameter of the original circle. Another arc is struck from the top of the original circle to merge with the previous two arcs. Arnaut gives the radius of this arc as 3. Söhne correctly points out that this is geometrically imprecise and claims that this is an example of 'the Pythagorean concept of numerical proportion' upon which Vitruvius had dwelt. But is it? The geometry dictates that the height of the body of the lute from the centre of the original circle is $3 - \sqrt{2}$ the maximum width. How does a practitioner deal with this surd? The usual rational convergent to $\sqrt{2} : 1$ is $7 : 5$. Using this value the height of the body is in the ratio $3 - \frac{7}{5} = \frac{8}{5}$ to the maximum width, the proportion that Arnaut gives in his text.[44] Söhne calls this a 'mathematical inexactitude', but it really is not in terms of the arithmetical rationalizations in use in this period. The total length of the body to the width is thus $\frac{13}{5} : 1$, or $13 : 5$. The bridge is placed one sixth of the full length from the bottom. The rose of the lute, Arnaut says, is centred at the midpoint between the bridge and the top of the body. This would place the centre $\frac{7}{12}$ of the height above the bridge. Söhne sees this at odds with the diagram which shows the rose centred between one of the 13 modules established by Arnaut's previous computation. The centre divides these 13 modules into $7\frac{1}{2}$ and $5\frac{1}{2}$, or a ratio of $15 : 13$. This is the same rational convergent to $\sqrt{4} : \sqrt{3}$ which Alberti appears to use later at Santa Maria Novella. It is based on the value $26 : 15$ for $\sqrt{3} : 1$. But note that $12 : 7$ is also a rational value to $\sqrt{3} : 1$. In this way the text and drawing are compatible: both $12 : 7$ in the text and $26 : 15$ in the drawing refer to the common idea of $\sqrt{3} : 1$. The $12 : 7$ ratio means that the centre of the rose divides the height into a ratio of $7 : 5$, or $\sqrt{2} : 1$, while the $26 : 15$ ratio gives $15 : 11$. Exactly this computation is involved in the design of Palladio's 'La Rotonda' more than a century later. (Fig. 11)

Any comparison of architectonic practice with music must take into account three aspects of music: the theoretical description and prescription of musical scales including the tetrachord; next the transfer of this knowledge to the tuning of instruments including the design of fretting arrangements; and finally the design of the instruments themselves. The relevance to architects and designers of musical and acoustical knowhow is surely most obvious at the level of physical design – of instruments and the placement of frets (and holes in the case of wind instruments). The only arguments for theoretical influence are two. Firstly, that the occurrence of ubiquitous ratios like $1 : 1$ and $2 : 1$ reflect the prime musical consonances of the unison and the octave, whereas almost anything will give rise to such a simple idea of something and its double – including music. Secondly, that the occurrence of ratios like $3 : 2$, $4 : 3$, $5 : 4$ and even $5 : 3$ confirm the usage of the secondary musical consonances of the perfect fifth, the perfect fourth, the major third and the major sixth, when they might simply arise from the employment of the 3, 4, 5 triangle to set out an architectural design.[45] Among the leading architectural writers of the Renaissance only Alberti argues the musical analogy with any conviction, and even that turns out to have more arithmetical reality than musical. Pythagorean musical theory is limited arithmetic: it really has remarkably little to do with musical practice,

Nuremberg, 1525, devotes seven pages to the Delic problem and illustrates Heron's method, Book II, Figure 51. However, Zarlino's construction seems to have a stronger resemblance to Barbaro's depiction of Archytas' method. Barbaro, *op. cit.*, p. 279.

42 In fact the diagram essentially takes the half division of the square and shows how to obtain the third division. Having fixed this third division on the side of the square a new diagonal may be drawn to obtain the quarter division. Recursive application produces a fifth division, sixth, seventh and so on. The diagram employs the properties of similar triangles. Geometry takes precedence over any musical interpretation.

43 *Op. cit.*, Lindley, Appendix 4, pp. 109–11.

44 Note that this Fibonacci-type ratio ($8 : 5$) does not spring from any consideration of the extreme and mean ratio but emerges from computations involving $\sqrt{2}$. Simple addition also give the height of the lute belly to the height above the diameter as $13 : 8$. Yet again this Fibonacci-type ratio is a coincidence of the geometric construction, not any imposition of the golden section.

45 There are three direct ratios from the 3, 4, 5 right triangle – $4 : 3$, $5 : 4$, $5 : 3$. The ratio $3 : 2$ may be derived from halving 4, or from doubling three. Many other ratios are possible, see 'Right Triangular Number', *supra*.

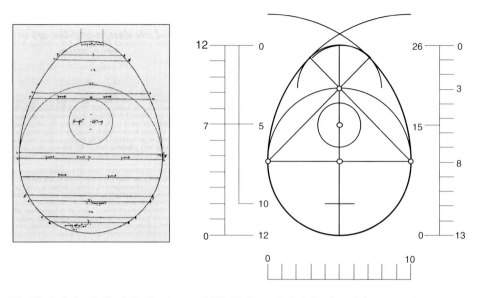

Fig. 11. Left, lute belly design by Arnaut *c*1440. Right, analytical drawing of the geometric construction compared with the arithmetic divisions used in Arnaut's text. The belly is 10 modules wide (bottom scale). The height of the belly is 13 of these modules (right-hand scale). The height of the centre of the rose is shown in Arnaut's drawing at the midpoint of the sixth module, dividing the height of the belly to the height of the rose centre in the ratio 26 : 15, a rational surrogate for √3 : 1. His text, however, divides the height of the lute belly into 12 divisions and places the bridge at one sixth of the height of the lute belly and the centre of the rose midway between the bridge and the top of the belly (left-hand scale). The ratio of the height of the belly to the height of the rose centre is 12 : 7, also a rational convergent to √3 : 1. But the ratio of the height of the rose centre to the distance of the centre to the top of the lute belly is 7 : 5, a rational convergent to √2 : 1 used by Arnaut to compute the height of the lute belly to its width.

or with harmonious sound. The musical analogy has been overstated and over-used by protagonists to the detriment of continued, searching inquiry into Renaissance architectonics, or the practice of design and computation in the age of humanism. Only proselytizers of the monotheistic dogma of the golden section have had a more deadening and corrupting effect on serious study.[46]

46 Starting with Luca Pacioli's comparison of the extreme and mean ratio with the threefold nature of God in Book I, *De divina proportione*, Venice, 1509.

XVIIII

PRISONERS OF NUMBER

When writing about the planning of temples, Vitruvius makes one statement that has intrigued and captivated generations of artists and architects: 'For without symmetry and proportion no temple can have a regular plan; that is, it must have an exact proportion worked out after the fashion of the members of a finely-shaped human figure.'[1] Vitruvius goes on to describe the ratios of members of the body to the total height including the foot which is one-sixth of the height. Painters and sculptors have made good use of such proportions. He then jumps back again to temples: 'In like fashion the members of temples ought to have dimensions of their several parts answering suitably to the general sum of their whole magnitude.'[2] Vitruvius is implying, it seems, that the proportioning of the human form is simply analogous to the design of a temple which has its own architectonic. And then follows the passage on a man stretched out with his back on the ground and his feet and hands spread: his navel will be found to be at the centre of a circle touching his extremities. 'Also a square will be found described within the figure, in the same way as a round figure is produced.'[3] The difficulties of reconciling circle and square with the same outstretched human posture is quickly avoided by the next statement in which the man is in an upright position with arms extended so that the height of the man is found to be equal to the span of his arms to the finger tips. Clearly, in such an attitude the man fits into a square. The ubiquitous presence of Leonardo da Vinci's sketch from sweatshirts to computer software testifies to the perennial appeal of this anthropocentric notion. The sketch has become the logo of our idea of the age of humanism.[4]

Attempts to reconcile the human form with Vitruvian arithmetic and geometry produced many solutions, and five definite, recognizable approaches between which compromises may be reached. (Fig. 1)

In the first approach the human figure is forced to conform to the geometry. Cesariano's man looks more like a victim of the Inquisition, or on closer inspection, a client of a dominatrix, than a model for universal harmony. In another approach, geometry is forced to fit the human frame. In Francesco di Giorgio's drawing the 'square' touches the top and bottom of the circle, but falls inside it at the sides and seems to have no relation to the outstretched hand. A compromise between the human figure and geometry is reached in Leonardo da Vinci's sketch. The third approach ignores the geometry and simply measures the human body. Alberti and Dürer appear to do this. A fourth approach ignores geometry and reduces the problem to predetermined arithmetic ratios. Francesco Zorzi takes this approach, but unfortunately his male lives in the body of an androgyne to achieve total conformity to *harmonia*

1 Vitruvius III i 1. '*Namque non potest aedis ulla sine symmetria atque proportione rationem habere compositionis, nisi uti ad hominis bene figurati membrorum habuerit exactam rationem.*' F. Granger trans, *Vitruvius: De Architectura*, Harvard University Press, Cambridge, 1931, I, p. 159.

2 *Ibid.*, III.1.3. '*Similiter vero sacrarum aedium membra ad universam totius magnitudinis summam ex partibus singulis convenientissimum debent habere commensus responsum.*' Granger, I, p. 161.

3 *Ibid.*, '*Non minus quemadmodum schema rotundationis in corpore efficitur, item quadrata designatio in eo invenietur.*' Granger, I, p. 161.

4 However, the sketch in Leonardo's private notebook would have been known to few in his own day.

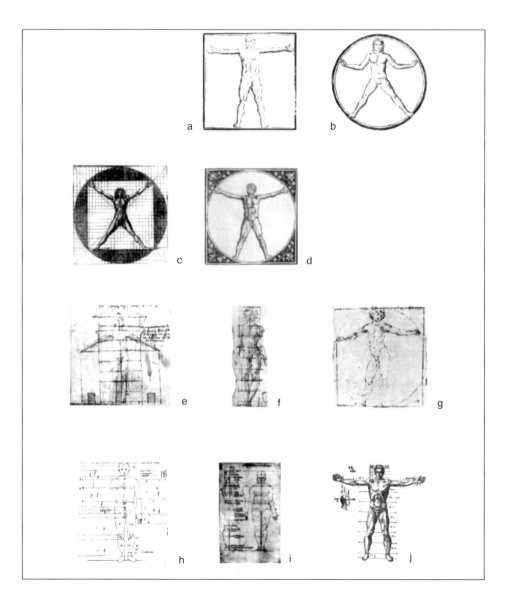

Fig. 1. Studies of the human figure. From left to right, top row a. from Fra Giocondo's edition of *Vitruvius* (Venice, 1511) and b. from Francesco Zorzi, *De Harmonia Mundi* (Venice, 1525); second row c. from Cesariano's edition of *Vitruvius* (Como, 1521), and d. from Fra Giocondo, *Vitruvius*; third row e., f. and g. from Francesco de Giorgio; bottom row h. from Alberti *De statua*, *c*1470, i. from Dürer – study for *Vier Bücher von Menschlicher Proportion*, *c*1523, j. from Girolamo Cardano, *De subtilitate* (Lyons, 1559) and reproduced in Daniele Barbaro's edition of *Vitruvius* (Venice, 1567).

mundi.[5] The fifth approach is to ignore the human aspect and apply geometry directly. Palladio, with his deep appreciation of Vitruvius, appears to follow this route. In doing so, as an architect, he is probably the most true to Vitruvius.

The Vitruvian project is confused from the beginning. It is derived from painters and sculptors who like Alberti and Dürer have a legitimate interest in gaining the knowledge required to represent the human form. Vitruvius makes an analogy between the proportionate relations of the human body and the kinds of proportions to be found in a well-designed temple. These need not be the same: Vitruvius never says so. Vitruvius does suggest that Nature's way is an example to be followed in the production of an artefact and that the ancients had observed 'an exact adjustment of the several members to the general pattern of the plan'.[6]

There is a second thesis to Vitruvius' analogy which is that architects and builders use measures derived from the human body: the finger, the palm, the foot and the

[5] F. Zorzi, *De Harmonia Mundi*, Venice, 1525, suggests that the human body is concordant with musical ratios; 9 : 8 the total height to the headless body, 4 : 3 the length of torso to the length of legs; 3 : 2 for the width of the hips to the width of the waist (many women would like to sport 30″ hips and a 20″ waist, but men?), and 2 : 1 the chest to the belly (measured how?) – all numbers and ratios from the Pythagorean lambda and Plato's *Timaeus*. See M. Fend, 'Musik-theoretisches in Francesco Giorgis Idee einer harmonischen Welt' in *Kongressbericht Bayreuth*, 1981.
[6] Vitruvius *op. cit.*, III.1.4.

cubit, or the length of the forearm.[7] Here the smallest unit, the finger, is compounded to produce larger measures, whereas in the first thesis Vitruvius takes the largest unit – the height of a man – and divides it into aliquot parts. Both these systems persist in the various reconstructions: Alberti takes a tiny unit which is one six-hundredth of the height, or a hundredth of a foot, and measures everything accordingly, whereas Cardano uses a unit based, it would seem, on picking his nose since the unit is the *nasiforamen*, the nasal passage.[8]

In *De statua*,[9] Alberti observes to an accuracy of one in six hundred the measurements of a sample of human bodies.[10] He then eliminates extreme measurements and arrives at their mean values. While some measures relate to others in the Vitruvian manner, at least as many do not. He could not have been captivated by Vitruvius' claim concerning proportionality except as a most general analogy. Relating the scale of a building to the human figure is clearly important. That the parts of the human figure are proportionately related is trivially true of any form – natural or artificial. Inexorably, any two dimensions selected from a form will be in ratio. The choice of dimensions is always arbitrary. It might be thought, in arriving at the 6 : 1 and 10 : 1 ratios, that Alberti was using maximum widths across the body: from shoulder to shoulder (1.5.0), or from the buttocks to the front (0.7.5).[11] Yet his own computations give ratios of 4 : 1 and 8 : 1 respectively for these measurements when compared to the full height. To obtain the 6 : 1 ratio, it is necessary to choose a measurement not across the hips, nor even across the shoulders, but the maximum width between sides above the hips (1.0.0).[12] The 10 : 1 ratio comes from the thickest part of the thigh (0.6.0).[13] The length of the body is divided in half, 2 : 1, by the height from the ground to the middle finger of the hand hanging down or the height of the bone below which hangs the penis (3.0.0).[14] Yet both the anatomically motile height to the testicles and the height to the base of the buttocks give the irreducible ratio 600 : 269[15]. Add 1/600 to this height and the ratio 600 : 270 :: 20 : 9 is obtained, a rational convergent to $\sqrt{5} : 1$.[16] Other dimensions hint at Alberti's possible interest in incommensurables. The full height of the figure (6.0.0) to the height from the ground to the bottom of the shoulder blades (4.2.5) is in the ratio of 24 : 17, or compared with the heights to the bone below which hangs the penis or to the wrist (3.0.0) the ratio 17 : 12. The ratio of the heights to the node of the neck or to the point of the shoulder (5.1.0), and the height to the navel (3.6.0) is also equal to 17 : 12. The ratio of the height from the ground to the elbow joint with the arm hanging down (3.8.5) to the height of the ear hole (5.5.0) is 10 : 7. All of these are rational convergents to $\sqrt{2} : 1$. Even the nipples compared to the full height, or to that bone below which the penis hangs, make a $\sqrt{2}$ relation.[17] The ratio of the full height (6.0.0) to the height to the chin (5.2.0) is in the ratio 15 : 13, or a rational convergent to $\sqrt{4} : \sqrt{3}$, and the chin (5.2.0) to the heights of the wrists and that bone above the penis (3.0.0) are in the ratio 26 : 15, the convergent to $\sqrt{3} : 1$. There are several $\sqrt{2} : 1$ relations among the measurements of the width of the body, at least two $\sqrt{4} : \sqrt{3}$ relations, and a $\sqrt{3} : 1$ ratio.[18] The ratio of the width of the waist (0.9.0) to the width at the kneebones (0.4.0) is a good rational convergent to the diagonal of the double square, $\sqrt{5} : 1$.[19] Many of these anatomical decisions seem prisoners of arithmetic necessity rather than the results of objective empirical observation: even Alberti's seemingly naturalistic scheme is impregnated with *ad quadratum* and *ad triangulum* relationships. Is this a demonstration that God geometrizes, or rather that man approaches his studies with geometrical and arithmetical preconceptions?[20]

7 *Ibid.*, III.1.5. The measures are the Roman *digitus* of which there are 4 in a *palmus*. There are 4 *palmus* in a *pes*, and 1½ *pedes* in a *cubitus*. The *uncia* was also used. There were 12 *uncia* in a *pes*. An excellent description of Roman measuring systems is given in T. Kurent, *The Modular Eurythmia of Aediculeae in Sempeter*, DM, Ljubljana, 1970, pp. 7–10.

8 There is surely a touch of Rabelaisian wit in this choice. G. Cardano, *De subtilitate*, Lyons, 1559, pp. 462–3. Barbaro use this figure in his edition of Vitruvius. P. H. Scholfield, *The Theory of Proportion in Architecture*, Cambridge University Press, Cambridge, 1958, p. 48 notes that Cardano starts with the smallest unit and shows that the height of man is 180 nasal passages, whereas Barbaro adheres to the division of the height by making the unit 1/180th of the height.

9 Cecil Grayson ed. and trans, *Leon Battista Alberti: On Sculpture* from the Latin, *De statua*, Phaidon, Oxford, 1972. Grayson, p. 23, comments: 'The main theme of *De statua* is the measurement of men or statues of men, with the object of reproducing their exact form. The methods he uses represent a complete departure from those of the past; they are untrammelled by the imposition of theoretical criteria of harmony ... [Alberti's] system ... is not based on Vitruvius.' Grayson, p. 20, suggests that *De statua* was most likely written after Alberti's manuscript on architecture, posssibly around 1452. Grayson's excellent introduction is advised.

10 About ⅛ inch, or 3mm.

11 *Ibid.*, pp. 134–39, 'Tables of measurements of man'. The measures are respectively '*maxima latitudo inter angulos scapularum*' and '*a pene ad prominentias in natibus*' p. 136. Alberti uses a place value system which almost defines the decimal system attributed to Simon Stevin a full century later. His triple (*p.q.r*) measures *p* feet, *q* degrees which are one-tenth of a foot, and then *r* minutes which are one-tenth of a degree, or one-hundedth of a foot. Arithmetically the choice of ratios is understandable given the privileged positions of the numbers 6 and 10, of the hexad and the decad, in the Pythagorean and classical traditions. St Augustine relates these ratios to the length and breadth, 6 : 1, and the length to height, 10 : 1, of Noah's Ark with which he compares the human form, Christ and the Church. 'The actual measurements of the ark, its length, height and breadth, symbolize the human body, in the reality of which Christ was to come, and did come, to mankind. For the length of the human body from the top of the head to the sole of the foot is six times its breadth from side to side, and ten times its depth, measured on the side from back to belly.' H. B. Withan trans, *St Augustine: City of God*, (first published 1467), Penguin Books, 1972, XV, 26, p. 643.

12 '*maxima latitudo inter ambo latera supra ischiam*', ibid., pp. 136–137.

13 '*crassitudo maxima in coxa*'.

14 '*ad longissimum digitum manus pendentis*', and '*ad os, sub quo pendet penis*' ibid., pp. 134–35.

15 '*ad nodum coxae, hoc est ischiam*'.

16 The ratio 600 : 239 is better than 20 : 9 and is just ½% over $\sqrt{5} : 1$.

17 The ratios are 40 : 29 and 29 : 20 which may be

derived from the 20, 21, 49 right triangle – the first rational triangle to approximate the right isosceles triangle, or half square.

18 Width between cheek bones : maximum width of foot :: 0.4.8 : 4.2.0 :: 8 : 7; maximum width at the knee bone : the widest point of the calf muscle :: 4.0.0 :: 3.5.0 :: 8 : 7; both rational convergents to $\sqrt{4}$: $\sqrt{3}$, the diameter of a circle to the side of the inscribed equilateral triangle. The maximum width of foot : the width between ankle bones :: 4.2.0. :: 2.4.0 :: 7 : 4, the standard convergent for $\sqrt{3}$: 1, or the side of an equilateral triangle to the radius of the circumscribed circle.

19 The maximum width at mid-thigh : the narrow part below the knee bone 0.5.5 :: 0.2.5 :: 11 : 5 is also a rational convergent to $\sqrt{5}$: 1. The maximum width between sides above the hips : width at waist :: 1.0.0 : 0.9.0 :: 10 : 9 which is an estimate for the diagonal of the double square to the long side, $\sqrt{5}$: $\sqrt{4}$.

20 One thing seems certain about Alberti's measurement is that the tell-tale rational convergents for the extreme and mean ratio – the golden section – are nowhere to be found.

21 J. R. Spencer, *Filarete's Treatise on Architecture*, Yale University Press, New Haven, 1965. This magnificent two-volume work carries an English translation and introductory essay in the first volume and a fascimile of the Milan copy in the second. Unfortunately, no other architectural treatises of this period have received such devoted attention in which English translation and scholarly annotation are found accompanied by the original. One only has to think of the various mediaeval and Renaissance editions of Vitruvius to realize how impoverished architectural studies remain in this respect. Music scholars are very much better served in their field. A convenient introduction to Filarete is J. Onians, *Bearers of Meaning: The Classical Orders in Antiquity, the Middle Ages, and the Renaissance*, Princeton University Press, Princeton NJ, 1988, pp. 158–170.

22 *Ibid.*, p. 6.

23 *Ibid.*, p. 7. That Filarete chooses these names is odd. He is aware of Alberti's treatise on architecture. Alberti allocates the dimension 7 to the Doric order, 8 to the Ionic and 9 to the Corinthian in terms of the module of the column width. In terms of character, the Doric may be seen to be the most masculine and Ionic the most feminine of orders: in this sense the names chosen by Filarete for the human figure may be seen to be appropriate.

24 *Ibid.*, p. 8. Spencer's note, n. 11 pp. 8–9, gives a succinct commentary on the Vitruvian proposal and its problems.

25 *Ibid.*, p. 9. Better known as Campanus whose thirteenth-century work provided the standard Latin translation of Euclid in circulation during the fifteenth century.

26 Grayson suggests that Alberti's *De statua* was not circulated widely. *Op. cit.*, p. 26.

Antonio di Pietro Averlino, also known as Filarete, is the next contributor to examine the Vitruvian proposal in his illustrated *Trattato di architettura,* the first significant treatise on architecture in a modern language.[21] 'As everyone knows', Filarete writes, 'man was created by God . . . the body [was] organized and measured and all its members proportioned according to their qualities and measure. Since man is made with the measure stated above, he decided to take the measures, members, proportions, and qualities from himself and to adapt them to this method of building.'[22] He then relates his understanding of the measures of man. There are five types of man: giant, large, normal, small, and dwarf. Measured by the head, giants are 10 heads tall, large men 9 heads, normal men 8, small 7 and dwarfs 6. Filarete discounts the extremes – giants and dwarfs – and attributes the name Doric to the large, the Corinthian to the common and Ionic to the small.[23] With arms stretched out, man 'is the same measure vertically and horizontally', he 'will be nine heads in either direction. Vitruvius says that the navel is in the middle of the figure of man. The navel would be the centre for the point of a compass that would circumscribe the man in a circle. From this the circle derives. It is good enough reason to confirm our proposition that all measures are derived from man. However, it does not seem to be exactly the middle, but the circle does remain round. The square and every other measure is derived from man'.[24] Filarete seems determined to derive geometry from the man, rather than accepting that man is being modelled after geometry. Indeed, he writes that he will only treat of those measures that he deems most useful, leaving others 'to those who wish to understand them better and at greater length. Let them read mathematicians and geometricians like Euclid, who wrote subtly about this, or Campano da Vigevano, who commented on him and demonstrated all the subtleties of measure'.[25] It is clear that Filarete does not acknowledge Alberti's findings in *De statua*, for the proportions he describes are very simple aliquot divisions of the head such as $\frac{1}{3}$ for the divisions of the face, or $\frac{1}{2}$ for the neck and the instep to the sole; or simple multiples of the head such as 1 for the chest, 2 for the chest to the groin, 4 for the groin to the instep.[26] The arm is $2\frac{1}{2}$ heads long. There is also a discussion of standard building measures such as the *braccio* and the *polisi*. Despite the fact that his treatise is well illustrated elsewhere, Filarete gives no drawing of the measures of the human figure.

Fra Gioconda illustrates the man in the circle and the man in the square separately in his edition of Vitruvius in 1511. Cesariano comes up with his disturbing image of the man in a square in a circle in a square for his edition of Vitruvius of 1521. The outside square is marked by a 30×30 mesh, the inside square is 21×21. The squares are in the ratio 10 : 7, or a rational convergent to $\sqrt{2}$: 1. Geometrically this is to be expected, but Cesariano stresses the arithmetic relationship explicitly by drawing in the mesh. Cesariano, true to his mediaeval roots, conforms man *ad quadratum*. Francesco Zorzi in *De harmonia mundi* illustrates man in a circle whose geometry is almost certainly pentagonal, which seems to be a novel configuration.

Today the most famous of these presentations is Leonardo da Vinci's portrayal. Perhaps because of his association with Luca Pacioli, commentators have seen the extreme and mean ratio in his construction of the square and the off-centred circle. A careful reconstruction suggests that the *ad quadratum* theme found in previous authors is still dominant. Leonardo's architectural investigations of centralized fabrics are almost all based on the octagon. He would have been very familiar with the *ad quadratum* relationships to be found in the regular octagon. The test comes in seeing just how the circle clips the top corners of the square. The extreme and mean construction comes too close to the corners, whereas the octagonal method seems to place the circle in the right relationship to the corners. The octagonal construction is surely correct given Leonardo's own interest and the continuing traditions of *ad quadratum*. In his written description, Leonardo even places an equilateral triangle within the scheme, suggesting familiarity with *ad triangulum*.[27]

Leonardo places a scale at the foot of the square showing 4 large divisions, each divided into 6 parts, which are further divided into 4. There are $4 \times 6 \times 4 = 96$ units. This division corresponds to Leonardo's reading: 'Vitruvius, the architect, has it in his work on architecture that the measurements of man are arranged by nature in the following manner: four fingers make one palm and four palms make one foot; six palms make a cubit; four cubits make a man, and four cubits make one pace; and twenty-four palms make a man; and these measures are those of his buildings.'[28] The unit is thus a *digitus*, 4 of which make a *palmus*, 6 of which combine to make a *cubitus*, and 4 of these give the height of man. This scale indicates that the diameter of the circle is 29 palms; the height of the navel is then 58 digits. 'The penis is at the middle of the man',[29] or the middle of the square at a height of 24 digits. The ratio 29 : 24 is related to the regular octagon: it is a rational convergent to the ratio of the half chord to the side.[30] Leonardo uses a range of aliquot divisions of the body height to describe the dimensions of its members: $\frac{1}{30}$, $\frac{1}{10}$, $\frac{1}{8}$, $\frac{1}{7}$, $\frac{1}{6}$, $\frac{1}{5}$, $\frac{1}{4}$, $\frac{1}{2}$. It is to be noted that divisions like a tenth, seventh and a fifth are incommensurable with the 96 digits of Leonardo's scale.[31] (Fig. 2.)

Henry Cornelius Agrippa summarizes the various models proposed before him in *De occulta philosophia*, 1533.[32] The first image shows a man standing with his feet together and arms apart in a circle. This seems to be original.[33] The second image shows the same postures with the arms now straight out touching the edges of a square defined by the man's height: one of the Vitruvian attitudes and not too dissimilar to one of Fra Giocondo's figure in his edition of Vitruvius.[34] The third image is similar to one by Francesco Zorzi, but Agrippa makes the pentagonal relationship explicit by overdrawing a pentagram; the centre of the pentagram is the penis, and the apex of an equilateral triangle based on a side marks the navel.[35] The fourth image shows the Cesariano posture, but just in a square without the circle.[36] The fifth image is similar again to one by Fra Giocondo although Agrippa's man seems less confortable within the circle. The text to this image also suggests some familarity with Leonardo's Vitruvian man. It is possible that the feet and the hands mark four vertices of a regular heptagon with the centre at the navel. An equilateral triangle on a side as base would then reach the penis. This geometry appears to be original to Agrippa.[37] The sixth image shows a man with his arms stretched above his head within a square, the centre of which is the man's navel.[38] (Fig. 3.)

Agrippa goes on to describe particular measures based on a man 4 cubits high – the same height chosen by Leonardo. There are yet further parallels in Agrippa's text to give rise to speculation that he was familiar with Leonardo's reconstruction of Vitruvian man. Agrippa also reiterates Alberti's comparison of the human body with the dimensions of Noah's Ark.[39]

Dürer returns to the tradition started by Alberti. He uses Alberti's methods of measurement, but without acknowledgement. He too searches for arithmetical relationships, but seems more content to let empirical observations dictate his conclusions. His attempt to use aliquot divisions leads to his use, at one time, of an harmonic *regula*: a rule divided into half, thirds, quarters, fifths, sixths, sevenths, eights, ninths and tenths.[40] What is special about Dürer is his measurements of

27 M. Kemp, *Leonardo on Painting*, Yale University Press, New Haven, 1989, p. 120. Leonardo writes, Urb 104v (McM 296), translated by M. Kemp and M. Walker: 'If you open your legs so that you lower your head by one-fourteenth of your height, and open and raise your arms so that with your longest fingers you touch the level of the top of your head, you should know that the central point between the extremities of the outstretched limbs will be the navel, and the space which is described by the legs makes an equilateral triangle.' Note that this sounds like the adjustment to the navel height that had bothered Filarete about Vitruvius' original proposal.

28 *Ibid.*, For a fuller discussion see 'Proportions', p. 119–29.

29 *Ibid.*, p. 122.

30 The computation is simple. Let the side be a unit length, 1. The chord will then be of length $1 + \sqrt{2}$. The half chord is half of this and its ratio to the side is thus $1 + \sqrt{2} : 2$. If the rational convergent 17 : 12 is used for $\sqrt{2} : 1$, the result 29 : 24 immediately follows.

31 The first number to satisfy aliquot divisions would be 840.

32 Book II xxvii. The seventeenth-century English translation by 'J. F.' is used here. H. C. Agrippa von Nettersheim, *Three Books of Occult Philosophy*, Gregory Moule, London, 1651.

33 *Ibid.*, p. 264. '. . . the whole measure of the body may be turned, and proceeding from roundness, is knowen to tend to it again.'

34 *Ibid.*, p. 265. 'Also the four square measure is the most proportioned body; for, if man be placed upright with his feet together, and his arms stretched forth, he will make a quadrature equilateral, whose center is the bottom of his belly.'

35 *Ibid.*, p. 266. 'But if on the same center a circle be made by the crown of the head, the arms let fall so far, till the ends of the fingers touch the circumference, as much as the fingers ends are distant from the top of the head; Then they divide that circle, which was drawn from the center of the lower belly, into five parts, and do constitute a perfect Pentagon; and the Heels of the feet, having reference to the navile, make a triangle of equal sides.'

36 *Ibid.*, p. 267. 'But if the Heels being unmoved, the feet be stretched forth on both sides to the right and left, and the hands lifted up to the line of the head, then the ends of the fingers and Toes do make a square of equall sides, whose center is on the navile, in the girdling of the body.'

37 *Ibid.*, p. 268. 'But if the hands be thus elevated, and the feet and Thighes extended in this manner, by which a man is made shorter by the fourteenth part of his upright stature [see n. 27 above], then the distance of his feet having reference to his lower belly, they will make an equilaterall Triangle; and the center being placed in his navile, a circle being brought about, will touch the ends of the fingers and toes.'

38 *Ibid.*, p. 269. 'But if the hands be lifted up as high as can be, above the head, then the elbow will be equal to the crown of the head, and if then the feet be put together, a man stands thus, he may be put into an equilateral square brought by the extremities of the hands and feet: the center of this square is the

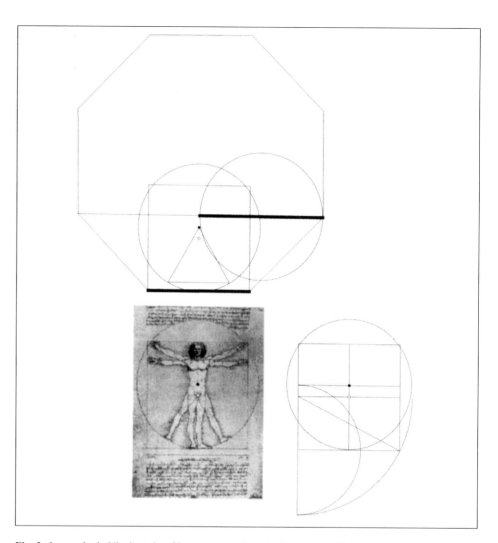

Fig. 2. Leonardo da Vinci, study of human proportions in the manner of Vitruvius, Venice, Accademia, 228, 29 (R343). Bottom right, suggested extreme and mean ratio reconstruction by R. D. Lawlor, *Sacred Geometry*, Thames and Hudson, 1982, p. 59. Top left, alternative reconstruction based on *ad quadratum* relationships in the regular octagon. The square stands on a base of the octagon, and the circle has a diameter equal to half the chord of the octagon.

navel, which is the middle betwixt the top of the head and the knees.'

39 *Ibid.*, p. 263. See n. 11 above. Agrippa modifies Alberti's protodecimal measuring scheme: 'some who have written of the Microcosme, or of man, measure the body by six feet, a foot by ten degrees, every degree by five minutes; from hence are numbred sixty degrees, which make three-hundred minutes, to which are compared so many Geometrical cubits, by which Moses describes the Arke ... '. Agrippa chooses to divide a degree into 5 minutes, instead of Alberti's 10, precisely to arrive at the number 300 for a direct comparison with the Ark.

40 Dürer would need to divide a rule into 2520 units to accomodate each of these aliquot divisions. It will be noted that this is half of 5040 ($7 \times 6 \times 5 \times 4 \times 3 \times 2 \times 1$), Plato's 'convenient number' of citizens in *Laws* V 737, presumably chosen because of its multiple aliquot divisibilty. See Schofield, *op. cit.*, p. 49.

41 See n. 8 above.

42 180 is a highly composite number which is a number that, counting from one, sets a record for the number of its divisors. In other words no smaller number has more divisors. Cardano's considerable mathematical intelligence probably suggested the usefulness of this number in terms of determining aliquot parts. He then would have had to look for a part of the body which would conform – the *nasi-foramen*. Note that Cardano, and therefore Barbaro, avoid the seventh division used by Leonardo. See note 2 above. The Cardano image is shown and acknowledged by D. Barbaro, *M Vitrvvii Pollionis: De Architectvra Libri Decem cvm Commentarivs ...* Venice, 1567, pp. 89–90, and *La Pratica della Perspettiva*, Venice, 1569, p. 180.

43 V. Scamozzi, *Idea dell'architettura universale*, Venice, 1615.

women and children in which proportions are often at considerable variance with those of the God-given ideal man. But perhaps the brilliant, but rakish, Girolamo Cardano also deflates – in Rabelaisian style – the arrogance of male perfection when he chooses to measure man by his nasal passage.[41] Daniel Barbaro deflects this barb by restoring the Vitruvian method of relating members to the body's height and converting Cardano's measures to aliquot parts: $\frac{1}{180}$, $\frac{1}{90}$, $\frac{1}{45}$, $\frac{1}{30}$, $\frac{1}{15}$, $\frac{1}{10}$, $\frac{1}{6}$, $\frac{1}{5}$. Barbaro also has to include $\frac{2}{15}$ since the height of man is 180 units (Cardano's nasal passages) and 180 is not divisible by 8.[42] (Fig. 4.)

Many of the arithmetical and geometrical preoccupations of the fifteenth and sixteenth centuries with the microcosmic order of the human body are summarized in a drawing from Vincenzo Scamozzi.[43] The drawing shows a man in a circle with both

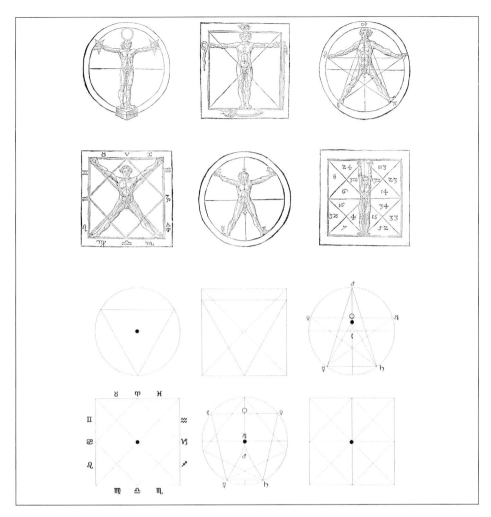

Fig. 3. Studies of the human figure from Henry Cornelius Agrippa, *De occulta philosophia*, 1533. Below, the anaylsis of the geometries involved. The *ad quadratum*, square within a square configuration, appears to have astrological significance. In any event it will be noted that signs of the zodiac and the signs of the planets accompany some of the figures.

a circumscribed and inscribed square. A third square is set between these as a mean. This male figure is surrounded by fifteen panels, thirteen of which display geometrical figures with rational arithmetic convergents. The remaining two panels depict human figures reclining on pediments: above are two females and below are two males. To appreciate the geometry of the circle and squares in the central panel, it is necessary first to inspect some of the strictly mathematical illustrations. (Fig. 5.)

In the top row, there are three triangles. The first is equilateral, the second is a 3, 4, 5 Pythagorean triangle, and the third is isosceles based on two back to back 5, 12, 13 Pythagorean triangles. The equilateral triangle is inscribed in a 15 : 13 rectangle – one of the common rational convergents to $\sqrt{4} : \sqrt{3}$, or the base to the altitude. The 3, 4, 5 triangle is given dimensions 18, 24, 30. A perpendicular from the right angle falls on the hypotenuse and divides it into 10⅘ and 19⅕. The altitude of the triangle is 14⅖.[44] The triangle sits in a 25 : 12 – almost double square

[44] This is an illustration of Euclid, VI.13 (T. L. Heath, *Euclid: the Thirteen Books*, II p. 216). The dimensions are more easily understood measured in fifths: they are respectively, 54, 96 and 72 fifths.

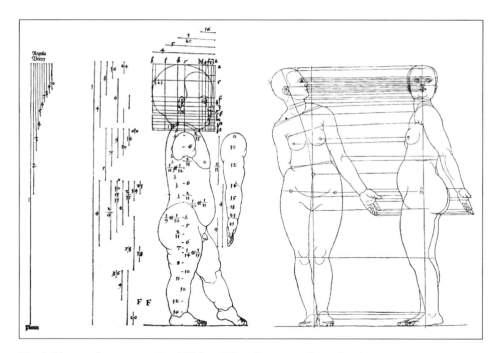

Fig. 4. Figures of a woman and a child from Dürer, *De symmetria partium humanorum corporum*, Nuremberg, 1532. To the left Dürer's harmonic *regula* used in proportioning the child.

– rectangle. Scamozzi erroneously computes the areas of the two triangular parts. The third triangle sits in a 12×10 rectangle. Scamozzi indicates correctly that the area of the isosceles triangle is 60, or half the area of the rectangle. On the next row down, Scamozzi shows circles and computes arc lengths and areas of sectors using $^{22}\!/_{7}$ as a rational convergent for π. To simplify his computations Scamozzi takes a circle of radius 7. On the next row appear two panels with computations related to the volumes of obelisks and columns with entasis. Below these are two more circles. One shows the 10×10 inscribed square in a circle of radius 7.[45] He calculates the areas of the four segments. The second figure on this row shows an equilateral triangle inscribed in the same circle. Scamozzi indicates that the altitude of the triangle divides the diameter of the circle (14) in the lengths $10\frac{2}{3}$ and $3\frac{1}{3}$. The side of the triangle is 12. Removing fractions it is easily seen that Scamozzi is using a poor $9:8$ rational convergent for $\sqrt{4}:\sqrt{3}$,[46] although this same incommensurable ratio of the diameter of the circle (14) to the side of the triangle (12) is better approximated by the ratio $7:6$. The bottom row deals with squaring the circle, and the measurement of cubes and spheres. A circle of radius 7 has an area of 154 using the $^{22}\!/_{7}$ value of π. A $12\frac{2}{5} \times 12\frac{2}{5}$ square, according to Scamozzi, also has an area of 154 – thus the circle is arithmetically squared.[47] The drawing to the right takes the previous square and computes numbers for surface areas and volume.[48] The surface area (1176) and volume (2744) of a cube of width 14 is shown next. Finally, the surface area (616) and volume of sphere ($1437\frac{1}{3}$) of radius 7 are computed.[49]

The squaring of the circle suggests a reason for the three concentric squares in Scamozzi's portrayal of Vitruvian man. He shows the beginning of the procedure which will lead to a value for squaring the circle. The circumscribed square is clearly

45 He is using the $7:5$ rational convergent to $\sqrt{2}:1$.
46 Using the better $8:7$ rational convergent the length would have been $10\frac{1}{2}$ and $3\frac{1}{2}$.
47 Actually $153\frac{19}{25}$.
48 The volume of a cube $12\frac{2}{5} \times 12\frac{2}{5} \times 12\frac{2}{5}$ is given as $1912\frac{1}{5}$ instead of the correct value $1906\frac{78}{125}$.
49 Scamozzi shows the volume as $1437\frac{1}{2}$, although the computation of $\frac{4}{3}\pi r^3 = \frac{4}{3}\cdot\frac{22}{7}\cdot 7^3$ clearly leads to a fractional third.

larger than the circle, and the inscribed circle is too small. The square with the same area as the circle must lie somewhere between. A reasonable guess would be at the arithmetic mean. This is what Scamozzi does. The three squares have widths 15, 18, 21 with areas 225, 324 and 441. The circle has an area of 346½. This is not a good estimate for squaring the circle, but it represents a stage in the procedure for reaching such an estimate.[50] Also the three squares are in ratio 5 : 6 : 7 from which the ratios $\sqrt{4} : \sqrt{3}$ (7 : 6), $\sqrt{3} : \sqrt{2}$ (6 : 5), and $\sqrt{2} : \sqrt{1}$ (7 : 5) may be derived.[51] The scheme is an ingenious one and combines most of the previous attempts to resolve the Vitruvian proposal. It also reinforces the observation that geometry and arithmetic have priority over the anthropometric investigations of most contributors during a period of 150 years with the possible exception of Dürer's studies.

Fig. 5. Diagram from Scamozzi, *Idea dell'architettura universale*, Venice, 1615.

50 It might have been thought that Leonardo, who was obsessed with the problem of squaring the circle, was trying to represent a square equal to the area of the circle in his icon, but this is not so.

51 Squaring demonstrates these rational convergents: 4 : 3 is close to 49 : 36 (48 : 36), while 3 : 2 is close to 36 : 25 (36 : 24), and 2 : 1 is close to 49 : 25 (50 : 25).

FOUNDATION

XVIIIII

JUDAIC HERITAGE

Noah's Ark

'God said to Noah, "The loathsomeness of all mankind has become plain to me, for through them the earth is full of violence. I intend to destroy them, and the earth with them. Make yourself an ark with ribs of cypress; cover it with reeds and coat it inside and out with pitch. This is to be its plan: the length shall be three hundred cubits, its breadth fifty cubits, and its height thirty cubits.'[1] This statement is transformed through proportion by St Augustine into a model of the microcosm that is man.[2] The ark is proportioned 30 : 5 : 3. This patriarchal authority is noted by Alberti in relating the dimensions of what were to become established as the five orders of architecture.[3] The Tuscan, or Italic, order has a height which is related to its diameter as 6 : 1 (30 : 5), while the Composite order is 10 : 1 (30 : 3). Alberti then argues that the Ionic order is the mean of 10 and 6 at 8 : 1, and that the Doric is the mean between the Tuscan and Ionic at 7 : 1 while the Corinthian stands in the same relationship between the Ionic and Composite at 9 : 1.[4] The other significant ratio to be derived from God's design for the ark is 5 : 3.

Bezazel's Tabernacle

Bezazel, Moses told the Israelites, had been specially chosen to execute the Lord's design for the tabernacle and all its accoutrements. 'He has filled him with divine spirit, making him skillful and ingenious, expert in every craft, and a master of design ... He has inspired both him and Aholiab ... to instruct workers and designers of every kind .... Bezazel and Aholiab shall work exactly as the Lord has commanded....'[5] Their principal task was to make the components for the tabernacle, a nomadic sanctuary. The structure was a tent. The covering comprised an inner lining of ten finely woven linen hangings. 'The length of each hanging was twenty-eight cubits and the breadth four cubits, all of the same size. They joined five of the hangings together, and similarly the other five....'[6] They fastened the two hangings together 'and the Tabernacle became a single whole'.[7] Each hanging was proportioned 28 : 4 :: 7 : 1. One might speculate as to whether the perfect number 28 was knowingly used. Five joined together make a rectangular covering of 28 cubits to 20 cubits, the tell-tale *ad quadratum* ratio 7 : 5 for $\sqrt{2} : 1$.[8] When the two halves are joined the proportion of the whole covering is 40 : 28 :: 10 : 7,

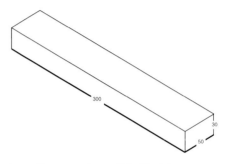

Fig. 1. The proportions of Noah's Ark.

1 Genesis 5: 6.13–16.
2 See 'Prisoners of Number', *supra*.
3 Alberti does not refer to St Augustine explicitly, but to 'the commentators of our sacred books'. Nor does he specifically mention the names of the two extreme orders in this discussion. J. Rykwert, N. Leach, R. Tavernor, *Leon Battista Alberti: On the Art of Building in Ten Books*, MIT Press, Cambridge, 1988, p. 309.
4 As Alberti writes, the ancients 'resorted ... to arithmetic' to determine the values between the extremes of 6 and 10. The Leone translation after Cosimo Bartoli's edition has the charming phrase 'vitious Extremes'. J. Rykwert ed., *Ten Books of Architecture by Leon Battista Alberti*, Alec Tiranti, London, 1953, p. 201.
5 Exodus 35: 30–35, 36: 1.
6 Exodus 36: 8–11.
7 Exodus 36: 13.
8 If this was actually made this way it places Plato's 'rational diagonal of the square' as common knowledge a millennium earlier. The written report of the Exodus, of course, is later than the time of Moses. For a recent discussion of dating and authorship, see R. E. Friedman, *Who Wrote the Bible?*, Summit Books, Simon & Schuster, New York, 1987.

9 Presumably the covering was made in two halves for ease of transport, but it is significant that each separate half is proportioned as the assembled whole.

10 Exodus 36: 14–19.

11 Each of the sloping sides of the tent – the sides of the triangle – would be 14-cubits long and hence the width of the groundplan – the hypotenuse – would be 20 cubits.

12 Pythagoras' theorem requires that $11^2 + 10^2 = 221$ and $15^2 = 225$ be equal. It is clearly a near miss.

13 1 Kings 7: 23–24. Outside Solomon's temple, the Sea of cast metal was 10 cubits wide and 'it took a line thirty cubits long to go around it'. This gives a value of $\pi = 3$ rather than the common and more accurate 22/7. The Rhind Mathematical Papyrus shows that the Egyptians had used a superior estimate for π as early as c1800BCE. The Chinese *Chóu-peë* uses the value 3 which was a value probably used as early as the twelfth-century BCE. As late as 628CE, the Hindu mathematician Brahmagupta used 3 as the 'practical' value.

14 Exodus 38: 9–16.

15 If $7 : 5$ is a rational surrogate for $\sqrt{2} : 1$, then $5 : 2$ stands for $1 : \sqrt{2} - 1$, which is equal to $1 + \sqrt{2} : 1$. This is an octagonal relation: the ratio of the width of an octagon between its sides to its side.

16 Exodus 36: 23. Each plank would have been about 18–20 inches (450–500 mm) wide and 15–17 feet (4.5–5.0m) long.

17 Exodus 36: 28. R. E. Friedman has reconstructed the tabernacle in quite another manner. There are several objections that can be raised against his reconstruction concerned with the manipulation of the dimensions of the inner lining (which he doubles in half to conform to his supposition about the acacia plank walls), and his neglect of the outer covering and how its dimensions might be accommodated. The long walls are not given any stability at the open end in Friedman's reconstruction, and it would seem that the proper place for the additional two planks would be at this end of the tabernacle. R. E. Friedman, 'The Tabernacle and the Temple', *Biblical Archaeologist* 43, 1980, also Friedman *op. cit.*, Chapter 10, 'The Sacred Tent', pp. 174–187. The problem with the reconstruction given here is that the Biblical account does not make any reference to the structural supports for the tent such as the ridge-pole. However, none of the subsequent conjectures undo the findings about the geometry of the inner and outer coverings themselves, no matter how they might have been deployed. Our proposal is similar to Le Corbusier's, with which architects will be familiar, shown in *Vers une Architecture Nouveau*, see J. Rykwert, *On Adam's House in Paradise*, MIT Press, Cambridge,1981, pp. 14–16.

18 Exodus 36: 31–34.

the conjugate value of $\sqrt{2} : 1$, which seems to confirm explicit appreciation of the properties $\sqrt{2}$.[9] This was the design of the inner lining of the tabernacle. The outer hangings were 'made of goats' hair, eleven in all, to form a tent over the Tabernacle; each hanging was thirty cubits long and four cubits wide, all eleven of the same size. They joined five of the hangings together and similarly the other six' and joined the two pieces together with fasteners 'to join up the tent and make it a single whole'.[10] One piece was proportioned $30 : 24 :: 5 : 4$ and the other piece had the ratio $30 : 20 :: 3 : 2$. Together the pieces made a whole in the ratio $44 : 30 :: 22 : 15$.

Given these ratios it seems a reasonable presumption that the inner covering, stretched over a ridge-pole, formed the sides of a 7, 7, 10 near-right isosceles triangle. This implies that the width of the ground plan below the covering was 20 cubits.[11] The proportion of the ground plan itself is then seen to be a double square 40-cubits long and 20-cubits wide. The outer covering was designed to extend beyond the inner lining. In length it extends an additional 2 cubits at both ends. In the width the sloping sides of the outer covering measure an additional 1 cubit. If the outer covering rests on the same ridge-pole as the inner lining then a 15, 11, 10 near-right triangle is implicated.[12] Note that the designers had arranged for the seams of the inner lining to be half overlapped by the seams of the outer covering.

The presence of 22 in these computations might suggest a circle relationship, but elsewhere the writer of the first Book of Kings confirms that a circle was considered to have a circumference just three times the diameter.[13] Instead it seems that Bezazel may have used an equilateral triangle to determine the dimensions of the outer covering. A rational equilateral triangle of base 60 cubits will be 52 cubits high. If a 30 cubit square (the width of the covering) is placed on the half base it will leave a length of 22 cubits. 30×22 cubits is exacly half of the outer covering. Further evidence that Bezazel was using what was later to be called *ad triangulum* comes from the observation that two 30-cubit equilateral triangles placed at either end of the outer covering overlap and precisely determine, rationally that is, the width of each of the hangings, 4 cubits. It truly suggests that these later masonic devices had Mosaic roots. The value for $\sqrt{3} : 1$ implied by Bezazel's design is $26 : 15$. This will be given the name Bezazel's ratio in future references.

The ground plan proportion of $2 : 1$ is reflected in the boundary to the court which was made from hangings of 'finely woven linen' and was 100-cubits long by 50-cubits wide.[14] On the East side of the court was the entrance. The hangings reached 15 cubits to the corners of the court either side of the entrance, making the entrance 20-cubits wide. The ratio of the width of the court to the entrance was thus $5 : 2$, the ratio achieved when a square is removed from a 7×5 rectangle. The ratio $5 : 2$ was later defined by Euclid as the separation of the ratio $7 : 5$.[15] The designer Bezazel appears to be using the ratios $2 : 1$, $\sqrt{2} : 1$ and $\sqrt{3} : 1$ to organize the principal components of the tabernacle: in fact, the numbers $\sqrt{1}$, $\sqrt{2}$, $\sqrt{3}$ and $\sqrt{4}$.

The walls of the tabernacle were built out of upright planks of acacia wood, 'each plank ten cubits long and a cubit and half wide'.[16] The planks were arranged 20 to each long side, 6 at the end and 2 'for the corners of the Tabernacle'.[17] The proportion of the walled part of the tabernacle under the tent is then $20 : 6$ in terms of plank units, $30 : 9$ in terms of cubits, and both equivalent to the root ratio $10 : 3$. This is half the ratio of each individual plank, $20 : 3$, so that plan and the elevational element are simple related architectonically. In fact, the Biblical description goes on to mention bars which joined the planks together at their midpoint, thus making the bottom and top half of the planks equal in ratio to the plan as a whole, $10 : 3$.[18]

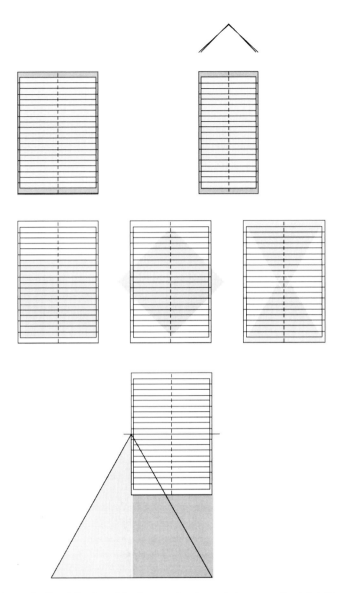

Fig. 2. The tabernacle. Top left, plan of the inner and outer coverings spread out flat. The outer rectangle is proportioned 22 : 15, the inner rectangle is 10 : 7. Top right, plan of the tent when erected giving a groundplan proportioned 2 : 1. The section of the tent showing inner and outer coverings is given above. Middle row: left, a square placed on the short edge of the inner lining; centre, the same square on the diagonal defines the length of the inner lining; right, equilateral triangles placed on the short edges of the outer covering intersect to define the width of each individual hanging. Bottom, an equilateral triangle and a square on the half base define the proportion of half of the external covering.

There is a play on combinations of the 5 : 3 ratio, the cross-sectional ratio of Noah's Ark. There may be support of a cabalistic kind in that the 30×9 cubit enclosure has at its core a $(30 - 8) \times (9 - 8) = 22 \times 1$ cubit rectangle which could possibly represent the number of letters in the Hebrew alphabet, and that the $20 + 6 = 26$ semi-perimeter of the enclosure measured in the number of planks is numerically

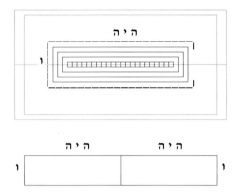

Fig. 3. Top, plan of the tabernacle showing the walled enclosure made of 20 vertical planks in length, 6 at one end and 2 to give stability at the entrance. Note that the 'core' of the 30 × 9 cubit enclosure is a 22 × 1 rectangle which may reflect the 22 letters of the Hebrew alphabet. The proportion of the enclosure spells out the Hebrew number-letters of God's name. Bottom, the individual planks double the proportion of the plan of the enclosure.

equivalent to the letters of **יהוה**.[19] It would surely have been appropriate for the tabernacle to have been blessed with God's name.[20] Read as numerals, the ratio **ה : י** is 10 : 5 :: 2 : 1 and the ratio **ו : י** is 10 : 6 :: 5 : 3 – two ratios which play a prominent part in Bezazel's design.[21]

Bezazel also designed the Ark of the Covenant and the altars. The Ark was 'a chest of acacia wood, two and a half cubits long, one cubit and a half wide, and one cubit and a half high'.[22] The Ark was proportioned 5 : 3 : 3, a play on the 5 : 3 ratio of the beam of Noah's ark. The cover for the Ark 'of pure gold, two and a half cubits long and one cubit and a half wide' was also in the ratio 5 : 3.[23] The acacia wood table was 'two cubits long, one cubit wide, and one cubit and a half high'.[24] That is to say, the length to height to width were in the arithmetic proportionality 4 : 3 : 2. Two other altars were the altar of incense whose proportions were square in plan and double square in elevation, 2 : 1 : 1, and the altar of full offering

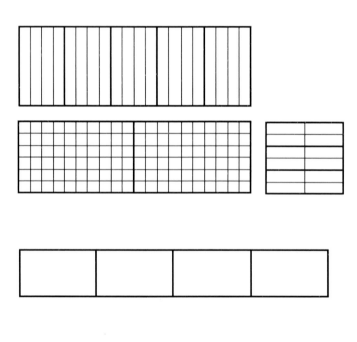

Fig. 4. The ratio 5 : 3 is a constituent of the main components of the tabernacle's enclosure. Top row, the long wall divides into five 5 : 3 rectangles. Second row, the plan is made from two 5 : 3 rectangles, and the end wall (shown turned on its side) from six. Third row, each plank is proportioned by four 5 : 3 rectangles. Bottom row, the 5 : 3 rectangle is easily constructed, with accuracy, using the 3, 4, 5 right triangle.

19 The number 22 also, in cubits, would be the width of the outer covering when erected as a tent. Its length, of course, is given as 2 × 22 = 44 cubits.
20 See *supra*, 'Occult Number'.
21 The Hebrew ratios are to be read from right to left. See text and footnote 42 below.
22 Exodus 37: 1.
23 Exodus 37: 6.
24 Exodus 37: 10.

which was square in plan but echoed, in elevation, the cross-section of Noah's Ark, 5 : 5 : 3.[25] All of these ratios and actual dimensions relate directly to the 3, 4, 5 right triangle which may well have been used to regulate the setting out of its individual components as well as the tabernacle as it was pitched during its travels.

Solomon's Temple

Four-hundred-and-eighty years after the Israelites had come out of Egypt, or so the scribe narrates, King Solomon began the building of 'the house of the Lord'.[26] The temple was 'sixty cubits long by twenty cubits wide, and its height was thirty cubits. The vestibule in front of the sanctuary was twenty cubits long, spanning the whole breadth of the house, while it projected ten cubits in front of the house. . . .'[27] The height of the colonnade to the vestibule was twenty cubits.[28] Solomon 'prepared an inner shrine in the furthest recesses of the house to receive the Ark of the Covenant of the Lord. This inner shrine was twenty cubits square and twenty cubits high. . . .'[29] The sanctuary before this inner shrine 'was forty cubits long'.[30]

There are four volumes to consider architectonically. On entry the vestibule is proportioned 2 : 2 : 1. The inner shrine is a cube, 1 : 1 : 1. The main volume of the temple is in the harmonic proportionality of 6 : 3 : 2. The sanctuary before the inner shrine is in the arithmetic proportionality 4 : 3 : 2. While the length of the sanctuary, 40 cubits, the length of the inner shrine, 20 cubits, and the depth of the vestibule, 10 cubits, are in the geometric proportionality 4 : 2 : 1, with the length of the inner shrine as the mean of the two extremes. The groundplan including the vestibule is 70-cubits long by 20-cubits wide, and the accessible area excluding the inner shrine is 50 × 20 cubits, the ratio of 5 : 2. The geometry of this plan is then quite intriguing. A square 50 cubits on each side has a rational diagonal of 70 cubits. The √2 : 1 ratio divides the inner sanctum from the whole. The length of the sanctuary itself, 40 cubits, is marked by the half base of an equilateral triangle of altitude 70 cubits. This implies the use of the 7 : 4 ratio for √3 : 1. The temple appears to be an example

Fig. 5. Left, the proportions of the Ark of the Covenant. Centre, the altar of full offering. Right, the acacia wood table.

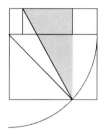

Fig. 7. The *parti* of the temple is generated by the geometry of the square and of the equilateral triangle.

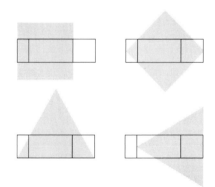

Fig. 8. Top row: left, a square based on the dimension from the front of the vestibule to the entrance to the inner shrine; right, the same square on the diagonal defines the full length of the temple. Bottom row: left, an equilateral triangle standing on the full width of the temple; right the same triangle rotated through a right angle defines the length of the temple that extends beyond the vestibule. The top row shows the *ad quadratum* relationship; the bottom row, the *ad triangulum*.

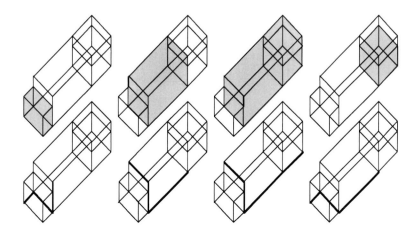

Fig. 6. The temple of Solomon. Top row: left, the vestibule; left centre, the sanctuary; right centre, the temple proper; right, the inner shrine. Bottom row: left, the arithmetic proportionality 3 : 2 : 1; left centre, the arithmetic proportionality 4 : 3 : 2; right centre, the harmonic proportionality 6 : 3 : 2; right, the geometric proportionality 4 : 2 : 1.

25 Exodus 37: 25 and 38: 1.
26 Solomon succeeded his father King David who died 960BCE. Solomon's reign lasted until 925BCE.
27 1 Kings 6: 1–4. Solomon flourished around 950BCE.

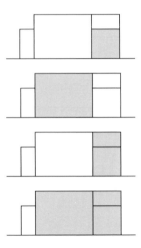

Fig. 9. The longitudinal section of the temple shows four 'consonant' proportions. Top, the inner shrine 1 : 1 (also the front elevation of the vestibule); below, the sanctuary 4 : 3; below again, the 'Most Holy Place' 3 : 2 (also the back elevation of the temple); bottom, the whole temple with the exception of the vestibule 2 : 1 (also the side elevation of the vestibule).

of the combined use of what was to become known as *ad triangulum* and *ad quadratum* proportioning. This is even clearer when a square is placed from the front of the vestibule to the front of the inner shrine. The diagonal of this same square then measures from the front of the vestibule to the back of the inner shrine. Similarly, an equilateral triangle based on the total length of the temple, when turned through 90° measures the length of the sanctuary and inner shrine combined. Certainly any mediaeval mason, or Renaissance architect, reading the Bible, would see these relationships and would appreciate the employment of the three traditional means: the arithmetic, the harmonic and the geometric. This structure built 400 years before Pythagoras also demonstrates in its elevational architectonics the four ratios of the 'musical' consonances usually attributed to him: namely the ratios 4 : 3, 3 : 2, 2 : 1, 1 : 1. Was music the source, or does architecture have priority over the origin of this tradition? Solomon practised in architecture what he preached about God's universe: order is brought about through number, weight and measure.[31] The evidence is lucent in the specifications of his architecture.

Solomon 'built the House of the Forest of Lebanon, a hundred cubits long, fifty broad, and thirty high, constructed of four rows of cedar columns, over which were laid lengths of cedar. It had a cedar roof, extending over the beams, which rested on the columns, fifteen in each row; and the number of beams was forty-five. . . . He made also the colonnade, fifty cubits long and thirty broad. . . .'[32] The ratio of the main volume is 10 : 5 : 3. In fact the size of the house was exactly one-sixth in length of Noah's ark. The plan of the colonnade and the cross-sections of both the ark and the house all share the ratio 5 : 3. But the layout of the columns is interesting. Four rows of cedar columns implies three intercolumniations and 3 into 50 does not lead to an aliquot division. In all there are 45 beams, meaning that there are 15 columns in each of the four rows and hence 14 intercolumniations in the length of the house. Fourteen does not form aliquot parts of 100. Assuming that the columns are equally distributed, each bay will be in proportion 50/3 : 100/14 or 7 : 3. Two adjacent bays would be in proportion 7 : 6, an *ad triangulum* relation. It means that an equilateral triangle may be placed on the length of one beam and the next but one beam would then be placed at the distance of the triangle's altitude. Even more it means that the Magen David may be inscribed in the plan of the house.[33] The symbolism is potent. It leads to speculations that the 45 beams and the 42 bays may have cabalistic significance even at this very early age. The Tetragrammaton and Moses' question 'What is the name of God?' have the same gematriot value 45. There is also the 42-letter name of God.[34] Whether or not his

28 2 Chronicles 3: 4.
29 1 Kings 6: 19, 20. The pilasters and the door posts at the entrance of the inner shrine were pentagonal.
30 1 Kings 6: 17.
31 Wisdom of Solomon 10: 20. It is interesting that the phrase 'thou has ordered all things in measure and number and weight' follows a lurid description of wild beasts, retribution and carnage. Yet the passage begins with Wisdom who 'prospered their works' while the godly nomads 'pitched tents' in the wilderness.
32 1 Kings 7: 2, 3, 6.
33 For a succinct history of the Magen David, known from the Bronze Age in many cultures and locations, see G. Scholem, *Kabbalah*, Dorset Press, New York, 1974, pp. 362–68.
34 See 'Occult Number', *supra*.

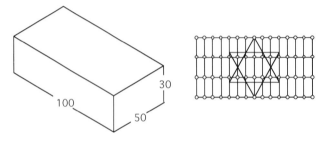

Fig. 10. The House of the Forest of Lebanon. Left, the cross-section is the same as Noah's Ark, but the length is one-sixth as long. Right, the groundplan and layout of columns and beams with the Magen David superimposed to indicate the underlying *ad triangulum* architectonic.

actual buildings were designed to the measurements stated by the scribes, their descriptions provide circumstantial evidence that gematria was in use when Solomon's achievements were recorded. The occurrence of Bezazel's ratio, with its Tetragrammaton connotations, in the design of the tabernacle takes the whole tradition back to Moses.

Ezekiel's Vision

The computations have clearly ignored the materiality of wall thicknesses and other corporalities. This is the architectonics of the ideal, of the written word. The actual execution of the building would involve compromise: the one is a mental artifice, the other is a physical artefact. Ezekiel's vision of a new temple is an ideal design, the description of which fired the imagination of the Jesuits Jeronimo Prado and Juan Bautista Villalpanda and had some connection with the design of the Escorial of Philip II.[35] Here only the temple will be examined not its elaborate precinct. As he is guided around the mountain top city, Ezekiel has in hand 'a chord of linen thread and a measuring rod. . . . The length of the rod which the man was holding was six cubits, reckoning by the long cubit which was one cubit and a hand's breadth'.[36] Having passed through gateways and courts, measuring all as he goes, Ezekiel arrived at the vestibule of the temple and measured 'the width of the gateway fourteen cubits and that of the corners of the gateway three cubits in each direction. The vestibule was twenty cubits long by twelve wide. . . .' Going into the sanctuary he found that the 'opening was ten cubits wide and its corners five cubits wide in each direction'. He measured the sanctuary 'its length; it was forty cubits, and its width twenty'. Then to the inner shrine, 'the Holy of Holies', the opening to which 'was six cubits, and the corners of the opening were seven in each direction'. Of the inner shrine itself, 'its length and its breadth were each twenty cubits'.[37]

The dimensions of the inner shrine and the sanctuary are those of Solomon's structure. The vestibule is widened to 12 cubits compared with Solomon's 10 cubits. This lengthens the temple to 12 + 40 + 20 = 72 cubits. The main difference in the descriptions is the care in which each opening is measured by Ezekiel – from the one into the vestibule, then the opening into the sanctuary and finally at the inner shrine. Each opening is set in a 20-cubit long wall. The description provides three distinct ways in which the 20 cubits may be divided. The vestibule opening may be represented 3 + 14 + 3, the sanctuary opening 5 + 10 + 5 and the opening to the inner shrine 7 + 6 + 7. The openings decrease in size towards the inner shrine in the arithmetic proportionality 7 : 5 : 3. The 7 : 5 ratio is a signal for *ad quadratum* organization and sure enough the dimensions of the vestibule sit comfortably within the traditional nested squares. A square spanning the vestibule (20 cubits), defines a square half its area which has sides equal to the opening into the vestibule (14 cubits). In turn, this square defines a smaller square which marks the opening into the sanctuary (10 cubits). The narrowing of the openings suggests a perspective effect. The geometry shows that the lines joining the edges of the openings intersect at a point 30 cubits inside the sanctuary and 10 cubits from the inner shrine, or 42 cubits from the front of the vestibule.

The 5 : 3 ratio is an early convergent to $\sqrt{3} : 1$. Two equilateral triangles span the vestibule *ad triangulum*. Another equilateral triangle with a base from the side wall to the opposite edge of the opening into the sanctuary may be used to define the

35 Ezekiel was exiled to Babylon after Nebuchadnezzar II burned Jerusalem in 581 BCE. The building of the Escorial, from 1563, is definitively presented in G. Kubler, *Building the Escorial*, Princeton University Press, Princeton, New Jersey, 1982. A good account of the Prado and Villalpanda reconstruction is given by J. Rykwert, *On Adam's House in Paradise*, MIT Press, Cambridge, 1981, pp. 120–40. G. Prado, J. B. Villalpanda, *In Ezechielem explanationes et apparatus Vrbis ac Templi Hiersolymitani: Commentariis et Imaginibvs Illvstratvs*, Zanetti, Rome, 1596–1604, especially Volume II.

36 Ezekiel 40: 3, 5.

37 Ezekiel 40: 48, 49 and 41: 1–4.

opening into the inner shrine when turned through a right angle. This triangle has a base of 15 cubits and a height of 13 cubits – Bezazel's ratio.

By stretching the temple to a length of 72 cubits, Ezekiel gives it the impress of the Tetragrammaton whose characters sum to 72:

$$
\begin{array}{cccc}
 & & & \text{י} \\
 & & \text{ה} & \text{י} \\
 & \text{ו} & \text{ה} & \text{י} \\
\text{ה} & \text{ו} & \text{ה} & \text{י}
\end{array}
$$

$$
\begin{array}{cccc}
 & & & 10 \\
 & & 5 & 10 \\
 & 6 & 5 & 10 \\
5 & 6 & 5 & 10
\end{array}
$$

As has already been observed the sum of the fourth line to the second line is the ratio 26 : 15, a convergent for $\sqrt{3} : 1$, while the sum of the third row to the second is 21 : 15, or 7 : 5, the rational surrogate for $\sqrt{2} : 1$. Ezekiel uses exactly both these convergents in the design. The point where the view lines intersect is 42 cubits into the temple. The name of God with 42 letters seems to be evoked.[38] The distance from the entrance to the inner shrine is 52 cubits which is the name of God in a trigonal number transformation $\triangle 5 + \triangle 6 + \triangle 5 + \triangle 1 = 15 + 21 + 15 + 1 = 52$.[39] Perhaps even more compelling is the fact that the dimensions of the entrance into the sanctuary would have been described using the Hebrew letters $\text{ה} + \text{י} + \text{ה}$, and of the opening to the inner shrine with the letter ו.[40] The name of God is definitely and unmistakably imprinted in Ezekiel's sanctuary. The names of the letters of the Tetragrammaton may be spelt out to obtain new values[41]

ה	הא	6 (1 + 5)
ו	וו	12 (6 + 6)
י	יוד	20 (4 + 6 + 10).

It will now be seen that the dimensions of the vestibule 20 cubits by 12 cubits are directly related to the letters forming God's name. Using these values יהוה sums to 44 (20 + 6 + 12 + 6), the length in cubits of the outer covering in Bezazel's design for the tabernacle. Further, the ratios 10 : 3, 5 : 3 and 2 : 1 which these names spell out, are the dominant proportions regulating the plans and planks of the tabernacle.[42]

The architectonics of Judaic architecture suggests that the deciphering of the numerical content of early Biblical literature may not be as delusional as the sceptic may otherwise think. In truth, the consistent employment of $\sqrt{2}$ and $\sqrt{3}$ surrogates in these Biblical accounts, and their encipherment in the Tetragrammaton, surely indicate remarkable architectonic achievement. An achievement which, knowingly or not, was to sustain and nourish western cultures for the next two millennia. The Hebrews did one remarkable thing: they wrote down the architectonic specifications of their most iconic buildings. The numbers are set in tablet and scroll, no longer in stone. There is no need for the archaeological measurement of sites and subsequent reconstructive interpretations. For Judaic architecture, in the ending is the word.

38 See 'Occult Number', *supra*.
39 The letter YOD י in the Tetragrammaton is frequently counted as 1 and not 10. Such transformations are a central feature of gematria.
40 The entrance to the sanctuary is measured in cubits with the Hebrew number-letter YOD י, or 10, which alone may stand for God. As Agrippa von Nettersheim records concerning 'Iod' – 'One Divine essence, the fountain of all virtues, and powers, whose name is expressed with one most simple letter'. H. C. Agrippa, *Three Books of Occult Philosophy*, trans 'J. F.', Gregory Moule, London, 1651, II, p. 176.
41 See the conversion table in 'Occult Number', *supra*.
42 The computation, shown *supra*, in which equilateral triangles define the width of the hangings in the tabernacle suggests that this may be so, since each of those triangles is 26-cubits high and that is the primary value of יהוה, 5 + 6 + 5 + 10. Even the division of the outer covering into two parts 24-cubits and 20-cubits long seems to be a bipartition of the encipherment 44 = (6 + 12 + 6) + (20).

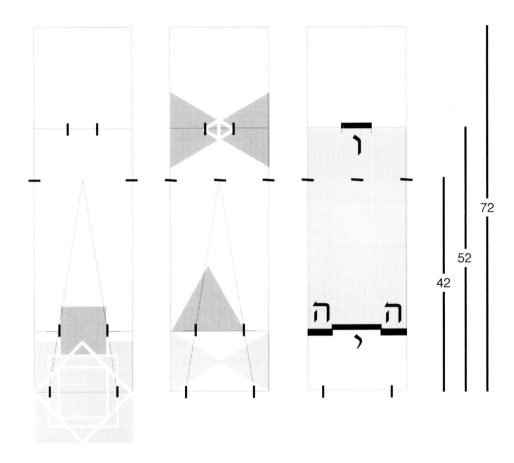

Fig. 11. Ezekiel's temple. Left, the *ad quadratum* organization of the entrance and the 'perspective' created by the entrances to establish a point in the sanctuary; centre, *ad triangulum* relationships; right, the dimensions of the opening in the sanctuary are marked with the name יהוה and the key longitudinal measurements of the temple reflect the use of gematria.

XX

GREEK EXPERIENCE

Temples at Silenus

In describing Greek temples, Vitruvius specifies the number of columns along the side and the number at the ends.[1] Vitruvius counts the corner columns twice. For the peripteral these numbers are 11 and 6, and for the pseudodipteral 15 and 8. The formula appears to be $4n-1$ and $2n$. Vitruvius does not give the number of columns along the sides of the dipteral for which there are 8 columns at each end, or the hypaethral with 10. Using the formula, it might be inferred that there are 15 and 19 columns, respectively, along each side in these two forms of temple. Given the written description of Vitruvius, how might someone reconstruct the arrangement of such a temple? One way would be to imagine a rectangular mesh divided into squares. The columns would be placed in the centre of each of the perimeter squares. This may even be how the original designers conceived of their schemes. Such schemata would allow subsequent adjustments to be made in the positioning of the columns within the mesh, such as making the intercolumniations at the corners somewhat less than in the middle, or increasing the intercolumniation in the centre of the end elevations. Three pairs of numbers are then involved: one pair describes the dimension of the outer rectangle for the mesh, the 'platform'; one pair describes the number of columns on the perimeter of the pteron; and one gives the dimensions of the number of intercolumniations. These three number pairs (ratios) are clearly related:

$$p + 1 : q + 1$$
$$p : q$$
$$p - 1 : q - 1.$$

The Vitruvian formula gives the proportion of the intercolumniations – sides to ends – as 2 : 1, but actual Greek temples rarely conform to the Vitruvian descriptions. Early Doric structures at Silenus in Sicily have column ratios of 17 : 6, 13 : 6, 17 : 8 and one, most exceptionally, has an even number of columns along the sides and at the ends, 14 : 6, or a ratio of 7 : 3.[2] None of these ratios agree with the Vitruvian models. Later structures such as the Parthenon, has a 17 : 8 arrangement, while the uncompleted hypaethral Temple of Apollo at Didyma has a 21 : 10 arrangement of columns, not the 19 : 10 prescribed by Vitruvius.[3] Architects who relied on the Vitruvian description alone would in many cases not be following Greek practice.

1 Vitruvius III ii 5–8. F Granger, *Vitruvius: De Architectura*, Harvard University Press, Cambridge MA, 1931, pp. 168–71.
2 A. W. Lawrence, *Greek Architecture*, Penguin Books, Harmondsworth, 1957 pp. 121–23.
3 *Ibid.*, pp. 202–6.

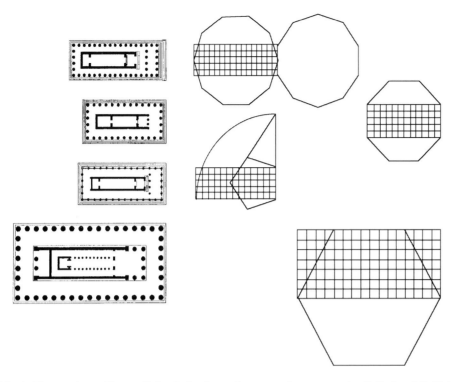

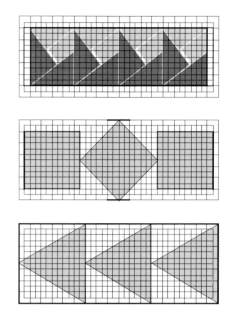

Fig. 2. Temple C at Silenus. Top row, the inner mesh is defined by the repeated application of the 3, 4, 5 right triangle to define a 16 by 5 rectangle. Second row, *ad quadratum* relationships. Bottom row, *ad triangulum* relationships.

Fig. 1. The temples at Silenus, Sicily. Left column, from top to bottom, temples C, D, F and G. Right, the temples related to the geometries of regular polygons.

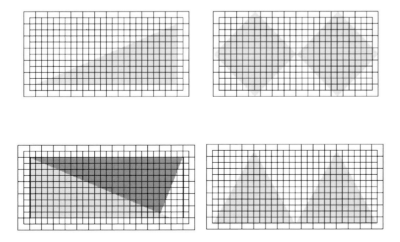

Fig. 3. Temples D and F at Silenus. Top row, left to right temple D, the 5, 12, 13 right triangle defines a 12 by 5 rectangle, and the double square. Bottom row, temple F, the 5, 12, 13 right triangle defines a 13 by 5 rectangle, and an *ad triangulum* rectangle.

125

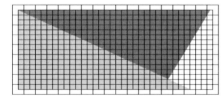

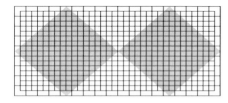

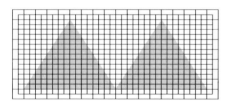

Fig. 4. Temple G at Silenus. Top, a 8, 15, 17 right triangle defines a 17 by 8 rectangle. Centre, a double square. Bottom, an *ad triangulum* rectangle. Note that this later temple combines the *ad quadratum* and the *ad triangulum* arrangements of temples D and F. This becomes the underlying architectonics for the Parthenon.

4 Apart from the octave, 2 : 1, the only other ratio which might have a musical connection is 15 : 8 although this does not seem to have any significance in Greek musical theory. Archytas, about 430–365BCE, might have recognized this ratio as the interval between the *nete* and the enharmonic *lichanos*.

5 Plato was born 20 years after the Parthenon was started in 427BCE, and Socrates whose knowledge Plato reports was 22-years old. It is known that Plato travelled to Sicily several times to visit the Pythagorean community at Tarentum. W. Burkert, *Lore and Ancient Pythagoreanism*, Harvard University Press, Cambridge MA, 1972, p. 201. It seems entirely plausible that persons responsible for the design of the Parthenon would also have made similar, but earlier, journeys, and have taken note of temple G at Silenus as an exemplar to be refined and surpassed.

Little is known about actual experience of Greek building in the Renaissance, and therefore just how influential their works were, or might have been.

The Sicilian Doric temples at Silenus were built in the sixth century BCE. They are usually identified by single letters. The pteron of temple C is 17 : 6; that of temple D is 13 : 6; temple F, 14 : 6; and temple G, 17 : 8, the arrangement to be found later in the Parthenon. Apart from temple F, the pterons at Silenus had columns arranged $4n + 1$ in length by $2n$ in width for values of $n = 3, 4, 5$, and this formula holds for the Temple of Apollo at Didyma, as well as the Parthenon. While in certain cases a distant musical analogy might be made, it seems very evident that architects practised an autonomous art.[4] Large structures had to be laid out. How might that have been done?

Taking the three ratios recognized above, the Silenius temples D and F have ratios 14 : 7, 13 : 6, 12 : 5 and 15 : 7, 14 : 6, 13 : 5 respectively. Now the last of these ratios, in each case, may be associated with the 5, 12, 13 right triangle and this would certainly enable the innermost meshes to be set up correctly. In the case of temple D the 'platform' is a double square, but for temple F the columns are centred on a rectangle defined by two equilateral triangles – using the 7 : 6 rational convergent for $\sqrt{4} : \sqrt{3}$. The three ratios associated with temple C are 18 : 7, 17 : 6, 16 : 5. The innermost mesh could be surveyed using the 3, 4, 5 right triangle repeatedly. The outer mesh may be inscribed with three equilateral triangles using the same rational convergent for temple F. There is also a potential *ad quadratum* relationship in this design employing the 7 : 5 rational convergent for $\sqrt{2} : 1$.

Temple G at Silenus, almost certainly the latest, looks forward to the architectonics of the Parthenon.[5] Both temples share the same column arrangement for the pteron, 17 : 8. The ratio 17 : 8 may be derived directly from the 8, 15, 17 right triangle. The rectangle circumscribing the 'platform' is a double square, 18 : 9; while two equilateral triangles may be inscribed in the inner rectangle of the mesh using the rational convergent 8 : 7 for $\sqrt{4} : \sqrt{3}$. The temples at Silenus suggest the use of right triangles for setting out the main elements of the plan, and also indicate that *ad quadratum* and *ad triangulum* relationships may have been a consideration in the architectonic design.

The ratio of intercolumniations of temple D, 12 : 5, suggest an octagonal relation since this ratio is a rational convergent for $1 + \sqrt{2} : 1$. The double equilateral triangles of temple G suggest a rational hexagonal relation. Is it possible that the other temples have polygonal associations. The intercolumniation ratio, 13 : 5, of temple F suggests a rational pentagonal relation. The ratio for temple C, 16 : 5, fits a rational decagon. The last two examples, make use of the rational convergents, 8 : 5 and 13 : 8, for the extreme and mean ratio $\tau : 1$.[6] Could lost Greek writings on temples have made such suggestions? If so, could this tradition, if it ever existed, be the source of Alberti's references to hexagonal, octagonal and decagonal temples? Is this why Vitruvius is so keen to distinguish between signifiers and signifieds at the beginning of his treatise which is generally presumed to have leaned heavily on Greek scripts which he had access to, but we do not?[7] The corporeal temple is rectangular, its mental progenitor is polygonal?

Temple of Apollo at Bassae

The hexastyle temple of Apollo at Bassae has a 15 : 6 pteron.[8] The 'platform' may be inscribed with the 8 : 7 equilateral triangle, while *ad quadratum* (7 : 5) relations define the inner and outer meshes. The three ratios for the later hypaethral temple of Apollo at Didyma are 20 : 9, 21 : 10, 22 : 11.[9] The 21 by 10 rectangle may be

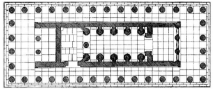

Fig. 5. The temple of Apollo at Bassae.

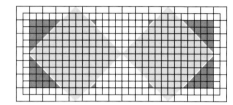

Fig. 6. The temple of Apollo at Bassae. Top, repeated applications of the 3, 4, 5 right triangle defines the column spacing, 15 : 6. Bottom, an *ad quadratum* arrangement.

precisely set out using the 20, 21, 29 right triangle since the ratio 21 : 10 is equivalent to (21 + 21):20. The 'platform' is a double square, and the inner mesh is 20 : 9, or a rectangle based on the rational diagonal of a double square, $\sqrt{5} : 1$.

Temple of Apollo at Didyma

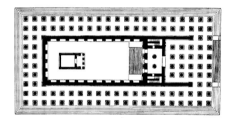

Fig. 7. The temple of Apollo at Didyma.

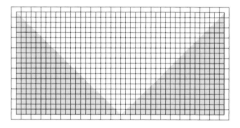

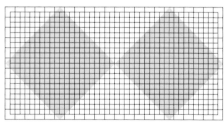

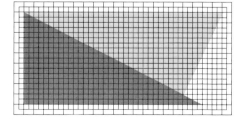

Fig. 8. The temple of Apollo at Didyma. Top, the 20, 21, 29 right triangle defines the column centres. Centre, a double square. Below, a rectangle defined by the diagonal of a double square, $\sqrt{5} : 1$.

6 The ratio 13 : 5 is a rational convergent for $\tau^2 : 1$ which may be derived from the pentagon. The isosceles triangle based on one side of the pentagon with its apex at the opposite vertex of the pentagon has sides in proportion to its base as $\tau : 1$. If the base is added to a side of the triangle the length $\tau + 1 = \tau^2$ is obtained by the extreme and mean relationship. This same isosceles triangle forms a tenth slice of the decagon, its sides correponding to the radius of the circumscribing circle. The diameter of the circle, and therefore the decagon, is twice the radius, and the ratio of the decagonal side to the diameter of the decagon is seen to be $2\tau : 1$. Substituting the rational convergent 8 : 5 for $\tau : 1$ gives 16 : 5.

7 Vitruvius I.i.3. See G. Hersey, *Pythgorean Palaces: Magic and Architecture in the Italian Renaissance*, Cornell University Press, Ithaca NY, 1976, pp. 21–25.

8 Joseph Rykwert discusses Ictinus' Doric order in this temple, *The Dancing Column: On Order in Architecture*, MIT Press, Cambridge MA, 1996, pp. 338–40.

9 Designed by Paionios of Ephesus and Daphnis of Miletus in the third century BCE, the temple was still under construction at the beginning of the Christian era. It was never completed. The actual 'blueprint' for the design has been carefully researched by L. Haselberger, 'The Construction Plans for the Temple of Apollo at Didyma', *Scientific American*, 253.6, December 1985, pp. 126–32.

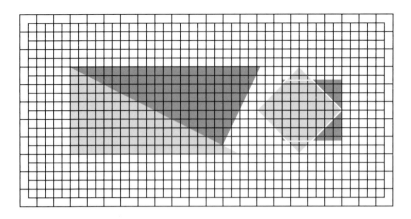

Fig. 9. The temple of Apollo at Didyma. Key elements of the inner sanctum and courtyard are defined by the diagonal of the double square and other *ad quadratum* relationships.

The Parthenon

The Parthenon was constructed from 447 to 438 BCE. What has been called here the rectangle of the inner mesh is in the ratio 16 : 7, proportioned by two rational equilateral triangles each 8 : 7. Architectonically, the same inner mesh defines the position of the dividing wall between the naos and the adytum, simultaneously *ad quadratum* (10 : 7) from the porch and *ad triangulum* (8 : 7) from the opisthodomus, a witful combination of the two world-making systems which awaited the arrival of Plato to recount in the following century. The 7 by 7 square, based on the intercolumniation of the portico, also marks the position of the pedestal for Phidias' chryselephantine Athena. The proportions of the naos and of the adytum are $\sqrt{2} : 1$ and $\sqrt{4} : \sqrt{3}$ respectively giving a square root transformation of the four numbers of the tetraktys, $\sqrt{1}$, $\sqrt{2}$, $\sqrt{3}$, $\sqrt{4}$. These are schematic positionings which the practicalities of construction compromise: this is the mental architecture of conception, not the physical issue of execution. The adjustments of physical necessity are clearly seen in the corner detailing of both the temple of Apollo at Bassae and the Parthenon where the regular conceptual meshes undergo shifts and ruptures visible in the paving

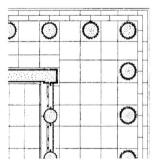 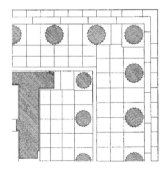

Fig. 10. Corners of the temple of Apollo at Bassae (left) and the Parthenon (right) showing the irregularities in the paving of the stylobate and a more regular pattern in two steps of the crepidoma.

of the stylobate to accommodate practical needs and refinements.[10] Surely this is one reason for Plato's admiration for the pure Idea and his anxieties about the corruptibility of the corporeal: architects, like Ictinus and Callicrates, had had to contend with this dilemma on each occasion of the designing and building process.[11]

The Parthenon, dedicated to Athena the goddess of Wisdom, may well be a mathematical text.[12] Consider approaching the temple from a corner. Twenty-three columns will present themselves to view without obstruction. There are two obvious parsings of these 23 columns. One parsing sees 16 columns along the side and 8 columns in front – a ratio of 2 : 1. Another parsing sees 17 columns along the side and 7 across the front – a ratio of 17 : 7.[13] The meaning of this becomes clearer when the total number of unobstructed columns is measured against those along the side – a ratio of 24 : 17. This is an excellent rational convergent to $\sqrt{2} : 1$, and 17 : 7 is seen to be the ratio $1 : \sqrt{2} - 1$, or as more commonly expressed, $1 + \sqrt{2} : 1$. These are ratios associated with the geometry of the octagon, the latter being the ratio of the chord length to the side of a regular octagon. The often-called 'Plato's problem' of the diagonal of the square had already been cast in stone in the century before his writing *Meno* and Book VIII of the *Republic*.[14] Ictinus' columns broadcast a better rational convergent than Plato's 7 : 5. That this was intentional on the designer's part becomes even more compelling when the ratio of all the external columns, including the 12 prostyle columns in the porch and the opisthodomus, are compared with the columns of the pteron. The ratio here is 29 : 23, a remarkably good rational convergent for $\sqrt[3]{2} : 1$, and an excellent practical solution to the God-given Delic problem.[15] Inside the adytum, the original Parthenon, or room of the virgin Athena, there are 4 columns on the ground, and another four above them – 2^2 and 2^3. Thus the Parthenon exhibits

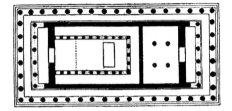

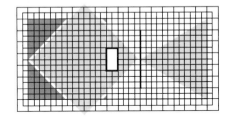

Fig. 11. The Parthenon. Schematic showing the combined use of *ad quadratum* and *ad triangulum* to define the wall dividing the naos from the adytum, and the location of the pedestal for the statue of Athena.

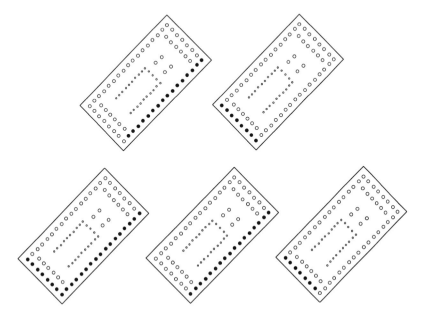

Fig. 12. The Parthenon. The arithmetic parsing of unobstructed columns viewed on an angle. Top row, 16 side columns to 8 across the front, a ratio of 2 : 1. Bottom row, 24 columns to 17 side columns, a ratio of 24 : 17, a rational covergent for $\sqrt{2} : 1$, and 17 side columns to 7 front columns, a ratio of 17 : 7, a rational convergent for the octagonal relation $1 + \sqrt{2} : 1$.

10 The lower steps of the crepidoma in these two cases show more regularity than the stylobate, and hint at the physical presence of the meshes discussed here.

11 This seems to be the import of Vitruvius' distinction between '*quod significat*' and '*quod significatur*', the building as signifier, and its description as the signified: one the '*praxis*' and the other '*theoria*'. Vitruvius I.i.3.

12 For a recent discussion of the Parthenon, see *The Parthenon: And its Impact on Modern Times*, Harry N. Abrams, New York, 1996, in particular M. Korres 'The Architecture of the Parthenon' pp. 54–97.

13 Ernest Flagg notes that for the Parthenon 'the key number was seven'. E. Flagg, *Le Naos du Parthenon*, Charles Scribner's Sons, New York, 1928, p. 23.

14 Plato's figure pictures a square with another square on the diagonal touching the midpoints of the sides, *Meno* 84d. The ratio 7 : 5 is implied in *Republic* VIII 546b–d.

15 *Supra*, 'Inexpressible Proportion'. The computation gives $29^3 = 24389$, $2 \times 23^3 = 24334$ which is in error by just over 0.2%.

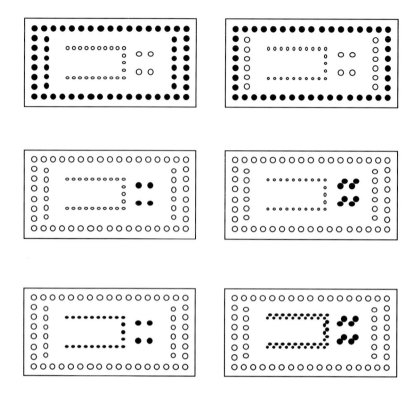

Fig. 13. The Parthenon. The arithmetic parsing of columns in plan. Top row, the ratio 29 : 23, a good rational covergent to $\sqrt[3]{2}$: 1. Middle row, the columns in the adytum: four, or 2^2, on the groundplan, and eight, or 2^3, on the two level. Bottom row, the internal columns number 27 on the ground, or 3^3, and this number is doubled in elevation.

beautiful transformations of the feminity of the dyad: $2^{1/3}$, $2^{1/2}$, 2^2, 2^3. Taking all the columns and piers into account on the plan of the naos and the adytum, there are in number $27 - 3^3$. This number is doubled by a second story of columns. Surely this is an unresolved evocation of the Delic problem of doubling of the cube.

Finally, did the architects attempt a solution of the third great classical problem involving the squaring of the circle? It is customary in classical arithmetic to imagine numbers as geometrical figures and to develop number series by the recursive addition of a gnomon. The outer mesh of the Parthenon is 18 : 9, a double square of area 162. Such a rectangle may be generated by the addition of gnomons from a 10 by 1 rectangle, which is very significant in its own right given the potent symbolism of the monad and the decad. The identity $10 + 12 + 14 + 16 + 18 + 20 + 22 + 24 + 26 = 162$ would be evident to a classical arithmetician. The last gnomon is valued at 26. Half the number of columns is 23. The ratio 26 : 23 is a very good estimate for squaring the circle – the square has a side length of 23 and the circle a diameter of 26.[16] This last computation may be stretched, especially to later Aristotelians who would object to the mixed categories, but in no way would its rejection undermine the previous observations. The generation of the rectangular 'platform' from its source in the monad and decad remains a powerful notion.

Does the architectonics of the Parthenon speak in other ways? Like Hebrew, the Greek language used letters of the alphabet to stand for numbers. Every word had

16 The radius of the circle is 13, using the rational convergent 22/7 for π, the area of the circle is $22 \times 13^2/7 = 3718/7$. The area of the square is 529. Compare $7 \times 529 = 3703$ with 3718. The error is close to 0.4%.

its pythmen, a number derived by adding together the numerical values of the letters in the word.[17] Is it a coincidence that the ideal area of the 'platform' as computed above, 162, is the number of Athena's other name Pallas – $\Pi\alpha\lambda\lambda\alpha\varsigma = 80 + 1 + 30 + 30 + 1 + 20 = 162$. By keeping the numbers within the decad, $\Pi\alpha\lambda\lambda\alpha\varsigma = 8 + 1 + 3 + 3 + 1 + 2 = 18$, which reduces to 9, like 162, when nines are cast out. The platform represents the enigmatic equation $\Pi\alpha\lambda\lambda\alpha\varsigma \times \Pi\alpha\lambda\lambda\alpha\varsigma = \Pi\alpha\lambda\lambda\alpha\varsigma$, or $18 \times 9 = 162$. There may well be other number-letter games, but speculation on this is hampered by the different spellings of Athena's name. Which would the designers have used? It may be no accident that the common root of all but the Doric form is $A\theta\eta\nu = 1 + 9 + 8 + 5 = 23$, a number which features not only in the 2×23 columns of the pteron, but also in the 23 groundplan columns and corner piers of the naos.[18] Nor may it be a coincidence that the total number of columns in the structure is 112 which is the area of the 16×7 rectangle defined by the intercolumniations.[19] The number $16 = 10 + 6$ reduces to the pythmen $1 + 6 = 7$, so that in a sense, the intercolumniations read in classical Greek as the square of seven. Recall that a 7 by 7 square determines the location of Athena's statue inside the cella. Athena was called the Hebdomad, the number seven.[20]

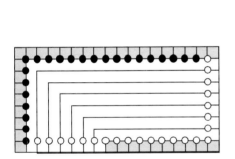
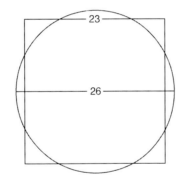

Fig. 14. The Parthenon. In the classical manner, the 18×9 platform may be generated from a 10×1 rectangle by successive gnomons, the last of which is 26. Half the number of columns in the pteron is 23. The ratio 26 : 23 is good rational estimate for squaring the circle.

17 Strictly speaking, a pythmen reduces the tens and the hundreds in Greek numeration to their unit equivalents. Thus $\kappa = 20$ is reduces to 2, $\tau = 300$ to 3, and so on. *Supra*, 'Occult Number'.

18 H. G. Liddell and R. Scott, *Greek-English Lexicon*, Oxford University Press, Oxford, 1996, gives five different spellings. One Attic spelling is $A\theta\eta\nu\alpha\iota\alpha$. The pythmenes $1 + 9 + 8 + 5 + 1 + 1 + 1$ sum to 26, the final gnomon of the 'platform'.

19 This observation accords with views expressed by George Hersey, *op. cit.*, who is inclined to imagine a rectangular array of columns from which some are deleted. In the case of the Parthenon, the columns are relocated without diminishing the number.

20 According to T. L. Heath *A History of Greek Mathematics*, Clarendon Press, Oxford, 1921, I, pp. 116–17, the use of the pythmen originated with the Pythagoreans. This would place the practice earlier than the building of the Parthenon. A late reference to 'the hebdomad Athena' is Plutarch fl.100CE. J. Gwyn Griffiths, *Plutarch's De Iside et Osiride*, University of Wales Press, Cambridge, 1970, [10, 354f] pp. 132–33. Recall that seven was understood to be a virgin number, *supra*, 'Theological Number', and Athena was *parthenos*, a virgin.

XXI

ROMAN WONDERS

Basilica at Fano

Vitruvius describes one building in detail. A basilica which he designed for the Julian Colony at Fano.[1] Vitruvius gives this written description:

> Its proportions and harmonies are as follows: There is a vaulted nave between the columns 120 feet long and 60 broad. The aisle between the columns of the nave and the outside wall, is 20 feet wide. The columns are of unbroken height, including the capitals, of 50 feet with a diameter of 5 feet. Behind them adjoining the aisle are pilasters 20 feet high, 2½ feet wide and 1½ feet thick. These carry the beams under the flooring. Above, there are pilasters 18 feet high, 2 feet wide and 1 foot thick, which take the beams which carry the principals of the main roof, and the roofs of the aisles which are lower than the vaulting of the nave. The space which remains in the intercolumniations, above the pilasters and below the tops of the columns, admits the necessary lighting. In the width of the nave counting the angle columns right and left, there are four columns at each end. On the side adjoining the forum, there are eight, including the angle columns. On the other side there are six, including the angle columns. The two columns in the middle are omitted, so as not to obstruct the view of the pronaos of the Temple of Augustus which is situated in the middle of the side wall of the basilica and faces the middle of the forum and the Temple of Jupiter. The tribunal which is in the former temple, is in the shape of the segment of a circle. The width of the segment in front is 46 feet; its depth is 15 feet; so that those who come before the magistrates may not interfere with persons on business in the basilica.

Most commentators have made attempts to reconstruct this building from Vitruvius' written description. Such reconstructions involve some calculations, and it is most likely that Palladio would have carried through such computations in reconstructing the basilica at Fano described by Vitruvius and illustrated by him in Barbaro's commentaries.[2]

The nave is 120×60 *pedes*, a double square. 120 *pedes* is 1 *actus*, so that the area of the nave is *actus quadratus*. These dimensions derive from basic surveying

1 Vitruvius V i 6–10. F. Granger trans, *Vitruvius: De Architectura*, Harvard University Press, Cambridge MA, 1931, I pp. 258–61.
2 D. Barbaro, *M Vitrvvii Pollionis De Architectura Libri Decem, Cvm Commentariis . . .* Venice, 1567, pp. 163–68.

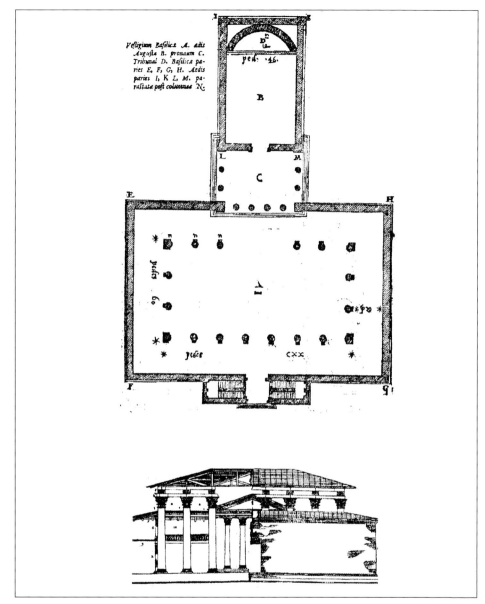

Fig. 1. Basilica at Fano. Plan, half elevation and half section of the Barbaro/Palladio reconstruction of the Vitruvius' design.

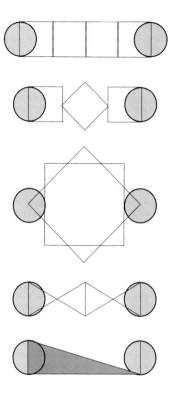

Fig. 2. Basilica at Fano. Reconstructions of the intercolumniations. Top, the intercolumniation at the ends is commensurable with the column diameter. Below, three different interpretations of the longitudinal intercolumniation. First, 7 + 10 + 7, the *ad quadratum* theme employing the 10 : 7 rational convergent; second an *ad quadratum* arrangement using the 24 : 17 rational convergent. Third, an *ad triangulum* configuration in which the 7 : 6 rational convergent for √4 : √3 is used. Bottom, the 7, 24, 25 right triangle exactly determines the longitudinal centre-to-centre dimensions with respect to the column diameter as module.

measures.[3] The number 120 = 1.2.3.4.5 is rich in aliquot parts: sixtieths, fortieths, thirtieths, twentieths, fifteenths, twelfths, tenths, eighths, sixths, fifths, fourths, thirds, and halves. But Vitruvius does not exploit this divisibility in setting out his plan. There is an aisle 20 *pedes* wide around the nave. The dimensions to the outer walls are thus 20 + 120 + 20 = 160 *pedes* and 20 + 60 + 20 = 100 *pedes* which evoke the earlier statement by Vitruvius concerning the special qualities of numbers 16, 10, and 6 (60 *pedes* for the width of the nave).[4] It is clear from these particular quantities that the measures must necessarily be taken to the centre line of the columns. Computations may then be made to determine the intercolumniations.[5]

3 O. A. W. Dilke, *Reading the Past: Mathematics and Measurements*, University of California/British Museum, 1987, pp. 26–27.
4 Vitruvius III i 8. Granger, *op. cit.*, I, pp. 164–65.
5 It seems from Palladio's drawing that he may have taken the measurement to the insides of the columns, which for reasons that will unfold does not seem correct.

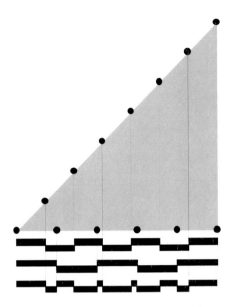

Fig. 3. Basilica at Fano. The 7 : 5 near-right triangle permits the division of a line into five and seven equal parts. The polyrhythmic division is the result of combining a divison of 5 with one of 7 — 5 + 2 + 3 + 4 + 1 + 5 + 1 + 4 + 3 + 2 + 5. This sums to $7 \times 5 = 35$.

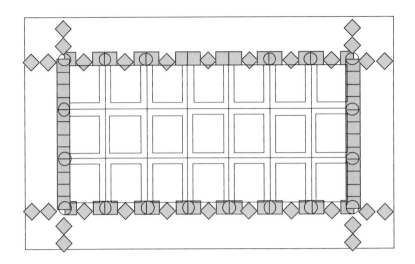

Fig. 4. Basilica at Fano. The main hall set out *ad quadratum*.

Palladio appears to accept that the central intercolumniation on each side is not differentiated. The equations are, for the long side, eight column diameters plus seven intercolumniations of equal length between centres plus one column diameter; and for the short side, four column diameters plus three intercolumniations of equal width between centres plus one column diameter. Let x be the intercolumniation in the length of the nave, and y be the intercolumniation in the width. The equations are, for the length:

$$8.5 + 7x = 120 + 5$$
$$7x = 85$$

whence

$$x = 12\frac{1}{7}.$$

For the width,

$$4.5 + 3y = 60 + 5$$
$$3y = 45$$

whence

$$y = 15.$$

Palladio's drawing indicates this difference in intercolumniations in length and width. The intercolumniations in length are puzzling: an aliquot division of 120 *pedes* might have been expected. However, the ratio of column diameter to intercolumniation is $12\frac{1}{7} : 5 :: 17 : 7$. Further, $17 + 7 = 24$, and it will be recalled that a

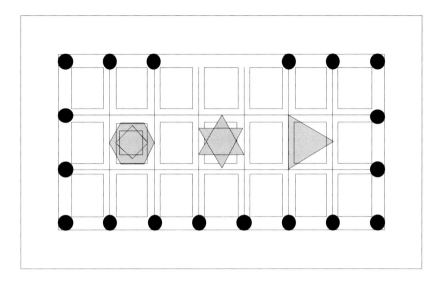

Fig. 5. Basilica at Fano. The ceiling coffers are determined by two distinct intercolumniations, one commensurable with the column diameter and the other incommensurable. They produce *ad triangulum* relations in the dimensioning of the coffers and beams.

rational convergent to √2 : 1 is 24 : 17, a convergent used later by Palladio in two of the rooms in the city house for Antonini.[6] The relationship of the intercolumniation along the length of the nave at Fano to the centre to centre distance between columns is thus seen to be *ad quadratum*. In the width, the equivalent relationship is 4 : 3. The sequence of convergent ratios leading to 24 : 17 is 2 : 1, 4 : 3, 10 : 7, 24 : 17, . . ., so that the 4 : 3 ratio in width of the centre to centre dimension with the intercolumniation is seen to have a familial relationship with the ratio 24 : 17 along the length through this process of convergence. The intermediate convergent 10 : 7, mentioned by Vitruvius as a discovery of Plato, is also apparent in the 7 + 10 + 7 longitudinal theme of columns and their spacing, proportional to the *ad quadratum* 1 + √2 + 1.[7]

This is one interpretation. Another arises from the observation that 12 : 7 is a good rational proxy for √3 : 1, and it is seen that four equilateral triangles, with bases the diameter of the column, span from centre to centre. The rational convergent 7 : 6 is employed here for the ratio of base to height of an equilateral triangle. The intercolumniations are then measured 6 + 6 + 6 + 6 in length, and 7 + 7 + 7 + 7 in width, potentially generating a triangular grid for the floor plan which might then have been laid out with hexagonal pavers.[8] Projecting the coffering across the nave from the columnar locations reinforces this reconstruction since the coffers appear to have *ad triangulum* proportions related to the equilateral triangle and the hexagon. A 7, 24, 25 right triangle exactly determines the centre-to-centre spacing of the longitudinal columns with respect to the diameter of the columns as module. The nave is a double square which means that a right isosceles triangle may be placed in one half. Roman surveyors are known to have used the Platonic convergent 7 : 5 for the ratio of the sides of such a triangle to its hypotenuse, and illustrated in Barbaro.[9] Thus a division of the length of the nave into sevenths, even though

6 Palladio II.4–5. R. Tavernor, R. Schofield, *Andrea Palladio: the Four Books on Architecture*, MIT Press, Cambridge MA, 1997, pp. 80–81. The ratio 24 : 17 is also the one explicated in the Parthenon, but there is no need to leap to conclusions. This tradition appears to be a longstanding one, probably involving the oral transmission of practical knowledge across generations and cultures as well as the constant renewal and rediscovery of the same information.
7 Vitruvius IX Preface 5. Granger, *op. cit.*, II, pp. 200–201.
8 *Supra*, 'Inexpressible Proportion.
9 *Op. cit.*, p. 270. Also see D. J. Watts, C. M. Watts 'A Roman Apartment Complex', *Scientific American*, 255.6, December 1986, pp. 132–39. They discuss the employment of rational convergents for √2 : 1 in Roman apartment construction and design.

not an aliquot division, is a simple projection of unit divisions along the hypotenuse of this right isosceles triangle. In fact, this particular process divides the length into fourteenths from which the seven centre lines for the columns along the length of the nave are easily determined. The surveyor needs no such device to set out the centre lines of the columns at each end of the nave where the diameter of the column is applied directly as module.

Is Vitruvius' basilica at Fano a description of an actual building, or a project – does it report on a signifier, or is itself the signified? There is something uncommon about the arithmetical structure of Vitruvius' name. Setting out the number equivalents of the Latin alphabet produces the following results:[10]

M	3	30	V	2	200	P	6	60
A	1	1	I	9	9	O	5	50
R	8	80	T	1	100	L	2	20
C	3	3	R	8	80	L	2	20
V	2	200	V	2	200	I	9	9
S	9	90	V	2	200	O	5	50
			I	9	9			
			V	2	200			
			S	9	90			

26		**44**		**29**		**99**	
⇓	**404**	⇓	**1088**	⇓	**209**	⇓	**1701**
8	⇓	8	⇓	11	⇓	18	⇓
⇓	**8**	⇓	17	⇓	11	⇓	18
8	⇓	8	⇓	2	⇓	9	⇓
	8		**8**		**2**		**9**.

His name is equivalent to 404 + 1088 + 209 = 1701 before reduction, and 26 + 44 + 29 = 99 when the letter-numbers are confined to single digits, as was the Greek custom. This latter gives the first clue to the artifice. Using just the initial letters M, V, P to stand for the whole names, M + V + P : M + V :: 99 : 70, is an excellent rational convergent for $\sqrt{2} : 1$. and M + V : P :: 70 : 29, is a very good rational convergent for $1 : \sqrt{2} - 1$, the octagonal relation. Further, M + V + P : V :: 99 : 44 :: 9 : 4 is a good value for the diagonal of the double square, $\sqrt{5} : 1$, while M + P : V :: 55 : 44 :: 5 : 4 is the first reasonable rational estimate for $\sqrt[3]{2} : 1$. Even more remarkable P : M :: 29 : 26 uses the fine rational convergent 29 : 13 for $\sqrt{5} : 1$ to deliver the ratio $\sqrt{5} : \sqrt{4}$. It seems most improbable that these precise ratios should arise by accident. Vitruvius designed his own name, or someone designed it for him.[11] That someone would have to be capable of constructing a name to match the references written about in Book IX of Vitruvius – the diagonal of the square and the Delic problem of doubling the cube – might well engage in other games. Take the Latin name for the community at Fano as it appears in Vitruvius: '*Coloniae Iuliae Fanestri*.'[12] Beyond Vitruvius' own remarks, there is no other independent documentary or archaeological evidence that such a basilica was ever built for this community. Applying the numbers to the Latin letter:[13]

10 See 'Occult Number', *supra*. Each letter is shown with two columns of numbers, the first gives number equivalences confined to single digits, and the second shows the full number in units, tens and hundreds. The numbers in bold at the foot of the table are summations of the columns. The ⇓ indicates successive summations such as 1088, MDXXXVIII, first goes to 17, I + V + III + V + III = XVII, and then is reduced to 8, I + V + II. The Latin equivalencies make M (1000), C (100), X (10) all equal to I (1), and D (500), L (50) equal to V (5). The numbers in bold on the right of the table are the summations of the rows. For example, 26 + 44 + 29 = 99.

11 The custom of constructing names to accord with auspicious numbers continues today in societies such as China and Korea where the number of strokes in a name may be significant. I owe this observation to my former student Dr Hyunho Shin. But even in Western societies the custom persists. The composer Arnold Schoenberg named his children according to number lore, and actually changed the spelling of Aaron in his opera, *Moses und Aron*, to avoid an unfortunate numerical occasion. See C. C. Sterne, with a foreword by John Cage, *Arnold Schoenberg: the composer as numerologist*, E. Mellen Press, Lewiston NY, c1993; also C. W. Ore, *Numbers and number correspondences in Opus 40 by Arnold Schoenberg: Pythagoras and the Quadrivium revisited*, microform, UCLA Library, 1986.

12 Vitruvius V.i.6. Granger, *op. cit.* 1 pp. 258–62.

13 Latin is an highly inflected language which means that depending on the role of a word in a sentence its endings may be changed. The clever arithmologist, like the poet, may exploit this to adjust his numerical, or poetical, purposes. 'Colonia' is a first declension femine noun. Four other cases of this noun have an added 'e', which is marked in parentheses in the table.

C	3	30	I	9	9	F	6	6		
O	5	50	V	2	200	A	1	1		
L	2	20	L	2	20	N	4	40		
O	5	50	I	9	9	E	5	5		
N	4	40	A	1	1	S	9	90		
I	9	9	(E)	5	5	T	1	100		
A	1	1				R	8	80		
(E)	5	5				I	9	9		
		178			**244**			**331**		**753**
	34	⇓		**28**	⇓		**43**	⇓	**105**	⇓
	⇓	**16**		⇓	**10**		⇓	**7**	⇓	**15**
	7	⇓		**10**	⇓		**7**	⇓	**15**	⇓
		7			**10**			**7**	⇓	**6**

6.

Quite magically, the *ad quadratum* theme of the basilica $7 + 10 + 7$, or $1 + \sqrt{2} + 1$, is unambiguously spelt out. There is also the palindromic symmetry of 34 and 43 about the perfect number 28. This is obvious in modern numerals. For a Roman, the symmetry would look different:

X X X I I I I

X X X X I I I

but would still be evident. The sum $178 + 244 + 331$ of unreduced numbers is 753 which, apart from its sequential series of odd digits, would be unremarkable, if it were not for the fact that the reduced form $34 + 28 + 43 = 105 = 7 \times 5 \times 3$. Again the arithmetic defies chance, and the arithmology becomes even more anfractuose when the full number of Vitruvius' name, 1701, is found to be

$$7 \times \underbrace{3 \times 3 \times 3 \times 3 \times 3}_{5},$$

or 7 times 5 multiplications of 3. What is difficult to dismiss is that the author's arithmological skills are seemingly at full play.

Arithmology was a subject that exercised the prolific and polymathic encyclopaedist, Marcus Terentius Varro (116–27BCE).[14] His *De Principiis Numerorum*, in nine books, is generally thought to have been a Pythagorean treatise on arithmology. In the *Hebdomades*, he celebrated the qualities of the number 7, and according to St Augustine, Varro mentions in the *Disciplinae* how the dactylic hexameter (12 half-feet) may be bisected into 7 and 5 half-feet respectively. In other words, a geometric division mimicking the rational diagonal of the square.[15] St Augustine, an early authority on Varro's work, specifically draws attention to the numerical structure of Varro's monumental *Antiquitates* with its 41 books divided into 'human matters' and 'divine matters' by the square numbers 25 and 16.[16] But 41 is affiliated with 5 (4 + 1), and both 16 and 25 reduce to 7 (1 + 6 and 2 + 5):

14 I am indebted to the late Elizabeth Rawson for her observations on Varro and Vitruvius, although she certainly did not hint at the possibility that they might be the same individual. An outstanding classical scholar of my generation and a former acquaintance of mine at Cambridge, she passed away too soon. E. Rawson, *Intellectual Life in the Late Republic*, The John Hopkins University Press, Baltimore, 1985. See particularly her chapters, 'The Mathematical Artes', in which she chiefly discusses Varro and Vitruvius, pp. 156–69, and 'Architecture and Allied Subjects', pp. 185–200.

15 *Ibid.*, p. 167.

16 J. O'Meara 'Introduction', H. Bettenson trans *St Augustine: Concerning the City of God against the Pagans*, Penguin Books, Harmondsworth, 1972, VI.3, pp. 230–31. St Augustine is severely critical of this philosopher of Paganism and cites Cicero's avoidance of praising Varro's eloquence or fluency 'for in truth Varro is seriously inadequate in this department' – as is Vitruvius judged by Ciceronian standards. But he does say that he was 'a man of pre-eminent, of unparalled erudition', succinctly and neatly described in one line of Terentian: 'Varro, that man of universal science; a man who read so much that we marvel that he had any time for writing, who wrote so much that we find it hard to believe that anyone could have read it all.' (pp. 229–30.)

once again the marriage of 7 with 5. In *Tubero de Origine Humana*, Varro espouses the musicality of the seven month, 210 day, birth. Elizabeth Rawson summarizes Varro concerning this birth which has 6, a perfect number, as its basis: 'for six days the seed is a milky liquid, for eight more it is blood; $6 + 8$ correspond to the musical interval of the fourth. For nine more days the seed is turning into flesh: $6 + 9$ make up the fifth in music. Then during twelve days the foetus is taking human shape: $6 + 12$ represents the octave. $6 + 8 + 9 + 12$ together make 35, and the foetus comes to birth in $6 \times 35 = 210$.'[17] Is it again a coincidence that the basilica is associated with the number $7 \times 5 \times 3$, and this seventh-month birth takes $7 \times 5 \times 3 \times 2$ days. Is the basilica a child to be born? Is it a coincidence that Marcus Terentius and Marcus Vitruvius have the same number of letters in their names, and that both sum to the numerical values of $26 + 44 = 70$, or the values $8 + 17$ (25) and $8 + 8$ (16), the very same numbers in Varro's opus magnum, *Antiquitates*, which divide the customs of men from those of the gods?

M	3	30	T	1	100	V	2	200
A	1	1	E	5	5	A	1	1
R	8	80	R	8	80	R	8	80
C	3	3	E	5	5	R	8	80
V	2	200	N	4	40	O	5	50
S	9	90	T	1	100			
			I	9	9			
			V	2	200			
			S	9	90			

26		**44**		**24**		**94**	
⇓	**404**	⇓	**629**	⇓	**411**	⇓	**1444**
8	⇓	**8**	⇓	**6**	⇓	**13**	⇓
⇓	**8**	⇓	**17**	⇓	**6**	⇓	**13**
8	⇓	**8**	⇓	**6**	⇓	**4**	⇓
	8		**8**		**6**		**4.**

Varro's name has a similar constitution to Vitruvius' in that, using initials again for the full names, $M + T : M + V :: 70 : 50$, a rational convergent for $\sqrt{2} : 1$, but it does not expand beyond that obvious and very Varronian relationship. The Vitruvian equations are far more complex, and would have had to have been composed by someone with considerable arithmological knowledge of the kind that Varro appears to have established over his long and prodigious career.

The author of the basilica at Fano gives two other critical sets of dimensions: the columns are 50 *pedes* high, with pilasters 20 *pedes* high to support the gallery, with 18 *pedes* high pilasters in the upper story, and the remaining space of 12 *pedes* to admit clerestory light; and the second dimensional set is for the important tribunal in the shape of a segment of a circle 46 *pedes* wide and 15 *pedes* deep. The number 50 could represent the name MARCVS VARRO ($26 + 24$), but it does not fit Vitruvius. It will also be noted that the dimensions of the columns, pilasters and the clerestory involve the proportion $25 : 10 : 9 : 6$, a mixture of two square numbers,

17 Rawson *op. cit.* pp. 161–62. Note Varro's use of 'the most perfect proportion' two or more centuries before Nicomachus, *supra*, 'Proportionality'.

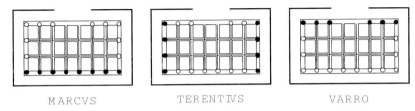

Fig. 6. Basilica at Fano. The column formation of the nave spells out the name MARCVS TERENTIVS VARRO.

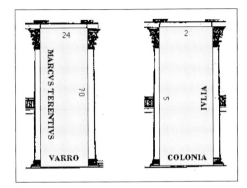

Fig. 7. Basilica at Fano. The proportion of the height and centre to centre spacing of the longitudinal columns spells out the name MARCVS TERENTIVS (26 + 44) and VARRO (24). The height may also be read as MARCVS VITRV-VIVS, but not the width – POLLIO is 29. The proportion of the side columns, 50 *pedes* by 20 *pedes*, agrees with IVLIA (5) and COLONIA (2).

25 and 9, and two (perfect) triangular numbers, 10 and 6; and consequently the Pythagorean values 25 = 16 + 9 associated with the 3, 4, 5 right triangle. As observed earlier, 25 (8 + 17) and 16 (8 + 8) are related to both names: MARCVS TEREN-TIVS and MARCVS VITRUVIUS. The extraordinary arrangement of the basilica with the tribunal placed in the long side leads to the omission of two columns on that side: 'In the width of the nave counting the corner columns there are four at each end' – 8. 'On the side of the forum, there are eight, including the angle columns' – 8. 'On the other side there are six, including the angle columns' – 6. Once more, the name MARCVS TERENTIVS VARRO, 8 + 8 + 6, is imprinted in the scheme, if you choose to see it that way. Examining more closely the columns and their different intercolumniations an even more exacting relationship is to be discovered. Longitudinally, the columns are spaced at 24 module centres, with the columns being 7 modules in diameter (equal to 5 *pedes*). This very Varronian 7 to 5 conversion makes each column 70 modules tall. The elevational proportion is thus 70 : 24, or spelt out: MARCVS TERENTIVS : VARRO (26 + 44 : 24). Down the sides of the basilica the proportion is different and there are no fractional parts of *pedes*. The columns are 50 *pedes* tall and centred at 20 *pedes*. This proportion, 5 : 2, might well stand for COLONIA : IVLIA.[18]

The tribunal specification gives a chord length 46 *pedes* and the sagitta 15 *pedes* – numbers which when reduced return to perfection: 4 + 6 = 10 and 1 + 5 = 6. The description begs the question: what is the diameter of the circle?[19] The computation requires a simple application of Pythagoras' theorem. The nearest rational solution is 50 *pedes*. Working backwards it can be seen that the centre of the circle is 10 *pedes* out from the opening. The right triangle formed by the radius 25 *pedes* as hypotenuse, and the half the chord 23 *pedes* and the distance to the centre 10 *pedes* as sides, must satisfy to a tad the Pythagorean condition. The square of 25 is 625. The sum of the square of 10 and 23 is 629. Not a bad fit: only now, 629 is exactly the unreduced number for TERENTIVS, while the diameter of the circle is 50, again MARCVS VARRO (26 + 24).

This is either a carefully crafted number game in which the names of the colony and of the author are cast into the architecture of the basilica, or it is not. Nothing is heard from Vitruvius after 27 BCE, the year of Varro's death. No contemporaries mention Vitruvius by name, or take note of any of his buildings. Nor do Roman architects of his own time seem to have shown any interest in his writings, if these were ever circulated. Only Frontius, a hundred years later, acknowledges an invention of Vitruvius' to do with gauging the flow of water, not his buildings, not his writings, not his life.[20] Varro had written on architecture, as a younger man, in his *Disciplinae*. As an old pedant did he concoct the fiction of the unseen, unheard and unidentified Vitruvius?[21] Was the superannuated author who produced this paper design declaring

18 The name of the colony in the nominative case. From the table the numbers are 34 − 5 = 29 for COLONIA which reduces to 2, and 28 − 5 = 23 for IVLIA which reduces to 5. Note, however, that 29 : 23 is an excellent rational convergent for $^3\sqrt{2} : 1$ – the Delic problem cited by Vitruvius.

19 It is to be noted that Varro had held various public offices, including tribune of the people and then praetor. The comment in Vitruvius 'that those who come before the magistrates may not interfere with persons on business' may be – if Varro is the author – reflect personal experiences of less well-planned basilicas. (Vitruvius V.i.8.)

20 See D. Wiebenson, 'Vitruvius', pp. 334–42. She cites Pliny the Elder as the first recorded person to refer to *De architectura* in his bibliography for *Historia naturalis*. However, this work is dedicated to Titus who became Caesar in 79CE, the year of Pliny's premature death by asphyxiation on approaching Mt Vesuvius, out of scientific curiosity, during the eruption which destroyed Pompeii. This first reference, then, must be dated a century later than *De architectura*.

21 Varro would have been 89-years-old when he died.

22 Varro had been proscribed by Mark Anthony, much of his property taken including his exceptional library of Greek and Latin works. He had spent the last fifteen years of his life in seclusion, writing until the very last. He had been a close personal friend of the assassinated Julius Caesar, and the design of the basilica at Fano appears to be in memory of more stoic times past.

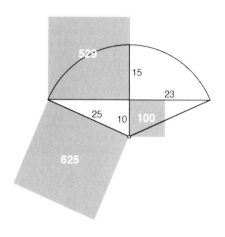

Fig. 8. Basilica at Fano. The Pythagorean geometry of the tribune reveals the name TERENTIVS (100 + 529 = 629) and the diameter of the circle defining the arc of the rear wall is 50, MARCVS VARRO (26 + 24).

his occult, Pythagorean contempt for the unphilosophic, materialistic hustlings of younger architects readying themselves for the Augustine building campaign?[22]

It perhaps is no accident that the Preface to Book V contains the passage about Pythagoras and the cube number 216: 'and they thought that no more than three cubes should be in one treatise.'[23] Three times 216 is 648, the very same numbers that spell out, in their most reduced form, Varro's names: VARRO (6), both MARCVS and TERENTIVS (8), and the full name MARCVS TERENTIVS VARRO (4). The number 648 is equal to

$$8 \times \underbrace{3 \times 3 \times 3 \times 3}_{4},$$

and it will be recalled that MARCVS VITRVVIVS POLLIO summed, in its unreduced form, to 1701 which is equal to

$$7 \times \underbrace{3 \times 3 \times 3 \times 3 \times 3}_{5},$$

or the familial, close relative

$$(8-1) \times \underbrace{3 \times 3 \times 3 \times 3 \times 3}_{(4+1)}.$$

This looks suspiciously like the final key to a fiendishly Pythagorean riddle.[24]

The Pantheon

The Pantheon was built by Hadrian and completed by 121CE.[25] There can be little doubt that this structure had a profound influence on architects in the Renaissance. Both Serlio and Palladio record it.[26] At a glance, the ground plan of the principal space is circular, and therefore centralized. On closer scrutiny, it will be seen that the rotunda plan is based on a 16-gon within its circular perimeter. The detailed execution of the plan makes use of the subsymmetries of the 16-gon which include the dihedral symmetries of the octagon, the square, and the oblong as well as simple bilateral symmetry. Subshapes of the design display all of these subsymmetries. Above, the cupola displays 28 radial divisons. Licht claims that the number 28 is derived from Euclid's definition of a perfect number: however, he finds 'no direct relation to the other proportioning of the building'.[27] Contemporary arithmeticians, Nicomachus and Theon of Smyrna, may also have been sources.[28] The source may just possibly be Vitruvius, or at least the traditional knowledge that Vitruvius had sought to preserve and which may have been part of an oral tradition. The number 16 was produced, according to Vitruvius by 'throwing' both the perfect numbers 6 and 10 together to make the most perfect number.[29] The number 28 counts the nights of the lunar cycle described in some detail by Vitruvius without noting its arithmetical perfection.[30] In sympathy with this, the number 16 may be derived from the disposition of the Roman winds. Vitruvius counts and names eight principal winds, but writes somewhat ambiguously about dividing the circle into sixteen parts.[31]

23 Vitruvius V Preface 3. Granger *op. cit.* pp. 252–53. Given Varro's friendship with Julius Caesar it is worth noting that IVLIVS is made up of three letters of value 2 and three of 9. The number cited in the Preface to Book V, 216, equals

$$\underbrace{2 \times 2 \times 2}_{3} \times \underbrace{(9 + 9 + 9)}_{3}.$$

It looks suspiciously like a covert encoding of Varro's murdered hero. The full number of Caesar's name is I (9) + V (200) + L (20) + I (9) + V (200) + (90) = 528, which misses by an acceptable unit the square on the half-opening to the tribunal, 529, but which also equals 5 + 2 + 8 = 15, the depth of the tribunal – the most august space in the whole basilica.
24 Or a most mistaken inference of the kind to be found in a story by Edgar Allan Poe.
25 H. Stierlin, *Hadrien et l'Architecture Romaine*, Office du Livre, Frieberg, 1984, pp. 80–111.
26 *Infra*, 'Centralized Design'.
27 K. de F. Licht, *The Rotonda in Rome: A Study of Hadrian's Pantheon*, Jutland Archeological Society Publications VIII, Copenhagen, 1968. Euclid VII, Definition 22.
28 *Supra*, 'Ethical Number'.
29 Vitruvius III.i.8. *Supra*, 'Shapeful Number'.
30 Vitruvius IX.i.8.
31 *Ibid.* I.vi.12.

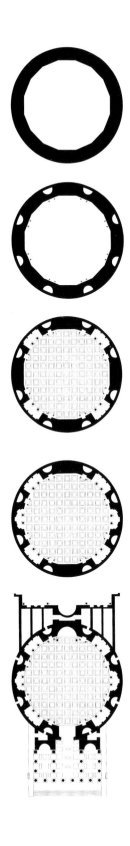

Fig. 9. The Pantheon (left). Deriving the full groundplan from the 16-gon, top. Next level, the eight inscribed niches in the outer wall and the eight double columns in front of the small rectangular niches provide octagonal symmetry. Below that, the four large exedrae, their double columns, and the circular and square floor design conform to the symmetry of the square. Then with the addition of two semi-circular exedrae the symmetry is further reduced to that of the oblong, bilaterally symmetrical in two orthogonal directions. Finally, bottom, the whole design with the portico and the principal exedra reduces to simple bilateral symmetry along the north-south axis.

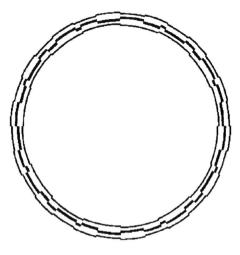

Fig. 10. The Pantheon. The interplay of the 16-fold symmetry of the groundplan and the 28-fold symmetry of the cupola creates a polyrhythmic cycle, $4 + 3 + 1 + 4 + 2 + 2 + 4 + 1 + 3 + 4$, which repeats itself in the four quarters of the interior.

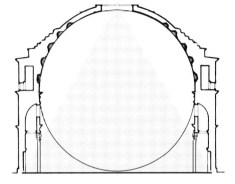

Fig. 11. The Pantheon. A cross section showing the relationship of the circle to the equilateral triangle. After Stierlin.

Varro, in *De ventis*, 'seems to have linked the sixteen directions from which his winds came to the rising or setting of the sun at different points in the year (solstice, equinox and so on). . . . A calendar, dividing the year astronomically into eight divisons, in which the farmer has different tasks, forms the basis of some chapters of Varro's *De rebus rusticus* . . .'.[32] The ground plan of the Pantheon is aligned to the compass points, with the entrance facing due north. This might be thought to support such a metereological interpretation.

The proportional relation between 28 and 16 is 7 : 4, a standard rational convergent to $\sqrt{3} : 1$, but 28 is itself 7×4, which is how Euclid determines that it is a perfect number according to the formula $(1 + 2 + 4) \times 4$. Ground plan and ceiling plan are thus related in the different perfections of their numbers. A circle of radius 4 circumscribes an equilateral triangle of side lengths 7. Such a figure is evoked by Vitruvius where he notes a question held in common between astronomers and musicians '*de sympathia stellarum et symphoniarum in . . . trigonis*', and again in describing the design of a Roman theatre based on four equilateral triangle inscribed in a circle '*in duodecim signorum caelestium astrologia ex musica convenientia astrorum ratiocinatur*'.[33] This is a musico-astrological reference to the 'trine' which Ptolemy develops in *Harmonics* written in Alexander most probably at the time the Pantheon was under construction in Rome.[34] Stierlin observes this triangular relationship in the cross-section of the Pantheon. The same theme may also be counted in the two freestanding column systems in the interior. There are 16 columns in the aedicules and 14 larger columns in front of the apses – a ratio of 8 : 7. More directly, there are 8 aedicules and 7 apses. Elizabeth Rawson cites an arithmological observation by Cicero: ' to give the Dream of Scipio at the end of *De Republica* a slightly archaic colouring (he believed there had been much Pythagoreanism in earlier periods in Rome); . . . he analyzes Scipio Aemilianus' age at his death, 56, as significantly made up of 7×8, two "full" or "complete" numbers, a term of Pythagorean origin'.[35] This 'fullness' and 'completeness' may be deliberate, or it may reflect the names of Hadrian: PVBLIVS ÆLIVS which in single digits reads $6 + 2 + 2 + 2 + 9 + 2 + 9 = 32$ and $1 + 5 + 2 + 9 + 2 + 9 = 28$, a ratio of 8 : 7, but also note the explicit and perfect value 28 of ÆLIVS, and that PVBLIVS is twice 16. There are 30 freestanding columns on the interior and 16 in the portico, making 46 in all. HADRIANVS is $8 + 1 + 4 + 8 + 9 + 1 + 4 + 2 + 9 = 46$. The architects honour their patron.

32 E. Rawson, *op cit.*, p. 164.
33 Vitruvius I.i.16 and V.vi.1.
34 A. Barker, *Greek Musical Writings, Volume II Harmonic and Acoustic Theory*, Cambridge University Press, Cambridge, 1989, pp. 380–91.
35 Rawson, *op. cit.*, p. 162.

XXII

CHRISTIAN WORKS

Twenty-eight years earlier Rome had been sacked by the Vandals, there had then followed the defeat of the Roman fleet off Cartagena, and a rapid succession of Western Roman Emperors to the very last of the breed, Romulus Augustulus, deposed by Odoacer who is proclaimed German king of Italy: Simplicius is Pope and the decision to build 'heaven on earth' is taken and the construction of Santo Stefano Rotondo based on the model of the Holy Sepulchre in Jerusalem begins.[1] Rome has gone and a new Christian era begins. Boethius is born too, a true Roman survivor, and classical learning is to hold on by the quill of his Latinate pen until the Renaissance. The great neo-Platonic philosopher, head of the Academy at Athens, Proclus – commentator on Euclid – dies, as the structure of Santo Stefano Rotondo rises above the ruins of a Roman military barracks and its temple to Mithras.

Santo Stefano Rotondo

Santo Stefano Rotondo has been described as the New Jerusalem.[2] It is certainly possible to attribute occult meaning to its controlling dimensions by reference in particular to the Book of Revelations. It is said that the diameter of the original circular enclosure was 144 cubits which is the number for 'the Holy Jerusalem' in Greek, and that the external platform has a diameter of 170 cubits equal to the name 'the New Jerusalem'. Dimensions are deceptive, but columns can be counted. There were 22 columns in the circumference of the innermost circle. The principal structure was supported on 8 T-sectioned piers. Between these piers alternate 4 and 5 columns to make $16 + 20 = 36$ columns in this ring. There is agreement about this disposition.[3] The reconstruction of the remaining two outer rings is more contentious, but the proposal by Sándor Ritz S.J. makes architectonic sense.[4] He proposes 16 more columns placed in pairs radially, and 8 more for the four doors into the temple in the next to last ring. The external wall has eight doors, making twelve doors in all to the temple.

The 22 columns almost certainly refer to St John's opening of his Gospel: 'In the beginning was the Word, and the Word was with God, and the Word was God.' The Word here is represented by the 22 letters of the Hebrew language.[5] But 22 columns arranged on the circumference give the circle a diameter of 7 intercolumniations. Seven representing, perhaps, the Seven Churches which John addresses at the beginning of the Book of Revelations, or any of the numerous other septenaries

1 For an unexcelled discussion of the migration of the iconic image of the Holy Sepulchre in mediaeval building see R. Krautheimer 'Introduction to an "Iconography of Medieval Architecture"' *Journal of the Warburg and Courtauld Institutes*, V, 1942, pp. 1–33. Krautheimer stresses the importance of number and of counting over measurements.

2 The comparison is elaborately detailed in S. Ritz SJ, *The Supreme Creation of the Past, Present and Future. The Everlasting Temple of Santo Stefano Rotondo in Roma. The New Jerusalem of the Book of Revelation,* mimeograph *c*1985. I am indebted to my former student James M. Schwentker for bringing this document to my attention.

3 The church was one of a number of restoration project undertaken by Pope Nicholas V for the Jubileee of 1450. Alberti is generally believed to have been consulted. The church was in a dilapidated state. Supervised by Bernardo Rosellino, the restorers walled up the second ring of columns. Commentators see this act as in conformity with Alberti's views on walls and columns. For a discussion, and further references, see F. Borsi, *Leon Battista Alberti*, Phaidon Press, Oxford, 1977, pp. 40–50.

4 This outer ring was demolished by the restorers, although much of it probably had already been destroyed.

5 *Supra*, 'Occult number'. St Augustine's, *De Civitate Dei* . . . is divided into 22 books. The pythmen of Λογος, logos, is also $3 + 7 + 3 + 7 + 2 = 22$.

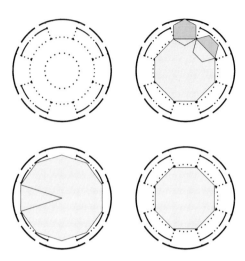

Fig. 1. Santo Stefano Rotondo. Top left, the reconstructed plan, after Sándor Ritz. Top right, the semi-regular octagon marking the centre positions of the piers is defined by the lengths of the diameter of a regular hexagon and its chord. Bottom right, the regular octagon defines the innermost edges of the piers in the openings with five columns. Bottom left, the side of a regular decagon marks the opening in the next to outermost ring.

6 The numbers 16, 20 and 36 are shapeful: 16 is ◇4, 20 is ▲4, and 36 is the first number to be both trigonal and tetragonal, △8 and ◇6. *Supra*, 'Shapeful Number'.

7 I am unaware of any evidence that generating sequences were used to determine rational values for the extreme and mean ratio prior to Kepler's seventeenth-century observations. Such a sequence conforms to the tenth classical proportionalities of Nicomachus, or the seventh of Pappus, *supra*, 'Proportionality'. It seems more likely that the extreme and mean ratio would be computed by substituting rational convergents for √5 : 1.

8 $\dfrac{20}{9} \times \dfrac{9}{4} = 5.$

9 An application of Pythagoras' theorem gives the diameter of the octagon as 94 cubits, that is to the face of the piers. Ritz gives the diameter of the second circle as 96 cubits, but it's unclear as to whether this is to the centres of the columns.

10 Ritz suggests that 62 is the number, in Greek, of the words 'Son' (of God) and 'logos'. The latter count is achieved by simply numbering the letters from 1 to 23 in sequence. It may also be no accident that the name of the Pope, SIMPLICIVS I, 9 + 9 + 3 + 6 + 2 + 9 + 3 + 9 + 2 + 9 + (1) also sums to 62.

that pepper that text. The Tetragrammaton has a value 36 when the numbers are confined to units only, and it may be parsed into 20 + 16 by summing alternate, leading diagonal rows, so that the second ring of columns may well stand for the Tetragrammaton.[6] On its own, **יהוה** sums to 17 and then reduces to 8. Among Christians, the eight Greek letter θ often appears at this time in the centre of a four-fold, or eightfold, cross.

,
ה י
 י ה ו
ה ו ה י

```
        1
      5   1
    6   5   1
  5   6   5   1.
```

The column configurations present a veritable library of arithmetical and geometrical knowledge cunningly arrayed. Simple groupings conjure up square roots, cube roots, squaring of the circle, and solutions to other classical problems. There are, in all, 82 columns according to Ritz's reconstruction. This relates very well, although he does not use this fact as part of his argument, with the known existence of 58 columns in the two inner rings. 82 : 58 :: 41 : 29 is an excellent classical rational convergent to the diagonal of the square. The 36 columns of the second ring make an extreme and mean ratio with the 22 columns of the inner circle, 18 : 11. In fact, as is to be expected with this ratio, the total number of columns in the two inner rings, 58, is in extreme and mean ratio with the 36 columns of the second ring, 29 : 18. The generating sequence is 1, 3, 4, 7, 11, 18, 29, . . ., and the values of √5 : 1 implied, or used, are 25 : 11 and the better 20 : 9, respectively.[7] The second ring of 36 columns to the 16 columns on the principal cross is in proportion 36 : 16 :: 9 : 4, the conjugate value of √5 : 1 for 20 : 9.[8] The ratio of the two sets of columns to one another in the second ring is 20 : 16 :: 5 : 4, a practical value for $^3\!\sqrt{2}$: 1, although another configuration of columns gives the much finer estimate 29 : 23. There are 22 + 16 = 38 columns in the centre ring together with those in the principal crossing. The ratio of these columns to the 22 columns in the centre is 38 : 22 :: 19 : 11, a good rational proxy for √3 : 1.

The eight piers are not equally spaced around the circle as is made plain by the alternating sets of four and five columns along the orthogonal and diagonal axes respectively. Ritz suggests that the sides of this octagon are 38 and 33 cubits between centers of the piers. If this is the case then the two side lengths may be defined by an hexagon of diameter 38 since its chord will be 33, using the value 19 : 11 for √3 : 1. Measuring to the inner corners of the piers where the five columns are, the octagon is regular with side of 36 cubits according to Ritz.[9] He also gives the radius to the next to outermost ring of the structure as 62 cubits.[10] A decagon of this radius will have a rational side of length 38, and this seems to be the dimension of the openings in the next to outermost ring which originally made room for four walled courtyards. This suggests that Santo Stefano Rotondo is architectonically founded on the regular polygons: the hexagon, the octagon and the decagon. The counting

Fig. 2. Santo Stefano Rotondo. Parsings of the columnar configurations provide rational convergents for inexpressible numbers.

82 : 58 :: 41 : 29
the diagonal of the square √2 : 1

58 : 46 :: 29 : 23
the Delic problem of doubling the cube, ³√2 : 1

20 : 16 :: 5 :4
the Delic problem of doubling the cube, ³√2 : 1

58 : 52 :: 29 : 26
the diagonal of the double square to its long side √5 : √4

36 : 16 :: 9 : 4
the diagonal of a double square to its short side √5 : 1

58: 36 :: 29 : 18.
the extreme and mean ratio.

36 : 22 :: 18 : 11.
the extreme and mean ratio.

28 : 22 :: 14 : 11.
area of the circumscribed square to the circle.

52 : 46 :: 26 : 23.
squaring the circle with a square of side 23 and a circle of diameter 26.

38 : 2 :: 19 : 11.
the chord of a regular hexagon to its side √3 : 1.

of columns certainly supports this hypothesis. The hexagon and decagon are hidden. The octagon is visible, but somewhat ambivalent in regard to its regularity. The potent geometries of the five world-making solids are seemingly brought together in this design through these associated polygons, and their arithmetic expression in rational convergents for $\sqrt{2}$, $\sqrt{3}$ and $\sqrt{5}$ is inevasible in parsings of the columnar configuration.[11]

Amiens Cathedral

The Chancellor of Amiens was Richard de Fournevall, known today for his satirical rendering *Bestaire d'Amour* of the *Physiologus*, some early Christian allegories using imagery from the animal kingdom. He had also been attributed with the authorship of the *Vetula*, an imitation of Ovid's *Ars Amatoria* which was reputedly found in the Roman's tomb four-hundred years after the poet's death. The *Vetula* makes mention of the game of rithmomachia:

O utinam ludus sciretur Rhythmimaciae!

ludus Aritmeticae folium, flos fructus et eius

gloria laus honor.[12]

Amiens cathedral has been measured in recent years by Niels Luning Prak. He throws down the gauntlet: 'It seems therefore more likely that the dimensional system was no more than a technical expedient, without any symbolic meaning.'[13] At the time, given the extraordinary interest in arithmology and the adamantine way that Joachamite number was believed to have over human destiny, it seems most unlikely that the architectonic design of Amiens is merely the result of technical expediency. The number game may not be musical, but then very little of the architectonic history related here has been musical. The musical analogy, in our judgement, has been no more than one sustained and clamorous cadenza to a vacuous score.

Quite properly, Prak converts his measurements into *pieds royaux*, the measure used during the cathedral's construction. In this way he finds that simple whole numbers were used to dimension the building over the fifty or so years of its construction. He notes the dominance of numbers which are multiples of 7 *pieds royaux*, and makes the reasonable assumption that this might have been the length of a standard measure. Almost all of his numbers for Amiens may be interpreted as shapeful, with a predominance of fifth, seventh, and tenth figurate numbers.[14] It is as if the game of rithmomachia, *ludus philosophorum*, 'nobilissimus et antiquissimum ludus Pythagoreus', has been lapidified.[15] Longitudinally, the 140 *pieds royaux* length of the nave is twice the seventh pentagonal number ⬠7, the width of the transept 98 *pieds royaux* is twice the seventh tetragonal number ◇7, the length of the choir 70 *pieds royaux* is twice the fifth pentagonal number ⬠5; the length of the five equal bays in the nave *pieds royaux* is the fourteenth trigonal number △14; and the length of the cathedral to the apse is the seventh heptagonal pyramid ●7.[16] Transversely, the width of the nave 45 *pieds royaux* is the ninth trigonal number △9; while the combined width of the two aisles 55 *pieds royaux* is the tenth trigonal number △10; the combined width of the nave and its two side aisles 100 *pieds royaux* is the tenth tetragonal number ◇10; while combined width

11 The equilateral triangular ($\sqrt{3}$), square ($\sqrt{2}$) and pentagonal($\sqrt{5}$) faces of the five regular polyhedra are, of course, embedded in the geometries of the regular hexagon, octagon and decagon.

12 Quoted in D. E. Smith *History of Mathematics*, Ginn, New York, *c*1923/5, n.4, p. 198.

13 N. L. Prak, 'Measurement of Amiens Cathedral', *American Society of Architectural Historians*, pp. 209–21. A more recent survey has been made by a team from Columbia University's Amiens Project under the supervision of Peter Murray. Architecturally speaking, more accurate measurements do little to disturb the underlying thesis. It is to be expected that the actual building will diverge from its mental plan.

14 *Supra*, 'Shapeful Number'.

15 H. J. R. Murray, *A History of Board-Games Other than Chess*, Clarendon Press, Oxford, 1952, pp. 84–87. Smith, *op. cit.* I, pp. 198–200. The quotation is the title of a book on rithmomachia by the French mathematician Claude de Boissière published in Paris, 1556. It reflects the long-standing tradition that the game was Pythagorean, possibly invented by Boethius.

16 308 = ○1 + ○2 + ○3 + ○4 + ○5 + ○6 + ○7 is the 7th 7-gonal pyramid.

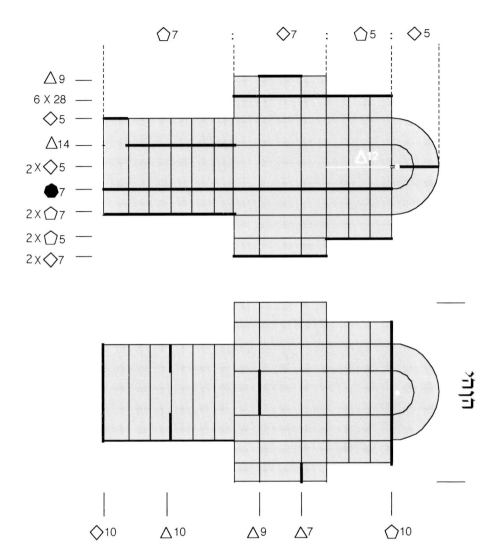

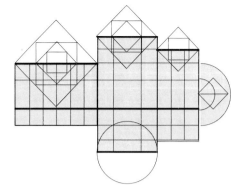

Fig. 4. Amiens cathedral. *Ad quadratum* relationships. Also the circumference of a circle with a diameter based on the width of the transept defines the length of the cathedral to the chevet.

Fig. 3. Amiens cathedral. Schematic plan showing dimensions and ratios as figurate numbers (after Prak).

of the choir and its four side aisles 145 *pieds royaux* is the tenth pentagonal number ⬠10; and the width of the additional bays of the transept 21 *pieds royaux* are each the sixth trigonal number △6. The space in medieval buildings was measured in bays. There are 6 × 3 = 18 bays in the nave, or ⬠3. There are 3 × 7 = 21 bays across the transept, or △6, and 3 × 5 = 15 bays in the choir, △5. It will be noted that the bays are in arithmetic progression 15 and 21 are the extremes and the nave is the mean 18. The chevet has a complex arrangement of non-rectangular bays, but each clearly defined by the vaulting pattern. There are 17 such bays or **יהוה** = 5 + 6 + 5 + 1 = 17 bays. That this is probably intentional is corroborated by the fact that the total number of bays is 18 + 21 + 15 + 17 = 71, the palindrome of 17. In Roman numbering this would have looked like:

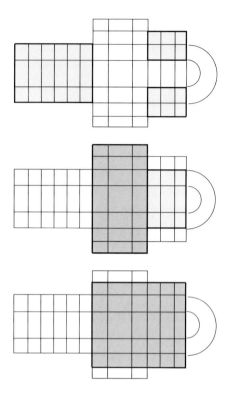

Fig. 5. Amiens cathedral. Top, bay areas define √2 : 1 rectangles using the 7 : 5 rational convergent. Centre, bay areas in the choir form a √2 : 1 rectangle using the 10 : 7 rational convergent. The bays of the transept define a rectangle with the transcendental proportion π : τ; where τ : 1 is the extreme and mean ratio. Bottom, the combined bay areas forming a rectangle between the choir and the transept is in the ratio √2 : ³√2, a meld of two classic problems – the diagonal of the square and doubling the cube.

17 V. F. Hopper, *Medieval Number Symbolism: Its Sources, Meaning, and Influence on Thought and Expression*, Cooper Square Publishers, New York, 1969, pp. 75–76 and p. 87. Barnabus, *Epistle* IV i Ante Nicene Christian Library X, 303–4.
18 Not only do the figurate numbers evoke 6 and 10, but the actual numbers 145 and 42 reduce to 10 and 6. The triangle and pentagon, as numbers 3 and 5, also have Christian significance. For the number 42, see n.22.
19 G. Ifrah, *From One to Zero: a Universal History of Numbers*, Viking Penguin, New York, 1985, p. 298.
20 For Hugo of St Victor see Hopper, *op. cit.*, pp. 100–103. Factorization is the sixth of his nine methods.

X	V	I	I
I	L	X	X

where the number 71 is read backwards, but the pattern is clear. Both 17 and 71 reduce to 8, the Ogdoad associated with God.

Beyond the public realm of the cathedral, the distance from the beginning of the choir to the radial centre of the chevet 78 *pieds royaux* is the twelfth trigonal number △12 – surely signifying the trinity and its multiple duodecanery associations, not least the twelve apostles. The offset of 8 *pieds royaux* from the end of the choir for the chevet's centre of turning gives a total length from this point of entry into the nave of 316 *pieds royaux*. A very well-known number in Christian tradition is 318, the supposed number of Bishops at the Council of Nicea, the number of servants of Abraham, and most significantly the number of Jesus on the Cross. Barnabus explains: 'And Abraham circumsized 10 and 8 and 300 men of his household. 'What, then, was the knowledge given to him in this? Learn the 18 first and then the 300. The 10 and 8 are thus denoted. Ten by I [iota], and 8 by H [eta]. You have Jesus [at least the first two letters of Ιησους]. And because the Cross was to express the grace by the letter T [tau], he says also "300"'.[17] Were the architectonic designers of Amiens torn between two possibilities, one satisfying a "glass bead" game and the other conforming to tradition; or is there some other significant measure in the length of Amiens satisfying this numerical imperative? If, from the 308 *pieds royaux* mark at its entrance to the choir, the chevet is half the width of the nave and its aisles – that is 50 *pieds royaux* – then the full length of the church would amount to 358 *pieds royaux*. The Gnostics had interpreted the phrase from Genesis 'Shiloh shall come' as the gematriot 358, prophetic of the coming Messiah whose number is also 358. The church would have been doubly blessed by Christ once by the vulnerable human being on the cross and again by the divine Messiah whose second coming was nearing (in 1260). If the major lengths of the cruciform are interpretable in this manner, what of its width? The full width of the transept is 145 *pieds royaux* for the choir and two additional bays each 21 *pieds royaux*, a full width then of 145 + 42, 10 + 6, or 187 *pieds royaux*. The dimension is potent with meaning and perfection.[18] The name **יהוה** may be evaluated in gematria, using the squares of the usual numbers, as 25 + 36 + 25 + 100 = 186. Adding unity – the divine monad – only reiterates the sacred name. It is also the case that the Hebrew word for 'place' has the same value.[19] To esoterics, as blazeningly as the Marlboro man plies nicotine to the man in the street, the Cathedral advertises that it is the place of God. At least the coming Messiah would surely spot the logo on his spanking new home.

So much for numbers. Does any of this translate into proportion? The application of *ad quadratum* is almost too obvious to mention. In length, there is the sequence 140 : 98 : 70, or 10 : 7 : 5. The length and breadth of the nave and the aisles, and each of the two double aisles in the choir are 7 : 5. The choir, without its two additional aisles on the nave, is 10 : 7. A rithmomachia player would yawn. But what is this? The length of the church from the entrance to the end of the choir is 140 + 98 + 70 = 308 *pieds royaux*; the most significant rupture to this length is the transept which is 98 *pieds royaux* wide. The ratio 308 : 98 is 22 : 7, the rational convergent for π : 1. The transept itself is proportioned, apparently, with total disregard for numerical niceties, 187 : 98. Factoring these numbers, as Hugo of St Victor instructs, the ratio becomes 17.11 : 14.7 or π : 28/17.[20] Now, this last fraction is a rational convergent to the extreme and mean ratio τ : 1 as the sequence 1, 5, 6, 11, 17, 28, ...

indicates to modern readers. It is more, in that this particular value combines the perfect number 28 as numerator, and **יהוה** = 17 as denominator. The transept is in the ratio $\pi : \tau$, a union of two transcendental inexpressibles. The rectangle embracing part of the transept and the choir is proportioned 70 + 98=168 *pieds royaux* in length and $22\frac{1}{2} + 100 + 22\frac{1}{2} = 145$ *pieds royaux* in width, a ratio of 168 : 145, or following Hugo's directions, 8.21 : 5.29. The numbers 29 and 21 immediately recall the 20, 21, 29 right triangle which is the closest 'small' triangle to look like an half square. The central crossing of the cathedral is 45 *pieds royaux* square, a powerful assertion of the Trinity when described in figurate terms, for 45 is the ninth trigonal number $\triangle 9$, nine is the third tetragonal number $\diamondsuit 3$, and three is the first trigonal number after unity. However, the whole crossing is dimensioned 100 *pieds royaux* to 98 *pieds royaux*, or a ratio of 50 : 49, a not-quite square. These are the very numbers that occur in the determination of the diagonal of the square with sides of length 5. Pythagoras' theorem gives the diagonal as $49 = 7^2$ and the sum of the squares on the two sides as $50 = 5^2 + 5^2$. They are also the numbers that occur if the 20, 21, 29 right triangle is used in laying out a ground plan, 20 + 29 = 49, 21 + 19 = 50. The likelihood is that this triangle was used to survey the site. Its rope would be 20 + 21 + 29 = 70 units long. All dimensions in Prak's survey are easily derived from it.[21] But now, back to the ratio 8.21 : 5.29: while there are several interpretations here, the one that is most appealing is that the antecedent 42/29 is taken for the value of a diagonal of a square in which the sacred number 42 appears, and that the consequent 5/4 is taken as the traditional arithmetic estimate for solving the Delic problem of doubling the cube.[22] The ratio may then be expressed 42/29 : 5/4, or in modern notation $\sqrt{2} : \sqrt[3]{2}$.[23] Yet another notable fusion of arithmetic knowledge worthy of being presented in the ineludable age of *spiritualis intelligentia*. The import of these exceptional mediaeval ratios, $\pi : \tau$ and $\sqrt{2} : \sqrt[3]{2}$, may perhaps be best appreciated if they are seen as the equivalents, for their time, of what Euler's relation $e^{i\pi} + 1 = 0$ was for the nineteenth century, or Einstein's $E = mc^2$ has been for the twentieth.[24]

21 In the manner described *supra*, 'Right Triangular Number'.

22 Hopper, *op. cit.*, p. 53. It may also refer to the 42-letter Greek name of God, *supra*, 'Occult Number'.

23 This is the kind of ratio that the French mathematician Nicole Oresme was to commend in the next century as being rational in its exponents: $2^{1/2} : 2^{1/3}$, that is 3 : 2. *Vide supra*, 'Empowered Proportion'.

24 Euler's relation brings together not only 1 and 0, the multiplicative and additive identities, but also Napier's number e, the imaginary unit $i = \sqrt{-1}$, and π.

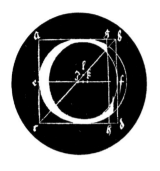

EDIFICE

XXIIII

CENTRALIZED DESIGN

Piero della Francesca

Georgio Vasari, in the quaint but literal 1912 translation of Gaston de Vere, writes of Piero della Francesca: 'He, having been held a rare master of the difficulties of drawing regular bodies, as well as arithmetic and geometry, was not yet able – being overtaken in old age by the infirmity of blindness, and finally by the close of life – to bring to light his noble labours and the many books written by him, which are still preserved in the Borgo, his native place. The very man who should have striven with all his might to increase the glory and fame of Piero, from whom he had learnt all that he knew, was impious and malignant enough to seek to blot out the name of his teacher, and to usurp to himself the honour that was due to the other, publishing under his own name, Fra Luca dal Borgo, all the labours of that good old man, who, besides the sciences named above, was excellent in painting'.[1] Vasari is referring to the man, better known to us, as Luca Pacioli.

Luca Pacioli

The relationship between Piero della Francesca's mathematical manuscripts and Luca Pacioli's printed publications of the late fifteenth and early sixteenth centuries has been well covered by Margaret Daly Davis.[2] She demonstrates very well the relationship between the two mathematical treatises, the *Trattato d'abaco*, which covers both arithmetical and geometrical problems, and the *Libellus de quinque corporibus regularibus* on the five Platonic solids; and the *De prospectiva pingendi* which is directed towards designers and painters in particular.[3] The algebraic part of the *Abaco* shows remarkable advances over the work of Leonardo Pisano, called Fibonacci. Whereas Fibonacci had treated six forms of algebraic equations, Piero adds a further fifty-five types.[4] Many of the problems require Piero to treat numbers which are rational in square as well as lines which are irrational according to Euclid. There seems little doubt that Piero worked from Campanus' translation of Euclid.[5] He is particularly interested in placing one regular body within another for which he needs to compute the ratio of sides.

Davis shows that Piero uses all of the Propositions 1–12 from Euclid's supposed Book XV to arrive at his results.[6] Piero also examines certain semi-regular figures such as the figure with four equilateral triangles and four regular hexagonal faces,

1 G. Vasari, *Lives of the Painters, Sculptors and Architects*, trans Gaston du C. de Vere, Alfred A. Knopf, New York, 1996, Volume 1, p. 397. The three surviving treatises are: *Trattato d'abaco* (Florence, Biblioteca Medicea Laurenziana, MS. Ashb. 280/359–291, *Libellus de Quinque corporibus regularibus* (Rome, Biblioteca Vaticana, MS. Vat.Urb.lat.632), and *De prospectiva pingendi* (Parma, Biblioteca Palatina, MS.1576, in Italian; Milan, Biblioteca Ambrosiana, Cod.Ambr.C.307, in Latin). See also E. Giusti, C. Maccagni, *Luca Pacioli e la Matematica del Rinascimento*, Giunti, Florence, 1994.
2 M. D. Davis, *Piero della Francesca's Mathematical Treatise*, Longo Editore, Ravenna, 1977, Appendix I, 'Luca Pacioli and the *Tratto d'abaco*', pp. 98–106 and Appendix II, 'Piero's Manuscripts and Pacioli's Adaptations: Textual Questions', pp. 107–18. *Vide*, Luca Pacioli, *Summa de arithmetica, geometria, proportioni, et proportionalità*, Paganino de Paganini da Brescia, Venice, 1494; and *De divina proportione*, Paganius Paganinus, Venice, 1509.
3 *Ibid.*, Davis p. 18, 'In fact we will see that the geometry section of Piero's *Trattato d'abaco* is closely related to his *De prospectiva pingendi*, and that it forms the basis of the *Libellus de quinque corporibus regularibus*. 'Unlike his *Abaco*, Piero's book on the five regular bodies . . . did not belong to a pre-existing genre. Instead, like the *De prospectiva pingendi*, it is original in conception and content. The *Libellus* presents for the first time a theme treated in many artists' manuals from the sixteenth-century onwards. Such manuals aimed, at least in part, to teach the construction and perspectival drawing of the regular bodies.'

Fig. 1. Piero della Francesca's studies of regular polyhedra inscribed in one another. Drawings from Pacioli, *De Divina Proportione*:
a. octahedron in a tetrahedron,
b. tetrahedron in a cube,
c. octahedron in a cube,
d. icosahedron in a cube,
e. cube in an octahedron,
f. tetrahedron in an octahedron,
g. cube in a dodecahedron,
h. tetrahedron in a dodecahedron,
i. octahedron in a dodecahedron,
j. icosahedron in a dodecahedron,
k. cube in an icosahedron,
l. tetrahedron in a icosahedron,
m. dodecahedron in an icosahedron.

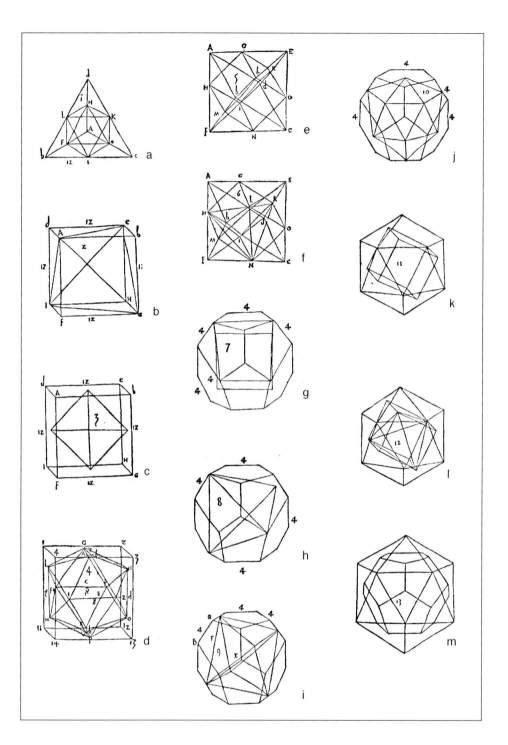

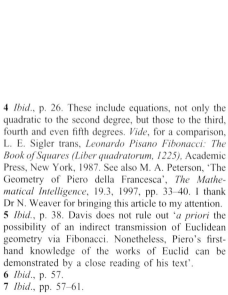

4 *Ibid.*, p. 26. These include equations, not only the quadratic to the second degree, but those to the third, fourth and even fifth degrees. *Vide*, for a comparison, L. E. Sigler trans, *Leonardo Pisano Fibonacci: The Book of Squares (Liber quadratorum, 1225)*, Academic Press, New York, 1987. See also M. A. Peterson, 'The Geometry of Piero della Francesca', *The Mathematical Intelligence*, 19.3, 1997, pp. 33–40. I thank Dr N. Weaver for bringing this article to my attention.
5 *Ibid.*, p. 38. Davis does not rule out '*a priori* the possibility of an indirect transmission of Euclidean geometry via Fibonacci. Nonetheless, Piero's first-hand knowledge of the works of Euclid can be demonstrated by a close reading of his text'.
6 *Ibid.*, p. 57.
7 *Ibid.*, pp. 57–61.

the truncated tetrahedron; and the irregular 72-sided solid of revolution included in Campanus' translation of Euclid's Book XII.[7]

Davis writes: 'The mathematical rules for the correct, scientific measurement of regular and irregular geometrical solids demonstrated in the *Trattato d'abaco* were in a way, preliminary and necessary to a thorough understanding of the *De prospectiva pingendi*. As Piero wrote, a painter needed to know the significance of lines and angles in order to understand perspective.'[8] Peterson sees this as an argument that Piero's geometry 'derives from his art and intends to be useful to artists, a view which seriously misunderstands what is going on mathematically . . .'. In standard accounts of the history of mathematics, 'Piero is still a footnote to Pacioli. More space is given, as a rule, to explaining that Leonardo da Vinci did no mathematics than is given to anything that Piero did. It may seem that no reassessment is necessary of the period generally, since these works were never lost, only mislabelled, but this is to underestimate the baleful influence of Pacioli, who is considered emblematic of the fifteenth century. There is a quality to his work which makes it difficult to believe it could contain anything of merit. When Piero's work is segregated from it and correctly identified as the work of a different author, it takes on an integrity and intensity which appears altogether different. . . . Beneath the surface, the thought is surprisingly deep. Piero was a real mathematician – one can say that without apology. . . . Piero worked ambitiously in mathematics, proved new theorems, and even formulated and completed a coherent research program, the arithmetization of the later books of Euclid'.[9] Piero's great achievement was this: the arithmetization of geometry. He showed how the inexpressible magnitudes of geometrical reasoning could be expressed, within working tolerances, as the multitudes of arithmetic computation. Shape reduced to rational number.

Always bearing in mind Vasari's comment, much of Piero della Francesca's theoretical work is still to be found in the more accessible and better known writings of Luca Pacioli, especially as these relate to painting and architecture, and not just everyday commerce.[10] Pacioli certainly made direct use of Campanus' Euclid, indeed he restored this mediaeval version in opposition to Bartolomeo Zamberti's modern, 'humanist', translation from the Greek.[11] Pacioli's *De Divina Proportione* owes much to Piero, but not everything. It is in many ways a paean to a Platonic Euclid who never actually existed, but which the age conjured into existence to satisfy its intellectual tendencies, in somewhat the same way that in promoting the *prisca theologia* Hermes Trimegistus suited their esoteric demands.[12] Pacioli shows a version, presumably from Piero della Francesca, of Euclid's diagram of the comparison of the lengths of sides of the five regular polyhedra inscribed in the same sphere.

Pacioli acknowledges Leonardo da Vinci as illustrator of the Platonic solids in his treatise.

Leonardo da Vinci

Leonardo's own studies of polyhedra are somewhat puzzling, since some are full of obvious errors.

They are not the sketches of someone as fully in command of the mathematics as was Piero della Francesca. Leonardo seems to have attempted to square the circle. He notes: 'The night of St Andrew, I finally found the quadrature of the circle; and as the light of the candle and the night and the paper on which I wrote were coming to an end, it was completed; at the end of the hour'.[13] Completed, but failed. Connected with this endeavour are many figures drawn within circles including some based on the square, some on the hexagon, and some on the octagon.

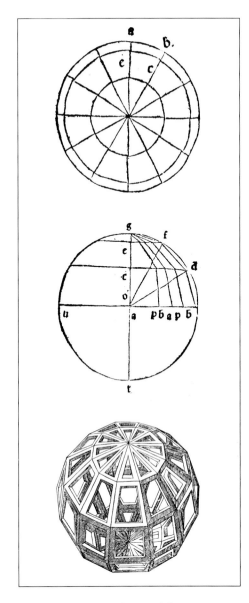

Fig. 2. 72-sided body from Pacioli, *De Divina Proportione*. The figure is associated with Euclid Proposition XII.17: 'Given two spheres about the same centre, to inscribe in the greater sphere a polyhedral solid which does not touch the lesser sphere at its surface'. Euclid's solution uses triangular and quadrilateral faces such as are depicted by Pacioli.

8 *Ibid.*, p. 43.
9 Peterson, *op. cit.*, pp. 38–40. He also gives an excellent account of how Piero's mathematical achievements were obfuscated.

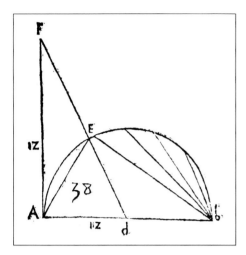

Fig. 3. Diagram in Pacioli (III.3, Figure 38) after Euclid's proposition XIII.18 showing a comparison of the lengths of sides of the five regular solids inscribed in the same sphere. The diameter of the sphere is the diameter of the semi-circle.

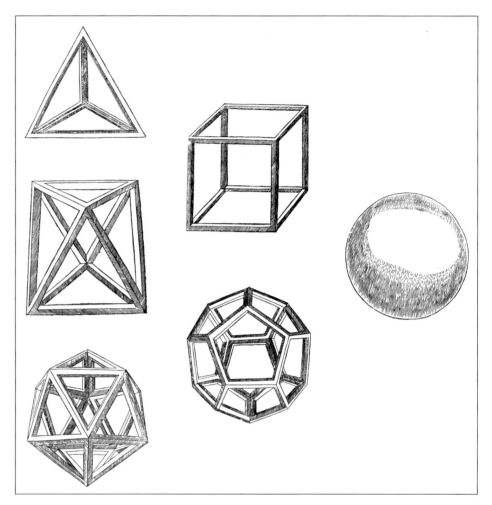

Fig. 4. The five Platonic solids and the sphere from Pacioli. The drawings are attributed to Leonardo da Vinci.

10 Cecil Grayson who has done so much to gather together Alberti's works has reported on a similar project for the writings of Piero della Francesca.
11 P. L. Rose, *The Italian Renaissance of Mathematics: Studies on Humanists and Mathematicians from Petrarch to Galileo*, Librairie Droz, Genève, 1975, pp. 50–52. 'Zamberti conflates Euclid the geometer with Euclid of Megara, the Platonist philosopher', a confusion that Pacioli perpetuates. Later, Rose, p. 144, quotes a letter accompanying Pacioli's 1509 edition of Euclid: 'Euclid infirm, pallid, shapeless, from the shadows of his ancient elegance. . . . These mathematical disciplines had lain in darkness for so many years. . . . Euclid's *Elementa* itself was so mutilated that Euclid himself would not have recognized it. But in our age Luca Pacioli has not only cleansed it but explicated it greatly.' *Vide*, Bartolomeo Zamberti ed., *Euclidis Megarensis philosophi platonici mathematicarum disciplinarum janitoris: habent in hoc volumine quicumque ad mathematicum substantiam aspirant: Elementorum libros XIII*, I Tacuini, Venice, 1505; and Luca Pacioli ed., *Euclidis Megarensis philosophi acutissimi . . . Opera*, Paganinus Paganinus, Venice, 1509.
12 *Vide*, F. A. Yates, *Giordano Bruno and the Hermetic Tradition*, Routledge & Kegan Paul, London, 1964.
13 *Codex Madrid II*, folio 112r. One of three great classical problems: doubling the square, squaring the circle, and doubling the cube. Squaring the circle is not possible with rule and compass, but this proof of impotence was not given until C. L. F. Lindemann, 1882. He was the first to show that π is a transcendental number. It follows that a Euclidean geometric construction is impossible. Some half-century earlier, A. M. Legendre had proved that π is neither rational,

Such designs have led to the idea that Leonardo systematically investigated the point groups of symmetry in the plane – a somewhat misleading claim given the evidence and intention of sketches similar to these.[14] Leonardo also arrives at an arithmetical approximation for doubling the cube, a problem noted by Vitruvius along with doubling the square.[15]

Another diagram indicates that Leonardo used the recursive, geometrical construction for square roots from $\sqrt{2}$ to $\sqrt{12}$ in setting out a series of twelve circles whose areas increase by the unit established by the smallest circle, so that the spaces between successive circles are each of unit area.[16]

Leonardo describes this art as 'the science of equiparation' in which different shapes are compared while some common property such as area, or perimeter, is kept invariant.

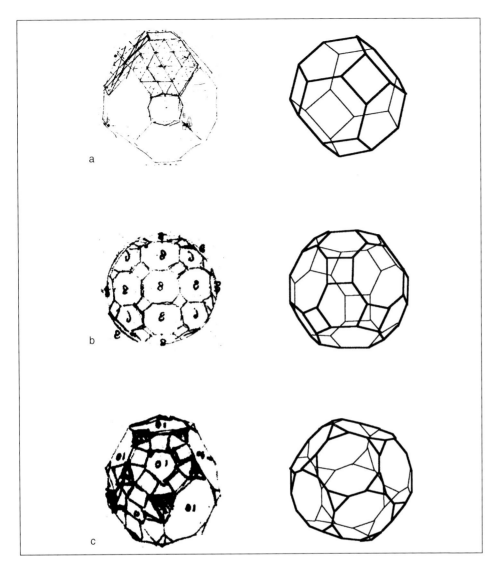

Fig. 5. Sketches (left) of polyhedra by Leonardo da Vinci after *Codex Atlanticus* 272v-b. On the right are the semi-regular figures most closely related to Leonardo's sketches:

a. Leonardo attempts to construct a truncated octahedron with square and hexagonal faces, but it is not possible for three hexagonal faces to coincide at a point without being flat. Each hexagon has an internal angle of 120° so that three angles sum to 360°, which is of course flat. Such an arrangement occurs in hexagonal pavement tilings. The drawing is incorrect, and the solid impossible.

b. Here Leonardo would seem to be sketching the great rhombicuboctahedron with square, hexagonal and octagonal faces. Once again he produces flat planes. Around the central octagonal face, Leonardo places four squares and four other octagons. Such a configuration produces the familiar square and octagon tiling to found in many floor designs. The result cannot be a solid.

c. Leonardo's design here is not necessarily incorrect. He appears to be inventing a new solid by building a pentagonal cupola upon the faces of a truncated dodecagon. The result is a solid with triangular, square and pentagonal faces. At the stage shown, with cupolae added to two adjacent decagonal faces, Leonardo has produced a polyhedron which is not convex. A design for a stellated cube, *exahedron elevatum vacuum*, in Pacioli, carries the tag 'Horum inventor Magister Lucas Paciolus de Burgo Sancti Sepulchri, Ordinia Minorum', indicating Pacioli's own interest in inventing and constructing non-convex forms.

nor rational in square. Leonardo's obsessive drawings show that he was not aware of Hippocrates' elementary theorem in which a 'lune' is rectified, a lune being the shape obtained when two circular segments of different radii, but each less than or equal to a semi-circle, both intersect. The resulting shape looks like a crescent moon. Whereas certain lunes can be rectified – that is their area can be reproduced in some figure with straight edges such as a triangle – there had never been a successful example of a segment being so reduced, and yet this is the hopeless approach that Leonardo takes.

14 H. Weyl, *Symmetry*, Princeton University Press, Princeton, New Jersey, 1952, p. 66. In his celebrated Louis Clark Vanuxem Lectures, Weyl sets out a table of two classes of central symmetry, and then writes that Leonardo's result 'is essentially our above table of the possible finite groups of rotations (proper and improper) in two dimensions'. *Vide infra*, 'Leon Battista Alberti'.

15 F. Granger, *Vitruvius: De Architectura*, II, pp. 199–201, 207. Vitruvius IX. Preface, gives the name 'Plato's theorem' to doubling the square. He names Archytas of Tarentum and Eratosthenes of Cyrene as providing theorems for doubling the cube. The solution of Archytas pictures the intersection of three surfaces of revolution, while that of Eratosthenes is a mechanical system. Leonardo does not use any of the classical methods. He observes that a cube of side-length 4 has a volume of 64, and that a cube of side-length 5 has a volume of 125 which is just less than twice 64, or 128. Leonardo remarks that the answer to doubling the cube of side-length 4, is '5 and a certain inexpressible fraction, which is easy to make but hard to say'. *Codex Antlanticus*, Folios 218 v.b, 58 r.a. *Vide*, A. Marinoni, 'The writer: Leonardo's literary legacy', in L. Reti ed., *The Unknown Leonardo*, Abradale Press, New York, 1988, pp. 56–85.

16 In the 1960s, this diagram received renewed relevance in land use and built form studies. Arranged as a series of concentric squares, and in ignorance of Leonardo's sketch, it was dubbed the Fresnel diagram after the French physicist's refraction circles. L. Martin and L. March eds., *Urban Space and Structures*, Cambridge University Press, Cambridge, 1972, p. 19.

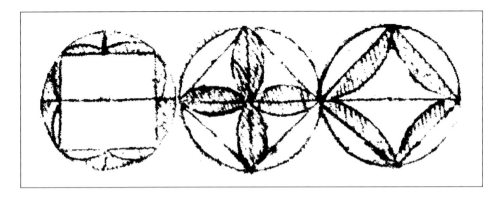

Fig. 6. Designs based on a square inscribed in a circle (after Leonardo, *Codex Atlanticus* 167r-ab).

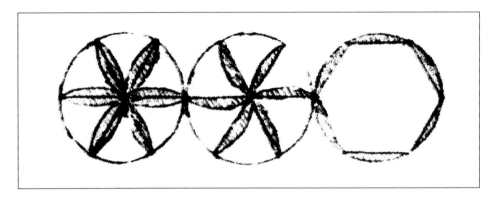

Fig. 7. Designs based on the hexagon inscribed in a circle (after Leonardo, *Codex Atlanticus* 106r-b).

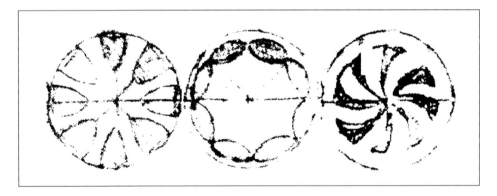

Fig. 8. Designs based on an octagon inscribed in a circle (after Leonardo, *Codex Atlanticus* 167r-ab).

Davis gives an analysis of the well-known portrait of Luca Pacioli attributed to Jacopo de' Barbari. The painting shows Pacioli dressed in his Franciscan habit standing before a table upon which are displayed an opened text of Euclid, a copy of Pacioli's *Summa*, surmounted by a model of a dodecahedron, and a slate with a

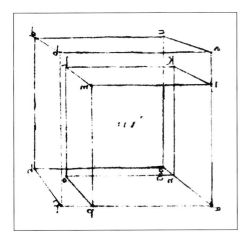

Fig. 9. Doubling the cube (after Leonardo, *Codex Atlanticus* 58r-a).

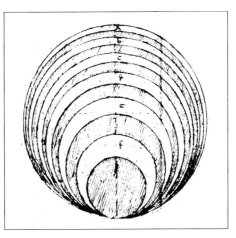

Fig. 10. A nest of circles increasing in area by a unit, the area of the smallest circle (after Leonardo, *Codex Atlanticus* 221v-b).

Fig. 11. Portrait of Luca Pacioli. Jacopo de' Barbari, 1495, Museo di Capodimonte, Naples.

mathematical figure. Suspended beside Pacioli is a translucent Archimedean semi-regular solid, a 26-face icosahexadron.[17]

Davis identifies the perspectival figure on the slate as an illustration of Euclid's Proposition XIII.12 since she reads the triangle as equilateral. A computer restoration shows that the figure is in fact the isosceles triangle which Euclid needs in his construction of a regular pentagon, which in turn is required to make a dodecahedron.[18]

Albrecht Dürer

It is not known from whom Albrecht Dürer learned perspective theory during his travels through Italy. His humanist friend in Nuremberg, Willibald Pirckheimer, received a letter from Dürer in Venice dated 13 October, 1506: 'I shall be finished here in another ten days. Then I shall ride to Bologna in order to learn more about the secret art of perspective, which someone there is willing to teach me.'[19] It is thought that Dürer met Luca Pacioli in Venice or Bologna when the latter was working on his edition of Euclid and *De divina proportione*. In 1507, Dürer himself purchased a copy of Zamberti's translation of the *Elements* in Venice two years after its publication. Strauss believes that Dürer acquired his knowledge of perspective from three sources: Piero della Francesca's manuscripts, for Dürer translates verbatim from *De prospectiva pingendi*; from Alberti's *De pictura*, a copy of which had been in the late Regiomontanus' library in what was to become Dürer's house in Nuremberg; and from Jean Pellerin's *De artificiale perspectiva* which had been published under the name Viator in 1505, and pirated under a German title in Nuremberg by 1509.[20]

It is not perspective theory that is of direct interest here, but Dürer's enthusiasm for regular figures – polygons and polyhedra – which was surely stimulated by the work of Piero della Francesca and its later promotion by Pacioli. Dürer, following both Alberti and Piero, believed that it was necessary for the painter to know

17 The 26-sided solid is almost certainly a cabalistic reference to the Tetragrammaton. See *infra*, 'Occult Number'.

18 T. L. Heath, *Euclid: The Thirteen Books of the Elements*, Cambridge University Press, Cambridge, 1926, II, pp. 96–100. Euclid Proposition IV.10: 'To construct an isosceles triangle having each of the angles at the base double the remaining one', that is, 36°, 36°, and 72°. Proposition IV.11 uses this triangle 'in a given circle to inscribe an equilateral and equiangular pentagon'. Proposition XIII.11 which immediately precedes the one cited by Davis deals not with an equilateral triangle, but with the regular pentagon: 'If in a circle which has its diameter rational an equilateral pentagon be inscribed, the side of the pentagon is the irrational straight line called minor'. The drawing on the slate seems to correspond to a partly completed figure 34 in *De Divina Proportione*, Part 3, Chapter 1. Although this figure was published after the portrait, it is in fact based on an earlier drawing from Piero della Francesca's *Libellus*.

19 W. L. Strauss trans, *The Painter's Manual: a manual of measurement of lines, areas and solids by means of compass and ruler, assembled by Albrecht Dürer for the use of all lovers of art with appropriate illustrations arranged to be presented in the year MDXXV*, Abaris Books, New York, 1977, p. 7. There could have been many teachers of perspective in Italy by this time. Strauss points to Pacioli as a likely candidate, pp. 30–31.

20 *Ibid.*, pp. 25–31.

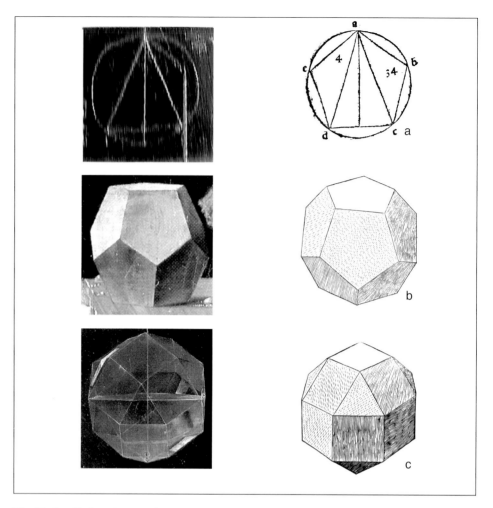

Fig. 12. Details from the portrait of Luca Pacioli compared with illustrations from *De divina proportione* after Piero della Francesca.

a. The drawing in perspective on the slate is restored by computer to show the original diagram. This may then be compared with the figure of an inscribed pentagon. Euclid's construction of the regular pentagon requires the prior construction of the isosceles triangle shown.

b. The dodecahedron with 12 faces, 20 vertices and 30 edges.

c. The icosahexadron. This solid is formed by cutting off the twelve edges of the cube to give twelve squares and eight equilateral triangles at the corners. The result is a solid which expresses the 26 semi-axes of the cube, the 6 from the centre through the faces, the 8 through the vertices and the 12 through the midpoints of the edges. Further it makes evident the symmetries of the cube. The threefold symmetry about axes through the vertices represented by the triangular faces; the fourfold symmetries about the square faces with four squares at their edges; and the two-fold symmetries of the squares with two triangles on opposite edges and two squares on the remaining edges. It should be noted that apart from having 26 faces, the icosahexadron has 72 edges and vertices taken all together.

precisely how to measure objects. In his introductory remarks to Willibald Pirckheimer, Dürer writes of contemporary German painters: 'They have . . . grown up in ignorance like an unpruned tree. Although some have achieved a skillful hand through continual practice, their works are made intuitively and solely to their tastes. Whenever knowledgeable painters and true artists had occasion to see such unplanned works, they smiled – not without reason – about the ignorance of these people. Nothing is more annoying to men of understanding than a blunder in a painting, no matter how diligently it may be executed. Because such painters have derived pleasure from their errors has been the sole reason that they never learned the art of measurement, without which no one can become a true artisan. It is the fault of their masters who themselves were ignorant of this skill.

'It is this skill which is the foundation of all painting. For this reason, I have decided to provide all those who are eager to become artists a starting point and a source for learning about measurement with ruler and compass.'[21]

Like Alberti in *De pictura*, Dürer starts his manual by distinguishing the nature of point and line for the mathematician and the artist. The mathematician's entities are invisible, but the painter must make marks to represent these.[22] There then follow definitions of surfaces and solids, constructions for spirals and plane curves of various kinds including the conic sections. Dürer knows that an ellipse is made by cutting through a cone within an appropriate angular range, but despite his own admonitions to young painters his intuition overrides mathematical knowledge and the ellipse is drawn egg-shaped, with the fatter end where the cut is made low down on the cone, and the pointed end where the cut is made higher up. The first book ends with designs of instruments to draw and copy in proportion.

Book 2 opens with a discussion of angles, triangles and quadrilaterals made of both straight and curved lines. Then Dürer launches into the construction of regular polygons from the equilateral triangle to a 16-sided figure inscribed in a circle.[23] Each construction is examined below.

Equilateral triangle. Dürer's construction derives from the regular hexagon, see 'hexagon' below. It is noteworthy that he does not use Euclid's very first proposition, I.1. Dürer shows how to determine an approximation to the length of side for the regular heptagon, the lengths marked with number 7.[24]

Square. A circle is drawn and a diameter struck. Through the centre a second diameter, perpendicular to the first is drawn. The four points where the diameters intersect the circle mark the vertices of the square.[25]

Pentagon. Dürer gives two constructions. Neither are Euclid's. One is derived from Pappus and is closely related to the construction of the decagon given by

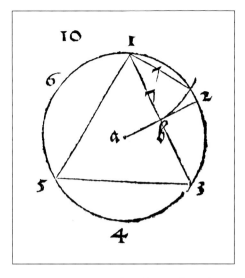

Fig. 13. Exact construction of an equilateral triangle inscribed in a circle by joining alternate vertices of a regular hexagon, 1, 3, 5. An estimate for the side of an heptagon derived from the triangle is marked 7 (from Dürer).

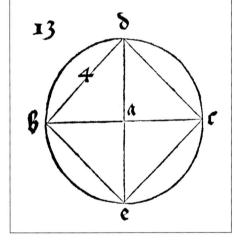

Fig. 14. Exact construction of a square inscribed in a circle (from Dürer).

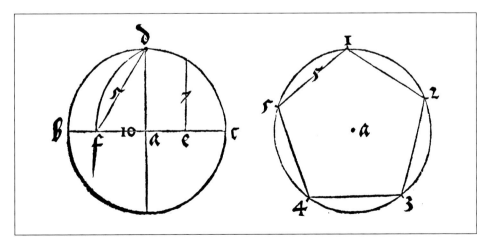

Fig. 15. Exact construction of a pentagon in a circle (from Dürer).

21 *Ibid.*, p. 37.
22 *Ibid.*, p. 41.
23 *Ibid.*, pp. 142–51.
24 *Ibid.*, pp. 142–43, Figure 10.
25 *Ibid.*, pp. 144–43, Figure 13.

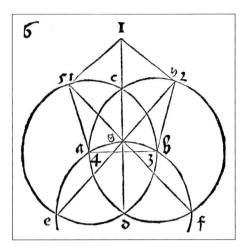

Fig. 16. Approximate construction of the pentagon (from Dürer).

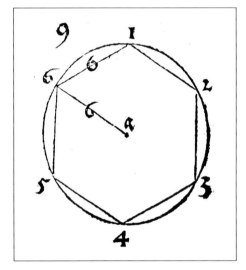

Fig. 17. Exact construction of a hexagon in a circle (from Dürer).

26 *Geometria Deutsch, aus der geometrey etliche nutzparliche stuck*, Nuremberg, *c* 1484–86.
27 *Vide infra* Fig. 19.
28 Note that the start of this construction bears similarities with that used by Euclid in Proposition I.1 to make an equilateral triangle on a line: a construction that Dürer curiously does not use in setting out an equilateral triangle. *Vide supra*, Fig. 13.
29 *Ibid.*, pp. 144–47, Figures 15, 16.
30 *Op. cit.*, Strauss p. 143.
31 *Vide infra* 'Alberti'.
32 It was arriving at this proof that moved the nineteen-year-old Carl Friedrich Gauss to take up

Alberti in *De re aedificatoria*, the other is an approximation based on craft knowledge recorded in *Geometria Deutsch*.[26] The first method takes a circle and its diameter. Through the centre a perpendicular is struck. From a point half-way along the radius on the diameter a line is drawn to the point of intersection of the perpendicular and the circle. The length of this line is laid out from the halfway point on the diameter through the centre of the circle and its end marked. From this mark to the point of intersection of the perpendicular and the circle is the length of side of the pentagon inscribed in the circle. Dürer notes this with the number 5. From the same mark to the centre of the circle is the length of the side of the decagon used by Alberti. Dürer notes this with the number 10.[27] Finally, from the half-way point, the perpendicular cuts the circle in a line whose length Dürer writes 'is equal to approximately one-seventh of the circle'.

The second method for the construction of the pentagon uses a fixed opening on the compass. Draw two circles that overlap and pass through each other's centre.[28] Connect the two centres with a straight line This line will be one of the edges of the pentagon. Also draw the perpedicular bisector of this line by joining the two points of intersection of the circles. At one of the two points where the circles intersect place the compass with the same opening and strike a circle through the first two centre points. Mark the points where this new circle cuts the first two. From these points draw two straight lines through the point where the perpendicular bisector cuts the new circle. Where these straight lines cut the original two circles mark two more vertices of the pentagon. 'Then erect', Dürer writes, 'two inclined lines of equal length [to the fixed radius of the circles] until they meet at the top. You will then have constructed a pentagon . . .'[29]

Hexagon. Dürer actually constructs this polygon first 'because it can be made without changing the opening of a compass'.[30] The construction is the same as used by Alberti and follows Euclid IV.15.[31] The equilateral triangle is formed by joining alternate vertices of the hexagon.

Heptagon. Dürer has already given two approximate ways of making a heptagon: from the equilateral triangle and from the construction of the pentagon. There is no straightedge and compass construction of the heptagon. A proof of impotence was not given until 1796.[32]

Octagon. The method used is to take a square inscribed in the circle and to erect the perpendicular bisectors of its sides. Where these cut the circle determines the remaining vertices of the octagon. Oddly, Alberti does not employ this direct method.[33]

Enneagon. With centres at the vertices of an equilateral triangle inscribed in a circle, and with the same fixed opening draw three *fischs blosen* (fish-bladders). Draw a radius through the original circle and divide this into three equal parts. One part is taken as the length of a new circle drawn concentric with the first. A line is drawn to join the points of intersection of this new circle with two of the *fischs blosen*. This line is the approximate side of the enneagon inscribed in the new circle.[34]

Decagon. See pentagon above.[35]

11-gon. Dürer takes a quarter of the diameter and extends it by one eight of its length, and uses this as the side of the 11-gon. He writes: 'This is a mechanical not a demonstrative method'.[36]

12-gon. The dodecagon is constructed by extending the perpendicular bisectors of the sides of the hexagon. Dürer does not show a construction, although one is given by Alberti.[37]

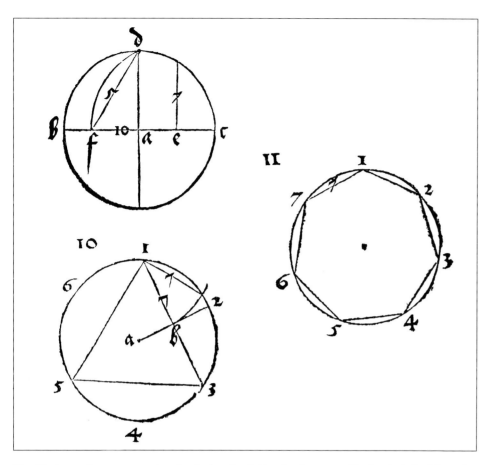

Fig. 18. Approximate constructions for the length of side of an heptagon. The first is derived from the construction of a pentagon and decagon, and the second from the equilateral triangle. In both cases the lengths are marked 7 (from Dürer).

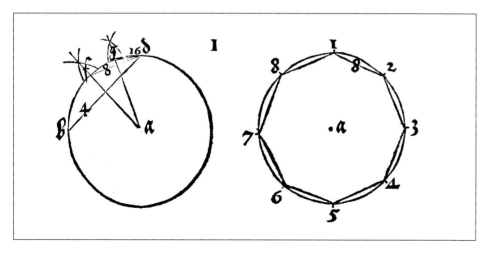

Fig. 19. Exact construction of an octagon by using the perpendicular bisectors of the sides of a square. This is a general method for doubling the number of sides of any inscribed polygon (from Dürer).

mathematics and not philology as his career. Gauss showed that rule and compass construction of odd-sided polygons is possible, if and only if the number of sides is either a Fermat prime of the form $2^{2^n} + 1$ or is made up of factors which are Fermat primes. The first three Fermat primes are 3 for $n = 0$, 5 for $n = 1$, and 17 for $n = 2$. Note that the 15-gon is constructible, as Euclid IV.16 shows, since 15 is the product of the first two Fermat primes. Polygons with 7, 9, 11 and 13 sides considered by Dürer are not then constructible by rule and compass, although he had no way of knowing that at the time. He shows approximate methods employed by craftsmen. Even-sided polygons are always constructible by rule and compass, if the root polygon is constructible. Thus, a 30-sided polygon is constructible, but a 26-sided polygon can only be approximated.

33 *Vide infra* 'Alberti'.
34 *Ibid.*, pp. 148–49, Figure 18.
35 *Ibid.*, pp. 144–46, Figure 15.
36 *Ibid.*, pp. 148–51, Figure 19.
37 *Vide infra* 'Alberti'.

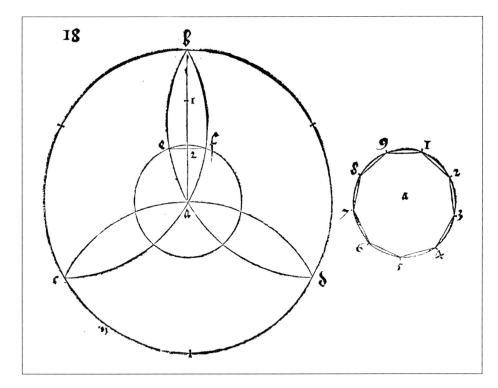

Fig. 20. Approximate construction of the enneagon (from Dürer).

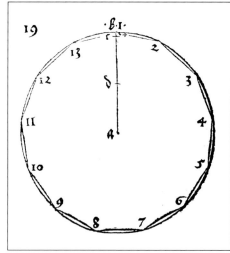

Fig. 22. Approximate construction of the 11-gon (from Dürer).

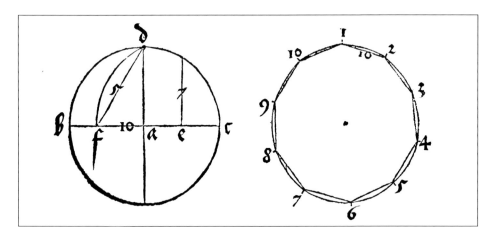

Fig. 21. Exact construction of the decagon following Pappus. The side of the decagon is marked 10. This is the same construction as used by Alberti (from Dürer).

Fig. 23. Approximate construction of the 13-gon (from Dürer).

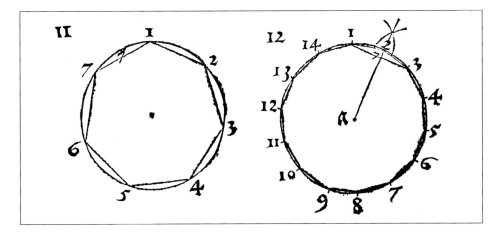

Fig. 24. Approximate construction of the 14-gon (from Dürer).

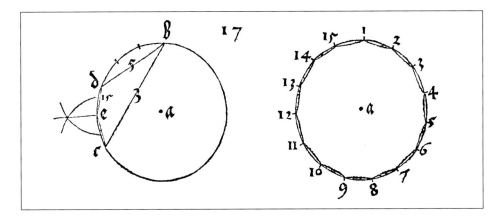

Fig. 25. Exact construction of the 15-gon following Euclid (from Dürer).

13-gon. Another approximate method. Dürer uses the half radius as side of the figure. His drawing shows that this is a rough approximation only.

14-gon. Dürer uses the perpendicular bisectors of the side of the heptagon. He mentions further recursions of this method 'to construct a figure with twenty-eight sides or twice as many'.[38]

15-gon. Dürer follows Euclid IV.16 and sets both an equilateral triangle and a regular pentagon to share a common vertex within the same circle. The length of side of the 15-gon is the shortest length between two distinct vertices.[39]

16-gon. Derived through recursive bisection from the octagon.[40]

Book 2 of *Underweysung der messung* continues with the development of planar patterns and designs: these include the construction of pointed stars, tiling patterns using triangles, squares, pentagons ... to octagons, some including designs which combine more than one tile type, examples of proportional increase of surface areas, and comparing areas of different figures, including the construction of a circle of the same area as a square, the *quadratura circuli*. Dürer demonstrates that only the equilateral triangle, the square, and the hexagon, among regular figures will tile

38 *Ibid.*, pp. 142–43, Figure 12.
39 *Ibid.*, pp. 146–49, Figure 17.
40 *Ibid.*, pp. 144–45, Figure 14.

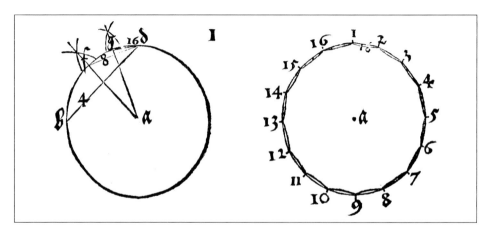

Fig. 26. Exact construction of the 16-gon (from Dürer).

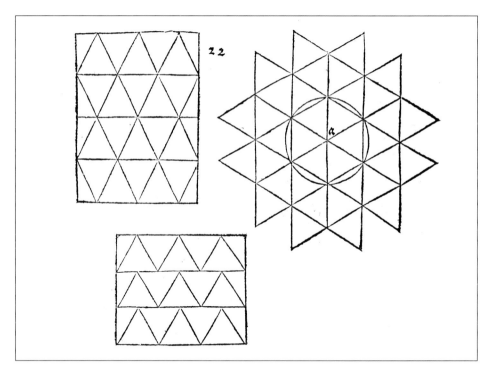

Fig. 27. Triangular plane-filling tilings (from Dürer).

41 *Ibid.*, p. 158ff, Figures 22, 23 and 25.
42 *Ibid.*, p. 160ff, Figures 24, 26, and 27.
43 *Ibid.*, p. 168, Figure 27. *Vide infra*, p. 172, for Barbaro's presentation of star polygons.
44 *Ibid.*, pp. 178–79, Figure 34. Dürer takes the diameter of the square and divides it into ten parts, he uses eight of these parts as the diameter of the circle. In terms of these parts, the square has an area of 50, and this is also the area of the circle if π is assumed to have the value 3 1/8.

the plane without gaps,[41] but decorative designs can be made using pentagons, heptagons, and octagons with filling elements.[42] He also shows some starlike polygons made by superimposing figures over one and other.[43]

In showing an approximate method for *quadratura circuli*, Dürer writes that it 'has not yet been demonstrated by scholars. But it can be done approximately for minor applications or small areas . . .'[44] He gives the general case of Pythagoras' theorem in which similar figures placed similarly on the sides of a right-angled triangle are related in area: the combined area of the two figures on the sides which

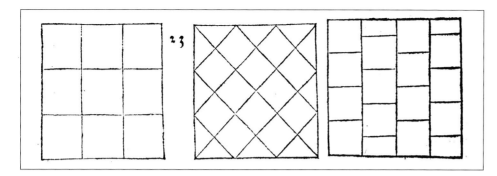

Fig. 28. Square plane-filling tilings (from Dürer).

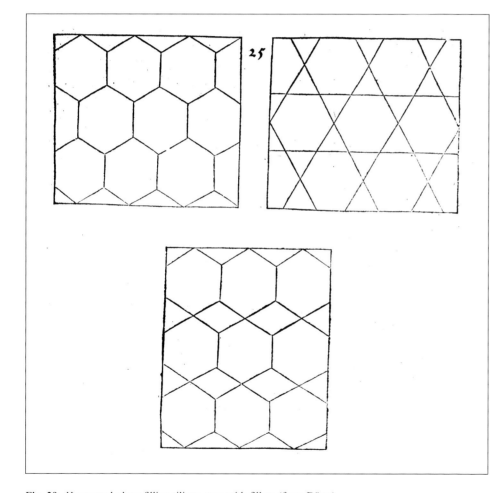

Fig. 29. Hexagonal plane-filling tilings, two with fillers (from Dürer).

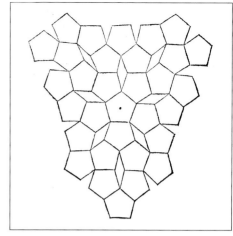

Fig. 30. A tiling using pentagons and fillers (from Dürer).

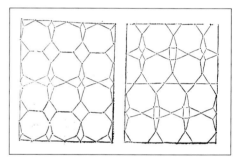

Fig. 31. Tilings using heptagons and fillers (from Dürer).

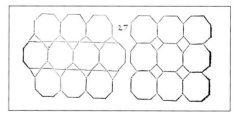

Fig. 32. Tilings using octagons and square and half-square fillers (from Dürer).

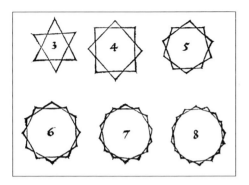

Fig. 33. Starlike polygons made by superimposition (from Dürer).

include the right-angle will be equal to the area of the figure on the side opposite the right-angle. In this form the theorem allows the designer to add areas, just as he may add line lengths.[45]

In Book 3, Dürer examines solid bodies such as columns and cones with circular and polygonal ground plans. He discusses the design of vaults, but gives only one example. This is of interest since it displays pinwheel symmetry.[46] There are instructions for the construction of sundials, followed immediately by the construction of both the classical Antiqua and the gothic Fraktur alphabets.[47] Book 4 deals with three topics. Firstly, the Platonic solids, the tetrahedron, the octahedron, the icosahedron, the cube, the dodecahedron, and the sphere, a few Archimedean solids,[48] an irregular design of his own comprising six dodecagonal faces and thirty-two triangles not all of which are equilateral, and the 72-faced solid from Piero della Francesca and Luca Pacioli.[49]

45 *Ibid.*, pp. 179–80, Figure 35.
46 *Ibid.*, pp. 190–91, Figure 4. A similar design is to be found in late 'gothic' manuals of the sixteenth century, F. Bucher, *Architector: the Lodge Books and Sketchbooks of Medieval Architects*, Abaris Books, New York, 1979. *Vide infra*, Fig. 47.
47 *Ibid.*, pp. 21–22 and nn. 39–41. Strauss cites Georg Dehio who in 1881 suggested that Dürer's most likely source for his alphabet designs, as with Pacioli's in *De divina proportione*, is an anonymous manuscript addressed to Piero de' Medici in which a letter by the 'learned Greek scholar Johannes Lascaris (1445?-1535) . . . stresses the importance of the introduction of the ancient, noble, and authentic letters of the alphabet'. The manuscript shows how to construct the Latin alphabet with each letter described and illustrated. The Greek and Hebrew alphabets are illustrated without commentary.
48 *Ibid.*, pp. 316–24 covers the five Platonic solids. Dürer's plan and elevation views of the solids are mostly incorrect since he shows their vertices touching the outer circumference of the orthographic view of the sphere. This is most obvious when the cube and octahedron are compared. The octahedron is drawn correctly, but the cube is shown with the same side lengths as the octahedron which cannot be. Six Archimedean solids are shown, pp. 330–43: the truncated tetrahedron, the cuboctahedron, the truncated octahedron, the rhombicuboctahedron, the snub cube, and the truncated cuboctahedron. In the edition of 1538, Dürer adds the truncated icosahedron and the icosidodecahedron, pp. 414–17.
49 *Ibid.*, pp. 417–18. This is not in the 1525 edition, but is added to the edition of 1538. E. Panofsky, *The Life and Art of Albrecht Dürer*, Princeton University Press, Princeton, New Jersey, 1955, p. 259 writes: 'Dürer treats seven – in the revised edition of 1538 even nine – of the "Archimedean" semi-regulars, plus several bodies of his own invention (for instance, one composed of eight dodecagons, twenty-four isosceles triangles and eight equilateral triangles), and instead of representing the solids in perspective or stereographic images, he devised the apparently original and, if one may say so, proto-topological method of

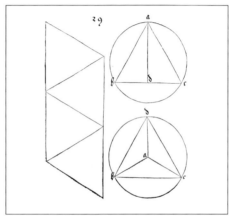

Fig. 34. Cutout for assembling a tetrahedron and supposed orthogonal views of the solid inscribed in a sphere (from Dürer).

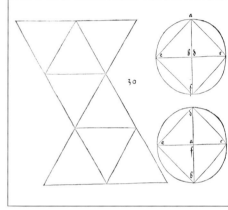

Fig. 35. Cutout for assembling an octahedron and correct orthogonal views of the solid inscribed in a sphere (from Dürer).

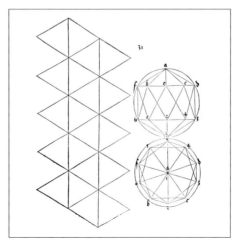

Fig. 36. Cutout for assembling an icosahedron and supposed orthogonal views of the solid inscribed in a sphere (from Dürer).

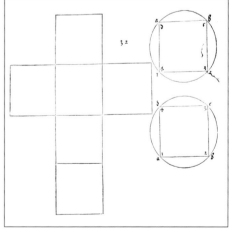

Fig. 37. Cutout for assembling a cube and supposed orthogonal views of the solid inscribed in a sphere (from Dürer).

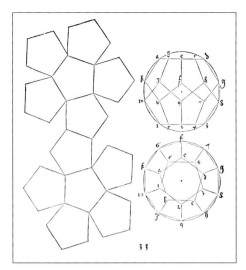

Fig. 38. Cutout for assembling a dodecahedron and supposed orthogonal views of the solid inscribed in a sphere (from Dürer).

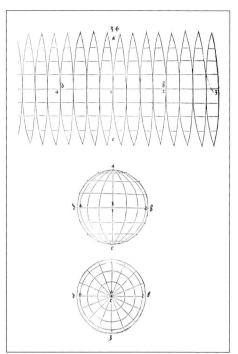

Fig. 39. Cutout for assembling a spherical solid based on a 16-gon at the equator (from Dürer).

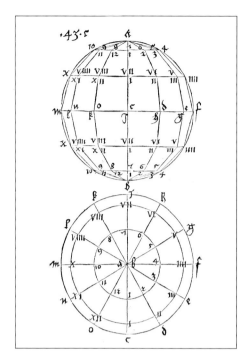

Fig. 40. Orthogonal views of a solid with 48 quadrilateral faces and 24 triangular faces (from Dürer).

Secondly, the Delic problem of doubling the cube which is generalized to some extent to include tripling and quadrupling.[50]

Thirdly, a section on perspective drawing with its well-known woodcuts of Dürer's instruments. The presentation of the regular figures is accompanied by Dürer's cutout designs which when folded produce the solid object.[51]

That Dürer had something to learn from a perspective master on his Italian jouney is now clear. To be a master of perspective it was necessary to draw the Platonic solids accurately. This was the ultimate test established by Piero della Francesca and those who followed him. To draw a room in perspective, a fireplace, a table was one level of achievement, but to construct the Platonic and Archimedean solids that was altogether something else. Dürer unfortunately seems to fail at the very first step – the precise representation of the solids in orthographic projection! If these are incorrect, then no reasonable perspective can be produced. It would seem that it was not the general scenic use of perspective that Dürer sought, but this highly specialized constructive method associated with the regular and semi-regular figures in particular. It is noteworthy that Dürer does not actually show any perspectives of the solids.[52]

Sebastiano Serlio

Serlio does not present such a systematic treatment of regular figures. He does, however, show constructions for a pentagon, a hexagon, an octagon, and an ennegon. In his discussion of the pentagon, Serlio again uses the Pappus construction found

developing them on the plane surface in such a way that the facets form a coherent "net" which, when cut out of paper and properly folded where two facets adjoin, will form an actual, three-dimensional model of the solid in question.'

50 Dürer uses the method of Pappus, *Synagoge* iii, pp64–68, viii, pp. 1070–1072. The method uses rule and compass, but also requires a straight edge which is turned about a given point until 'certain intercepts which it cuts off between two pairs of lines are equal'. T. L. Heath, *A History of Greek Mathematics*, Clarendon Press, Oxford, 1921, I pp. 266–68. Strauss, *op. cit.*, p. 349, notes that the duplication of the cube was described by Dürer's contemporary, Johannes Werner, *Libellus Verneri Nurembergen*, Nuremberg, 1522.

51 Strauss, *op. cit.*, pp. 316–47.

52 *Ibid.*, p. 29–30. There is the stone polyhedron in *Melancholia I*, a cube truncated on two opposite corners to produce a solid with two equilateral triangular faces and six nonregular pentagonal faces. W. M. Ivins Jr, *On the Rationalization of Sight*, Metropolitan Museum of Art Papers 8, New York, 1938, argues that Dürer failed to understand his predecessors' theoretical contributions to perspective theory. This explains, argues Strauss, why 'although not apparent at first glance, the stone is a perfect cube, seen in Dürer's own peculiar perspective'. Dürer's novel polyhedron has 18 edges, 12 vertices and 8 faces, a geometric proportion of 9 : 6 : 4.

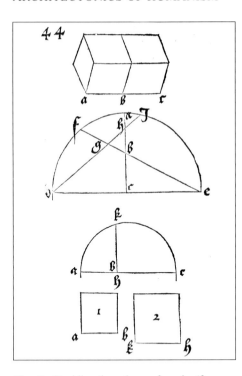

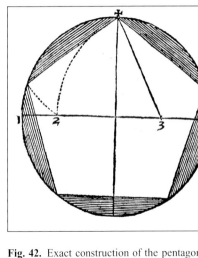

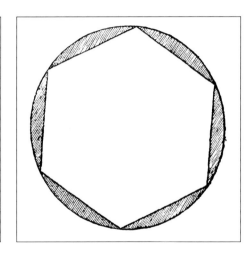

Fig. 42. Exact construction of the pentagon and decagon (from Serlio).

Fig. 43. Exact construction of the hexagon (from Serlio).

Fig. 41. Doubling the volume of a cube (from Dürer).

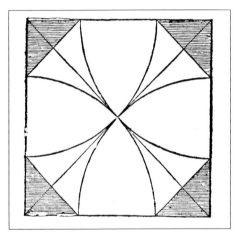

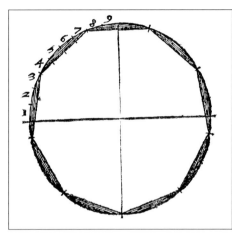

Fig. 44. Exact construction of the octagon (from Serlio).

Fig. 45. Approximate construction of the enneagon (from Serlio).

in Alberti, and points to the concomitant evaluation of the length of side of the decagon. He does not make use of the value for the side of the heptagon suggested by Dürer, but he suggest that the dimension marked 1 to 2 is a side of the 16-gon, which it is not – at least not precisely. Dürer has already demonstrated an exact method for this.[53] If Serlio was referring to Dürer in this brief section he would surely have used the latter's construction for the octagon, when in fact he uses Alberti's second method. Serlio's primary source seems to be Alberti.

Like Dürer, Serlio acknowledges craft methods. He gives a general method for approximating the division of the circumference of a circle 'into any number of parts required, regardless of how large that number may be, even if it is odd'. The method takes the quarter circumference and divides that into the appropriate number of parts by eye, and then four of these parts are the divisions required for the whole circle.[54] The example he gives is the enneagon.[55] Serlio rehearses the doubling of

53 V. Hart, P. Hicks, *Sebastiano Serlio: On Architecture*, Yale University Press, New Haven, 1966, p. 29 n. 51, suggest that this construction for a 16-sided figure is derived from Dürer, but I find no evidence for this.
54 *Ibid.*, p. 29.
55 Note that Serlio does not use Dürer's construction for the enneagon, nor his approximations for the 11-gon and 13-gon. Serlio does mention Dürer in Book I *Tutte l'opere d'architettura et prospetiva*, Hart and Hicks *op. cit.*, p. 24, in connection with the drawing of an egg-shaped line for the design of vases.

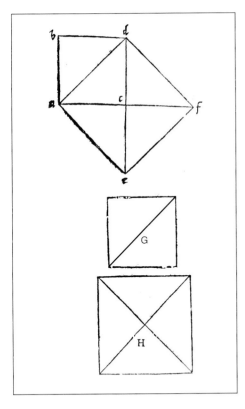

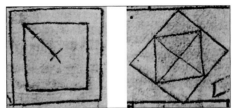

Fig. 47. (Above) Doubling the area of a square (after Villard de Honnecourt):.
a. 'In such a way one makes the galleries and the garden a cloister'. The galleries cover the same area as the open quadrangle.
b. 'In this way one partitions a stone so that its two halves are square'.

Fig. 48. (Right) Doubling the circle (after Serlio).

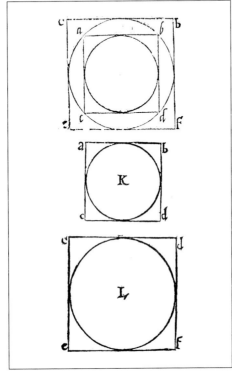

Fig. 46. (Above) Doubling the area of a square (after Serlio).

the square in a way that is reminiscent of Villard d'Honnecourt's demonstration in the thirteenth century, suggesting that mediaeval methods lived on.[56]

He also gives a way of doubling the circle.

These matters deal with the the problem identified by Vitruvius as 'Plato's theorem' where the sides of the squares, or the diameters of the circles, are in the ratio $1 : \sqrt{2}$.

Daniele Barbaro

Daniele Barbaro's *La pratica della perspettiva* followed new editions of his celebrated commentaries on Vitruvius.[57] Barbaro had made a point of excluding perspectival drawing from the legitimate representations to be employed by the architect. The Aristotelian scholar found it difficult to reconcile the distortions of perspectival drawing with that category of drawing in which measurements were

56 Hart and Hicks, *op. cit.*, p. 9.
57 Daniele Barbaro, *La pratica della perspettiva di Monsignor Daniele Barbaro Eletto Patriarca D'Aquileia, opera molto profittevole a pittori, scultori, et architetti*, Camillo & Rutillo Borgominieri fratelli. Venice, 1569. Concerning Daniele Barbaro, *vide infra*, 'Andrea Palladio'.

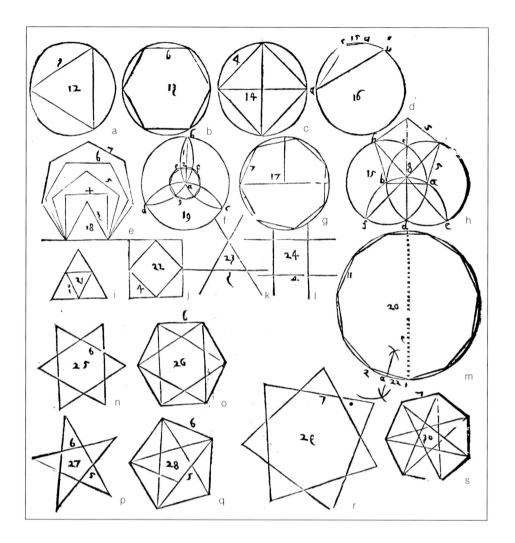

Fig. 49. Diagram from Barbaro, *La pratica*, showing regular figures in the plane:

a. equilateral triangle inscribed in a circle,
b. hexagon in a circle,
c. square in a circle,
d. construction for a 15-sided figure, after Euclid,
e. nested polygons on the same base from the equilateral triangle to the regular heptagon,
f. an approximate construction for the enneagon, after Dürer,
g. heptagon in a circle,
h. an approximate construction for the pentagon, after Dürer,
i. quadrupling areas of nested equilateral triangles,
j. doubling areas of nested squares,
k. plane filling triangle,
l. plane filling square,
m. 11-gon in a circle. Also indicated is the bisection to create a 22-gon,
n. star hexagon, two disjoint equilateral triangles,
o. star hexagon in a circle,
p. star pentagon,
q. star pentagon in a circle,
r. star heptagon based on every second vertex,
s. star heptagon based on every third vertex inscribed in a regular, convex heptagon.

58 F. J. Laven, *Daniele Barbaro: Patriarch Elect of Aquileia*, PhD Dissertation, University College London, 1957, comments on this, pp. 386–87: 'The first two of these types of drawing, plan and elevation drawn to an identical scale, caused no bother. But the third – Vitruvius' "scaenographia" – greatly embarrassed Barbaro. Indeed, he expatiated upon the matter on two occasions, repeating the arguments of the "Commentaries" in the "Perspective", so worried was he by this Vitruvian aberration. Barbaro's objection to the inclusion of "scaenographia" as part of disposition was based on the demands of Aristotelian logic. The three types of drawing had, in Barbaro's view, to conform with each other in so far as they were all species of the same aesthetic genus, disposition. . . . Disposition could only be usefully and logically conceived by the architect in terms of plan, elevation and cross-section with perhaps the addition of a model. All of these could, and always the first three should, be made as proportionate representations of the proposed work.'
59 *Vide supra*, Fig. 57.

correctly shown, as in orthographic views of plan, elevation and section.[58] A separate volume preserved this distinction. A distinction which Andrea Palladio honours in *I quattro libri dell'architettura*, where his drawings are all, with just one exception, orthographic. Palladio does not show perspectival views such as those commonly featured in Serlio.

It is clear that Barbaro owes much to Dürer. He reprints the woodcut of Dürer's perspectival apparatus,[59] but he does also make reference to Serlio, showing his three theatrical settings for the tragic, the comic and the rustic. Much of *La pratica della perspettiva* is devoted to Piero della Francesca's programme: the construction of the regular Platonic solids and their semi-regular Archimedean derivatives for the purpose of educating the artist in perspective drawing. Barbaro employs Dürer's cutout technique for assembling models, but he also gives correct, see-through, orthographic plans and elevations of the solids from which perspective views may be accurately constructed. This is the theory that Dürer sought during his earlier visit to Italy, and if he had actually learned the techniques they would have surely been exploited in *Underweysung der messung*. He does not. The evidence suggests, then, that he did not acquire this particular knowledge during that visit. There is a world of difference – the humanists' world – between Dürer's treatment of solid figures and Barbaro's precise opticality. Barbaro's theoretical contributions remain underestimated, perhaps because he never was a practitioner. Today both Piero della Francesca and Albrecht Dürer are valued as painters more than theoreticians, and even Alberti's texts – aloof from everyday craft – excite interest, in part, because of his built works.

Barbaro summarizes his knowledge of regular, planar figures in a single plate at the beginning of Part 2 of *La pratica della perspettiva*, which illustrates Chapter 1: '*Pratica di descrivere le figure di molti anguli in uno circolo*'.

It is remarkable that Barbaro does not use the exact construction of the pentagon familiar to Alberti, Dürer and Serlio, but repeats Dürer's approximate, second method. He gives Dürer's approximate construction for the enneagon and 11-gon, which he takes by bisection to the 22-gon. Barbaro illustrates some star polygons, the 5, 6, and 7-pointed stars, including the two distinct stars that can be formed from the heptagon by joining every second, or every third, vertex.[60] He indicates the plane filling properties of the square and the triangle (from which the hexagon follows). Two figures show the doubling series of square areas and the quadrupling series of triangular areas. Perhaps, for the first time, Barbaro produces a diagram in which the regular polygons are nested on the same base.[61]

Part 3 of *Pratica della perspettiva* deals with the 'mode of elevating solid bodies from their plans'. It is by far the longest section of Barbaro's treatise.[62] Systematically, he treats of the perspective representations of the Platonic solids, giving cutout patterns for models of the polyhedra. The cutout patterns for the octahedra and dodecahedron differ in layout from those shown by Dürer. Barbaro then turns to the semi-regular solids. First, the truncated tetrahedron with triangular and hexagonal faces, then the cuboctahedron, the truncated cube with triangular and octagonal faces, the 26-faced small rhombicuboctahedron which had been shown as a translucent body in the portrait of Luca Pacioli.[63] His list includes the truncated dodecahedron with triangular and decagonal faces, and indeed all thirteen Archimedean semi-regular solids with the exception of the two snub forms.[64] Barbaro includes a number of cutouts for convex polyhedra with regular polygonal faces apparently of his own invention including three with dodecagonal faces.[65] He also shows two stellated polyhedra formed by elevating the faces of a dodecahedron and icosahedron with pentagonal and triangular pyramids respectively.[66]

A third stellated form places tetrahedra on the triangular faces of the icosidodecahedron leaving its pentagonal faces exposed. Barbaro concludes Part 2 with a figure showing a stellated torus, or 'mazzocco'.[67]

This theme is taken up in Part 3, '*La perfetta descrittione del mazzocco*'. Here, Barbaro shows his indebtedness to Piero della Francesca's programme in *De prospectiva pingendi*, as a comparison of illustrations indicates clearly.

Part 4 deals with techniques for drawing architectural elements in perspective and concludes with the illustrations of stage designs lightly adapted from Serlio's Book II. In Part 5 Barbaro briefly rehearses the '*secreta parte di perspettiva*'. Barbaro illustrates these principles with a perspectival tour-de-force, a stellated spherical object with 180 faces based on the twentyfold longitudinal division of the sphere.

In Part 6, '*Spiegatura, descrittione, et digradatione della sphera*', Barbaro employs Dürer's unfolding of the sphere as a flat cutout. He also takes the pole of a sphere marked with longitudinal and latitudinal lines as viewpoint and projects the lines onto the plane upon which the sphere rests. He then produces zodiacal diagrams.

60 G Molland trans, *Thomas Bradwardine: Geometria Speculativa*, Franz Steiner Verlag, Stuttgart, 1989. Bradwardine (c1300–1349), sometime Chancellor of St Paul's Cathedral and then Archbishop of Canterbury, writes, p. 37: '. . . discussion about them is rare, and I have not seen a discussion of them, except only by Campanus, who only casually touches on the pentagon a little.' Mollond notes, p. 11(7), 'Luca Pacioli lifted many of the comments in his edition of Campanus's version of Euclid verbatim and without acknowledgement from the *Geometria*'; and also 'the humanist Juan Luis Vives ranked Bradwardine with Archimedes and Ptolemy among those authors not necessary to students who were studying mathematics as a preparation for the arts'.

61 This figure is rescusitated in the twentieth century as the basis for the theme in Max Bill's lithographs, *Quinze variations sur un même thème*, Editions des Chroniques du Jour, Paris Ve, 1938. Bill adds the octagon and nests the polygons in a spiral.

62 D. Barbaro, *M. Vitruvii Pollionis De architectura libri decem, cum commentariis*, Franiscum Franciscium Senensem and Ioan. Crugher Germanum, Venice, 1567, pp. 43–128.

63 *Vide supra*. Fig. 12.

64 The snub cube and the snub dodecahedron are not found by truncation, but by translating the faces of the cube and dodecahedron outwards, rotating them and then filling in the space between with equilateral triangles. Unlike the other eleven Archimedean figures which exhibit bilateral symmetry about their axes, the two snub solids are handed and possess rotational symmetries only.

65 Attempts to construct polyhedra from Barbaro's cutouts will show that some are derived from prior cutouts, but that they are in fact impossible solids. In one case Barbaro requires six hexagons to surround a seventh. Like Leonardo he ends up with a flat tiling, not a polyhedral surface. In another case, an arrangement of squares and triangles around a hexagon also ensure a flat surface. Today, we know that only regular polygons with 3, 4, 5, 6, 8, 10 faces will be found in uniform polyhedra, that is, those convex solids all of whose faces are regular polygons. *Vide*, B. Grünbaum and N. Johnson, 'The faces of a regular-faced polyhedron' *Journal of the London Mathematical Society*, 40, pp. 577–86, 1965. Barbaro's cutouts include regular polygons with 12 sides which simply cannot be. It seems that the patrician's intellectual fabrications were untouched by manual demonstration and never put to the ultimate pragmatic test: make it!

66 The elevated icosahedron imitates the *icosahedron elevatum* shown in Pacioli, *De Divina Proportione*, *op. cit.* Figures XXV, XXVI. But, whereas Pacioli's *dodecahedron abscisum elevatum* shows both triangular and pentagonal pyramids, Barbaro's figure elevates just pentagonal pyramids on each pentagonal face of the dodecahedron. It is not clear from the drawings that Barbaro appreciated that both of these figures can be constructed by intersecting star pentagons. Today, the first is known as the small stellated dodecahedron and the second as the great stellated dodecahedron. They comprise two out of four Kepler-Poinsot polyhedra.

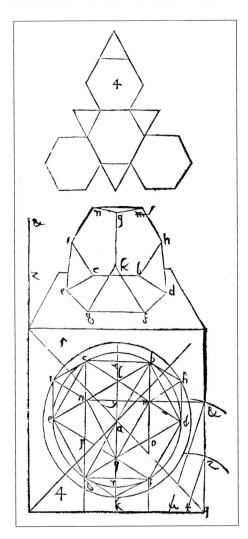

Fig. 50. Cutout, plan and perspective of the truncated tetrahedron (from Barbaro, *La pratica*).

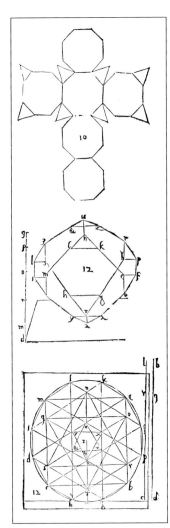

Fig. 51. Cutout, plan and perspective of the truncated cube (from Barbaro, *La pratica*).

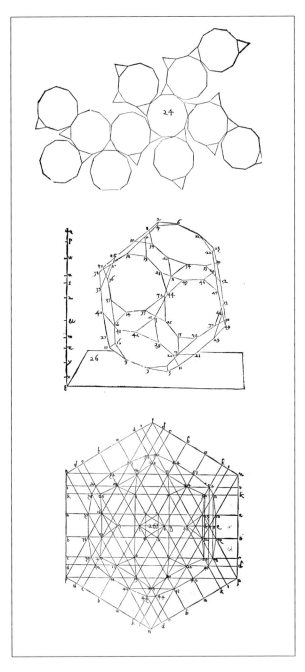

Fig. 52. Cutout, plan and perspective of the truncated dodecahedron (from Barbaro, *La pratica*).

67 Named after 'mazzocchio', the decorated Florentine cap. The drawing is remarkably similar to a toroidal object in Wenzel Jamnitzer, *Perspectiva corporum regularium*, published in Nuremberg, 1568, one year before Barbaro's book. Both designs are based on a sixteenfold division of the circle. Jamnitzer's work makes explicit reference to 'die fünff Regulirten Cörper, darvon Plato in Timeus und Euclides inn sein Elementis' in its extended title.
68 Girolamo Cardano, *De subtilitate*, Lyons, 1559, Book XIII. Barbaro uses the same figure in his Vitruvian commentaries, *vide infra*.

Part 7 deals with light, shade and colour, and is illustrated by casting the shadow of a cube. Part 8, '*Misuratione del corpo humano*', makes reference to Vitruvius, but is illustrated by the figure of a man from Girolamo Cardano.[68] Barbaro illustrates methods for drawing the human head which echo those used by Dürer, but

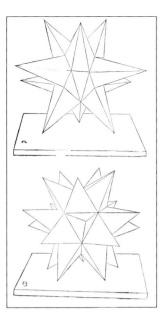

Fig. 53. Two stellated polyhedra
(from Barbaro, *La pratica*).

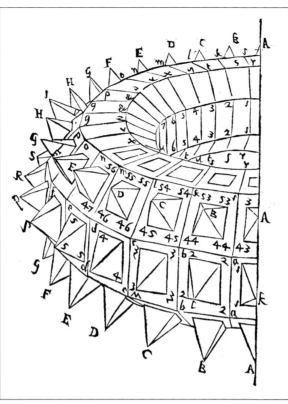

Fig. 54. Half of the thirty-two-sided, studded 'mazzocco'
(from Barbaro, *La pratica*).

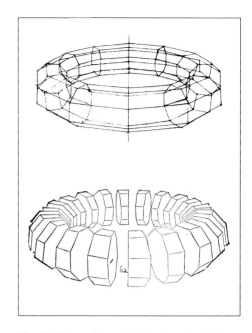

Fig. 55. Comparison of designs by Piero della
Francesca and Daniele Barbaro:
a. Torus with an octagonal cross-section
(from Piero della Francesca).
b. Fragmented torus made of octagonal prisms
(from Barbaro, *La pratica*).

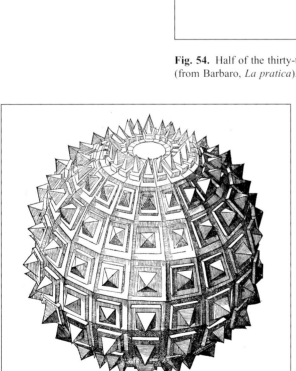

Fig. 56. Perspective drawing of a studded spherical object
(from Barbaro, *La pratica*).

Fig. 57. Instrument for constructing perspectives:
a. Woodcut of the second method (from Dürer).
b. Adaptation of Dürer's woodcut (from Barbaro, *La pratica*).

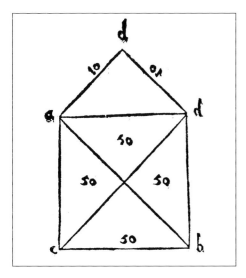

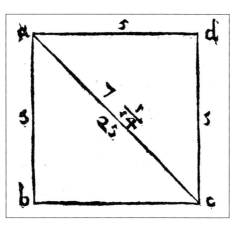

Fig. 58. Doubling the area of a square of side length 10. The square on the diagonal has an area of 100, and the orthogonally oriented square has an area of 200 (from Barbaro, *Vitruvius*).

Fig. 59. In a square of side length 5. the diameter is approximately 7 1/14. This gives a rational convergent of 99 : 70 for √2 : 1 (from Barbaro, *Vitruvius*).

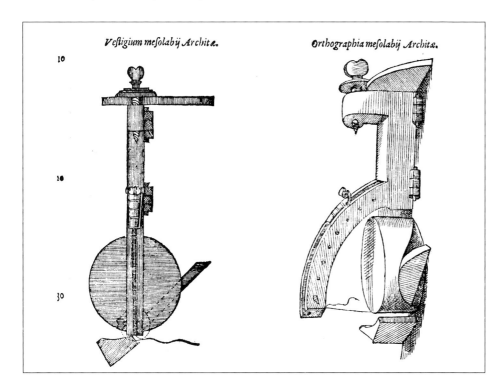

Fig. 60. Instrument for applying the method of Archytas for doubling the volume of cube (from Barbaro, *Vitruvius*).

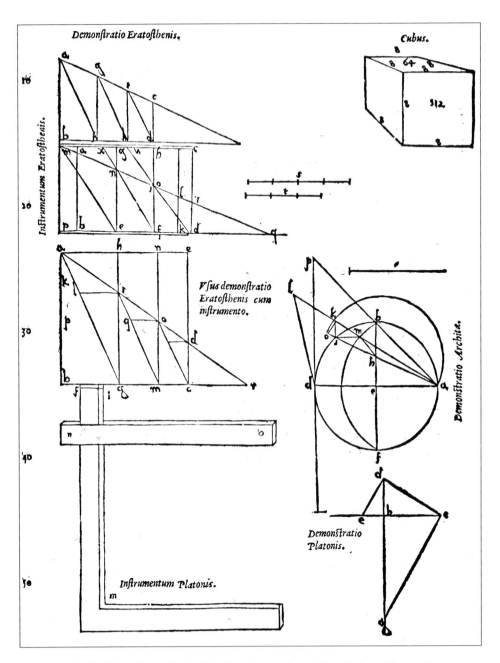

Fig. 61. Method of Eratosthenes for doubling the volume of cube (from Barbaro, *Vitruvius*).

without acknowledgement.[69] Part 9 proposes a design for a sun globe, '*horario universale*', before concluding with an adaptation of Dürer's woodcut of one of his instruments for constructing perspective drawings.[70]

In Barbaro's commentaries on Vitruvius the problems of doubling the square and the cube are addressed.[71] He gives two diagrams related to doubling the square. One follows Serlio, but, in the text, Barbaro gives dimensions 10, 10 and 14 for the right

69 Albrecht Dürer, *Vier Bücher von Menschlicher Proportion.*
70 *Op. cit.*, Barbaro, *La pratica*, p. 191. 'Lo instrumento di Alberto Durero da pigliare in perspettiva'.
71 *Op. cit.*, Barbaro, *Vitruvius*, Book IX.

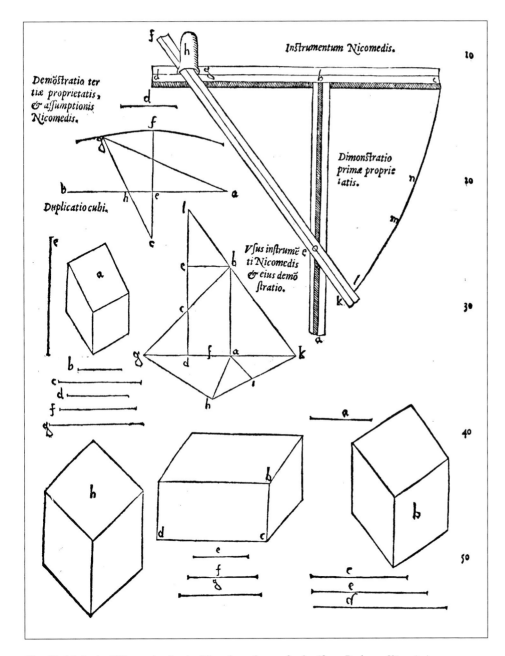

Fig. 62. Method of Nicomedes for doubling the volume of cube (from Barbaro, *Vitruvius*).

isosceles triangle, a quarter of the square. The area of each quarter square is thus 50. In adopting 14 as the length of the hypotenuse, he uses the rational approximation 7 : 5 for $\sqrt{2}$: 1. The small square has an area of 100. The larger square has an area of 196, close to 200. But if the hypotenuse had been 15 the area would be 225, and certainly more than double.[72] Another diagram uses the finer approximation 99 : 70.[73]

72 *Ibid.*, Figure, p. 279. Barbaro, p. 268, cites Vitruvius: '*Id autem numero nemo potest inuenire; nanque si 14, constituerentur, etunt multiplicati pedes 196, si quindecim, pedes 225.*'
73 *Ibid.*, pp. 268–70.

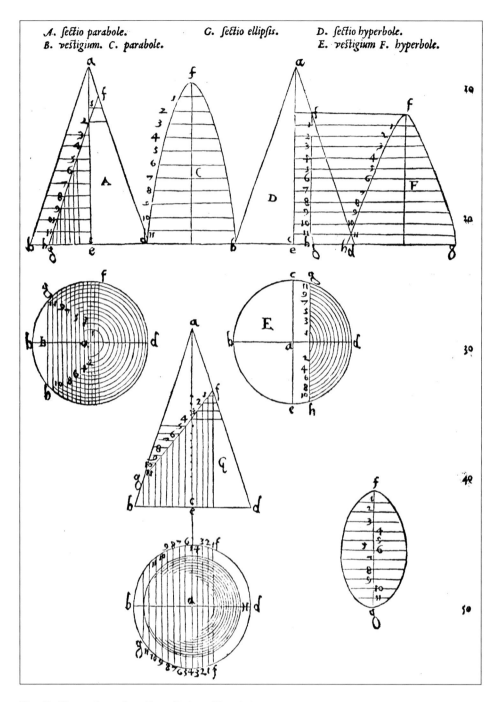

Fig. 63. The conic sections (from Barbaro, *Vitruvius*).

For the duplication of the cube, the Delic problem, Barbaro explicates and illustrates the methods of Archytas[74] and Eratosthenes[75] mentioned by Vitruvius, but adds the concoidal method proposed by Nicomedes.[76] In his commentary of Vitruvius IX.7 on sundials, Barbaro sets out the conic sections. Following Dürer he repeats the same error, but less obviously, of making the ellipse an egg-shape.[77] Palladio was surely familiar with Barbaro's geometrical investigations. The Renaissance tradition of central design based on regular polygons is seen to have been continued into the seventeenth century by Vincenzo Scamozzi.[78]

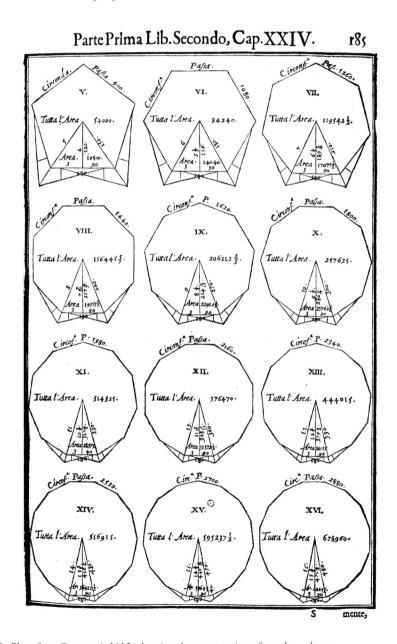

Fig. 64. Plate from Scamozzi, 1615, showing the construction of regular polygons.

74 *Ibid.*, p. 270–81, Figure, p. 277.

75 *Ibid.*, Figure, p. 279.

76 *Ibid.*, Figure, p. 280.

77 *Ibid.*, Figure, p. 304.

78 Palladio's younger contemporary, his jealous rival, and executor of his architectural testament – most notably the cupola of La Rotonda and extensions to Teatro Olimpico. Vincenzo Scamozzi *L'Idea dell'Architettura Universale . . .* Venice, 1615. In Germany, Daniel Specklin also shows the construction of regular polygons in *Architectura von Vestungen* Strassburg, 1589. Specklin's book is considered to be 'second in importance and in date only to Albrecht Dürer's *Unterricht zur Befestigung'*. T. Besterman ed. *The Printed Sources of Western Art 5, Daniel Specklin: Architectura von Vestungen,* Collegium Graphicum, Portland OR, 1972.

LEON BATTISTA ALBERTI

During his time in the court of Nicholas V, Alberti gave architectural advice to his friend on the renewal of Rome.[1,2,3] Among the church buildings, which would have been familiar to him, were the Pantheon, known as Santa Maria Rotonda; Santa Costanza; Santo Stefano Rotondo; and the Lateran Baptistery. All of these exhibit centralized plans: the first three are essentially circular, the last is octagonal. The circular plans are subdivided radially: the Pantheon is divided sixteenfold at ground level, but its hemispherical dome is divided into twenty-eight; Santa Costanza is twelvefold in plan; and Santo Stefano Rotondo is based on a division of twenty-two columns in its inner circle and forty-four in the next ring.

In Alberti's day, Santo Stefano had already had its inner circle divided in half so that only twenty of the original columns stood free. It is believed that Alberti may have advised that the outer ring of forty-four columns be incorporated as pilasters in a new outer wall, reducing the extent of the structure considerably.[4]

Although these buildings were in Christian use in the fifteenth century, it is generally thought that they were all identified in the fifteenth and sixteenth centuries as

1 Tommaso Parentucelli was born in 1398. He was a fellow student of Alberti's acquaintance at the University of Bologna. He became Pope in 1447 as Nicholas V.

2 Born in 1404, Battista Alberti was the natural child of a Genoese widow, fathered by Lorenzo Alberti, a member of a powerful Florentine merchant-banking family then living in exile in Genoa. He died in 1472, twenty years before Piero della Francesca's death.

3 For an overview of Alberti's involvement, see J. Gadol, *Universal Man of the Early Renaissance*, The University of Chicago Press, Chicago, 1969, p. 93ff. Also F. Borsi, *Leon Battista Alberti*, Phaidon, Oxford, 1975, p. 29ff. Both authors make use of T. Magnuson, 'The Project of Nicholas V for Rebuilding the Borgo Leonino in Rome', *Art Bulletin*, 36, 1954, pp. 91–115. Magnuson does not promote Alberti's contributions as much as other commentators. See also C. W. Westfall, *In this Most Perfect Paradise; Alberti, Nicholas V, and the Invention of Conscious Urban Planning in Rome, 1447–55*, Pennsylvania State University Press, Philadelphia, 1974.

4 Borsi, *op. cit.*, pp. 41–50. *Vide supra.* 'Christian works'.

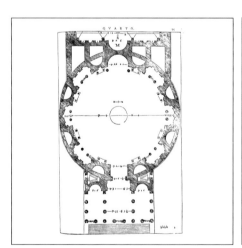

Fig. 1. Pantheon, Santa Maria Rotonda. Plan (after Palladio, Plate LI). Note the 16 diametral axes locating the entrance, the apses, and the niches.

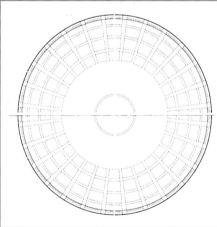

Fig. 2. Pantheon, Rome. Ceiling plan of the dome, showing the division of the circle into 28 coffers.

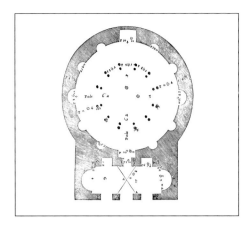

Fig. 3. Santa Costanza, plan (after Palladio, Plate LXI). Note the 12 diametral axes for the entrance, and the apses.

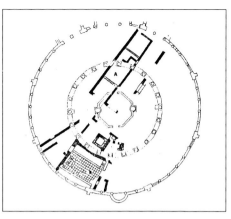

Fig. 4. Santo Stefano Rotondo showing earlier Roman foundations. Note the 44 columns built into the outer wall, and the 22 diametral axes for the 22 original columns, two of which have been replaced later by piers, defining the – now bisected – inner circle.

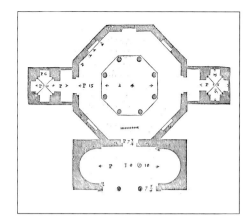

Fig. 5. Lateran Baptistery. Plan (after Palladio, Plate XLII). Note the 8 diametral axes centred on the sides of the octagon for the entrance and the apses; and the 8 diametral axes joining opposite vertices of the octagon which locate the position of the inner ring of columns.

Fig. 6. The Old Sacristy of San Lorenzo, Florence. Dodecagonal ceiling plan of the dome.

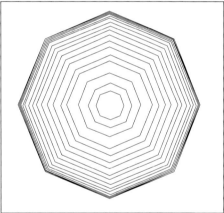

Fig. 7. The Duomo, Santa Maria del Fiore, Florence. Octagonal plan. Based on a photogrammatic diagram of the inner shell (after Battista).

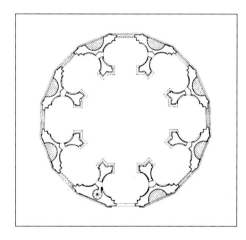

Fig. 8. Santa Maria degli Angeli, Florence. Brunelleschi's octagonal plan.

original pagan temples.[5] In fact, only Hadrian's Pantheon (118–128CE), believed to be an earlier Augustan monument, was not built specifically for Christian practice. Santa Costanza was built by the Christian convert, Emperor Constantine, as a mausoleum for his daughters Costanza and Elena (*c*377–350CE). The Lateran Baptistery was originally founded by Constantine, but assumed its present form under Pope Sixtus III (432–440CE).

Between 1428 and 1443, Alberti had occasion to spend time in Florence. There he would have seen the astonishing contributions of Filippo Brunelleschi (1377–1446): the Old Sacristy of San Lorenzo, its twelve ribbed dome and hexagonal lantern; the unprecedented construction of the octagonally framed Duomo of

5 For a discussion of circular and polygonal forms in the mediaeval period see R. Krautheimer, 'Introduction to an "Iconography of Medieval Architecture"', *Journal of the Warburg and Courtauld Institute*, 5, 1942, pp. 1–33. Among the centralized churches, the author mentions Santa Costanza, Santo Stefano, and the Lateran Baptistery.

Fig. 9. The Galluce, Rome. Decagonal plan (after Palladio, Plate XXIV). Now known as the Temple of Minerva Medica, Rome. The side apses, based on an 18-gon, are a later addition.

6 E. Battista, *Filippo Brunelleschi: the Complete Work*, Rizzoli International, New York, 1981. The outside walls form the sides of a 16-gon.

7 Borsi, *ibid.*, pp. 277–88.

8 J. Rykwert, N. Leach, R. Tavernor trans, *Leon Battista Alberti: On the Art of Building in Ten Books*, MIT Press, Cambridge MA, 1988. This text is based on the critical edition of G. Orlandi, *Leon Battista Alberti, L'architettura (De re aedificatoria)*, Edizioni il Polifilo, Milan, 1966.

9 J. Leoni trans, *Leon Battista Alberti: The Ten Books on Architecture*, from the Italian translation by Cosimo Bartoli, ed. Joseph Rykwert, Alec Tiranti, London, 1955.

10 *Ibid.*, IX.7, Rykwert, Leach, Tavernor, p. 196: 'All temples consist of a portico and, on the inside, a *cella*; but they differ in that some are round, some quadrangular, and some polygonal. It is obvious from all that is fashioned, produced, or created under her influence, that Nature delights primarily in the circle. Need I mention the earth, the stars, the animals, their nests, and so on, all of which she has made circular? We notice that Nature also delights in the hexagon. For bees, hornets, and insects of every kind have learned to build the cells of their hives entirely out of hexagons.

'The round plan is defined by the circle. In almost all their quadrangular temples our ancestors would make the length [of the plan] one and a half times the width. Some had a length one and a third times their width, and others a length twice their width. . . .

'For many-sided plans, the ancients would use six, eight, or even ten angles. The corners of all such plans must be circumscribed by a circle'.

Santa Maria del Fiore which had reached the base of the lantern by 1436; and the site works for Santa Maria degli Angeli, a centralized project generated from an octagon, begun in 1434, but abandoned in 1437.[6]

Some years were to pass before Alberti himself became involved in another centralized project in Florence. The Annunziata design was inititated by Michelozzo di Bartomeleo (1396–1472) around mid-century, but during the course of construction disputes ensued in which Alberti is cited as an authority supporting the central, decagonally generated plan.[7] This project derives from the Temple of Minerva Medica in Rome and would have represented, for Alberti and his contemporaries, the first major centralized structure of their day to be based on a pre-Christian exemplar.

Sometime around 1450, Alberti presented an unillustrated manuscript of his architectural treatise, *De re aedificatoria*, to Nicholas V. Further manuscript copies were soon in circulation, some with illustrations by the copyists. The first printed version was published posthumously in 1486. Nevertheless, its magisterial influence was felt before its widespread distribution, and well before a printed translation from Latin into Italian was published in 1546.[8]

Fig. 10. Decagonal plan of Michelozzo's Church of the Annunziata, Florence.

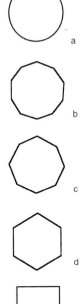

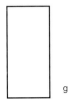

Fig. 11. Alberti's canon of seven temple 'platform' types:

a. circle,
b. decagon,
c. octagon,
d. hexagon,
e. square and a third,
f. square and a half,
g. double square.

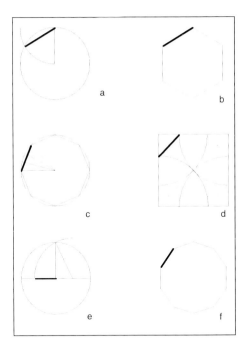

Fig. 12. Alberti's geometrical constructions:

a. the side of an inscribed hexagon,
b. the hexagon,
c. the octagon inscribed in a 24-gon,
d. the side of the regular octagon inscribed in a square,
e. constructing the side of an inscribed decagon,
f. the decagon.

Citing 'our ancestors' and 'the ancients', Alberti describes the forms of temples, or in Leoni's translation, their 'platforms'.[9,10] Seven recommended platforms may be classed in three distinctive types : one circular, three rectangular, and three polygonal.

A circle is a circle, it is one of a kind. However, there is no limit to the differences between rectangles, or the varieties of polygons. Alberti selects just three of each for special attention. Among the rectangles he chooses a square and a third, a square and a half, and the double square. Among the polygons he chooses those that are regular, that are both equiangular and equilateral. Of these he selects only those that are even-sided, and then only the six-sided hexagon, the eight-sided octagon, and the ten-sided decagon. The square alone is a member of both the set of rectangles and the set of regular polygons. It is noteworthy that the square is conspicuously absent from Alberti's seven recommended shapes.[11]

11 R. Wittkower, *Architectural Principles in the Age of Humanism*, Academy Editions, London, 1998, p. 17, counts nine basic forms. Along with the seven, he adds the square and the dodecagon. These two shapes do occur later in the text, but are not specifically recommended for temples. Indeed, Alberti's text makes it clear that these shapes may be required to construct some of his prescribed polygons. These 'may be plotted exactly using the circle. For half the diameter of the circle will give the length of sides of the hexagon. And if you draw a straight line from the centre to bisect each of the sides of the hexagon, it is obvious how to construct a dodecagon. From a dodecagon it is obvious how to derive an octagon, or even a quadrangle.' Then, Alberti gives an alternative method of constructing an octagon, deriving it from the inscribed square. This is followed by the construction of the regular decagon. These constructions are examined more closely below, as is the counter-example of Alberti's use of a square in the plan of San Sebastiano, Mantua. *Vide infra*, p. 200.

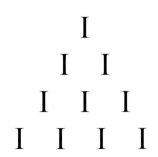

Fig. 13. The *tetraktys*.

12 V. Hart, P. Hicks, *Sebastiano Serlio: On Architecture*, translated from the Italian *Tutte L'Opere D'Architettura et Prospetiva*, Books I–V, Yale University Press, New Haven, 1996, p. 30. R. Tavernor, R. Schofield, *Andrea Palladio: The Four Books of Architecture* translated from the Italian *I Quattro Libri dell'Architettura*, MIT Press, Cambridge MA, 1997, p. 27. *Infra*, Appendix I 'Canons of Proportion'.

13 M. D. Davis, *Piero della Francesca's Mathematical Treatise: The 'Trattato d'abaco' and 'Libellus de quinque corporibus regularibus*", Longo Editore, Ravenna, 1977.

14 Pappus, *Synagoge*, or *The Collection*, V.3, 'Digression on the Semi-Regular Solids of Archimedes', cited in T.L. Heath, *A History of Greek Mathematics*, Clarendon Press, Oxford, 1921, II, p. 394.

15 Pappus writes of the bees: 'Presumably because they know themselves to be entrusted with the task of bringing from the gods to the accomplished portion of mankind a share of ambrosia in this form, they do not think it proper to pour it carelessly on ground or wood or any other ugly and irregular material; but, first collecting the sweets of the most beautiful flowers which grow on the earth, they make from them, for the reception of the honeycombs, (with cells) all equal, similar and contiguous to one another, and hexagonal in form. And that they have contrived this by virtue of a certain geometrical forethought we may infer in this way. They would necessarily think that the figures must be such as to be contiguous to one another, that is to say, to have their sides in common, in order that no foreign matter could enter the interstices between them and so defile the purity of their produce. Now only three rectilineal figures would satisfy the condition, I mean regular figures which are equiangular and equilateral; for the bees would have none of the figures which are not uniform . . . . There being then three figures capable by themselves of exactly filling up the space about the same point, the bees by reason of their instinctive wisdom chose for the construction of the honeycomb the figure which has the most angles, because they conceived that it would contain more honey than either of the two others.'

What possible pattern is there in this selection. Alberti puts forward seven temple forms – not at all the same seven as the Greek forms described by Vitruvius. Later Serlio and Palladio each select seven, but not identical, preferred room shapes.[12] In setting down their canons, the number seven probably carries some numerological significance for these authors. The lengths and breadths of the rectangular platforms are in the ratios 4 : 3, 3 : 2, 2 : 1, which correspond to ratios between successive lines of the Pythagorean *tetraktys*.

The ratio 1 : 1, associated with the square, would sit uncomfortably in such a pattern requiring, as it would, a comparison of not one line with another, but of a line to itself.

The polygons can be associated with just those three that emerge from truncations of the five regular polyhedra, the Platonic solids which so fascinated Alberti's younger acquaintance, Piero della Francesca (*c*1410–1492).[13] The Greek mathematician Pappus (*c*300CE) reports in the *Synagoge* that Archimedes studied these semiregular derivatives, enumerating thirteen polyhedra, all but two of which result from truncations of the Platonic solids.[14] Alberti may have had access to Pappus' work. The remarks concerning bees and the hexagonal formation of the honeycomb made by Alberti in introducing the topic of platform types, reflect words on the sagacity of bees by Pappus which preface his isoperimetric comparison of regular polygons and his enumeration of the thirteen Archimedean solids.[15] Heron of Alexander (*c*250) also includes a list of the Archimedean semi-regular polyhedra in his *Definitiones*.[16] In *Metrica* Heron systematically studies the regular polygons from the equilateral triangle to the regular, twelve-sided dodecagon, including the hexagon, the octagon and the decagon, giving various dimensions derived from the length of a side.[17] Both Pappus and Heron could be mathematical sources for Alberti's interests in regular polygons, a subject that was further developed in Piero della Francesca's mathematical manuscripts.

The primary polygons associated with the Platonic solids are easily determined from Alberti's set by adjoining alternate vertices: the equilateral triangles of the four-faced tetrahedron, the eight-faced octahedron, and the twenty-faced icosahedron come from the hexagon; the squares of the six-faced cube come from the octagon; and the pentagons of the twelve-faced dodecahedron come from the decagon.[18]

The number sequence 3, 4, 5, of sides of the triangle, square and pentagon evoke the side lengths of the Pythagorean triangle. Indeed, the numbers 6, 8, 10, themselves are sides of a very special Pythagorean triangle since it is one (of just two) whose perimeter shares the same number with its area, namely 24. The other triangle is 5, 12, 13, for which perimeter and area amount to 30.

In *De re aedificatoria*, Alberti refers to the 'ancient' use of 6 and 10 as extremes in an argument that produces 8, the arithmetical mean, as the height of the Ionic column in modules of its diameter.[19] In this argument 6 and 10 are ostensibly derived from the human figure. Full frontal, the width of the figure to its height is reckoned to be 1 : 6, while in a side view the width, from front to back, to the height is 1 : 10. In the Bible[20], the beam, 50 cubits, to the length of Noah's ark, 300 cubits, is 1 : 6, and its height, 30 cubits, to length is 1 : 10. This is Alberti's reluctant genuflection to the Vitruvian anthropometric analogy.[21] No squares. No circles. No wretched being crucified on the axes of unyielding geometry.[22]

What seems to have attracted Alberti's attention is the concern for 'perfection' to be found in the numbers 6 and 10 in Vitruvius' Book III. Six, because its factors 1, 2, 3, sum to itself, is said to be arithmetically perfect. A number such as eight,

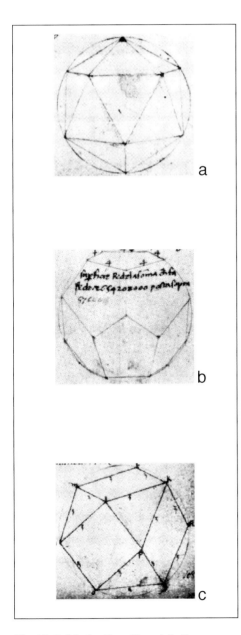

Fig. 14. Polyhedra (from Piero della Francesca, *Trattato d'abaco* a, c, and *Libellus de quinque corporibus* b):

    a. icosahedron.
    b. dodecahedron.
    c. cuboctahedron.

Fig. 15. Deriving the faces of the regular polyhedron from the hexagon, octagon and decagon.

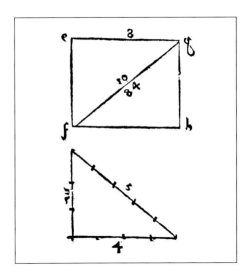

Fig. 16. The 6, 8, 10 Pythagorean triangle (from Barbaro).

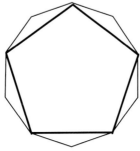

'Bees, then, know just this fact which is of service to themselves, that the hexagon is greater than the square and the triangle and will hold more honey for the same expenditure of material used in constructing the different figures'. Heath, *ibid.*, II, pp. 389–90.

    Nicholas V was actively engaged in commissioning translations of Greek mathematical texts. It is thought that a Greek codex of the Pappus was in private circulation from 1424 although it was not lodged in the Vaticana until the early 1500s. P.L. Rose, *The Italian Renaissance of Mathematics*, Libraire Droz, Genève, 1975, p. 28.

16 Heath, *op. cit.*, II, p. 315 cites Heron of Alexandria, *Definitiones*, Definitions 95–97.
17 *Ibid.*, II, p. 317, pp. 326–29 citing Heron of Alexandria, *Metrica*, I, 17–25.
18 It is significant that Alberti derives the construction of the decagon from Ptolemy and not Euclid. Alberti does not specifically give a construction for the pentagon, although the two constructions are intimately related. Ptolemy's construction is described in his *Syntaxis*, I, *ibid.*, Heath, II, pp. 277–78. In preparation for developing a Table of Chords, required for his astronomical observations, Ptolemy gives a lemma for finding the side lengths of a pentagon and decagon, or the chords subtending arcs of 18° and 36°. In his proof, Ptolemy makes use of Euclid's Propositions 9 and 10 from Book XIII (T. L. Heath, *Euclid: The Thirteen Books of The Elements*, Cambridge University Press, Cambridge, 1926, III, pp. 455–61); Euclid's construction for the constituent isosceles triangles forming a regular pentagon is given in Proposition 10, Book IV, (*ibid.*, Heath, II, pp. 96–100).
19 Rikwert, Leach, Tavernor, *op. cit.*, IX.7, p. 309. 'When they [the ancients] considered man's body, they decided to make columns after its image. Having taken the measurements of a man, they discovered that the width, from one side to the other, was a sixth

with factors 1, 2, 4, which sum to less than 8, is said to be deficient; while a number such as 12 with factors 1, 2, 3, 4, 6, which sum to more than 12 is said to be abundant.[23] The number 10 is not arithmetically perfect, it is easy to see that it is deficient, its factors summing to 8. Nevertheless, because the Pythagoreans had marvelled at the fact that 1 the monad, 2 the dyad, 3 the triad, and 4 the tetrad, summed to

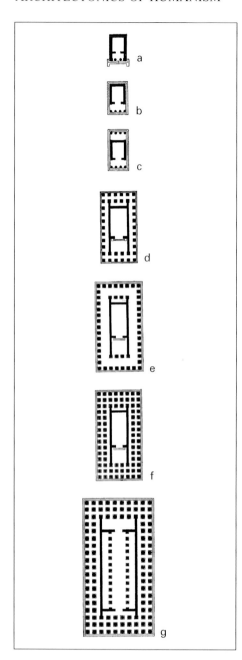

Fig. 17. The seven Vitruvian temple forms (after Warren, in Morgan):

a. *in antis*,
b. *prostyle*,
c. *amphiprostyle*,
d. *peripteral*,
e. *pseudodipteral*,
f. *dipteral*,
g. *hypaethral*.

10 the decad, and had enshrined this into the *tetraktys*, by which they swore, the number 10 assumed theological, if not arithmetical perfection.[24] Vitruvius, in effect, canonizes these two numbers. Further, he conjoins them to make a third 'perfect' number by summing the first two, $6 + 10 = 16$.[25] Yet it is transparent that 16 is deficient too, its factors summing to 15. Vitruvius seems to be drawing attention to the figurate nature of number. The numbers 6 and 10 are triangular numbers. Pebbles can be arranged to form triangular figures in both cases. It is a theorem of figurate numbers that two successive triangular numbers, such as 6 and 10, sum together so that a square arrangement of pebbles may be formed; that is to say, the sum of triangular numbers 6 and 10 is 16, a square number.[26] These reasons and sources give pattern to Alberti's selection of platform shapes. The choice shows a strong theoretical mind in which observation is subordinate to idea.

In describing the planning of temples, Vitruvius refers primarily to rectangular plans.[27] He casts these into seven types.

No proportions are given for the platforms of *in antis*, prostyle, or amphiprostyle temples.[28,29,30] Vitruvius then describes four temple forms with columns all round the *cella*. The peripteral has six columns in front and back, and eleven down each side with the corner columns repeated; the pseudodipteral has eight columns front and back, and fifteen along the sides.[31,32] Given equal intercolumniations, both these temple forms have a platform in 2 : 1 ratio. The dipteral temple has eight columns in front and back but it has a double row of columns all round.[33] The hypaethral temple has ten columns back and front, 'for the rest it has everything like the dipteral'.[34] Vitruvius does not specify the number of columns along the sides of these last two temple forms.[35] With but one exception, Vitruvius does not recommend temple platforms less than 2 : 1, such as the 4 : 3 and 3 : 2 ratios suggested by Alberti. Exceptionally, the Etruscan temple described by Vitruvius is set on a platform 6 : 5.[36] This ratio is not in his canon, but Alberti does make a separate note of the Etruscan scheme.[37] Nor does Vitruvius specifically recommend circular or polygonal temple platforms.[38] Although Alberti would have experienced such temple-like buildings in Rome, it is probable that many, if not most, were built after Vitruvius. Such was the case with the Pantheon, for example. The inclusion of such forms in Alberti's canon does not arise then from Vitruvius, but from empirical observation tempered by theoretical interests. The existence of such centralized forms allowed their inclusion as a type in Alberti's canon, but the choice of hexagon, octagon and decagon is truly not derived from observation alone.[39]

Many of the centralized building with which Alberti might have been familiar exhibit more radial divisions than ten – as many as forty-four in the case of the Santo Stefano Rotondo. In Florence, Alberti would have been familiar with Brunelleschi's contemporary use of the hexagon in the lantern of the Old Sacristy of San Lorenzo, the octagon of the Duomo and its lantern, and the use of the decagon in the cathedral's exhedrae, and in the plan of Santa Maria degli Angeli. In Rome, the octagon of the Lateran Baptistery and the decagon of the Temple of Minerva Medica would have presented Alberti with more ancient precedents. Yet these, and other, centralized buildings were overwhelmed in number by the very much larger set of rectangular temples in Rome, and by the dominance of the basilica plan of most Christian churches including St. Peter's, whose reconstruction had so exercised Nicholas V.

'Of the arts the ones that are useful, even vital, to the architect are painting and mathematics. I am not concerned whether he is versed in any others.' Alberti then

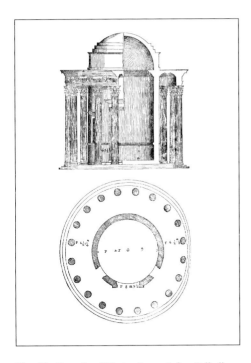

Fig. 18. Temple of Vesta, Rome (after Palladio, Plate XXXIV).

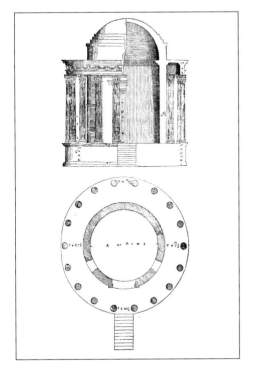

Fig. 19. Temple of Vesta, nr. Tivoli (after Palladio, Plate LXV).

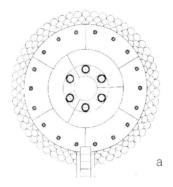

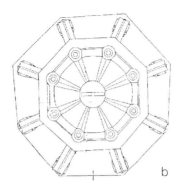

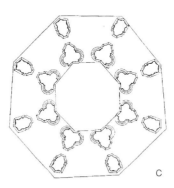

Fig. 20. Plans of Brunelleschi's lanterns (after Battista):

a. the hexagonal arrangement of columns at the Old Sacristy of San Lorenzo.

b. octagonal plan of the original model of the lantern of Santa Maria del Fiore viewed from above.

c. groundplan of model.

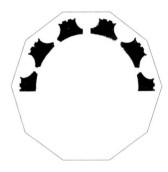

Fig. 21. Exhedra, Santa Maria del Fiore, Florence, set out within a decagon.

of the height, while the depth, from navel to kidneys, was a tenth. The commentators of our sacred writings also noted this and judged that the ark built for the Flood was based on the human figure.' The 'commentator' is probably St Augustine, *vide supra*, 'Prisoners of Number', n. 11.

20 Genesis 6.15.

21 Even then, Alberti attributes these anthropometric notions to the ancients, and specifically to their application in determining the height of the Doric, Ionic and Corinthian orders. Alberti avoids the Vitruvian overarching statement that the ancients 'collected from the members of the human body the proportionate dimensions which appear necessary in all building operations'. F. Granger trans, *Vitruvius: On Architecture* from the Latin *De architectura*, Harvard University Press, Cambridge, MA, 1931, III.i, p. 161.

22 *Vide supra*, 'Prisoners of Number'.

23 M.L. D'Ooge trans, *Nicomachus of Gerasa: Introduction to Arithmetic*, trans from the Greek, with studies in Greek arithmetic by F. E. Robbins and L. C. Karpinski, University of Michigan Press, Ann Arbor, 1937, I xiv, xv, xvi, pp. 207–12. Alberti, IX.10, mentions Nicomachus (Rykwert, Leach, Tavernor *op. cit.*, p. 317).

24 *Ibid.*, II, xxii, p. 267. Nicomachus enumerates the number of means 'making up the number ten, which, according to the Pythagorean view, is the most perfect possible.' Footnote 1 reads: 'The sacredness of the number 10 was a favorite theme of the Pythagoreans. 10 symbolized for them the universe, and by the *tetraktys* (1 + 2 + 3 + 4 = 10) their most sacred oath was taken.' Aristotle *Metaphysics*, I.5.986, is sceptical: 'And all the properties of numbers and scales which they could show to agree with the attributes and parts and the whole arrangement of the heavens, they collected and fitted into their scheme; and if there was a gap anywhere, they readily made additions so as to make their whole theory coherent. E.g. as the number ten is thought to be perfect and to comprise the whole nature of numbers, they say that the bodies which move through the heavens are ten, but as the visible bodies are only nine, to meet this they invent a tenth – the "counter-earth"' (R. McKeon ed., *The Basic Works of Aristotle*, Random House, New York, 1941, p. 698). Nicomachus, and Pappus, *Synagoge*,

III.2, both cite ten means, but each shows one that the other does not. There are in fact eleven classical means. Yet both authors, setting aside Aristotle's scepticism, fit the number to meet the perfection of ten by discarding one. *Vide supra*, 'Proportionality'.

25 Vitruvius, II.i., Granger, *op. cit.*, pp. 163–65: 'Now while in the two palms with their fingers, ten inches are naturally complete, Plato considered that number perfect, for the reason that from individual things which are called *monades* among the Greeks, the decad is perfected. ... But mathematicians, disputing on the other side, have said that the number called six is perfect for the reason that this number has divisions which agree by their proportions with the number six. ... But afterwards they perceived that both numbers were perfect, both the six and the ten; they threw both together, and made the most perfect number sixteen [*fecerunt perfectissimum decusis sexis*].'

26 Nicomachus, II.viii, ix. D'Ooge, *op. cit.*, pp. 241–43. *Vide supra*, 'Shapeful numbers' and 'Prisoners of Number'.

27 Vitruvius, III.ii. Granger, *op. cit.*, pp. 166–71. *Vide supra*, 'Roman wonders'.

28 *Ibid.*, p. 166, n. 1, *naos en parastasin*, 'temple in pilasters'.

29 *Ibid.*, n. 2, 'with columns in front'.

30 *Ibid.*, n. 3, 'with columns on both fronts'.

31 *Ibid.*, n. 4, 'with columns all round'.

32 *Ibid.*, p. 167, n. 5, 'with columns all round set at a distance from the temple walls'.

33 'double columns all round'.

34 *Ibid.*, p. 167, n. 6 'with interior open to the sky'.

35 M. H. Morgan, *Vitruvius: The Ten Books on Architecture*, Harvard University Press, 1914, p. 75–78, assumes that these forms would also have 2 : 1 platforms in terms of the intercolumniations.

36 Vitruvius, IV.vii, Granger *op. cit.*, pp. 238–41.

37 Alberti, VII.4, Rykwert, Leach, Tavernor, *op. cit.* p. 197: 'These temples are laid out as follows: In plan their length, divided into six, is one part longer than their width.'

38 Vitruvius, VII.viii, Granger, *op. cit.*, pp. 240–47: 'Circular temples are also built . . .' reads like an afterthought, more than a commendation. Vitruvius does not describe the division of the circle, or the number of columns encircling the temple. This aspect of centralized planning seems not to attract his attention. The remainder of this Chapter returns to a discussion of quadrangular temples, including a mention of the Parthenon.

39 Alberti did not illustrate *De re aedificatoria*. Borsi, *op. cit.* p. 329–30 shows ilustrations by an unknown copyist for Book VII.4 describing temple forms.

40 Alberti, IX.10, *op. cit.*, Rykwert, Leach, Tavernor, p. 317.

41 C. Grayson, *Leon Battista Alberti: On Painting and On Sculpture*, edition and translation of *De pictura* and *De statua*, Phaidon Press, London, p. 61.

42 D'Ooge, *op. cit.*

43 For example, T. Taylor, 1983, *The Theoretic Arithmetic of the Pythagoreans*, Samuel Weiser, York Beach, Maine, first published in London in 1816.

44 *Op.cit.*, 1988, p. 317.

argues against the necessity of the architect being an expert in such subjects as law, astronomy, music, and oratory. 'Yet he should not be inarticulate, nor insensitive to the sounds of harmony', nor should he be unaware of orientation marked by the stars, nor regulations governing property rights and building codes. 'I would not criticize him for being better educated. But he should forsake painting and mathematics no more than the poet should ignore tone and metre. Nor do I imagine a limited knowledge of them enough.' 'For all this I would not expect him to be Zeuxis in his painting, or a Nicomachus in arithmetic, or an Archimedes in geometry.'[40]

Alberti refers to the classical Greek painter Zeuxis in his *De Pictura*.[41] Nicomachus flourished around 200CE and his *Introduction to Arithmetic* became the principal theoretical text on the subject and survived as such in Platonic circles into the nineteenth century.[42,43] It is interesting that Alberti attributes geometry to Archimedes and not Euclid. Having mentioned Archimedes, Alberti writes that the architect should have 'sufficient knowledge of Mathematics for practical and considered application of angles, numbers, and lines, such as that discussed under the topic of weight and the measurement of surfaces and bodies . . .'.[44] His interest, as it is in his *Ludi rerum matematicarum* is in practical use, and many of the problems addressed by Archimedes are of this nature.[45] However, the speculative arithmetic of Nicomachus is far from practical, especially when compared with the *abbaco* books of the fourteenth and fifteenth centuries which were the staple of the *scuola dell'abbaco*, the training ground for craftsmen and artists.[46] It is certain that Alberti was aware of Euclid. His younger acquaintance, Piero della Francesca, had used Campanus' translation of Euclid in presenting geometrical problems in his *Liber abbaci* around 1450.[47] His *Libellus de quinque corporibus regularibus*, on the five Platonic polyhedra, based on Euclid's Book XIII, and the pseudo- Euclid Books XIV and XV, were written after Alberti's death. A Greek manuscript of Euclid was acquired by the Biblioteca Vaticana during Alberti's mission as *familiare* to Nicholas V at the Vatican.[48,49,50] The Pope, however, was more enthusiastic about Archimedes whose works he had Jacobus Cremonensis translate in 1450 or so. This endeavour is known to have piqued the interest of Nicholas' humanist circle including Cardinals Cusanus and Bessarion.[51] Although Alberti did not count in this hierarchy, his life-long friendship with the new Pope suggests that he too would have been excited by the Archimedean texts at the very time he was writing *De re aedificatoria*.[52] Archimedes, then, would have been Alberti's geometer of choice.

Alberti argues that there are three principal components in his theory of beauty: number, outline and position.[53] A fourth quality, concinnitas, brings the individual parts into a harmonious whole. Our concern here is with number and outline.

In Book IX, Alberti rehearses the theology of arithmetic associated with the decad, the numbers from one to ten. He takes the odd numbers first, and then the even numbers.[54] Following the Pythagorean tradition the numbers one and two are not mentioned. The monad and the dyad are not, in this tradition, strictly numbers, they are seen as the prime genitors of number.[55] The numbers properly start with three, the triad, generated by the union of the male monad with the female dyad. Alberti associates the numbers, among other things, with five fingers on a hand, seven planets in the heaven, nine orbs in the sky, the 'holy fourfold' oath, and the dire consequences of a stillbirth, or of coition during pregnancy, in the eighth month. The numbers six and ten are described as 'perfect'. Six because it is the sum of its factors, and ten because 'its square equals the cubes of the first four numbers'.[56]

The treatment of the numbers six and ten illustrate the difference between modern arithmetic and calculation, and the classical system within which Alberti operated. Not only were numbers imbued with extranumeric qualities, but they were often visualized as geometric figures, combinations of which generated other figures. The square of four is seen as two successive triangular numbers, six and ten:[57]

I I I I
I I I I
I I I I
I I I I.

A square number conjoined to its immediately preceding triangular number, makes a pentagonal number; a pentagonal number conjoined to its immediately preceding triangular number makes an hexagonal number; and so forth.[58] A modern student who ignores such number attributes will fail to appreciate the nicety of their usage in the Renaissance, and particularly in a work such as Alberti's.

In introducing $12 : 9 : 8 : 6$ as an example of the 'most perfect proportion', Nicomachus explains that it is 'three dimensional'. This proportion is called 'harmony', and Nicomachus reminds us, 'the cube is harmony'.[59] For Alberti: 'The cube is a projection of the square. The primary cube, whose root is one, is consecrated to the Godhead, because the cube of one remains one; it is, moreover, said to be the one solid that is particularly stable and that rests equally sure and fast on any of its sides.'[60] 'In establishing dimensions, there are certain natural relationships that cannot be defined as numbers, but that may be obtained through roots and powers.' Alberti takes as his model the cube whose side is two. This gives a face area equal to four, and a volume of eight. He introduces 'the relationships that cannot be defined as numbers' by considering the 'diameter' of a square face, and the 'diameter' of the cube. From the first, he obtains the square root of eight; from the second he derives the square root of twelve. Neither of these have a known 'numerical value'.

This is an application of Euclid's Proposition II.10 which effectively addresses the question of the diameter of the square, or Proposition XIII.14 which directly relates the square on the side of a square with the square on the diameter of the circle within which it is inscribed; and of Proposition XIII.15: 'To construct a cube and comprehend it in a sphere; and to prove that the square on the diameter of the sphere is triple of the square on the side of the cube.' While there are no exact numerical values for these lengths, which in today's language are "irrational", Piero della Francesca was, nevertheless, interested in giving numerical estimates, or convergents, for such magnitudes in the regular polygons and polyhedra.[61]

Is there any evidence that Alberti employs these or other convergents? If he had taken a cube of side 15, the diameter of the face would be close to 21 (7 : 5 ratio for the diameter to the lateral dimension, $\sqrt{2} : \sqrt{1}$), and the diameter of the cube would be close to 26 (26 : 15 ratio is a good convergent to $\sqrt{3} : 1$). An equilateral triangle of side 30, would have a half side of length 15 and an altitude close to 26 in height. The rational proportion 30 : 26 : 21 : 15 is, then, a good surrogate for $\sqrt{4} : \sqrt{3} : \sqrt{2} : \sqrt{1}$, and provides an arithmetic interpretation of Alberti's cubic geometry.

45 R. Rinaldi, *Leon Battista Alberti: Ludi matematici*, Ugo Guanda Editore, Milan, 1980 (original title *Ludi rerum mathematicarum*) from C. Grayson's edition *Alberti: Opere volgari III*, G. Laterza, Bari, 1973. I am grateful to Dr Hyunho Shin, University of California, Los Angeles, for his English translation of this text.

46 M. Baxandall, *Painting and Experience in Fifteenth Century Italy*, Oxford University Press, London, 1972.

47 M.D. Davis, *Piero della Francesca's Mathematical Treatises*, Longo Editore, Ravenna, 1977, pp. 21–43.

48 The Euclid manuscript is Vat.Gr.1040. Almost forty years after the completion of *De re aedificatoria*, Giovanni Pico della Mirandola could write in his *Conclusiones Nongentae*: 'Nothing is more harmful for a theologian than frequent and assiduous exercises in the mathematics of Euclid.' P. L. Rose, *The Italian Renaissance of Mathematics*, Libraire Droz, Genève, 1975, p. 9.

49 *Ibid.*, Rose, pp. 36–37.

50 F. Borsi, *Leon Battista Alberti*, Phaidon, Oxford, 1977, who cites G. Mancini, 1911, *Vita di Leon Battista Alberti*, Florence.

51 Rose, *op. cit.*, p. 39.

52 As a Florentine intellectual, Alberti would almost certainly have been familiar with the Rinuccio affair in which an Archimedean manuscript was reputed to have been brought back from Byzantium in the 1420s. One of the humanists interested in this event was Tommaso Parentucelli, later Nicholas V (Rose, *op. cit.*, p. 31–32).

53 Rykwert, Leach, Tavernor, *op. cit.*, p. 302.

54 R. Waterfield trans, *The Theology of Arithmetic*, Phanes Press, Cedar Rapids, Michigan, 1988. This work on the theology of arithmetic is attributed to Iamblichus (4th century CE), but is most likely a version of a work by Nicomachus: *Theologumena Arithmeticae*, D'Ooge, *op. cit.*, p. 126. Alberti points out that, in a building, elements such as columns are even in number, while the openings between them are odd. Even and odd coexist in such configurations. *Vide supra*, 'Theological Number' where the full quotations from Alberti are given.

55 W. Burkert, *Lore and Science in Ancient Pythagoreanism*, Harvard University Press, Cambridge, 1972, p. 432.

56 Rykwert, Leach, Tavernor, *op. cit.*, p. 304. Alberti's treatment of this relationship has already been given *supra*, 'Shapeful Number'.

57 D'Ooge, *op. cit.*, p. 247. Nicomachus shows how a triangular number and its immediate successor produce a square number. This seems to be the import of Vitruvius' remark that mathematicians had 'perceived that both numbers were perfect, both six and ten; and they threw both together and made the most perfect number sixteen'. Vitruvius III.1, Granger, *op. cit.*, pp. 162–62. *Vide supra*, 'Shapeful Number'.

58 D'Ooge, *op. cit.*, pp. 243–44.

59 *Ibid.*, pp. 284–85.

60 The monad is identified with the Godhead by Nicomachus, who is cited for this opinion in *Theologia Arithmetica* attributed to Iamblichus, see Waterfield, *op.cit.*, p. 37. That Alberti identifies the Godhead with the unit cube is interesting. For

Platonists the cube is associated with the element earth, *Timaeus*, 56-D. One possibility is that Alberti is referring to a cabalistic interpretation. G. Scholem, *Kabbalah*, Dorset Press, New York, 1974, p. 27, mentions the statement found in the *Sefer Yezirah*, I.13, in which the extremities of the world are sealed by the six permutations of the abbreviated Hebrew Name of God, Yod-Hay-Waw. The extremities of the world correspond to the upper and the lower; East and West, North and South. An appropriate model for this would be the six faces of a cube.

61 L. Pacioli, *De Divina Proportione*, Venice, 1509, presents much of Piero's earlier manuscript material. An exercise in Book II, iii, 2, covers the same ground concerning dimensions in the cube as Alberti does. It is noteworthy that Alberti does not explicitly explore the pentagon. Euclid X, Definition 2, makes it very clear that 'straight lines are commensurable in square when the squares on them are measured by the same area'. The lines are then said to be 'rational'. This relationship does not hold for sides and diameters in the pentagon. For Euclid, XIII.11, these are 'incommensurable', and the lines are 'irrational'. Alberti shows little interest, at least overtly, in the extreme and mean ratio, the golden section. Euclid, Proposition XIII.13, concerns the relationship of the square on the side of an equilateral triangle to the square on the radius of the circle within which it is inscribed. In the course of the proof Euclid shows that the square on the diameter to the square on the side of the equilateral triangle is in the ratio 4 : 3, so that the lengths involved are in the ratio $\sqrt{4}$: $\sqrt{3}$. *Vide supra*, 'Inexpressible Proportion'.

62 H. Burns, 'A Drawing by L. B. Alberti', *Architectural Design*, 49, 5–6, 1979, pp. 45–56, and R. Tavernor, 1985, 'Concinnitas in the Architectural Theory and Practice of L.B. Alberti,' PhD Thesis, University of Cambridge, p. 25, n. 23.

63 This ratio does not appear in Fowler's list. It is derived by combining two ratios that he does cite: namely 7 : 5 :: 21 : 15 for $\sqrt{2}$: 1 and 26 : 15 for $\sqrt{3}$: 1.

$$21 : 15$$
$$\times$$
$$26 : 15$$
$$\overline{26 : 21.}$$

Note that the overall dimension of the 'solid', 3 + 8 + 3 = 14, to the opening into the small chapel, 8, is in the ratio 7 : 4, also a rational surrogate for $\sqrt{3}$: 1.

64 This would favour Cadioli over Tavernor. However, Alberti may be thinking of another geometrical problem, that of squaring the circle. Taking Tavernor's measurements, the ratio $7\frac{1}{3}$: $15\frac{1}{3}$ is produced. This reduces to 26 : 23, a good arithmetical rationalization for the side of the square to the diameter of the circle when both figures have equal area. The square has an area of 529 and the circle an area a tad less than 531. Such a game is fully in agreement with the tendency of Alberti's arguments. He did not have to spell everything out in writing. His readers could be expected to be sympathetic to his direction.

65 D'Ooge, *op. cit.*, p. 183.

Sant'Andrea

The $\sqrt{2}$: $\sqrt{1}$ ratio is the generator of the *ad quadratum* series, and the $\sqrt{4}$: $\sqrt{3}$ ratio is the generator of the *ad triangulam* series. The use of the first of these series is well vouched for by Howard Burns and Robert Tavernor in studies of San Sebastiano, Mantua.[62] Is there other evidence of Alberti's use of root relationships? Robert Tavernor gives the dimensions of the side chapels in Sant' Andrea, Mantua. The sequence of dimensions in Mantuan braccia along the side of the nave is:

$$3 \; 8 \; 3 \; 17\frac{1}{3} \; 3 \; 8 \; 3 \; 17\frac{1}{3} \; 3 \; 8 \; 3 \; 17\frac{1}{3} \; 3 \; 8 \; 3.$$

The 3, 8, 3, dimensions refer to the sold-void-solid features of the small side chapels, which act as the 'solid' structural elements separating the arcuated voids of the principal side chapels whose widths between pilasters are each $17\frac{1}{3}$ braccia. This produces a void to 'solid' ratio along the nave of $17\frac{1}{3}$: 14 (= 3 + 8 + 3), or removing fractional terms, 52 : 42. This is none other than the ratio 26 : 21, the rational surrogate for $\sqrt{3}$: $\sqrt{2}$ derived above.[63] Here, then, is some evidence that Alberti occasionally, at least, employs the kind of arithmetic rationalization that so absorbed Piero della Francesca in his *Liber abacci* exercises. Tavernor's measurement for the opening into the principal side chapel is $15\frac{1}{3}$ braccia, although a previous surveyor, Giovanni Cadioli, measures this distance as 15 braccia. Taking the width of the entrance to the chapel between pilasters, and comparing this to the opening given by Cadioli, gives a ratio of $17\frac{1}{3}$: 15, or removing fractions, 52 : 45. This seems unpromising until the ratio is decomposed into two ratios, 3 : 2 and 26 : 15, the surrogate for $\sqrt{3}$: 1. Whence the ratio 52 : 45 is seen to be 26 x 2 : 15 × 3, a rational estimate for $\sqrt{3}$ x 2 : 1 × 3, or simplifying, once again, $\sqrt{4}$: $\sqrt{3}$.[64]

Measurement requires discretion. Between what points are the measurements to be taken, with what measures, and with what tolerances? Counting, except of crammed crowds and huge heaps, is less contentious. This distinction arises from the classical definitions of multitude and magnitude.[65]

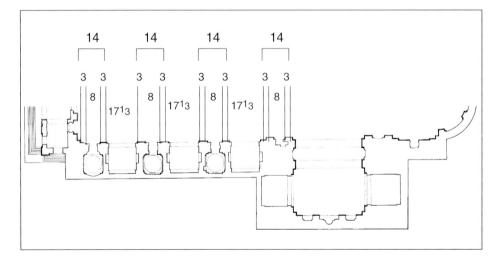

Fig. 22. Sant'Andrea, Mantua. Half plan showing Tavernor's measurements in Mantunian braccia.

Santa Maria Novella

The façade of Santa Maria Novella serves as an example of proportion in number. Count the number of black stripes in the lower pilasters, there are fifteen. Count the number in the upper pilasters, there are thirteen. The ratio is 15 : 13, or 30 : 26, a rational surrogate for $\sqrt{4} : \sqrt{3}$. Count the white stripes, there are fourteen and twelve, a ratio of 7 : 6, another rational surrogate for $\sqrt{4} : \sqrt{3}$. Now count the elements in the two great rosettes, principal components of the volutes buttressing the upper storey: the outer circle contains twenty-six repeating elements, the inner circle, thirty repeating elements. The ratio of repeating elements in the inner circle to the outer is 30 : 26 :: 15 : 13, or the same relationship found in the stripes of the lower and upper pilasters: 15 black stripes below and 13 black stripes above. In a deliberate break with symmetry, the central motif in each rosette differs. On the right there is a design based on eight florets, and on the left there is a design based on seven equal circles: a ratio of 8 : 7 – the rational surrogate for $\sqrt{4} : \sqrt{3}$ used *ad triangulum* in Milan Cathedral – but also the ratio of stripes in the side columns: 16 white stripes below and 14 white stripes above.[66]

The numbers 26, 21, 15 are related to the Tetragrammaton and may have something to do with Alberti's usage here. His own Latin name LEO BAPTISTA ALBERTVS, adopted *c*1450, sums to $12 + 30 + 30 = 72$ in the standard nine chambers encoding of the Latin alphabet. The terms of the Tetragrammaton, representing the name of God, also sum to 72.[67] It is surely noteworthy that the sunburst in the

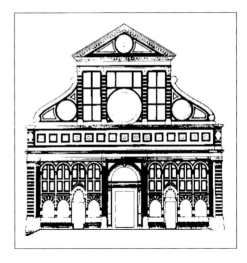

Fig. 23. Santa Maria Novella, Florence. Elevation (after Borsi).

Fig. 24. Santa Maria Novella, Florence. The left and right volute rosettes. The outer circles are divided into 26, the intermediate circles into 30. The centre designs vary. The left rosette has a centre based on the hexagon, a small circle surrounded by six others. The right rosette has a centre based on the octagon.

66 J. S. Ackerman, ' "Ars Sine Scientia Nihil Est": Gothic Theory of Architecture at the Cathedral of Milan', *The Art Bulletin*, 31, pp. 84–111, 1949, reprinted with postscript in J. S. Ackerman, *Distance Points: Essays in Theory and Renaissance Art*, MIT Press, Cambridge MA, 1991, pp. 209–268. In his celebrated essay, Ackerman gives Gabriele Stornaloco's arithmetical rationalization for the width of the cathedral to its height as 96 braccia to 84 braccia so as to contain these dimensions within the bounds of an equilateral triangle, *ad triangulum*. The ratio reduces to 8 : 7, the standard rational convergent for $\sqrt{4} : \sqrt{3}$ that any tiler of hexagonal paving would have known. It is difficult not to imagine that the powers-that-were could have found this result out from any jobbing mason, but like their modern-day corporate counterparts they had to consult at the highest level to arrive at what must have been to the men on the job a plain and simple result.

67 *Vide supra*, 'Occult Number'.

pediment (the zodiacal LEO – the name that Alberti adds to his birth name) has twelve rays, and that each volute contains an intermediate cycle of thirty, $30 + 12 + 30 = 72$.[68] Setting up a division of the circle into thirty requires the construction to begin with 'a fifteen-angled figure which shall be both equilateral and equiangular'.[69] Any regular polygon may have its sides doubled through bisection. However, the regular thirteen-angled figure required to cut the circle into 26 divisions is not constructible by Euclidean straight edge and compass methods.[70]

Given these difficulties, Alberti 's choice of 26 divisions would seem to be very deliberate. The number 26 enumerates the axes of the cube (or equivalently the sum of its faces, edges and vertices, $6 + 12 + 8 = 26$), but it is also in Hebrew gematria, one of the numbers of the Name of God, HAY(5)+WAW(6)+HAY(5) +YOD(10) = ‏יהוה‎ (26). Has Alberti signed his work with the blessing of God? Remember, Alberti was the author of 'the first modern work of cryptography', *De compendis cifris*.[71] David Kahn cites a passage from near the beginning of 'the succinct and suggestive work that earned [Alberti] the title Father of Western Cryptography':

'Dato and I were strolling in the Supreme Pointiff's gardens at the Vatican and we got to talking about literature as we so often do, and we found ourselves greatly admiring the German inventor who today can take up to three original works of an author and, by means of movable type characters, can within days turn out more than 200 copies. ... And so we went from topic to topic marvelling at the ingenuity that men showed in various enterprises, till Dato gave expression to his warm admiration for those men who can exploit what are called "ciphers"'.[72] In this art, Alberti showed himself to be the very best.

Note also that $10+5+6=21$, and $10+5=15$ from which $26 : 15$ and $21 : 15 :: 7 : 5$ are directly derived to evoke Alberti's cubic measures, $\sqrt{3}$ and $\sqrt{2}$.[73] These more cryptic forms of the Name of God are an essential part of Hebrew gematria: in particular, the constitution of the Tetragrammaton where $10+15+21+26=72$, the seventy-two angels – and, not surprisingly, the auspicious numerical value of Alberti's modified name.[74] Why else would Alberti modify his birth name?

$$L(2)+E(5)+O(5) = \text{LEO}(12 \Rightarrow 3),$$

$$B(2)+A(1)+P(6)+T(1)+I(9)+S(9)+T(1)+A(1) = \text{BAPTISTA}(30 \Rightarrow 3),$$

$$A(1)+l(2)+B(2)+E(5)+R(8)+V(2)+S(9) = \text{ALBERTVS}(30 \Rightarrow 3).$$

In its most reduced form the name is the Trinity of Trinities $3 + 3 + 3$. This is the name that appears on the Matteo de' Pasti commemorative medallion in the National Gallery, Washington DC. The medallion in the Bibliothèque Nationale, Paris, shows the same two first names, but only the shortened AL for the family name. $A(1)+L(2) = AL(3)$ preserves the Trinity of Trinities. Using units, tens and hundreds, Alberti's name comes to $75 + 363 + 498 = 936$. This number factorizes into 26×36, both numbers associated with the Tetragrammaton.[75] The Matteo de' Pasti medallion carries the motto QVID TVM? which Alberti adopted at the same time that he modified his name:

$$Q(7)+V(2)+I(9)+D(4) = \text{QVID}(22), \quad T(1)+V(2)+M(3) = \text{TVM}(6),$$

a combination of the 22 letters in the Hebrew alphabet and the three potencies that make the first perfect number 6. The whole phrase QVID TVM? sums to the perfect number 28. What next, indeed.[76]

68 If this cabalistic interpretation is correct it removes some of the force of originality from Giovanni Pico della Mirandola's promotion of the Kabbalah, and suggests that the ideas were abroad enough in Florence to have already been inlaid in marble.

69 Euclid, Proposition IV.16, Heath, *op. cit.*, I, p. 110.

70 Dürer gives an approximate construction, *vide supra*, 'Centralized Design in the Renaissance', which almost certainly came from established craft practice.

71 J. Gadol, *Leon Battista Alberti: Universal Man of the Early Renaissance*, The University of Chicago Press, Chicago, 1973, pp. 207–11, and D. Kahn *The Codebreakers the Story of Secret Writing*, Scribner, New York, 1996, Chapter 4, 'On the Origin of a Species', p. 125ff).

72 Kahn *op. cit.*, p. 125.

73 Is it not remarkable that these ratios are the very same ones found in Bezazel's work for the Tabernacle?

74 M. Jarzombek, *On Leon Baptista Alberti: His Literary and Aesthetic Theories*, MIT Press, Cambridge MA, 1989, p. 177, is 'so bold as to suggest' that the fifteen marble inlays across the front of Santa Maria Novella 'might stand for the fifteen letters of his name: BAPTISTA ALBERTI'. They might also stand for the patron's name IOHANNES RVCELLARIVS which sums, in units, to $96 \Rightarrow 15$.

75 *Vide supra*, 'Occult Number' and 'Christian Works'.

76 In his introductory essay, Joseph Rykwert speculates on the circumstances surrounding Alberti's modification of his name and the adoption of the motto. J. Rywert, N. Leach, R. Tavernor *op. cit.*, p. xvi.

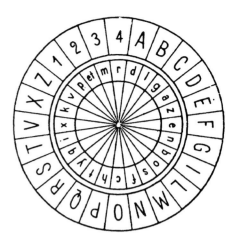

Fig. 27. Alberti's cipher disk.

Fig. 25. Obverse. Commemorative medallion of Alberti by Matteo de' Pasti (National Gallery of Art, Washington). The name is spelt out around the edge in Latin: LEO BAPTISTA ALBERTVS.

Fig. 26. Reverse. Commemorative medallion of Alberti (National Gallery of Art, Washington). The motto QVID TVM is below the winged eye.

Cappella Rucellai

Both at Santa Maria Novella and at the Cappella Rucellai in San Pancrazio, Alberti has fun with point symmetries. There are 30 marble inlaid roundels at the Shrine of the Holy Sepulchre in the Cappella Rucellai, divided from the entrance into $3 + 9 + 9 + 9$ sets, surely a play on the architect's name. Alberti's name in reduced form is $3 + 3 + 3 = 9$, but also note that $3^2 + 3^2 + 3^2 = 9 + 9 + 9$ is an allowable cabalistic transformation of his name. This might be interpreted as an extremely egotistical act when the tomb is for someone else. But, of course, as well, the numbers evoke the Trinity in multiple ways. Even more, they relate to the patron's given name:

I(9)+O(5)+H(8)+A(1)+N(4)+N(4)+E(5)+S(9) = IOHANNES(45 $\Rightarrow$ 9).

The family name on the tomb causes some difficulty since, although perfect, it does not reduce to 3 or 9:

R(8)+V(2)+C(3)+E(5)+L(2)+L(2)+A(1)+R(8)+I(9)+V(2)+S(9)

= RVCELLARIVS(51 $\Rightarrow$ 6).

Is that why the family name is modified to ORICELLARIVS across the façade of Santa Maria Novella?

O(5)+R(8)+I(9) = ORI(22), while
R(8)+V(2) = RV(10).

IOHANNES RVCELLARIVS

Fig. 28. The name IOHANNES RVCELLARIVS as it appears on Alberti's Shrine of the Holy Sepulchre, Cappella Rucellai, San Pancrazio, Florence.

IOHĀNES·ORICELLARIVS

Fig. 29. The name IOHANES ORICELLARIVS as it appears on Alberti's façade of Santa Maria Novella, Florence. Note the absence of the second N in the given name and the elision mark above.

This is the only difference between the two renderings of the name. The difference in numerical value is $22 - 10 = 12$, so that the Santa Maria Novella version sums to $51 + 12 = 63 \Rightarrow 9$. In some way then the number 9 is related to the patron, to the architect and to the Trinity. Ambivalence and ambiguity are essential elements of this game. One of the key techniques of cryptography, at the time, was to send a message saying one thing to most people, but informing the targeted recipient – in possession of the key – something entirely different. Cryptography, it might be said, was the obsession of the age.[77]

The roundels themselves show a command over the geometry of regular polygons and their symmetries. There are two kinds of point symmetry: dihedral symmetry in which the design exhibits bilateral symmetries about its axis of rotation and cyclic symmetry where it does not.[78] The distinguished physicist Hermann Weyl delivered lectures on symmetry to students at Princeton and attributed these two groups to Leonardo da Vinci. The notation Weyl uses is:

$$C_1, C_2, C_3, \ldots; D_1, D_2, D_3, \ldots$$

for the cyclic and dihedral groups respectively, where the subscripts indicate the rotation required to bring the design back to itself. Subscript 1 means that one whole turn is required, subscript 2 that a halfturn will do, and 3 that a threefold turn is implied. Since Weyl, some mathematicians have called them Leonardo's groups. Weyl delivered his lectures in the spirit of breaking down barriers between the 'two cultures', but his claims concerning Leonardo were greatly exaggerated. 'Leonardo da Vinci engaged systematically in determining the posssible symmetries of a central building and how to attach chapels and niches without destroying the symmetry of the nucleus. In abstract modern terminology, his result is essentially our above table of the possible finite groups of rotations (proper and improper) in two dimensions'.[79] But it was not. Leonardo's church designs are all octagonal and exhibit only dihedral symmetry. In no way is this a systematic study of the symmetry groups. Leonardo does show examples of cogwheels which naturally employ cyclic symmetry, but then anyone drawing cogwheels with different numbers of cogs could be said to be exploring cyclic symmetry. It is inevitable. The case with Alberti is different. He is at full imaginative play, unrestrained by any functional restrictions.

[77] The extraordinary care taken to compute such cryptographic and hermetic devices is matched by the singular attention that the design of each individual letter in the inscriptions received. Borsi, *op. cit.*, p. 112, but particularly R. Tavernor, 'I caratteri albertiani dell'iscrizione del sepolcro Rucellai a Firenze', pp. 402–407 and 'Concinnitas, o la formulazione della bellezza', pp. 300–315 in J. Rykwert, A. Engel *Leon Battista Alberti*, Olivetti/Electa, Milan, 1994.

[78] For mathematically rigorous presentations see J. A. Baglivo, J. E. Graver, *Incidence and Symmetry in Design and Architecture*, Cambridge University Press, Cambridge, 1983; A. V. Shubnikov, V. A. Koptsik, *Symmetry in Art and Science*, Plenum Press, New York, 1974. Also L. March, P. Steadman, *The Geometry of Environment: An Introduction to Spatial Organization in Design*, RIBA Publications, London, 1971; and most recently A. N. Economou, *Architectonics of Symmetry in Twentieth Century Architectural and Music Theories*, PhD Dissertation, University of California, Los Angeles, 1997.

[79] H. Weyl, *Symmetry*, Princeton University Press, Princeton, New Jersey, 1952.

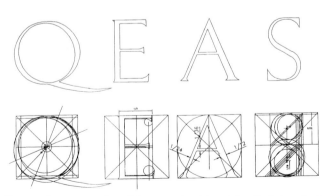

Fig. 30. Robert Tavernor's reconstruction of the geometry determining the letters for the inscriptions on the Shrine of the Holy Sepulchre, Cappella Rucellai, San Pancrazio, Florence.

An analysis of the symmetries used in the 30 roundels shows that Alberti uses 12 distinct patterns, but that beneath these patterns lie the symmetries of regular polygons: the dodecagon, the decagon, the octagon; as well as the hexagon, the square and the equilateral triangle. The subsymmetries of the first three cover the symmetries of the last three.[80] While most of the designs exhibit dihedral symmetry, five are cyclic and two have no symmetry. The presence of these last two is significant mathematically because such patterns are representative of the identity in a symmetry group.[81] It is as if Alberti had an intuitive appreciation of this, long before the mathematics of group theory was formalized in the eighteenth and nineteenth centuries.[82] Equally the combination of both cyclic and dihedral symmetries in the same design programme parallels the mathematical structure of symmetry. In most roundels, Alberti sets one figure inside another: a hexagon inside a dodecagon, a pentagon inside a decagon, a square inside an octagon, which indicates an intuitive – a designer's – appreciation of the nature of a subgroup. This is somewhat similar to working with the factors of a number as submultiples. The five cyclic designs illustrate eightfold, sixfold, fourfold, and threefold rotational symmetries. Only one design shows simple bilateral symmetry. The 'identity' designs are Rucellai family crests.

A comparison of these roundels with those to be seen on the façade of Santa Maria Novella is instructive. Alberti actually plays with combination symmetrical designs in which one polygon is not a submultiple of the other: a triangle inside a pentagon, a pentagon inside an octagon, a hexagon inside a decagon and an octagon inside a dodecagon. Such designs are equivalent to ratios: $5:3$, $8:5$, $10:6$, $12:8$. Curiously these designs illustrate the root ratios $3:2$, $5:3$, $8:5$ in a Nicomachean tenth mean series (better known today as the Fibonacci sequence). How conscious is this? If Albert uses this sequence elsewhere, especially in a different context, then it might be reasonable to draw a positive inference. Designs with dihedral symmetry exhibit twice the number of axes radiating from the rotorcentre than the number of rotations. Thus a square has 4 quarterturns, but 8 axes – four to each corner from the centre, and four to the midpoints of each side. Alberti uses this property in those designs where a single polygon is employed: for example, a square on the inside is on the diagonal to the one on the outside, and similarly for the pure pentagonal, hexagonal and octagonal designs. Two designs have a circle in the centre which is reminiscent of the conversations that Alberti might have engaged in with Nicolas Cusanus over the nature of the infinite.

80 J.-H. Park, 'Subsymmetry Analysis of Architectural Designs: Some Examples', *Planning and Design*, 25, 1998.

81 L. March, P. Steadman, *op. cit.*, p. 107.

82 The principal authors of mathematical group theory – curiously associated in its origins with the idea of letter substitution familiar to cryptographers – were Joseph-Louis Lagrange (1736–1813) and Augustin-Louis Cauchy (1789–1857). Later, in the work of Felix Klein (1845–1925), the symmetries of the Platonic solids were shown to form a group.

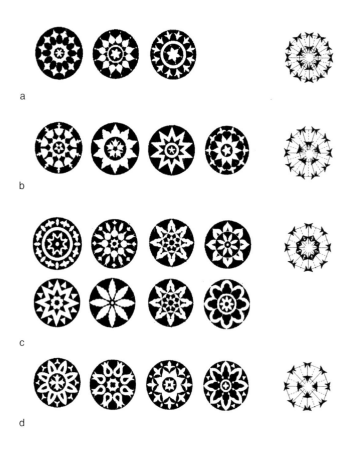

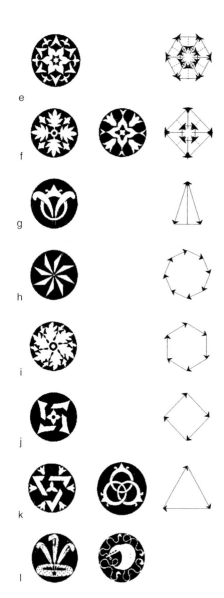

Fig. 31. Cappella Rucellai in San Pancrazio. Thirty inlaid marble roundels on the sides of Alberti's Shrine of the Holy Sepulchre. The designs are organized according to their order of symmetry:

a. three designs based on the regular dodecagon with a hexagonal interior;
b. four designs based on the regular decagon with a pentagonal interior;
c. eight designs based on the regular octagon with an octagonal interior;
d. four designs based on the regular octagon with a square interior;
e. one design based on the regular hexagon;
f. two designs based on the square;
g. one simple bilateral design;
h. an eightfold rotational design;
i. a sixfold rotational design;
j. a fourfold rotational design;
k. two threefold rotational designs;
l. two 'identity' designs with no symmetry.

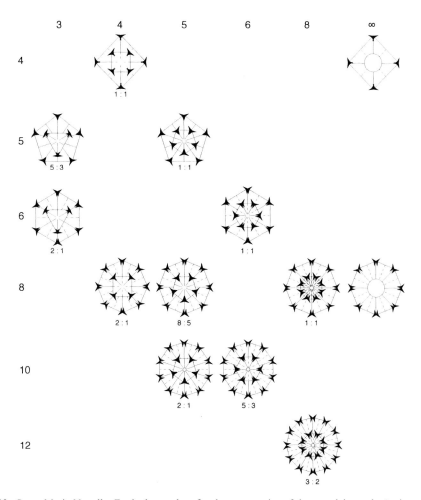

Fig. 32. Santa Maria Novella. Equivalence class for the symmetries of the roundels on the 'string-course' of the façade. These are tabulated with the inside *n*-gon numbers across the top, and the outside *m*-gon numbers down the left. The ratio shown under each figure is the root value of *m* : *n*.

San Sebastiano

Alberti's work for San Sebastiano in Mantua has been the subject of scholarly dispute in recent years.[83] Much of the argument is to do with his involvement in the construction. There seems to be agreement that the plan drawn by Antonio Labacco in the sixteenth century is a copy from an original sketch by Alberti.[84] It is possible to develop an architectonic argument based on this sketch without becoming embroiled in discussions about the building itself. In doing so it is worth recalling Alberti's own words: '. . . the whole matter of building is composed of lineaments and structure. All the intent and purpose of lineaments lies in finding the correct, infallible way of joining and fitting together those lines and angles which define and enclose the surfaces of building. It is the function and duty of lineaments, then, to prescribe an appropriate place, exact number, a proper scale, and a graceful order for whole buildings and for each of their constituent parts, so that the whole form

83 The dispute is well covered in R. Tavernor, *op. cit.*, Appendix II, 'San Sebastiano in Mantua', pp. 121–35.
84 The drawing from the Uffizi. Cabinetto Disegni e Stampe, Florence, is reproduced in Borsi, *op. cit.*, p. 207, and in Rykwert, Engel, *op. cit.*, p. 253.

85 Alberti, I.1, Rykwert, Leach, Tavernor, *op. cit.*, p. 7, nn. 3–6 for discussion of the various problems involved in translating 'lineamenta', 'structura', 'numerum' and 'modum'.

86 Alberti, Prologue, *ibid.*, p. 5.

87 Plotinus, *Enneads*, 1.6.3. E. Panofsky, *Idea: A Concept in Art Theory*, translated from the German, J. J. S. Peake, Harper & Row, New York, 1968, p. 29. There is another passage in Plotinus, also from Book I, in which a musician, a lover, and a philosopher are compared, I.3.1–3. 'The philosopher is naturally ready to respond and "winged" we may say, and in no need of separation like the others. He has begun to move to the higher world . . . he must be given mathematical studies to train him in philosophical thought and accustom him to firm confidence in the existence of the immaterial – he will take to them easily, being naturally disposed to learning. . . .' (A. H. Armstrong, *Plotinus*, Allen & Unwin, London, 1953). The reference to 'winged' reminds us of Alberti's motif 'the winged eye'. Armstrong sees a link to Socrates' second discourse in the *Phaedrus*. Although Ficino made his translations and commentaries of Plato and Plotinus later, starting some ten or more years after *De re aedificatoria*, it is difficult to imagine that the contents of the Plato dialogues and works by Plotinus – in Greek – were not generally appreciated in intellectual circles before then. In commissioning Marsilio Ficino, how else would Cosimo de' Medici have known that these were significant works to be translated into Latin? Ficino's translations of Plato have a Plotinian cast, and it is his translations that probably come closest to how Plato was received in fifteenth-century Florence. Professor M. J. B. Allen, University of California, Los Angeles, is responsible for the most recent critical editions of Ficino's Platonic commentaries. His essay, 'Icastic Art', in M. J. B. Allen, *Icastes: Marsilio Ficino's Interpretation of Plato's Sophist*, California University Press, Los Angeles, 1989, refers to the possible influence of Florentine architecture on Ficino's thinking, pp. 117–67. Ficino delivered some of his public lectures on Plato and Plotinus in Santa Maria degli Angeli.

and appearance of the building may depend on the lineaments alone. Nor do lineaments have anything to do with material, but they are of such a nature that we may recognize the same lineaments in several different buildings that share one and the same form, that is, when the parts, as well as the siting and order, correspond with one another in their every line and angle. It is quite possible to project whole forms in the mind without any recourse to the material, by designating and determining a fixed orientation and conjunction for the various lines and angles. Since that be the case, let lineaments be the precise and correct outline, conceived in the mind, made up of lines and angles, and perfected in the learned intellect and imagination'.[85] Alberti is even more succinct in the Prologue: '. . . first we observe that the building is a form of body, which like any other consists of lineaments and matter, the one the product of thought, the other of Nature; the one requiring the mind and the power of reason, the other dependent on preparation and selection; but we realized that neither on its own would suffice without the hand of the skilled workman to fashion the material according to the lineaments.'[86] Such remarks suggest the influence of Plotinus who writes (in Panofsky's translation): 'How can the architect adjust the externally apparent house to the internal ειδος, divided of course with regard to the mass of matter, but indivisible in essence, even though appearing in multiple form.'[87]

In examining Labacco's sketch, it is the ειδος that is of interest. It has been seen that the Greeks and Romans seemed to encode into columnar arrangements certain mathematical ideas, a tradition which the early Christians appear to continue. With the late mediaeval work – sometimes known as proto-Renaissance – such as Amiens cathedral, there is a move from the solidity of the column towards the spaciousness of the bay as a countable object of significance. It seems that in San Sebastiano this spatial sense is abstracted even further. Internally, there are no columns or piers. The space is unified. However, the 'lineaments' delineate a precise eidetic mesh according to Labacco's record: a eidetic mesh that, on close examination, is a computational device. The eidetic mesh represents the ειδος.

The eidetic mesh is 9×9 in its divisions. The numbers have Christian significance in terms of the empowerment of the Trinity, but they also remind us of the name of the designer. If a centre line is added the eidetic mesh is 10×10 which is 'monadic' and God-like.

The dimensions of the eidetic mesh, as shown by Labacco, include the numbers 12, 8, 7, 6. These may be expressed as figurate numbers. In particular it will be observed that the full width of the church is 66 Mantunian braccia and that 66 is the sixth hexagonal number – a potent concentrate of sextuple perfection.

Burns and Tavernor have remarked on the *ad quadratum* nature of the dimensional design. This is very apparent in the eidetic mesh, where several rational convergents to the diagonal of the square are present: 10 : 7, 17 : 12, 24 : 17, 41 : 29. Indeed, there is a case to be made that the eidetic mesh is set out using the 20, 21, 29 right triangle, The width of the transepts is $6 + 8 + 6 = 20$ braccia. Measured from the opening of the transept into the central square space, $7 + 6 + 8 = 21$ braccia defines the furthest corner of the opening to one of the chapels. The diagonal length of 29 braccias ensures that everything is square. The half transept proportion 29 : 20 is clearly a proportion derived from the 20, 21, 29 right triangle. To a rithmomachy player this would be obvious and somewhat dull. The arrangement has to be more entertaining.

From previous historical examples, it might be expected that *ad triangulum* relations would be fused with those that are *ad quadratum*. Worldmaking requires

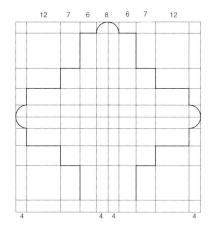

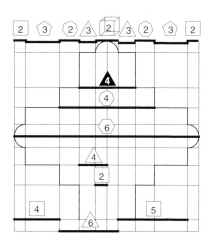

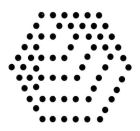

Fig. 35. The sixth hexagonal number, 66.

Fig. 33. San Sebastiano, Mantua. The eidetic mesh derived from Antonio Labacco's sketch with his dimensions, top. The dimensions at the bottom are extrapolated.

Fig. 34. San Sebastiano, Mantua. The dimensions of the eidetic mesh expressed as figurate numbers. The full width of the church is the sixth hexagonal number, 66 Mantunian braccia.

more than the geometry of the square. The ratio 12 : 7 is a rational convergent to √3 : 1, and both 8 : 7 and 14 : 12 :: 7 : 6 are rational convergents to √4 : √3. From the centre line to the extremity of the eidetic mesh is 33 braccia, while the dimension from the end of one transept to the nearest flank of the other is 19 braccia: 33 : 19 is an excellent rational convergent to √3 : 1. The ειδος is impregnated with *ad triangulum* relationships. Alberti has achieved one of the classic unions: the contrary traits of square and triangle brought into harmony: in his terms the diagonals of the God-evoking cube.

Another play on the eidetic mesh produces a 29 : 13 rectangle, or a very good rational convergent for √5 : 1, the diagonal of the double square and the first move in Pappus' construction of the decagon and pentagon. To be complete, worldmaking geometry requires the pentagon to construct the dodecahedron. It then transpires that

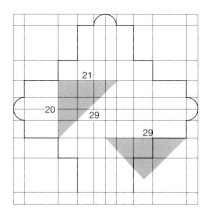

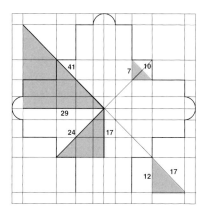

Fig. 36. San Sebastiano, Mantua. The 20, 21, 29 right triangle defines key dimensions.

Fig. 37. San Sebastiano, Mantua. Some of the *ad quadratum* relations.

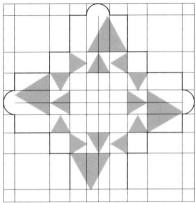
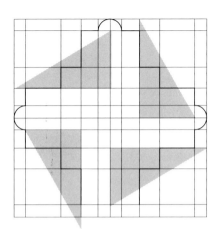

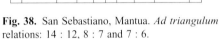

Fig. 38. San Sebastiano, Mantua. *Ad triangulum* relations: 14 : 12, 8 : 7 and 7 : 6.

Fig. 39. San Sebastiano, Mantua. An *ad triangulum* relation: 33 : 19.

the eidetic mesh is swarming with decagonal/pentagonal relationships. In fact the Nicomachean tenth mean sequence is very much present:

$$34 : 21, \; 21 : 13, \; 13 : 8, \; 8 : 5, \; 5 : 3, \; 3 : 2, \; 2 : 1, \; 1 : 1.$$

The ratios were almost certainly derived by substituting successive rational convergents for $\sqrt{5} : 1$

$$1 : 1, \; 3 : 1, \; 2 : 1, \; 7 : 3, \; 11 : 5, \; 9 : 4, \; 29 : 13, \; 47 : 21$$

in the Euclidean formula for the extreme and mean ratio, and not from the modern Fibonacci sequence. This application seems to confirm that Alberti's use of these ratios, in the totally different context of the Santa Maria Novella roundels, was no accident.

The central square and its 7 braccia offsets to the transept provides an excellent arithmetical solution to the Delic problem: the width of the square is 34 braccia. Less one offset the dimension is $34 - 7 = 27$ braccia.

$$34^3 = 39304 \text{ and } 2.27^3 = 2.19683 = 39366.$$

The arithmetic is an overestimate by one sixth of a per cent. Even more compelling is the external arrangement in the four corners of the eidetic mesh. Here the dimensions for the arithmetic solution to the Delic problem uses the immediately prior convergent 29 : 23.

$$29^3 = 24389 \text{ and } 2.23^3 = 2.12167 = 24334.$$

The arithmetic is an underestimate by one tenth of a per cent. The symmetry of the arrangement for these two Delic solutions surely indicates calculated intentionality on Alberti's part. Even the configuration seems designed to suggest the notion of a gnomon – the additional amount required to double the cube is represented by the 7 braccia wide L-shaped strip.

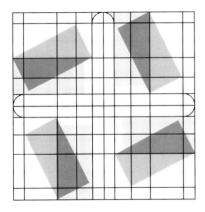

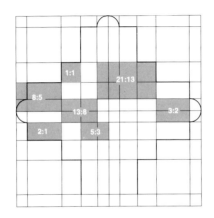

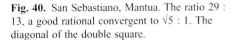

Fig. 40. San Sebastiano, Mantua. The ratio 29 : 13, a good rational convergent to √5 : 1. The diagonal of the double square.

Fig. 41. San Sebastiano, Mantua. A series of ratios in the tenth Nicomachean sequence. The width of the central square is 7 + 6 + 8 + 6 + 7 = 34, so that a 34 : 21 rectangle is also present.

Angles and lines define the lineaments. The profile of the quarter plan for San Sebastiano serves as good illustration of Alberti's applied mathematical skills. Each corner offset forms a 7 × 7 braccia square. A regular hexagon with a side length of 7 braccia has a rational chord of length 12 braccia, the depth of the transept from the central square. A 5, 12, 13 right triangle defines the side, a chord and diameter of a regular octagon. 13 braccia is the orthogonal distance from the side of the central square to the opening into a chapel. To round things out a decagon of side length 8 braccia – the width of the chapel opening – has a radius of 13 braccia. All of Alberti's ideal polygons for temples are represented in this profile: such is the incredible ingenuity of Alberti's eidetic mesh. Classical matters have been brilliantly addressed, but what of Christianity?

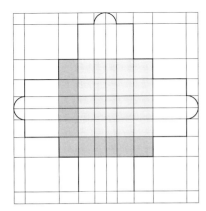

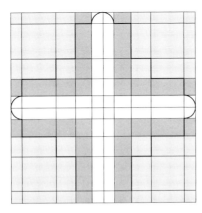

Fig. 42. San Sebastiano, Mantua. Central square displays an arithmetic solution to the Delic problem of doubling the cube using the rational convergent 34 : 27.

Fig. 43. San Sebastiano, Mantua. Corner squares of the eidetic mesh define another solution to the Delic problem using the rational convergent 29 : 23.

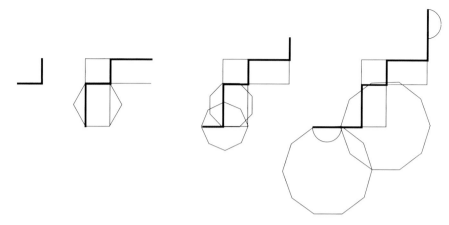

Fig. 44. San Sebastiano, Mantua. Left, the offset corner of the central square, 7 braccia square. Left centre, a regular hexagon defines the depth of the transept, 12 braccia, from the corner with respect to the length of the offset to central square, 7 braccia. Right centre, a regular octagon defines the distance, 13 braccia, to the opening to the chapel with respect to the depth of the transept, 12 braccia, from the central square. Right, a decagon measures the width, 8 braccia, of the opening to the chapel with respect to its orthogonal distance, 13 braccia, from the corner of the central square.

An exact calculation shows that a diagonal line which is tangential to the side chapels forms one side of a square whose diameter is:

$17/3 + 58 + 17/3 = 208/3 = (26 \times 8)/3$, a divine equation by the rules of Hugo of St Victor's:

$$\frac{Tetragrammaton \times Ogdoad}{Trinity}.$$

The wall length of the corner that falls outside this tangential line is 26/3 braccia, the closely related divine equation:

$$\frac{Tetragrammaton}{Trinity}.$$

San Sebastiano speaks to the intelligibles and is divinely blessed. It is yet another astonishing triumph of Christian art of the kind previously seen in Santo Stefano Rotondo and at Amiens.

An attempt has been made here to relate Alberti's discussion of architectural proportion to Renaissance mathematical literature. Arithmetic reigns sovereign over geometry in the quadrivium. The remaining two subjects are dependent upon these: music is governed by arithmetical relationships; astronomy by geometrical ones.[88] A renaissance architect like Alberti had direct access to arithmetic and geometry for his architectonics. Alberti's use of the musical analogy applies only to one of his systems, and then in ways that do not make musical sense. He appears to use music mainly for didactic reasons, given that Boethian musical theory was readily available and widely understood.[89] Alberti's other system is geometrical and would seem to make use of the arithmetization of geometry to be found, for example, in Piero della Francesca's mathematical tracts. The influence of Archimedes in this

88 D'Ooge, *op. cit.*, pp. 187–88.
89 *Vide supra*, 'Scales of Proportion'.

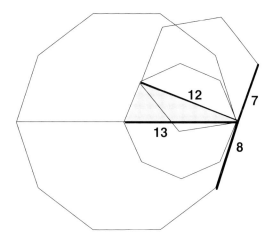

Fig. 45. San Sebastiano, Mantua. The relationship of the numbers 7, 8, 12 and 13 (7 + 6) to the regular hexagon, octagon and decagon.

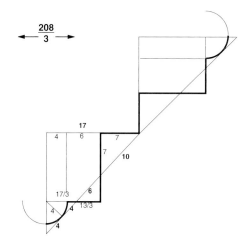

Fig. 46. San Sebastiano, Mantua. The profile of the quarter plan is set along a diagonal line tangential to the semi-circular chapels. The diagonal cuts the end of the transept in the ratio 17 : 13 as shown, using the ratio 17 : 12 for √2 : 1 on the right isosceles triangle whose side is the radius of the chapel (4 braccia). The diameter of the square formed by the diagonal lines as sides is then exactly computable as 208/3 braccia. The two sides of the corner external to the diagonal line have a length of 26/3 braccia.

aspect of Alberti's work is not apparent.[90] Alberti's rehearsal of arithmetic is somewhat Pythagorean and much derives from Nicomachus, but the geometry is Platonic and reflects a working knowledge of Euclid. In selected cases it appears that Alberti consciously applies Euclidean 'rational in square' ratios to his architectural works. These give evidence of the practical employment of rational convergents for otherwise incommensurable magnitudes associated with classic problems such as the diagonal of the square and the doubling of the cube, as well as the arithmetization of the regular polygons such as the hexagon, the octagon and the decagon. Alberti explores and exploits the symmetry properties of the regular polygons in his decorative designs.[91] His remarkable skills as a cryptographer are revealed in his choice of numbers, related either to personal names, or to Christian kabbalah and arithmology. Roger Bacon's words come to mind: 'A man is crazy who writes a secret in any other way than one which will conceal it from the vulgar.'[92] In true neo-Platonic fashion, it is the ειδος of his work that stands as an incorruptible monument to his architectonic genius.

90 E. O'Brien, *The Essential Plotinus*, Hackett, Indianapolis, 1986, p. 55: 'Geometry, as the science of intelligible entities, has a place in the intelligible realm.'

91 *Ibid.*, p. 55. 'Skills such as those of architect and carpenter, exercised though they are upon sense objects, draw their principle and patterns from the intelligible realm to the extent that symmetry is their goal. But to the extent that they bring them into contact with the realm of sense, the principles and patterns are not wholly of the intelligible except, again, as contained in the mind of man'.

92 From R. Bacon, *Secret Works of Art and the Nullity of Magic*, quoted in Kahn, *op. cit.*, p. 90. Bacon repeats the sentiments of Iamblichus who describes the esoteric ways of the Pythagoreans who 'used modes recondite and unintelligible to the uninitiated, and concealed from others through symbols their thoughts and discourses'. T.M. Johnson trans, *Iamblichus: The Exhortation of Philosophy*, Phanes Press, Grand Rapids MI, 1988, p. 94. Ficino expressed something similar in a letter to Lorenzo de' Medici, dated 14 April 1477: 'I have not spoken openly of that about which men are not permitted to speak; I have not given what is holy to dogs or pigs for it to be torn into shreds. On the other hand, it certainly seems to me that I have revealed to men like Oedipus as many secret things as I myself have seen; however, to all the ignorant I have given them completely veiled.' *The Letters of Marsilio Ficino III*, Ginko Press, New York, 1985, p. 15.

XXV

SEBASTIANO SERLIO

Serlio shows ten centralized designs for temples in Book V and two basilica-style buildings. There are two circular designs, an oval design, and designs which use the geometries of the square and oblong, and the regular pentagon, hexagon, and octagon. Out of the necessity to accommodate a principal entrance to the temple, the symmetries of these regular figures are consistently eroded to the bilateral symmetry of the basilica-style form. Nevertheless, axes derived from the higher order symmetries of the regular polygons control the location of chapels following Alberti's prescription. In fact, Serlio provides designs for an hexagonal, octagonal and decagonal temple as Albert recommends. The symmetry of the octagon implies the symmetry of the square, and that of the decagon the symmetry of the pentagon. Serlio gives exact dimensions for elements of his temple designs.

Hexagonal Temple[1]

The 'diameter' of the hexagon is 25 feet. Serlio means by this the chord length between alternate vertices. The wall thickness is 5 feet. The overall width of the temple is thus $5 + 25 + 5 = 35$ feet. The ratio of the external width to the internal width, $35 : 25$, is $7 : 5$, the standard rational convergent for $\sqrt{2} : 1$. The external hexagon is thus twice the area of the internal hexagon. An equilateral triangle can be inscribed in the outer hexagon and its sides will each be 35 feet. An estimate for the altitude of this triangle is 30 feet, based on the rational convergent $7 : 6$ for $\sqrt{4} : \sqrt{3}$.[2] The difference between the side length and the altitude $35 - 30 = 5$ feet is the thickness of the wall. Thus Serlio accommodates both *ad quadratum* and *ad triangulum* considerations in the same computation for the wall thickness. What is the side length of the outside wall? Using the standard $7 : 4$ ratio for $\sqrt{3} : 1$, the exterior side wall will be $\frac{4}{7} \cdot 35 = 20$ feet. The interior side wall will be $\frac{4}{7} \cdot 25 = 14\frac{2}{7}$ feet. For major elements, Serlio uses dimensions to the nearest half foot in his descriptions and it seems likely that he would have rationalized this dimension as $14\frac{1}{2}$ feet.[3]

The opening to each of the chapels is 10 feet. The ratio of the wall width to the chapel opening is thus $29 : 20$ – two dimensions of the 20, 21, 29 right near-isosceles triangle – a rational estimate for $\sqrt{2} : 1$. Using the 20, 21, 29 right triangle measured in palms the ends of the window are exactly located in the rear wall at points $20 + 20 - 29 = 11$ palms from the side walls, that is by $2\frac{3}{4}$ feet.[4] Inside each chapel

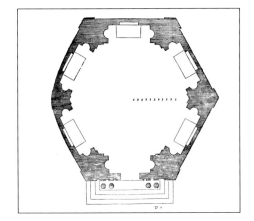

Fig. 1. Hexagonal temple from Serlio, 1545.

1 V. Hart, P. Hicks, *Sebastiano Serlio: On Architecture*, Yale University Press, New Haven, pp. 406–7.
2 Using the rational convergent $7 : 4$ for $\sqrt{3} : 1$.
3 If he had made the interior width of the temple 26 feet instead of 25 feet, he could have chosen the rational convergent $26 : 15$ and made the length of the internal sides 15 feet.
4 Note that such a rope is the width of the temple to its exterior walls. The dimension of 30 feet used to determine the wall thickness *ad triangulum* is found from the rope: $29 + 21 - 20 = 30$. There are 4 palms to a foot. This avoids fractions.

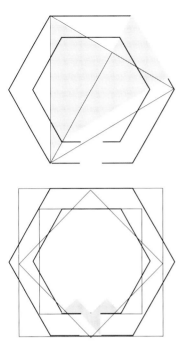

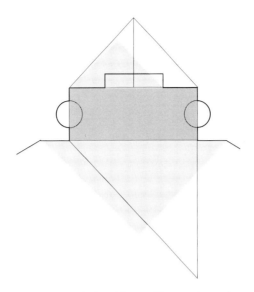

Fig. 3. Typical chapel layout. The opening to the chapel is defined by a 20, 21, 29 near-isosceles right triangle as is the window in the rear wall. The main 5 : 2 rectangle of the chapel is the Euclidean separation of the rational convergent 7 : 5 for √2 : 1. With respect to the semi-circular niches, the ratio of their diameter to the length of the side wall is 2 : 1 , and of their depth is 4 : 1.

Fig. 2. Top, *ad triangulum* derivation of wall thickness using the sides and hypotenuse of the half-equilateral triangle. Bottom, the exterior and interior hexagons defined within two squares in *ad quadratum* relationship, and the entrance dimension marked by 20, 21, 29 near-isosceles right triangle.

there is a window 4½ feet, or 18 palms wide. The ratio of the window width to the rear wall is 20 : 9, a good rational convergent to √5 : 1. The depth of each chapel is 4 feet, making a rectangular space in proportion to 5 : 2. This proportion is derived from the √2 rectangle by subtracting a square, Euclid's separation, from a 7×5 rectangle.[5] The ratio of the interior side wall of the hexagon to the width of each chapel window: 29 : 9 :: 2τ : 1 is a relation derived from the pentagon.[6] The entrance to the temple is 5 feet wide set in the wall of a potential chapel. The width of the door to the 'chapel' opening is in the ratio 2 : 1, but its width compared to the interior side wall of the hexagon is 29 : 10 which may again be set out using the 20, 21, 29 right triangle.

In this temple Serlio employs not only values derived from *ad triangulum* computations which are clearly associated with the hexagonal geometry, but also *ad quadratum* measures based on proportions found in the the 20, 21, 29 right triangle, the diagonal of a square, and the diagonal of the double square. The Euclidean 'rational in square' numbers involved in this design are √2, √3 and √5. Once again, these evoke the world-making proportions of the Platonic solids with their triangular, square and pentagonal faces. Other ratios include the rational empowerments R^2 2 : 1 (4 : 1), R^1 2 : 1 (2 : 1), $R^{1/2}$ 2 : 1 (7 : 5, 29 : 20), and $R^{3/2}$ 2 : 1 (29 : 10) which introduce proportions based on the rational powers 2, 1, ½ and ¾ in the manner of Oresme and Cusanus. (Figs. 1, 2, 3.)

5 5 : 7 − 5.
6 Using the value 20 : 9 for √5 : 1, the extreme and mean ratio τ : 1 :: 1 + √5 : 2 is 29 : 18.

Octagonal Temple[7]

Serlio states that the diameter of the octagonal temple is 43 feet. This is the interior dimension measured from wall to opposite wall, not corner to corner. At first glance 43 is a most unlikely number. A simple computation delivers the number directly. The ratio of a chord of an octagon to the side, as was seen in the case of Alberti's San Sebastiano, is in proportion to $1 + \sqrt{2} : 1$. Serlio does not specify the interior side length of the octagonal chapel. Let this be x. The rule of three requires that the equation $43 \div x = (1 + \sqrt{2}) \div 1$ be satisfied, or that $x = 43 \div (1 + \sqrt{2})$. Serlio has used the rational convergent $7 : 5$ in the hexagonal temple. Substituting this same value, $x = (5 \times 43) \div 12 = 215 \div 12$. Now, $18 \times 12 = 216$ and thus $x = 18$ is an excellent rational solution.[8] It is most likely that Serlio worked backwards from a side length of 18 feet to determine the width of the octagon as 43 feet in the expectation that a contemporary reader would be able to figure this out using the rule of three and some well-known knowledge about rational values of inexpressible numbers.

The chapels are of two kinds – oblong and semi-circular alternating according to Alberti's prescription. Each chapel is 12 feet wide by 5 feet deep. These are the dimensions of the 5, 12, 13 right triangle which may be used to fabricate an octagon.[9] The ratio $12 : 5$ is also the Euclidean separation of the rational convergent $17 : 12$ for $\sqrt{2} : 1$.[10] Serlio places a vaulted altar in the centre of the temple which is defined by lines extended from the chapel openings. The altar octagon is 12 feet wide. Again, using the ratio $1 + \sqrt{2} : 1$, it is easy to compute that the sides of the octagon are 5 feet long.[11] Each chapel has semi-circular niches which are 4 feet wide. In the oblong chapels these niches are set in a wall which is 5 feet long – a ratio of $5 : 4$, and a common rational convergent to $\sqrt[3]{2} : 1$.[12] The window in each of the three semi-circular chapels is described in some detail. The windows are as wide as the chapels themselves – 12 feet. Each window has two circular columns $6\frac{1}{2}$ feet high and $\frac{3}{4}$ foot in diameter – a ratio of $26 : 3$, and there are two half columns on the side. The central intercolumniation is given as $4\frac{1}{2}$ feet. Measuring in palms, the width of the window is 48 palms.[13] Each column is 3 palms across, and the total width of the two columns and the two half columns is 9 palms. The central intercolumniation is 18 palms. The two side intercolumniations are then computed to occupy 21 palms together. The distance of the window opening between the half columns is $48 - 3 = 45$ palms. The height of the window in palms is 26. Now, the ratio $45 : 26$ is an excellent rational convergent to $\sqrt{3} : 1$.[14] The proportion of the central opening including half of each of the central columns – that is, measuring in the same way that the previous opening was measured – is 26 palms high to a width of $18 + 3 = 21$ palms. The ratio $26 : 21$ is associated with the Tetragrammaton.[15] It is a good rational convergent to $\sqrt{3} : \sqrt{2}$ – the altitude of a half equilateral triangle with a unit short side to the diagonal of a unit square. This is the perfect union of *ad triangulum* and *ad quadratum*.

The proportion of the column may have occult significance. Although divided, the window has three full columns which might together represent the Trinity, yet there is the presence of four apparent columns suggesting perhaps the relationship with the four Evangelists. The numbers corroborate such an interpretation. The number 26 is the name of God in the Tetragrammaton and 3 is the Trinity so that each column, proportioned $26 : 3$, contains within itself the triune Godhead. But

7 V. Hart, P. Hicks, *op. cit.*, pp. 408–9.
8 Note that this computation involves the Vitruvian number 216, or the perfect number 6 solidified, 6^3.
9 See discussion of Francesco di Giorgio's construction in 'Prisoners of Number', *supra*.
10 $12 : 17 - 12$. A semi-circle of diameter 12 feet suggests that the chapel ought to be 6 feet deep, but Serlio appears to strike a straight window across the back thereby shortening this dimension.
11 Using the rational convergent $7 : 5$ for $\sqrt{2} : 1$, if the side is 5 feet, then the width of the octagon $5(1 + \sqrt{2})$ will be 12 feet as required.
12 A reference to the Delic problem set by the God's to double the size of an altar, cited by Vitruvius, would not be out of place in a sacred chapel.
13 Four palms to a foot. Fractions are avoided.
14 It is the conjugate to the more usual $26 : 15$. The ratio $45 + 26 : 26 + 15 = 71 : 41$ is used by Serlio in the oval temple.
15 Previously mentioned in relation to Alberti's Santa Maria Novella, *supra*.

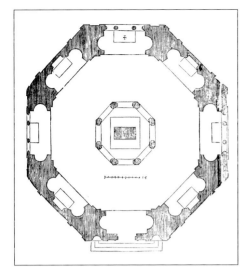

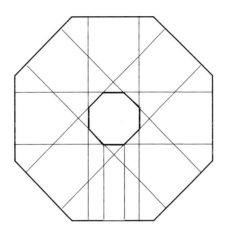

Fig. 5. The dimensions of the chapel openings determine the central octagonal altar. The side of this central octagon gives the size of the door-opening.

Fig. 4. Octagonal temple from Serlio, 1547.

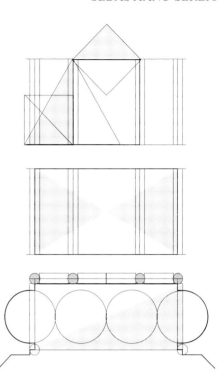

Fig. 6. Details of the oblong chapel. Top, the central opening of the tripartite window is measured by the altitude of a half-equilateral triangle standing on a unit base and the diagonal of an unit square combining both *ad triangulum* and *ad quadratum* methods (26 : 21). Centre, the window opening is proportioned *ad triangulum* in the ratio 45 : 26. Bottom, plan of the chapel showing the 5, 12, 13 right triangle.

further, the number 45 is also the name of God, so that the window opening to the light is doubly blessed with God's name in its proportion 45 : 26.[16] Only the most detailed attention to Serlio's instructions, read with the *mentalitè* of his times, reveals such semantics beyond mere syntactical architectonic elaborations. Even the fact that 26 reduces to 2 + 6 = 8 is surely no accident in this octagonal structure.

Decagonal Temple[17]

Serlio actually refers to this in the first place as a pentagonal temple, but immediately acknowledges the difficulties 'because if the door is built in one of the sides there will be a corner opposite it, something which is unsuitable in worthy architecture. Nevertheless, because I wanted to use this form, I made the exterior of V sides and the interior of X. This turns out rather well because one of the larger chapels is in the side opposite the door'.[18] The diameter of the chapel is 62 feet, meaning this time the distance between opposite corners of the decagonal interior.[19] The relationship of the radius of a decagon to its side is the extreme and mean ratio, $\tau : 1$. What then is the length of side in this case where the radius is 31 feet? An application of the rule of three leads to the equation $x = (2 \times 31) \div (1 + \sqrt{5})$. A good rational convergent to $\sqrt{5} : 1$ is 9 : 4.[20] Substituting this value in the equation gives $248 \div 13$. Now $19 \times 13 = 247$ and it follows that the side length is rationalized at 19 feet.[21] Serlio specifies the opening to the chapels as 15 feet. The three semi-circular niches in the larger square chapels have diameters of 10 feet. The single semi-circular niche in the smaller chapels has a diameter of 13 feet. The entrance is 7½ feet across. A lantern is placed at the apex of the vault which mimics the design as a whole with an internal decagon of diameter 12 feet.

The radius of the decagon to the side wall is 31 : 19. The next nearest values to this relationship are 19 : 12 and 12 : 7 in descending order and 50 : 29 ascending. All indications are that Serlio uses the 12 : 7 proportion for the lantern making its

16 See 'Occult Number' *supra*. The number 45 may also be derived from the Tetragrammaton, see G. Scholem, *Kabbalah*, Dorset Press, New York, 1974, p. 132. Use of these numbers in a tripartite window is particularly significant since the doctrine of 'three lights', which Scholem indicates originated in the thirteenth century, had aroused a great deal of speculation, especially among Christian kabbalists. *Ibid.*, pp. 95–96, also Scholem, *Les Origines de la Kabbalah*, 1966, pp. 367–75.

17 V. Hart, P. Hicks, *op. cit.*, pp. 404–5.

18 Serlio's use of the pentagon may have influenced Vignola in his design of the Villa Farnese at Caprarola near Viterbo, started prior to 1559, but the tradition of pentagonal fortresses is a more probable source.

19 This confirmed by the scale provided in the drawing and the fact that this diameter is marked specifically on the drawing with radial lines.

20 The conjugate to the ratio 20 : 9 previously employed by Serlio in the octagonal temple.

21 Surely corroborated by the height of the pilasters which frame each side which Serlio gives as 19 feet.

interior sides 7 feet, and the 50 : 31 ratio appears to be the ratio of the width of the exterior pentagon to the wall length of each of its five sides. This suggests that Serlio had made the connection at least with Nicomachus' tenth mean and the extreme and mean ratio. It's worthy of remark that Serlio does not use the Fibonacci sequence. The generators of Serlio's sequence are the numbers 2 and 5 – 2, 5, 7, 12, 19, 31, 50 ... The sequence relates common rationalizations for $\sqrt{2}:1$ (7 : 5) and its separation (5 : 2), as well as for $\sqrt{3}:1$ (12 : 7) and progressively improving values of the extreme and mean ratio $\tau:1$ (12 : 7, 19 : 12, 31 : 19, 50 : 31).[22] The plan is coordinated with these critical measurements.

Moving clockwise from the entrance the following proportional relationships are found. At the entrance itself, once past the portico, the dimensions 7½, 15 and 19 feet provide ratios 19 : 15, an excellent rational surrogate for the Delic $\sqrt[3]{2}:1$; the proportion 15 : 7½ or the duple 2 : 1; and 38 : 15 which is $2^3\sqrt{2}:1$. These may be written in the spirit of the period as $\mathbb{R}^{1/3}2:1$, $\mathbb{R}^{1}2:1$ and $\mathbb{R}^{4/3}2:1$ expressing the rational relation 1, 3, 4. Next clockwise, each large square chapel is the equality 1 : 1. Then the smaller chapels display the Albertian ratio 15 : 13 derived both from the Tetragrammaton and the ratio of the side of an equilateral triangle to its altitude, $\sqrt{4}:\sqrt{3}$. The extreme dimensions of the large chapel to the interior of the niches is (5 + 15 + 5) feet in width to (5 + 15) feet in depth – a ratio of 5 : 4, an early practical rationalization of the Delic $\sqrt[3]{2}:1$. Following this, the next small chapels indicates the Albertian ratio 15 : 13 again, but now in a different configuration. The large chapel opposite the entrance demonstrates the ratio 19 : 15 – the Delic $\sqrt[3]{2}:1$ – first found on entry. To its immediate right the equality 1 : 1 is established for the small chapel when the ratio of its opening to its extreme depth to the back of the niche is measured. Finally, the radius of the chapel's interior compared to its decagonal side is the extreme and mean rationalization 31 : 19.

Serlio describes the portico in detail, but with some discrepancies which seem to indicate conflicting and unresolved demands of his arithmetical ingenuity. In the

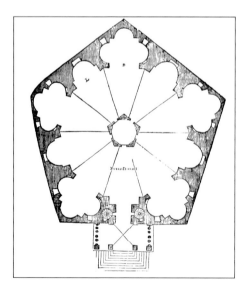

Fig. 7. Plan of decagonal temple from Serlio, 1547.

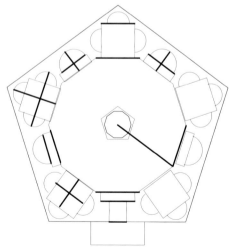

Fig. 8. Plan of Serlio's temple based on the decagon and pentagon. The diagram indicates the dimensions compared in the accompanying text.

22 Note that the ratio 12 : 7 may be read as either $\sqrt{3}:1$ or $\tau:1$. This is true of the primitive ratio 5 : 3 which appears early on in the generative sets see *supra*, 'Inexpressible Proportion'.

description accompanying the plan the portico is described as being 24 feet long and 10 feet wide. There is no conflict here, this is the proportion 12 : 5 – the Euclidean separation of the rationalization 17 : 12 for √2 : 1, and easily set out with the 5, 12, 13 right triangle. The columns are described as square and 2 feet wide. The central intercolumniation is 10 feet and between the side columns 3 feet. The dimensions are consistent with the overall length, 2 + 3 + 2 + 10 + 2 + 3 +2 = 24 feet. The commingling of ratios is a play on the rational diameter of the square, √2 : 1 –

$$(2 + 3 + 2) : 10 : (2 + 3 + 2) :: 7 : 10 : 7$$
$$(2 + 3 + 3) : (2 + 3) :: 7 : 5.$$

However, an equilateral triangle spanning the two central columns may be divided in half and reassembled to span the whole length of the portico –

$$(2 + 3 + 2 + 10 + 2 + 3 + 2) : (2 + 10 + 2) :: 12 : 7$$

thus introducing the *ad triangulum* relationship 12 : 7, a rationalization of √3 : 1. Once again Serlio brings the two systems into union.

In the description of the exterior elevation, Serlio gives the height of the columns to the portico as 14 feet. Given that the length of the portico is 24 feet, the rectangle containing the columns is seen to have the same *ad triangulum* relationship as the

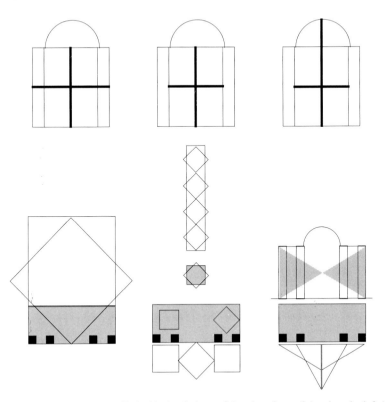

Fig. 9. Top row, ratios used by Serlio in his decriptions of the elevations of the chapels; left 1 : 1, centre 19 : 15, right 5 : 3. Middle, the proportion of a column in the portico. Bottom row, plan of the portico; left and centre *ad quadratum relations*, right, *ad triangulum* relations in plan and elevation.

columns and their intercolumniation do in plan, namely 12 : 7. But in announcing that the columns are 14 feet high, Serlio changes their thickness from 2 feet to 2½ feet without accounting for how this change is accommodated by the inter-columniations.[23] What is Serlio attempting to do? It seems that he would like to design the column itself *ad quadratum*, By changing its proportion from 7 : 1 to 14 : 2½, or 28 : 5 he not only extracts the perfect number 28 as an auspicious over-ture, but defines the column in the ratio $4\sqrt{2} : 1$, or $\mathbb{R}^{5/2}2 : 1$ – thus providing the initial numbers 5 and 2 for his extreme and mean generating sequence.[24] Serlio gives dimensions for the chapel elevations. The pilasters are 19 feet high so that the side of the decagonal interior containing a chapel is in an equality relationship with its height. Between the pilasters the ratio of height to opening is the Delic rational-ization 19 : 15 for $^3\sqrt{2} : 1$. Serlio, however, has changed the width of the pilasters to 3 feet which would upset all of the computations. Certainly the width of the opening to the chapel would have to change and this seems very unlikely.[25] Or the diameter of the temple is not 62 feet which would imply that the whole scheme has to be thrown out for the sake of a change to the pilaster. A similar problem arises with the height of the vault in the chapels which Serlio gives as 25 feet. If the pilasters, including the capitals, are 19 feet tall and they are surmounted by a semi-circular arch of diameter 15 feet and height 7½ feet, then the combined height exceeds Serlio's 25 feet. The 25 feet figure gives a nice round ratio of 25 : 15 ::5 : 3 of height of vault to width of opening, but seems incompatible with previous computations.

Oval Temple

'Following the circle in perfection, oval shapes are the next closest'.[26] Serlio then gives the internal dimensions of the interior space. It is 66 feet in length and 46 feet wide. These dimensions turn out to be the result of applying a precise algo-rism – a method of determing rational convergents to a square root known as the rule by defect.[27]

Suppose a value a_0 is a convergent to $\sqrt{A}$ and that it misses A by an amount r_0 – its defect – then the rule gives the next best convergent as:

$$a_1 = a_0 + \frac{r_0}{2a_0 + 1}.$$

Take 1 as the first convergent to $\sqrt{2}$, then $1^2 = 1$ is defective by 1. That is to say $a_0 = 1$, $r_0 = 1$. By the rule, the next convergent is:

$$a_1 = 1 + \frac{1}{2.1 + 1} = 1 + \frac{1}{3} = \frac{4}{3}.$$

Now $(4/3)^2 = 16/9$ which falls short of 2 by the new defect 2/9. For the next iteration the values $a_1 = 4/3$, $r_1 = 2/9$ are substituted in:

$$a_2 = a_1 + \frac{r_1}{2a_1 + r_1}.$$

23 If the central intercolumniation is maintained at 10 feet, then the side intercolumniations each reduce to 2 feet which is certainly inconsistent with Serlio's drawing of the elevation. A reduction of the central intercolumniation would also be inconsistent with the dimension of the doorway.
24 This may seem far-fetched, but Serlio's involve-ment with the mathematically sophisticated and occultist French court should not be taken lightly.
25 It would imply in the small chapels that the semi-circular niche is the same width, 13 feet, as the new opening. The drawing contradicts this.
26 V. Hart, P. Hicks, *op. cit.*, pp. 402–3.
27 Smith attributes the method to Arabic sources. D. E. Smith, *History of Mathematics*, Constable and Company, London, 1925, II, pp. 253–57.

This gives:

$$a_2 = \frac{4}{3} + \frac{2/9}{2.4/3 + 1} = \frac{4}{3} + \frac{2}{2.3.4 + 9} = \frac{4}{3} + \frac{2}{33} = \frac{46}{33}.$$

If 46/33 is a rational value for $\sqrt{2}$, then so is its conjugate 66/46, since $46/33 \cdot 66/46 = 2$. Thus Serlio's dimensions are the precise outcome of a particular and contemporary computation for $\sqrt{2}$. The oval temple, despite superficial appearances, is nicely embedded *ad quadratum*.

The walls of this temple are 8 feet thick. The dimensions of the exterior oval are thus $8 + 66 + 8 = 82$ feet and $8 + 46 + 8 = 62$ feet, a ratio of 41 : 31. What construction for the oval does Serlio use. In his Book I on geometry, he gives four related methods. Two are based on an armature of equilateral triangles and two on squares.[28] In this case Serlio uses the construction based on equilateral triangles. It is not difficult to show that if the oval is based on two equal circles which pass through one another's centres, then two overlapping equilateral triangles result – indeed two regular hexagons emerge.[29] A simple application of Pythagoras' theorem shows that if the length of such an oval is $3s$, where s is the length of a side of an equilateral triangle, then the width of the oval will be $(4 - \sqrt{3})s$. The ratio is thus $3 : (4 - \sqrt{3})$. Substituting the rational convergent 71 : 41 in this expression gives $3 \cdot 41 : 164 - 71 = 3 \cdot 41 : 93 = 41 : 31$, exactly the proportion that Serlio uses. Serlio shows in the other construction using equilateral triangles how to draw concentric ovals of which the interior oval is one. Figure 11 shows sequentially the graphic construction of the outer and inner ovals. First, two overlapping hexagons are drawn from an assembly of ten equilateral triangles. Each triangle has a length proportional to 41.[30] The width of this scheme is then proportional to 71. Two circles circumscribe the hexagons. Centre points are taken at the ends of the common chord and circles are struck of radius proportional to 82, or twice the side of one of the ten equilateral triangles. These circles extend the common diameter by a distance proportional to $2 - \sqrt{3}$ at both ends. The overall width of the oval is thus $(2 - \sqrt{3}) + \sqrt{3} + (2 - \sqrt{3}) = 4 - \sqrt{3}$. Substituting the rational value 71 : 41 for $\sqrt{3} : 1$ gives the result obtained above, namely the ratio 41 : 31. The width of the outer oval is divided into 62 parts. Using the same centres at the ends of the common chord of the hexagons two more arcs are struck passing through points 8 parts in

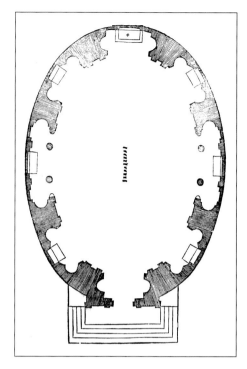

Fig. 10. Oval temple from Serlio, 1547.

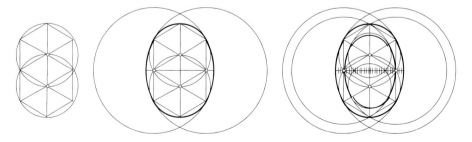

Fig. 11. Geometrical construction of the ovals. Left, overlapping hexagonal armature with two circles struck each passing through the other's centre. Centre, two more circles are drawn using the diameter of the hexagons as radius. Right, the width of the oval is divided into 31 parts (62 feet) and the interior oval is formed by striking arcs through the same centres as before, but now with radii reduced by 4 parts (8 feet).

28 Hart and Hicks, *op. cit.*, pp. 26–27.
29 Serlio reiterates Euclid's definitions from Book I of *The Elements*, and it is not surprising that this construction of two overlapping circles is the basis for Euclid's very first proposition showing how to construct an equilateral triangle.
30 In fact, two-thirds of 41 feet.

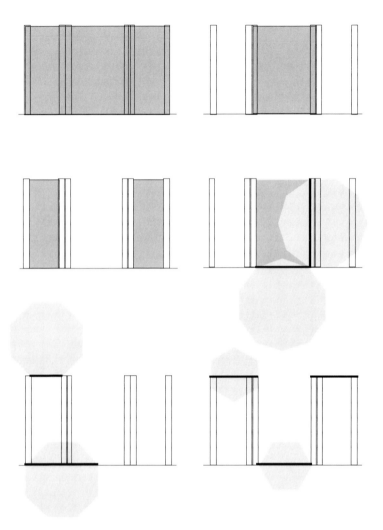

Fig. 12. Elevation of the principal chapels. Top left, the overall proportion is 41 : 24, an *ad quadratum* proportion. Top right, the proportion of the central opening to the centre line of the columns is 4 : 3 defined by the 3, 4, 5 right triangle. Middle left, the side openings between the columns is 48 : 17, another *ad quadratum* proportion. Middle right, the central opening between the columns is 8 : 5, an exteme and mean ratio related to the decagon and pentagon. Bottom left, the half width of the chapel to the side intercolumniation is in an octagonal (*ad quadratum*) relationship 41 : 17. Bottom right, the central intercolumniation to each of the residual distances on either side is in the hexagonal (*ad triangulum*) ratio 15 : 13.

on the extended chord. These arcs are merged with two other arcs struck from the centres of the hexagons. This completes the construction of the inner oval.

Serlio details the internal elevation and especially the columned openings to the largest chapels at the sides. The opening is framed by two half columns 3 palms wide.[31] There are two full columns 6 palms in diameter. The central intercolumniation is 30 palms. The two side intercolumniations are each 17 palms. The total width of the opening is 82 palms and is thus directly proportionate to the total length of the temple, 82 feet. The height of the columns is 48 palms. The proportion of the diameter to the height of the columns is $8 : 1$.[32] The height to the side inter-columniation is in the ratio $48 : 17$, or $2\sqrt{2} : 1$ which is the empowerment $\sqrt{8} : 1$ of the columns' proportion, $8 : 1$. The ratio of the breadth of the opening to the height is thus $41 : 24$, or $1 + \sqrt{2} : \sqrt{2}$ using the $24 : 17$ rational convergent. This is the Euclidean inverted composition of $\sqrt{2} : 1$ and is to be found in the geometry of the octagon.[33] The central opening to the midpoint of the columns is 36 palms so that the ratio of the opening to its height is $4 : 3$. The width of the central opening to the lengths on either side is in the Albertian proportion $(3 + 17 + 6) : 30 : (36 + 17 + 3) :: 13 : 15 : 13$, or a rational surrogate for $\sqrt{3} : \sqrt{4} : \sqrt{3}$ – an empowered echo of the proportion of the central opening. *Ad triangulum* and *ad quadratum* come together in these elevations with a hint of the Tetragrammaton in the numbers 36, 26 and 17. The significant proportion of the height of the central opening itself to its intercolumniation is $48 : 30 :: 8 : 5$. A rational decagon can be drawn with an inscribed pentagon defining chords of length 8 and 5 using this rational convergent to the extreme and mean ratio. Perhaps this is an acknowledgement of Pacioli's earlier paean to the divine, but it also completes the references to Alberti's ideal polygonal platforms for temples – the hexagon $(15 : 13)$, the octagon $(41 : 24)$, and the decagon $(8 : 5)$, all embodied in these elevations to the two principal chapels.

Yet again outward appearances are deceptive. Behind appearance is hidden structure. The oval seems not to have anything to do with rectilinearity and regular polygons. Nevertheless, its construction is based on the equilateral triangle and the hexagon which includes it. This provides the geometrical basis for *ad triangulum* construction. Further, the overall dimensions of the interior relate to the diagonal of the square and are thus *ad quadratum*. Once more, a fine union of the these two established systems. In the principal chapel elevations, Serlio combines the geometries of the hexagon, octagon and decagon which hold the world-making code to create the Platonic solids. In these temple designs, Serlio displays a consistent architectonic sensibility and especially that inconspicuous erudition which is the hallmark of genius in his time.

31 The conversion of 4 palms to the foot is done to avoid fractions. Serlio presents the information in feet.
32 This is a somewhat inelegant proportion for the Corinthian order which Serlio specifies.
33 See *supra*, p. 208.

XXVI

ANDREA PALLADIO

Scheme Mocenigo on the Brenta[1]

That the drawings of buildings and projects shown in Palladio's second book often show inconsistencies between dimensions and the drawn image, or the drawing and the building as built, is an observation made by many authors. Even an unbuilt project such as the Mocenigo scheme on the Brenta, the project with which Palladio brings his second book to a close – 'il fine del secondo libro', cannot be read without dimensional contradiction. Take the ground-floor great hall in which columns are proposed 'to make the length and breadth proportional to the height'. The length of the great hall is given as P76[2]. Its width as P30. There are six columns to each side, and therefore seven intercolumniations. From centre to centre the columns would be spaced at an average interval of just less than P11. The drawing indicates what look like square bays between the columns and the side walls. P22 would be taken up by such bays, leaving P8 as the width of the great hall between opposite rows of columns. This is architecturally absurd, and either the drawing is incorrect, or the given measurements are wrong, or perhaps both.

The dimensions are at least consistent with others shown in the plan. The length of the great hall is given by the dimensions of the front, octastyle loggia. From the elevational drawing Palladio gives the column diameter as P4, the side intercolumniations as P6 and the centre intercolumniation as P8. The sum of dimensions is thus:

$$4 + 6 + 4 + 6 + 4 + 6 + 4 + 8 + 4 + 6 + 4 + 6 + 4 + 6 + 4 = 76$$

which is the length of the great hall, P76. This suggests that, for Palladio, plan dimensions may sometimes be determined by those of the principal loggia which acts as an overture to the fabric. This will be further illustrated in other schemes examined below.

The dimensions of the portico in the main courtyard are P75 and P59. What is to be made of these numbers? In elevation, Palladio indicates that the columns on the ground floor are P22½ high with a diameter of P2½ so that the ratio of height to diameter of the Ionic order is the canonic 9 : 1.[3] From the drawing two equations can be set up given certain assumptions:

1. That the intercolumniation dimensions in the length and width of the courtyard are the same;

1 A. Palladio, *I Quattro Libri dell'Architettura*, Domenico de' Franceschi, Venice, 1570, II, p. 66. The page number is incorrect and the proposal actually follows p. 77. R. Tavernor, R. Schofield, *Andrea Palladio: The Four Books on Architecture*, MIT Press, Cambridge MA, 1997, pp. 156–57.
2 P. Stands for 'piede Vicentino', Palladio, *op. cit.*, II, p. 4.
3 *Ibid.*, I, p. 28, *op. cit.*, Tavernor, Schofield, p. 32.

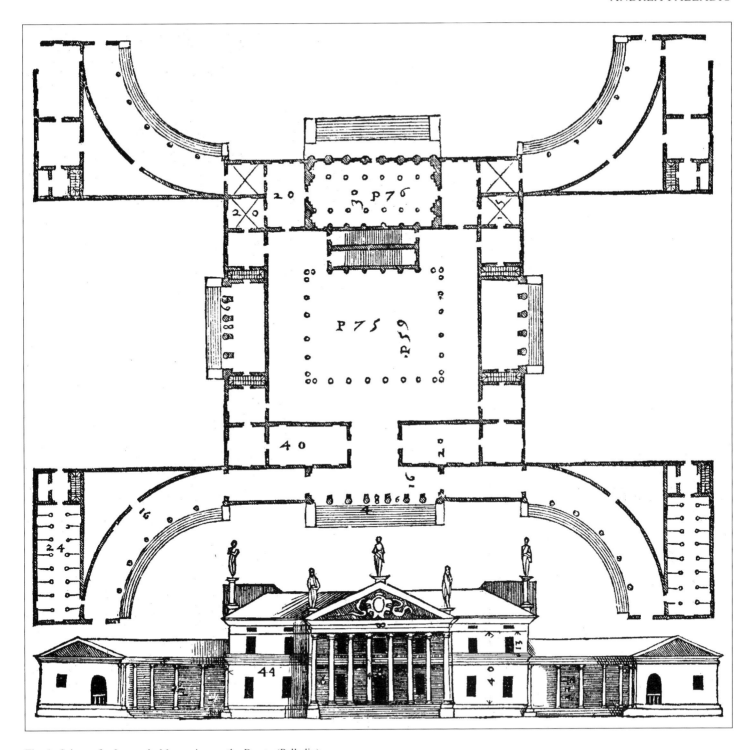

Fig. 1. Scheme for Leonardo Moncenigo on the Brenta (Palladio).

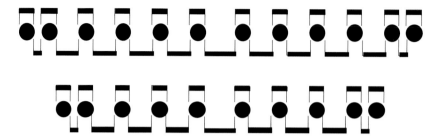

Fig. 2. Scheme for Leonardo Moncenigo on the Brenta (Palladio). Column distribution in the courtyard. Above, the length; and below, the width.

2. That the intercolumniations are Px in the corners, Py to the sides of the centre, and Pz in the centre;

3. That the dimensions P75 and P59 are to the inner face of the columns in the courtyard.[4]

The equations are:

$$x + 2\tfrac{1}{2} + y + 2\tfrac{1}{2} + y + 2\tfrac{1}{2} + y + 2\tfrac{1}{2} + z + 2\tfrac{1}{2} + y + 2\tfrac{1}{2} + y + 2\tfrac{1}{2} + y + 2\tfrac{1}{2} + x$$
$$= \quad 2x + 6y + x + 20$$
$$= \quad 75.$$
$$x + 2\tfrac{1}{2} + y + 2\tfrac{1}{2} + y + 2\tfrac{1}{2} + z + 2\tfrac{1}{2} + y + 2\tfrac{1}{2} + y + 2\tfrac{1}{2} + x$$
$$= \quad 2x + 4y + z + 15$$
$$= \quad 59.$$

We thus have two simultaneous equations

$$2x + 6y + z = 55$$
$$2x + 4y + z = 44$$

from which it is evident that

$$y = 5\tfrac{1}{2}$$

and

$$2x + z = 22.$$

This last equation cannot be solved with architecturally satisfactory values. It is possible that Palladio's dimensions shown on the drawing refer to measurements to the outer faces of the columns in the portico. In this particular context, these measurements would be consistent with that of the loggia measured to include the outermost column diameters (see above), even though this is not Palladio's practice for courtyards. It will be easily seen that this leads to the same value for y, and to a new equation relating the other two unknowns:

$$2x + z = 17.$$

4 Palladio's usual measurement.

If x were equal to y – an architecturally acceptable arrangement, but not that indicated by the drawing – then the central intercolumniation z would be 6. This value too would be acceptable. For example, the private house of the ancient Romans shows a courtyard in which the central intercolumniation is P6 and the side intercolumniations are P5.[5] The Roman courtyard, however, shows the typical arrangement of a corner cluster of three closely packed columns such as is to be seen in the Mocenigo drawing. Structurally, the maximum span that the central intercolumniation in this project might assume is unlikely to have been more than P10, which would make the space between the corner columns each P3½ – larger than might be expected. Also the fact that the central intercolumniation in this arrangement is almost double that of the intervals on either side is architecturally unlikely: the ratio is excessive and not to be found elsewhere in Palladio's work.

No matter how the dimensions are taken in the Mocenigo project, the drawing cannot be made to conform. This is not the case for the courtyard in the Trissino project where dimensions and drawing are compatible.[6] Using the same notation, the Trissino equations reduce to:

$$2x + 6y + z = 42 \text{ (62 less 20 for the aggregate diameters of eight columns)}$$

and

$$2x + 4y + z = 31 \text{ (46 less 15 for the aggregate diameters of six columns)}$$

whence again

$$y = 5\frac{1}{2}$$

but now

$$2x + z = 9$$

which gives reasonable values for x and y such as half the column diameter for spacing between columns in the corner cluster $x = 1\frac{1}{4}$, with a central intercolumniation $z = 6\frac{1}{2}$.

Palladio frequently uses the pilaster system described by Vitruvius at Fano in which a column rising through two stories is adjoined by pilasters supporting the intermediate floor and the roof.[7] Specifically, he does so in the scheme on the Brenta for Mocenigo to support the second-story loggia. The ratio of the diameter to the height of the columns in the Fano nave is 10 : 1 which should have suggested to Palladio the use of the Composite order, but his, or Barbaro's, reconstruction illustrates the Corinthian order. From the information given by Vitruvius, the section of the nave is divided into P20 for the height of the ground floor, P18 for the mezzanine and the remaining P12 for the clerestory lighting to make up the full height of P50. As will be discussed later, these same dimensions are rhetorically quoted in the plan of the Villa Maser, as are those of the basilica in the house of the ancient Romans, P72 and P36. Even the dimension of the opening to the tribunal at Fano P46 is evoked in the side wings of the villa at Maser.[8]

To complete the analysis of the scheme on the Brenta for Leonardo Mocenigo, it pays to examine the two principal ratios 76 : 30 for the great hall, and 75 : 59 for

5 *Ibid.*, II, pp. 33–35, Tavernor, Schofield, pp. 109–11.
6 *Ibid.*, II, pp. 73–74, Tavernor, Schofield, pp. 151–52.
7 *Vide supra*, 'Roman Wonders'.
8 *Vide infra*, p. 138.

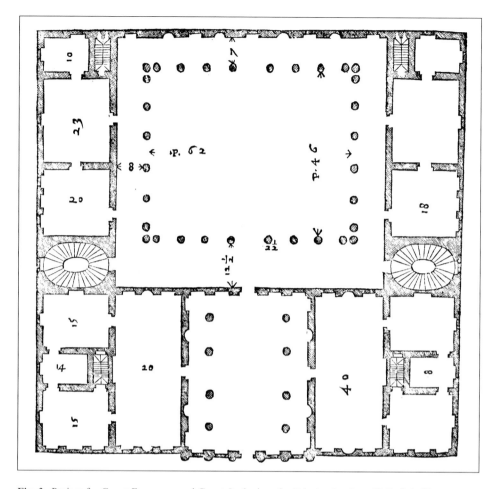

Fig. 3. Project for Count Francesco and Count Ludovico, the Trissino brothers (Palladio). Plan.

the courtyard. It will be noted that in the text Palladio refers to the proportion of the great hall as 'due quadro, e mezo' which would give the ratio 5 : 2. This would be the case if the great hall was P75 and not P76 long. Why does Palladio insert this dimensional change in the drawing? Again, if the width of the courtyard had been P60, its proportion would have been simply 5 : 4. The great hall and the court-yard would then have shared the common ratio 5 : 4, the great hall being two 5 : 4 rectangles placed end to end. Given the very schematic nature of the proposal, it is very surprising that this was not done. P76, and not P75, is the length of the prin-cipal loggia at the entrance, and this significant measure is reinforced by employing the same dimension in the great hall, but why not the courtyard? The great hall is P76 long. The number 76 is 4.19. The number 19 suggests a rational convergent for $\sqrt{3} : 1$, namely 19 : 11. In turn $19 + 11 = 30$, and P30 is the width of the great hall. The great hall might then divide itself into a central hall between the two rows of columns with dimensions P76 long and P19 wide, a 4 : 1 space, and two aisles each P5½ wide. Given the proximity of 77 to 76, it then appears that the aisle bays are very close to being double squares P11 × P5½, and not the squares illustrated in the woodcut. If the columns in the great hall have a diameter of P2 and their height

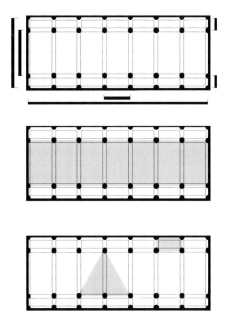

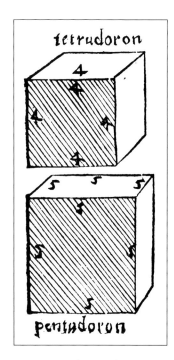

Fig. 4. Scheme for Leonardo Moncenigo on the Brenta (Palladio). Top, the dimensions of the great hall. The width is P30 divided into two side aisles P5½ – together P11 – and a central hall P19. The length is P76, or 4 × 19 , and each bay is very close to being P11 wide. 19 : 11 is a rational convergent for √3 : 1. Centre, the central hall between the columns is P76 × P19, a ratio of 4 : 1. Bottom, two bays are *ad triangulum* using a 22 : 19 rational equilateral triangle (P22 base and P19 altitude). The side aisle bays are double squares, P11 × P5½.

Fig. 5. *Tetradoron* and *pentadoron* bricks showing an early solution to the Delic problem of doubling the cube (from Barbaro).

is P19 'to make the length and breadth proportional to the height', then it might be surmised that Palladio intended to use the Corinthian order giving a canonic height to diameter ratio of 9½ : 1.[9]

The question of the courtyard proportion is prised open by its approximation to 5 : 4. A musical analogy, such as Wittkower's, would relate this to the major third.[10] A geometrical, and Vitruvian interpretation, would be found in Book IX where, in the Preface, Vitruvius discusses the Delian problem of finding the cube root of two.[11] Barbaro gives some attention to this problem in his own commentary and Palladio – presumably – illustrates the classical instruments by which the cube root may be found.[12] Arithmetic convergence gives 5 : 4 as an early approximation. Barbaro and Palladio illustrate two Greek bricks, the *tetradoron* of dimensions $4 \times 4 \times 4$ palms and the *pentadoron* of dimensions $5 \times 5 \times 5$ palms.[13] These blocks are mentioned by Vitruvius:[14]

'Now the Greeks call the palm *doron*, because the giving of gifts is called *doron*, and this is always done by means of the palm of the hand. Thus the brick that is of five palms every way is called *pentadoron*; of four palms, *tetradoron*. Public buildings are erected with the former; private buildings with the latter.'

The ratio of volumes of these two bricks is $5^3 : 4^3$ or 125 : 64. The ratio 128 : 64 :: 2 : 1, so that one brick is approximately double the volume of the other. If the *tetradoron*

9 *Ibid.*, II, pp. 37–42, Tavernor, Schofield, *op. cit.*, pp. 41–46.

10 R. Wittkower, *Architectural Principles in the Age of Humanism*, Academy Editions, London, 1998, pp. 123–29.

11 Vitruvius IX, Preface 13. F. Granger, *Vitruvius: De Architectura*, Harvard University Press, Cambridge MA, 1931, pp. 206–7: 'For they satisfied, each by his own method, the demand which Apollo had imposed upon Delos: namely, that the number of cubic feet in his altar should be doubled, and that thereby the residents of the island should be freed from a religious scruple.'

12 *Vide supra*, 'Centralized Design in the Renaissance'.

13 D. Barbaro, *M Vitrvvii Pollionis: De Architectura Libri Decem Cvm Commentariis . . .*, Venice, 1567, p. 54.

was slightly smaller, the two bricks could be in an exact 2 : 1 volumetric relationship. This would seem to be approximated by adopting the ratio 75 : 59 rather than the proportion 75 : 60 :: 5 : 4. However, there is a remarkable relationship that produces the precise ratio 75 : 59. A sequence of best rational convergents to the cube root of 2 is 4 : 3, 5 : 4, 9: 7, 14 : 11, 19 : 15, 24 : 19,. . . . Note that the first term in this series is the proportion of the four rooms on either side of the great hall, 20 : 15 :: 4 : 3, which is itself preceded by the ratio of the width of the utility buildings and the curved colonnades, namely 24 : 16 :: 3 : 2. Some of these ratios will give values larger, when cubed, in excess of 2, and others will be deficient.[15] It is a fact that summing the antecedents and comparing them with the sum of the consequents produces:

$$(4 + 5 + 9 + 14 + 19 + 24) : (3 + 4 + 7 + 11 + 15 + 19) :: 75 : 59.$$

That is to say, an averaging out of values in the sequence produces the exact ratio that Palladio employs. There is no way of confirming that this procedure was actually used by Palladio from available evidence, but the coincidence is compelling.

The arithmetic games that Palladio entertains is surely confirmed by the information given in the elevation. On the elevational drawing of the scheme on the Brenta, Palladio gives a dimension of P13 to the height of the second storey. How does this measure relate? Possibly to the height of the curved colonnades which he gives as P22½. These two dimensions are brought together in the proportion 22½ : 13 :: 45 : 26 which is a rational convergent to $\sqrt{3}$: 1. Already, it has been shown that the loggia is P76 wide. The 'wings' on either side of the loggia are given as P44. The proportion of these two dimensions is 76 : 44 :: 19 : 11, another very good rational convergent to $\sqrt{3}$: 1 corresponding to the dimensions used by Palladio in four rooms in the Palazzo Della Torre which is analysed below, and present in the great hall of the Mocenigo scheme itself.[16] There would seem to be no doubt about Palladio's intentions here. At the same time, the height of these 'wings' is given as P40. The proportion of height to width of the 'wings' is thus 44 : 40 :: 11 : 10. Now 11 : 5 is an early rational convergent to $\sqrt{5}$: 1, the diameter of the unit double square, so that 11 : 10 is a rational convergent to $\sqrt{5}$: 2, or $\sqrt{5}$: $\sqrt{4}$.

$$
\begin{array}{ll}
2 : 1 & R^{1/2}4 : 1 \\
\times & \times \\
\underline{11 : 5} & \underline{R^{1/2}5 : 1} \\
11 : 10 & R^{1/2}5 : R^{1/2}4.
\end{array}
$$

If 5 : 4 is an arithmetic surrogate for $R^{1/3}2$: 1, the cube root of two, then $\sqrt{5}$: $\sqrt{4}$ is a surrogate for $R^{1/6}2$: 1, or the sixth root of two. Remember, the courtyard itself may be read as having a proportion which is a rational convergent to $R^{1/3}2$: 1. The proportion of the great hall, 76 : 30 :: 38 : 15, may also be read as a two cube root of two spaces placed end to end since 19 : 15 is a good rational convergent $R^{1/3}2$: 1 (also used by Palladio in two rooms for the Palazzo Della Torre):

$$
\begin{array}{ll}
19 : 15 & R^{1/3}2 : 1 \\
|\ | & |\quad | \\
\underline{2 : 1} & \underline{2\ :\ 1} \\
38 : 15 & R^{4/3}2 : 1.
\end{array}
$$

14 Vitruvius, II, iii 3. F. Granger, *op. cit.*, I, pp. 92–93.
15 *Vide supra*, 'Inexpressible Proportion'.
16 *Op. cit.*, Palladio, II, p. 11, Tavernor, Schofield, p. 87.

Is it possible that Palladio is playing with fractional powers of two: already established in the mathematical literature, but something that musicians were to grasp only later in the century as they moved towards equal temperament? If so, he shows advanced mathematical ability for his time.[17] Significantly, more than one interpretion of the proportion of the great hall have now been given, and these polysemic readings with multiple archaic references seemingly enrich the scheme. It is my belief that Palladio understood this, but there is no way of knowing whether our interpretations here have any validity with respect to the author's intentions. None are in conflict, however, with the knowledge that Palladio possessed, as recorded in his writings, drawings and collaborative work with Barbaro, or with other works to which he might have had contemporary access.

All the dimensions shown in the scheme on the Brenta have now been related, but the nexus of relationships is evidently not musical. On the contrary, the scheme seems to be pervaded by geometrical and arithmetical harmonies associated with $\sqrt{3}$, $\sqrt{4}$, $\sqrt{5}$ (evoking the Pythagorean triplet 3, 4, 5) and with rational transformations of the Delian $\sqrt[3]{2} : 1$. These are all Pythagorean and Platonic themes touched upon by Vitruvius, encouraged by Alberti, and commented upon by Barbaro in collaboration with Palladio. Despite some obvious inconsistencies between dimensions and drawing, on discriminating examination, the Mocenigo scheme concludes the second book with exacting harmonic and penetrating geometric play.

Reconstructing the ceiling plan in the entrance of a scheme for a site in Venice[18]

Palladio rarely gives ceiling plans for actual projects, although he usually indicates vaulting patterns. Such a plan is given for an unbuilt project sited in Venice. The only dimensional information given is that the entrance is P45 by P37½, the column diameter is P2½, and that the inner opening into the house is P11, or twice the intercolumniations on the façade. Assuming that the central ceiling coffer is P11 wide as suggested in the drawing, and that eight of the corner coffers are square, all the remaining dimensions can be computed. The last assumption might be questioned since some corner coffers look more square than others in the woodcut, but reference back to the ceiling plan for the atrium with four columns suggests that this assumption is at least reasonable.[19] Let the width of the square coffers be Px and the length of the long coffers be Py. Then the following equations may be set up to insure dimensional consistency. In length:

$$x + 2\tfrac{1}{2} + x + 2\tfrac{1}{2} + 11 + 2\tfrac{1}{2} + x + 2\tfrac{1}{2} + x = 4x + 21 = 45$$
$$x = 6.$$

And in the width:

$$6 + 2\tfrac{1}{2} + y + 2\tfrac{1}{2} + 6 = 37\tfrac{1}{2}$$
$$y = 20.$$

Multiplying all dimensions by two to eliminate fractions, the following six numbers are involved in the design:

5, 12, 22, 41, 75, 90.

17 Recall that Nicole Oresme had found an ally in Nicholas Cusanus in recommending exponents as rational entities, *Vide supra*, 'Empowered Proportion'.
18 *Ibid.*, II, p. 72, Tavernor, Schofield, pp. 150–51.
19 *Ibid.*, II, pp. 27–28, Tavernor, Schofield, pp. 103–4.

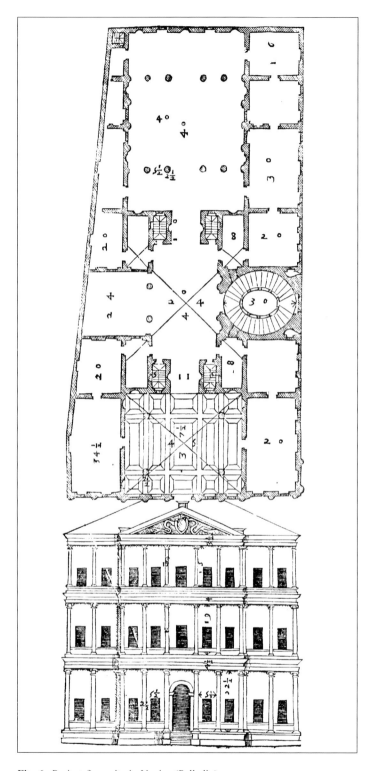

Fig. 6. Project for a site in Venice (Palladio).

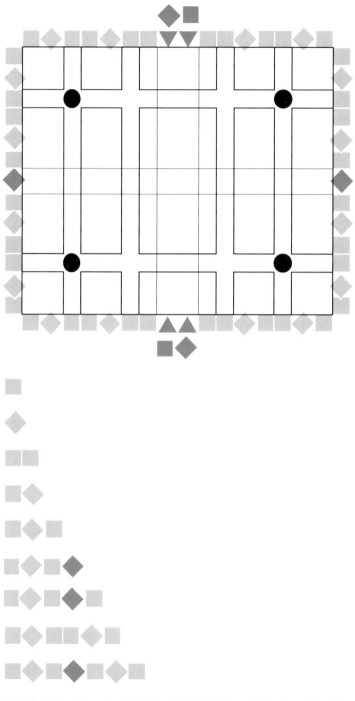

Fig. 7. Project for a site in Venice (Palladio). The mesh for the ceiling plan is formed *ad quadratum*. Note the caesurae in the centres of the sides (darker modules) where the 5 + 7 + 5 rhythm is broken. The mesh provides a host of *ad quadratum* dimensions: from top to bottom, 5, 7, 10, 12, 17, 24, 29, 34, 41.

The first four are elementary dimensions, the last two are aggregates. The numbers 5, 12 and 41 all relate to the algorism for generating rational convergents for $\sqrt{2}$, and it would seem reasonable to explore the possibility that Palladio is using *ad quadratum* methods to generate the ceiling plan, perhaps in the way that Vitruvius might have planned the basilica at Fano.[20] The nave of the basilica can be laid out using a square module placed both orthogonally and diagonally, given that the side of the square is the diameter of the column P5, and that the diameter of the square is taken to be P7½; that is, to assume the ratio 10 : 7 for a convergent to $\sqrt{2}$: 1. In the case of Palladio's project, the convergent 7 : 5 appears to have been used. Unlike the regularity to be seen in the Vitruvian scheme, Palladio introduces caesuræ both in length and breadth by breaking the regular rhythm of orthogonal and diagonal application.

It will be observed that a range of convergents to $\sqrt{2}$: 1 are embedded in the dimensional design resulting from the intersection of the two elementary numbers 5 and 7 and their aggregates 10, 12, 14, 17, 24, 29, 34, 41, 48. Through the caesaræ introduced by Palladio, the ceiling provides a brilliant sampler of rational solutions to the Platonic problem of doubling the square:

7 : 5, 14 : 10;

10 : 7;

17 : 12, 34 : 24;

24 : 17, 48 : 34;

41 : 29.

The number 11 in the original set of solutions suggests that the equilateral triangle may not be entirely absent since 19 : 11 is a rational convergent to $\sqrt{3}$: 1. The aggregates $5 + 5 + 7 + 5 = 22$ and $7 + 5 + 7 = 19$ give dimensions for the base and height, respectively, of an arithmetically determined equilateral triangle. Recall that these numbers are the double of the actual dimensions in *piedi*. The central coffer appears to be P20½ by P11. It may therefore be considered to be composed of a square P11 by P11 and an equilateral triangle P11 by P9½, proportionate to 22 : 19, which is the same ratio used in the great hall of the Mocenigo project on the Brenta. That Palladio is intentionally using the $\sqrt{3}$ relationship is corroborated by the dimensions of the two side rooms at the front. Their dimensions are P34½ by P20, or a ratio of 69 : 40. The ratio 7 : 4 is a standard rational convergent for $\sqrt{3}$: 1, but it is a tad too large. 70 : 40 is proportionate, and by reducing the antecedent to 69 Palladio compensates for the overestimate. The rational convergents to $\sqrt{3}$: 1 may be set out in two rows, in which the lower row are conjugate values, the result of inverting and tripling the upper row, in the process that has been explained earlier.[21]

2 : 1	**5 : 3**	7 : 4	**19 : 11**	**26 : 15**	71 : 41
	3 : 2	9 : 5	**12 : 7**	33 : 19	45 : 26

By summing the antecedents and the consequents of the emboldened ratios, some of the underestimates and the overestimates are averaged out,

$$(5 + 7 + 12 + 19 + 26) : (3 + 4 + 7 + 11 + 15) :: 69 : 40,$$

20 *Vide supra*, 'Roman Wonders'.

21 Note that the ratio 5 : 3 is an early convergent for $\sqrt{3}$: 1. It is often assumed to be a proxy for the golden section. In this context, the former interpretation seems more reasonable.

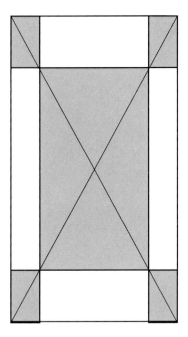

Fig. 8. Project for a site in Venice (Palladio). One of two principal rooms adjoining the entrance hall showing its dimensions compounded from a 45 × 26 rectangle and four 12 × 7 rectangles – all proportionate to rational convergents for √3 : 1.

and the exact proportion of the side rooms is determined. Perhaps a more design directed approach would be to extend a 45 : 26 rectangle by 12 : 7 rectangles placed at the corners:

$$(12 + 45 + 12) : (7 + 26 + 7) :: 69 : 40.$$

The number 11 also suggests a possible relationship with the circle and the common rational convergent to π : 1 with a value 22 : 7. Indeed, where the caesura cuts the central coffer the ratio 22 : 7 is implicit. The length of the semi-circle on a circle whose radius is determined by the caesura, gives the width of the central coffer and of the inner entrance to the house. An equilateral triangle inscribed in this circle provides the construction for Euclid's Proposition XIII.12:[22] 'If an equilateral triangle be inscribed in a circle, the square on the side of the triangle is triple of the square on the radius of the circle.'

In fact, the side of this particular equilateral triangle measures the caesura in the long side of the entrance, so that the intersection of the caesuræ is a 12 : 7, a rational surrogate for a √3 : 1 rectangle. The four rectangles which fill out the coffer are rational surrogates for a √2 : 1 rectangle: two have ratios 17 : 12 and two 7 : 5. The central coffer is potent with arithmetic and geometric relationships.

The overall proportion of the entrance is 45 : 37½ :: 6 : 5, evoking the proportion of the Etruscan temple, but also an early convergent to the base and height of the equilateral triangle, so that the whole entrance space circumscribes an equilateral triangle, implicating *ad triangulum*.[23] Even the coffers which abut the central coffer on the main axis, share a proportionate similarity with it since their dimensions P11 by P6 may be decomposed, like the central coffer, into a square P6 by P6 and an

22 T. L. Heath, *Euclid: The Thirteen Books of the Elements*, Cambridge University Press, Cambridge, 1921, pp. 466–67.

23 Vitruvius, IV, vii 1, Granger, *op. cit.*, I, pp. 238–39. Also Alberti, VII 4, Rykwert, Leach, Tavernor, p. 197 and n. 65. For further discussion, R. Tavernor, 'Concinnitas, o la formulazione della bellezza', pp. 300–335, and G. L. Hersey, 'Alberti e il tempio etrusco. Postille a Richard Krautheimer', pp. 216–23, in J. Rykwert, A. Engel, *Leon Battista Alberti*, Olivetti/Electa, Milan, 1994.

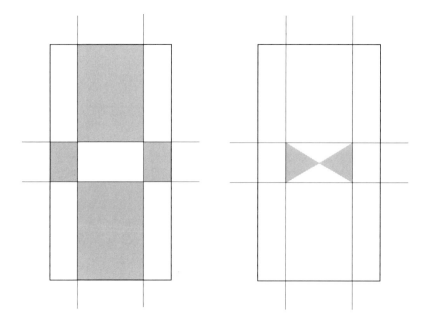

Fig. 9. Project for a site in Venice (Palladio). Left, the central coffer in the ceiling is proportionate to: (5 + 7 + 5 + (7) + 5 + 7 + 5) : (5 + (12) + 5) :: 41 : 22. The intersection of the caesura is surrounded *ad quadratum* by 7 : 5 and 17 : 12 'panels'. Right, the caesura is 12 : 7, an *ad triangulum* relation.

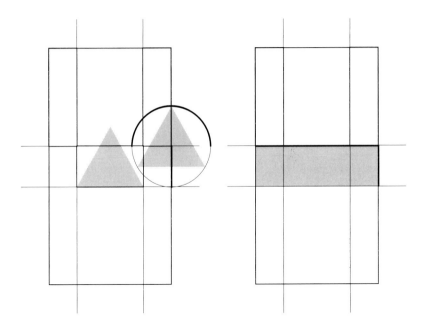

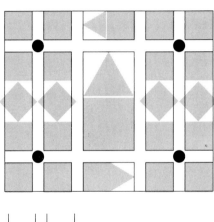

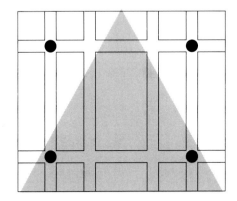

Fig. 10. Project for a site in Venice (Palladio). Right, one caesura creates a 'panel' in the mesh proportionate to 22 : 7, or π : 1. Left, a rational equilateral triangle inscribed in a circle of radius P7 has a base of length P12 – the width of the other caesura. The semi-circumference of the circle is P22 – the width of the central coffer.

Fig. 11. Project for a site in Venice (Palladio). The dimensions of the coffers in the ceiling of the entrance hall are determined by *ad quadratum* and *ad triangulum* relations. Bottom left, even the detailed centring of the columns and the beams follow an *ad quadratum* regime.

equilateral triangle with a base P6 and and height P5: the latter replicating at a small scale the proportion of the whole entrance. This overlay of *ad quadratum* and *ad triangulum* is immanent in the Vitruvian scheme at Fano, and is apparent to anyone who studies it with care, as Palladio surely did.

Atria

The atrium with four columns²⁴

The coffering of the entrance hall above shares the same schema with the Palladio's notion of the classical atrium with four Corinthian columns. Palladio provides the following dimensions in the drawing: P3¼ for the column diameter, P6½ for the side passages, the length of the atrium is P52½, and the width between columns is P35. The written description reads: 'The following design illustrates the atrium with four columns, the breadth of which is three-fifths of the length. The side passages are a quarter of the length of the atrium. The columns are Corinthian and their diameter is half the breadth of the side passages; the unroofed part is one-third of the breadth of the atrium; the tablium is half as broad as the atrium and the same in length.'

Looking at the drawing, the tablium is shown with dimensions P17½ and P16, not 'the same in length' as Palladio describes. It is, however, 'half as broad as the atrium'. Even more glaring, is the fact that the atrium as drawn and dimensioned is not as broad as 'three-fifths of the length'. Three-fifths of the length P52½ would

Fig. 12. Project for a site in Venice (Palladio). The overall proportion of the entrance hall is *ad triangulum* using the rational equilateral triangle with a base 6 and altitude 5. The tinted triangle is an exact equilateral and shows the degree of error involved in taking 5 : 3 as a rational convergent for √3 : 1.

24 *Op. cit.*, Palladio, II, pp. 27–28, Tavernor, Schofield, pp. 103–4.

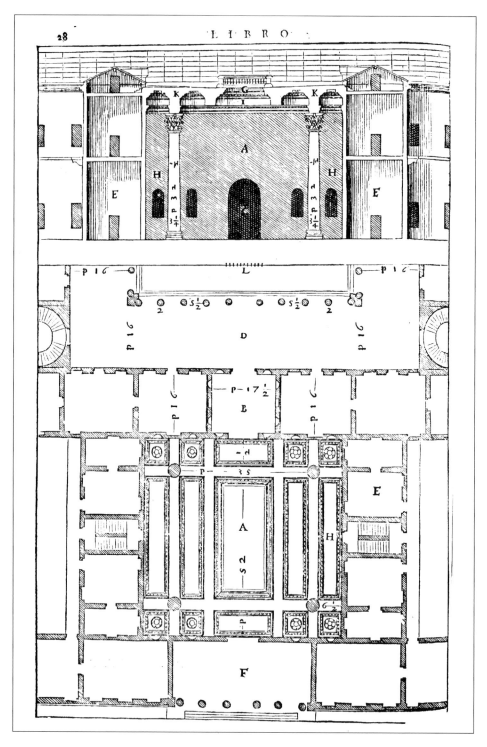

Fig. 13. The atrium with four columns (Palladio). Plan and section.

be P31½, not P35. The other dimensions pan out if the length is taken as P52. The side passages together take up a width of P13, or P6½ each. The columns are half again of this, or P3¼. If the numbers are quadrupled to remove fractions, the atrium is controlled by the set 13, 26, 140, 210. It is then clear that, between the columns, the proportion of the atrium is 210 : 140 :: 3 : 2, not 5 : 3 as Palladio writes. The presence of the numbers 26 and 13 suggest the Bezazel relationship which Alberti employed in Santa Maria Novella: namely, 26 : 15 for √3 : 1, and 15 : 13 for the base of an equilateral triangle to its height.

The unknowns are the width of the central ceiling coffer x and the measure between the columns in the direction of the main axis y. The defining equations are:

$$26 + 13 + x + 13 + 26 = 140$$
$$26 + 13 + y + 13 + 26 = 210$$

from which $x = 62$ and $y = 132$. Remember these numbers are quadruple the actual dimensions in *piedi*. From these, centre to centre numbers between columns may be derived, namely 153 and 145. The underlying dimensional mesh to the centre lines of columns and beams is then given by the intersection of two orthogonal partitions:

$$(26 + 6½) + (6½ + 26 + 6½) + (6½ + 62 + 6½) + (6½ + 26 + 6½) + (6½ + 26)$$
$$= 32½ + 39 + 75 + 39 + 32½$$

across the atrium, and:

$$(26 + 6½) + (6½ + 132 + 6½) + (6½ + 26)$$
$$= 32½ + 145 + 32½$$

in length.

Within the tolerances of arithmetic rationalizations, the ceiling plan may then be set out by a combination of squares and equilateral triangles. The squares are 32½ by 32½, and the equilateral triangles are mostly proportional to 37½ : 32½ :: 15 : 13, although some less precise 39 : 32½ :: 6 : 5 triangles are also used.

The number 153 is $13^2 - 4^2$ and therefore a number associated with a Pythagorean triangle. The other side is 2.4.13 = 104, and the hypotenuse is $13^2 + 4^2 = 185$. That one side is a multiple of 13, a number which pervades the atrium, is intriguing. The length of the atrium is P52½, a number which when doubled is 105. It suggests that Palladio may have used the 104, 153, 185 Pythagorean triangle to set out the atrium and to ensure its precise rightness.

But why does Palladio not make the length of the atrium P52? Why the extra six inches? The addition is required to make the proportion of the atrium between the columns along the main axis exactly 3 : 2. Also with the fine dimensioning of centre lines for the beams of the ceiling using the more precise 15 : 13 equilateral triangle, the additional six inches is required. Using the quadrupled numbers, the sequence of side lengths of the squares and equilateral triangles gives:

$$32½ + 32½ + 37½ + 37½ + 37½ + 32½ + 32½ + 37½ + 37½ + 37½ + 32½ + 32½ = 210$$

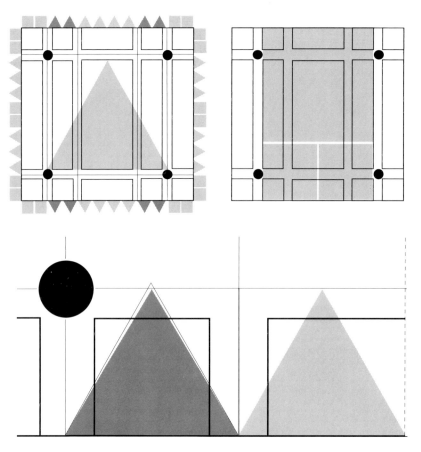

Fig. 14. The atrium with four columns (Palladio). Top left, the mesh for the ceiling is defined by square and triangular modules. The centre lines and edges of the beams are defined by a 15 : 13 rational equilateral triangle. Top right, the atrium between the columns is a 3 : 2 space. Bottom, detail of coffering along the sides showing use of two rational equilateral triangles: dark, 6 : 5 with margin of error indicated; and light, the improved 15 : 13 value for $\sqrt{4} : \sqrt{3}$.

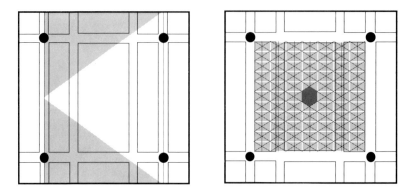

Fig. 15. The atrium with four columns (Palladio). Left, the 104, 153, 185 right triangle sets out the principal dimensions of the atrium. Right, the central area between the columns may be paved with hexagonal tiles.

which implies the actual dimension of P52½, a quarter of 210. Adding six inches does not invalidate the surveying method used to set out the atrium, and seems to confirm the architectonic hypothesis presented here.

The area between the four columns is defined by the numbers 153 − 13 = 140 and 145 − 13 = 132, a proportion of 140 : 132 :: 35 : 33. This near-square ratio may be interpreted as a compound ratio:

$$
\begin{array}{cc}
11 : 7 & \pi : 2 \\
\times & \times \\
\underline{5 : 3} & \underline{\mathrm{R}^{1/2}3 : 1} \\
35 : 33 & 2\mathrm{R}^{1/2}3 : \pi.
\end{array}
$$

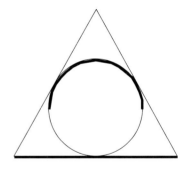

Fig. 16. The atrium with four columns (Palladio). The ratio 35 : 33 as a rational convergent for $2\sqrt{3} : \pi$ is the ratio of the side of an equilateral triangle to the semi-circumference of the inscribed circle. Compare Fig. 10.

Again, Palladio seems to be implying a Euclidean relationship. This time the relationship is between an equilateral triangle and the inscribed circle. The area between the columns has the potential for being divided by a mesh of eleven by seven 5 : 3 rectangles, each of which may be subdivided into two rationally convergent 6 : 5 equilateral triangles. It is tempting to think that it is this implicit use of the 5 : 3 ratio that Palladio is recalling in his written statement, where he mistakenly attributes the ratio to the length and breadth of the atrium itself. The mesh shows that the area might be covered nicely with hexagonal pavers.[25] Having analysed the atrium with four columns, it is very difficult not to imagine that this prototypical design did not receive this kind of exacting consideration by the architect.

House of the Ancient Romans[26]

That such techniques were familiar to Barbaro and Palladio is clear from their drawing in which the right isosceles triangle is given more precise rationality with sides of length 5 and a hypotenuse of length 7¼, a ratio of 99 : 70.[27]

Such a ratio is implied by Palladio in the house of the ancient Romans where the inner courtyard is shown as being P99 square with a portico P20 wide surrounding it: a ratio of almost 140 : 99 (139 : 99) for the dimensions to the outer bounds of the portico to those of the inner courtyard, making the area of the inner courtyard just half of that of the whole with the portico included.[28] This is what Euclid had defined as being 'rational in square'. That Palladio is interpreting Vitruvius is clear from the text. He specifically mentions that the atrium is 'è lungo per la diagonale del quadrato della larghezza', that is based on the diagonal of the square. Exceptionally, the drawing marks this explicitly with a diagonal line. With a width of P48 and the rational convergent 17 : 12, the length of the atrium would be P68. The difference generates the P20 for the width of the surrounding rooms.[29] Palladio then describes the tablium, directly across the atrium from the entrance, as being two-fifths of the breadth of the atrium. This would make the proportion of the tablium:

20 : ⅖.48 :: 25 : 24,

a tad off a perfect square. In the detail drawing, Palladio amends the dimensions of the atrium to P83 ∂4 in length and P50 in width, or in proportion 83⅓ : 50 :: 5 : 3, which is no longer proportionate to the diagonal of the square, but which would make

25 *Vide supra*, 'Inexpressible Proportion'.
26 *Ibid.*, II, pp. 33–35, Tavernor, Schofield, pp. 109–11.
27 Barbaro, *op. cit.*, p. 270.
28 Where exactly Palladio takes his measurements is not clear. The columns are P2½ and there is plenty of room for tolerance. Given Barbaro's use of the 99 : 70 rational convergent for $\sqrt{2} : 1$, it seems reasonable to suppose that Palladio is making use of the conjugate value 140 : 99.
29 68 − 48 = 20.

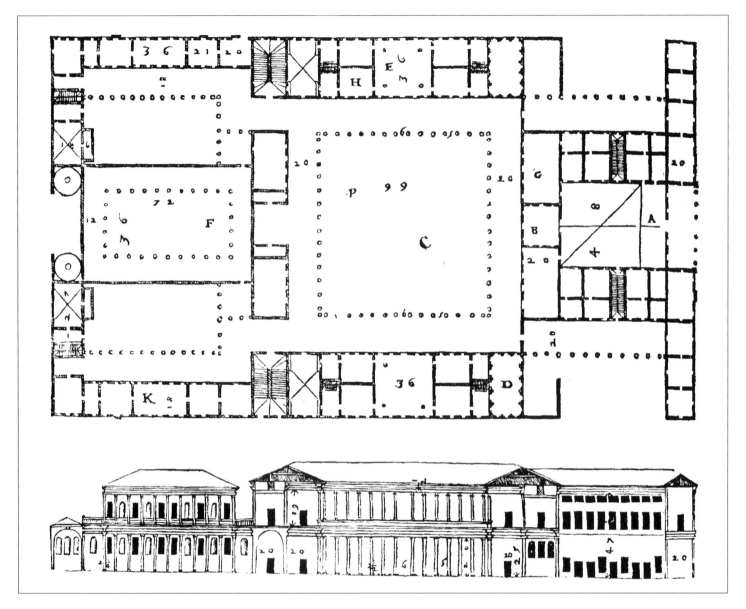

Fig. 17. House of the ancient Romans (Palladio). Plan and section.

the tablium precisely P⅗50 by P20, or P20 square in accordance with the dimensions shown on the small scaled plan; but this time, Palladio, in the detailed plan, has decided to change the width of the rooms to P21 to break again its perfect square-ness. The room exhibits the proportions of the first Pythagorean triangle to approximate the right isosceles triangle, namely the 20, 21, 29 triangle. The use of such a triangle in setting out the tablium would allow the builders to make the room perfectly right angled. Here Palladio is shown to be balancing the demands of dimensioning of proportional harmony against those of practical construction.

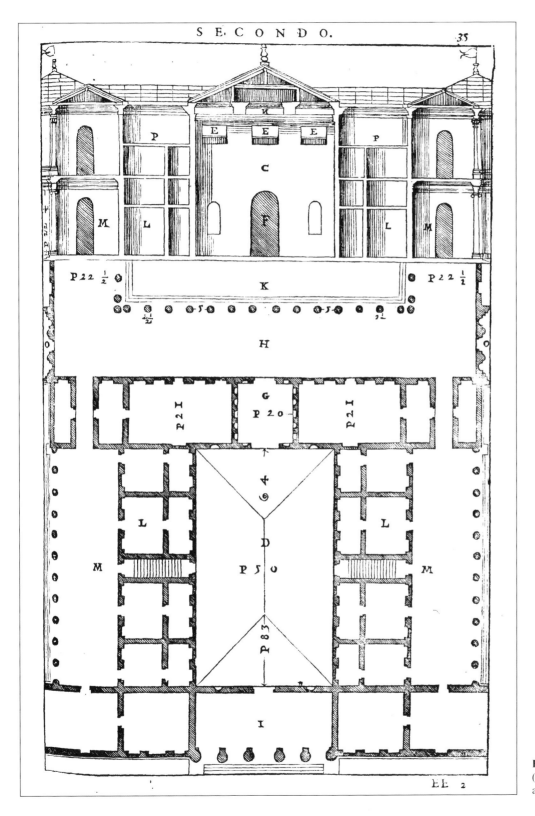

Fig. 18. House of the ancient Romans (Palladio). Detailed plan and section of atrium.

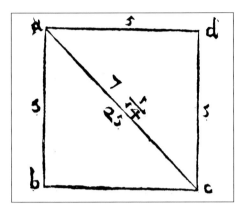

Fig. 19. The diagonal of the square as the ratio 7¼: 5 :: 99 : 70 (from Barbaro).

Across the plan is the basilica, which precisely echoes the same proportions as Vitruvius' basilica at Fano: 72 : 36 :: 2 : 1 for the nave and 96 : 60 :: 8 : 5 to the outer walls. Indeed, Palladio's basilica is exactly five-thirds the size of Vitruvius'. That Palladio reinforces this fact by his detailed amendment of the proportion of the atrium to 5 : 3 seems entirely plausible.[30]

The atrium in the convent of the Carità[31]

Palladio writes: 'I endeavoured to make this house like those of the ancients and so I built there a Corinthian atrium, which is as long as the diagonal of the square of its breadth. The corridors at the side [**ala**] are two-sevenths of the length; the columns are of the Composite order, three-and-a-half feet wide [**grosso**] and thirty-five feet long. The unroofed part in the middle is a third the breadth of the atrium. . . .' This text is accompanied by a plan, a section and a detail 'on a large scale'.

The plan shows dimensions of P54 for the length of the atrium and P40 for the width between columns. The corridors are each P8 wide, and together occupy P16 which does not agree with the computation ⅔.54. It would have agreed, if the length of the atrium had been P56. This would also have made the proportion of the atrium compatible with the diagonal of the square, 56 : 40 :: 7 : 5, the rational proxy for √2 : 1. The column diameter is P3½, and the intercolumniation is P8, including the distance of the end columns from the wall.[32]

This information confirms the length of P54, and not P56:

$$8 + 3\tfrac{1}{2} + 8 + 3\tfrac{1}{2} + 8 + 3\tfrac{1}{2} + 8 + 3\tfrac{1}{2} + 8 = 54.$$

The proportion of the atrium, between the columns, is thus the compound ratio 54 : 40 :: 27 : 20:

$$
\begin{array}{cc}
5 : 3 & \sqrt{3} : 1 \\
\times & \times \\
9 : 4 & \sqrt{5} : 1 \\
\hline
27 : 20 & \sqrt{5} : \sqrt{3}.
\end{array}
$$

The width of the walled space, including the corridors, is given by the equation:

$$8 + 3\tfrac{1}{2} + 40 + 3\tfrac{1}{2} + 8 = 63$$

so that the proportion of the walled enclosure is 63 : 54 :: 7 : 6, or *ad triangulum*. The defining mesh of the atrium includes both squares and 4 : 3½ :: 8 : 7 equilateral triangles. It will also be noted that the width between opposite rows to the height of the columns is in proportion 40 : 35 :: 8 : 7, also *ad triangulum*. Since 5 : 3 is a rational surrogate for √3 : 1, the proportion of the atrium √5 : √3 represents an arithmetical transformation of this characteristic *ad triangulum* root: in fact, the fractional power $3^{1/4} : 1$.

30 *Vide supra*, 'Roman Wonders'.
31 *Op. cit.*, Palladio, II, pp. 29–32, Tavernor, Schofield, pp. 105–8.
32 *Ibid.*, II, p. 31, Tavernor, Schofield, p. 107.

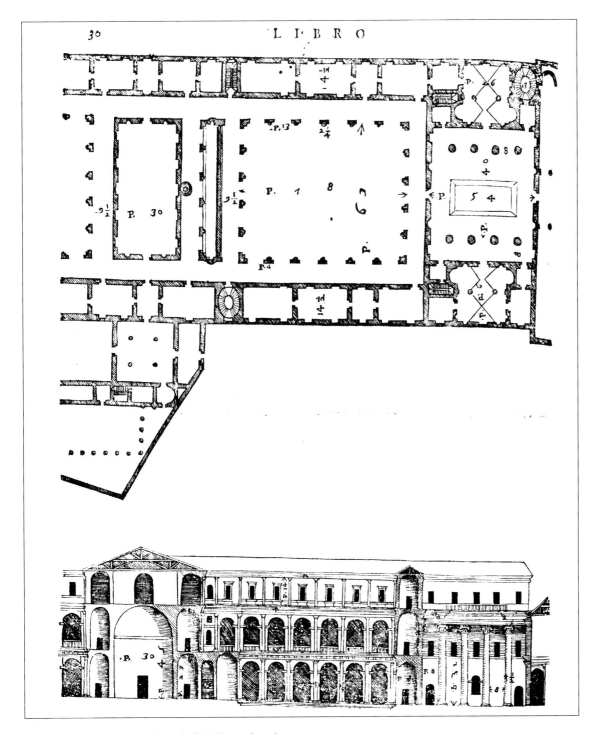

Fig. 20. Convent of the Carità (Palladio). Plan and section.

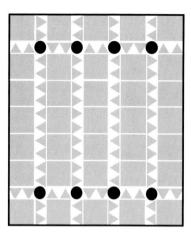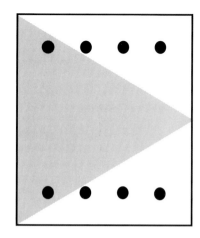

Fig. 21. Convent of the Carità (Palladio). Left, the atrium showing combination of *ad quadratum* for the bays between the columns and *ad triangulum* for the beams. Right, the whole space is *ad triangulum* using the 7 : 6 rational convergent for √4 : √3.

Palazzo Antonini, Udine[33]

Built according to Puppi around the time when Barbaro and Palladio were working on the Vitruvius commentaries, this scheme is the first to be presented in Book II of *I Quattro Libri dell'Architettura*. It patently does not fit the musical model of harmonious proportions attributed to some of the later works. Indeed, most of the schemes shown at the beginning of Book II do not agree with such a model. The atrium-style room with four columns is P32 by P28 – a proportion of 8 : 7 which is a rational convergent for √4 : √3. The two middle rooms at each side are P24 by P17 – a good rational convergent for √2 : 1. These two rooms play a variation on the theme of the tetraktys: √4, √3, √2, √1. The two rooms in the front are P28 by P17. This is a ratio that was used at Amiens and is related to the extreme and mean ratio in the regular pentagon.[34] The relationship is easily grasped to modern eyes by the generating sequence: 1, 5, 6, 11, 17, 28, . . . , which in classical arithmetic is a sequence of terms in Nicomachus' tenth proportionality. In these three principal spaces, then, Palladio commemorates the worldmaking geometries of the Platonic solids: their regular triangular, square and pentagonal faces.

There is an alternative interpretation of the proportion of the two front rooms as a composite ratio:

$$
\begin{array}{ll}
24 : 17 & P_\phi^{1/2}2 : 1 \\
\underline{\;\;7 : 6\;\;} & \underline{P_\phi^{1/2}4 : P_\phi^{1/2}3} \\
28 : 17 & P_\phi^{1/2}8 : P_\phi^{1/2}3.
\end{array}
$$

This would be a play on the Pythagorean lamda – another Platonic theme from the *Timaeus* – of which the four numbers of the tetraktys are a subset. The two side rooms at the top of the drawing are drawn as rectangles, but the dimensions suggest that they should be square rooms. Here is another mismatch between drawing and dimensions. It is unlikely that Palladio intended these rooms to be square since this

33 *Op. cit.*, Palladio, II, pp. 4–5, Tavernor, Schofield, pp. 78–80. Also L. Puppi, *Andrea Palladio: The Complete Works*, Electa/Rizzoli, New York, 1973, pp. 148–49.

34 *Vide supra*, 'Christian Works'. It may have the occult meaning of *Perfection : Tetragrammaton* since 28 is a perfect number and 17 is the gematriot for the Name of God. Bless this house!

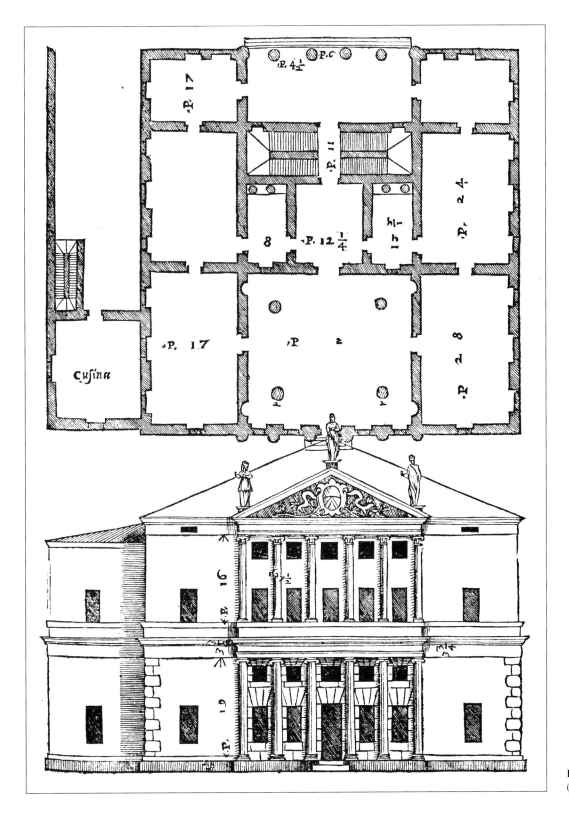

Fig. 22. Palazzo Antonini, Udine (Palladio). Plan and elevation.

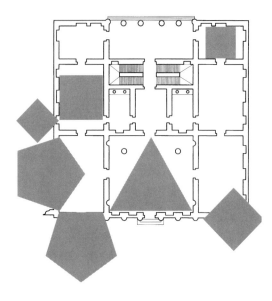

Fig. 23. Palazzo Antonini, Udine (Palladio). Regular polygons define the principal proportions.

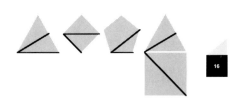

Fig. 24. Palazzo Antonini, Udine (Palladio). Key arithmeticized ratios determined from the equilateral triangle, the square and the pentagon – faces of the Platonic worldmaking solids – and the 3, 4, 5 right triangle. Far left, hall with four columns, 32 : 28 :: 8 : 7; centre left, the two middle side rooms, 24 : 17; middle and centre right, the two principal rooms, 28 : 17 – as a pentagonal relation or as a relation between a square and a triangle; far right, the two inner rooms, 25 : 16.

Fig. 25. (Right). Palazzo Antonini, Udine (Palladio). Ratios derived from the columns and intercolumniations of the portico define basic rational convergents.

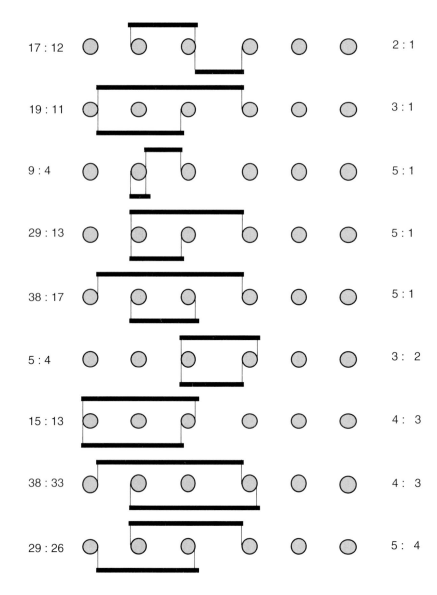

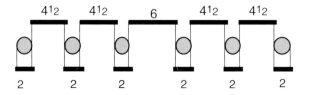

would make the proportion of the portico too deep. If the proportion of the back rooms is based on the diagonal of the square, then P17 should read P12. This would make the porch P32 by P12 – in proportion to 8 : 3. It would then be related to the two large side rooms which, in the second interpretation, are rationally proportionate to $\sqrt{8} : \sqrt{3}$.

At the heart of the plan are three spaces. In the centre is a space that is not quite square by 3 inches, P12½ by P12¼, proportionate to the superparticular ratio 50 : 49. This ratio is also to be found in Amiens in the crossing of the cathedral. This is not to suggest a direct link, but it may well indicate a continuance of an oral tradition among stone masons. Palladio was a master mason. The ratio evokes the so-called theorem of Plato cited by Vitruvius in the book that Palladio and Barbaro were working on together at that time.[35] The two side spaces are dimensioned P12½ and P8 – a ratio of 25 : 16 which strongly suggests another reference to the Pythagorean theorem through the 3, 4, 5 right triangle.[36]

The columns and intercolumniations of the portico produce multiple relationships, many of which include fine rational convergents for $\sqrt{5} : 1$ (9 : 4 and 29 : 13), $\sqrt{3} : 1$ (19 : 11 and 26 : 15), $\sqrt{2} : 1$ (17 : 12), and $\sqrt{5} : \sqrt{4}$ (29 : 26), $\sqrt{4} : \sqrt{3}$ (38 : 33), $\sqrt{3} : \sqrt{2}$ (5 : 4).[37] It is surely this multiplicity of readings that make Palladio's architecture so enduringly interesting. It cannot be reduced to a dogmatic system. The overwhelming architectonic impression is that the Palazzo Antonini is replete with arithmeticized metaphors of classical geometry and Platonic mathematics.

Palazzo Della Torre, Verona[38]

The number 19 is a most unmusical number, yet it pervades the Palazzo Della Torre. Palladio shows four rooms around a corner proportionate to the ratio 19 : 11, a rational convergent to $\sqrt{3} : 1$. This ratio occurs in the great hall of the project for Leonardo Mocenigo studied earlier. It is clearly a convergent that Palladio is happy to employ. The corner rooms are square to preserve the P19 width in both directions. Next to the P19 by P11 rooms in the main block are rooms with dimensions P19 by P15 and P30 by P19, one the double of the other.

The ratio 19 : 15 is a good rational value for a solution to the Delic problem $\sqrt[3]{2} : 1$.[39] The ratio 30 : 19 is then $2 : \sqrt[3]{2}$, or using the fractional powers introduced by Nicole Oresme in the fourteenth century the ratio $2^{2/3} : 1$. Behind these larger rooms are two with dimensions P22½ and P18, a ratio of 5 : 4. This may either be interpreted as an early convergent to the Delic problem, or as a value of $\sqrt{3} : \sqrt{2}$. At the end of the two wings there are rooms that are dimensioned P19 by P17. How can the ratio 19 : 17 relate to the others? The ratio happens to be a rational convergent for $\sqrt{5} : \sqrt{4}$.[40] Start with the estimate 1 : 1 –

$$\sqrt{\frac{5}{4}} \quad \frac{1}{1} \rightarrow \frac{1 + \frac{5}{4}}{1 + 1} = \frac{9}{8} \rightarrow \frac{9 + \frac{5}{4} \cdot 8}{9 + 8} = \frac{19}{17}.$$

The ratio 5 : 4 is a rational convergent for the cube root of two $\sqrt[3]{2} : 1$, or $2^{1/3} : 1$; so that $\sqrt{5} : \sqrt{4}$ is a rational convergent for the sixth root of two $\sqrt[6]{2} : 1$, or $2^{1/6} : 1$. Such mathematical concepts were current in Palladio's day, although notational devices for representing roots were still evolving.[41] The covered entrance court before

35 Vitruvius, IX, Preface 4. *Op. cit.*, Granger, pp. 198–99, and Barbaro, p. 268. A right isosceles triangle (half square) of sides 5 has an hypotenuse of $\sqrt{50}$, but $\sqrt{49} = 7$ is a close rational value.

36 Vitruvius, IX, Preface 6. *Ibid.*, Granger, pp. 200–201, and Barbaro, pp. 268–69.

37 There are 22 distinct lengths that can be extracted from the portico. There are therefore 22!//2!.20! = 231 ratios (pairs) that can be determined, although these may not all be distinct because of common factors (22 and 231 are cabalistic numbers, *vide supra*, 'Occult Number', but this is almost certainly coincidental in this situation). That some of these ratios are familiar is not surprising: not shown in the figure are extreme and mean ratios 5 : 3, 13 : 8, 21 : 13, 34 : 21, nor ratios related to π. Chance is at play here, and it would be a mistake to infer that such ratios are intentional – but some might be.

38 *Op. cit.*, Palladio, II, p. 11, Tavernor, Schofield, p. 87. Also L. Puppi, *Andrea Palladio: The Complete Works*, Electa/Rizzoli, New York, 1973, pp. 182–83.

39 *Vide supra*, 'Inexpressible Proportion'.

40 *Vide supra*, 'Inexpressible Proportion'.

41 F. Cajori, *A History of Mathematical Notation*, Open Court, Chicago, 1928–29, I, pp. 360–70. Girolamo Cardano, cited by Barbaro in his Vitruvian commentaries, presents the cases of equations in an unknown to the *n*th power, the solution of which is the *n*th root. T. R. Witmer, *Girolamo Cardano: The Great Art, or the Rules of Algebra* (1545), MIT Press, Cambridge MA, 1968, Chapter II, 'On the Total Number of Rules'.

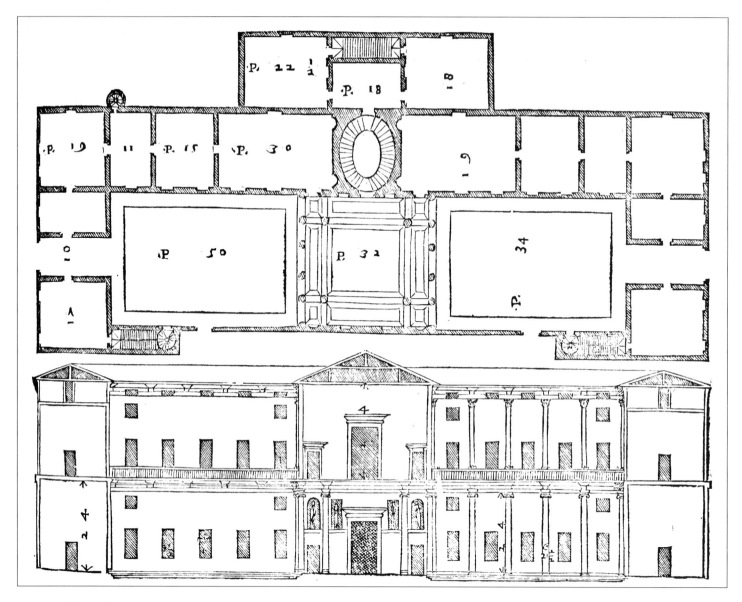

Fig. 26. Palazzo Della Torre, Verona (Palladio). Plan and section.

the great staircase has dimensions p34 by P32 according to the drawing, a ratio of 17 : 16. This happens to be a rational value for √9 : √8. Again starting with 1 : 1 –

$$\sqrt{\frac{9}{8}} \quad \frac{1}{1} \rightarrow \frac{1 + \%}{1 + 1} = \frac{17}{16}.$$

From the previous derivation √5 : √4 has a first convergent of 9 : 8, and thus √9 : √8 is in fact the twelfth root of two $^{12}\sqrt{2}$: 1, or $2^{1/12}$: 1. Remarkably, Palladio appears to be rehearsing the very same arguments that musicians were to become involved in concerning equal temperament: that the semitones should all be

42 The matter is discussed by C. V. Palisca, *Humanism in Italian Musical Thought*, Yale University Press, New Haven, 1985. Puppi dates the Palazzo Della Torre as after 1561.

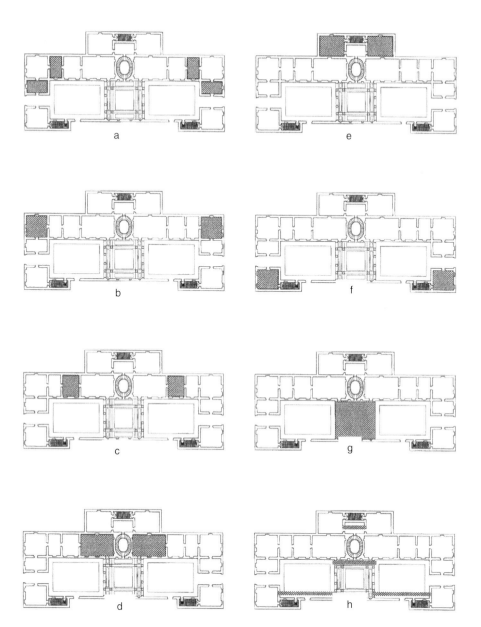

Fig. 27. Palazzo Della Torre, Verona (Palladio). a. $\sqrt{3}$: 1 (19 : 11) rooms; b. 1 : 1 (19 : 19) corner rooms; c. $\sqrt[3]{2}$: 1 (19 : 15) rooms; d. $\sqrt[3]{2^2}$: 1 (30 : 19) rooms; e. $\sqrt[3]{2}$: 1 (5 : 4); f. $\sqrt[6]{2}$: 1 (19 : 17) rooms; g. $\sqrt[12]{2}$: 1 (17 : 16) space; h. the length of the courtyards P50, the width of the entrance area P32, and the grand staircase lobby P18 – in proportion to 25 : 16 : 9.

proportional to the twelfth root of two in order to provide an equal division of the octave into twelve semitones.[42] In the cross-section through the courtyards, the width is P34 and the height of the groundfloor columns is marked P24, a ratio of 17 : 12, or $2^{1/2}$: 1. The section shows that the floor to floor height are both P24 so that the full height of the courtyard is P48 giving the conjugate value 24 : 17 for $2^{1/2}$: 1. Consequently, in this scheme, Palladio has used rational convergents for five fractional powers of two:

$2^{2/3} : 1 \ (30 : 19)$, $2^{1/2} : 1 \ (17 : 12, 24 : 17)$, $2^{1/3} : 1 \ (19 : 15, 5 : 4)$, $2^{1/6} : 1 \ (19 : 17)$, $2^{1/12} : 1 \ (17 : 16)$.

Looked at through the eyes of Oresme and Cusanus, these are rational powers with exponents in the proportion $8 : 6 : 4 : 2 : 1$ from the Pythagorean lamda. Architecturally, this may be considered to be a mannerist variation played upon traditional methods. Another way of looking at the familial relations between the proportions is to observe that the courtyard is P50 long, the covered entrance is P32 across, and the main staircase lobby is P18 wide: the characteristic 3, 4, 5 right triangular squares on the side relation $25 : 16 : 9 :: 5^2 : 4^2 : 3^2$. Entering the palazzo is a Pythagorean experience. The following empowerments of $5 : 4$ are found in the scheme – using our quasi-Renaissance notation to give a sense of how this might have been appreciated at the time – $R^2 5 : R^2 4 \ (25 : 16)$, $R5 : R4 \ (5 : 4)$, $R^{1/2}5 : R^{1/2}4$ $(19 : 17)$, $R^{1/4}5 : R^{1/4}4 \ (17 : 16)$.

There is another reason to look at the near square, P32 by P34, covered entrance and that is Palladio's assumed name. His name was concocted at a time he was under the mentorship of Count Giovanni Giorgio Trissino. Palladio's original name was Andrea di Pietro dalla Gondola.[43] There has been much speculation about his new appellation – Palladio – but this is not our concern here. Once again let us examine the numbers. But what spelling? Moving in humanist circles it would be appropriate to take the name in Latin. Carved in the frieze of the chapel at Maser, it reads: ANDREAS PALADIVS.[44]

A	1	1		P	6	60
N	4	40		A	1	1
D	4	4		L	2	20
R	8	80		A	1	1
E	5	5		D	4	4
A	1	1		I	9	9
S	9	90		V	2	200
				S	9	90

32		34		66	
⇓	221	⇓	385	⇓	606
5	⇓	7	⇓	12	⇓
	5		16	⇓	12
			⇓	3	⇓
			7		3.

Fig. 28. Tempietto Barbaro, Maser (Palladio). Frieze detail showing Palladio's name: ANDREAS PALADIVS.

Immediately it will be noticed that the P32 by P34 covered entrance is signed with the architect's name: ANDREAS (32) PALADIVS (34). The area of this space is $32 \times 34 = 1088$ which is VITRVVIVS (1088) and the two names are intimately related: Palladio was created to be the modern Vitruvius.[45] Palladio's full name has the double perfection of summing to the sixth hexagonal number, the 6th 6-gon, and of multiplying together to be VITRVVIVS. It is a very auspicious name. Even more, when spelt out in full, his name is equivalent to the numbers 221, 385, or according to Hugo of St Victor's sixth method, 17.13, 11.7.5 – a sequence of prime numbers, each of which has the oddity of maleness and the monadicity of the divine according to the theology of numbers. The sum is 606, or 6.101.

Towards the end of Johann Reuchlin, *De Arte Cabalistica* (1517), Simon discusses the creation of the world: the emergence of intellectual power along with light and the birth of Ideas on the first day, and the creation of the angels deputed to minister on the second day – angels who, in neo-Platonic understanding, are conveyors of intelligible Ideas, especially to human intelligence.[46] At the end of the second day God said ‏ויהי נ‎: 'And it was so'.

Reuchlin writes: 'So in the creation of sensible things, God uses this symbol of the intelligible, ‏ויהי נ‎, to designate the angels created to attend on natural things, all signified together by the one name Michael, which is like a descriptive name for the angelic species. Michael is signified by this phrase ‏ויהי נ‎ which is recited in the account of the following five days' work, and which is the symbol for Michael according to the first part of the Kabbalistic art of numerical equality. By this we are informed that all the angels are of the same species and, besides, that everybody, whether in heaven or earth, has its own guide of its powers to control its activities, whether it be a rational body like the heavens, the stars, and men, or irrational like the beasts and the elements.' Both ‏ויהי נ‎ and the Hebrew for Michael, ‏מיכאל‎, sum to 101 which is then seen to be equivalent to 'angelos', or messengers: for ‏ויהי נ‎ 'designates the prince and high priest called Michael – clear evidence of the state of the angels, which consist of one added to a hundred'.

ANDREAS PALADIVS – 6.101 – is the perfection of six in union with the daemonic powers of creative intelligence. Such concepts, strange to us today, were current in the post-Ficinian world of the sixteenth-century intelligentsia. It was a daemonic world. The intellectual connections are elaborate and Manfredo Tafuri goes some way to establish possible links in which Domenico Grimani plays an important role, and in which Francesco Zorzi, who was involved in discussions for the rebuilding of San Francesco dell Vigna, carries much of Reuchlin's work into Venetian society through *De harmonia mundi*.[47] It is also recorded that Ermolao Barbaro was an acquaintance of Reuchlin's in Rome.[48] All of these connections tie back to the Barbaro family who were to become Palladio's leading patrons; but before that time arrives, is it possible that Trissino was also part of this same intellectual nexus at a time when the name Palladio was composed? Was the name designed to be full of such occult, but providential, meanings?

It should be noticed that in its most reduced form ANDREAS PALADIVS reads numerically as $5 + 7 \Rightarrow (12) \Rightarrow 3$, the odd primes in the decad and partitions of the 12 unit long 3, 4, 5 right triangular rope. The derived ratios $A : P :: 7 : 5$, $A : AP :: 5 : 3$ and $P : AP :: 7 : 3$, where A and P are understood to be fully spelled out, are early rational convergents to $\sqrt{2} : 1$, $\sqrt{3} : 1$ and $\sqrt{5} : 1$ respectively.

43 Puppi, *op. cit.*, p. 29.

44 With one 'L'. The name ANDREAS PALLADIVS appears in a contemporary portrait. The effect of adding the extra 'L' lessens the occult value of the name. It is possible that the 'L' is omitted precisely to give more content to it. PALLADIVS sums to 405, or 36, both of which reduce to 9. However, such flexibility is typical of the game. Several documents are also signed 'Paladivs'.

45 *Vide supra*, 'Roman Wonders'.

46 M. Goodman, S. Goodman, *Johann Reuchlin: On the Art of the Kabbalah, De Arte Cabalistica*, Abaris Books, New York, 1983, pp. 342ff.

47 M. Tafuri, *Venice and the Renaissance*, MIT Press, Cambridge MA 1989, p. 129ff. Also F. A. Yates, *The Occult Philosophy in the Elizabethan Age*, Routledge & Kegan Paul, London, 1979, particularly Chapter II, 'The Occult Philosophy in the Italian Renaissance: Pico della Mirandola', Chapter III, 'The Occult Philosophy in the Reformation: Joannes Reuchlin', and Chapter IV, 'The Cabalist Friar of Venice: Francesco Giorgi [Zorzi]'.

48 L. Geiger, *Johann Reuchlin sein Leben und seine Werke*, B. De Graaf, Nieuwkoop, 1964 (1870), p. 33.

Villa Ragona[49]

This villa is an elegant design again lacking primary musicality in plan: that is to say, the ratios in Palladio's stated canon 1 : 1, 4 : 3, 3 : 2, 5 : 3, 2 : 1 do not occur.[50] The diagonal of the square does.[51]

The central room at the back of the villa has dimensions P21¼ by P15, or a ratio of 85 : 60 :: 17 : 12. This is a standard rational convergent for $\sqrt{2} : 1$. The four corner rooms are each P15 by P12, or a ratio of 5 : 4 which has been interpreted above as a rational proxy for $\sqrt[3]{2} : 1$.[52] On either side of the central stairwell are two rooms which are not quite square, P18 by P17. In a previous discussion of musical proportion it was noted that this ratio was in regular use, at the time, by lutenists who wished to place their frets at equal intervals on the instrument.[53] The ratio was the Boethian minor semitone. Mathematically it is the conjugate of 17 : 16 used by Palladio in the Palazzo Della Torre.[54] It is a rational convergent for $\sqrt[12]{2} : 1$.

The stairwell in the centre of the villa occupies a space that can be easily computed assuming all the internal walls are the same thickness. The equation

$$12 + 21\tfrac{1}{4} + 12 = = 17 + x + 17$$

must be satisfied, that is $x = 11\tfrac{1}{4}$. The proportion of the central stairwell is thus 18 : 11¼ :: 8 : 5. This might be taken as a rational convergent for the extreme and mean ratio (the golden section), but in this particular architectonic context it is probably best to read it as the double of 5 : 4, that is as $2 : \sqrt[3]{2}$ which occurred previously in the Palazzo Della Torre. The Villa Ragona, like the Palazzo Della Torre, seems to be proportioned according to rational convergents of the roots of two:

$$2^{2/3} : 1 (8 : 5), \quad 2^{1/2} : 1 (17 : 12), \quad 2^{1/3} : 1 (5 : 4), \quad 2^{1/12} : 1 (18 : 17).$$

Again, a mannerist play on classical methods since the exponents fall proportionately on the Pythagorean lamda: 8 : 6 : 4 : 1.

The elevation is in part sympathetic to the plan relationships, and in part tells another story. The main columns of the portico are P25 high and P2½ in diameter, a ratio of 10 : 1 which implies the use of the Composite order.[55] The colonnade in the courtyard has columns P15 high and of diameter P2, a ratio of 7½ : 1 suggesting the Doric order.[56] A comparison of the two diameters renders the ratio 5 : 4 which relates to the use of this same ratio in plan. A comparison of the heights gives the proportion 25 : 15 :: 5 : 3. Together the numbers of the 3, 4, 5 right triangle are suggested, and 5 : 3 might be read as one of Palladio's signatures A : AP. The height of the base of the villa is P12 and this is proportionate to the columns of the colonnade, 5 : 4. The actual intercolumniation is P8 wide and the height of the column is P15: the 8, 15, 17 right triangle comes to mind as rectangular matrix. The dimension of the intercolumniation in the colonnade together with the diameters of two columns is P12 (2 + 8 + 2) and this too relates in a 5 : 4 ratio with the height of the columns. Taking the columns of the main portico however a different game emerges. Here, the relationship of the central intercolumniation to the column diameter is a rational convergent for $\sqrt{5} : 1$, this time 11 : 5. This is the immediate predecessor to 9 : 4 used in the side intercolumniations of the portico for the Palazzo Antonini. Now, however, the dominant relationship is rational convergents for $\sqrt{5} : 1 - 11 : 5, 9 : 4, 29 : 13, 47 : 21$ – and extreme and mean ratios derived from

---

49 *Op. cit.*, Palladio, p. 57, Tavernor, Schofield, p. 135. Also L. Puppi, *Andrea Palladio: The Complete Works*, Electa/Rizzoli, New York, 1973, pp. 138–40. The actual building is something of a mystery. Palladio's description has 'been denied by every successive fact which has come to light; furthermore, not a trace of the building now stands'. Puppi, p. 138.
50 *Vide infra*, 'Canons of Architectural Proportion', Appendix I.
51 Musically this can be interpreted as the tritone, an interval that is not considered harmonious by musicians in the Renaissance, or by most today. It clearly has greater significance geometrically, than musically.
52 Although, again, a musical interpretation is possible as the major third.
53 *Vide supra*, 'Scales of Proportion'.
54 The major semitone. 9 : 8, the whole tone, but a ratio that Palladio never once uses.
55 *Op. cit.*, Palladio, I, pp. 44–47, Tavernor, Schofield, pp. 48–51.
56 *Ibid.*, Palladio, I, pp. 22–27, Tavernor, Schofield, pp. 26–31.

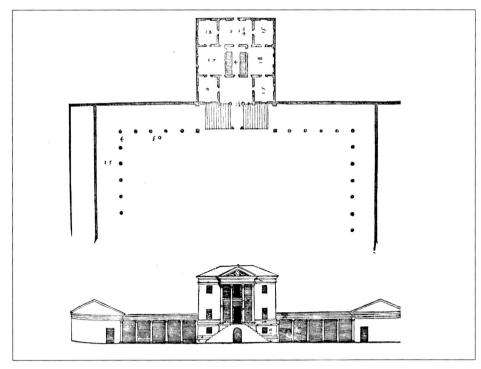

Fig. 29. Villa Ragona (Palladio). Plan and elevation.

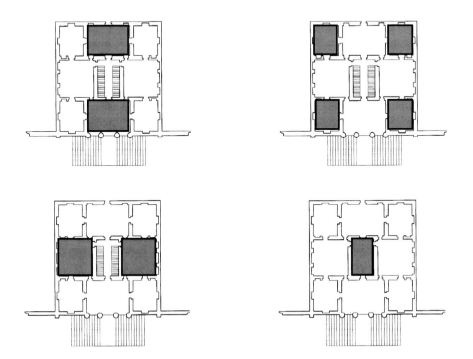

Fig. 30. Villa Ragona (Palladio). Top left, the $2^{1/2}$: 1 (17 : 12) spaces. Top right, the $2^{1/3}$: 1 (5 : 4) spaces. Bottom left, the $2^{1/12}$: 1 (18 : 17) spaces. Bottom right, $2^{2/3}$ (8 : 5) spaces.

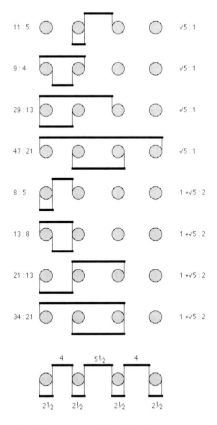

Fig. 31. Villa Ragona (Palladio). The rhythmic structure of the portico showing the characteristic play of rational convergents for $\sqrt{5}$: 1 and for the extreme and mean ratio $1 + \sqrt{5}$: 2.

them – 8 : 5, 13 : 8, 21 : 13, 34 : 21. This tetrastyle portico is an ingenious calculating machine whose only connection to the plan is the 8 : 5 proportion of the central stairwell.[57] Again, we see that Palladio probably intends his proportional programme to be read in more than one way.

Before leaving the Villa Ragona, look again at the central stairwell. Its dimensions are P18 by P11¼ giving a floor area of 202½. Removing fractions the number 405 is obtained – PALLADIVS.[58]

La Rotonda, Vicenza: Plan[59]

With *Architectural Principles in the Age of Humanism*, Rudolf Wittkower established a line of thought concerning the ratios used by Palladio to give proportion to his designs. While acknowledging Alberti's analogy between musical harmony and architectural proportion, Wittkower recognized in Palladio's work a development which took into account sixteenth-century musical theory. Specifically, whereas Alberti had based his musical analogy in *De re aedificatoria* on archaic, Pythagorean principles, Palladio – or so Wittkower would have us believe – adapted those harmonic investigations of his time which culminated in Zarlino's magisterial *Le Istitutioni Harmoniche* of 1558. 'If we take this new development into consideration', Wittkower claims, 'most of the problematic ratio in Palladio's buildings become intelligible'.[60] Howard and Longhair dispute this claim, demonstrating that no more than half of the ratios explicitly shown in Book II of *I Quattro Libri dell'Architettura* can be said to be 'harmonic'.[61] The cases examined here so far have not exhibited musicality, but then they have been chosen deliberately as counter examples to Wittkower's thesis.

The most notable of Palladio's inventions is 'La Rotonda', the Villa Almerico, in Vicenza. None of the room ratios found in the Book II depiction of this building are in compliance with Wittkower's musical thesis. 'La Rotonda' is exceptional among Palladian villas. Does it also have to be excepted from a comprehensive theory of Palladian proportional practices? This prime example will serve to redirect attention to aspects of architectural proportion which have a non-musical source. It provides an exemplar of the established pattern by which ideal geometrical forms are represented arithmetically, and some numbers are given geometric, figurate forms. This tradition has classical roots, as has been shown earlier, in the arithmetic of Nicomachus and Theon of Smyrna and the geometry of Euclid and Pappus, among others; and the tradition had been revived in the late fifteenth and early sixteenth centuries by Piero della Francesca and widely publicized in print by Luca Pacioli, especially in applying arithmetic to Euclid's geometrical propositions of Books X–XIII. Evidence has been given earlier to show that Alberti, Cesariano, Serlio and Palladio all used rational convergents in giving measurements to otherwise incommensurable geometrically determined magnitudes, in particular, dimensions associated with the ideal geometrical figures from Plato's *Timaeus*: the equilateral triangle, the square and the regular pentagon.

Take the numbers in the plan of 'La Rotonda' as presented by Palladio, dislocate them, and arrange them in descending order:

30   26   15   12   11   6.

57 There are 13 distinct dimensions, and therefore 13!/11!.2! pairs which can form ratios. Because of symmetry and common factorization this number will be reduced considerably. Even so it should be noted that the ratios selected are arbitrary from among a larger set.

58 n. 13, *supra*.

59 *Op. cit.*, Palladio, II, pp. 18–19, Tavernor, Schofield, pp. 94–95. Also L. Puppi, *Andrea Palladio: The Complete Works*, Electa/Rizzoli, New York, 1973, pp. 69–70, 222–26.

60 Wittkower, *op. cit.*, p. 124.

61 D. Howard, M. Longhair, 'Harmonic Proportion and Palladio's *Quattro Libri*', *Journal of the Society of Architectural Historians*, 41, pp. 116–43.

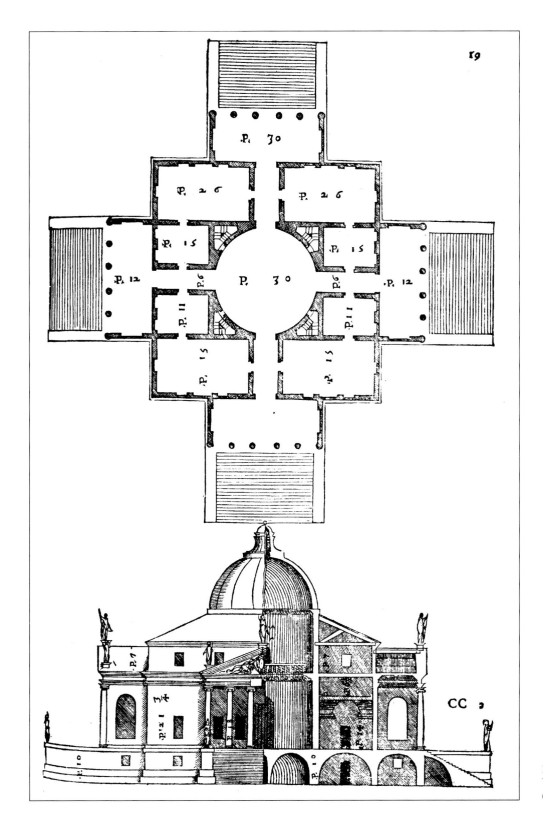

Fig. 32. Villa Almerico, 'La Rotonda', Vicenza. Plan, elevation and section (Palladio).

There are six distinct numbers, with 6 the lesser extreme and 30 the greater. The hexad, 6, is the premier perfect number whose factors 1, 2, 3 sum to the number itself, $1 + 2 + 3 = 6$. Vitruvius enshrines it, Alberti rehearses it, and Barbaro explicates the general concept of the perfect number in his Vitruvian commentaries.[62] Palladio's acquired Latin name is doubly perfect as the sixth hexagonal number.

From the sextuple, there are two pairs in double ratio, $2 : 1$:

$$| \; 30 \quad 26 \quad 15 \; || \; 12 \quad 11 \quad 6 \; |$$
$$\lfloor \qquad 2:1 \quad \rfloor\lfloor \qquad 2:1 \qquad \rfloor$$

The extremes of the sextuple are in the proportion $5 : 1$,

$$| \; 30 \quad 26 \quad 15 \quad 12 \quad 11 \quad 6 \; |$$
$$\lfloor \qquad\qquad 5:1 \qquad\qquad \rfloor$$

the two central terms are in proportion $5 : 4$,

$$30 \quad 26 \; | \; 15 \quad 12 \; | \; 11 \quad 6$$
$$\lfloor \; 5:4 \; \rfloor$$

while the greater extremes of the triples, and the lesser extremes are in proportion $5 : 2$,

$$| \; 30 \quad 26 \quad 15 \quad 12 \; | \; 11 \quad 6$$
$$\lfloor \qquad 5:2 \qquad \rfloor$$

$$30 \quad 26 \; | \; 15 \quad 12 \quad 11 \quad 6 \; |$$
$$\lfloor \qquad 5:2 \qquad \rfloor$$

The ratios $5 : 1$ and $5 : 4$ are present in Euclid's proof of Proposition XIII.11 in which he shows that the side of a regular pentagon inscribed in a circle whose diameter is rational is 'the irrational straight line called minor'.[63] The ratio $5 : 2$ is an early rational convergent for $\sqrt{6}$ since $1 : 5^2 = 25$, $6 \times 2^2 = 24$.

It is significant that the terms in the sextuple sum to one hundred:

$$\underbrace{30 + 26 + 15 + 12 + 11 + 6}_{100}.$$

In the theology of number, 100 is the monad of the third course: the monad itself, 1, being the first, and the decad, 10, being the second. Unity is thus brought into the plan dimensions even before their spatial distribution: they express a partition of the 'one' into a 'perfect' six parts.[64] This does not appear to be accidental. Dividing the six measures into triples,

$$\underbrace{30 + 26 + 15}_{71} \quad \underbrace{12 + 11 + 6}_{29}$$

two sub-sums emerge. A Renaissance arithmetician would be alerted, interpreting these numbers in a familiar geometrical context. An arithmeticized equilateral triangle with a semi-base 41 has a rational altitude of 71; while an arithmeticized square with a rational diameter 41 has sides 29. These are classical, rational convergents to the otherwise inexpressible, incommensurables roots, $\sqrt{3}$ and $\sqrt{2}$, respectively. Setting out the ratios as Barbaro does to form products,

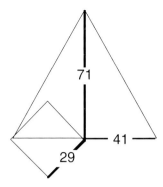

$$71 : 41 \qquad\quad \text{R}^{1/2}3 : 1$$
$$\underline{41 : 29} \qquad\quad \underline{\text{R}^{1/2}2 : 1}$$
$$71 : 29 \qquad\quad \text{R}^{1/2}6 : 1.$$

Fig. 33. Villa Almerico, 'La Rotonda', Vicenza. The equilateral triangle and the square define the ratio 71 : 29.

it is seen that the triples divide the monad of the third course in the ratio of $\text{R}^{1/2}6 : 1$.[65]

Barbaro comments at length on the perfection, in one sense, of the decad, 10, and the perfection, in another sense, of the hexad, 6. In the same passage he describes both the derivation of powers: the square and the root of a number.[66] It can now be seen that Palladio has squared the decad, $\text{R}^{2}10$, to arrive at the sum of his sextuple, 100, and uses a rational convergent square root of the hexad, $\text{R}^{1/2}6$, to arrive at the bipartition of 100.

The first triple, 30, 26, 15, occurs when inscribing an equilateral triangle of rational sides 26 in a circle of diameter 30, radius 15. It is as if Palladio arithmetically embeds Euclid's Proposition X.12 – 'If an equilateral triangle be inscribed in a circle, the square on the side of the triangle is triple the square on the radius' – in the triple.[67] The arithmetic approximation is close: $26^2 = 626$, $3 \times 15^2 = 625$. The central hall of 'La Rotonda' has a diameter of P30 and the length of the principal rooms is P26.

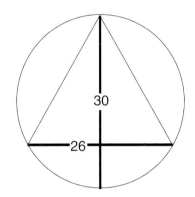

Fig. 34. Villa Almerico, 'La Rotonda', Vicenza. The central hall with inscribed equilateral triangle showing the ratio 30 : 26.

Alberti, in what appears to be a commentary on Euclid's Proposition XIII.15 in which it is proved that 'the square on the diameter of the sphere is triple of the square on the side of the [inscribed] cube', refers to 'certain natural relationships that cannot be defined as numbers, but that may be obtained through roots and powers'. He describes a $2 \times 2 \times 2$ cube. The diameter of the cube and the diagonals across the face of the cube are in in proportion $\sqrt{3} : \sqrt{2}$. Alberti continues: 'Lastly, there is the line in the right-angled triangle whose two shorter sides are joined by a right-angle, one being the square root of four, the other the square root of twelve. The third and longest line, which is subtended by the right angle, is the square root of sixteen.'[68] These are the sides of a triangle formed by bisecting an equilateral triangle. In modern notation, the sides are in incommensurable proportion $\sqrt{4} : \sqrt{3} : \sqrt{1}$, but for Euclideans they are 'commensurable in square'. As noted earlier, Alberti evokes Bezazel's proportion 30 : 26 : 15 as a rational convergent to the sides of this triangle in Santa Maria Novella. An explicit diagram of the equilateral triangle with these rational dimensions appears in Vincenzo Scamozzi's volume where he also refers to his earlier involvement with the building of 'La Rotonda'.[69]

The leading triple may also indicate that Palladio was aware of the rule published in 1484 by Nicholas Chuquet for computing square roots, most recently referred to by David Fowler, in his reconstruction of the mathematics of Plato's Academy, as the rule of Parmenides.[70] In this case, if 26 : 15 is an overestimate for $\sqrt{3}$ (which it is), then the conjugate ratio derived from the identity $\sqrt{3} : 1 :: 3 : \sqrt{3}$, namely 45 : 26 is an underestimate. The Chuquet rule makes the ratio formed from the sum of the antecedents to the sum of the consequents, in this instance,

$$(26 + 45) : (15 + 26) :: 71 : 41,$$

62 *Vide supra*, 'Ethical Number'.
63 Heath, *op. cit.*, III, pp 461–66.
64 *Vide supra*, 'Theological Number'.
65 *Vide supra*, 'Inexpressible Proportion'.
66 Barbaro, *op. cit.*, p. 91.
67 Heath, *op. cit.*, III, pp. 34–35.
68 *Vide supra*, 'Leon Battista Alberti'.
69 *Vide infra*, Appendix I.
70 *Vide supra*, 'Inexpressible Proportion'.

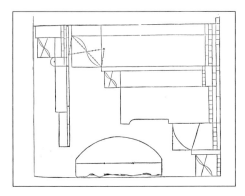

Fig. 35. Detail of an invention for a cornice (Palladio). Showing the use of the 6, 7, 6 isosceles triangle to set out arcs.

a better convergent to √3 than either of its constituent ratios. This computation corresponds directly to the sum of the leading triple to the sum of its last two terms,

$$\underbrace{30 + \overbrace{26 + 15}^{41}}_{71} \quad 12 \quad 11 \quad 6.$$

The second triple, 12, 11, 6, suggests the side of a square and its rational diameter

$$30 \quad 26 \quad 15 \quad \overset{12}{\overline{12}} \quad \underbrace{11 + 6}_{17}.$$

This particular value for $R_x^{1/2}$ 2 : 1 :: 17 : 12 is used elsewhere by Palladio, for example, in the Palazzo Antonini and Villa Ragona.

In Book I, Palladio employs a 6, 7, 6 isosceles triangle in the graphic construction of cyma moldings.[71] Five of these triangles make up a regular pentagon of side length 7 and chord length 11, inscribed in a circle of diameter 12, or radius 6. The second triple of the plan dimension, 12, 11, 6, is closely associated, then, with the pentagon. The computation involves the use of 20 : 9 as a rational convergent for √5 : 1. From Euclid XIII.10, in modern notation, the side of a pentagon inscribed in a circle of radius r is given by the expression:

$$\frac{r}{2}\sqrt{10 - 2\sqrt{5}}.^{[72]}$$

Substituting the rational value for √5 and letting $r = 6$, the side of the pentagon is determined

$$\frac{6}{2} \cdot \sqrt{10 - 2 \cdot \frac{20}{9}} = 3\sqrt{\frac{90 - 40}{9}} = \sqrt{50},$$

but as with the computation for the diagonal of the square √50 ≅ 7. Thus the arithmetical relationships between 12, 7, 6 are established. The chord of a pentagon with sides 7 is given by

$$7 \cdot \left(\frac{1 + \sqrt{5}}{2} \right).$$

Using 15 : 7 an early rational convergent for √5 : 1, the conjugate value to 7 : 3, the chord is found to be 11. In this way the triple 12, 11, 6 is established as pentagonal.[73] It is also noteworthy, given the cubic form of the main mass of 'La Rotonda' that this triple relates to the rational ratio 29 : 23 associated with the Delic problem of doubling the cube, since $29^3 = 24389$, $2 \times 23^3 = 24334$. An early approximation for the Delphic problem, used by Palladio on other occasions, is 5 : 4 – the proportion of the central two terms of the sextuple. In this case $5^3 = 125$, $2 \times 4^3 = 128$.

71 *Op. cit.*, Palladio, I, p. 57; Tavernor, Schofield, pp. 62–63.
72 Heath, *op. cit.*, III, pp. 457–61.
73 *Vide supra*, 'Inexpressible Proportion' for rational convergents to √5 : 1.

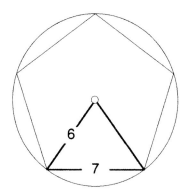 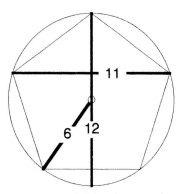

Fig. 36. Villa Almerico, 'La Rotonda', Vicenza. The pentagonal geometry defining the proportion 12 : 11 : 6.

$$30 \quad 26 \quad 15 \quad \underbrace{\overbrace{12 + 11}^{23} + 6}_{29} \ .$$

The other classic problem of squaring the circle is to be found in the ratio which relates the sub-sum 23 in this second triple to the 26 in the first triple.

$$30 \quad \underset{26}{\underline{26}} \quad 15 \quad : \quad \underset{23}{\underline{12 + 11}} \quad 6.$$

A circle of diameter 26, radius 13, has very nearly the same area as a square of side 23, here

$$\pi.26^2 \cong \frac{22}{7} \cdot 626 = 531\tfrac{1}{3}, \ 23^2 = 529.^{74}$$

The second triple displays each of the uncompounded ratio types discussed in Barbaro's Vitruvian commentaries. Multiplex ($n : 1$) is represented by $12 : 6 :: 2 : 1$, the duplex; superparticular ($n + 1 : n$) is represented by $12 : 11$; and superpartiens ($2n + 1 : n + 1$) is represented by $11 : 6.^{75}$

$$\begin{array}{cccc}
|\ 12 \quad 11 \quad 6\ | & 12\ |\ 11 \quad 6\ | & |\ 12 \quad 11\ |\ 6 \\
[\quad \ \ 2 : 1 \quad] & [\ 1\tfrac{5}{6} : 1\ ] & [\ 1\tfrac{5}{11} : 1\ ].
\end{array}$$

The sextuple is grounded at its extremities by two heteromecic numbers $n(n + 1)$

$$(5.6 = 2 + 4 + 6 + 8 + 10 = 30) \quad 26 \quad 15 \quad 12 \quad 11 \ (6 = 4 + 2 = 2.3).$$

The bracketed expressions, in each case, show the derivation of heteromecic numbers from sums of successive even numbers as set out in the classical texts.[76]

[74] *Vide supra*, 'Leon Battista Alberti', who uses the same value for the Delic problem, and 'Christian Works', where both ratios 29 : 23 and 26 : 23 are apparent in Santo Stefano. This is very suggestive of 'the migration' of numerical symbolism as an extension of the migration of pictorial images, R. Wittkower, *Allegory and Migration of Symbols*, Thames and Hudson, London, 1977.
[75] *Vide supra*, 'Relative Proportion'.

Alberti writes: 'Aristotle thought the tenth the most perfect number of all; perhaps, as some interpret, because its square equals the cube of four consecutive numbers':[77]

$$1^3 + 2^3 + 3^3 + 4^3 = 100 = 10^2.$$

The sum of the sextuple is 100. The sextuple sums to 100 in no haphazard manner. The central two numbers sum to the cube of 3:

$$30 \quad 26 \quad \underbrace{15 + 12}_{27} \quad 11 \quad 6$$

and the central four terms sum to the cube of 4:

$$30 \quad \underbrace{26 + 15 + 12 + 11}_{64} \quad 6.$$

The extreme numbers sum to 36 which number itself may be expressed as the sum of the cubes of the first three numbers:

$$1^3 + 2^3 + 3^3 = 36 = 6^2$$

– the perfect hexad empowered. Subsequent to the monad, 36 is the first number which in classical terms is circular, tetragonal and trigonal. A circular number is one which when multiplied by itself gives a number whose end digit is the same: $6 \times 6 = 36$; a tetragonal number can be set out as a square figure; and a trigonal number can be set out as a triangle.

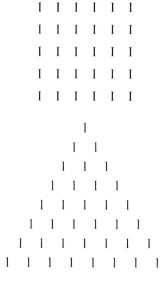

Once again, the Platonic motifs of circle, square and triangle are evoked, but this time through geometricized arithmetic.

76 *Vide supra*, 'Shapeful Number'.
77 *Vide supra*, 'Shapeful Number'.

The triple of square numbers 36, 64, 100 – 6^2, 8^2, 10^2 – is derived from the squares on the Pythagorean triangle with sides 6, 8, and hypotenuse 10. This is the triangle that Barbaro introduces in his commentary on the Vitruvian passage in which the common 3, 4, 5 right triangle is discussed.[78] The beauty of this 'doubled' triangle is that its extremes are the Vitruvian perfect numbers, 6 and 10, and that the area of the triangle and its perimeter have the same value, 24. This is one of two such Pythagorean triangles, the other being 5, 12, 13 where the area and perimeter answer to the value 30, the greater extreme of the 'Rotonda' sextuple.

Palladio illustrates determinations for three means: the arithmetic, geometric and harmonic. He does so both numerically and diagrammatically.[79] Earlier classical texts enumerate six means, later texts list ten. Since it is apparent that the 'Rotonda' sextuple is cunningly designed, is it possible that it makes use of these additional means? It does not, however, use the three most familiar proportionalities.[80]

The leading triple 26, 15, 11 illustrates the tenth Nicomachean mean, where the ratio of the difference between the greater extreme and the mean (26 – 15 = 11), and the difference between the greater and lesser extremes (26 – 11 = 15) is in proportion to the ratio between the lesser extreme and the mean (15 : 11). This is the classical definition; it amounts to the simple notion that the greater extreme is the sum of the mean and the lesser extreme. Modern writers have a habit of confusing this with the generating scheme for terms in a Fibonacci sequence. Unfortunately, this is to commit an anachronism:

$$\begin{array}{lll} 30 & 12 & 6 \\ \underbrace{26 \quad 15 \qquad\quad 11}_{X}. \end{array}$$

The triple 30, 26, 6 which spans the sextuple is an example of the fourth Nicomachean mean, the subcontrary to harmonic. Here, the ratio of the difference between the greater extreme and the mean (30 – 26 = 4) and the difference between the mean and the lesser extreme (26 – 6 = 20) is in proportion to the ratio of the greater extreme to the lesser (30 : 6 :: 20 : 4). In the harmonic this latter ratio is inverted, hence the qualification 'sub-contrary':

$$\begin{array}{lll} & 15 \quad 12 \quad 11 & \\ \underbrace{30 \quad 26 \qquad\qquad\qquad 6}_{IIII}. \end{array}$$

Finally, the triple 15, 12, 6 exemplifies the fifth Nicomachean mean. Indeed, it is proportional to the example given by Nicomachus: 5, 4, 2. This mean is fashioned, like the sixth, after the geometric, and is sometimes called sub-contrary to geometric, or contra-geometric. In this case, the ratio of the difference between the greater extreme and the mean (15 – 12 = 3) and the difference between the mean and lesser extreme (12 – 6 = 6) is in proportion to the ratio between the lesser extreme and the mean (6 : 12 :: 3 : 6). In the geometric mean this latter ratio is inverted:

78 Barbaro, *op. cit.*, p. 270.
79 Palladio, I, pp. 53–54; Tavernor, Schofield, pp. 58–59.
80 *Vide supra*, 'Proportionality'.

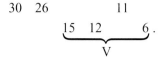

These three triples of extremes and means cover the sextuple.

To recapitulate. The six distinct numbers, 30, 26, 15, 12, 11, 6, employed in the groundplan of 'La Rotonda' sum to the monad of the second course, 100. The primary division into two triples is by the square root of six, $(30 + 26 + 15) : (12 + 11 + 6) ::$ $71 : 29 :: R^{1/2} 6 : 1$. The first triple $30 : 26 : 15$ is a rational convergent to the incommensurable proportion $\sqrt{4} : \sqrt{3} : \sqrt{1}$; while the second triple implies the ratio $17 : 12$ as a rational convergent to $\sqrt{2} : \sqrt{1}$. The sextuple as a whole implicates the rational roots, $R^{1/2} 1$, $R^{1/2} 2$, $R^{1/2} 3$, $R^{1/2} 4$, of the constituents of the tetraktys, 1, 2, 3, 4. The sextuple also evokes the primary Platonic figures: the circle, the regular pentagon, the square, and the equilateral triangle; and the classical problems of doubling the cube and squaring the circle. The 'Rotonda' sextuple is intricately fabricated in itself, showing abundant associations and multiple relationships. Just how much it was intended for anyone to read into these numbers must remain an unanswered and unanswerable question, but none of the interpretations are exceptional in the terms of classical arithmetic and practical geometry as understood in Palladio's day.

So far the sextuple has been examined in its own right, abstracted from the distribution of the numbers as dimensions in the plan. Now consider how the numbers are applied. The circular hall has diameter P30, and the marked hallway which leads to it has width P6. The extremes of the sextuple are found at the heart of the scheme. An equilateral triangle inscribed in the circle would have rational sides P26. This side length and the radius of the circle determine the dimensions of the principal rooms which are proportioned as a rational convergent $26 : 15 :: R^{1/2}3 : 1$. If a square is subtracted from such a $R^{1/2}3 : 1$ rectangle, the remaining rectangle will be proportioned $15 : 11$, the ratio of the smaller rooms. If a square is subtracted from a $R^{1/2}3 : 1$ rectangle with rational dimensions $12 : 7$, the remaining rectangle will be a rational convergent $R^{1/2}2$, or $7 : 5$. By analogy, it can be argued that $15 : 11$ stands for $R^{1/2}2 : 1$. Since the rational convergent $7 : 5 :: R^{1/2}2 : 1$ is in proportion to $14 : 10$, the propinquity of $15 : 11$ can be appreciated. The implication is that, within practical tolerances, a square of side P22 can be inscribed in the circle of diameter P30. The large rooms thus become associated with the inscribed triangle,

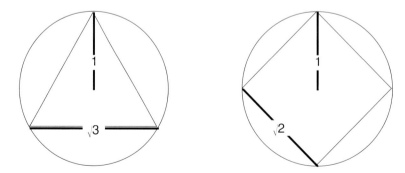

Fig. 37. Villa Almerico, 'La Rotonda', Vicenza. Inscribed equilateral triangle and square. If the circle has a radius 15, or diameter, the rational side of the triangle will be 26 and of the square 22.

and the smaller rooms with the inscribed square of the circular hall. These primal figures – triangle, square, circle – are imprinted on the plan of 'La Rotonda' as surely as they illustrate texts, bracketing its construction, by Piero della Francesca, Pacioli, and Dürer before and by Barbaro after. Some years later, Scamozzi reveals the scheme in his depiction of Vitruvian man.[81]

La Rotonda, Vicenza: Section and Elevation

Palladio's woodcut for the elevation and cutaway section of 'La Rotonda' shows another six distinct dimensions. Here the dimensional set is:

55   21¾   18   10   7   6½

or, removing fractions, the set is proportionately

220   87   72   40   28   26.[82]

The most important number in the elevational set is surely 55, the height of the domed, central hall, whose diameter is P30. The hall is thus proportioned 11 : 6, a superpartiens ratio earlier found between the least terms in the sextuple of the plan which may be identified with an inscribed pentagon.[83] While the pentagon is not physically present in the dome, it must be noted that the balustrade around the balcony in the hall is formed from 100 elements, 20 posts and 80 balusters. Their position is graphically determined through a pentagon, giving a five-fold division, and a square, giving a four-fold division, which together locate the $5 \times 4 = 20$ posts. To return to the number 55 itself. In classical texts it is remarkable for having so many guises. It is the tenth triangular number:

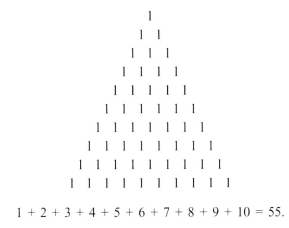

$$1 + 2 + 3 + 4 + 5 + 6 + 7 + 8 + 9 + 10 = 55.$$

Ten is the perfect *tetraktys*, the fourth triangular number,

81 *Vide supra*, 'Prisoners of Number'.
82 In classical arithmetic, the whole numbers are the source of the fractional variety and removing fractions seems an appropriate thing to do.
83 Just one of many relationships between the plan set and the elevational set, see further discussion below.

and thus 55 may be read as perfection empowered, as a metamorphosis of the decad which is reconstituted by summing its digits $5 + 5 = 10$. The affinity with the width of the hall P30 is apparent from the odd and even partition of the decad which sums to 55: $25 + 30$,

$$1 + 3 + 5 + 7 + 9 \ = 25$$
$$2 + 4 + 6 + 8 + 10 = 30.$$

In another guise 55 is the sum of the first five square numbers,

$$1^2 + 2^2 + 3^2 + 4^2 + 5^2 = 55,$$

but now note a new affinity with the width of the hall P30,

$$1^2 + 2^2 + 3^2 + 4^2 = 30.$$

Such figurate presentations are known in classical arithmetic as pyramids: the fourth tetragonal pyramid ◆ 4 and the fifth ◆ 5.

The sum of the extremes in the sextuple for the plan is $30 + 6 = 36$. The factors of the empowered hexad, 6^2, sum to 55:

$$1 + 2 + 3 + 4 + 6 + 9 + 12 + 18 = 55.$$

Undoubtedly the most remarkable property of the number 55, also celebrated in classical arithmetic, is that its square is the sum of the first ten cubes:

$$1^3 + 2^3 + 3^3 + 4^3 + 5^3 + 6^3 + 7^3 + 8^3 + 9^3 + 10^3 = 55^2.$$

This is tellingly demonstrated by setting out the first 55 odd numbers as a triangular figure according to the procedure by which the cube numbers are found in successive sequences of odd numbers: $1 = 1$, $3 + 5 = 8$, $7 + 9 + 11 = 27 \ldots$

```
                        1
                     3    5
                  7    9   11
              13   15   17   19
           21   23   25   27   29
        31   33   35   37   39   41
     43   45   47   49   51   53   55
  57   59   61   63   65   67   69   71
73   75   77   79   81   83   85   87   89
91  93  95  97  99  101  103  105  107  109
```

Such characterizations make the number 55 extremely potent as Anatolius describes. He also points out that in Greek the number 55 is written εν, ε = 5, ν = 50. The word is Greek for 'one' and divinely endowed.[84]

84 *Vide supra*, 'Theological Number'.

Another significant number in the elevation is 18, the height of the Ionic columns. The height of column to podium base is 18 : 10 :: 9 : 5, or an early rational convergent to ℞^{1/2} 3 : 1. The proportion of the column to the wall height between the base and the attic is 87 : 72 :: 29 : 24. The numbers 29 and 24 appear as close companions in the Chuquet derivation of convergents for √2 : 1.[85] As has been previously noted, 17 : 12 is a good convergent, but a little too large. The conjugate ratio 24 : 17 is a convergent which is a little too small. The Chuquet procedure sums the antecedents and forms a ratio with the sum of the consequents,

$$(17 + 24) : (12 + 17) :: 41 : 29,$$

a better convergent, in which 29 is seen to relate to 24. The relationship may be illustrated even more pertinently in Euclid's algorism starting with the ratio 41 : 29.

1. 29 is subtracted from 41 once: 41 − 29 = 12;
   12 is the remainder.
2. 12 is subtracted from 29 twice: 29 − 24 = 5;
   5 is the remainder.
3. 5 is subtracted from 12 twice: 12 − 10 = 2;
   2 is the remainder.
4. 2 is subtracted from 5 twice: 5 − 4 = 1;
   1 is the remainder.
5. 1 is subtracted from 2 twice: 2 − 2 = 0;
   there is no remainder.

The anthyphairesis once, twice, twice, twice, twice [1, 2, 2, 2, 2] is another description of the ratio 41 : 29. In the second recursion the close affinity of 29 and 24 is apparent. The algorism can be best seen in a diagram in which successive squares are subtracted from a rectangle of proportion 41 : 29. The relationship of the two heights is then transparent. More obvious is the proportionality between the base height and the roof height over the porticoes: 10 : 7 :: ℞^{1/2} 2 : 1.

The height of the piano nobile 21¾ may be compared with the dimensions of the principal P26 by P15 rooms in the proportion 26 : 21¾ : 15 −

$$\overbrace{\underbrace{26 \quad 21\tfrac{3}{4} \quad 15}_{\sqrt3\,:\,1}}^{\sqrt3\,:\,\sqrt2}$$

$$\underbrace{\overbrace{26 \quad 21\tfrac{3}{4} \quad 15}^{\sqrt2\,:\,1}}_{\sqrt3\,:\,1}.$$

The proportion 21¾ : 15 :: 29 : 20 is a convergent to ℞^{1/2} 2 : 1 derived from the Pythagorean triangle of sides 29, 21, 20 which is the first rational approximation to the right isosceles triangle. The principal room is in proportion to 26 : 15 :: ℞^{1/2} 3 : 1. Thus the length of this room to the height of the piano nobile to the room width is in the proportion ℞^{1/2} 3 : ℞^{1/2} 2 : ℞^{1/2} 1 fractional powers of the triad, the dyad and the monad.[86]

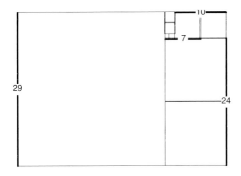

Fig. 38. Villa Almerico, 'La Rotonda', Vicenza. Anthyphairetic diagram showing the ratios 29 : 24 and 10 : 7 taken from a 41 : 29 rectangle (√2 : 1).

85 *Vide supra*, 'Inexpressible Proportion'.
86 Palladio, II, p. 18 writes that the height of the principal rooms is determined by the first mode of proportionality, that is to say, the arithmetic mean of P26 and P15 which would be P21½. The drawing suggests that the ceiling height might actually be P21¾, or 15 inches higher. If it is, then the main rooms have the Albertian cubic proportion √3 : √2 : √1, or at least an arithmetic version of it.

La Rotonda, Vicenza: Portico

The internal width of each portico is P30, the column height is P18, and the depth is P12:

$$30 : 18 : 12 :: 5 : 3 : 2.$$

This is an example of the tenth mean of Nicomachus, but these derivations of the rational convergents for $\sqrt{2} : 1$,

$$1:1, \quad \mathbf{3:2}, \quad 7:5, \quad 17:12, \quad 41:29,$$

and $\sqrt{3} : 1$,

$$1:1, \quad 2:1, \quad \mathbf{5:3}, \quad 7:4, \quad 19:11, \quad 26:15,$$

suggest that $3:2$ and $5:3$ may also be understood as embryonic rational roots for $\mathbb{R}^{1/2}\, 2:1$ and $\mathbb{R}^{1/2}\, 3:1$, while the ratio $5:2$ is an embryonic $\mathbb{R}^{1/2}\, 6:1$ as this calculation demonstrates:

$$
\begin{array}{ll}
3:2 & \mathbb{R}^{1/2}2:1 \\
\mid\ \mid & \quad \mid\ \ \mid \\
\dfrac{5:3}{5:2} & \dfrac{\mathbb{R}^{1/2}4:1}{\mathbb{R}^{1/2}6:1.}
\end{array}
$$

These embryonic convergents found in the external porticoes of 'La Rotonda' serve to introduce, as in an overture, the motif which is developed and elaborated in the interior.

Passing through the central columns of the hexastyle portico, the width of the marked entrance halls is P6 (the unmarked hallways are wider, but not specifically dimensioned), and the relationship of portico depth to column height is

$$18 : 12 : 6 :: 3 : 2 : 1.$$

The primal theme could not be more directly stated in the material world of three dimensional directions: up and down (column), front and back (portico depth), and the left to right (hallway width). The ratios both assert the monadic, dyadic, triadic grounding of numbers and their incorporation into the architectural scheme. The triple, 1, 2, 3, is the example given by Nicomachus for both the first mean – the arithmetic – and the tenth mean.[87] The monad and the decad are thus recalled, along with the perfection of the hexad expressed by its factors, 1, 2, 3. The numbers 18, 12, 6, in themselves are means in the Pythagorean lambda. As Plato asserts, there is one mean between two square numbers, for example, the mean between 4 and 9 is 6. Whereas there are two means between cube numbers, for example between 8 and 27 there is 12 and 18.[88]

$$
\begin{array}{ccccc}
& & 1 & & \\
& 2 & & 3 & \\
& 4 & \mathbf{6} & 9 & \\
8 & \mathbf{12} & \mathbf{18} & 27. &
\end{array}
$$

87 *Vide supra*, 'Rational Proportion'.
88 F. M. Cornford, *Plato's Cosmology: The 'Timaeus' of Plato translated with a running commentary*, Routledge & Kegan Paul, London, 1937, pp. 66–72. Cornford writes of the numbers in this lamda: 'Modern commentators seem not to have taken sufficient notice of the fact that this decision [to stop the lamda at the cube numbers 8 and 27] has nothing whatever to do with the theory of musical harmony.' He argues that it has to do with arriving at three-dimensional solidity.

A closer examination of the hexastyle is revealing. It obviously pays tribute to the hexad. The internal length of each portico is P30. Canonically, for a eustyle portico such as Palladio uses, Vitruvius gives the dimensions 3 modules for the central opening and 2¼ modules for the side openings, a proportion of 4 : 3 between inter-columniations, with the column diameter as unit module.[89] This produces an overall dimension of

$$1 + 2¼ + 1 + 2¼ + 1 + 6 + 1 + 2¼ + 1 + 2¼ + 1 = 18.$$

The order is Ionic and canonically the height to diameter is in the ratio 9 : 1. The height in this instance is P18 so that proportionately the diameter of the columns is P2 and the total length of the eustyle should be P36. Instead the total length is P34, adding two columns diameters to the inside dimension to accommodate the two outer columns. To reduce the width between the outer columns of the eustyle to P30, and yet to maintain proportionately between the central opening x and the side openings y, the following equations must be satisfied.
    Conservation of length between the outer columns:

$$x + 2 + x + 2 + y + 2 + x + 2 + x + 2 = 30, \text{ or}$$
$$4x + y = 22.$$

Conservation of ratio between the central and side intercolumniations:

$$4x = 3y.$$

The solution is $x = 11/2$ and $y = 33/8$. Multiplying throughout to remove fractions, the dimensions of the portico are: column diameter 16, central opening 44, side openings 33, and length of portico between outer columns 240.

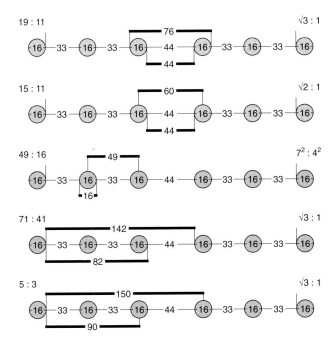

Fig. 39. Villa Almerico, 'La Rotonda', Vicenza. Column and intercolumniation arrangement of the porticoes showing ratios related to the design.

89 Vitruvius III, iii 6. Granger, *op. cit.*, pp. 172–75.

Look first at the central opening and its adjacent columns. The ratio of the distance inclusive of columns to the distance between columns is

$$(16 + 44 + 16) : 44 :: 76 : 44 :: 19 : 11.$$

This is the rational convergent to $\sqrt{3} : 1$ immediately preceding the ratio $26 : 15$ for the principal rooms. The ratio of the distance from centre to centre of the columns adjacent to the central opening and the opening is

$$(8 + 4 + 8) : 44 :: 60 : 44 :: 15 : 11,$$

precisely in proportion to the smaller rooms. Again with the side openings, the ratio of the centre to centre distance between adjacent columns to the column width itself is

$$(16 + 33) : 16 :: 49 : 16 :: 7^2 : 4^2.$$

An early rational convergent for $\sqrt{3} : 1$ is $7 : 4$ and the test for its closeness is to compare $7 \times 7 = 49$ with $4 \times 4 = 16$ and to see that the one goes into the other 3 times except for a unit which is an acceptable deviation. Even more cunningly, summing the dimensions on either side of an adjacent column to the central opening and measuring to the centre of the last column in each case

$$33 + 16 + 33 + 16 + 44 + \frac{16}{2} = 150$$

$$33 + 16 + 33 + \frac{16}{2} = 90$$

the ratio of the one to the other is

$$150 : 90 :: 5 : 3,$$

but if the measurement is to the inside of the columns the ratio is

$$142 : 82 :: 71 : 41.$$

Both of these ratios are rational convergents to $\sqrt{3} : 1$, the one a relatively crude convergent and the other a refined rational value. In fact, 'La Rotonda' is pervaded by the ειδος of $\sqrt{3} : 1$

$$\{1 : 1, \ 5 : 3, \ 7 : 4, \ 19 : 11, \ 26 : 15, \ 71 : 41, \ \ldots\}.$$

La Rotonda, Vicenza: Occult Significance

That Palladio crafted the dimensions, ratios and proportionalities of 'La Rotonda' to exploit a knowledge of contemporary arithmetic seems almost certain. But how probable is it that the architect computed the design in this manner? To lend plausibility to these speculations an attempt must be made to elicit intentions beyond those of playing games with numbers. The context of Renaissance arithmetic is essentially neo-Platonic and Pythagorean. Arithmetic is sovereign over geometry; music theory comes from arithmetic, astronomy comes from geometry. These four are the quadrivium, and their foundation is arithmetic. This argument is well made by both Nicomachus and Theon of Smyrna.

Michael Allen has recently drawn attention to the commentary of Marsilio Ficino on arithmetic constructions in Plato's *Republic*.[90] The significance of the hexad and decad are clear, the circularity of 36 is noted, and the powers of 10, especially 100, are given emphasis. The ratio 17 : 12 is given as a rational square root of 2, following Theon's earlier commentary.

The height of the dome from the ground, P65, the length of the principal rooms, P26, and the vaults of these rooms, P6½, are in proportion 10 : 4 : 1. The tenth division in elevation recalls the dimensions of Vitruvian man where 'the face from the chin to the top of the forehead and the roots of the hair is tenth part' of the full height.[91] St Augustine, following his description of the perfection of the hexad as the first number made up of aliquot parts, points to four being 'a part of ten, but no fraction indicates which part, whereas one is an aliquot part of ten because it is one tenth'.[92] The sequence 10, 4, 1, is the first three triangular pyramid numbers

$$1$$
$$1 + 3$$
$$1 + 3 + 6.$$

Transformed, the proportion 10 : 4 : 1 may then be read as 'triangular pyramid three to pyramid two to pyramid one' in nice symmetry with the triad, dyad and monad: ▲ 3 : ▲ 2 : ▲ 1.

The significant number 26 does not occur in Ficino's text, but it is most significant in a later humanist text, Johann Reuchlin's *De Arte Cabalistica*.[93] Reuchlin dedicates this book to Pope Leo X in 1517, making reference to the Pope's Medici heritage and his father's support of among others, Ficino. In the elevation set multiplied through by 4, the numbers 26 and 72 suggest cabalistic interpretations. Further, 26 is the only number common to both plan and elevation sets. As has been observed several times before, 26 is the well known number for Yahweh יהוה while 72 is the sum of the Tetragrammaton and the number of angels:

Johann Reuchlin writes: 'Any Hebrew letter you take stands for a particular number. Thus, in this way, יהוה equals seventy-two; YOD י means ten, HE ה five, VAV ו six, HE ה five again. Put together arithmetically, י is ten, יה fifteen, יהו twenty-one, יהוה twenty-six. Now add ten, fifteen, twenty-one and twenty-six and the answer is seventy-two.'[94]

This interpretation gives added meaning to the numbers 26 and 15 in the sextuple of the plan, indicates that there is a divine presence in both plan and elevation in

90 M. J. B. Allen, *Nuptial Arithmetic: Marsilio Ficino's Commentary on the Fatal Number in Book VIII of Plato's Republic*, University of California Press, Los Angeles, 1994.

91 *Vide supra*, 'Prisoners of Number'.

92 H. Bettenson trans, *St Augustine: Concerning the City of God Against the Pagans*, Penguin, Harmondsworth, 1984, XI, 31, p. 465.

93 M. Goodman, S. Goodman trans, *Johann Reuchlin: On the Art of the Kabbalah; De Arte Cabalistica*, Abaris Books, New York, 1983.

94 *Ibid.*, p. 267 (Latin and Hebrew, p. 264).

the number 26, יהוה , and the ratio 72 : 26 in elevation surrounds God with a host of angels. Such heavenly and divine presences are surely appropriate for Canon Paolo Almerico, 'referendario di due Sommi Pontefici Pio IIII, & V' who commissioned 'La Rotonda'.[95] The villa is sanctified through number.

The height of the dome to the ground is P65 (55 + 10). Again Reuchlin interprets: 'God was ineffable before the creation. In the creation he was named Elohim. After the creation, living in the world as if in his Temple, he was called Adonai. Hence it is written in Psalm 11: 'Tetragrammaton in his sacred temple. Tetragrammaton who has his throne in the heavens, who is the Lord in his works.' He is, as Scripture says (Deuteronomy 10): 'God of gods and Lord of lords, great El.' Thus the temple is denoted in Kabbalah by Adonai and vice-versa through their equal numerical value. Just as the ineffable Tetragrammaton is to be worshipped in Adonai אדני as if in his own הילכ (Temple), so God is to be loved in God in accordance with the three-fold world (Jeremiah 7), 'Temple of the Lord, Temple of the Lord, Temple of the Lord.'[96]

In gematria, Temple הילכ (ה = 5, י = 10, ל = 20, כ = 30) has the same numerical value as Adonai אדני (א = 1, ד = 4, נ = 50, י = 10): 5 + 10 + 20 + 30 = 1 + 4 + 50 + 10 = 65. Numerically equivalent to the height of the dome of 'La Rotonda' from the ground.[97]

In this interpretation 'La Rotonda' is an ideal 'Temple of the Lord'. This claim is strengthened by the sequence of values 1 for the module, 10 for the podium height from the ground, 100 for the division of the gallery, 20 for the posts in the gallery and 55 for the height of the dome. In gematria, all these numbers represent YOD י the first letter of יהוה.[98]

Even more remarkable is a passage which follows this where Reuchlin uses gematria to interpret the sense of the word חלמה; '. . . which is wisdom in all the commands of God, for when you pronounce the four letters of that word all written out in full – HETH, KAPH, MEM, HE – you get from them the number 613, which is the number of the commands of God, which our sages call Tharyag.'[99]

The four letters (HETH = 418, KAPH = 100, MEM = 80, HE = 15) sum to 613. Is it coincidental that the ground plan sextuple sums to KAPH, 100? And that the remainder, 513, is the sum of the elevational set when fractions are multiplied out:

$$220 + 87 + 72 + 40 + 40 + 28 + 26 = 513?$$

Does God, יהוה 26, emanate his wise commands, חלמה 613, through an angelic host,

י
ה י
ה ו
ה י
ה ו י
ה ו ה י

72, upon 'La Rotonda' as the Neoplatonic doctrine of creativity requires? Does La Rotonda partition the number for wisdom into two unequal parts, even 100, for the plan and odd 513, for the elevation. The vertical dimension from ground to dome, 65, secretly informs that 'La Rotonda' is a Temple of Adonai, הילכ of אדני . The

95 Palladio, *op. cit.*, I, p. 18.
96 *Op. cit.*, Goodman, Goodman, p. 397 (Latin and Hebrew, p. 304).
97 *Vide supra*, 'Occult Number'.
98 The primary value of YOD is 10. This may be reduced to 1 in the usual nine chambers way. Its tetragonal value is 100 and its trigonal value is 55, both of which are legitimate transformations. When YOD is spelt out as דו' , 4 + 6 + 10, its value is 20. That one letter stand for a whole word is not unusual. Reuchlin specifically mentions this in a statement that is peculiarly modern: '. . . they say that Vergil wrote this in his verse. "Yes" and "no" are monosyllabic words common to everyone. With these removed, human conversation could not keep going; therefore almost all human discourse is encapsulated in "yes" and "no". So no one should doubt that a complete word may be contained in one letter or a sentence in one word or that, conversely, a particular word may be stretched out and denoted by a sentence.' Goodman, Goodman, *op. cit.*, p. 313 (Latin 'est & nō' p. 310).
99 *Op. cit.*, Goodman, Goodman, pp. 309–11 (Latin and Hebrew pp. 306–8).

Trinity is then invisibly present in the occult triangle set in the circle of diameter 30, whose sides are 26, יהוה .

If, however, each of the fractional numbers of the elevation set is reduced to its simplest whole number form, that is,

$$21\tfrac{3}{4} \xrightarrow{\;\times 4\;} 87$$

$$6\tfrac{1}{2} \xrightarrow{\;\times 2\;} 13,$$

it will be seen that together they sum to 100. The remaining whole numbers 55, 18, 10, 7 sum to 90. But here Palladio provides a seemingly redundant 10 to inform us twice that the podium for 'La Rotonda' is P10 high. So that the whole numbers also round out to 100. Together these two monads of the second course sum to 200.

Seemingly, the plan responds to the 'one' through the monad of the third course 100, and the elevation responds to the 'other' through the dyad of the third course 200. As Reuchlin reminds his readers:

> The most useful precept on the question of the basis of nature will be 'One and Two', because when we want to examine the causes and origins of the universe, it is these that come most quickly to mind. Upon first sight one sees that something that is identical with itself is not something else, and so we grasp mentally the fact that 'same' and 'other' are 'one' and 'two'. . . . Plutarch wrote 'Pythagoras takes number for mind.' The metaphor is not a bad one. In the realm of the incorporeal, nothing is more divine than mind; and with particular things there is nothing more absolute than number. There is nothing that can be thought to resemble mind more, and from this source of everlastingness the Pythagorean 'One and Two' has flowed in streams and channels, which from eternity has been, will be and always is in that boundless source, the enormous sea, welling up in abundance. . . . As 'One' is the origin of the mental world, so 'Two' is the beginning of the corporeal world.[100]

The two dimensional plan is a mental construct which cannot be realized materially until it is elevated into three dimensional space. It is appropriate that the plan is identified with 'One' (100), and the elevation with 'Two' (200). The 'boundless source', the 'enormous sea, welling up in abundance' are surely metaphors for both divine and human creativity founded in number. The multiple relationships between numbers, the individual constitutions of number, the overlapping taxonomies among numbers, and the dual role of letters as numbers in Greek and Hebrew, provide the Renaissance humanist with a model of the mental and corporeal worlds, of possible worlds and the actual world, of divine worlds and the mundane world. The human creative act, seeded by prolific number and polysemous word, aspires to the divine in the making of its own designs. Reuchlin, in a passage on the perfection of the decad, suggests an ethical principle: 'The world is more perfect, the more it contains many modes of numbering: equality, inequality; squares, cubes; length and area; primes or compound numbers.'[101]

This concept of perfection does not promote the view that small numbers and their ratios guarantee beauty, nor the concept of similitude and the repetition of a single ratio such as the golden section throughout a work. Rather this ethical principle seeks to maximize variety of content, and yet so to weave a web of relationships

100 *Ibid.*, selected from pp. 189–205 (Latin pp. 188–204).
101 *Ibid.*, p. 191 (Latin p. 190).

between numbers that a sense of unity is fostered in the whole. It is as if the starting point is the 'One', that this oneness is then partitioned into a plurality of contrary and opposite elements only to be reconstituted as a new creative unity. Nicomachus writes that 'things are made up of warring and opposite elements and have in all likelihood taken on harmony – and harmony always arises from opposites; for harmony is the unification of the diverse and the reconciliation of the contrary-minded. . . .'[102]

Palladio does not confine proportion in 'La Rotonda' to simple musical ratios, but instead exploits the taxonomies of and relationships between numbers familiar in classical texts. Barbaro in his Vitruvian Commentaries illustrates architectural proportioning with the full range of ten distinct forms of arithmetic ratio. There is the briefest mention of musical harmony, and Barbaro does not recommend the analogy between Pythagorean music and architecture which Alberti had made efforts to establish a century earlier.[103]

The patron of this magical structure is both a humanist and a man of God. His architect is no mean mathematician. In 'La Rotonda' they reach out to perfection and come as close as humanity can to achieving that end. To commemorate their achievement, is it possible that their names are enciphered in 'La Rotonda'? The Latin name of the patron is PAVLVS ALMERICVS. The first name sums to 571 and the second to 438. By tradition, these numbers may be reduced to 5 + 7 + 1 = 13 and 4 + 3 + 8 = 15, by adding digits. The names are in the ratio of the diameter of the domed hall, to the length of the principal rooms:

$$15 : 13 :: 30 : 26.$$

Together the two names sum to 28, the perfect number, and may be further reduced to the decad, 2 + 8 = 10; both numbers which occur in the elevational sets. In single digit enumeration PAVLVS (6 + 1 + 2 + 2 + 2 + 9 = 22) and ALMERICVS (1 + 2 + 3 + 5 + 8 + 9 + 3 + 2 + 9 = 42) the full name comes to 64. It is surely no accident that the volume of the main body of the villa when the fabric is taken into account is a P64 cube.

The architect will be found inscribed in the portico. The total length of the portico including columns is 272 units when fractions are eliminated. The length from the centres of the outside columns is 256. The ratio 256 : 272 is 32 : 34, or as noted earlier, in the Palazzo Della Torre, ANDREAS : PALADIVS. The number 272 is even more potent:

$$68 \xleftarrow{\div 4} 272 \xrightarrow{\times 4} 1088.$$

Through the Tetrad (4) it reaches down to ANDREAS PALLADIVS (68) and through the Tetrad again up to VITRVVIVS (1088).[104]

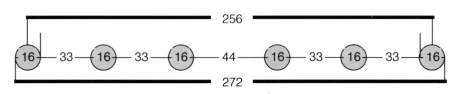

Fig. 40. Villa Almerico, 'La Rotonda', Vicenza. The ratio 256 : 272 :: 32 : 34, or ANDREAS : PALADIVS. Or 64 : 68, PAVLVS ALMERICVS : ANDREAS PALLADIVS.

102 M. L. D'Ooge, *Nicomachus of Gerasa: Introduction to Arithmetic*, University of Michigan Press, Ann Arbor, 1938. Nicomachus II, xix.
103 P. J. Laven, 'Daniele Barbaro, Patriarch Elect of Aquileia with Special Reference to His Circle of Scholars and to His Literary Achievement', PhD University of London. Laven's study of Barbaro's Vitruvian commentaries shows that the musical material was strictly reserved for acoustical matters. The architect perforce used geometry and hence the incommensurable ratios associated with magnitudes which make no sense in music. He also took exception to Vitruvius' musical authority, Aristoxenus, who was more interested in the practice of music than the theory. See Laven's Chapter, 'Harmony', p. 512.

La Rotonda, Vicenza: Conclusion

It is most unlikely that all of the associations and relationships uncovered in this analysis were consciously designed, although none would have surprised contemporaries, and most would have delighted any esoteric audience of the period. The mathematics was familiar to humanists of the period, neo-Platonism was a way of life, and the Kabbalah may not have been as esoteric as might otherwise have been expected, especially in the acceptable Pythagorean terms presented by Reuchlin. For Christians the Kabbalah offered proof that Christ was the Messiah. The syncretic tendency, by mid-sixteenth century, may have become prescriptive: it was no longer sufficient to take note of differences, but it had become necessary to demonstrate that *harmonia est discordia concors* by creating new syntheses. The more foreign and alien the elements that could be drawn together into harmonious coexistence, the more ethical the achievement: for architecture, this moral dimension was sovereign over the aesthetic. 'La Rotonda' is surely an exemplar. Palladio could do this the more easily in Book II of *I Quattro Libri dell'Architettura*, by selecting just those dimensions, just those numbers, that display *symmetria* without regard to those measurements which otherwise might be required for construction purposes. Palladio takes the next step in abstraction from Alberti's eidetic mesh in San Sebastiano by freeing the numbers from physical space, relating them one to another initially as abstract sets regardless of their ultimate destination. Such abstraction is pure neo-Platonic speculation aspiring to the realm of the intelligibles first, before turning to the practicalities and material requirements of the natural world. Reuchlin, again, puts the matter plainly: '. . . no one should be so bleary-eyed in his examination of sacred matters as to despise the recondite, nor so indulgent to aural delights in hearing about the divine as to venerate, praise and follow only those things that are pleasant to the senses, pretty to the eyes, soft to the touch and seductive in their intonation. Man should grasp the spiritual rather than the physical, the constant rather than the fickle and the real rather than the counterfeit.'[105]

This study shows that the harmony expressed in 'La Rotonda' by the architect and patron is not in tune with the limited and restrictive harmonic intervals of musical theory, but is shaped by the more permissive possibilities of arithmetic and the rational measurement of geometric figures in the world of 'Thynges Mathematicall'.[106] Certainly, as in music, simple numbers are the grounds and generators for this harmony, be they the numbers 1, 2, 3, 4; or the threeness of the triangle, the fourness of the square, the fiveness of the pentagon; or the $\sqrt{4} : \sqrt{3} : \sqrt{2} : \sqrt{1}$ relationships of Alberti's cube. Number is key, each an individual with syntactic possibilities and manifold semantic potential. Relative number, proportion and proportionality, provide the discourse between the individual numbers. Yet it is through the metamorphoses of number, in forms of potency such as roots and powers, or through rational convergents to incommensurable ratios, or the ciphers of number-letter correspondences, that these simples find their composite, often occult, expression.

> The great inventions of men have so much good, more so when they are ingeniously proportionate. The most effective thing is in the mixture. One can say that the character of numbers for reasons of comparison among them is divine. One can see that they are the most abundant thing in the fabric of this universe, that what we call convenient in the world is from weight, number, and measure.   DANIELE BARBARO[107]

104 The full width of the portico is P34 and PALADIVS sums to 34.

105 Goodman, Goodman, *op. cit.*, p. 335 (Latin, p. 332).

106 A phrase used by John Dee to describe a world between supernatural things which are 'immateriall, simple, induisible, incorruptible, & vunchangeable' and natural things which are 'materiall, compoundeed, diuisible, corruptible, and chaungeable'. Mathematical things have a 'meruaylous newtralitie' and a 'straunge participation betwene thinges supenaturall, immortall, intellectuall, simple and indiusile: and thynges naturall, mortall, sensible, compounded and diuisible'. Quotations from 'Mathematicall Praeface' to Euclid, 1570, cited in N. H. Clulee, *John Dee's Natural Philosophy: Between Science and Religion*, Routledge, London, 1988, p. 150. Dee visited Venice in June 1563 and met with Federico Commandino (an acquaintance of Daniele Barbaro) in Urbino in September. Given his interest in architecture as one of the mathematical arts – he had copies of Alberti (cats. 607, 1040, 2152) – it is tempting to imagine that he visited Barbaro: he owned copies of Barbaro's 1567 edition of Vitruvius (cat. 41) and his 1569 *Pratica della Perspettiva* (cat. 98). It appears he did not own a copy of Palladio, although he did possess Silvio Belli's books on measurement and proportion (cats. 2125, 2126). J. Roberts, A. G. Watson, *John Dee's Library Catalogue*, The Bibliographical Society, London, 1990.

107 D. Barbaro, *I dieci libri dell'architettura di M. Vitruvio traduitti et commentati da Monsignor Barbaro eletto patriarca d'Aquileggia*, Francesco Marcolini, Venice, 1556, p. 57. Translation Cynthia Maya. It is possible that Barbaro is reciting S. Bonaventura *Breviloquium* which he had studied during his sojourn as Venetian Ambassador in London. During his tenure he had corresponded monthly with his aunt, Cornelia Barbaro, a nun at the convent of Santa Chiara at Murano, concerning his reading of *Breviloquium*. S. Bonaventura writes: 'The whole of the cosmos machine was produced in time and from nothing, by one principle only who is supreme and whose power, though immense, still arranges all things according to a certain weight, number and measure'. *Doctoris seraphici S. Bonaventurae opera omnia*, Ad Claris Aquas (Quaracchi): Ex typographia Colegii S. Bonaventurae, 1882–1902, V p.219.

Villa for the Most Reverend Patriarch-elect of Aquileia and the magnificent Marc'Antonio, the Barbaro brothers, Maser. Andrea Palladio, *I Quattro Libri Dell'Architettura*, Dominico de' Franceschi, Venice, 1570, p. 51. Courtesy The Elmer Belt Library of Vinciana, University of California, Los Angeles.

EPILOGUE

In the Prologue, I mentioned an examination question concerning Palladio's theory of proportion. My answer had made use of the Villa Malcontenta upon which Wittkower had commented in 1949.[1] The ratio of the length of the cross-shaped hall to its width, 46½P to 32P, could not be explained in terms of simple numbers. Only at the end of my researches on this book, as I sat down to draft this Prologue, do I have a possible answer to the question I asked myself some forty years ago. If the cross is parsed into five rectangles, the following dimensions are found: 8P by 16P, 16P by 16P, 8P by 16P for the spaces from side to side of the cross; and from front to back, 17P by 16P, 16P and 16P again in the centre, and 13½P by 16P.[2] The areas of the three rectangles from front to back provide the numbers 272, 256, 216:

$$
\begin{array}{ccc}
 & 216 & \\
128 & 256 & 128 \\
 & 272. &
\end{array}
$$

The numbers 272 and 256 were found in the porticoes of La Rotonda.[3] There, they were shown to be proportional to ANDREAS : PALADIVS, 256 : 272 :: 34 : 32 when divided through by 4. If, however, 272 is multiplied by 4 it gives 1088 which is the number for VITRVVIVS. The remaining number, at the head of the cross, is 216 which both Vitruvius and Barbaro had occasion to comment on, not least because $3^3 + 4^3 + 5^3 = 6^3 = 216$.[4] The total area of the cross gives the number 1000 – the monad of the fourth course with its own perfection. Thus the head of the cross is seen to have an area which is the cube of the arithmetically perfect number 6, and the whole cross has an area which is the cube of the Vitruvian perfect number 10.[5]

'However', Wittkower writes of his own studies, 'the reader may doubt whether Palladio's inscribed figures are really so full of implications. In spite of our close adherence to his own figures we may be accused of the error, so often made by modern writers on proportion, of interpreting into a building relations which were never intended by the architect. Yet nobody can deny that Palladio's numbers were meant to be indicative of certain ratios, and it is not this fact but only the degree of interpretation which may be questioned'. These are cautionary words which must be taken seriously. The understanding of number that I have attempted is based on contemporary sources which I have described comprehensively in part A, GROUND. The architectural interpretation of these ideas about number, in many ways so unfamiliar to us today, is surely debatable, but I hope not unreasonable.

1 R. Wittkower, *Architectural Principles in the Age of Humanism*, Academy Editions, London, 1998, pp. 121–22.

2 8 + 16 + 8 = 32 and 17 + 16 + 13½ = 46½. The dimension 17P is arrived at from the width of the adjoining rooms – 16P – with the wall thickness – 1P – added. The dimension 13½P is the residual required to satisfy Palladio's overall length.

3 *Supra*, p. 264.

4 D. Barbaro, *M Vitruvvii Pollionis De Architectvra Libri Decem Cvm Commentariis*, Venice, 1567, p. 157, cites this formula in his discussion of Vitruvius' introduction to Book V. The formula is a kind of three-dimensional extension of Pythagoras' more familiar equation. Multiplied by 8, the number 1728 is reached. At the end of his life and the fifteenth century, Ficino determined this to be Plato's fatal number, M.J.B. Allen, *Nuptial Arithmetic: Marsilio Ficino's Commentary on the Fatal Number in Book VIII of Plato's Republic*, University of California Press, Los Angeles, 1994. My former student, Dr Hyunho Shin, has pointed out that the major side rooms in the Palazzo Antonini – the first project in Palladio's second book – have the dimensions 17P by 28P which possibly reflect some acknowledgement of Ficino's speculations, H. Shin, *Pythagorean Number Theory and Proportional Designs in the Second Book of Andrea Palladio's I quattro libri dell'architettura*, PhD Dissertation, UCLA, 1996. I have given another interpretation, *supra*, p. 236.

5 It may be no accident that the product of the two dimensions of the cruciform hall 46½ × 32 = 1488 = 3.496. Theologically, 3 shows primary perfection because it is the first number to have a beginning, middle and end, and 496 is the third perfect number in the strict arithmetical sense. *Supra*, 'Theological Number', and 'Ethical Number'. The number 496 is specifically mentioned in D. Barbaro, *op. cit.*, p. 91.

After these words, Wittkower immediately moves on to discuss the relationship between Palladio and Barbaro: 'Any unease about Palladio's intentions can be resolved by reading the relevant chapters of the Commentary to Vitruvius by Daniel Barbaro ...' in examining the application of architectural principles, and proportion in particular, Barbaro urges the reader to look beyond appearances.[6] The villa at Maser commissioned from Palladio by the Barbaro brothers should be examined with this injunction in mind. Remember that numbers, ratios and proportionalities carry many evocations. The eidetic mesh of the central section of the villa is 72P by 36P.[7] Immediately the numbers conjure up the Tetragrammaton: one using the full number-letter evaluation and the other using the single digit values only:

$$
\begin{array}{cccc}
 & & & 10 \\
 & & 5 & 10 \\
 & 6 & 5 & 10 \\
5 & 6 & 5 & 10
\end{array}
$$

which sums to 72, and

$$
\begin{array}{cccc}
 & & & 1 \\
 & & 5 & 1 \\
 & 6 & 5 & 1 \\
5 & 6 & 5 & 1
\end{array}
$$

which sums to 36. Marked by its cruciform hall, this principal part of the villa seems powerfully blessed with Judaeo-Christian significance as would befit Daniele Barbaro, at least, as Patriarch-elect of Aquilea and prominent representative at the Council of Trent. He was heir to his great uncle Ermolao Barbaro's exceptional library and literary estate. Ermolao Barbaro had mentored Johann Reuchlin in Latin.[8] It seems highly probably that Reuchlin's *De Arte Cabalistica*, dedicated to Pope Leo X, would have been known to the Barbaro brothers. In any event, Agrippa von Nettersheim's popular exposition of the occult philosophy was widely circulated.[9] The Asclepian programme of the grotto at Maser with which Marc Antonio Barbaro is associated also suggests that the dimension 36 might signify the all-important godlike Decans in the Hermetic theogony.[10]

The side room proportions in the central block of the Villa Barbaro are 5 : 3, 2 : 1, 20 : 9 and, in the centre overlooking the nymphaeum, the Sala dell'Olimpo, 10 : 9. The ratio 5 : 3 is said by Palladio to be his favourite.[11] The ratios 20 : 9 and 10 : 9 may be derived from 5 : 3 by composition of the kind illustrated by Barbaro:

$$
\begin{array}{cc}
3 & 2 \\
 & \times \\
5 & 3 \\
\hline
10 & 9
\end{array}
$$

6 *Op. cit.*, p. 127.

7 D. Barbaro, *I Dieci Libri Dell'Architettura di M Vitruvio*, Venice, 1665, p. 97: 'Pèro se alcuno sia, che voglia vedere piu a dentro, à ritrovare la verità cose,. ...'

8 Recall that I have defined the eidetic mesh as one in which material thicknesses, such as walls, are ignored.

9 L. Geiger, *Johann Reuchlin sein Leben und seine Werke*, B. De Graaf, Nieuwkoop, 1964, p. 33.

10 The Barbaro family church was San Francesco della Vigna for the rebuilding of which the Franciscan friar, Francesco Zorzi, had supplied an occult, arithmetic programme. This was also the Grimani family's church and Domenico Grimani had been a defender of Johann Reuchlin's cabalistic interests. It is commonly supposed that Giovanni Grimani was instrumental in promoting Palladio's first executed church commission – the façade of San Francesco della Vigna.

11 D. Lewis, 'Classical Texts and Mystic Meanings: Daniel Barbaro's Program for the Villa Maser' in *Klassizismus: Epoche und Problem. Feschrift für Erik Forssman zum 70. Geburtstaf*, Georg Olms, Hildesheim, 1987. Lewis, like most scholars, attributes the programme to Daniele, but I am inclined to give weight to Marc Antonio, especially in regard to the nymphaeum cut into the hillside. For the Asclepius myth, see B. Copenhaver, *Hermetic and the Latin Asclepius in a New English Translation*, Cambridge University Press, Cambridge, 1996.

and

$$\begin{array}{cc} 4 & 3 \\ & \times \\ 5 & 3 \\ \hline 20 & 9 \end{array}.$$

In this way four of the five rational ratios in Palladio's canon are accounted for $- 2:1, 5:3, 3:2, 4:3$. These could be given a musical interpretation as the octave, the major sixth, the fifth and fourth respectively. The ratio $10:9$ itself is the minor tone, but since Palladio nowhere uses the major tone $9:8$, it would be curious for him to employ this ratio with this musical interpretation in the most important room of the villa. Immediately on either side of the central block are square rooms, $1:1$, thus completing the rational canon.

There is another possibility. The ratio $20:9$ is a rational convergent for $\sqrt{5}:1$.[12] The ratio $2:1$ can be represented as $\sqrt{4}:1$, while $5:3$ is an early convergent for $\sqrt{3}:1$. The side rooms from back to front then read in sequence as $\sqrt{3}$-, $\sqrt{4}$-, $\sqrt{5}$- rectangles. The Sala dell'Olimpo in this interpretation is thus $\sqrt{5}:\sqrt{4}$. The crossing of the hall, surprisingly not square, is 14P by 12P, a ratio of $7:6$, or $\sqrt{4}:\sqrt{3}$. The crossing is marked by the proportion of the *Magen David*, or star of David.[13] In this interpretation the Pythagorean triangle numbers 3, 4, 5 are evoked in their root transformation. The same numbers are the factors of the width, 60P, of the fishpond which lies before the nymphaeum $- 3.4.5 = 60$. The two connecting elements between the central block and the wings each have an eidetic length (without walls) of 50P, the main rooms in the two wings are 32P long, and the Sala dell'Olimpo is 18P wide: the same $50:32:18$ relationship previously seen in the Palazzo Della Torre based on the squares on the hypotenuse and sides of the Pythagorean triangle $25:16:9$. This interpretation of numbers used by Palladio as rational convergents also has a geometric depiction in terms of the world-making regular polygons of Plato: the equilateral triangle, the square and the pentagon. These are the objects of consuming interest to Daniele Barbaro in his *La Pratica della Perspettiva*.[14] But it is not so much the geometry that is expressed as the arithmetic associated with that geometry.

There are two full eidetic lengths of the villa to consider. One is 228P through the stables and wine cellars,

46   50   36   50   46

and the other is 224P through the rooms in the side wings,

16   12   16   50   36   50   16   12   16.

The second number, $224 = 32.7$ is equivalent to ANDREAS.PALADIVS, but the first is 228 which when multiplied by two (brothers?) is equivalent to BARBARVS $(2 + 1 + 80 + 2 + 1 + 80 + 200 + 90 = 456)$.[15]

The linear dimensions from back to front read

⌊20   12⌋   6   ⌊14   20⌋.

---

12 One possibility for this might be the frequent, but implicit, citation of the ratio $5:3$ in the Old Testament, *supra* 'Judaic Heritage'.

13 *Supra* 'Judaic Heritage'.

14 *Supra* 'Central Design'.

15 *Supra* 'Occult Number'.

Thus about the perfect number 6 – equivalent to the family name BARBARVS – are the two numbers 32 and 34, ANDREAS PALADIVS, while the width 36 reads PALLADIVS in the alternate spelling. The central crossing of the cruciform hall is in the ratio 7 : 6 which encodes the names of both brothers, DANIEL (7) BARBARVS (6) and MARCVSANTONIVS (7) BARBARVS (6). The dimensions from front to back of the side wings are 12P, 32P and 20P. These are in proportion 3 : 8 : 5, but 385 is the full number of PALADIVS.

The music analogy is really secondary to the arithmetical and geometrical grounds upon which music and the visual arts were both seen to stand. Aristides Quintilianus, translated from the Greek for Gaffurius at the end of the fifteenth century, advocates the use of arithmetic in music by reference to other arts such as painting: 'It will be evident, when we have looked over the arts, how much benefit they collect from numbers. If one should wish consider painting, he will discover that it does nothing without numbers and proportions, but rather captures the symmetries of bodies and blending of colours through numbers and from these, creates beauty in the paintings.'[16] He then goes on to discuss the use of numbers and proportioning in medicine. There is also an aspect of music which is rarely mentioned – rhythm. The classical theory of rhythm which studies the possible divisions of time has, surely, a more direct relation to the divisions of space than do the vibrations of a string.[17]

Among the twentieth-century architects, Rudolph Schindler makes a compelling comparison between rhythm in music and architectural proportion.[18] Frank Lloyd Wright appears to make good use of geometrically determined ratios such as $\sqrt{2}$, $\sqrt{3}$ and $\sqrt{5}$ and their combinations.[19] Hans Scharoun seems to employ rational right triangular systems in generating his apparently free forms.[20] Wittkower himself praised Le Corbusier and *Le Modulor*, but I have expressed elsewhere some scepticism concerning the classical provenance of this method.[21] I do not think that 'proportion is dead'. Proportion cannot be avoided. The architect can be conscious of it and work with it, or ignore its inevitable presence whenever and wherever two quantities are compared. These may be perceived in the same visual field as modern psychology demands, or as I have shown in humanist work, they may only be apparent beyond appearances – in the realm of the intelligibles.[22]

That there is a difference between my approach and Wittkower's is a matter of time. I like to think – I could be wrong – that he would have appreciated the investigations I have undertaken using the accumulated knowledge of half a century in this area. He not only had the task of developing his thoughts on humanist architectural principles, but also of introducing the architecture of Alberti, Serlio and Palladio to a readership that had been somewhat less than careful over history in its quest to be modern. That is a task I am fortunate to be free from given the excellent studies that have subsequently been made by scholars and specialists. I have been at liberty to concentrate on the architectonics of the period – the period before the first moderns.[23]

To me, architectonics is to architecture as musicology is to music. Musicology, however, is a twentieth-century term taken into the English language from the French. It refers to music scholarship – all those studies other than performance and composition. Architectonics describes the 'science' of architecture in contradistinction to the 'art'.[24] It is a term introduced in the seventeenth century by the Cambridge Platonist, Henry More, who placed it beside music and letters, but music to a neo-Platonist was first and foremost its theory. It was not the practice of music that found a place in the quadrivium, but its theory. Architectonics is the theoretical study of architecture. In

16 BARBARVS is associated with the numbers 456, 33 and 6; DANIEL with 79, 25 and 7; MARCVS ANTONIVS with 934, 61 and 7. Both brothers share the same reduced number form 7, 6. ANDREAS is associated with the numbers 221, 32 and 5; PALADIVS with the numbers 385, 34 and 7; and the alternate spelling PALLADIVS with 405, 36, 9. *Supra* 'Occult Number'.

17 T.J. Matheisen, *Aristides Quintilianus. On Music in Three Books: Translation, with Introduction, Commentary, and Annotations*, Yale University Press, New Haven CT, 1983, p. 172.

18 There is one striking exception. J. Onians, *Bearers of Meaning: the Classical Orders in Antiquity, the Middle Ages, and the Renaissance*, Princeton University Press, Princeton NJ, 1988, quotes Francesco di Giorgio Martini: 'And as music has its long and very long intervals, its breves and semibreves which correspond in their proportions, so too the same is necessary in a building.' (p. 181).

19 R.M. Schindler, 'Reference Frames in Space', pp. 57–61 and L. March, 'Proportion is an alive and expressive tool. . . .' pp. 88–101, in L. March, J. Sheine, eds., *R M Schindler: Composition and Construction*, Academy Editions, London, 1994.

20 L. March, 'Sources of Characteristic Spatial Relations in Frank Lloyd Wright's Decorative Designs' in L. Nelson, *Frank Lloyd Wright: the Phoenix Papers II. The Natural Pattern of Structure*, University of Arizona Press, Tucson AZ, 1995, pp. 12–48.

21 G. Fusco, R. Mattei, *Griglie Pitagoriche: Nuovi Campi di Forme per la Progettazione Modulare*, Guida Editori, Naples, 1979.

22 *Op. cit.*, March 1994.

23 J. Rykwert, *The First Moderns. The Architects of the Eighteenth Century*, The MIT Press, Cambridge MA, 1980. The opening chapters of Rykwert's book are concerned with seventeenth-century developments, and I use 'first moderns' to include these. 'Before' means sixteenth century and earlier in this context.

24 Architectonics also has a philosophical sense as in W. Watson, *The Architectonics of Meaning: Foundations of the New Pluralism*, Chicago University Press, Chicago IL, 1985.

these essays I am using the term in a specific and narrow sense, parallel, perhaps, to a division of musicology dealing with rhythm and metrics. There are many other divisions that might be developed in equal depth.

Whereas music has a long tradition as a university subject, architecture only came to a few universities in the nineteenth century and has spread to more in the twentieth. Academically, it remains an awkward youngster. It has been reluctant to admit to a division of labour between those who practice its arts and those who reflect upon its products and processes. The 'reflective practitioner' requires that theoretician and practitioner are one, but a 'reflective profession' divides the responsibilities and pursues each direction to the limits.[25] Engineering and medicine are, perhaps, the most developed of the 'reflective professions' in which the pretence that its individual members, with a few notable exceptions, should be both has been set aside.

There was a moment at the turn of the fifteenth and sixteenth centuries when theory in the visual arts, especially perspective theory (prospectiva), was promoted as equal, or superior, to music in the quadrivium. It was suggested that either it should be added to make a fifth discipline, or should displace music to create a new quadrivium: arithmetic, geometry, prospectiva, astronomy.[26] The movement did not gather force for the simple reason that the scholastic paradigm of the quadrivium was about to be replaced, in the wake of the Galilean revolution, by the embryonic form of our modern letters and sciences. The visual arts, and architecture in particular, now have a new opportunity to assert their intellectual grounding as reflective, scholarly disciplines; and, in doing so, mathematical and computational issues will again play a significant part. To persuade you that they once did, at a high point of western culture, has been my aim in these essays on the architectonics of humanism.

25 D.A. Schoen, *Educating the Reflective Practitioner: Toward a New Design for Teaching and Learning in the Professions*, Jossey-Bass, San Francisco CA, 1987. Schoen's emphasis is on the education of the individual, not on the institutional development of professions as learned societies.

26 *Op. cit.*, Onians, pp. 216–19. Luca Pacioli, Leonardo da Vinci and Francesco di Giorgio all spoke out on this matter in favour of the visual arts which combine arithmetic and geometry, unlike music which was seen to be dependent on arithmetic alone.

APPENDICES

CANONS OF PROPORTION

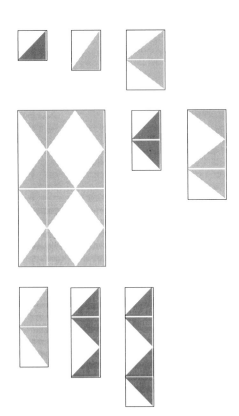

Fig. 1. Alberti's nine canonic ratios which mimic Pythagorean musical systema. Top row, 1 : 1, 4 : 3, 3 : 2. Middle row, 16 : 9, 2 : 1, 9 : 4. Bottom row, 8 : 3, 3 : 1, 4 : 1. The simple geometry of the square and of the 3, 4, 5 right triangle describe these ratios without any need for a musical reference.

Renaissance architects provided evidence of proportional preferences, or canons. Such proportional canons typically referred to room plans and sometimes the elevations of rooms. In practice these canonic proportions were more often neglected than honoured. It is as if they had become part of some masonic catechism to be recited without pragmatic consequence. Proportional schemata were also established in detail for the orders.

Alberti sets out two distinct canons. One may be said to mimic musical systema; the other has a geometrical base, but is executed using rational arithmetical terms.[1] Apart from the ratios 1 : 1, 2 : 1, 3 : 2, 4 : 3, none of Alberti's five other Pythagorean musical proportions find written favour with architects who follow him.

The second canon of Alberti's is related to the geometry of the cube. Within the cube a regular tetrahedron may be placed giving rise to ratios related to the equilateral triangle, or alternatively, it is possible to dissect a cube along an hexagonal face so that the same proportions, but now associated with the regular hexagon, are generated. There are six discernible ratios in this canon: 1 : 1, the sides of the cube, the sides of the tetrahedron, or the sides of the regular hexagon; $\sqrt{2} : 1$, the diagonal of the face of the cube (a side of the inscribed tetrahedron) to the side of the cube; $\sqrt{3} : \sqrt{2}$, the diagonal of the cube to the diagonal of the face of the cube; $\sqrt{3} : 1$, the diagonal of the cube to the side of the cube; $\sqrt{4} : \sqrt{3}$, the diameter of the hexagon to its chord; and $\sqrt{4} : 1$ (2 : 1) the diameter of the hexagon to its side. Four of the six ratios are inexpressible except as rational convergents.

Francesco di Giorgio shows a range of rectangular temple proportions and room shapes. It appears that he largely follows Alberti's Pythagorem system apart from the 7 : 4 intercolumniations of one of his temples which may stand for a rational convergent to $\sqrt{3} : 1$.[2] A plate in Cesare di Lorenzo Cesariano's vernacular edition of Vitruvius is particularly revealing.[3] The problem is to define the ceiling heights of rooms of different plan proportions: a square room, 1 : 1; a double square room, 2 : 1; and a room of ratio 4 : 3. In the case of the double square room, the room is marked by tenth divisions to the unit – call them 'feet' so that room is 20 feet long. The height of the room may be determined by placing a 3, 4, 5 right triangle with a base of 12 feet against the long wall. Its height is the height of the room 16 feet and its hypotenuse is 20 feet, the length of the room. The long wall is proportioned 5 : 4, and the short wall is in the ratio 8 : 5. These proportions introduce the number 5 into the discussion breaking the Pythagorean tradition, just as di Giorgio's 7 : 4 ratio had done earlier. These numbers were the cause of heated debate in musical

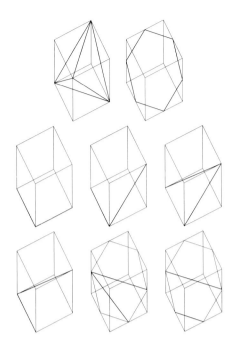

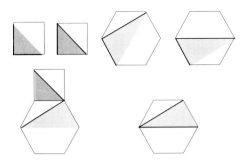

Fig. 3. Geometrical constructions in the plane for Alberti's cubic ratios. Top row, left to right, 1 : 1, √2 : 1, √3 : 1, √4 : 1. Bottom row, √3 : √2 (left) and √4 : √3 (right). The dark grey triangle is a right isosceles, the light grey triangle is an half equilateral.

Fig. 2. Alberti's cube. Top row, showing the inscribed tetrahedron (left) and the hexagonal dissection face (right). Second row, from left to right, 1 : 1, √2 : 1, √3 : √2. Bottom row, √3 : 1, √4 : √3, √4 : 1 (2 : 1).

circles during the sixteenth century, for example, Gaffurio holding to the the Pythagorean ratio 81 : 64 in preference to 5 : 4 for the ditone proposed by the mathematician Ramos de Pareja in 1482. Zarlino accommodates number 5 in his *senario* – the numbers from one to six – from which he constitutes the consonances of his system. He has a ready excuse in admitting the minor sixth with a ratio 8 : 5 which lies outside the limiting number 6. But he dare not extend the numbers to 8 since this would necessarily include the number 7 leading to ratios, as Palisca says, 'falling outside the circle of consonances'.[4] It is not clear whether Cesariano was familiar with the earlier musical debate. It is certain that Francesco di Giorgio felt able to use the ratio 7 : 4 and the number 7 in architectural practice well before this ever became an issue in music. It is most likely that these were independent developments in the two arts.

Cesariano shows six variant ceiling heights for a square room. Each is constructed by striking arcs. The first arc defines a √2 : 1 rectangle, its long side to the square. Then, two arcs, each the length of the square, define a rectangle in which an equilateral triangle may be inscribed. Next, the arcs continue to define a square. From the corners of the original square, arcs are struck of radius equal to the diagonal – where these arcs cross is the height of the ceiling. The arcs continue and mark a √2 : 1 rectangle, its short side to the original square. Finally, a semi-circle is drawn on the second square to create a ratio of 3 : 2 for the wall of the square room. The ratios of the wall height to the room length follow the sequence: √2 : 1, √4 : √3, 1 : 1, √4 : √7, 1 : √2, 2 : 3. Only two of these ratios are commensurable, the other four are rational in square, and the ratio √4 : √7 is somewhat exceptional. The heights vary by a factor of two.

The third example Cesariano gives is based on a 4 : 3 room in which a 3, 4 5 right triangle may be inscribed. The ceiling height is first set by the ratio of the

1 *Vide supra*, 'Inexpressible Proportion' and 'Scales of Proportion'.
2 Di Giorgio's approach is well described by G. Hersey, *Pythagorean Palaces: Magic and Architecture in the Italian Renaissance*, Cornell University Press, Ithaca, NY, 1976, pp. 40–43, using an illustration, figure 1.3, from a manuscript by di Giorgio in The Beinecke Rare Book and Manuscript Library, Yale University.
3 C. Di L. Cesariano, ed., *Di Lucio Vitruvio Pollione: De architectura libri decem traducti de latino in Vulgare affigurati: Comentati: & con mirando ordine insigniti*, Gotardus de Ponte, Como, 1521.
4 C.V. Palisca, *Humanism in Italian Renaissance Musical Thought*, Yale University Press, New Haven NJ, 1985, Chapter 9, 'Gaffurio as humanist', pp. 191–225, and Chapter 10, 'The Ancient *Musica speculativa* and Renaissance Musical Science', pp. 225–79.

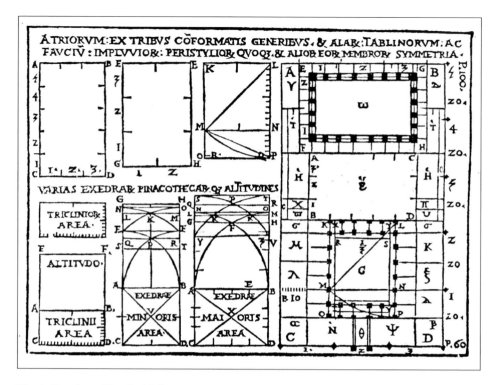

Fig. 4. Cesariano, *Vitruvio*, 1521.

length of the room to its height, 4 : 3, thus making a square end wall. Then, an equilateral relation defines the ceiling height, √4 : √3 for the long wall and √3 : √4 for the end wall. Next, the long wall is square 1 : 1, making the end wall 3 : 4. Striking arcs through the corners of the first ceiling height, three new ceiling heights are determined. One provides the strange relation 5√39 : 32 : 24 of ceiling height to long wall to short side, another the relation √21 : 4 : 3, and a final relation, the pure right triangular relation 5 : 4 : 3. Only the last of these three fits into any of the accepted canons: the other two are wild.

Cesariano explicitly illustrates the 17 : 12 rational convergent for √2 : 1 as well as the value 7 : 5 which he uses in two distinct orientations in the courtyards of a scheme for a palace. He also illustrates rooms which are 3 : 2 and 5 : 3 in ratio. In this diagram of floor plans his set of six ratios is thus 1 : 1, 4 : 3, √2 : 1, 3 : 2, 5 : 3, 2 : 1. The inexpressible ratio √2 : 1 is rationalized as 7 : 5 or 17 : 12. This is the core set for both Serlio and Palladio in their canons. Both authors extend the number of desirable room shapes to seven. Serlio in 1545 adds the ratio 5 : 4 which gives him three superparticulars, rather than Cesariano's two – 5 : 4, 4 : 3. 3 : 2. By adding 5 : 4, it also rounds out the set of three ratios derivable from the sides of the 3, 4, 5 right triangle 5 : 4, 5 : 3, 4 : 3. It would be difficult to argue that this addition results from advances in contemporary musical theory, given this excellent architectonic reason for its inclusion. Palladio, perhaps not to be seen to follow Serlio, does not add the 5 : 4 ratio, but adds the wholly architectonic circle – a shape with no intervallic analogue in music. For rectangular rooms he preserves the same set of ratios Cesariano extracts from Vitruvius. In the plan of a Roman house, Vitruvius notes three kinds of atria with ratios of length to breadth given as 5 : 3,

5 Vitruvius, VI.iii.3–8.

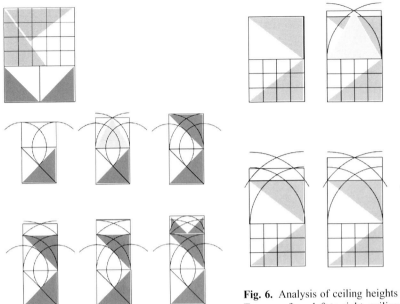

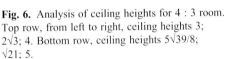

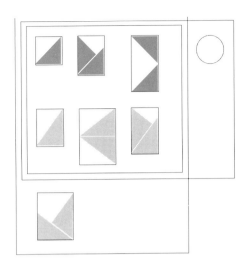

Fig. 5. Analysis of ceiling heights for a double square and square rooms. Top, the double room has a ceiling height determined by the 3, 4 5 right triangle. Next two rows, the square room has ceiling heights determined by the intersection of pairs of arcs. The heights are, second row from left to right, $1/\sqrt{2}i$; $\sqrt{3}/\sqrt{4}i$; 1; and third row, $\sqrt{7}/\sqrt{4}i$; $\sqrt{2}i$; 3/2.

Fig. 6. Analysis of ceiling heights for 4 : 3 room. Top row, from left to right, ceiling heights 3; $2\sqrt{3}$; 4. Bottom row, ceiling heights $5\sqrt{39}/8$; $\sqrt{21}$; 5.

Fig. 7. The architectural canons. The inner rectangle shows the six Vitruvian ratios illustrated by Cesariano. Top row, three ratios based on the right isosceles triangle: the square, 1 : 1; the $\sqrt{2}$: 1 rectangle; the double square, 2 : 1. Bottom row, rectangles derived from the 3, 4, 5 right triangle – 4 : 3 rectangle, 3 : 2 rectangle, 5 : 3 rectangle. The vertical rectangular outline marks Serlio's seven ratios and includes, at the bottom, the ratio 5 : 4. The horizontal rectangular outline embraces Palladio's seventh room shape – the circle.

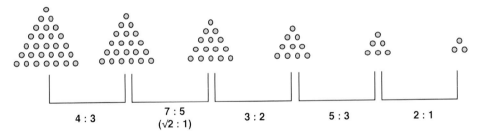

Fig. 8. Ratios between successive trigonal numbers are in agreement with the five inequalities in the core canon, including the common rational convergent for $\sqrt{2}$: 1.

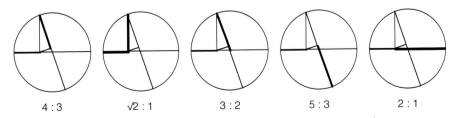

Fig. 9. The common means between 2 and 1 define four canonic ratios, including $\sqrt{2}$: 1 itself. The ratio of the extremes provides the fifth inequality, 2 : 1.

$3:2$, and $\sqrt{2}:1$. The *triclinia*, or dining room, is to be $2:1$, and the peristyles 'should be one-third wider than they are deep', that is in the ratio $4:3$.[5] Vitruvius does not refer to the ratio $5:4$, and nor does Palladio.

What has been described as the core set has special properties in regards to classical arithmetic theories. If the trigonal numbers are set out from $\triangle 2$ to $\triangle 7$, 3 to 28, successive pairs provide the five inequalities of the core set, $4:3$, $7:5$, 3, $5:3$, $2:1$. The pairwise ratios give only one rational convergent for $\sqrt{2}:1$, namely $7:5$. Alternatively, if the common proportionalities between 2 and 1 are constructed geometrically or arithmetically – then $\sqrt{2}:1$ is found explicitly as the geometric mean of 2 and 1. The harmonic mean is $4:3$, the arithmetic mean is $3:2$, the counter harmonic mean is $5:3$, and $2:1$ is the ratio of the extremes.[6] If Serlio's ratio of $5:4$ were to be included these patterns would be disrupted. In the case of the trigonal numbers, the ratio $\triangle 8:\triangle 7::36:28::9:7$ would intervene before the ratio $\triangle 9:\triangle 8::45:36::5:4$ was reached. With the proportionalities, none of the eleven classical means produce the ratio $5:4$ for extremes 2 and 1.[7]

6 *Supra*, 'Proportionality', above. Silvio Belli, Palladio's mathematician friend, specifically mentions the counterharmonic mean.

7 $8:5:4$ is not a proportionality. This is easily seen. Ratios between the differences $(8-5)=3$, $(5-4)=1$, $(8-4)=4$, do not match the ratios between the numbers.

RATIOS USED IN PLANS BY PALLADIO

Table 1 Ninety ratios used by Palladio in his second book of *I Quattro Libri Dell'Architettura* arranged in increasing order from the square, 1 : 1, to ratios greater than the double square, 2 : 1. The ratios have been derived from rooms, porticoes and courtyards. Fractional dimensions have been multiplied out; in bold are the canonic ratios including three rational convergents for √2 : 1 – 7 : 5, 17 : 12 and 24 : 17.

1 : 1	98 : 83	18 : 13	25 : 16	30 : 17	29 : 12
57 : 56	6 : 5	31 : 23	30 : 19	9 : 5	112 : 45
50 : 49	11 : 9	27 : 20	27 : 17	214 : 115	5 : 2
21 : 20	26 : 21	15 : 11	8 : 5	32 : 17	38 : 15
18 : 17	5 : 4	**7 : 5**	13 : 8	61 : 32	18 : 7
17 : 16	19 : 15	**24 : 17**	28 : 17	23 : 12	8 : 3
35 : 32	397 : 390	**17 : 12**	53 : 32	**2 : 1**	14 : 5
10 : 9	75 : 59	93 : 64	83 : 50	29 : 14	17 : 6
19 : 17	9 : 7	25 : 17	**5 : 3**	21 : 10	54 : 19
8 : 7	85 : 66	**3 : 2**	27 : 16	20 : 9	32 : 11
23 : 20	13 : 10	307 : 204	12 : 7	9 : 4	27 : 8
37 : 32	21 : 16	56 : 37	69 : 40	25 : 11	108 : 31
7 : 6	33 : 25	445 : 292	19 : 11	23 : 10	18 : 5
41 : 35	**4 : 3**	43 : 28	26 : 15	57 : 24	15 : 4
128 : 109	83 : 60	37 : 24	7 : 4	12 : 5	49 : 11

Table 2 Ninety ratios used by Palladio in his second book of *I Quattro Libri Dell'Architettura* arranged in alphanumeric order. In bold are the canonic ratios including three rational convergents for √2 : 1 − 7 : 5, 17 : 12 and 24 : 17.

1 : 1	9 : 5	18 : 17	25 : 16	32 : 17	61 : 32
2 : 1	9 : 7	18 : 5	25 : 17	33 : 25	69 : 40
3 : 2	10 : 9	18 : 7	26 : 21	35 : 32	75 : 59
4 : 3	11 : 9	19 : 11	26 : 15	37 : 24	83 : 50
5 : 2	12 : 5	19 : 15	27 : 16	37 : 32	83 : 60
5 : 3	12 : 7	19 : 17	27 : 17	38 : 15	85 : 66
5 : 4	13 : 10	20 : 9	27 : 20	41 : 35	93 : 64
6 : 5	13 : 8	21 : 10	27 : 8	43 : 28	98 : 83
7 : 4	14 : 5	21 : 16	28 : 17	49 : 11	108 : 31
7 : 5	15 : 11	21 : 20	29 : 12	50 : 49	112 : 45
7 : 6	15 : 4	23 : 10	29 : 14	53 : 32	128 : 109
8 : 3	**17 : 12**	23 : 12	30 : 17	54 : 19	214 : 115
8 : 5	17 : 16	23 : 20	30 : 19	56 : 37	307 : 204
8 : 7	17 : 6	**24 : 17**	31 : 23	57 : 24	397 : 390
9 : 4	18 : 13	25 : 11	32 : 11	57 : 56	445 : 292

ACKNOWLEDGMENTS

This book has its beginnings in the School of Architecture and the History of Western Art at Cambridge University: its themes were broached by my teachers and fellow students. In particular Leslie Martin supported my mathematical investigations of architectural phenomena, Sandy Wilson inspired the thought that number and architecture had cryptic affinities, Colin Rowe illustrated one approach to such studies following the path set down by Rudolf Wittkower, Bruce Martin was deeply involved in European policy issues of modular coordination, and my supervisor David Wynn Roberts transmitted that special Welsh passion for intellectual enquiry. Among students, my contemporary Christopher Alexander shared a common background in the Mathematical Tripos and blazed the way towards formal approaches to architectural studies. My association with musicians at the time, especially Leon Lovett and Brian Trowell, had a profound influence on my subsequent interests. Conversations with the composer Alexander Goehr have lingered with me as pointing to conceivable analogies between the arts of music and architecture. Other close colleagues (some former students) must be mentioned for maintaining my intellectual buoyancy during some stormy years: Patricia Apps, Michael Batty, Catherine Cooke, Helen Couclelis, Christopher Earl, Chuck Eastman, Marcial Echenique, Julie Eizenberg, Diane Favro, Terry Knight, Dean Hawkes, Bill Hillier, Ed Hoskins, Frank Israel, Jeff Johnson, Ray Matela, John Meunier, Bill Mitchell, Patricia Patkau, Judith Sheine, Philip Steadman, George Stiny, Philip Tabor. In the past, Sergio Los has translated our ideas for Italians, and Manuel de Solà-Morales did something similar in Spanish. Among recent doctoral students, I thank Hendrika Buelinckx, Athanassios Economou, Djordje Krstic, Hyunho Shin, Jin- Ho Park, and Sukru Yuksel for their various insights and contributions. Research assistants who have prepared translations for me include: Angelique Gulermovich, Cynthia Maya, and Taina Rikala de Noriega.

My thoughts on Alberti were first tested in Architectural Research Quarterly with the encouragement of its editor, Peter Carolin. I have been further encouraged by Robert Tavernor's enthusiastic response to this earlier paper and his support for the current project. A special thanks must go to Maggie Toy at Academy Editions who commissioned this book, and Mariangela Palazzi-Williams who has steered it so ably through its editorial currents.

Most figures were drawn by the author, but the base drawings for figures 23, 27 and 30 in essay XXVI were made by Khary Knowles. Apart from figure 11 in essay XXIII which is from the collection Lessing/Art Resources NY, and figures 25, 26 in essay XXIIII from the National Gallery of Art, Washington DC, all other historic materials come from University of California, Los Angeles, libraries: The Elmer Belt Library of Vinciana; Special Collections, University Research Library; and the William Andrews Clark Memorial Library. Special thanks to librarians Alfred Willis, Joyce Ludmer and Steve Tabor for their assistance, and to Andreanna Adler at the Office of Instructional Development, Photographic Services.

I acknowledge generous research support from the UCLA Senate, the Center for Medieval and Renaissance Studies, and valuable assistance from Claudia Mitchell-Kernan, Vice-Chancellor for Academic Affairs and Dean of Graduate Studies. Maureen Mary suffered my obsessive fixations, but enticed me away on a sufficient number of loving occasions to keep me fed and to put me to bed.

INDEX

A

Ackerman, J S x, 194
Actus quadratus 132
Ad pauca respicientes 6, 92
Ad quadratum, ad triangulum
    105ff, 115ff, 125ff, 133ff, 143ff,
    192ff, 206ff, 216ff
Adonai 262
Aethelhard 85
Agrippa, Henry Cornelius 38ff,
    108–9, 122
Aholiab, see Bezazel
Al-Khindi, Ya'qub ibn Isbaq 6,
    78ff
Alberti, Leon Battista vii, 4, 7, 9,
    13, 79, 85, 91–3, 101–3, 126,
    143, 182ff, 223, 246, 252, 274
Alberti, Lorenzo 182
Alchindo, see al-Khindi
Alchindus, see al-Khindi
Allen, M J B viii, 5, 6, 19, 48, 200,
    261, 269
Almerico, Paolo 262
Alphabets: Greek, Hebrew, Latin
    38ff
Amiens Cathedral 146ff, 204, 239
Anatolius 37, 256
Annunziata 184
anthyphairesis 9
Antiquitates 67, 137
Antonio di Pietro Averlino, see
    Filarete
Aquarius 44
Archimedean solids, see Semi-
    regular solids
Archimedes 4, 85–86, 190
Archytas 65, 93, 125, 177,
Areae 93–94
Aries 44
Aristides Quintilianus 272
Aristotle 15, 20, 22, 189, 252
Aristoxenus 5, 93
Arithmetic, classical 3ff
Arithmetic, cosmogonic 13ff
Arithmetic, Euclidean 9ff
Arithmeticall Militare Treatise,
    named Stratioticos 24
Ark of the Covenant 118
Ark, see Noah's Ark
Armstrong, A H 200
Arnaut, Henri 101

Athena 126
Atria 227–231
Augustine, St 67, 105, 137, 143, 261

B

Bacon, Roger 205
Baglivo, J A 196
Bailey, K xi
Barbari, Jacopo de' 158
Barbaro, Daniele 5, 6, 10, 34, 52,
    63, 65, 78ff, 82, 96ff, 108, 132,
    171ff, 221, 249, 266, 269
Barbaro, Emerlao 270
Barbaro, Marc'Antonio 270
Barker, A 5, 59, 92, 142
Barozzi, Francisco 50, 52
Bartoli, Cosimo 8, 10, 115
Basilica at Fano 132ff, 219, 234
Battista, E 184
Batty, M vii
Baxandall, M x, 191
Beckenbach, E F 73
Bell, E T 26
Belli, Silvio 8, 61, 77, 82
Bellman, R 73
Belt, E vii
Benedetti, Giovanni-Battista
    8, 79,
Bessarion, Cardinal 85, 190
Bettenson, H 261
Bezazel 115
Bezazel's ratio 116, 194, 249
Bezazel's Tabernacle 115
Bill, M 173
Boethius, Anicius Manlius
    Severinius 6, 58, 73, 76, 91,
    143
Boissière, Claude de 52
Bonaventura, St 266
Boncompagni, D J B 5
Borsi, F x, 86, 143, 182, 196
Boucher, B x
Boucher, F 168
Boulez, P xi
Bower, C 6, 58, 99
Braccio 106
Bradshaw, M C 92
Bradwardine, Thomas 6, 22, 52, 63,
    70, 173
Brunelleschi, Filippo 85, 91, 183
Bruno, Giordano ix

Bryce, J 8
Buelinckx, H 63
Burkert, W 15, 29, 37, 126, 191
Burns, H x, 192

C

Cadioli, G 192
Cage, J 136
Cajori, F 38, 70, 79, 93, 239
Callicrates 129
Calliope 42
Campanus of Novaro 85, 106, 153,
    173
Cancer 44
Canon 10
Canons of proportion 274–8
Capnion, see Reuchlin
Cappella Maggiore, San Francesco,
    Arezzo 7
Cappella Rucellai 195–8
Capricorn 44
Cardano, Girolamo 7, 52, 80, 99,
    104, 174, 239
Cauchy, A-L 26, 197
Cesariano, Cesare 103, 246,
    274–7
Chuquet, Nicholas 7, 65ff, 70, 92,
    249, 257
Cicero 137, 142
Claudius Ptolemaeus, see Ptolemy
Clio 42
Clulee, N 5, 265
Commandino, Frederico 6, 79
Conic sections 180
Constantine, Emperor 183
Contarini, Jacopo 79
Convent of the Carità 234–5
Convergent, rational 65ff
Conway, J H 21, 25
Copenhaver, B P viii, 270
Copernicus 85
Cornford, F M 10, 22, 68, 86, 93,
    258
Cosmos 38
Cremonensis, Jacobus 85
Critchlow, K 31
Crosby Jr, H L viii, 6, 22, 63
Cube 67, 154ff, 168, 186
Cubitus 107
Cusanus, Nicholas 7, 14, 85, 91,
    190, 223, 241

D

D'Ooge M L 5, 13ff, 20ff, 58ff, 67,
    73, 189–191, 264
Daphnis of Miletus 127
Davis, M D viiin, 7, 153ff, 186
De architectura x, xi see also
    M Vitruvius
De arte cabalistica ix, 44, 243, 261
De aspectibus 6
De Boissière, Claude 52
De caelo et mundo 22
De civitate Dei . . . 67, 105, 137, 143
De compendis cifris 194
De divina proportione 7, 67, 102,
    159, 192
De harmonia mundi 104, 243
De harmonia musicorum
    instrumentorum opus 52, 80,
    93
De hominis dignitate 45
De institutione arithmetica 58, 76
De institutione musica 91, 99
De Iside et Osiride 53
De l'Orme, P 52
De Morgan, A 87
De occulta philosophia 38ff, 44,
    122
De pictura 159
De prospectiva pingendi 153, 173
De proportionibus proportionum 6,
    92
De re aedificatoria 85, 93, 99,
    184
De rebus rusticus . . . 142
De Republica 142
De statua 104
De solidorum elementis 28
De subtilitate 104, 174
De triangulis 7
De ventis 142
De verbo mirifico 44
Decad 36
Decagon 125, 162, 186
Dee, John 265
Definitiones 186
Del modo di misure 8, 10
Delic problem, see doubling the
    cube
Della proportione et
    proportionalità 61, 82
Descartes, René 28

Diagonal of a square, see doubling the square
Diapason 92
Diapason diapente 92
Diapente 92
Diatesseron 92
Digges, T & L 24
Digitus 107
Dilke, O A W 133
Disciplinae 137
Disdiapason 92
Diversarum speculationem liber 8, 80
Dodecahedron 154ff, 169, 186
Doubling the cube 11, 65ff, 100–101, 159, 169, 177–9, 202–3, 208, 212, 221, 254
Doubling the square 171, 177
Dürer, Albrecht 8, 42, 99, 103ff, 153, 159ff, 254
Dyad 31, 263
Dyad, indefinite 15

E

Earl, C vii
Eaton, C C 49
Eco, U ix
Economou, A N 196
Eidetic mesh 200
Eidos 200, 260
Eidetic mesh 200ff
Elders, W viii, 92
Elements, The 9ff, 79, 85ff, 213
Enchiridon 5
Engel, A 196, 226
Ennead 36
Enneads 200
Enneagon 162, 170
Equilateral triangle 39, 161, 186, 236, 238, 254
Erato 42
Eratosthenes 18, 65, 178
Escorial 121
Euclid 4, 9ff, 67, 70ff, 82, 85ff, 95, 143, 153, 156, 191, 246, 249, 265
Euclidean regular figures 85ff
Euterpe 42
Evans, R xi
Ezekiel 121
Ezekiel's Vision 121ff

F

Fibonacci, see Leonardo Pisano
Ficino, Marsilio viii, 44, 48, 205, 261
Field, J V xi
Filarete 106
Filelfo, Francesco 96
Finè, Oronce 8, 52
Flagg, E 129
Flegg, G 7, 66, 70
Fokker, A D 6, 9, 98
Fournevall, Richard de 52, 146
Fowler, D H viii, 65, 87, 249

Fra Giocondo 104
Francesco di Giorgio Martini 103, 272, 273–5
Friedman, R E 115
Frisius, Gemma 8
Fusco, G 272

G

Gadol, J 182, 194
Gaffurio, Franchino 52, 80, 93, 272, 275
Galilei, Galileo 79
Galilei, Vincenzo 99
Gauss, C F 26, 162
Geiger, L 44, 270
Gematria 47
Gemini 44
Geographia 6
Gerbert, Pope Sylvester II 52
Gherard of Cremona 85
Gillings, R J 53
Ginzburg, C viii, 7, 85
Giusti, E 8
Gnomon 25
Godwin, J viii, 44
Goehr, A viii
Gogava, Antonio 5
Goodman, M & S 41, 261
Granger, F 26, 65, 98, 103, 157, 189, 226, 259
Grant, E 6, 70, 91
Graver, J E 196
Grayson, C 92, 156, 190
Grendler, P F viii
Griffiths, J Gwynn 53, 131
Grünbaum, B 173
Guthrie, W K C 87
Guy, R K 21, 25

H

Hadrian 140ff
Harary, F vii
Harmonics 5, 98
Hart, V x, 86ff, 170, 186, 206ff
Haselberger, L 127
Hay, C 7, 66,70
Heath, T L 4, 9, 15, 38, 53, 58, 64ff, 79, 87, 169, 187, 226, 249
Hebdomad 130
Hebdomades 137
Helikon 99
Helmoltz, H 56
Heptad 34
Hermannus, Archbishop of Colonia 44
Heron of Alexandria 5, 65, 186
Hersey, G viii, 127, 131, 226, 275
Hexad 33
Hexagon 125, 158, 162, 170, 186
Hicks, P x, 86ff, 170, 186, 206ff
Hippolytus, St 38
Hodges, A ix
Hopper, V F 148
House of the Ancient Romans 231–4

House of the Forest of Lebanon 120
Howard, D 246
Hugo of St. Victor 148, 204, 243
Hypate meson 94

I

I dieci libri dell'architettura di M Vituvii traduitti et commentati . . . 78ff, 270
I quattro dell'architettura x, 8, 12, 70, 172
Iamblichus 5, 20, 31ff, 44, 205
Icosahedron 154ff, 168, 186
Icosahexahedron 159
Ictinus 129
Ifrah, G viii, 38, 148
Introduction to Arithmetic 4, 13ff, 20ff, 22ff, 58ff, 86, 93, 140, 190
Ivins Jr, W M 169

J

Jamnitzer, Wenzel 174
Jarzombek, M 194
Jayawardene, S A 7
Jeans, J 56
John, St 143
Johnson, N 173
Johnson, T M 205
Joseph, G G 53, 115ff
Judaic heritage 115ff
Julian Colony at Fano 132ff
Jupiter 33, 42

K

Kabbalah 38ff, 45, 67, 194, 205, 209, 243, 262, 265
Kahn, D 194
Kaplan, A 38ff
Kemp, M xi
Kepler, Johannes 5
Klein, F 197
Klein, J 15
Knight, T W xi
Koptsik, V A 196
Korres, M 129
Krautheimer, R 143, 183, 226
Krstic, D 74
Kubler, G 121
Kurent, T 105

L

L'idea dell'archittetura universale 108, 111
La pratica della perspettiva 6, 108, 171, 271
Labacco, Antonio 199ff
Lagrange, J-L 197
Lambda , Pythagorean 76, 96
Lampugnani, V M vii
Laritsmethique nouellement . . . 7
Lateran Baptistery 182, 188
Laven, F J 171, 264
Lawlor, R and D 5, 13, 58, 65, 73, 91

Lawrence, A W 124
Laws 108
Le Corbusier x, 116, 272
Le institutioni harmonische 246
Leach, N x, 15, 24, 31ff, 44, 67, 86, 92, 115, 184ff, 226
Lee, D 87
Lefèvre, d'Etaples 52
Legendre, A M 197
Leibniz, G W 28
Leo 44
Leo Baptista Albertvs, see Alberti
Leo X, Pope 44, 261
Leonardo da Vinci vii, 8, 59, 63ff, 103ff, 155–9, 273
Leonardo Pisano 5, 101, 153
Leoniceno, N 5
Levi, F R 6
Lewis, D x, 270
Libellum sex quantitatum 6, 80
Libellus de locorum describendorum ratione 8
Libellus de quinque corporibus regularibus 7, 153, 190
Liber abacci 5, 192
Liber quadratorum 5
Libra 44
Libro del mesurar con la vista 8
Lichanos hypaton 94
Lichanos meson 94
Licht, K de F 140
Liddell, H G 131
Lightbown, R 7, 86
Lindberg, D L 6
Lindemann, C L F 156
Lindley, M 92, 99
Lines, commensurable and incommensurable in square 89
Lines, rational and irrational 89
Lohr, C H 14, 92
Longhair, M 246
Lovett, L vii
Ludi Matematici 7–10, 190
Ludi rerum mathematicarum see *Ludi matematici*
Ludus philosophorum, *see* rithmomachia

M

M.Vitrvvivs Pollionis De architectura libri decem commentariis 34, 63, 78ff, 82, 96, 108, 132 221, 269
Maccagni, C 8
Magen David 120, 271
Magic squares 41
Magnitude 9
Magnuson, T 182
March, L vii, 157, 196, 272
Marcvs Terentivs Varro, *see* Varro
Marcvs Vitrvvivs Pollio, *see* Vitruvius
Marinoni, A 66, 157
Mars 33, 42
Martin, L vii, ix, 157

Masi, M 6, 73
Matteo de' Pasti 194
Matheisen, T J 272
Mathematics Useful for Understanding Plato 5, 13, 65, 91
Mattei, R 272
Maya, C 266
Mazzocco 173
McClain, E G 44
McKeon, R 189
Mean
  arithmetic 72,97, 253
  geometric 73, 97, 253, 277
  harmonic 73, 97, 253, 277
  Nicomachus VII, VIII, VIIII, X 73, 96, 253, 277
  Pappus 7, 8 , 9, 10: 73, 96
  subcontraries to the geometric ratio 73, 253, 277
  subcontrary to the harmonic 73, 253, 277
Means, see Proportionality
Melencholia I 42, 169
Melpomene 42
Memoria technica 47
Menelaus 79
Menninger, K 38
Meno 9, 86, 129
Mensula Jovis 42
Mercury 33, 42
Mese 93
Metamorphosis 52
Metaphysics 15, 189
Metrica 5, 186
Metropolitan of Nicea, *see* Bessarion
Meyer, L B xi
Michelozzo di Bartomeleo 184
Miller, C A 80, 93
Millon, H A viii
Molland, G 6, 173
Monad 31, 263
Monas 38
Moon 42
More, Henry 272
Morgan, M H 190
Moses x
Moss, B 7, 66, 70
Müller, Johann *see* Regiomontanus
Multiple, multiple superparticular, multiple superpartient 58ff
Multitude 9
Murray, H J R 49ff

N

Name of God, *see* Tetragrammaton
Nasiforamen 105
Nelson, L 272
Nete diezeugemenon 92
Nete hyperboleon 92
Nicholas V, Pope 5, 85, 143, 182–4

Nicomachus 4, 13ff, 20ff, 22ff, 58ff, 86, 93, 140, 190, 246, 261
Nicomedes 65, 179
Nine chambers 38
Noah's Ark x, 44, 105, 115, 186
Notarikon 47
Numbers
  beam 22
  brick 22
  circular 24
  cube 22
  deficient, perfect, superabundant 20
  ethical 20ff
  even, even-times even, odd-times even 15
  gendered 15ff
  heteromecic 27
  oblong 22
  occult 38ff
  odd 15, 17ff
  odd composite 17
  playful 49ff
  polygonal 24ff
  prime 18,
  Prisoners of 103ff
  pyramidal 27
  relative 58ff
  right triangular 53ff
  scalene 22
  shapeful 22ff
  spherical 24
  square 22
  theological 31ff
Numbering systems
  Greek 24
  Hebrew 38ff
  Hindu 5, 38
  Roman 24

O

O'Brien, E 205
O'Meara, D J O 5, 20, 31, 37, 137
Octad 35
Octagon 125, 144, 158, 162, 170, 186
Octahedron 154ff, 168, 186
Olympic Academy 8
Onians, J 106, 272, 273
Orders
  Composite 115, 219, 234
  Corinthian 106, 115, 219, 221
  Doric 106, 115
  Ionic 106, 115, 216
  Tuscan 115
Ore, C W 136
Oresme, Nicole 6, 52, 70, 91, 149, 223, 241
Ovid 52, 146

P

Pacioli, Luca 7, 59, 65ff, 70, 102, 153ff, 173, 192, 254, 273
Paionios of Ephesus 127

Palazzo
  Antonini 83, 236–9, 250
  Della Torre 99, 222, 239–242, 244, 271
  Valerio Chiericati 83
Palisca, C V viii, 91, 93, 241, 275
Palladio, Andrea x, 8, 10, 12, 70, 98, 133, 140, 172, 186, 216ff, 269, 276–8
Palladio, ratios used by (Tables) 279–280
Pallas, *see* Athena
Palmus 107
Panofsky, E x, 42, 168, 200
Pantheon 140ff, 182
Pappus 6, 67, 73, 169, 186, 246
Pappus' algorithm 75
Paramese, paranete diezeugemenon 92
Parentucelli, Tommaso, *see* Nicholas V
Park, J-H 197
Parmenides 67
Pars 70
Partes 70
Parthenon 128ff
Parthenos 131
Pedes 132
Pedretti, C viii
Peirce, C S ix
Pellerin, Jean (Viator) 159
Pentad 33
Pentadoron 221
Pentagon 39, 153, 170, 186, 236, 238
Pentagrammaton 44
Peterson, M A 154–5
Philip II 121
Philolaus 15
Photius 31
Pico della Mirandola, Giovanni 44, 191, 194
Piede Vicento 216
Pieds royaux 146
Piero della Francesca viii, 7, 67, 86, 153, 173, 186–7, 192, 246, 254
Pirkheimer, Willibald 159
Pisces 44
Pius II, Pope 86
Plato viii, 9, 86, 97, 125, 246, 261
Platonic solids, see Regular figures, Platonic
Pliny the Elder 139
Plotinus 44, 200
Plutarch 16, 53, 131
Polihymnia 42
Polisi 106
Polygons, star 168
Polygraphiae libri sex, Ioannis Trithemii . . . 44
Porphyry 44
Practica arithmeticae generalis 80
Practica arithmeticae, & mensurandi singularis 7
Practica geometriae 5, 85

Prado, Jeronimo 121
Prak, N L 146ff
Proclus 10, 44, 143
Proportion,
  composite 78
  empowered 70ff
  inexpressable 65ff
  rational 58ff
  scales of 91ff
  the most perfect 75–77, 96, 138
Proportionality 72ff
Proportione, et Proportionalità 8, 59
Proslambanmenos 92
Protomathesis 8
Psellus 20, 31
Ptolemy 5, 93ff, 142, 186
Puppi, L x, 236, 244
Pvblivs Aelivs Hadrianvs, *see* Hadrian
Pythagoras x, 44–5, 67, 91, 93, 116
Pythmen 38ff, 130–1

Q

Quadrivium 14

R

Rabelais, François 52
Raphael 28, 96
Ratio 9ff, 58
Ratio: composition, conversion, inverse, inverse composition, separation 10
Rawson, E 137ff
Recorde, Robert 23
Regiomontanus 6, 7, 85, 91
Regula 107
Regula sex quantitatum 79
Regular figures, Euclidean 85ff
Regular figures, Platonic 85, 90, 146, 153
Republic 9, 44, 261, 129
Reuchlin, Johann x, 41, 44, 243, 261ff, 270
Right rectangular triangles 53ff
Rinaldi, R 191
Rithmomachia 49ff, 146
Ritz SJ, S 143ff
Roche, Estienne de la 7, 65
Rose, P L viii, 79, 85, 91, 156, 187
Rosellino, Bernardo 143
Rotonda, La, *see* Villa Almerico
Rowe, C vii
Rykwert, J x, 15, 24, 31ff, 44, 67, 86, 92, 115–6, 121, 127, 184ff, 196, 226, 272

S

Sagittarius 44
San Francesco della Vigna 270
San Lorenzo 183, 188–9
San Petronio, Bologna 5
San Sebastiano 199–205, 208
San Stefano Rotondo 143, 182–3, 188, 204, 251

Sant'Andrea 192
Santa Costanza 182–3
Santa Maria degli Angeli 183, 188
Santa Maria del Fiore 183, 189
Santa Maria Novella 83, 193–5, 199, 208
Santa Maria Rotonda, *see* Pantheon
Saturn 42
Scamozzi, Vincente 109ff, 180–1, 249, 255
Scharoun, H 272
Schelling, F W J ix
Scheme
    for a site in Venice 223
    for Leonardo Mocenigo on the Brenta 216–223
    for the Trissino brothers 220
Schiller, F ix
Schindler, R M 272
Schoen, D A 273
Schoenberg, A 136
Schofield, R x, 134, 216ff
Scholem, G 38ff, 67, 120, 192, 209
Scholfield, P H 105
School of Athens 28, 96
Scorpio 44
Scott, R 131
Sectio Canonis 93
Sefir Yetzirah 39, 44, 67, 192
Semi-regular solids 159, 173, 186
Sephiroth 44
Serlio, Sebastiano 85, 101, 140, 169ff, 186, 206ff, 246, 276–8
Sesquialtera, sesquioctavus, sesquitertia 92
Sheine, J 272
Sherwood, John 52
Shin, Hyunho 191, 269
Shubnikov, A V 196
Sieve of Eratosthenes 18
Sigler, L E 5, 154
Simplicius I, Pope 143ff
Sixtus IV, Pope 7
Smith, D E 49, 53, 80, 212
Söhne, G 101
Solomon x, 48, 119
Solomon's Temple xi, 119ff
Specklin, D 181
Spencer, J R 106

Square 39, 158, 161, 186, 236, 238, 254
Squaring the circle 7, 110
Steadman, P vii, xi, 196
Steganographica 44
Sterne, C C 136
Stevin, Simon 6, 98–99
Stierlin, H 140
Stiny, G vii, xi, 87
Stornaloco, Gabriele 194
Strauss, W L 159ff
Submultiple, submultiple superparticular, submultiple superpartient 58ff
Subsuperparticular, subsuperpartient 58ff
Summa de Arithmetica, Geometria, Proportioni et Proportionalità 61, 70, 153
Sun 42
Superparticular, superpartient 58ff
Symmetria 70
Synagoge 6, 96, 169, 186
Syntaxis 5, 186
Systema 91ff

T

Tabernacle, see Bezazel's Tabernacle
Tafuri, M x, 79
Taurus 44
Tavernor, R x, 15, 24, 31ff, 44, 67, 86, 92, 115, 134, 184ff, 192, 196, 216ff, 226
Taylor, Thomas 13, 190
Teatro Olimpico 181
Temple
    Apollo at Bassae 126–7
    Apollo at Didyma 127–8
    Minerva Medica 184, 188
    Vesta 189
    decagonal 209–212
    hexagonal 206–7
    octagonal 208–9
    oval 212–5
    at Silenus 124–6
Temurah 47
Terpsichore 42
Tetrabiblos 5
Tetrachord 98

Tetrad 32
Tetradoron 221
Tetragrammaton 40, 44ff, 121, 144, 194, 209, 215, 262
Tetrahedron 154ff, 168, 186
Tetraktys 28, 186
Thalia 42
Theaetetus 9
Theologumena Arithmetica 5–6, 31ff, 67, 191
Theon of Smyrna 5, 13, 65, 91, 140, 246, 262
Thomas, I 65
Tiles, hexagonal 69, 167
Tiles, square 69, 167
Tiles, triangular 166
Timaeus 10n, 22, 44, 68, 85, 91ff, 97, 246
Tonus 70, 92
Toscanelli, Paolo 85, 91
Tractatus de proportionibus 6, 70
Trattato d'abaco 7, 153
Trattato di architettura 106
Traversari, Ambrogio 96
Triad 32
Triparty en la science des nombres 7, 65ff
Trissino, Giangiorgio 242
Trithemius, Abbott John 44
Tubero de origine humana 138
Turner-Smith, R 92

U

Underweysung der Messung 8, 99, 159ff, 172
Ungers, O M xi
Urania 42

V

Varro xi, 67, 137ff
Vasari, Georgio 7, 153
Vendler, H xi
Venus 33, 42
Vere, Gaston de 153
Vetula 146
Victoria excellentissima, victoria magna, victoria major 52
Vier Bücher von Menschlicher Proportion 104
Vignola, Giacomo Barozzi da 209

Villa
    Almerico 'La Rotonda' 101, 246–266
    Barbaro at Maser 84, 270–2
    Farnese at Caprarola 209
    Malcontenta vii, 269
    Pisani 84
    Pogliana 99
    Ragona 99, 244–6, 250
Villalpanda, Juan Bautista 121
Villard de Honnecourt 171
Virgo 44
Vitruvius xi, 5, 26, 34, 53, 67, 94, 98, 103, 124–5, 132ff, 157, 171, 189, 219, 239, 259, 269

W

Walker, D P 44
Waterfield, R 6, 31
Watson, A G 265
Watson, W 272
Watts, C M 135
Watts, D J 135
Watts, P M 7
Weaver, N 154
Wertheim, M 16
Westfall, C W 182
Weyl, H 157, 196–7
Whetstone of Witte, The 23
White, J xi
Wiebenson, D 139
Wilkinson, E M and L A ix
Wilson, St J C A vii
Wind, E x
Withan, H B 105
Witmer, T R 239
Wittkower, R vii, x, 8, 25, 80, 98, 185, 221, 246, 251, 269, 272
Wren, C vii
Wright, F L 272

Y

Yates, F A viii, 39, 156
Yahweh, *see* Tetragrammaton

Z

Zamberti, Bartolomeo 155
Zarlino 98, 246
Zeuxis 86, 190
Zodiac 44
Zorzi, Francesco 104, 106
Zorzi, G x, 243, 270